# TEACHING FOR DIVERSITY AND SOCIAL JUSTICE

# TEACHING FOR DIVERSITY AND SOCIAL JUSTICE

second edition

Edited by

Maurianne Adams ♦ Lee Anne Bell ♦ Pat Griffin

Routledge
Taylor & Francis Group
New York London

Routledge
Taylor & Francis Group
270 Madison Avenue
New York, NY 10016

Routledge
Taylor & Francis Group
2 Park Square
Milton Park, Abingdon
Oxon OX14 4RN

Printed in the United States of America on acid-free paper
10 9 8 7 6 5 4 3 2 1

International Standard Book Number-10: 0-415-95200-X (Softcover) 0-415-95199-2 (Hardcover)
International Standard Book Number-13: 978-0-415-95200-2 (Softcover) 978-0-415-95199-9 (Hardcover)

**Library of Congress Cataloging-in-Publication Data**

Teaching for diversity and social justice / Maurianne Adams, Lee Anne Bell, and Pat Griffin. -- 2nd ed.
     p. cm.
   ISBN-13: 978-0-415-95199-9 (hb)
   ISBN-10: 0-415-95200-X (pb)
   1.  Critical pedagogy--United States. 2.  Social justice--Study and teaching--United States.
3.  Multicultural education--United States. 4.  Teachers--Training of--United States. I. Adams, Maurianne. II. Bell, Lee Anne, 1949- III. Griffin, Pat.

LC196.5.U6T43 2007
370.11'5--dc22                                                                          2006031606

**Visit the Taylor & Francis Web site at**
**http://www.taylorandfrancis.com**

**and the Routledge Web site at**
**http://www.routledge.com**

# Contents

## Part I  Theoretical Foundations and Principles of Practice

## Part II  Curriculum Designs for Diversity and Social Justice

# List of Figures and Tables

# List of Appendices

All appendices are on the CD that accompanies this volume.

## Chapter 10. Transgender Oppression Curriculum Design

## Overview. Religious Oppression

No appendices.

## Chapter 11. Religious Oppression Curriculum Design

## Chapter 12. Antisemitism and Anti-Jewish Oppression Curriculum Design

## Chapter 13. Classism Curriculum Design

## Chapter 14. Ableism Curriculum Design

## Chapter 15. Ageism and Adultism Curriculum Design

## Chapter 16. Knowing Ourselves as Social Justice Educators

No appendices.

## Chapter 17. Knowing Our Students

No appendices.

# Acknowledgments

This book reflects more than 30 years of collaboration among several "generations" of faculty, graduate, and undergraduate students, originally all at the University of Massachusetts Amherst, but now in many academic and community locations. The development of the theory and practice described in this volume has truly been a collaborative and ongoing endeavor. A very special acknowledgment goes to Bailey Jackson, whose original thinking, vision, and inspired teaching and mentorship have been an indispensable foundation for much in this volume.

We owe a tremendous debt to those colleagues and friends who generously took time, under tight deadlines, to review new chapters and answer questions. Many thanks to John Alessio, John Bell, Mark Chesler, Henry Goldschmidt, Miguel Guajardo, Eric Hamako, T. Aaron Hans, John A. Hunt, Zander Krieg, Jerry Levinsky, Christoper MacDonald-Dennis, Shahanna McKinny-Baldon, Todd Nelson, Camille O'Bryant, K. Ravishankar, Francesca Rheannon, Dilys Schoorman, Suzanne Soohoo, Sonny Suchdev, Maria Elena Torre, Elaine Whitlock, Frank Yamada, and Jasmin Zine.

Mary McClintock and Janice Reyes provided invaluable and highly skilled work to insure consistency and accuracy as we completed revisions and new chapters. Jennifer Becerra graciously helped with figures. Mary McClintock's particular genius with libraries, computers, and databases of all sorts; her humor, patience, and sound judgment; and her formidable knowledge of the field of social justice education put her in a class by herself.

We want to acknowledge and give heartfelt thanks to the authors who contributed to the designs in the earlier edition (1997). Their work provided a firm basis for the revisions and changes developed, in many cases, by new teams of authors in this new edition. In particular we want to thank for their earlier work Charmaine L. Wijeyesinghe on Racism, Diane Goodman and Steve Shapiro on Sexism, Gerald Weinstein and Donna Mellen on Antisemitism, Laura Rauscher and Mary McClintock on Ableism, and Linda Marchesani on the Multiple Issues Course Overview that has now been integrated into the revised and updated chapter 4, "Designing Social Justice Education Courses." We also acknowledge our debt to Stephen Botkin, Georganne Greene, Elinor Levine, and Valerie Young whose early work contributed to several of the revised and updated curriculum designs.

We continue to learn and be inspired by the graduate students in the Social Justice Education Program at the University of Massachusetts Amherst School of Education who teach the courses described in this and the earlier volume, and who have, over the years, become treasured colleagues and friends. Their creativity, resourcefulness, and passion for teaching have contributed greatly to this approach and sustained us in our ongoing learning about forms of oppression and approaches to social justice education.

We want to thank the authors who contributed to this new edition for their thoughtful, painstaking, creative approaches to their subjects, and for the examples they set of dedication to social justice education as a life project.

We are blessed with an amazing editor at Routledge, Catherine Bernard, who encouraged and supported us in reenvisioning this new edition and the CD that accompanies the book.

Finally, we want to appreciate each other. Our collaboration as an editorial and writing team has been as generative, energizing, and rewarding as the first time around. The ongoing conversation in preparation for the work before us challenged and stretched our understanding of social justice education, and was nourished by the laughter and wonderful meals we shared in Amherst, Belchertown, New Paltz, and New York City as we shaped this new edition.

# Preface

*Teaching for Diversity and Social Justice*, second edition, provides a unified framework for helping people understand and critically analyze multiple forms of oppression. Our approach to social justice education includes both an *interdisciplinary conceptual framework* for analyzing multiple forms of oppression and *a set of interactive, experiential pedagogical principles* to help learners understand the meaning of social difference and oppression both in the social system and in their personal lives. In an increasingly abrasive and polarized American society, we believe that social justice education can play a constructive role in helping people develop a more sophisticated understanding of diversity and social group interaction, more critically evaluate oppressive social patterns and institutions, and work more democratically with diverse others to create just and inclusive practices and social structures.

As social justice educators, our goal is to help people identify and analyze dehumanizing sociopolitical processes, reflect on their own position(s) in relation to these processes so as to consider the consequences of oppressive socialization in their lives, and think proactively about alternative actions given this analysis. We believe that traditional lecture methods do not sufficiently invite the active involvement necessary to reach this goal. We draw upon multiple pedagogies to help participants consider information about various forms of oppression in light of their own personal experiences in ways that we hope foster critique, self-assessment, and more conscious choices about the actions they take in the world.

When we wrote the first edition of this book 10 years ago, social justice education was a newly emerging field. We wrote the book we wished had been available to us when we began teaching courses on issues of oppression in the late 1970s and early 1980s. Since then, interest in research, writing, and teaching about social justice education has proliferated. The use of the term *social justice* within the American Educational Research Association (AERA) is illustrative. We (Jackson, Griffin, Bell, and Adams) first presented a session on our approach to social justice education at AERA in 1995. At that point, ours was one of very few, if not the only session listed under the descriptor *social justice*. In the program for the recent 2006 annual meeting, fully 112 sessions were listed under that descriptor, and AERA now has a director of social justice, a Social Justice Action Committee, a special interest group (SIG) on Educators for Social Justice, and another newly formed SIG on Leadership for Social Justice.

Although it is exciting to see so much interest in social justice education and gratifying to have our book play a role in expanding awareness and knowledge about the field, we worry about *social justice education* becoming a buzz term, used uncritically and lacking the analytic perspective and personal engagement that we believe are its indispensable features. We have tried to situate our work so that readers who hold different perspectives from ours can locate us in a broader body of work on the theory and practice of antioppression and social justice education.

Our approach to social justice is necessarily collaborative. We feel that change cannot happen without ongoing cross-fertilization and exchange of ideas about practice. As social justice education gains currency and visibility, we hope that various communities of practitioners and researchers will acknowledge and build upon each other's work to better prepare all of us to engage the problems we face as a society in committed, sustained, and radically creative ways.

We have learned a great deal since the publication of the first edition of *Teaching for Diversity and Social Justice* in 1997 and would like to note here the most significant changes in this second edition. First, we acknowledge the potential problems with artificially highlighting one form of social injustice in each design, given that in real life they interact in multiple ways that are not so easily represented through a single-issue focus. Although we continue to find it pedagogically useful to foreground one ism at a time, we have more systematically integrated examples into each curriculum design to acknowledge the ways in which multiple issues overlap in real life.

Second, we see the creation of hierarchy to divide and rank social groups, to delineate arbitrary but sociopolitically potent binaries, is a hallmark of oppression and we use this construct to analyze how individuals and groups are positioned differently within each form of oppression. At the same time, we know that relationships among individuals and groups are multiple and cross-cutting, and that people continuously struggle to challenge, redefine, and invent anew more meaningful ways to name and describe our lived experiences of the world. These tensions and contradictions make our work challenging as we call upon constructs for analysis that inevitably do not contain or represent the much richer and messier terrain of lived experience. We have tried in this new edition to note the tension between curricular foregrounding of single issues and isms, and real-life interations of multiple identities and isms in the way we represent models and constructs. The map is not the territory, but a map is nonetheless useful in finding our way.

Third, we have noticed in our teaching that participants often lack sufficient historical knowledge to make sense of the maintenance and reproduction of oppression in contemporary life. Therefore, we have stressed more strongly the importance of historical knowledge and awareness of the legacies in which oppression is rooted. We provide new overview chapters and introductions to each curriculum that situate the issues historically, and we provide activities, readings, and resources that explore information and knowledge of history and the social sciences within each curriculum. Most of these resources are on the CD that accompanies this volume. We hope this information can help prepare facilitators who are new to the material to develop the background knowledge they will need to emphasize this learning with their students.

Fourth, our work with a wonderfully diverse range of students has continually challenged us to account for new forms and novel ways of looking at processes of oppression. This has prompted us to both revise the original curriculum designs and to add new designs that address ideas and forms of oppression that are more visible to us now than they were a decade ago. We have significantly revised our approach to teaching about racism to more directly address white privilege/advantage and the very different experiences among diverse communities of color and national origin. As we read and thought about the powerful role of religion in international and domestic conflicts, we decided to contend with the relationship between religion and oppression/liberation. We have also learned the importance of distinguishing among biological sex, gender identity/expression, and sexual orientation to acknowledge the diversity of experiences of gender expression and sexual orientation. Finally, we have examined the oppression of youth and elders in a society that holds very narrow ideas about maturity and capacity. We are grateful to our students who pushed us to think about how issues change, emerge, and are reframed through struggle. This text is enriched by the additions and changes they encouraged us to make.

One last issue concerns the globalized world in which we live. In the past 10 years, dramatic demographic changes have occurred in the United States that challenged our thinking about the U.S.-centered focus of our earlier designs. It no longer makes sense, if it ever did, to think of U.S.-based issues as discrete. The multinational, multiethnic, multicultural, and diasporic dimensions of the topics we teach, and their impact on the way every ism plays out, make the systematic study of oppression ever more complex, at the same time that our experience teaching mainly in U.S. classrooms inevitably shapes our perspective. We have tried, however imperfectly, to show global issues and connections in the examples and analyses provided in this new edition.

*Teaching for Diversity and Social Justice*, second edition, is divided into three parts. Part I, "Theoretical Foundations and Principles of Practice," consists of five chapters that lay out the theoretical and pedagogical foundations and frameworks upon which our approach to social justice education is based and the principles of design and facilitation that shape our practice as social justice educators. Chapter 1 situates our understanding of oppression and social justice within the broader historical and theoretical discourses, while Chapter 2 positions our pedagogical approach within broader communities of practice concerned with teaching social justice. Chapter 3 develops the specific conceptual foundations for our curriculum and lays out a plan for teaching the introductory material that is foundational to all of the designs in the book. We strongly encourage users to teach the introductory material before proceeding to the specific designs that follow, or to find ways to incorporate this introductory material in their curricular designs. Chapter 4 describes the principles of design we use to construct social justice education curricula in the hope that these principles will make it easier for facilitators to tailor material to their own teaching contexts. Chapter 5 considers specific facilitation issues that arise in social justice teaching and suggests practical strategies to address them.

Part II, "Curriculum Designs for Diversity and Social Justice," includes 10 curriculum designs (Chapters 6–15) that exemplify our approach. Revised and updated from the first edition are designs for teaching about racism, sexism, heterosexism, antisemitism, ableism, and classism. Four completely new designs are added: Racism and Immigration, Religious Oppression, Transgender Oppression, and Ageism and Adultism. We have clustered three sets of designs that are related in content and framed these clusters with overview essays that highlight the connections between and among the designs in each cluster. The first overview describes racism in the twenty-first century to frame Chapter 6, "Racism and White Privilege," and Chapter 7, "Racism, Immigration and Globalization." The second overview looks at the connections among gender, sex, and sexuality to frame Chapter 8, "Sexism"; Chapter 9, "Heterosexism"; and Chapter 10, "Transgender Oppression." The third overview defines religious oppression and frames Chapter 11, "Religious Oppression," and Chapter 12, "Antisemitism and Anti-Jewish Oppression." These clusters of designs are followed by Chapter 13, "Ableism"; Chapter 14, "Classism"; and Chapter 15, "Ageism and Adultism." As with the original volume, we explore the parallels and interconnections among these various isms.

Part III, "Conversations Among Facilitators," raises additional questions and challenges for SJE. Chapter 16 explores what we need to know about ourselves as facilitators, whereas Chapter 17 discusses what we need to know about our students as participants in our classes, in order to be effective social justice teachers. These two chapters use examples from our own practice to illustrate problems and issues that arise in social justice teaching and provide suggestions for how to address them based on what we have learned over time.

Rather than present a fixed curriculum, we provide guidelines, tools, and information that can help users adapt our designs to their own needs and contexts. We offer the curriculum designs in a format that includes four 3–4 hour modules, underscoring that information in the introductory modules in Chapter 3 be used first to prepare the foundation for each design. We hope that this format enables facilitators to flexibly integrate the material into semester-long courses as well. Because our approach to facilitation is primarily active and experiential, we have endeavored to provide sufficient instructions that someone experimenting with this pedagogy for the first time can be successful. Each design includes sections on facilitation issues for this purpose. We have also integrated theory and practical examples throughout to help facilitators better understand the roots of our approach and more effectively adapt our strategies. We have tried to balance recommended activities with flexible alternatives, to be descriptive rather than prescriptive, and to provide sufficient detail that those new to social justice subject matter or pedagogical process will be able to tailor curriculum designs to fit their own circumstances.

A new feature is the addition of a user-friendly CD that includes all of the needed handouts, PowerPoint presentations and lecture notes for facilitators, historical timelines, suggested homework and reading assignments for participants, resource lists and other supplementary material, all of which are in formats that can be easily duplicated/copied. Much of the handout material that readers of our 1997 edition will remember from the book text now appears in PDF form on the CD, more readily accessible to facilitators and participants. The CD also provides substantive background information that expands on facilitation notes in the book text to support preparation by facilitators who are teaching topics that may be new to them and to provide new perspectives for those who are more familiar with the curricular topics.

Some notes on language: We capitalize but do not hyphenate specific ethnicities (African American, Asian American) and capitalize racial designations only when used as proper nouns (Blacks, Latinos/as, Whites). We want to point out that the racial designations Black, Latino/a, Native American, Asian/Pacific Islander, and White are not really parallel terms, in that they conflate race, ethnicity, and pan-ethnicity. When we move to global, diaspora immigration issues, racial/ethnic descriptors become even more problematic. As much as possible, we use terms that are specific to national/geographic origin (people of South Asian descent, for example). We also want to note the use of gender-neutral pronouns (hir, ze) as an option for facilitators. We have asked authors of each curriculum design to address other considerations of language usage in their respective chapters.

We recognize that any terminology we use to describe human beings within the phenomenon of oppression will be problematic. The binary terms *oppressor* and *oppressed*, for example, may raise resistance from participants who cannot reconcile themselves as *oppressors* when they feel personally quite powerless, or who resist the term *oppressed* as one that denies them agency. On the other hand, we struggle to find other language that doesn't trivialize the power and harm of the oppressive system we want to expose. After wrestling with various terms, we have decided to primarily use the terms *advantaged* and *targeted* to connote the relative positions of individuals and groups within a hierarchical system.. We believe these terms, while not perfect, enable a more invitational rather than confrontational approach by highlighting the function of unequal roles in a system rather than attributes of individual people or social groups. Not all of our contributors agree on uniform terminology, and readers will notice the use of different terms in different design chapters. However, all of us do agree on the importance of attending to the systemic features that perpetuate inequality and injustice in our society and of the possibility for individuals to work from wherever they are positioned to challenge and change the system to be more equitable and just.

Our guiding principle is to adopt terms preferred by people from targeted groups to name themselves: *people of color* rather than *non-white*; *gay, lesbian,* and *bisexual* rather than *homosexual*; *people with disabilities* rather than *handicapped*. We also note the reclaiming by targeted communities of previously negative terms such as *queer, crip, girl,* and *trannie,* which reframes slurs as positive. We know that naming is a necessarily fluid and sometimes confusing process as people/groups insist on defining themselves rather than acquiesce to names imposed by others. We encourage people to recognize that such terms will continue evolving and to appreciate the significance of the power to name oneself as an important aspect of group identity and resistance.

We have been disappointed by the tendency of libraries, reviewers, booksellers, and scholars who cite our work to name the first author only, as in "Adams, et al (1997)." This practice does not adequately acknowledge and may even discourage collaborative work since academic rewards and professional visibility tend to accrue primarily to first authors, often presumed to be senior or primary. We have struggled with the question of how to represent the participation of all members of a collaborative team such that both academic rewards and professional visibility are credited equally to all whose ideas, creativity, and writing contribute to the final product. Any line of names, however arranged, suggests a ranking order and we regret that we have found no successful alternative to the convention of alphabetical order in listing editors and contributors. As a step in this direction, we place a statement at the beginning of each mulitiply-authored chapter honoring the nature and value of our collaborative work with a request that people who cite us include the full names of all authors. We have followed our own preferred practice by including all names in the works we cite within our chapters.

In the past 10 years, we have received feedback from hundreds of people throughout this country and abroad who use *Teaching for Diversity and Social Justice* and find it a valuable resource. Their comments and critiques have guided us as we developed this new edition. We are gratified to know that our book has been used successfully in academic departments (Black Studies, Women's Studies, Ethnic Studies, Teacher Education, Multicultural Education, Sociology, Psychology), as well as in student affairs, adult formal and nonformal education, workplace diversity and staff development programs, diversity curricula for general education, and upper-level high school courses.

Given the challenges to justice in the world today and the dynamically evolving social justice movements around the world, we expect that the theory, language, and practice of social justice education will continue to evolve as it has in the 10 years since the first edition of *Teaching for Diversity and Social Justice*. We hope we have given voice to some of these challenges and possibilities in this new edition and that our curriculum can inspire new generations of educators and activists in the cause of social justice. We look forward to a continuing dialogue with those who use this book and to the inspiration they give to our ongoing work in social justice education.

Maurianne Adams, Lee Anne Bell, Pat Griffin

# PART I

# Theoretical Foundations and Principles of Practice

# Theoretical Foundations for Social Justice Education

## LEE ANNE BELL

This chapter contextualizes the approach to oppression and social justice taken throughout this book. It provides a framework for readers who approach oppression and social justice from other positions to see what approaches we share, and where we differ. Our intention is to foster a broad and continuing dialogue among the many people who struggle, as we do, to find more effective ways to challenge oppressive systems and promote social justice through education.

The chapter examines the enduring and the ever-changing aspects of oppression by tracing ways in which "commonsense" knowledge and assumptions make it difficult to see oppression clearly. We underscore the value of history for discerning patterns, often invisible in daily life, that reflect systemic aspects of oppression as it functions in different periods and contexts. We propose concepts that enable us to freeze and focus on specific forms of oppression in our teaching while staying cognizant of the shifting kaleidoscope of dynamic and complex social processes in which they are embedded.

## What Is Social Justice?

We believe that social justice is both a process and a goal. The goal of social justice is full and equal participation of all groups in a society that is mutually shaped to meet their needs. Social justice includes a vision of society in which the distribution of resources is equitable and all members are physically and psychologically safe and secure. We envision a society in which individuals are both self-determining (able to develop their full capacities) and interdependent (capable of interacting democratically with others). Social justice involves social actors who have a sense of their own agency as well as a sense of social responsibility toward and with others, their society, and the broader world in which we live. These are conditions we wish not only for our own society but also for every society in our interdependent global community.

The process for attaining the goal of social justice, we believe, should also be democratic and participatory, inclusive and affirming of human agency and human capacities for working collaboratively to create change. We do not believe that domination can be ended through coercive tactics, and we agree with Kreisberg (1992) in a "power with" versus "power over" paradigm for enacting social justice goals. This book focuses on developing educational processes for reaching these goals within a framework we name social justice education.

The definition of *social justice education* we present in this book includes both an *interdisciplinary conceptual framework* for analyzing multiple forms of oppression and *a set of interactive, experiential pedagogical principles* to help learners understand the meaning of social difference and oppression both in the social system and in their personal lives. The goal of social justice education is to enable people to develop the critical analytical tools necessary to understand oppression and their own socialization within oppressive systems, and to develop a sense of agency and capacity to interrupt and change oppressive patterns and behaviors in themselves and in the institutions and communities of which they are a part.

We realize that developing a social justice process in a society and world steeped in oppression is no simple feat. For this reason, we need clear ways to define and analyze oppression so that we can understand how it operates at individual, cultural, and institutional levels, historically and in the present. Although inevitably an oversimplification of a complex social phenomenon, we believe that the conceptual frameworks presented here can help us make sense of and, hopefully, act more effectively against oppressive circumstances as these arise in our teaching and activism.

## Why Social Justice Education Needs a Theory of Oppression

Practice is always shaped by theory, whether formal or informal, tacit or expressed. How we approach social justice education, the problems we identify as needing remedy, the solutions we entertain as viable, and the methods we choose as appropriate for reaching those solutions are all theoretical as well as practical questions. Theory and practice intertwine as parts of the interactive and historical process that Freire calls "praxis" (1970).

Articulating the theoretical sources of our approach to social justice education thus serves several important purposes. First, theory enables us to think clearly about our intentions and the means we use to actualize them in the classroom. It provides a framework for making choices about what we do and how, and for distinguishing among different approaches. Second, at its best, theory also provides a framework for questioning and challenging our practices, and remaining open to creating new approaches as we encounter inevitable problems of co-optation, resistance, insufficient knowledge, and changing social conditions. Ideally, we keep coming back to and refining our theory as we read and reflect upon the emerging literature on oppression, and as we continually learn through practice the myriad ways oppression can alternately seduce our minds and hearts or inspire us to further learning and activism. Finally, theory has the potential to help us stay conscious of our position as historical subjects, able to learn from the past as we try to meet current conditions in more effective and imaginative ways.

## Defining Features of Oppression

### Pervasive

We use the term *oppression* rather than discrimination, bias, prejudice, or bigotry to emphasize the pervasive nature of social inequality woven throughout social institutions as well as embedded within individual consciousness. The term *oppression* encapsulates the fusion of institutional and systemic discrimination, personal bias, bigotry, and social prejudice in a complex web of relationships and structures that shade most aspects of life in our society. For example, we present a new chapter (Chapter 7) that examines how immigrants of color are racialized and subordinated through history, law, foreign and economic policy, social custom, and educational practice. Woven together through time and reinforced in the present, these patterns provide an example of the pervasive nature of oppression.

### Restrictive

On the most general level, oppression denotes structural and material constraints that significantly shape a person's life chances and sense of possibility. Oppression restricts both self-development and self-determination (Young, 1990b). It delimits who one can imagine becoming and the power to act in support of one's rights and aspirations. A girl-child in the United States in 2006, for example, especially if she is poor or of color, is still unlikely to imagine herself as president since, unlike many other countries, we have yet to elect a woman to this high office. 140 years after the abolition of slavery, African Americans as a group have still not achieved full equality and cannot even rely on their government for basic human treatment and aid in a time of crisis, as in the recent scandalous government desertion of the victims of Hurricane Katrina. Despite rhetoric that anyone can get ahead if they work hard enough, a father's economic status continues to be the best predictor of the status of his offspring, a situation that worsens as economic inequality grows and the possibilities for social mobility steadily decline (*The Economist*, 2004; Hertz, 2006).

### Hierarchical

Oppression signifies a hierarchical relationship in which dominant or privileged groups reap advantage, often in unconscious ways, from the disempowerment of targeted groups (Frye, 1983; Johnson, 2006; McIntosh, 1992; Miller, 1976; Wildman, 1996; Young, 1990b). Whites, for example, gain privilege as a dominant group because they benefit from access to social power and privilege, not equally available to people of color. As a group, Whites earn more money and accumulate more assets than other racial groups, hold the majority of positions of power and influence, and command the controlling institutions in society (Hacker, 1992; Oliver & Shapiro, 1997). White-dominated institutions restrict the life expectancy, infant mortality, income, housing, employment, and educational opportunities of people of color (Smelser, Wilson, & Mitchell, 2001).

### Complex, Multiple, Cross-Cutting Relationships

Power and privilege are relative, however, because individuals hold multiple complex and cross-cutting social group memberships that confer relative privilege or disadvantage differently in different contexts (Collins, 1990). Identity is not simply additive but multiplicative (Wing, 2003). An upper-class professional man who is African American, for example (still a very small percentage of African Americans overall), may enjoy economic success and professional status conferred through male, class, and perhaps dominant language and citizenship privilege as an English-speaking native-born citizen, yet face limitations not endured by white, male and female, or foreign national coworkers. Despite economic and professional status and success, he may be threatened by police, be unable to hail a taxi, and endure hateful epithets as he walks down the street (Cose, 1993; Feagin & Sikes, 1994; Petillo-McCoy, 1999). The constellation of identities that shape his consciousness and experience as an African American man, and his varying access to privilege, may fluctuate depending upon whether he is light or dark skinned, Ivy League–educated or a high school dropout, incarcerated, unemployed, or a tourist in South Africa, Brazil, or Europe.

### Internalized

Oppression not only resides in external social institutions and norms but lodges in the human psyche as well (Fanon, 1968; Freire, 1970; Miller, 1976). Oppressive beliefs are internalized by victims as well as perpetrators. The idea that poor people somehow deserve and are responsible for poverty, rather than the economic system that structures and requires it, is learned by poor and affluent alike. Homophobia, the deep fear and hatred of homosexuality, is internalized by both straight and gay people. Jews as well as Gentiles absorb antisemitic stereotypes.

How do we capture such complex social phenomena in clear and understandable terms that neither oversimplify nor rigidify processes that are lived by diverse human beings in historically specific and individually particular ways? What connects the experiences of a poor woman on welfare with a professional woman facing a glass ceiling at work? What commonalities are shared by African Americans segregated in northern cities and beltway suburbs and gay, lesbian, and transgender people harassed or beaten on the streets? In what ways do Native Americans on reservations and Jews and Arabs stereotyped in the media face a similar threat? How are avoidance and isolation of people with disabilities connected to assumptions that people who speak English with an accent are ignorant? In what ways is it possible, or even desirable, that these examples be subsumed under a unified theory of oppression?

### Shared and Distinctive Characteristics of "Isms"

In grappling with these questions, we have come to believe in the explanatory and political value of identifying both the particular histories and characteristics of specific forms of oppression such as ableism or classism, as well as the patterns that connect and mutually reinforce different oppressions in a system that is inclusive and pervasive. In this book we examine the unique ways in which oppression is manifested through racism, white privilege, and immigrant status; sexism, heterosexism, and transgender experiences; religious oppression and antisemitism; and classism, ableism, and ageism/adultism.

We look at the dimensions of experience that connect these "isms" in an overarching system of domination. For example, we examine the roles of a dominant or advantaged group and (a) subordinated or targeted group(s) in each form of oppression and the differentials of power and privilege that are dynamic features of oppression, whatever its particular form. At the same time, we try to highlight the distinctive qualities and appreciate the historical and social contingencies that distinguish one form of oppression from another. In this model, diversity and the appreciation of differences are inextricably tied to social justice and the unequal ways that power and privilege construct difference in our society (see Chapter 3).

From our perspective, no one form of oppression is the base for all others, yet all are connected within a system that makes them possible. We align with theorists such as Young (1990b) who describe distinctive ingredients of oppression without prioritizing one over another. We also share with Young the view that eradicating oppression ultimately requires struggle against all its forms, and that coalitions among diverse people offer the most promising strategies for challenging oppression systematically. Therefore, we highlight theory and practice that demonstrate interconnections among different forms of oppression and suggest common strategies to oppose it collectively.

## Learning From History

Knowledge of history helps us trace the patterns that constitute oppression over time and enables us to see the long-standing grievances and legacies of differently situated social groups in our society and in the world. Current debates on issues such as affirmative action or reparations, for example, cannot be fully understood without acknowledging the historical debts from slavery, legal and de facto segregation, relocation, and racial violence that have advantaged Whites as a group while locking African Americans out of positions that would allow their collective, rather than token, economic and social advancement (Katznelson, 2005). Similarly, stereotypes of Jews can only be explicated in the context of identifiable historical cycles in a 3,000-year history of exploitation, exclusion, and expulsion. Historical context is vital for understanding how stereotypes develop in one context with particular meanings and continue as unquestioned fact down through the ages.

Critical historical methods can "demarginalize" (Davis & Wing, 2000) the roles that people of color, working-class people, immigrants, and women of all groups have played in challenging oppression (Lerner, 1986; Zinn, 1980/1995, 2004). The concealed and resistance stories of marginalized groups challenge stock stories (Bell & Roberts, unpublished manuscript) and provide hope as well as evidence that oppressive circumstances can change through the efforts of human actors. Through history, we learn how groups organized and struggled to abolish slavery, extend suffrage to women, sustain unions to improve working conditions for laborers, challenge anti-immigrant policies, and advocate for gay, lesbian, and transgender rights, to name a few examples (Aptheker, 1993; D'Emilio, 1983; Zinn, 1980/1995). Historical examples suggest strategies for acting in the present to address current problems and learn from past mistakes. For example, the coalitions and ruptures between suffragists and abolitionists of the 19th century have been instructive for a 20th-century women's movement that seeks to be inclusive (Lerner, 1986), and the successes and failures of that movement have likewise informed more current efforts within global feminism (Wing, 2003).

Revisionist historians who look more closely at the 1950s for the roots of various liberation movements in what is popularly known as a quiescent period in U.S. history, show that "conservative" period sowed the seeds for mass movements that sprang up in the 1960s and 1970s (Marcus, 1992). As we encounter today a period in many ways like the 1950s, we need to recognize the seeds and lessons for similar activist movements now and in the years ahead. We can also learn from studying connections among movements that may not have been as clearly visible as they are now in hindsight. For example, newer historical studies illuminate ways in which the Civil Rights movement and African American struggles for equality and self-determination inspired Native Americans, Asian Americans, Puerto Ricans, and Chicanos (Marabel, 1984; Oboler, 1995; Okihiro, 1994); the New Left and antiwar movements (Gitlin, 1987); feminists (Evans, 1979; Russo, 2001); gay, lesbian, bisexual, and transgender rights activists (Feinberg, 1997; Zames & Zames, 2001); disability rights movements (Marcus, 1992; Morris, 1991; Shapiro, 1993); and, most recently, blossoming youth activism and hip hop (Rose, 1994; Watkins,2006) and immigrant rights movements (Chacon & Davis, 2006). These examples help us think about how to connect lessons from across movements and learn from the perspectives and leadership of those who have been marginalized to build more inclusive and enduring coalitions.

## Constructing an Inclusive Theory of Oppression

We touch on concepts from writing and activism in the Civil Rights, New Left, and women's liberation movements of the 1960s and 1970s, and from more recent movements for equality and social change, to discern lessons about oppression that provide a conceptual framework for understanding its operations. Tracking the history of ideas developed in these movements grounds our theoretical understanding in lived experience and highlights the contradictions and conflicts in different approaches to oppression and social justice as these are lived out in practice over time and place. Here, we highlight broad themes drawn from rich and well-developed academic and social movement traditions to which we are indebted.

## Racism

The social science literature on racism and insights about racism that emerged from the Civil Rights movement of the late 1950s and early 1960s profoundly shaped the way scholars and activists have come to understand oppression and its other manifestations. The Civil Rights movement fired the imagination of millions of Americans, who applied its lessons to an understanding of their particular situations and adapted its analyses and tactics to their own struggles for equality. For example, Native American, Chicano, and Puerto Rican youth styled themselves after the African American youth in the Student Nonviolent Coordinating Committee (SNCC) and Black Panther Party (Oboler, 1995). The predominantly white student antiwar movement drew directly from the experiences of the black freedom struggles to shape their goals and strategies (Gitlin, 1987). Early women's liberation groups were spawned within SNCC itself, as black and white women applied the analyses of racial inequality to their own positions as women (Echols, 1989; Evans, 1979; Sayres, 1984), as did Latinas within the Puerto Rican Youth (Hurtado, 1997; Oboler, 1995). The gay liberation and disability rights movements credit the Civil Rights movement as a model for their organizing and activism (Marcus, 1992; Shapiro, 1993), and poor people's and welfare rights movements likewise drew upon this heritage (Piven & Cloward, 1982) as do immigrant (Gordon, 2005) and youth activists today (Sherrod, 2005; Welton & Wolf, 2001).

Of the many valuable legacies of the Civil Rights movement and the academic traditions focusing on racism, we highlight here two key themes. One is the awareness that racism is a system of oppression that not only stigmatizes and violates the targeted group (Fanon, 1968; Freire, 1970; Memmi, 1967/1991), but also does psychic and ethical violence to the dominator group as well (Bowser & Hunt, 1981; McIntosh, 1992; Terry, 1975). The idea that oppression affects, albeit in different ways, both those advantaged and those targeted by oppression has been useful to many other groups as a way to make sense of their experiences of oppression.

The second broad theme is that racism functions not only through overt, conscious prejudice and discrimination but also through the unconscious attitudes and behaviors of a society that presumes an unacknowledged but pervasive white cultural norm (Frankenberg, 1990; Omi & Winant, 1986; Said, 1993; Segrest, 1994). Racial images and ideas are embedded in language and cultural practices promoted as neutral and inclusive (Bell, 2002). However, the alleged neutrality of social patterns, behaviors, and assumptions in fact define and reinforce a form of cultural imperialism that supports white supremacy. Identifying unmarked and unacknowledged norms that bolster the power position of advantaged groups is an important strategy for examining other forms of oppression as well. Feminists, for example, use the idea to examine practices of male supremacy and patriarchy (Bennett, 2006; Johnson, 2005; MacKinnon, 1991), and gay and lesbian rights activists use it to analyze heterosexual privilege (Frye, 1983; Rich, 1979).

The concept of racial formation has become an important analytic tool (Omi & Winant, 1986). This concept is useful for thinking about the ways in which racism is constructed and reconstructed in different contexts and periods. It works against the tendency to essentialize current social relations as given and encourages ideas about alternative ways to frame and understand human relations against systems of oppression. Critical race theory (Delgado & Stefanik, 1999, 2001; Wing, 2003; Yosso, 2006), Lat Crit theory (Solòrzano & Bernal, 2001), and Whiteness studies (Hill, 1997; Rothenberg, 2004) offer other important tools for analyzing oppression through the use of story to represent how racism operates and to invent alternative scenarios of possibility. They also focus on the idea of "interest convergence" both for analyzing how racism and White supremacy operate and for strategizing about how to interrupt and change racist conditions (Bell, 1992).

### Classism

The New Left movements of the late 1960s and early 1970s espoused ideals of political democracy and personal liberty and applied their political energy to make power socially accountable (Bowles & Gintis, 1987; van Gosse, 2005). New Left critiques of power built on Marxist theory to examine issues of domination and exploitation and to focus on the structural rather than individual factors that maintain oppressive economic and social relations. They also exposed and critiqued normative assumptions that conflate democracy with capitalism and its role in suppressing the exploration of alternative economic and social arrangements.

New Left analyses examine how power operates through normalizing relations of domination and systematizing ideas and practices that are then taken as given. These analyses remind us to continually ask the question "In whose interest do prevailing systems operate?" The question of power and the interests it serves has been a useful analytic tool for examining oppression in all of its multiple forms. Asking who benefits and who pays for prevailing practices helps to expose the hierarchical relationships as well as the hidden advantages and penalties embedded in a purportedly fair and neutral system.

Postcolonial scholars and activists have extended these questions to an analysis of the power dynamics within global relations of transnational capital and their impact on labor, migration, gender and ethnic relations, environmental issues, and national development around the globe (Dirlik, 1997; Mohanty, 2003; Sandoval, 2000; Shiva, 2005). These analyses of how power circulates alert us to the evershifting ways in which power maintains itself in support of the status quo and to the flexibility and persistence necessary to continually challenge its operations.

### Sexism

The women's liberation movement developed important theoretical and analytic tools for a general theory of oppression and liberation (Evans, 1979). Through consciousness-raising groups, women collectively uncovered and deconstructed the ways that the system of patriarchy is reproduced inside women's consciousness as well as in external social institutions, and challenged conventional assumptions about human nature, sexuality, family life, and gender roles and relations (Chodorow, 1978; Dinnerstein, 1976; Firestone, 1970). Consciousness-raising groups developed a process for naming how members of targeted groups can collude in maintaining an unequal system, identifying the psychological as well as social factors that contribute to internalizing oppressive beliefs, and exploring how to raise consciousness to resist and challenge such systems both inside our own consciousness and externally in the world (see Chapter 2). Feminist practice also sought to create and enact new, more liberated ways of thinking and behaving. Insights from feminist theory and practice have been fruitfully used by other groups to raise consciousness, develop analyses of psychological and social assumptions and practices of their group(s) as these collude in maintaining oppression, and experiment with alternative practices.

## Multiple Issues

Women of color, lesbians, Jewish feminists, and poor and working-class women brought forth critiques from within the women's movement to critique unitary theories of feminism, stressing the multiple and diverse perspectives, needs, and goals of women from different social groups (Collins, 1990; Hull, Scott, & Smith, 1982; Moraga & Anzaldúa, 1981/1983). These challenges have been used to critique unitary theories of class, race, and gender and to generate a range of analyses and ideas about oppression(s) that take into account both the multiple identities people hold and the range of experiences of oppression lived within any given group (Kumashiro, 2001; Spelman, 1988). Women of color who are lesbian and poor, for example, experience oppression in multiple and distinctive ways that demand more complex analyses of the mechanisms of oppression in the lives of diverse groups of people (Lorde, 1984). Global feminism (Mohanty, 2003) and global critical race feminism (Davis & Wing, 2000) both critique and add to the strategies and theories developed by previous feminists, highlighting the leadership of women at the margins, building transnational consciousness of shared and distinctive problems women face under postcolonial systems and U.S. imperialism, and developing strategies and solutions locally to address the particularities of their national contexts (Dirlik, 1997).

Postcolonial studies and postmodern theories, and ongoing discussions among people in various social movements, continue to challenge binary categorization such as black/white, heterosexual/homosexual, male/female, and notions that essentialize, or treat as innately given, the groupings created within an oppressive social order (Mohanty, Russo, & Torres, 1991; Trinh, 1989). The inadequacy of defining the experience of individuals and groups in simplistic binary terms is reflected through challenges within the gay and lesbian movement raised by bisexual, transsexual, and transgender people (Butler, 2004). The range of experiences of people holding multiple identities and diverse social group memberships poses continuing challenges that theories of oppression account for their experiences.

## Individual and Group Identity

Thinking broadly about the intersection of individual and group identity(ies) is complicated by the ways in which identities are co-constructed and assigned meaning within oppressive systems. In the United States, we are socialized to view life in individual terms; our Constitution and public ethos enshrine and celebrate the rights of individuals. Yet, in what meaningful sense can we say that a self "stands free from history and social affiliations" (Young, 1990b)? As members of human communities, our identities are fundamentally constructed in relation to others and to the cultures in which we are embedded (Bakhtin, 1981; Epstein, 1987; Rogoff, 2003; Vygotsky, 1978). In a very real sense, it is impossible to separate our individual identities from our socialization within various social groups and communities.

Oppression cannot be understood in individual terms alone, for people are privileged or oppressed on the basis of social group status. Group memberships coexist within individuals and among members of a particular social group, and their coexistence inevitably generates diverse and often conflicting personal meanings. People may affirm their group identity(ies) as a source of sustenance, pride, and personal meaning while also feeling victimized by the advantaged group's characterization of their group in ways they experience as oppressive and reject as invalid.

One of the privileges of advantaged group status is the luxury to simply see oneself as an individual. A white man, for example, is rarely defined by Whiteness or maleness. If he does well on his job, he is acknowledged as a highly qualified individual. If he does poorly, the blame is attributed to him alone. Members of targeted groups, however, can never fully escape being defined by their social group memberships. A Puerto Rican woman, for example, may wish to be viewed as an individual and acknowledged for her personal talents and abilities. Yet she can never fully escape the dominant society's assumptions about her racial/ethnic group, language, and gender. If she excels in her work, she may be seen as atypical or exceptional. If she does poorly, she may be seen as representative of the limitations of her group. In either case, she rises or falls not only on the basis of individual qualities alone, but always also partly as a member of the social group(s) with which she is identified.

This does not mean that all members of a particular social group will necessarily define themselves in exactly the same way. A person's self-defined group identity may be central, as religious identity is to a traditionally observant Jew. Or it may be mainly background, only becoming salient in certain interactional contexts, as Jewish identity may become for an assimilated Jew when confronted with antisemitism (Young, 1990b). Either way, both must struggle for self-definition within their shared burden as targets of antisemitism.

Group identity(ies) are also historical and contextual. Latinos in the United States, for example, are an extremely diverse group comprising people from many different countries of origin, speaking various languages, and from divergent racial, ethnic, and socioeconomic groups, who arrive in the United States under widely different conditions of immigration, colonization, or slavery over different time periods (Anzaldúa, 1987; Hurtado, Gurin & Peng, 1994; Oboler, 1995). The label *Latino/a* may include a Spanish-speaking, upper-class white man from Cuba as well as a Mayan-speaking Indian woman from Mexico or Guatemala. The dominant society lumps these individuals together in a group labeled *Hispanic* to which certain stereotypes are applied. On one level, they thus could be said to share a common group experience of oppression in a historical U.S. context, and, indeed, this is often the basis for political organizing across different groups self-named as *Latino/as*. On another level, their experiences are so divergent as to have little in common at all except when compared to the experiences of non-Latino/as.

The popular view of the United States as a "melting pot" posits that immigrants from all the various groups that enter the country ultimately merge together to create one unified cultural blend. Those who promote this view often point to the assimilation of successive waves of European immigration in the 18th and 19th centuries as evidence. They ignore, however, the Anglo-American conformity that required white immigrant groups such as the Germans, Irish, Italians, Greeks, and Scandinavians to divest themselves of their native ethnic cultures and languages and adopt Anglo-European, middle-class cultural norms and values (McLemore, 1993; Steinberg, 1989). They also overlook the continued exclusion of "non-white" groups, particularly Native Americans and those of African, Caribbean, and Asian descent, considered "unmeltable" ethnics.

One of the most invidious mechanisms of oppression is the eradication of targeted group cultures through the imposition of the advantaged group's culture and language. The ideal of assimilation rests on the assumption of a "supposedly unitary majority culture" (Omi & Winant, 1986; Said, 1993), which in fact is Anglo-European. In such a context, individuals and groups gain equality by becoming as much like the privileged group as possible, automatically marginalizing those who can never "pass" into the dominant culture by virtue of race, gender, or other noticeable difference and stripping people of cultural aspects they value and prefer to maintain. At its worst, this process has justified the near extermination of the native people of this continent (Churchill, 1995; Stannard, 1992; Wright, 1992).

The tension between individual and group identity(ies) is complicated further by the fact that group identity is also for many people self-consciously chosen and affirmed as a fundamental aspect of self-definition. Self-ascription, "belonging to a group with others who similarly identify themselves, who affirm or are committed together to a set of values, practices and meanings," is an important concept to many in our society (Young, 1990, p. 34). The emergence of black consciousness, gay pride, feminist solidarity, disability rights, the Gray Panthers, Red Power, La Raza, hip hop radicals, trannies, and others demonstrates the significance of self-ascribed group status for resisting devaluation by the dominant culture.

Finally, neither individual identities nor social groups are homogeneous or stable. Individuals are formed partly through group relations and affinities that are "multiple, cross-cutting, fluid and shifting" (Young, 1990b, p. 48). Postmodern writers have argued persuasively against the notion of a unitary subject and essentializing notions of group identity that ignore the fluid and changing ways that people experience themselves both as individuals and as members of different social groups over the course of a lifetime (Anzaldúa, 1987; Mohanty et al., 1991). "Despite our desperate, eternal attempt to separate, contain, and mend, categories always leak" (Trinh, 1989, p. 94).

## Hegemony, Reproduction, and the Operations of Power

Gramsci put forth the idea of hegemony to explain the way in which power is maintained not only through coercion but also through the voluntary consent of those who are subjugated by it (Gramsci & Forgacs, 2000; Morrow & Torres, 1995). Through hegemony, a dominant group can so successfully project its particular way of seeing social reality that its view is accepted as common sense, as part of the natural order, even by those who are in fact disempowered by it (Tong, 1989). Hegemony helps us understand power as relational and dynamic, something that circulates within a web of relationships in which we all participate, rather than as something imposed from top down (Foucault, 1980). Through hegemony we understand that power operates not simply when persons or groups unilaterally impose their will on others, but rather through ongoing systems mediated by well-intentioned people who, usually unconsciously, act as agents of oppression by merely going about their daily lives (Young, 1990b).

Political movements for equality over the past few decades have succeeded in challenging some of the most glaring abuses of power. Yet, although advances have been made, the basic relations of domination have been remarkably resistant to change and surprisingly resilient in adapting new forms (Pharr, 1996; Winant, 2004). General patterns of inequality recur, even in the face of deliberate efforts to change them, through entrenched norms, practices and policies (Young, 1990b).

The exclusion of people with disabilities from many jobs, for example, does not require overt discrimination against them. "Business as usual" is sufficient to prevent change. Physical barriers to access go unnoticed by those who can walk up the stairs, reach elevator buttons and telephones, use furniture and tools that fit their bodies and functional needs, and generally move in a world that is designed to facilitate their passage, and thus support and maintain policies that seem perfectly natural and fair from a privileged vantage point.

Hegemony is also maintained through "discourse," which includes ideas, texts, theories, and language. These are embedded in networks of social and political control that Foucault called "regimes of truth" (1980). Regimes of truth operate to legitimize what can be said, who has the authority to speak, and what is sanctioned as true (Kreisberg, 1992). Oppression operates through everyday practices that do not question "the assumptions underlying institutional rules and the collective consequences of following those rules" (Young, 1990b, p. 41). For example, until women began speaking about spousal abuse, a husband's authority to physically control his wife often went unchallenged, rendered invisible through the language of family privacy and assumptions about sexual consent in marriage. One important mechanism for challenging oppression, then, is to make visible and vocal the underlying assumptions that produce and reproduce structures of domination so that we can collectively begin to imagine alternative possibilities for organizing social life (Freire, 1970).

For example, assumptions of heterosexual privilege are often invisible in our society. Social norms, rituals, and language, as well as institutional rules and rewards, presume the existence of exclusively heterosexual feelings and relationships. The language and symbols of love, attraction, family, and sexual and emotional self-development largely ignore the existence of homosexual, bisexual, transgender, and other possibilities of human potential. Well-meaning heterosexual people may bemoan gay bashing and hate-based assaults on gays and lesbians, but assume that the system is basically fine as it is. They only see extreme examples of prejudice and live their lives unaware of the daily exclusions, insults, and assaults endured by those who are not heterosexual. Heterosexism also conceals how this regime operates not only to oppress gay, lesbian, bisexual, and transgender people but to constrain and limit heterosexuals to narrowly gender-defined rules of behavior and options for self-expression as well.

## Privilege and Penalty: Internalized Domination and Subordination

Conditions of oppression in everyday life become normal when we internalize attitudes and roles that support and reinforce systems of domination without question or challenge. As Audre Lorde so eloquently put it, "[T]he true focus of revolutionary change is to see the piece of the oppressor inside us" (1984, 123). Both those who are advantaged and those who are targeted play roles, albeit different ones, in maintaining systems of oppression.

When members of targeted groups accept and incorporate negative images of themselves fostered by the dominant society, they wittingly or not support the system of oppression (Fanon, 1968; Freire, 1970; Lipsky, 1977; Memmi, 1967/1991; Miller, 1976; Sennett & Cobb, 1972). Members of targeted groups collude in maintaining systems of oppression both because they internalize the false belief that the system is correct or inevitable, and as a means of survival. Internalized subordination includes such

feelings as inferiority and self-hatred and often results in self-concealment, resigna-
tion, isolation, powerlessness, and gratitude for being allowed to survive (Pheterson,
1990). Women, for example, may actively accept the belief that men are more capable in
politics and business and women more naturally suited to housework and child care,
and unquestioningly adopt assumptions about female limitations and negative stereotypes of women as weak, overemotional, and irrational. Or they may reject such stereotypes but support male advantage anyway as a means of survival, because to challenge
means risking jobs, relationships, and physical security.

Internalized acceptance of "the way things are" by members of targeted groups
can also lead them to turn on those who do challenge the status quo. Such horizontal
hostility (see Chapter 3) blocks solidarity among group members and prevents organizing for change. For example, gay and lesbian people who stay in the closet and pass
as heterosexual in order to survive may resent activists who insist on being open and
actively challenging discrimination against their group. This division within the community helps to maintain the system of heterosexism by preventing solidarity and collective action for change.

Members of dominant or advantaged groups also internalize the system of oppression and can operate as agents of the system by perpetuating oppressive norms, policies, and practices. Internalized domination includes feelings of superiority and, often,
self-consciousness, guilt, fear, projection, and denial (Frankenberg, 1990; McIntosh,
1992; Pharr, 1988). Through internalized domination, individuals in the advantaged
group incorporate and accept prejudices against others and assume that the status quo
is normal and correct. They learn to look at themselves, others, and society through a
distorted lens in which the structural privileges they enjoy and the cultural practices
of their group are represented as normal and universal.

The privilege of dominant groups is reinforced through both language and material practices. For example, despite rhetoric that the United States is a secular nation,
Christian symbols, holidays, and rituals are routinely integrated into public affairs and
institutions. Other religious and spiritual traditions held by large numbers of Americans, including Jews, Muslims, Hindus, Sikhs, and Native Americans, are invisible
or marginalized, so much that when members of these groups protest, they are often
viewed as challenging the American (Christian) way of life (see Chapter 11). Similarly,
even the most modest proposals to change the economic system to more equitably distribute goods and services are taken as challenges to the American (capitalist) way of
life (see Chapter 13 on classism).

Members of advantaged groups may also engage in horizontal hostility toward
members of their own group who defy the status quo. For example, white people who
openly name and critique racist practices may be labeled by other Whites as troublemakers, extremists, or bleeding hearts. Pressure against rocking the boat or "making
trouble" can discourage dominants from challenging inequality and discrimination
and lead them to block change. Ultimately, people from advantaged groups can perpetuate the status quo by simply doing nothing.

Freire (1970) argued that people in both targeted and advantaged groups are dehumanized by oppression. A goal of social justice education is to engage people from all
groups in recognizing the terrible costs of maintaining systems of oppression. The impetus for change more often comes from members of oppressed groups because those
who are oppressed by a system usually have the most incentive to change it. Their lived
experiences often allow them to see more clearly the contradictions between myths
and reality and lead them to develop a critical perspective on the dominant society
(Collins, 1990; Freire; Hartsock, 1983; Harding, 1991). These "subjugated knowledges" of

oppressed groups, those truths and insights about the social world that are suppressed, define the world and possibilities for human existence differently and offer valuable alternative visions of what is possible (Collins, 1990; Wing, 2003). Thus, listening to and learning from the analyses and experiences of members of targeted groups can help us all get a clearer understanding of how oppression operates and suggest more imaginative alternatives for socially just relationships and institutional patterns.

Those advantaged by the system have an important role to play in challenging oppression as well. Throughout our history, there have always been people from advantaged groups who used their power to actively fight against systems of oppression (Aptheker, 1993; Colby & Damon, 1992; Daloz, Keen, Keen, & Parks, 1996; Wigginton, 1992; Zinn, 1980/1995). White abolitionists, middle- and upper-class antipoverty crusaders, and men who supported women's rights are models for us today. Those who are advantaged can expose the social, moral, and personal costs of maintaining privilege so as to develop an investment in changing the system by which they benefit, but for which they also pay a price. Some argue this commitment comes through friendship (Spelman, 1988), while others insist that it comes only through mutual struggle for common political ends (Mohanty, Russo, & Torres, 1991; Sleeter, 1993). In either case, those who are advantaged need to understand the role they play in maintaining the system and contend with the high moral and societal costs of privileged status in an unequal system (Thompson, Schaefer, & Brod, 2003).

For example, when millions of Americans are homeless and hungry, those who are comfortable pay a social and moral price. Enjoying plenty while others starve corrodes our ability to view ourselves as decent people and to claim our society as just. It also prevents us from examining underlying structural problems in the economic system that ultimately make all Americans vulnerable in a changing international economy that disregards national boundaries or allegiances. The productive and creative contributions of people who are shut out of the system are lost to all of us. Rising violence and urban decay make it increasingly difficult for anyone to feel safe on city streets. Reduced social supports, limited affordable housing, and scarcities of food and potable water loom as a possible future for all who are not independently wealthy, particularly as we reach old age.

## Consciousness, Agency, and Resistance

Given how systems of domination saturate both the external world and our individual psyches, how do we challenge and change them? In a context where we are all implicated, where we cannot escape our social location(s), how do we find standpoints from which to act (Lewis, 1993)? A commitment to social justice requires a moral and ethical attitude toward equality and possibility and a belief in the capacity of people as agents who can act to transform their world (Freire, 1970; Weiler, 1991). Hegemony is never complete; it is always open to contestation (Morrow & Torres, 1995). Raising up the contradictions between espoused social principles and lived experience offers one place to begin.

Our approach to social justice education begins with people's lived experience as the ground for developing a critical perspective and actions directed toward social change (Bell & Schniedewind, 1987; Kreisberg, 1992; Lewis, 1993). We take the position that people in both advantaged and targeted groups have a critical role to play in dismantling oppression and generating visions for a more socially just future. The specific standpoints of particular social groups are valuable places to begin. Groups of people who share targeted status can build solidarity, articulate an analysis of power from the particular vantage point of their group, use this to analyze policies and practices that support oppression, and generate alternatives to the status quo. Coalitions among different groups can then develop these strategies further by drawing on the energies differential insights and diverse avenues to power of coalition members.

The Civil Rights movement illustrates well the potential of a coalition between empowered people in a targeted group working with allies from advantaged groups. Each member of the coalition brought its own perspective and moral commitment to the struggle. Black Americans brought a collective personal integrity and willingness to risk their lives that forced American society as a whole to confront the ugly truth of racism. Jews, who were the largest group of Whites to participate, drew on their own experiences of oppression to mobilize support and commitment in white communities and in the courts, along with Christians for whom equality was intrinsic to their religious faith. Whites with access to power and privilege not available to most black Americans acted as allies, passing laws in Congress, using the media to publicize the struggle, and joining actions where white lives were more likely to gain police protection. Together, they forged a coalition for change that, despite setbacks and problems within those coalitions that were later exposed, inspires social movements to this day.

We can also learn from studying the factors that led to the demise of the Civil Rights movement in order to be more effective allies in coalition work with others, without erasing or suppressing difference in the name of false unity (Albrecht & Brewer, 1990; Kaye/Kantrowitz, 1992; Reagon, 1983). As individuals and as groups, our visions can only be partial. Coalitions bring together multiple ways of understanding the world and analyzing the oppressive structures within it. Specific skills of perspective taking, empathic listening, and self-examination are useful to this process. So are practicing and sharing effective ways to be allies and to work against individual isolation and the suppression of political culture. Through dialogue, we can encourage each other to begin to "imagine otherwise" (Lather, 1991). Social justice courses are one arena for sharing knowledge, practicing such skills and developing collective strategies for change (Tatum, 1994).

## Conclusion

As historical circumstances change and newly emerging social movements take up issues of oppression in the United States and throughout the world, new definitions and understandings will evolve. Through highlighting the historical and contextual nature of this process here, we hope to avoid the danger of reifying systems of oppression as static or treating individuals as unidimensional and unchanging. History illustrates both how tenacious and variable systems of oppression are and how dynamic and creative we must continue to be to rise to the challenges they pose. The concepts and processes we present in this text are also continuously evolving. We hope the work presented in this second edition will contribute to an ongoing dialogue about social justice education theory and practice in ways that can have more potent and sustained impacts for justice, fairness and equality in our world.

# 2

# Pedagogical Frameworks for Social Justice Education

## MAURIANNE ADAMS

We know that ... changing *what* we teach, means changing *how* we teach.

Culley and Portuges (1985, p. 2)[1]

The social justice curricula in this volume propose numerous pedagogical challenges to established ways of teaching and learning and illustrate an approach that challenges dominant pedagogical assumptions. In this chapter, we turn our attention to social justice educational teaching practices, in order to consider *how* we teach as distinct from *what* we teach, and to examine the foundations for what we believe to be core frameworks of social justice education practice. These frameworks are as follows:

1. Establish an equilibrium between the emotional and cognitive components of the learning process.
2. Acknowledge and support the personal and individual dimensions of experience, while making connections to and illuminating the systemic dimensions of social group interactions.
3. Pay explicit attention to social relations within the classroom.
4. Make conscious use of reflection and experience as tools for student-centered learning.
5. Reward changes in awareness, personal growth, and efforts to work toward change, understood as outcomes of the learning process.

Educators whose work involves social justice and social change have been exploring the affective, personal, social, and experiential dimensions of teaching and learning for many decades in both academic and activist contexts. Their work draws upon traditions as far-ranging as adult literacy education, Black Studies/ethnic studies, community organizing, conflict resolution, counseling, critical pedagogy, critical race theory, developmental education, educational administration, experiential education, higher education, intergroup dialogue, international education, laboratory and T(raining)-group education, multicultural education, teacher preparation, and women's studies. This chapter builds upon the description of these pedagogical communities in the earlier edition of this volume 10 years ago (Adams, Bell, & Griffin, 1997), when social justice educational practice was not well acknowledged and too often dismissed as "touchy feely." In the decade since 1997, active learning and interactive pedagogy have been accepted by educators in schools and colleges, so that the cutting-edge innovations proposed by social justice education no longer need justification.

Nonetheless, although active learning and interactive pedagogies have become more generally accepted, the range and variability within social justice education approaches and strategies (as illustrated by the curricula in this volume) can seem daunting to practitioners unaware of the extensive theoretical, descriptive, and empirical literature that supports and validates this practice. Social justice education practice, like "traditional" teaching and learning, also has a long and distinguished "tradition," and it is the purpose of this chapter to describe some of the educational communities that have contributed to this tradition and to suggest some of the new directions explored during the past decade. We hope that readers will be able to situate themselves within one or more of these broad teaching and learning traditions, and find that key practices with which they are already familiar can be reinforced or elaborated by others with which they are less familiar.

In this chapter, we describe some of the convergent frameworks from various traditions that enrich social justice educational practice. These are organized under headings related to broadly defined communities of pedagogical theory and practice, and we note the many examples of cross-fertilization and intersections among them.

## Social Identity and Cognitive Development Frameworks

It will be clear to readers of this revised edition and its 1997 predecessor that social identity and cognitive developmental models are foundational to social justice education practice. In the aftermath of the Black Civil Rights movement and the context of Black Power, analyses of social identity and consciousness informed social change movements (Hurtado, 1997; Sherif & Sherif, 1970; Young, 1990b) and guided educators, behavioral scientists, and activists in facilitating and assessing educational interventions and personal change (Jackson, 2001). The pedagogical dimensions of social justice education are anchored in a conceptual framework that describes the dynamics of oppression at personal and systemic levels of social analysis (see Chapter 3). Based on this conceptual framework, social identity development models describe the perspectives of learners who hold different social identities at different levels of awareness, knowledge, and openness to change.

As social justice education facilitators, we draw in this volume upon Hardiman and Jackson's social and racial identity development models (1992, 1997; Jackson, 2001) as foundational elements for our pedagogical practice. The Hardiman-Jackson Social Identity Development Model appears on the CD that accompanies this volume, in Appendix 2A. This developmental approach to social identity enables us as facilitators to address differences and support transitions in the worldview and understanding of participants, based on attention to the following: *How does the learner understand her- or himself in relation to the dynamics of oppression described in our classes? What are her or his processes of understanding and meaning making about these social justice issues? What are the effects of different classroom contexts and social groupings, or of different dynamics in group or interpersonal communication and interaction in the classroom or community, in relation to these issues?*

## Social Identity Development Theories

Educational theorists and psychologists have long turned to psychosocial and social-cognitive developmental theory for guidance in understanding transitions in meaning making or consciousness for learners across the life span (Erikson, 1968a, 1968b, 1968c; Oser, Andreas, & Patry, 1992; Pascarella & Terenzini, 1991). But this body of theory has not paid sufficient attention to inequalities of social status or social position, differences in cultural contexts, or the ways in which oppression and cultural context together may shape the worldview and the interactions of participants in our courses.

Erikson acknowledged the formative and socializing role played by social groups significant to an individual's development (1964, 1968), but failed to question the assumptions behind his own normative, gendered, and racialized western concepts of self and social environment. Social identity *development* models, whether focusing upon racial, sexual, class, or gendered identities or the intersections among them, describe a person's awareness and understanding of oppression in the social environment (and also "within" every person) as part of the developmental process. These theories describe differences in the ways that learners may incorporate, resist, or redefine specific manifestations of social oppression (racism and sexism, for example) in the context of his or her own (racial or gendered) identity development. They also provide conceptual organizers that highlight and explain the developmental processes that participants in our courses are likely to move through as they engage with each other in the context of social justice curricula (Hardiman & Jackson, 1997; Jackson, 2001).[2]

Social identity development models[3] have been influenced during the past quarter of a century by social liberation movements such as the Black Civil Rights and Black Power movements (Cross, 1971, 1991, 1995; Jackson, 1976, 2001), "coming out" models of gay liberation (Cass, 1996; Cox & Gallois, 1996), feminist identity models in the women's movement (Bargad & Hyde, 1991; Downing & Roush, 1985), and ethnic and racial identity development models that reflect the ethnic/racial complexities of identity for immigrant communities of color (Duany, 1998; Hurtado, Gurin, & Peng, 1994; Kim, 2001). More recently, intersectional approaches to social identity development (using metaphors such as *fluidity, co-construction, indeterminacy,* and *braiding*) have captured the ways in which identity is simultaneously or interactively raced, classed, gendered, and sexed (Chan, 1995; Cramer & Gilson, 1999; Das Gupta, 1997; Goldschmidt & McAlister, 2004; Hurtado, 1997; Lee & Bean, 2003; Snow & Anderson, 1987; Zandy, 1996).

Social identity development models share several key assumptions: (a) individuals of all social identity groups are affected by pervasive and interacting multiple oppressions, and may respond to situations differently, depending on their consciousness levels and worldview; (b) manifestations of social identity respond in different ways to interpersonal, organizational, and/or societal contexts, and also reflect psychosocial and cognitive development; (c) social identity development theory provides a way of tracking one's progress away from internalized subordination or internalized domination, toward a liberated social identity; (d) interpersonal interactions within groups as well as between groups are affected by developmental differences and different levels of conscious awareness of oppression; and (e) developmental terms such as *stage, phase,* or *worldview* provide convenient metaphors for differentiating levels of consciousness or experiences of identity (see Cross, 1991; Cross & Phagen-Smith, 2001;

Cross, Smith, & Payne, 2002; Hardiman & Jackson, 1997; Helms, 1990, 1995; Wijeye-singhe & Jackson, 2001).

For example, we acknowledge that facilitators as well as participants bring to the classroom an array of unexamined assumptions and implicit worldviews that have been affirmed in their everyday interactions with family, peers, and communities (Rogoff, 2003; see also Chapters 16 and 17). These established worldviews are aspects of identities that help participants feel centered and in control. Not surprisingly, they may be vigorously defended against discordant information or experiences presented in the social justice classroom. Understanding the processes of social identity development as well as the manifestations of different levels of consciousness helps facilitators design curricula that will engage participants at various points of entry in the social justice education process.

Our goal as facilitators is to offer new perspectives and thoughtfully designed learning environments that take into account the participants' current worldviews as well as their potentially more inclusive ways of making meaning. Although we as facilitators may feel a responsibility to challenge and contradict stereotypic beliefs or attitudes held by participants, we need to remember that the decision to shed these beliefs or attitudes belongs to the participant, not to us (Jackson, 2001). We acknowledge the importance of understanding that human beings are never "in" a stage, but that *stage* or *level* is a metaphor for growth or change, and that *lens, worldview, perspective,* and *consciousness level* are equally appropriate metaphors. What "develops" is a person's increasingly informed, differentiated, and inclusive understanding of within-group and between-group commonalities and differences, and a personalized awareness of how these understandings bear on one's everyday behaviors. Beverly Tatum uses the metaphor of a spiral staircase: "As a person ascends a spiral staircase, she may stop and look down at a spot below. When she reaches the next level, she may look down and see the same spot, but the vantage point has changed" (Tatum, 1992, p. 12).

## Cognitive Development Theory

There are a number of factors that suggest why social justice education would pose cognitive developmental challenges for participants, as well as the challenges to social identity described above. These *cognitive* factors include the values, beliefs, and biases that both participants and facilitators bring to social justice education classes; the tenacity of stereotypes and entrenched modes of thinking; and the unexpectedly emotional attachments to beliefs and thought processes rooted in trusted home, school, and religious communities (Bidell, Lee, Bouchie, Ward, & Brass, 1994; King & Shuford, 1996). Theories of college student and adult cognitive development illuminate the evolution of momentous shifts in thinking from concrete to abstract, simple to complex, external authority to internal agency, and from insistence upon clear-cut certitudes to the acknowledgment of doubt and uncertainty (Baxter-Magolda, 1992; Belenky, Clinchy, Goldberger, & Tarule, 1986; King & Kitchener, 1994; Kitchener, 1982; Perry, 1970, 1981).

In the past decade, empirical studies have examined the role of cognitive and affective skill levels for participants in diversity and social justice education classes, especially in the domains of complex thinking, self-reflection, tolerance for uncertainty and ambiguity, and ability to take on multiple and divergent perspectives (Antonio, Chang, Hakuta, Kenny, Levin, & Milem., 2004; Engberg, 2004; King & Shuford, 1996; Lopez, Gurin, & Nagda, 1998; Nagda, Gurin, & Lopez, 2003; Nelson-Laird, 2005). These skills and ways of thinking suggest thresholds for effective participant engagement with social justice education. The curricula presented in this volume call for many of the qualities described in the developmental literature on critical thinking, such as openness to conflicting perspectives from readings or classroom discussions and the ability to reflect upon one's experiences, prior beliefs, and feelings, from one's own as well as another's perspective.

The processes of cognitive development outlined by Perry (1970, 1981) and Belenky, Clinchy, Goldberger, & Tarule (1986) map movement through qualitatively different understandings of knowledge, from a preference for clear certainties to an acceptance of ambiguity and uncertainty, and then toward degrees of comfort with relativistic or contextual thought. Thus, facilitators may find it challenging to facilitate the interaction between participants who insist upon concrete either/or answers and their peers who may appear comfortable balancing several both/and possibilities. Pedagogical strategies are offered in the cognitive development literature to emphasize approaches that are concrete, personal, and experiential, to help concrete either/or thinkers process contradictory information, to provide explicit course structure and support, and to devise open-ended questions for which there may be no "correct" answers. These and other strategies help facilitators anticipate participant resistance to multiple perspectives and provide opportunities for participants to practice the cognitive, social, and reflective skills needed in an emotionally charged, personalized, and complicated domain such as social justice education.

## Laboratory, Training-Group, and Organizational Frameworks

Structured experiments in group process that took place in the 1940s among interracial community leaders and social psychologists provided one of the key precursors to social justice education. Kurt Lewin (1948, 1951), a German Jewish refugee from Nazism, was studying intergroup prejudice and devising methods for direct action in community settings in 1944. His experiments with training groups ("T-groups") and action research (Benne, 1964; Lippitt, 1949; Marrow, 1969) combined the personal with structured group interactions and used simulations and role plays in a set of procedures called "laboratory training" that examined interracial conflicts and provided opportunities to "get into the shoes of the other" (Lippitt, 1949).

From those beginnings, laboratory training has developed structured and facilitated ways that enable participants in groups and organizations to learn about themselves in group-based social situations that focus on the following (adapted from Golembiewski & Blumberg, 1977). Many of these strategies and approaches are notable in the social justice curricula presented in this volume, and include

- *presentation of the self*: opportunities to disclose attitudes, beliefs, and behaviors for the purposes of feedback and learning;
- *feedback*: information from others that enables participants to understand the impact of what they say or do;
- *climate*: a learning environment that provides trust and nondefensiveness, so that participants can change and correct language and behavior that are inappropriate;
- *cognitive organizers or maps*: models derived from research and theory that help participants to organize and generalize from experiences within the group; and
- *experimentation, practice, and application*: opportunities to try out and practice new patterns of thought and behavior, in order to transfer them to back-home situations.

Reflective practices such as *processing* and *feedback* are central to social justice education. *Processing* enables participants to make personal meaning of curricular activities that may be open to multiple interpretations. *Feedback* helps participants understand their impact on each other across differences of culture, social identity, and social status. It helps frame interpersonal and intergroup miscommunication and brings undercurrents of conflict and criticism out into the open where they can be constructively addressed (Lippitt, 1949). Small-group simulations and structured interactions provide specific, socially situated examples of otherwise elusive abstractions about racism, classism, and other oppressions that can then be interpreted and analyzed ("processed") from various perspectives. These ideas have been enriched by raising questions about participants' status and positionality (Bell, 1995; Ellsworth, 1994).

The laboratory tradition also provides methods for generating data on attitudes, stereotypes, and misinformation. These data reflect the affective "inside" of interracial or cross-gender miscommunications as they emerge in the here and now of intergroup communication in the classroom. Such data can be presented by facilitators in their role of participant–observer through sensitive and respectful feedback to defuse difficult situations and enhance participant learning. The group dynamics literature provides many useful ideas about staging simulations and conducting process observation and feedback that can be adapted to social justice topics (Bradford, Gibb, & Benne, 1964; Eitington, 1984; Golembiewski & Blumberg, 1977; Pfeiffer & Jones, 1974). Lewin's insistence (1948) upon the necessary interaction among education, research, action, and explicit transfer from the laboratory situation to daily experience is also evident in social justice education.

## Multicultural Organization Development

Researchers and practitioners from within the laboratory and training group tradition (organization development, or OD), concerned with issues of social diversity and social justice, brought a diversity and social justice focus to the study of organizations and educational institutions through a new multicultural organization development (MCOD) framework of analysis and intervention (Jackson, 2005; Hardiman & Jackson,1994; Jamison, 1978; Miller & Katz, 2002). The MCOD framework uses a developmental continuum from monocultural to multicultural to assess policies and practices that bear upon social exclusion and inclusion within organizations. It enables MCOD professionals "to guide the identification of change strategies that are consistent with the developmental readiness of the educational system" using an MCOD change process (Jackson, 2005, p. 8). This change process involves all parts of our schools, campuses, organizations, and communities in a systems analysis of the barriers to full inclusion and the opportunities for lasting systemic change (Carlisle, Jackson, & George, 2006; Chesler, Lewis, & Crowfoot, 2005; Marchesani & Jackson, 2005).

## Intergroup, Intercultural, and International Training Models

Throughout the 1940s and 1950s, in the aftermath of World War II and the increased awareness of racism in the United States, the interpersonal and group dynamics insights from laboratory training and T-groups were applied to structured intergroup consciousness-raising groups and black-white sensitivity-training groups (American Council on Education, 1949; Cook, 1954; Williams, 1947). These applications were based in part on the belief that awareness and knowledge would be sufficient to reduce prejudice. They were used in 1950s school and military desegregation, antiracism training pioneered by the Southern Christian Leadership Conference (SCLC) and Student

Nonviolent Coordinating Committee (SNCC), and affirmative action and equal opportunity staff development programs of the 1970s and 1980s (Hayles, 1978; York, 1994). These efforts were designed largely to increase intergroup respect and improve cross-cultural communication.

Sociological analyses of race relations at the systemic level brought a more comprehensive grasp of systemic power differentials to the conception and design of change efforts (Hayles, 1978), and supported taking broader systems perspectives on interventions that had previously been focused primarily on individual and personal change (Nieto, 2004; Sleeter & Grant, 1994; Suzuki, 1984).

In this way, intergroup and antiracist training programs became informed by an emerging social science literature of race relations that described specific intervention strategies (Argyris, 1970, 1975), analyzed resistance to change (Coch & French, 1948; Mill, 1974), focused upon the dominance and privileges of the white majority (Hardiman, 2001; Segrest, 1994; Terry, 1975; Wellman, 1977), and generated research concerning conditions under which intergroup contact might reduce or exacerbate racial tensions and prejudice (Amir, 1969; Pettigrew, 1998; Sherif, 1967). The influence of laboratory training and T-groups continues in antioppression workshops within organizations and communities, as well as in course syllabi in schools and colleges (Cross, Klein, Smith, & Smith, 1982; Freedman, 1994; Katz, 1978; Sherover-Marcuse, 1981). In the multicultural classroom and in diversity professional development programs, these intergroup approaches converge with multicultural education pedagogies (Brewer & Brown, 1998) as an outgrowth of Black Studies and ethnic studies, discussed below.

## Cross-cultural and International Training

Cross-cultural training programs, more internationally oriented than domestic intergroup education efforts (Noronha, 1992), also began in the 1950s through study-abroad programs (Batchelder & Warner, 1977), the Peace Corps (Chaffee, 1978; York, 1994), and overseas work by U.S. businesses and government agencies and nongovernmental organizations (Downs, 1978; York, 1994). Given the importance of international staff and participants' being able to adapt to and act within unfamiliar and often ambiguous social situations, it is not surprising that international and cross-cultural training also favored group- and experience-based learning, feedback, application, and transfer strategies that had been pioneered by laboratory education, as discussed above, and that would also become intrinsic to experiential education, discussed below. The pedagogies developed within international and cross-cultural education were necessarily designed to enable participants to effectively handle feelings elicited by emotionally laden real-world situations and events (Condon, 1986). These pedagogies also valued cultural reciprocity among culturally different communication and learning styles, in tandem with the evolving learning style literature (Adams, 1992; Anderson & Adams, 1992), and with teacher-training programs concerned with culturally relevant pedagogy (see below).

## Intergroup Dialogue and Intergroup Relations

Intergroup dialogue (IGD) and intergroup relations programs (IGR) have emerged in schools, colleges, workforces, government, the military, neighborhoods, and communities in recent years as programs designed to bridge social and cultural difference and inequality, and to help resolve intergroup conflict (Schoem & Hurtado, 2001). The IGD process gained national attention as part of President Bill Clinton's "Initiative on

Race" with dialogues in varied formats. At its core, IGD provides face-to-face, interactive, structured, and facilitated learning experiences that bring together participants from two or more social identity groups for a sustained exploration of commonalities and differences, and positions of relative advantage and disadvantage (Zúñiga, Nagda, Chesler, & Cytron-Walker, 2007). IGD fosters intergroup communication, resolves conflict, builds bridges, enhances mutual understanding, and forges action coalitions and networks among participants from different racial, ethnic, gender, sexuality, class, religious, and/or national backgrounds. IGD's foundational theories derive from a substantive research literature on intergroup stereotype, bias, contact, and interaction (summarized in Stephan & Stephan, 2001). It draws upon virtually all of the pedagogies that contribute to social justice education as described in this chapter—and also contributes to the growing body of theory, research, and practice.

Since 1993, theorists, researchers, and practitioners from IGD and IGR programs nationwide began to describe and document their best practices, frameworks for design and implementation, diverse dialogue settings and participants, activities, and interactions, informed by theory and substantiated by research (Schoem, Frankel, Zúñiga, & Lewis, 1993; Schoem & Hurtado, 2001; Stephan & Vogt, 2004). Specific studies explain for practitioners the IGD process model, pedagogical foundations, and principles of design (Zúñiga, Nagda, Chesler & Cyrton-Walker, 2007; Zúñiga, Nagda, & Sevig, 2002) and explore evidence of learning and behavior outcomes (Gurin, Dey, Hurtado, & Gurin, 2002; Nagda, Gurin, & Lopez., 2003).

One of the challenges that IGD/IGR researchers have addressed is the documentation of curricular and pedagogical outcomes to these programs. A finding of great importance to social justice education practitioners concerns the ways in which different types of IGD/IGR interventions reduce different aspects of bias (Dovidio, Gaertner, Stewart, Esses, ten Vergert, & Hodson, 2004). Similarly, researchers continue to explore the affective, behavioral, and cognitive outcomes of structured intergroup classroom interactions (Chang, Hakuta, & Jones, 2002; Gurin, Dey, Hurtado & Gurin, 2002; Gurin, Lehman, & Lewis, 2004; Nelson-Laird, 2005; Orfield & Kurlaender, 2001; Zirkel, Lopez, & Brown, 2004).

## Black Studies, Ethnic Studies, and Multicultural Education

Black and ethnic studies, which emerged from the Civil Rights and Black consciousness movements (Banks, 1996; Cole, 1991; Moses & Cobb, 2001; Suzuki, 1984), fused pride with social action and insisted that education be made relevant to real-world problems of racial inequality and injustice. The movement incorporated a powerful critique of university educational curricula, questioning "*what* is taught in the liberal arts curricula of America's colleges and universities; *to whom* and *by whom* it is taught; *how* it is taught; and *why* it is taught" (Cole, 1991, p. 134, author's italics).

The pedagogies of Black Studies paralleled and also were informed by[4] Freire's vision of agency and empowerment within a real-world and activist teaching and learning process (McWhorter, 1969; Rachal, 1998). Bob Moses and Charlie Cobb (2001, p. 119) describe a pedagogy (in their Algebra Project) that relies in part on "a version of experiential learning [that] starts where the children are, experiences that they share," and then asks that they reflect and form abstract conceptualizations from their reflections, before testing their conceptualizations against their experience. This circular process of "clocking" (imagined by the children as a circle or clock where noon is the experience, quarter past is the reflective meaning making, half past is the conceptual work, and 15 before the next hour is testing against experience), echoes learning style models (see Chapter 4), and informs practice that "is not only experiential, but *culturally* based" (Moses & Cobb, 2001, p. 120). It is important to note that this pedagogical revolution continues to influence social justice pedagogies in math and science education, through the innovative use of cultural and historical examples for students who do not possess the specific kinds of cultural capital assumed by traditional teaching approaches (Bazin, Tamez, & the Exploratorium Teacher Institute, 2002; Gutstein & Peterson, 2005; Powell & Frankenstein, 1997) and who bring different cultural resources to the classroom..

This emphasis on real experience and reflection emerges in feminist pedagogy as well (Butler, 1985; Howe, 1984, see below). Other pedagogical concerns in Black Studies are the relationship of the classroom to everyday experience in community and the rootedness of theory in action (Bunch & Powell, 1983; James & Farmer, 1993). Black feminist pedagogies have elaborated these concerns for a "methodology that places daily life at the center of history" (Russell, 1983, p. 272) and in which "the classroom is the first step in [students'] own transformation" (Coleman-Burns, 1993, p. 141). Barbara Omolade (1987), for example, writes about connecting the personal with the political or historical "to empower students, drawing them out, helping them to make sense of what they already know and have experienced" while creating with her students "an intellectual partnership [that] lessens the power imbalance and class differences ... yet reinforces the knowledge that can be received from the instructor, the readings, and the discussion" (p. 35).

The pedagogical commitment to draw upon different cultural experiences for meaningful classroom examples, to establish the social relevance of what is to be learned and how it might be applied, and to take a critical or oppositional stance to received knowledge all of them elements of Black/ethnic studies not surprisingly have become hallmarks of "culturally relevant teaching" (Gay, 2000; Irvine, 2002; Ladson-Billings & Tate, 1995; Villegas & Lucas, 2002). Culturally relevant teaching affirms everyone's membership in a larger community, envisions teaching as a way to give back to one's community, and uses a Freirean "mining" rather than "banking" approach to teaching (Ladson-Billings & Tate, 1995, pp. 478–479). Culturally relevant teachers maintain equitable and reciprocal teacher–student relations within which student expertise is highlighted, teachers encourage their entire classes rather than singling out individual learners, and students share responsibility for each others' classroom success. Culturally relevant teachers see knowledge as doing, discuss their pedagogical choices and strategies with their students, and teach actively against a "right-answer approach" (Ladson-Billings & Tate, 1995, p. 482).

Culturally relevant teachers are also "caring" teachers, and dare to use the language of love in their writing (Duncan, 2002; Nieto, 2005). This aspect of shared humanity, kept alive in the classroom as a learning community, is also a powerful dimension in feminist pedagogy, especially in the work of Noddings (1999a, 1999b, 2003). Noddings (1999a, p. 17) argues for an ethic of care to compensate for limitations that inhere in an ethic of justice—for example, she would examine "the adequacy of conditions to respond to the needs of those for whom the practice exists." Gay (2000, pp. 45–46) affirms that "teachers demonstrate caring for children as *students* and as *people*" and that students, in response, "feel obligated to be worthy of being so honored" (author's italics).

## Multicultural Education

Multicultural education theorists and practitioners such as Suzuki (1984), Banks (1991), Banks and Banks (1995), Nieto (2004), Grant (1992), and Sleeter and Grant (1994) have enormously enriched pedagogical practices. Suzuki (1984), for example, proposes principles that integrate an experiential, personal focus with collaborative and democratic classroom processes, attention to social identity, sociocultural and historical context, and community-based experiments for change. Nieto (2004) stresses decision-making and social action skills and invokes Freire's call for a critical pedagogy based on the student experiences and viewpoints, not an imposed culture. Sleeter and Grant (1994) describe education that is multicultural and social reconstructionist to empower young people to make social changes.

These writers pose important distinctions between human relations approaches that do not focus on social power and oppression, and those that integrate personal awareness with a systemic change orientation. They bring an analysis of social inequality and institutional power into their discussions of effective classroom pedagogical practice. Nieto especially (1999, 2004) coordinates a systemic analysis of the sociopolitical and institutional contexts for education with passages that vividly convey the individual voices and experiences of teachers and students, with concrete accounts of actual pedagogical practice.

Increasingly, the personal experiences of teachers and students have become pedagogical texts in their own right. They embody first-person narratives—often from specific racial, ethnic, class, disability, and gender perspectives, not only for the purposes of recognition and connection (Nieto, 2003b, 2005) but also, more notably, as a source of inspiration for social justice educators (Allen, 2005; Ayers, Hunt, & Quinn, 1998; Berlak & Moyenda, 2001; Darling-Hammond, French, & García-Lopez, 2002; Ensign, 2005; Howard, 1999; Irvine, 2002; Oyler, Hamre, & Bejoian, 2006; Peña, 2005; Regenspan, 2002). This inspiration, buttressed by detailed pedagogical narrative or description, has enabled social justice pedagogical practice to be carried out in different academic disciplines (Kumashiro, 2004; Ouellett, 2005; Vincent, 2003).

## Social Justice Teacher Education

In the decade since the last edition of this volume, a substantial pedagogical literature has emerged in the field of teacher education, as noted above, and more recently, in educational leadership (Marshall & Oliva, 2006). Areas of pedagogical convergence from among multicultural education, Black Studies, and feminist pedagogies have made the "personal story" of social justice teacher-educators and classroom participants into a way of documenting and communicating "important happenings" and significance in the social justice teacher-education classroom (Gay, 2000, pp. 2–7). The literature expresses concern at the absence of an explicit social justice emphasis in teacher-preparation that draws upon accessible, effective pedagogies; "it teaches against the grain" (Cochran-Smith, 2004, pp. 28–36); and takes the institutional context of schools and schooling into account (Ouellett, 2005; Villegas & Lucas, 2002). This last characteristic is related to work being done in MCOD (see above).

Several writers in social justice teacher education have been noted already (Ayers, Hunt, & Quinn,, 1998; Cochran-Smith, 2004; Kumashiro, 2000, 2004; Nieto, 2005; Villegas & Lucas, 2002). The explicit, intentional emphases on *social justice* and on *social justice education* can be seen in recent discussions of social justice education frameworks for teacher and faculty practice (Adams & Love, 2005; Enns & Sinacore, 2005; Hackman, 2005; Kumashiro, 2000, 2002, 2004; Marshall & Oliva, 2006). New work describes strategies for "Action in social justice in education" (Griffiths, 2003) or for "Developing social justice allies" (Reason, Broido, Davis, & Evans, 2005). Often, these new pedagogies focus upon strategies and materials for teaching by, to, for, and about underrepresented, targeted groups in education—students and teachers of color

(Berlak & Moyenda, 2001; Bolgatz, 2005; Johnson, Delgado Bernal, Ramirez Wiedeman, & Knight, 2002; Tusmith & Reddy, 2002); gay, lesbian, bisexual, and transgender students and teachers (Griffin, 2003; Kumashiro, 2002; McCarthy, 2005); disabled students and teachers (Oyler, Hamre, & Bejoian, 2006; Pliner, 2004); and working-class, rural and raised-poor students and teachers (Anderson, Cavanagh, & Lee, 2000; Collins & Yeskel, 2005; Giecek, 2000; Heintz & Folbre, 2000; Lui, Robles, Leondar-Wright, Brew, & Adamson, 2006; Pittelman & Resource Generation, 2004). White researchers and practitioners have used teaching narratives and personal stories to describe the language and dynamics of advantage, privilege, and color blindness (Bell, 2003a, 2003b; Bell & Roberts, unpublished ms.; Howard, 1999; Roberts, Bell, & Murphy, unpublished ms.; Rodriguez & Villaverde, 2000).

Ongoing accounts of social justice pedagogy, ethnographies of classroom practice, and narratives of teacher preparation and experience appear regularly in education journals such as *American Educational Research Journal; Equity & Excellence in Education; Harvard Educational Review; Race, Ethnicity and Education; Educational Studies;* and *Teachers College Quarterly*—as well as in Women's Studies journals, Black Studies/ethnic studies journals, journals on the teaching of sociology or psychology, and journals on social issues (for recent citations, selected for their social justice education focus, see Adams, Abraham, Burrell, & Whitlock, 2003; Adams, Briggs, Catalano, Whitlock, & Williams, 2005; Adams Briggs, Catalano, Nuñez, Wagner, & Whitlock, 2004, 2006; McCarthy & Whitlock, 2002).

## Critical Race Theory

Disappointment, frustration, and outrage over the unremitting and savage inequalities in school funding and facilities, and, despite the 1954 *Brown v. Board of Education* decision, dramatic school resegregation (Kozol, 2005; Orfield & Eaton, 1996), have led educational theorists and researchers such as Ladson-Billings and Tate (1995) to refocus attention onto the centrality of racism to U.S. sociopolitical, legal, and educational systems. They draw on the work of critical race legal scholars Derrick Bell (1987, 1992) and Richard Delgado (1984, 1995; see Crenshawe, Gotanda, Peller, & Thomas, 1995).

In addition to offering a focused analysis of systemic racism, critical race theory (CRT) offers educators an innovative approach to "voice" by posing argument through the use of metaphorical tales, chronicles, and "counternarratives" synthesized from multiple historical, sociological, and personal , anecdotal, familial sources. These "counternarratives" dramatize and give voice to the experiences of peoples of color, from the perspective of peoples of color (Solórzano & Yosso, 2002). They thus "counter" the hegemonic majoritarian narratives and challenge unexamined assumptions in personal ways. From the outset, critical race theory has focused on multiple communities of color, with counternarratives on the achievement gap, desegregation, tenure, and promotion (see Love, 2004; Lynn & Adams, 2002; Lynn, Yosso, Solórzano, & Parker, 2002; Parker, Deyhle, & Villenes, 1999). Yosso's recent (2006) counterstories present experiences from along the Chicana/Chicano educational pipeline. A recent critical race theory collection provides pedagogical support and guidance for social justice education practitioners (Dixon & Rousseau, 2006). Critical race theory, extended by LatCrit (from the perspective of Latinos/as) and other group-specific writers who draw on critical race theory, provides both the theoretical framework and concrete criteria for counternarratives that challenge the hegemonic master narratives of race and racism that otherwise remain uncritically read both by Whites and people of color (Bell, 2003a, 2003b; Fernandez, 2002).

## Experiential Education Frameworks

A core premise that can be traced through the pedagogies discussed thus far—social identity development, laboratory, intergroup, Black Studies, multicultural and teacher education, and critical race theory—is the assumption that "all learning is experiential" and that most formal, traditional classrooms focus too much on the content at the expense of the process (Joplin, 1995). The primary impetus behind experiential education can be found in the legacy of John Dewey (Griffin & Mulligan, 1992; Hunt, 1995; Kolb, 1984). Dewey introduced the concept of "reflective experience" into educational discourse to refer to the process by which the personal and social meanings of experience interact and become one (Hunt, 1995). The interaction of reflection with experience is core to the work of experiential educators (and also noted earlier in the quotation from Moses & Cobb, 2001).

Except for the work of Kolb (1984), much of the writing on experiential education, remains undertheorized and devoted primarily to practical and pragmatic concerns. Experiential pedagogies usually start from a structured experience and focus the learner's reflections upon that experience. "Experience alone is insufficient to be called experiential education, and it is the reflection process which turns experience into experiential education" (Joplin, 1995, p. 15). Joplin's "action-reflection" cycle grounds experiential education in reflective analysis of a "challenging action," which is preceded by a "focus" and followed by a "debrief" (a process that we call "processing" in the curriculum designs in this volume).

The field of outdoor experiential education (or outdoor adventure) has proven especially challenging and fruitful for social justice education practice—challenging because of its associations with leisure and race/class/gender privilege, in which the "knapsack of privilege" becomes more than a metaphor (McIntosh, 1998; see Appendix 11M), but fruitful because of the opportunities presented by the increased numbers of urban children of color and women participating in outdoor experiential programs (Warren, 2005). Many of the hands-on cooperative activities developed within outdoor experiential education have made their way into social justice education .

The core principles and practices (Proudman, 1995) of experiential education, however, lead to questions of social status and social position concerning "the embodied location of experience and the social organization of the process" (Bell, 1995, p. 9):

> We talk about concrete experience, but I do not know what this means. To me experience "exists" through interpretation. It is produced through the meanings given it. Interpretations of lived experiences are always contextual and specific. Experiences are contingent; interpretations can change... . Perhaps remembering an experience recomposes it so that its meaning changes. (Bell, 1995, pp. 10, 15)

Experiential education has begun to identify core social justice education principles (Koliba, O'Meara, & Seidel, 2000) in order to help participants frame social identity, social status, and social position as important concerns within experiential education (Warren, 1996), in tandem with the questions raised within feminist pedagogy, as discussed below.

## Feminist Frameworks

The centrality of pedagogy to the women's movement can be seen in accounts of its originating descriptions of consciousness raising by women activists in SNCC and

Students for a Democratic Society (SDS) (Evans, 1979; Howe, 1984). Consciousness raising, however, was not all that new as a movement strategy. Florence Howe (1984) traced her own understanding that "all education is political" and her experiments with teaching that "turns upside down" the traditional roles of teacher and learner to her experiences in Mississippi's 1968 Freedom Schools. Howe described the use, in the Mississippi Freedom Schools, of a pedagogy designed to raise the consciousness among black students, a pedagogy that

> begins on the level of the students' everyday lives and those things in their environment that they have either already experienced or can readily perceive, and builds up to a more realistic perception of American society, themselves, the conditions of their oppression, and alternatives offered by the Freedom Movement. (Howe, 1984, p. 10)

This is the pedagogy that, in the women's movement, came to be known as consciousness raising and allowed personal experiences to serve as legitimate sites of knowledge. This core dimension of feminist pedagogy includes the analysis of personal experience to both illustrate and explore larger societal patterns of patriarchal domination and female subordination. Two other features that link feminist pedagogy to pedagogies pioneered during the Civil Rights Movement include the attention to process to ensure inclusive, egalitarian, and empowering learning environments, and the identification of strategies for individual and collective action toward change (Larson, 2005; Rachal, 1998).

## Consciousness Raising

Feminist pedagogy is rooted in the consciousness raising process, directed to social transformation (Bricker-Jenkins & Hooyman, 1986). Consciousness raising starts from the telling of women's individual stories, and then moves to discussion of commonalities among women's experiences in areas such as childhood, jobs, motherhood, or sexual relationships. Consciousness raising involves a "process of transformative learning" that awakens personal awareness, leads to critical self-reflection and analysis, discovers group commonality among a "class" of situations, and provides "an ongoing and continuing source of theory and ideas for action" (Sarachild, 1975, p. 147). Twenty-five years later, this strategy has been successfully used in a variety of contexts including work with elementary school girls (Bell, 1990). Consciousness raising remains a key feminist strategy (Hart, 1991; Larson, 2005), with its postmodern emphasis on "personal stories [which] gain new readings both by the teller and by the other group members" (Damarin, 1994, p. 35). Estelle Freedman (1994) describes her use of peer-facilitated "small groups" to create safe spaces in which her students discuss their personal reactions to classroom learning and integrate the personal with the academic. A similar site, although differently named, can be recognized in the leaderless and often overlapping "affinity groups" described by Elizabeth Ellsworth (1994) as "safer home bases" for support, clarification, common language, and the basis for dialogue among differently situated social groups. The process recurs through the pedagogies described in this chapter, in critical race theory and in multicultural and teacher education, for example.

Several chapters in this volume illustrate the use of homogeneous caucus groups (or fishbowls, in some cases) to generate shared identity-group themes and concerns for discussion, to provoke self-reflection and generate action strategies that can then be discussed by the class as a whole. Homogeneous caucus groups may be leaderless, although structured by guiding questions, or joined by a facilitator who shares the social identity of the group.

With parallels to the Freirean *conscientization* (from the Portuguese *conscientização*), feminist *consciousness raising* has suffered from the feminist backlash and is generally not accorded the same foundational status to social justice education practice as its Freirean counterpart (see Larson, 2005, pp. 136–139). At the same time, feminist educators and theorists continue to enrich both feminism and their own practice by exploring the many areas of connection among these pedagogies—feminist, Freirean, critical race theory, and multicultural—and the resulting convergence has led to powerful new pedagogies for use by social justice educators (see, for example, Enns & Sinacore, 2005; Felman, 2001; Fernandez, 2002; Luke & Gore, 1992; Weiler, 1991).

## Interactive Learning and Teaching

Some of the impetus behind the cooperative, interactive, and dialogic teaching emphasis within social justice education derives from research examining the reasons for women's silence in traditional classrooms (Lewis, 1993; Sadker & Sadker, 1992; Sandler & Hall, 1982) or from research on the relational and emotional dimensions of women's socialization and experience (Clinchy, 1993; Belenky, Clinchy, Goldberger, & Tarule., 1986; Maher, 1985). Here, feminist affirmation of student-based, active learning in collaborative small groups converges with pedagogical traditions of Freirean and experiential practice.

Facilitators who draw upon interactive and collaborative pedagogies find that they can engage participants as active co-investigators who more easily take multiple perspectives on their own prior knowledge and beliefs, on each others' viewpoints, and on the course content (see Maher, 1985). In this sense, "voice" relates to reciprocity and interaction: "Who speaks? Who listens? And why?" (hooks, 1994, p. 40). Because "it is one thing for students to know about cooperation, and another for them to experience it," feminist educators will often structure experiences that hold students accountable for cooperation, help students practice the requisite communication and shared leadership skills, and reward interdependence (Schniedewind, 1985, 1993).

## Being "Other" in the Classroom

Analysis of who is "Other" in the women's studies classroom directs our attention to differentials in power and status for both participants and facilitators (Butler, 1985; De Danaan, 1990; hooks, 1984; Washington, 1985). As the dynamics of power, positionality, and authority play out, silences among and between students of the socially advantaged European American, heterosexual, middle-class groups and students targeted and marginalized by racial or ethnic, gay, lesbian, or bisexual group identities dampen what Spelman (1985, p. 241) calls "the heart of the educational exchange ... the lively exchange among students." Felman's feminist pedagogical narrative (2001) juxtaposes anecdotes that illustrate the complicated dynamics among advantaged and targeted social groups, in a narrative of classroom teaching that explores social advantage and disadvantage based on gender and sexuality, race and ethnicity, religious identity and social class. Interactive feminist classroom pedagogies do not always or necessarily have the desired effects, and the feminist pedagogy literature also documents the not surprising reproduction, within hypothetically democratic classrooms, of social advantage and social marginalization (Crumpacker & Vander Haegen, 1987).

How to bring participants who are silent into a discussion is a complicated question for feminists, who note that in diverse ethnic communities as distinct from traditional classrooms, women have not always or necessarily been silent. "For Black women, our struggle has not been to emerge from silence to speech but to ... make a speech that compels listeners, one that is heard" (hooks, 1989, p. 6). Similarly, silence may not be the result of "voicelessness" so much as a result of "not talking in their authentic voices... . What they/we say, to whom, in what context ... is the result of conscious and unconscious assessments of the power relations and safety of the situation" (Ellsworth, 1994, p. 313). Participants from both advantaged and targeted social groups maintain silence in the classroom for many reasons -- fear of being patronized or polarizing the class; anger, anxiety, or hostility; ignorance of each others' life experiences; resistance to being forced to speak; or lack of skills or practice in intergroup communication or background for understanding their different cultural styles (De Danaan, 1990; hooks, 1984; Kochman, 1981; Spelman, 1985).

Maher and Tetreault's (1994) ethnography suggests that students and teachers can and do struggle to remain aware that their viewpoints are partial and oppositional. Although facilitators may "challenge and undermine the social structures they inhabit ... they cannot completely step outside them" (Maher & Tetreault, 1994, p. 203). "What is perceived as marginal at any given time depends on the position one occupies" (Laurie Fink, quoted in Maher & Tetreault, 1994, p. 164). Sandra Harding's exploration of the epistemological dimensions of "standpoint theory" provides a context within which to challenge traditional classroom practice based on the presumption of neutrality and objectivity (1993).

## Power, Authority, Voice

Feminists have pointed to two sources of asymmetry in the classroom, the one based on the facilitator's institutional power, status, and authority, and the other on gender, class, age, or other social status relative to the participants.

> Do we know what powers we do have and want to have? Do we know what powers our students have, and what powers we hope they might come to have? Are we *clear* about the powers, *wanted and unwanted*, that we as teachers have? (Spelman, 1985, p. 244; author's italics)

Feminists who have been asking how best to use teacher-power and position-authority present a range of options. Some say that "the teacher's power should be abandoned, but not her skills and knowledge" (Hoffman, 1985, p. 148), suggesting a distinction between the traditional teacher–student hierarchy and a place where women's expertise can be recognized. Others use her authority as a bridge, explaining that as students accept the instructor's authority ("I mean the authority of her intellect, imagination, passion"), they can also begin to "accept the authority of their own like capacities" (Culley, 1985, p. 215). And Barbara Omolade (1987) argues that this "authority with, not authority over," is complicated by the multiple ways in which teacher and students are both alike and not alike. She says, "I *am* just like my students" in relation to white male privilege and white female and black male status. "But as an employed intellectual who uses my mind and my skills to instruct others, I have greater status than my sister students in the classroom and in the society" (Omolade, 1987, p. 34; author's italics). Lisa Delpit adds a further alternative, to teach "the culture of power" (1988) as a way of bringing participants from targeted social groups into an understanding of the classroom codes that reflect the culture of those who have power.

## Safety, Emotions, Empathy, and Caring in the Classroom

Classroom safety is integrally tied to respect and the expression of emotion, especially emotions perceived as negative, such as fear, discomfort, threat, pain, anxiety, hostility, and anger. Throughout social justice education, running as a strong undercurrent, is the view that participants must feel that their comments will be treated with respect whether or not the facilitator or other participants agree with them. Participants need to feel confident that facilitators will intervene, if necessary, to prevent statements from provoking attacks by participants who may find them offensive. Striking the optimal balance between the creation of safe spaces and the obligation to subject blatantly false or stereotyped beliefs to thoughtful criticism is no easy task (Rothenberg, 1985, pp. 124–125). Toward this end, feminist facilitators recommend establishing explicit classroom norms to ensure respect and confidentiality, to help participants differenti-ate between willingness to move outside their comfort zones and experiencing threats to their safety, and to guide the handling of conflict and "triggers" (see Chapter 3 and Appendices 3A and 3B; Cannon, 1990; Rothenberg, 1985; Tatum, 1992; Thompson & Disch, 1992).

The feminist themes of process, voice, positionality, safety, power, and authority are related in feminist pedagogy to validating women's feelings and experience. The "connected" way of knowing described by Belenky, Clinchy, Goldberger, & Tarule (1986) combines feeling with thought, and emotion with ideas. Believing that emotions in feminist education guide the exploration of feminist beliefs and values, Fisher (1987) uses student experiences as a basis for improvisation, simulation, dialogue, and ques-tioning, in order to integrate emotion with thought. This valuing of emotion and feel-ings has led social justice educators to appreciate a process orientation as well.

> [We] know that it isn't information alone that educates people.... Our experience is that, when we focus on process in the teaching of oppression, learning occurs at an unusually deep level. The information students gain through the experiences of con-nection, empathy, and identification is not readily forgotten. (Romney, Tatum, & Jones, 1992, pp. 98, 107)

## Social Action

How to live out their new awareness of contradictions, reshaped beliefs and values, and shifts in direction or identity are momentous considerations for participants. "Action is the natural antidote to both denial and despair" (Romney, Tatum, & Jones, 1992, p. 107; see Tatum, 1994). Beverly Tatum has said pointedly that raising awareness without also exploring the possibilities for change "is a prescription for despair. I consider it unethi-cal to do one without the other" (1992, pp. 20–21).

Social justice educators make these connections between awareness and action by helping participants recognize various spheres of influence in their daily lives; ana-lyze the relative risk factors in challenging discrimination or oppression in intimate relations, friendship networks, and institutional settings; and identify personal or small-group actions for change (see Adams & Love, 2005; Bell & Schniedewind, 1987; Griffiths, 2003; Pittelman, 2005; Reason, Broido, Davis, & Evans, 2005). (Examples appear in module 4 of Chapters 6–15, this volume.)

## Critical Pedagogical Frameworks: Paulo Freire

The purpose of Freire's pedagogy is to enable the oppressed to understand that oppres-sive forces are not part of the natural order of things, but rather the result of historical and socially constructed human forces that can be changed by humans. The goal of this understanding is *praxis* (connecting theory and practice) on the part of the oppressed who thus become actors in their own history. Freire notes the role of internalized oppression (see Chapter 3, this volume), by which he means "the duality which has established itself" inside the consciousness of the oppressed:

> They are at one and the same time themselves and the oppressor whose consciousness they have internalized.... Only as they discover themselves to be "hosts" of the oppressor can they contribute to the midwifery of their liberating pedagogy. (Freire, 1970/1994, pp. 32–33)

Liberatory pedagogy not only envisions the recovery of the voices, experiences, and perspectives of socially targeted participants from their "internalized oppression," but also empowers the facilitator to use facilitator-status authority on behalf of the "truth claims" of these marginalized experiences. One key element in Freire's pedagogy, of tremendous value to social justice educators, is his contrast between banking education and problem-posing or dialogic education.

> A Freirean critical teacher is a problem-poser who asks thought-provoking questions and who encourages students to ask their own questions. Through problem-posing, students learn to question answers rather than merely to answer questions. In this pedagogy, students experience education as something they do, not as something done to them. (Shor, 1993, p. 26)

Because dialogue requires critical thinking, it can also generate critical thinking. In this sense, dialogue is not a "technique, a mere technique, which we can use to get some results" (Shor & Freire, 1987, p. 13); rather, as a communicative process that reflects social experience in order to understand the social and historical forces at work, it enables participants to develop "critical consciousness." This process enables participants to name and discuss "coded situations" to uncover "generative themes": "Problem-posing is a group process that draws on personal experience to create social connectedness and mutual responsibility" (Wallerstein, 1987, p. 34; see Freire 1970/1994, 1973; Shor, 1992, 1987 for accounts of these processes).

The facilitator's role in Freirean pedagogy is to provide structure and ask questions until participants begin asking questions of themselves and of each other, to generate the data for critical thinking. Chairs arranged in circles rather than in rows facing a teacher's desk reinforce the imagery of co-learners and co-facilitators. Small groups provide spaces for group listening or action brainstorming. The democratic classroom becomes, in effect, a laboratory for democratic social practice.

The critical and pedagogical writing inspired by Freire has grown internationally as well as in U.S. schools and colleges. Freire's writing, and the writing stimulated by his example, is both theoretical and practical, generative and applied. *Pedagogy* in this sense reaches beyond the basic distinction made at the beginning of this chapter, between process and content, the *how* and the *what*. Rather, pedagogy becomes a metaphor for the process of interrogation, inquiry, and action, especially as applied to the scholarship that examines links between racism and schooling, and the socioeconomic frameworks for liberatory education (see Fischman, McLaren, Sünker, & Lankshear, 2005; Grande, 2004; Leonardo, 2005). Several works on critical pedagogy can ease the access for social justice education practitioners wanting to understand the *how* of critical pedagogical practice: Freire (1970/1994), Horton and Freire (1991), Kanpol (1994), Shor (1987, 1992), Shor and Freire (1987), and Wink (2000). Educators have documented practices that integrate Freirean with feminist practice (Weiler, 1991), and with critical race theory (Smith-Maddox & Solórzano, 2002).

Social justice educators and activists in schools, colleges, workplaces, and various open public spaces have been exploring the pedagogical impact of Freirean-inspired theater, drawing on Boal's *Theater of the Oppressed* (1985) to open up actor–audience dialogues about oppression and liberation, using fluid, permeable scenarios that dramatize oppression while providing opportunities for "spec-actors" (active spectators) to engage in this slice of real life (whether or not active spectators know that this is theater rather than "real life"). Boal's *Games for Actors and Non-Actors* (1992) provides instruction and detail for activities, games, and structured exercises "designed to uncover essential truths about societies and cultures without resort, in the first instance, to spoken language" (p. xix) that can be used in what Boal calls Image Theater, Invisible Theater, and Forum Theater to generate situations of oppression and generate possibilities for political awareness and liberation (Kershaw, 1992; Mindell, 1995). Invisible Theater, for example, sidesteps the proscenium, so that the dramatization does not take place in a theatrical space, agent provocateur actors mingle with the spectators to stimulate reactions, and the audience does not know, in most cases, that it *is* an audience. Forum Theater presents a social justice issue or problem in an unsolved form, so that audience/spect-actors might suggest and enact alternative resolutions. These approaches overlap in current usage, and the games and activities designed by Boal and colleagues have also been incorporated into social justice courses as ice-breakers, dramatized scenarios, and problem–resolution simulations (Rohd, 1998; Schutzman & Cohen-Cruz, 1994).

## Frameworks for Social Justice Education Practice

As social justice educators, we juggle multiple goals. As facilicators, we hope for interactions that are safe and respectful for all participants at the same time that we engage them with information and questions that are likely to elicit emotional as well as thoughtful reflective reactions. We try to be aware of participants' advantaged and targeted social identities and their likely responses from various social identity, cognitive, and experiential positions. We believe that we ignore at our peril as well as theirs the beliefs and assumptions participants bring into our social justice education classes. It is our aim to help them develop credible sources of information, honest personal reflection, comfort with questioning their prior beliefs and assumptions, and sustained critical thinking, as the bases for a larger and more adequate view of their social roles and responsibilities as social agents.

Most, but not all, of the pedagogies presented in this chapter are rooted in academic and activist traditions that have been nourished from a variety of sources and perspectives. The convergence of these traditions is not accidental, in that they share goals of using education to promote positive social change. These distinctive traditions have provided a synthesized body of social justice education that includes the following principles for practice:

1. *Balance the emotional and cognitive components of the learning process*: facilitation that pays attention to personal safety, classroom norms, and guidelines for group behavior.
2. *Acknowledge and support the personal (the individual student's experience) while illuminating the systemic (the interactions among social groups)*: facilitation that calls attention to the here and now of the classroom setting and grounds the systemic or abstract in an accumulation of concrete, real-life examples.
3. *Attend to social relations within the classroom*: faciliation that helps participants name behaviors that emerge in group dynamics, understand group

process, and improve interpersonal communications, without blaming or judging each other.

4. *Utilize reflection and experience as tools for student-centered learning*: facilitation that begins from the student's worldview and experience as the starting point for dialogue or problem posing.

5. *Value awareness, personal growth, and change as outcomes of the learning process*: facilitation that balances different learning styles and is explicitly organized around goals of social awareness, knowledge, and social action, although proportions of these three goals change in relation to student interest and readiness.

These social justice education principles of practice suggest new roles, challenges, and opportunities for facilitators to encourage participants to take responsibility for their own learning and interaction in learning groups, to respect each other, to avoid blame or snap judgment, and to give themselves and each other room to make mistakes while learning. This pedagogy encourages participants learn to look critically at messages about the "Other" coming from the media and other sources of cultural information, practice new behaviors and communication skills, and develop social change scenarios.

The ideas and possibilities presented here may seem overwhelming to someone who is just starting out as a social justice educator, or a classroom instructor who has been socialized and skilled within the traditional lecture-and-discussion mode of higher education. It is encouraging to know that these principles of social justice education echo principles of effective college teaching for *all* participants (Chickering & Gamson, 1987; Hatfield, 1995; Meyers & Jones, 1993). It is our hope that in the chapters that follow, the curricular overviews, designs, resources, and facilitation notes will provide support and encouragement as well as inspiration and new possibilities for novice and experienced social justice educators.

## Notes

1. Authors' italics.
2. The foundational essay on social identity development by Hardiman and Jackson (1997) is located on the CD that accompanies this volume, as Appendix 2A, for the convenience of facilitators and participants.
3. This chapter differentiates *social identity development* models (Cross, 1991; Helms, 1990; Wijeyesinghe & Jackson, 2001) from a similar but distinctive body of theory known as *social identity theory* (Abrams & Hogg, 1990; Hogg, 1995; Stephan & Stephan, 1996). Examples of the application of *social identity theory* to specific social groups can be seen in the work of Cox & Gallois (1996) and Hurtado (1997).
4. See Rachal (1998) for an account of the convergence of these pedagogies in the 1960s and 1970s. Howe (1984) writes of the influence of the Freedom Schools on early feminist pedagogy. The convergence and interrelationship among Myles Horton, Highlander, the Freedom Schools, and Freire are noted in the "talking book" by Horton and Freire (1991), *We Make the Road by Walking: Conversations on Education and Social Change*, and their convergent pedagogical influence can be seen throughout SJE teacher education, for example Cochran-Smith (2004).

# 3

# Conceptual Foundations for Social Justice Education

## CONCEPTUAL OVERVIEW: RITA HARDIMAN AND BAILEY JACKSON

## INTRODUCTORY MODULES: PAT GRIFFIN*

### Conceptual Overview

*Rita Hardiman and Bailey Jackson*

Chapter 1 places social justice education within a broad framework of historically situated discourses on oppression and liberation. Chapter 2 describes the pedagogical frameworks that situate our approach to social justice education. This chapter lays out the conceptual foundation for the curriculum designs presented in this book. In the first part of this chapter, we describe our model of social oppression showing the linkages among different manifestations of oppression that undergird the practices and curricula presented here. The second part of the chapter presents introductory modules that apply these concepts in the classroom. These introductory modules provide participants in social justice education classes with a basic understanding of the con-

---

\* We ask that those who cite this work always acknowledge by name all of the authors listed rather than either only citing the first author or using "et al." to indicate coauthors. All collaborated on the conceptualization, development, and writing of this chapter.

cepts and models that form the foundation for all of the curriculum designs in Chapters 6–15.

During the late 1970s and early 1980s, we (Jackson and Hardiman) were developing and teaching courses on racism, cultural bias, and the impact of race and racism on counselor education and other helping professions (Hardiman & Jackson, 1992, 1997; Wijeyesinghe & Jackson, 2001). Our interactions with colleagues and students engaged in the women's movement, gay liberation, and disability rights movements, and our colleagues who were developing workshops on antisemitism and classism, led us to see striking parallels and commonalities in the manifestations of different forms of social oppression. With this observation in mind, we developed an experimental course on oppression in education that examined the similarities and differences among forms of oppression and explored several disciplinary lenses through which to study oppression, including psychology, economics, political science, sociology, and education.

Our goal became to recognize, describe, and understand generic characteristics of oppression and examine how different forms of oppression are linked together. One of the significant challenges to understanding oppression in contemporary contexts is that systems and manifestations of oppression vary from country to country and in different cultural contexts. There are both active, visible systems of oppression such as the recent apartheid regime in South Africa and the genocide of people in the former Yugoslavia, Darfur, and Rwanda, as well as more sophisticated, invisible systems of oppression. Although connected to these other forms, in this chapter we focus on oppression as it is manifested in the United States.

Our thinking on these issues was originally informed by the work of Fanon (1967, 1968), Freire (1970/1994, 1973), Memmi (1967/1991), Goldenberg (1978), and Miller (1976). Rather than ask historical questions, such as "How did oppression come to be?" or "Which manifestations of oppression are foundational to other forms?" we wanted to describe the dynamics of oppression as an overarching phenomenon with many different manifestations. Our intention was to develop a conceptual framework upon which to base our efforts to help students understand how systems of oppression are constructed and maintained so that they could more readily begin to challenge these systems in their personal and professional lives.

## Oppression as an Overarching Social Phenomenon

Social oppression is distinct from brute force in that it is an interlocking system that involves domination and control of the social ideology, as well as of the social institutions and resources of the society. In this section, we identify six key characteristics of oppression: (a) Oppression is pervasive and systematic, (b) oppression has multiple manifestations, (c) oppression has consequences for everyone, (d) oppression operates on multiple levels and dimensions, (e) we are socialized to accept systems of oppression as normal, and (f) the system of social oppression co-opts the social categories used to describe the differences among and between social groups.

### Oppression Is Pervasive and Systematic

Oppression is not simply the assertion of one group's superiority over another. Nor does it consist solely of random acts of violence, harassment, or discrimination. Oppression provides the base from which oppressor groups define reality and determine what is "normal," "real," or correct. Gramsci (Femia, 1987) describes this as hegemony, or the empowerment of certain cultural beliefs, values, and practices to the submersion and partial exclusion of others. Hegemony controls the ways that ideas become "naturalized" in a process that informs notions of common sense.

Violence, discrimination, exploitation, marginalization, and other forms of differential and unequal treatment are institutionalized and systematic (Young, 1990b). Once institutionalized, these acts often do not require the conscious thought or effort of individual members of oppressor groups but are part of normalized practices, policies, and beliefs that become embedded in social structures.

The oppressed group's culture and history can be misrepresented, discounted, erased, or appropriated by the dominant group. History is presented from the perspective of the oppressor group, and culture is defined by standards and norms that benefit the oppressor group(s). Systems of oppression are woven into the social fabric so that their processes and effects become normalized. Because of the pervasiveness of oppression in all aspects of a society, it is difficult to see the system for what it is: a socially constructed ideology that perpetuates a particular set of hierarchical relationships among different groups. Systems of oppression make it difficult to step outside the system to see it from a different perspective. Additionally, systems of oppression provide explanations for social inequities that are based on assumptions about the naturalness and the inevitability of things as they are. Invisible systems of domination and control are not less damaging. Instead, the more institutionalized, sophisticated, and embedded they become, the more difficult it is to identify, analyze, and challenge them.

## Oppression Has Multiple Manifestations

One of the key assumptions we make about oppression is that the overall dynamics of oppression are similar, but there are multiple manifestations of it. Moreover, these different manifestations of oppression are interconnected and cross-cutting. Almost everyone benefits from some manifestation(s) and is disadvantaged by others. We also experience each manifestation differently according to our multiple memberships in a variety of different social groups.

We believe, as did Audre Lorde (1983), that there is "no hierarchy of oppressions." Each of them dehumanizes us all and affects every one of us in some way. Because of this interrelatedness, addressing one manifestation is inadequate to achieve the goal of a socially just society.

The manifestations of social oppression in the United States that are focused on in this book are (a) ableism, (b) ageism/adultism, (c) antisemitism, (d) classism, (e) heterosexism, (f) racism, (g) religion oppression, (h) sexism, and (i) transgender oppression. For each of these manifestations of social oppression, some groups benefit and others are oppressed.

## Systems of Oppression Have Consequences for Everyone

Social oppression perpetuates the belief that some social groups are superior or normal and establishes systems of advantage and privilege for these groups while simultaneously defining other social groups as inferior and deserving of disenfranchisement, exploitation, and marginalization. The oppressors are members of dominant social groups privileged by birth or acquisition, who knowingly or unknowingly exploit and reap unfair advantage over members of oppressed groups. Members of oppressor groups are also trapped by the system of social oppression that benefits them, and are confined to roles and prescribed behavior for their group. Freire (1970/1994) observed the paradox that in a system of social oppression, oppressor groups are also dehumanized because they have engaged in a process of stealing the humanity of others.

Several authors have explored the phenomenon of privilege to describe the benefits of oppression to advantaged group members (Jensen, 2005; McIntosh, 1988; Rothenberg, 2004; Winant, 1997). We use *privilege* here to denote exclusive advantages or benefits afforded to certain people, based on their group identity or status (Johnson, 2006; McIntosh; Wildman, 1996). These advantages are largely unearned and are often invisible to the people enjoying them. For example, a white heterosexual man who feels safe walking alone at night does not necessary experience this as privilege. He may be unaware that women, gay men, or men of color do not share his assumptions of safety. Privilege, in some cases, is also visible and embraced by those enjoying it. When laws or institutional policies limit access or participation to certain groups, those receiving the benefits often feel entitled to them and believe that other groups are not similarly deserving. For example, laws limiting civil marriage to unions between men and women are often justified with this rationale. Privilege also can involve exempting some classes of people from rules and standards that are applied to others. This privilege of exemption can be seen when those who have wealth or special standing in their communities, for a variety of reasons (race, gender, social, and political connections), break the law. People from privileged groups who are caught speeding, possessing marijuana, vandalizing a neighbor's property, or committing even more serious crimes are sometimes not searched or arrested and may even be released from custody or not charged with having violated a law and receive only a warning from police. In such cases, police use their discretionary power to privilege certain people based on group membership or status.

Much like modern warfare, in which pushing computer buttons can launch missiles from afar, thus keeping soldiers away from the damage inflicted, systems of oppression keep privileged groups distant from the effects of the oppression. Privileged group members can therefore have a more passive involvement in carrying out discrimination, or benefiting from the advantages that accrue to the dominant group, without recognizing their participation in an interlocking system.

At the same time, oppression limits the access, mobility, resources, and self-definition of other people who are members of groups that are thought to be inferior or undeserving. Oppressed groups are those that, in Goldenberg's (1978) terms, are subject to containment, restricted movement, and limited choices. They are treated as expendable, without an individual identity apart from the group; and are compartmentalized into narrowly defined roles. Young (1990b) described the oppressed as people subjected to the "five faces of oppression": exploitation, marginalization, powerlessness, cultural imperialism, and violence. The oppressed or stigmatized people are kept in their place by dominant ideology that is supported by the societal structures. Part of oppressive ideology is denial that oppression exists. Instead, oppressed groups are blamed for their limited circumstances (Ryan, 1972). Memmi (1967/1991) argued that oppression, if it lasts long enough, becomes so familiar to oppressed people that they accept it and cannot imagine recovery from it.

## Choice of Labels for Oppressor and Oppressed Groups

There are currently many terms that are used to describe oppressed and oppressor groups and the individual members of those groups. Oppressed groups are variously referred to as *targets, the targeted, victims, disadvantaged, subordinates,* or *the subordinated.* Oppressor groups are often referred to as *advantaged, dominants, agents,* and *privileged.* The reasons for choosing one term over another vary depending on a number of theoretical, political, pedagogical, and strategic considerations. Indeed, none of these terms is universally accepted. As educators, we must be careful, however, not to trivialize the effects of oppression by the terms that we use in describing this serious

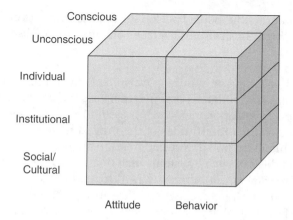

**Figure 3.1**   Multiple Dimensions of Oppression

social condition and the roles individual people play in the maintenance of this social system. We use the terms *oppressor group* and *oppressed group* because they are most closely aligned with the phenomenon of social oppression on which we are focusing.

Other chapters in this book use *advantaged* to refer to oppressor groups and *targeted* to refer to oppressed groups. This choice of terminology is an effort to place the emphasis on the effects of the system of oppression rather than on the social groups and the individual members of those groups who are in the position of oppressor and oppressed in the social system, oppression. These terms highlight the notion that the system of oppression has the effect of providing "advantages" for some social groups and "targets" others to be disadvantaged. We encourage readers to choose terminology based on their own philosophical and educational commitments and local political contexts.

## Oppression Operates on Multiple Dimensions

Oppression is an interlocking, multileveled system that consolidates social power to the benefit of members of privileged groups and is maintained and operationalized on three dimensions: (a) contextual dimension, (b) conscious/unconscious dimension, and (c) applied dimension (see Figure 3.1).

The contextual dimension consists of three levels: (a) individual, (b) institutional, and (c) social/cultural. The conscious/unconscious dimension describes how oppression is both intentional and unintentional. The applied dimension describes how oppression is manifested at the individual (attitudes and behaviors), institutional (policies, practices, and norms), and societal/cultural (values, beliefs, and customs) levels. The conscious/unconscious and the applied dimensions will be discussed further within the descriptions of each of the three contextual levels below:

### Individual Level

Oppression is maintained at the individual level by attitudes or behaviors of individual persons. These attitudes and behaviors can be conscious or unconscious, but their effects are equally destructive. Examples of individual actions or attitudes include the belief that women are not as capable of making reasonable, rational decisions as men are (conscious attitude); a male employer making unwanted sexual comments to a female employee in the workplace (conscious behavior); a white person automatically taking extra care to protect personal belongings when in the presence of black or Latino people (unconscious attitude); or a temporarily able-bodied person speaking loudly or slowly and using simple terms when addressing a physically disabled person (unconscious behavior).

### Institutional Level

Social institutions such as the family, government, business and industry, education, the legal system, and religious organizations are major participants in a system of oppression. Social institutions codify oppression in laws, policies, practices, and norms. As with behaviors and attitudes at the individual level, institutional policies and practices that maintain and enforce oppression are both intentional and unintentional. Examples of the less visible systems include the structural inequality of school funding in the United States, or tax benefits, health care benefits, and similar privileges that are available only to heterosexual couples through the institution of marriage. Other examples of institutional attitudes include the following: lack of an exit interview policy with faculty person of color who take positions elsewhere to determine how a university can improve its ability to retain faculty of color in a predominantly white university (unconscious institutional norm), a business that decides not to provide bereavement leave to a lesbian employee whose partner dies (conscious institutional policy), and a state legislature that passes a law barring illegal immigrants from accessing public services (conscious institutional law).

Institutions fail to address discrimination and inequality or fail to see the discriminatory consequences of their policies and practices as often as they intentionally act to support, maintain, or advocate social oppression: for example, failing to enforce existing sexual harassment policies or deciding to hold an organizational social event in an inaccessible space without thinking that this decision might preclude the participation of members with mobility impairments.

### Societal/Cultural Level

Society's cultural norms and patterns perpetuate implicit and explicit values that bind institutions and individuals. In an oppressive society, the cultural perspective of dominant groups is imposed on institutions by individuals and on individuals by institutions. These cultural norms include philosophies of life, definitions of good and evil, beauty, normal, health, deviance, sickness, and perspectives on time, just to name a few. Cultural norms often serve the primary function of providing individuals and institutions with the justification for social oppression. Examples of these cultural beliefs or norms that influence the perspective of individual and institutional actions and attitudes include the assumption that the definition of a family is a heterosexual nuclear family (can be either conscious or unconscious norm) and the belief that anyone can achieve economic stability in the United States if they are willing to work hard and take personal responsibility for their own achievements (conscious norm).

### We Are Socialized to Accept Systems of Oppression as Normal

We are socialized into a system of social oppression through interactions with individuals, institutions, and culture. We learn to accept systems of oppression as normal through interactions with parents, peers, teachers, and other influential individuals in our lives as they, intentionally or unintentionally, pass on to us their beliefs about oppressor and oppressed groups. We also learn to accept oppression as normal through our experiences in schools and religious organizations, and our encounters with health care, criminal justice systems, and other institutions that affect our daily lives. We may not recognize how our embeddedness in particular cultural norms and values affects our views of oppressor and oppressed groups because of the pervasive presence of oppressor ideology. When viewed as a whole, our socialization into acceptance of oppressive systems, through our interactions with individuals, institutions, and cultural norms and values, constitutes a cycle of business as usual until we are able to interrupt it with information or experiences that call into question the truth of what we have learned about the power relationships among different social groups and our own position vis-à-vis these dynamics. At this point, we can choose to interrupt our socialization, to step out of the cycle of socialization with new awareness, information, and action.

### The System of Social Oppression Co-opts the Social Categories Used to Describe the Differences Among and Between Social Groups

Our social identities/group memberships and the relationships among these identities and memberships have been co-opted, exploited, and distorted to serve the system of social oppression and its manifestations. The system of social oppression uses our membership in various social groups as a vehicle for designating groups that are oppressor and those that are oppressed.

We all have memberships in multiple social identity groups. That is to say, we can be described by our sex, race, sexual orientation, gender, religion, class, age, and ability. Naming our social group memberships/differences serves as a means of naming/describing our social/cultural groupings. They are primarily a way to describe our social group differences. However, the social system/disease of social oppression uses or co-opts the social identity structure to assign dominance/oppressor and subordinate/oppressed status to all individuals and groups in the society. The awarding of unearned or unjust privileges and the enforcement of disadvantages associated are assigned to each social identity group based on a corrupted social identity group membership structure. Though we experience our social group memberships as material, tangible identities (for example, woman, Black, heterosexual), we also inherit status associated with these identities in a system of oppression. In this way, oppression co-opts identities by attaching meaning and status to them that support the system of social oppression. The pervasive and systematic nature of oppression normalizes the redefined nature of the differences associated with social identity and transforms them into oppressed and oppressor social group identities at the expense of more neutral or alternative conceptions of identities and status (see Figure 3.2).

Members of oppressed groups are often more acutely aware of their membership because they experience the daily effects of oppression. Members of oppressor groups, on the other hand, are often unaware of themselves as members of a privileged group because the system of oppression enables and encourages them to view the accomplishments and achievements of their group members as deserved, the result of hard work, virtue, or natural superiority. At the same time, members of oppressor groups often blame the struggles, failures, and anger of members of oppressed groups on their inability, deficiency, or refusal to accept things as they are.

We are born into some of our social identities (e.g., race and ethnicity), and others either can be present at birth or can change or be acquired during our lifetime (e.g., age, class, religion, or physical/development ability). For some social group memberships, such as sexual orientation, the debate over whether we are born into or choose our sexual orientation has political consequences for the struggle for gay, lesbian, and bisexual rights. Opponents of gay rights in part base their arguments on the belief that homosexuality and bisexuality are sinful, immoral, and psychologically disturbed behavior choices. Many, but not all, gay rights proponents insist that sexual orientation is not a choice, but a characteristic with which we are

| Examples of Manifestations of Social Oppression | Examples of Oppressor Groups (US-Based) | Examples of Oppressed Groups (US-Based) |
| --- | --- | --- |
| Classism | Owning Class, Upper Middle Class, Middle Class | Working Class, Poor |
| Heterosexism | Heterosexuals | Lesbians, Bisexuals, Gay Men |
| Ableism | Physical/Developmentally/Psychologically Able-Bodied People | Physically/Developmentally/Psychologically Disabled People |
| Racism | Whites | African American; Asian American; Latina/o; Native American; Multi-Racial People |
| Religious Oppression | Christians | Jews, Hindus, Buddhists, Muslims, Atheists |
| Sexism | Men | Women |

**Figure 3.2**   Examples of Multiple Manifestations and Oppressor and Oppressed Groups

born. Similarly, the transgender rights movement has challenged beliefs about the immutability of sex and gender assigned at birth, calling for a more fluid, nonbinary conception of gender and sex.

Most of us have social identities that are disadvantaged by some forms of oppression and privileged by others. Because our membership in oppressor or oppressed groups can change during our lifetime, our relative status in relationship to our multiple identities is not static. For example, a white man who becomes disabled, a Latina with working-class roots who becomes the CEO of a large corporation, or any of us as we grow old and experience changes in our status associated with aging, declining economic status, or disability experience changes in social status related to group memberships.

Some forms of oppression are closely correlated; thus, if our social identities change and we become targeted by one form of oppression, we are also likely to acquire memberships in other groups where we will experience other forms of oppression as well. Although we are hesitant to say that some forms of oppression "cause" others, we do note the correlations among them. For example, if one is poor in the United States, whether destitute or among the working poor or chronically unemployed, one is more likely to experience illness and impairments that lead to disability due to the lack of access to health care. Similarly, acquiring a disability is closely correlated with being unemployed, being underemployed, or otherwise living on the economic margins of society without adequate access to health care.

The paradigm of "intersectionality," emerging from the fields of sociology, cultural studies, and critical race theory, informs our understanding of the complexities of how people experience privilege and disadvantage based on their social group memberships (Kirk & Okazawa-Rey, 2003; Ritzer & Goodman, 2003). Intersectionality suggests that markers of difference do not act independent of one another. Instead, our various social identities interrelate to negate the possibility of a unitary or universal experience of any one manifestation of oppression. An Asian or Latino gay man experiences the privilege of sexism in different ways than a white European heterosexual man because his experience of male privilege is muted by his identity as a man of color in a racist society and a gay man in a homophobic society.

For pedagogical purposes, this volume examines each manifestation of oppression separately in the designs described in Chapters 6–15. Because our lived experience of the interactions of multiple identities, some privileged and others disadvantaged, cannot be separated, it is important to examine the effects of individual manifestations of oppression in the context of each person's mosaic of multiple identities.

The list of possible social identities is necessarily incomplete as our understanding of systems of oppression and liberation continues to evolve. Because the list of categories of social groups and the descriptions and types of social group change and expand over time with the heightening of our social consciousness, it is necessary that we acknowledge the limitations of current conceptualizations. For example, sexual orientation (gay, lesbian, bisexual, or heterosexual) was not a distinct identity until the late 19th century (Katz, 1995). Likewise, transgender and intersex identities as well as many emergent associated identities like "genderqueer" have only entered the lexicon of oppression in the last 15 years (Nestle, Howell, & Wilchins, 2002).

### Border Identities

No attempt to describe the complex dynamics of oppression can be completely all-encompassing of lived experience. Some social identities do not clearly fit into a binary model of oppressed/targeted or oppressor/advantaged. We acknowledge this limitation with the designation *border identities*. Examples of border identities include people of mixed racial backgrounds, and persons who are bicultural by virtue of being born or raised in one country or culture and moving to a new country and cultural milieu. Adopted children of one race who are raised by persons of a different race may also occupy bordered space. Some social identities that could at one time be characterized as targeted identities have, over time, migrated to the advantaged side of the binary or at least moved out of the targeted category as oppressors rename and redefine targeted groups for their own benefit. For example, Roman Catholics were historically subjected to discrimination and violence, but are now integrated into the fabric of mainstream religions in the United States with considerable political power.

Some individuals with border identities may experience both privilege and disadvantage due to their status, for instance a bisexual man who is in a heterosexual marriage is both privileged by having access to rights only enjoyed by heterosexuals, and also potentially targeted by his identity as a bisexual in a binary system of sexual orientation. A transgender or transsexual man may intentionally or unintentionally benefit from male privilege after transitioning yet still be discriminated against by health care, criminal justice, or other social institutions because he is transgender. Similarly, children of color who are adopted by white families may have access to both race or class privilege from their parents, but are also targeted by racism due to their appearance and cultural characteristics.

### Disadvantaged by Association

Another group that does not fit within the binary notion of oppressed/advantaged or oppressed/targeted are those who occupy an intermediary or gray space due to their relationship to family members or significant others in their lives. These persons might include parents, spouses/partners, or family members of people with disabilities; parents or siblings of lesbians, gays, bisexual, or transgender people; or white people who are married or partnered to people of color, or have children of color. For example, able-bodied parents of a disabled child may have privilege as nondisabled people, yet their life circumstances are profoundly affected by their relationship to a disabled individual—their child. Their child's targeted status affects the family's income, housing, ability to travel, employment, and social interactions in their community. They may have to deal with the stereotypes or stigma attached to their child or other family member.

Similarly, a white member of a mixed-race couple or a white parent of mixed-race children is affected by racism in a secondary way and has less clear access to systems that advantage Whites in a racist society, due to this relationship. The mixed-race family's ability to find housing, social acceptance, employment, and safety is affected by racism, and this therefore has an impact on the white member of the family as well as the family members who are people of color. People in these situations are "disadvantaged by association" and live a dual existence: having access to privilege and resources in some capacities due to their personal dominant status, but also being a target of discrimination and other manifestations of oppression due to their family status. Individuals who are disadvantaged by association, however, do not automatically become allies. Many individuals in these relationships continue to support or participate in the system of oppression to which their loved one, and indeed they, are subjected by encouraging assimilation or other strategies that collude with oppression.

## Relationships Among and Between Oppressor and Oppressed Groups in a System of Oppression

Though participants in our classes often assume that oppression is maintained primarily by the intentional actions of members of the oppressor groups, oppressive systems depend on active and passive relationships between and among oppressor and oppressed groups. These relationships are described here as (a) internalized relationships, (b) vertical relationships, and (c) horizontal relationships. To help participants understand how oppression is manifested at the individual level by oppressor groups that dominate in interaction with oppressed groups that collude, we developed the model of vertical, horizontal, and internalized relationships presented here. This model draws from Fanon (1968) and Freire (1970/1994) regarding horizontal aggression and violence.

This model requires placing one social identity membership in the foreground, for the sake of analysis, while putting other social identities in the background. For example, to represent a male–female relationship in the context of sexism, as one of a privileged male and disadvantaged female, we must also take into account that the male may be gay, or a person of color, or disabled, and the woman may be heterosexual, white, or able-bodied. Though we foreground sex in this example, we also understand the complexities of examining relationships between privileged and disadvantaged groups while also taking into account the ways that other identities mediate privilege and disadvantage. Although we acknowledge that this single-identity focus has limits and represents neither the lived complexity of any one person's multiple identities nor the reality of a person's different advantaged and disadvantaged identities, we use this model to highlight the hierarchical relationship between oppressor groups and targeted groups.

### Internalized Subordination and Domination

Oppressive systems work most effectively when both advantaged and targeted group members internalize their roles and accept their positions in the hierarchical relationship between them.

*Internalized subordination* refers to ways in which the oppressed collude with their own oppression. Targeted social groups can live within a system of oppression that injures them or deprives them of certain rights without having the language or consciousness. Freire (1970/1994) used the term *conscientization* to name the oppression or to understand their situation as an effect of oppression rather than the natural order of things. Memmi (1967/1991) described this process as *psychological colonization* when disadvantaged groups internalize their oppressed condition and collude with the oppressive ideology and social system. Freire (1970/1994) refers to this process as oppressed groups playing host to the oppressor.

People who have been socialized in an oppressive environment, and who internalize the dominant group's ideology about their group, have learned to accept a definition of themselves that is hurtful and limiting. They think, feel, and act in ways that demonstrate the devaluation of their group and accept themselves as members of an inferior group. For example, internalized subordination is operating when oppressed group members question the credentials or abilities of members of their own social group without cause, yet unquestioningly accept that members of the oppressor group are qualified, talented, and deserving of their credentials. Internalized subordination also operates when target group members curry favor with dominant group members and distance themselves from their own group.

Conscious collusion occurs when oppressed group members knowingly, but not necessarily voluntarily, go along with their own mistreatment to survive or to maintain some status, livelihood, or other benefit, as when a person of color silently endures racist jokes told by a boss. Such collusion is often seen by the targeted group member as necessary to "live to fight another day." The more insidious form of collusion is unconscious, not knowing that one is collaborating with one's own dehumanization: for example, when a woman blames herself for the actions of her rapist or batterer or when gay and lesbian people, in order to gain acceptance from heterosexuals, exclude members of their community who look or act "too gay."

*Internalized domination* refers to the behaviors, thoughts, and feelings of oppressor group members who, through their socialization as members of the dominant group, learn to think and act in ways that express internalized notions of entitlement and privilege. Members of oppressor groups are socialized to internalize their dominant status so that it is not seen as privileged, but is experienced as the natural order of things, as rights, rather than as a consequence of systems that provide them with advantages not readily available to other groups.

Examples of internalized domination include men talking over and interrupting women in conversation, while simultaneously labeling women as chatty. Privileged groups learn to expect to be treated well and to be accommodated, as when English-only-speaking people in the United States get irritated when English language learners speak English with an accent. Extreme examples include the "erasure" of targeted group members by failing to acknowledge their existence or importance. For example, historical presentations that Columbus discovered America erase the existence of native peoples who preceded him by several thousand years.

## Vertical Relationships

The relationship between advantaged and targeted can be viewed as a one-up and one-down pattern, with advantaged people operating out of internalized privilege in a manner that is oppressive to targeted people, who simultaneously collude to some degree out of their own internalized subordination. Vertical interaction involves conscious and unconscious dehumanization and denial of rights of the targeted group by the advantaged group: for example, a male supervisor harassing a female employee, a white person refusing to be examined by a doctor of color, or a school principal supporting an athletic participation fee for students without considering the inability of some families to pay the fee.

Though individual targeted group members may also harbor prejudice against advantaged group members, this prejudice does not have institutional or cultural support that characterizes the actions of an advantaged group member toward a targeted group member. The terms *reverse racism* or *reverse sexism* are sometimes used to describe the prejudicial actions of targeted group members toward advantaged group members. However, the lack of institutional and cultural "backup" for this prejudice highlights the inequality in social power supporting the actions of privileged groups and targeted groups. For example, individual people with disabilities can harbor prejudice or even hatred toward able-bodied people, but there is a lack of institutional and cultural support for the prejudices of people with disabilities in an ableist society.

### Horizontal Relationships

We use the term *horizontal* to describe relationships and interactions among members of the same social group, who, at least on one dimension of social identity, are "equal" in status. This term comes from the terms "horizontal violence" or "horizontal hostility," used by Pharr (1988) to refer to the phenomenon of oppressed people misdirecting their rage at other members of their group or at other groups also oppressed by a particular form of oppression rather than directing their anger outward toward the more dangerous and powerful members of advantaged groups. Horizontal relationships may take two forms: *targeted-to-targeted horizontal oppression* and *advantaged-to-advantaged horizontal oppression*

#### Targeted-to-Targeted Horizontal Oppression

Targeted-to-targeted horizontal oppression is the conscious and/or unconscious attitudes and behaviors exhibited in interactions among members of the same targeted group that support and stem from internalized subordination (for example, women who ostracize or label other women who do not conform to traditional gender roles).

One of the strategies used to institute and maintain oppression is that of divide and conquer within groups of oppressed people. Dividing people who share common cause is a way to maintain control by fomenting strife among the targeted groups so that their energy is diverted to fighting among themselves rather than challenging the dominant group. Horizontal violence or aggression like this occurs when oppressed people lash out at each other in the same identity group or another similarly targeted identity group. In the early years of the U.S. labor movement, fear, stereotypes, and misinformation about ethnic and racial groups were used to break up unionizing efforts by poor and working-class workers in mills and factories.

Creating buffer groups and extending privileges to one or more targeted groups are other dimensions of the divide-and-conquer strategy, for example, pitting racial groups like Asians and Blacks against each other so that resentment and anger are directed at other oppressed racial groups who have slightly more resources or access. This occurred during riots in Los Angeles in 1992, when businesses owned by Asians were vandalized by Blacks and Latinos.

#### Advantaged-to-Advantaged Horizontal Oppression

This refers to the conscious and/or unconscious punishments that oppressor groups bestow on other members of their group who violate the ideology of the oppressive system (for example, men teasing and hazing other men who share equal responsibility for child care and household maintenance with their female partners). Another example is the case of Anne Braden, an antiracist activist in the United States in the 1960s. Anne and her husband participated in numerous actions challenging racism, and when they sold their home to a black family, they were tried on obscure sedition charges (treason against the state) and jailed (see Braden, 1991; Fosl, 2002).

Advantaged-to-advantaged relationships also include conscious or unconscious rewards given to those who actively support or passively accept the oppressive system: for example, membership in an informal social group of white men at work in which valuable information is shared about career opportunities that is not available to women or people of color in the organization. Horizontal oppression is also at work when members of advantaged groups physically attack, criticize, or ostracize other group members who work with disadvantaged groups to dismantle oppression, for example, when white people who challenge racism are called racial slurs or when the sexuality of heterosexual people who challenge heterosexism is questioned.

## Individual and Social Change

Now that we have described the characteristics of social oppression and the dynamics that serve to maintain oppressive systems, we turn our attention to an equally important topic in our courses: fostering individual and social change. The focus of the curriculum designs in this book is on the examination of individual participants' attitudes, beliefs, and actions in the context of an understanding of oppression in all of its dimensions—intentional and unintentional actions and attitudes on the individual, institutional, and social/cultural levels—and then to encourage action to eliminate oppression. To be able to envision oneself as a change agent, it is necessary to have language that describes this role. We use the terms *ally* for advantaged group members and *empowered targeted group members* to refer to these change agent roles.

### Allies

Allies are members of the advantaged group who act against the oppression(s) from which they derive power, privilege, and acceptance. Individuals who choose to ally themselves with people who are targeted by oppression may have different motivations for their actions. Some allies may be motivated by an understanding that their privileges come at a cost, and working against oppression can be in one's self-interest. For example, understanding how eliminating architectural barriers that limit people with disabilities' access to buildings can also benefit temporarily able-bodied people as they themselves age or become disabled. Other allies may be motivated to act by altruistic feelings or by a moral or spiritual belief that oppression is wrong. Another source of motivation may come from one's experience as a person who is "disadvantaged by association" with people who are targeted. For example, having a child who is disabled or having a family member "come out" as lesbian or gay can spur family members to become allies against the oppression that is targeting their loved ones, and themselves by extension. Whatever the motivation for allies, their role as change agents, working with other privileged group members or in coalition with targeted group members to challenge systems of oppression, is an essential aspect of eliminating inequality.

### Empowered Targeted Group Members

Empowered targeted group members reject the inferior status assigned to them in a system of oppression. They work to overcome the internalized aspects of oppression they were socialized to accept. They have pride in their group identity and enjoy a sense of community with others from their social identity group. Feminist conscious-raising groups and gay pride marches are two examples of these efforts. Most importantly, they develop a liberatory consciousness that leads them to become actively involved in efforts to eliminate oppression. These efforts include working in coalition with allies or working with other targeted group members. Finally, empowered targeted group members understand the interconnections among different manifestations of oppression and the importance of challenging them all, not only the ones that affect them most directly.

Efforts to challenge oppressive systems are most effective when guided by a conceptual analysis of social justice issues. Likewise, efforts to educate about oppression and social justice must be grounded in a clear conceptual understanding of the characteristics and dynamics of oppression. The conceptual model described here forms the foundation for our classes.

## Introductory Modules

*Pat Griffin*

This section of the chapter describes the introductory modules for each of the curriculum designs courses described in Chapters 6–15. The activities in these modules introduce participants to the conceptual framework for understanding oppression described in the first section of this chapter. These modules introduce basic vocabulary, key concepts, and the overall theoretical perspectives upon which each of the curriculum designs is based. For example, participants learn and practice using interaction guidelines followed in all of the curriculum designs. Participants also learn that, though there are multiple levels on which oppression operates, in these courses we focus on developing individual awareness, knowledge, and action plans. Because these introductory modules describe oppression as an overarching phenomenon, participants also begin to understand the interconnections and interactions among the different forms of oppression. By examining their own identities and experiences, participants begin to explore key concepts that form the conceptual foundation for all of the curriculum designs described in this book.

## Single-Issue Focus

In the course curriculum designs described in Chapters 6–15, we examine one form of oppression at a time, designed generally for classes of 25–30 participants. In each design, we discuss parallels and interconnections among the different forms of oppression, and course readings are chosen to help participants understand these connections. We teach these single-issue courses from a "multicentered" perspective that recognizes the interactions of other social group memberships with the one under study in the single-issue design. For example, in a racism course we encourage participants to talk and think about how their gender, sexual orientation, religion, class, and ability interact with their racial identity in affecting their life experiences.

There are advantages and disadvantages to this single-issue approach. Focusing on one issue at a time can simplify a complex and difficult process. Participants can think about one social identity and concentrate their attention on understanding the dynamics of one form of oppression at a time. For participants who have never given much thought to oppression, this focus can facilitate learning. Focusing on one form of oppression at a time also enables that form of oppression to be explored in greater depth than would be possible in a multiple-issue approach. One of the disadvantages of the single-issue approach is the danger of disregarding the impact of other social group memberships on the dynamics of the topic under study. For this reason, it is important to address the impact of other social group memberships in class discussions and readings as well as to invite participants to examine the impact of other social group identities on their experiences and perspectives.

## Essential Introductory Content

The introduction described here consists of two modules, each requiring 3 hours to complete. Depending on the course format and flexibility, selected parts of these introductory modules can be covered in several sessions or in one or two in-depth sessions. Course facilitators can choose to present selected parts of this introduction if time constraints do not allow for completion of both modules. We believe, however, that all introductory modules should include the following fundamental parts *prior* to (or incorporated into) the beginning of the single-issue curriculum designs described in Chapters 6–15:

1. Individual introductions of participants and course goals
2. Identification of discussion guidelines
3. Review of course outline, evaluation criteria, and other administrative information
4. Introduction to a conceptual framework for understanding oppression
5. Introduction to basic conceptual vocabulary
6. Exploration of participant targeted and advantaged social group memberships

In the instructional format we use, participants enrolled in all curriculum designs meet together for the introductory modules; then each course meets separately from 9 a.m. to 5 p.m. on a Saturday and Sunday during the semester. For example, racism, sexism, heterosexism, classism, ableism, and antisemitism all meet on different weekends. Each weekend course is 1 credit. Typically, 25–30 participants are enrolled in each weekend course. Participants may enroll in one or more weekends during the semester, but they take the introductory sessions only once. We find that spending 2 days together focusing on social justice issues enables participants to reach a depth of self-exploration and examination that is more difficult to achieve in a more traditional course format where participants meet together for 1 or 2 hours, two or three times a week. During the introductory sessions, we present the information described here. With this format, all participants during the semester have been introduced to the same basic foundational information about the dynamics of oppression.

For differently organized classes, such as semester-long courses, there are numerous options for organizing the activities from the introductory modules and the curriculum designs that follow. For example, this material can be presented over an extended time with shorter class periods similar to traditional courses that meet two or three times a week for the entire semester (see alternative formats described in Chapter 4). Though we have chosen to present introductory information to all participants enrolled in any single-issue course during a separate class session, this material could also be integrated into each curriculum design. We encourage social justice education teachers to choose how to present introductory information based on the specific characteristics of a teaching situation, but to address these key issues in some way at the beginning of the course.

These introductory modules introduce theoretical concepts and vocabulary that are used in each of the curriculum designs (see Table 3.1). Within the curriculum

**Table 3.1**  Structure of Curriculum Designs

| Introductory Modules | |
|---|---|
| Module 1 | Module 2 |
| Module 3 | Module 4 |

designs, Module 1 typically includes activities designed to help participants build community. Module 1 also reviews concepts presented in the introductory module, reviews discussion guidelines, previews the specific course agenda, and begins introductory work on the topic for that course. The second and third modules usually focus on developing a more in-depth understanding of how the particular form of oppression works and give participants an opportunity to engage in more discussion and exploration. The fourth module helps participants begin to think about how what they have learned can be integrated into their lives outside the course. Participants identify action plans and develop support networks among classmates, or make plans for continuing their learning about social justice issues.

In addition to the in-class activities described in Chapters 6–15, we require participants to complete selected readings for each course and integrate these readings into written reactions to the readings and the course. *Readings for Diversity and Social Justice* (Adams, Blumenfeld, Castañeda, Hackman, Peters & Zúñiga, 2000) is an excellent source of readings to accompany many of the single-issue curriculum designs in this book.

## Key Concepts

Several key concepts guide and structure course activities. These are conceptual organizers that we use in the curriculum designs described in Chapters 6–15.

- Social Diversity and Social Justice
- Social Oppression and Liberation
- Social and Individual Change
- Social Identity Categories
- Social Group Memberships: Advantaged and Targeted Identities
- Social Power
- Privilege and Disadvantage
- Social Construction
- Stereotypes
- Socialization
- Prejudice
- Collusion
- Internalized Dominance and Subordination
- Historical Context (social construction of identities and oppression)
- Multiple Levels: Personal, Institutional, and Cultural
- Horizontal and Vertical Oppression
- Advantaged Role: Becoming an Ally
- Targeted Role: Becoming Empowered
- Parallels, Interconnections, and Uniqueness of All Forms of Oppression
- Multiple Identities
- Partiality of Knowledge and Experience
- Individual and Collective Action
- Organizational Change

These key concepts provide guidance for choosing learning activities and help facilitators identify conceptual themes that cut across multiple manifestations of oppression. Each learning activity is designed to help participants understand one or more of these concepts. Because we conceptualize oppression as an overarching phenomenon with many different manifestations, most of the activities in the curriculum designs are interchangeable in that, with modification, any learning activity can be used to teach about several different forms of oppression.

The courses described in Chapters 6–15 address social justice issues in the United States. Although acknowledging that international events affect the experiences of social groups in the United States and that addressing oppression in other parts of the world is important, it has been our experience that an effective way to begin to explore social justice issues is through participants' experiences in the United States. Racism in Great Britain, South Africa, or Japan, for example, although related to racism in the United States, involves different social groups in different sociohistorical contexts. In addition, an explicit U.S. focus enables participants to explore their participation in perpetuating social injustice and acting to eliminate it. Though our courses focus on the United States, international students enrich class discussions by sharing experiences they have had both in their home cultures and in the United States.

Moreover, it has been our experience that a rich mix of different social identities, experiences, perspectives, and awarenesses creates the most productive learning environment for all participants. The role of the facilitators is to help create a class environment in which participants can share their experiences, express their beliefs, ask questions, and listen respectfully to the experiences and questions of others.

Over the past few years, the mainstream media and conservative educators and politicians have raised concerns about "political correctness" on college campuses. These critics charge that political correctness generates intolerance for the expression of views that contradict a progressive party line, stifles debate, and violates basic principles of free speech. Critics sometimes claim that social justice education courses indoctrinate students in a class atmosphere that discourages dissent and the free expression of all beliefs.

Although it is accurate to say that our courses present a definite perspective on social justice, we believe it is essential that participants are encouraged, rather than discouraged, to express their beliefs and to talk about their experiences. They are also encouraged to be critical of and reexamine their experiences and beliefs in light of other perspectives presented in class. However, no one is evaluated on the congruence of their beliefs with the perspectives presented by other participants or the facilitators. (See Chapter 4 for student evaluation information.)

## Underlying Assumptions

Several underlying assumptions create a philosophical foundation for our social justice education practice. Facilitators who plan to use this sourcebook should be aware of these assumptions. We also share these assumptions with our participants.

### It Is Not Useful to Argue About a Hierarchy of Oppressions

We believe that little is gained in debating which forms of oppression are more damaging or which one is the root out of which all others grow. Though we acknowledge that some participants believe that there is an urgent need to address one form of oppression over others, we present the perspective that each form of oppression is destructive to the human spirit. We do, however, identify ways in which specific forms of oppression are similar or different, but do not rank the differences identified. Our courses are based on the belief that even if we could eliminate one form of oppression, the continued existence of the others would still affect us all.

## All Forms of Oppression Are Interconnected

In addition to our use of an underlying conceptual framework to understand the dynamics of all the forms of oppression, we also recognize that each participant in our courses is a collage of many social identities. Even though a course is focused on sexism, for example, each participant's race, class, religion, sexual orientation, ability, and gender affect how that participant experiences sexism. We encourage participants to explore the intersections of their different social group memberships and also to understand the similarities in the dynamics of different forms of oppression.

## Confronting Oppression Will Benefit Everyone

Most people can understand how confronting sexism will benefit women or how addressing ableism will benefit people with disabilities. We also believe that men and nondisabled people will benefit from the elimination of sexism and ableism. Unfortunately, some participants react to social justice education as if engaged in a conflict in which one group wins and another loses. However, when people are subjected to oppression whatever their social group membership, their talents and potential achievements are lost and we all suffer from this loss. Moreover, we all have spheres of influence and connections that link us to people who are directly affected by oppression. Even if we are not members of a particular disadvantaged social group, we have friends, coworkers, or family members who are. In addition, we might become members of disadvantaged social groups in the future if, for example, we become disabled or have a change in economic circumstances. Another way we are hurt by oppression is that many people who are members of groups that benefit from oppression live with a burden of guilt, shame, and helplessness and are never sure whether their individual accomplishments are earned or the result of advantages received due to their social group membership. Confronting oppression can free members of all social groups to take action toward social justice. The goal in eliminating oppression is an equitable redistribution of social power and resources among all social groups at all levels (individual, institutional, and societal/cultural). The goal is not to reverse the current power inequity by simply interchanging the groups in power positions.

## Fixing Blame Helps No One; Taking Responsibility Helps Everyone

We present the perspective that there is little to be gained from fixing blame for our heritage of social injustice. We are each born into a social system in which we are taught to accept things as they are. Nothing is gained by feeling shame about what our ancestors did or what our contemporaries do to different groups of people out of fear, ignorance, or malice. Taking responsibility, in contrast, means acting to address oppression. Rather than becoming lost in a sense of helplessness, our goal is to enable participants to understand how they can choose to take responsibility in their everyday lives for confronting social injustice.

## Confronting Social Injustice Is Painful *and* Joyful

Most participants do not want to believe that they harbor prejudices about groups of people. Confronting these prejudices in themselves and others is difficult. Participants need to open themselves to the discomfort and uncertainty of questioning what is familiar, comfortable, and unquestioned. Facing the contradictions between what participants have been taught to believe about social justice and the realities of the experiences of different social groups is complex. Participants learn that some of what they were taught is inaccurate. Some necessary information was not part of their education. Participants need to be assisted through this process with hope and care. At the same time, we believe that understanding social oppression and taking action against it can be a joyful and liberating experience. Some participants' lives are changed in exciting and life-affirming ways as a result of their experiences in social justice education courses. They find ways to act on their beliefs and make changes in their personal lives that profoundly affect their personal and professional relationships.

## Overview of Introductory Modules

| Introductory Module 1: Orientation and Theoretical Framework (3 hours) | Introductory Module 2: Application to Our Experience (3 hours) |
|---|---|
| 1. Introductions (30 min.) | 1. Multiple Identity Wheel and Critical Incident Review (60 min.) |
| 2. Course Description (15 min.) | 2. Exploring Privilege and Disadvantage (60 min.) |
| 3. Class Participation Guidelines (20 min.) | Break (15 min.) |
| 4. Comfort Zones, Learning Edges, and Triggers (25 min.) | 3. What Is an Ally? What Is Empowerment? (20 min.) |
| Break (15 min.) | 4. Closing the Introductory Module and Preparing for Curriculum Designs (25 min.) |
| 5. Introduction to Oppression Dynamics Conceptual Framework (35 min.) | |
| 6. Exploring the Social Group Membership Profile (30 min.) | |
| 7. Closing (10 min.) | |

## Introductory Module 1

Time needed: 3 hours

### Goals

- Identify group participation guidelines.
- Develop a common vocabulary.
- Develop a common conceptual understanding of oppression dynamics.

**Key concepts**: social diversity education, social justice education, oppression, social group memberships (advantaged and targeted), multiple identities, interconnections of manifestations of oppression, privilege, prejudice, social power, socialization, stereotype, levels and types of oppression, vertical oppression, horizontal oppression, internalized oppression

### 1. Introductions (30 minutes)

Ask participants to find a partner, and then ask each person to take 2 minutes to share (a) their name, (b) what they are studying in school or what their work is, (c) what led them to take this course, (d) an expectation they have about the course, and (e) what other social justice–related courses or workshops they have attended previously. Return to the whole group, and ask each person to briefly introduce themselves to the group by giving their name and what they hope to learn from the course. Introduce yourself and other co-facilitators. Describe your interest in and commitment to social justice education. Sometimes, a personal story about the first time you attended a social justice education course or workshop helps to ease participant anxiety and also models the kind of personal sharing that is encouraged in the course.

## 2. Course Description (15 minutes)

Describe the course outline, work requirements, and grading information, and attend to other administrative matters.

## 3. Class Participation Guidelines (20 minutes)

Because the course content is challenging and the class process is experiential and interactive, participants need some basic discussion guidelines in order to develop trust and safety. Ask the participants to identify guidelines that would help them participate fully in class activities. This can be accomplished in groups of three to five and then shared with the whole group or brainstormed as a whole-group activity. Some of the guidelines we find helpful include the following:

- Set own boundaries for sharing
- Speak from experience, and avoid generalizing about groups of people
- Respect confidentiality (do not share personal information shared in class outside the class)
- Share air time
- Listen respectfully to different perspectives
- No blaming or scapegoating
- Focus on own learning
- Respect different experiences and perspectives

As each guideline is proposed, ask the participants to identify benchmarks or indicators of each guideline so that the meaning of the guideline becomes understood and shared. For example, how will they will "know" if respect or listening is happening, or what safety means? Allow discussion about each item, and before proceeding to the next one, make sure that each participant understands the meaning.

Once a set of guidelines has been proposed, review each item; ask for clarification, additions, or changes. Explain that once these guidelines are agreed to, each person is responsible for adhering personally as well as in relation to the group process.

### Facilitation Issues

As various guidelines are offered, the facilitators may identify cultural, linguistic, generational, or gendered differences that are embedded in the conversation about guidelines. The indicators of listening, for example, may vary within and between cultures. It is important to begin to note how our various "identity lenses" impact what we see and how we make sense of what we see. Facilitators may also need to pose questions in relation to some guidelines to clarify meaning. For example, if safety is mentioned, note that there is a difference between being safe and being comfortable so that the group does not confuse experiencing tension or confusion with not being safe. Depending on the length of the course, use these guidelines as a reference point for processing group interaction. Periodically through the course, ask how successful the group has been in adhering to the guidelines; ask if there are other guidelines to add, delete, modify or clarify. Additionally, be careful not to have too many guidelines that limit or restrict communication, honesty, and difference of expression (based on culture, language, age, gender, etc.).

## 4. Comfort Zones, Learning Edges, and Triggers (25 minutes)

The concepts of comfort zones, learning edges, and triggers can serve as guides to help participants understand and explore their reactions to class activities and other participants' perspectives. Present the following information to participants (see Appendix 3A).

*Comfort zone*: We all have zones of comfort about different topics or activities. Topics or activities we are familiar with or have lots of information about are solidly inside our comfort zone. When inside our comfort zone, we may not be challenged and we may not be learning anything new. Often, when we participate in a discussion or activity focused on new information or awareness, or the information and awareness we have or are familiar with are challenged, we may find ourselves out of our comfort zone or on its edge. If we get too far outside of our comfort zone, we may tend to withdraw or resist new information. One goal in this course is to learn to recognize when we are on the edge of our comfort zone.

*Learning edge*: When we are on the edge of our comfort zone, we often are in the best place to expand understanding, take in a new perspective, and stretch awareness. We can learn to recognize when we are on a learning edge in this course by paying attention to internal reactions to class activities and other people in the class. Being on a learning edge can be signaled by feelings of annoyance, anger, anxiety, surprise, confusion, or defensiveness. These reactions are signs that our way of seeing things is being challenged. If we retreat to our comfort zone, by dismissing whatever we encounter that does not agree with our way of seeing the world, we may lose an opportunity to expand understanding. The challenge is to recognize when we are on a learning edge and then to stay there with the discomfort we are experiencing to see what we can learn.

Ask participants to take 2 minutes each to share with a partner a time they can remember being on a learning edge with new information or a new skill. Provide some examples of your own to model self-disclosure and to help participants to understand what you are asking them to identify. For example, talk about learning a new sport skill or dance, taking a difficult academic course, or being in another country where you were not familiar with the culture or language. Ask participants to respond to this question: What internal cues will alert you that you are on a learning edge in this course? Encourage participants to recognize pounding hearts, sweaty palms, butterflies in the stomach, excited focused attention, confusion, fear, or anger as cues to recognize personal learning edges.

*Triggers*: Triggers are words or phrases that stimulate an emotional response because they tap into anger or pain about oppression issues (Obear, 2000). The term *trigger* connotes an instantaneous response to stimuli without accompanying conscious thought. Typically, triggers convey, consciously or unconsciously, a stereotypical perception or an acceptance of the status quo (see Appendix 3B). Examples of statements that some people may experience as triggers include the following:

"I don't see differences; people are people to me."

"What do you people really want anyway?"

"I think men are just biologically more adapted to leadership roles than women."

"I feel so sorry for people with disabilities. It's such a tragedy."

"If everyone just worked hard, they could achieve."

"Homeless people prefer their life."

"I think people of color are blowing things way out of proportion."
"If women wear tight clothes, they are asking for it."

Invite participants to identify a process for naming triggers and learning edges in ways that encourage open and respectful dialogue. This could be as simple as inviting participants who feel triggered or on a learning edge to say so. This can be a significant learning opportunity for everyone in the course and often is a "breakthrough" experience when the learning is "real time" because it is happening right in the class. Ask participants who are triggered or are on a learning edge to explain why. If participants are triggered by a comment by someone else, invite participants who triggered someone else to listen and try to understand what was upsetting about their comment. Ask them to listen rather than defend their comment. Encourage participants to view these discussions as "food for thought" rather than attempts to change individual participant's views on the spot. No one can focus effective attention on personal learning when they feel defensive or chastised.

## Facilitation Issues

Many participants come into social justice education courses with some fear that they will "make a mistake" by triggering someone else. Encourage participants to look at triggers as learning opportunities for everyone. Though members of privileged groups are usually more likely to say something that triggers targeted group members in a class, anyone, regardless of social group membership, can trigger another person. Sometimes members of privileged groups are triggered by what other members of their own group say, and targeted group members can be triggered by someone from their group as well.

### Break (15 minutes)

### 5. Introduction to Oppression Dynamics Conceptual Framework (35 minutes)

This lecture introduces participants to Jackson and Hardiman's conceptual model, which was presented in the Overview section of this chapter. This conceptual model forms the foundation for the course curriculum-designs presented in this volume. Although it is not the only way to understand oppression, we find it helpful in introducing participants to key concepts and helping them to develop an introductory understanding of how oppression works. It is important to stress that this model is one attempt to take a snapshot of dynamic and complex phenomena for the purposes of understanding and identifying a common vocabulary. In this spirit, invite participants to raise questions about the model and identify its limitations as well as its usefulness in helping us to understand social oppression. Describe to participants that oppression is an overarching phenomenon with individual manifestations based on different social identity categories (see explanations in Chapters 1, 2, and the Overview section of this chapter). After this introduction, give a lecture using the visual aids provided in Appendices 3C through 3I to explain the conceptual framework underpinning the curriculum designs in Chapters 6–15. (Note that the oppression lecture PowerPoint slide show in appendix 3I.)

### Oppression Framework Lecture

**Post some social identity groups on newsprint, an overhead transparency, or PowerPoint (see Table 3.2).**

**1. Define *social group*:**    a group of people who share a range of physical, cultural, or social characteristics within one of the social identity categories. We are focusing here

**Table 3.2**   Examples of Social Identity Categories

Sex
Class
Sexual orientation
Physical, developmental, and psychological ability
Race
Religion
Age
Gender
Ethnicity

**Table 3.3**   Examples of Social Identity Categories and Social Groups

| Examples of Social Identity Categories | Examples of Social Groups |
| --- | --- |
| Race | Black, White, Latino/a, Native American, Asian, biracial, multiracial |
| Sex | Female, male, intersex |
| Gender | Women, men, transgender, genderqueer |
| Religion | Jewish, Buddhist, Muslim, Christian, Hindu |
| Sexual orientation | Lesbian, heterosexual, bisexual, gay |
| Class | Owning class, working class, poor, middle class |
| Ability | Able-bodied, disabled |
| Age | Elders, adults, young people |

on social identity groups and the social group memberships typically included in discussions of social justice and oppression. Write the examples of social groups shown in Table 3.3 on newsprint, an overhead transparency, or PowerPoint.

**2. Social groups have different statuses:**   Describe the meaning of different statuses: *These social group memberships are not neutral differences. Within each social identity category, some people have greater access to social power and privilege based upon membership in their social group. We call this group the advantaged group. We call groups whose access to social power is limited or denied the targeted group. Other descriptors for these two groups include the following:*

- *Advantaged: agent, dominant, oppressor, privileged*
- *Targeted: target, subordinate, oppressed, disadvantaged*

*Social groups are afforded different status in the United States based on a multiplicity of historical, political, and social factors. These different statuses affect the abilities of people in the different groups to access needed resources. Some social group members are afforded an advantage, whereas other social groups are disadvantaged based on their social group memberships.*

*These status differences, and the social identities themselves to some extent, are socially constructed. We define social construction as taken for granted assumptions about the world, knowledge, and ourselves assumed to be universal rather than historically and culturally specific ideas created through social processes and interactions. For example, the concept of race and the assignment of people to racial categories are based on political, social, and historical dynamics that change across time and culture. These racial differentiations are institutionalized to maintain an imbalance of power and status among different social groups. Similar examples of social construction apply to sexual orientation, disability, and other categories of identity."*

Put the "Matrix of Oppression" (Appendix 3C) on newsprint, an overhead transparency, or PowerPoint. This chart describes differences in status among various social groups. *The groups in the "Privileged" column are typically afforded an advantage because of their social group membership. The groups in the "Targeted" column are typically disadvantaged by group membership. The groups in the "Border" column are groups that may or may not be privileged or disadvantaged or were disadvantaged in the past.1 Including the border social groups column is a way to illustrate that not all social group memberships are easily categorized as either privileged or tarketed. Determining who has privilege or disadvantage is complex because cultural, social, and historical changes affect which groups are privileged and which ones are not. Some people inhabiting border social groups are able to "pass" as members of the privileged group to avoid being disadvantaged by their social group memberships. Others are accorded uninvited privilege because others assume they are members of an advantaged group. For example, a bisexual person, a targeted social group membership, in a heterosexual relationship is often assumed to be heterosexual and treated according to this assumption. Moreover many identities are fluid in that people's group memberships can change through choice, accident, or other circumstances. Gender identity, physical ability, and social class are examples of this fluidity. Changes in group status also occur over time. Social groups once routinely discriminated against in the United States, for example Roman Catholics, are now accepted into mainstream society, and the Catholic Church has significant social influence.*

**3. Differentiate between *social diversity education* and *social justice education*:**    as a way to help participants understand the importance of social group status in social justice education. Emphasize that social diversity education is an important part of education about social differences, but we will be focusing on social justice education and issues of inequality and social hierarchy in this course.

- *Social diversity education*: focuses on *appreciating* social differences without an emphasis on power dynamics or differential access to resources and institutional support needed to live safe, satisfying, productive lives.
- *Social justice education*: focuses on understanding the *social power* dynamics and social inequality that result in some social groups having privilege, status, and access, whereas other groups are disadvantaged, oppressed, and denied access. *Social power* can be defined as access to resources that enhance one's chances of getting what one needs or influencing others in order to lead a safe, productive, fulfilling life.

**4. Define *oppression*:**    a system that maintains advantage and disadvantage based on social group memberships and operates, intentionally and unintentionally, on individual, institutional, and cultural levels.

- I*ndividua*l: attitudes and actions that reflect prejudice against a social group (intentional and unintentional).
- *Institutional*: policies, laws, rules, norms, and customs enacted by organizations and social institutions that disadvantage some social groups and advantage other social groups. These institutions include religion, government, education, law, the media, and the health care system (intentional and unintentional).
- *Societal/cultural*: social norms, roles, rituals, language, music, and art that reflect and reinforce the belief that one social group is superior to another (intentional and unintentional).

Provide some examples of the different levels and types of oppression, such as those in the following list, and invite participants to identify other examples:

Individual unintentional:

- A high school teacher assumes all of her students are interested in dating classmates of the other sex.
- A teacher who prides himself on being fair to all of his students calls on boys to answer questions three times more often than he calls on girls.

Individual intentional:

- Someone uses racial slurs to refer to Blacks and Puerto Ricans.
- A parent asks to have his child moved out of a gay teacher's classroom.

Institutional unintentional:

- Students celebrate Christmas in school, but not other winter religious holidays.
- A town hall building does not have an entrance that is accessible to people using wheelchairs.

Institutional intentional:

- A state adopts a law prohibiting the legal recognition of lesbian and gay relationships.
- An employment agency steers Blacks toward low-paying, domestic, or custodial positions.

Societal/cultural unintentional:

- Standards of beauty for women are based on white norms: blond, fine hair; blue eyes; and fair skin.
- A belief in individual merit and hard work being rewarded by economic success leads to an assumption that poor people are lazy and undeserving.

Societal/cultural intentional:

- English is designated as the "official" language in the United States.
- European culture is assumed to be superior to other cultures.

Encourage participants to identify examples from each of the manifestations of oppression discussed. Clarify any examples that are unclear. Call attention to the misconception among many people that oppression operates only on the individual level, and note that this is often what is most obvious in day-to-day interactions. Many people perceive racism, sexism, or other forms of oppression to be individual acts of meanness or hatred only. To fully understand oppression, it is essential that participants recognize that it operates on multiple levels. Differentiate individual prejudice from oppression, and emphasize that it is only one of the three levels on which oppression operates.

**5. Define** *privilege***:**    unearned access to resources (social power) only readily available to some people as a result of their advantaged social group membership. Provide some examples of privilege:

- Feeling physically safe in most places in your everyday life
- Having connections through friends or family that facilitate reaching your career goals
- Having access to health care
- Having your family legally sanctioned and protected through marriage
- Sharing similar dominant cultural expectations with others in your school or workplace
- Being seen by others as an individual rather than stereotyped as a member of a particular social group

**6. Oppression is an overarching concept with many different manifestations**   (see Appendix 3D). Note that racism, sexism, classism, religious oppression, heterosexism, and the other isms are manifestations of oppression.

**7. We are socialized into systems of belief.**   Help participants understand how oppression depends on socialization into systems of belief that mask injustice and promote dominant "commonsense" rationales for accepting social injustice as part of the natural order, the result of meritocracy, hard work, or individual talent. Use the "Cycle of Socialization" in Appendix 3E to describe how we learn to accept oppression as "the way things are" through our interactions with individuals, social institutions, and cultural practices and beliefs. *We were each born without prejudice into a world that has systematically taught us to accept an oppressive system. We learned this from people who love and care for us: parents, teachers, or friends. What we learn is reinforced in schools and by the media as well as other institutions with which we interact. To change how this system operates, it is necessary to take individual and collective action for social change.* Use the "Cycle of Liberation" (Appendix 3F) to illustrate the process of change. Invite participants to look at this course as an opportunity to critically examine assumptions and beliefs they have learned, to develop a different perspective that incorporates some of the social justice perspectives presented in the course, and to identify actions they can take to make the world a more socially just place for all.

**8. Oppression is based on negative stereotypes of targeted groups**   that are familiar to members of advantaged and targeted groups.

Describe that within each form of oppression, members of both advantaged and targeted groups can usually readily identify negative stereotypes of the targeted groups, whether they believe in these stereotypes or not. Define *stereotypes* as generalizations about the attributes of a particular social group that disregard individual diversity within the group. Stereotypes are sometimes based on historical information that is taken out of context, and stereotypes of targeted groups are often assumed not to apply to advantaged groups or are reframed as positive characteristics when applied to advantaged groups. Moreover, advantaged group members' knowledge of stereotypes is frequently not related to actual experience with targeted groups. Instead, they are learned from sources such as parents, other adults, or distorted media images (see Appendix 12C).

Ask participants to quickly call out a few stereotypes of men and women to illustrate how easily we can generate lists of stereotypes for different social groups. Make it clear that calling out stereotypes does not indicate one's agreement with them.

**9. Oppressive systems are maintained by different dynamics among and within social groups.**

**Vertical dynamics of oppression:**   Vertical oppression occurs in interactions between advantaged groups and targeted groups that maintain and reinforce oppression (see Appendix 3G). Actions of the advantaged group that affect the targeted group are the most easily identified oppression dynamic:

- An able-bodied person refusing to hire a person with a disability because of a belief that they could not "do the job" or that they would make others in the workplace uncomfortable
- A group of white men beating up a man of color while calling him racial epithets

- White male legislators passing laws negatively affecting women and people of color
- Heterosexual people harassing or make fun of lesbians and gay men

Actions by members of a targeted group against a member of an advantaged group, however, are more complicated and are not equivalent to the actions of a member of an advantaged group against a member of a targeted group. Point out that both members of advantaged and targeted groups are capable of prejudice, abuse, violence, and hatred, but only the advantaged groups have the institutional and cultural power to back up their prejudices against targeted groups. For example, individual people of color might feel or express prejudices against white people, just as individual women might have prejudices against men, but as a group, neither people of color nor women hold many positions of power in major institutions in the United States that would enable them to turn their prejudices into widely held institutional and social policy. Claims of "reverse racism" or "reverse sexism" fail to take this power dynamic into account.

**Horizontal dynamics of oppression:**    Explain that interactions among advantaged group members as well as interactions among targeted group members can maintain and reinforce oppression (see Appendix 3G).

Examples of horizontal oppression among members of an advantaged group include the following:

- Men ridicule other men who are pro-feminists.
- Gentile parents discourage a daughter's romantic interest in a Jewish man.
- Boys who don't conform to traditional "masculine" interests and behaviors are harassed by other boys.

Examples of horizontal oppression among members of targeted groups:

- Blacks who harass a Korean shop owner
- Lesbians and gay men who exclude other gay men who act "too effeminate" or lesbians who look too "butch"
- Working-class people who call other working-class people "white trash"

**Internalized dynamics of oppression:**    Internalized oppression occurs when members of advantaged and targeted groups adopt the dominant ideology about their own groups that maintains and reinforces oppression (see Appendix 3G). As part of the socialization process, members of both groups internalize social messages about their own groups as well as messages about other groups.

*Internalized domination*: when members of the advantaged group accept their group's socially superior status as normal and deserved. Examples include the following:

- A heterosexual who believes only heterosexuals are good parents
- A man who considers only men qualified for a management position
- Christians who believe that their spiritual practices are best for everyone

*Internalized subordination*: when members of targeted groups internalize dominant social messages of inferiority about their group. Examples include the following:

- A person with a learning disability who believes that she is unable to attend college or feels ashamed of the need to use disability services on campus
- A person from a working-class background who believes he is not smart enough to attend college or feels out of place among students from middle-class backgrounds

**10. Complexities of multiple identities:**    Conclude the lecture by reminding participants that, because we all have multiple identities, oppression is a complicated and
dynamic phenomenon (see Appendix 3H): We each have a sex, gender, sexual orientation, race, ethnicity, socioeconomic class, ability/disability, religious or spiritual perspective, and age. Even though we may focus on one manifestation of oppression, how
we experience disadvantage or privilege is related to our other social group memberships. How a woman of color experiences the disadvantage of sexism is intensified by
being a member of another targeted group because of her race. How a white gay man
experiences the disadvantage of heterosexism is softened by being a member of an
advantaged group because of his race. Most of us have some social group memberships
that provide us with privileges and other memberships in which we experience disadvantages. Our multiple identities interact to intensify or "soften" the effects of oppression and the consequent privileges and disadvantages we experience. A wealthy white
man with a disability has access to resources that can mediate the effects of his disability because he can buy assistive technology or personal care services that a Black, poor
woman with a disability could not afford.

## Facilitation Issues

Although no visual representations can capture the complexity or human reality of
oppression, the charts and models accompanying this lecture provide a way to illustrate and examine the relationships among groups within a power dynamic. Facilitators might want to use the border social groups in the "Matrix of Oppression" (see
Appendix 3C) to highlight changing power dynamics and positionality of individuals
and groups in different historical and geographical contexts.

### 6. Exploring the Social Group Membership Profile (30 minutes)

Using the "Social Group Membership Profile" in Appendix 3J, ask participants individually to indicate their social group memberships for each social identity category
listed. Tell them they will be describing their profile to one other person who they
choose. Stress that the social group memberships listed are examples and not exhaus-
tive. Invite participants to add other social group memberships that best describe
themselves. Ask participants to fill in the membership column first. After participants have completed the membership column, ask them to complete the status column for each of their memberships. Post or refer them to the "Matrix of Oppression"
(see Appendix 3C) to identify the status, either advantaged or targeted, for each of
their social group memberships.

    After participants have completed their individual profile, ask them to choose a
partner and discuss the following questions, which you write on the chalkboard, newsprint, or PowerPoint:

- Which of your social group memberships were easiest to identify?
- Which of your social group memberships were most difficult to identify?
- What questions are raised for you about your social group memberships?
- Which of your social group membership statuses were easiest to identify?
- Which of your social group membership statuses were most difficult to identify?
- What questions are raised for you in trying to identify your social group
  membership statuses?

After 15 minutes, bring their attention back to the large group, and ask for volunteers to
give their answers to the questions discussed in pairs.

## Processing

Point out that everyone belongs to multiple social groups, though most of us are more aware of some group memberships than others. Ask them what they think accounts for our being more aware of some social group memberships and statuses and less aware of others. Ask participants how this activity enabled them to think about themselves in new ways. Describe some of your own social group memberships and statuses. Note that we are often more aware of our targeted social group memberships and less aware of our advantaged social group memberships. This is part of the dynamics of oppression that can obscure its effects on both advantaged and targeted groups.

## Facilitation Issues

This framework often raises questions about the names used to represent different social groups. Emphasize that this framework is flexible. It changes in different historical contexts, geographical locations, and preferred usage by targeted groups at different times. Its purpose is to provide participants with a common understanding, not to rigidly impose particular language. Stress that the issue of self-definition is extremely sensitive, open to interpretation and contradiction, and constantly in flux. Invite participants to describe different names they prefer for their social groups and to ask questions about how other groups name themselves.

Participants might also have questions about which groups are included within each identity category. For example, Jewish participants may identify as being members of an ethnic or racial group rather than exclusively as a religious group. Invite participants to use the model in ways that feel most comfortable for their own self-definitions and experience. These issues can be taken up in more detail in the single-issue curriculum designs that follow.

This profile also raises questions about how to identify social group memberships that are not clearly differentiated. For example, biracial and multiracial participants might have difficulty categorizing themselves. Encourage these participants to self-identify by indicating the racial heritages of both their parents. Participants typically ask questions about how to define different age cohorts or social class membership. Provide participants with some initial (and flexible) guidelines for making these decisions, and emphasize that these categories are arbitrary, to be revisited and examined in more detail in the single-issue courses. For age, we recommend that participants think of ages 1–17 as young people, 18–29 as young adults, 30–65 as adults, and 65 on as elders. Participants who are 18–25 years old or younger can think of their parents' or caregivers' occupations and incomes when identifying social class. These guidelines help participants identify their social group memberships without having to get too deeply into any one topic at this point. Make sure participants know that they can leave blank any social group memberships they choose not to disclose, and may control what they wish to disclose and with whom they wish to share this information.

Identifying social group status is also a challenge for some participants. For men in the class who do not have any targeted identities, ask them to think about their experience as young children and recall feelings about the absence of power and privilege available to young people. Some participants resist assigning themselves privileged status because they don't want to associate themselves with an oppressor role. Others do not want to call themselves disadvantaged because they feel empowered by their targeted group memberships. Remind participants that in this model, the status of their social group memberships is related to larger social and historical dynamics and is not necessarily reflective of how they view themselves. Invite participants to see themselves as members of several social groups, some of which receive privileges and some of which do not. Asking participants to be aware of how their personal collage of social group memberships interacts can be a challenge for those who have not previously thought about having multiple identities. Encourage participants to hold onto their questions and explore them further in the curricula to follow.

### 7. Closing (10 minutes)

Ask for volunteers to share one thing they learned during Introductory Module 1. Also invite participants to identify questions that were raised for them during the module. Prepare participants for the second introductory module by previewing the goals of that module, as described below.

### Introductory Module 2

Time needed: 3 hours

### Goals

- Explore social group memberships and experiences.
- Explore personal experiences of privilege and disadvantage.
- Practice group participation guidelines.

**Key concepts**: multiple identities, advantaged and targeted group memberships, socialization, privilege, ally, empowerment

### 1. Multiple Identity Wheel and Critical Incident Review (60 minutes)

The purpose of this activity is to provide a vehicle for participants to further explore their social group memberships and to identify how they experience privilege and disadvantage. Provide each participant with the "Identity Wheel" in Appendix 3K. Using the social group profile created in the first introductory module (see Appendix 3J), ask participants to create an identity wheel. Have them divide the wheel into different sections, with each section representing one of their social group memberships. Instruct participants to indicate awareness of their different social group memberships by the size of the segment they allot to it. Group memberships of which they are more aware will be a larger slice of the circle, and memberships of which they are less aware will be smaller slices. Use the sample identity wheel in Appendix 3K to explain the process. In the sample identity wheel, the participant has indicated that she is much more aware of being black, a woman, and working class than she is of being able-bodied, gender conforming, or a young adult. Next, have participants color code or in some way differentiate their advantaged identities and their targeted identities.

Participants will now use the identity wheel activity as a foundation for further exploring the various social group memberships they have indicated on their identity wheel. Ask participants to find one or two others in the class with whom they would like to spend time discussing their social group membership experiences further. Distribute the critical incident inventory questions (Appendix 3L) to focus this discussion.

After 30 minutes, bring the group back together, and ask if anyone would like to share something they learned about their own identities. Make sure that respondents honor the confidentiality of the small-group discussion by only sharing from their own identity wheel and not from those of other members in their group.

## 2. Exploring Privilege and Disadvantage (60 minutes)

The purpose of this activity is to provide an opportunity for participants to deepen their understanding of the effects of social group memberships on their experience of privilege and disadvantage. Give participants the "Privilege and Disadvantage Inventory" in Appendix 3M. Ask them to take 10 minutes to complete the inventory individually. When everyone is finished, ask participants to gather in discussion groups of four to five people, and instruct them to use the following questions to guide a discussion of the inventory. Encourage participants to form small groups with people with whom they have not worked in other small groups.

### Small-Group Discussion Questions

1. What are your reactions to the process of doing the activity?
2. What are your reactions to identifying some of the privileges and disadvantages associated with some of your social group memberships?
3. What statements were particularly striking to you? Why?
4. What questions about privilege and disadvantage are raised for you?
5. How was your experience of privilege and disadvantage the same or different from others in your discussion group?

After 30 minutes of small-group discussion, invite participants to take a 15-minute break, and then return to discuss the inventory with the whole class.

## Break (15 minutes)

When the class has reconvened, invite participants to share responses to the following questions:

1. What did you learn about your own privileges and disadvantages?
2. What questions were raised for you about privilege and disadvantage?
3. How did this activity help you better understand the dynamics of oppression?

### Facilitation Issues

This activity can be revealing for participants who have never thought about the ways in which they are privileged. For participants who are already aware of the ways in which they are disadvantaged by some of their social group memberships, it is an important insight to realize that they also have privileges based on their other social group memberships. Some participants resist seeing their own or their family's accomplishments as partly due to privilege. Acknowledge that this realization can be confusing. Encourage them to remain open to further exploration of the effects of their social group memberships and to listen to the experiences of other participants who differ from their own identities and experiences. Invite them to continue to explore these questions in the curriculum designs to follow.

## 3. What Is an Ally? What Is Empowerment? (20 minutes)

The purpose of this activity is to introduce the concepts of *ally* and *empowerment*. Both of these concepts are important parts of developing an action-oriented, change-oriented focus in the course. Participants need to be able to see how change can happen and how they can play a role in creating a more socially just world. Begin the activity by displaying the following definitions on a chalkboard, newsprint, or PowerPoint:

Targeted Person as Empowered

When targeted group members refuse to accept the dominant ideology and their subordinate status, and take actions to redistribute social power more equitably

Working-class and poor mothers organize to fight cuts to welfare benefits and demand better child care programs

Students with disabilities sue a school to gain access to all buildings and programs

Advantaged Person as an Ally

A member of an advantaged group who rejects the dominant ideology and takes action against oppression out of a belief that eliminating oppression will benefit everyone, not only targeted groups

A man objects to sexist jokes told in the men's locker room

White people join an organization addressing racism in the workplace Coalition

When a form of oppression has multiple targeted groups, as do racism, ableism, and heterosexism, targeted group members can work in coalition with other targeted social groups they are not part of (e.g., lesbians can be allies to bisexual people, African American people can work in coalition with Native Americans, and blind people can be allies to people who use wheelchairs).

Ask participants to review their identity wheel from the first activity in this module. Ask them to write the word *ally* next to each of their advantaged memberships and *empowered* next to each of their targeted social group memberships. Encourage them to think about how their perspectives as allies or empowered are important parts of beginning to address manifestations of oppression discussed in the course. Remind them that their experiences in each of the curriculum designs to follow will be affected by their various memberships in advantaged and targeted social groups and will differ depending on the focus on the course. Encourage them to think about how they can become allies and feel more empowered to challenge social injustice. Distribute the "Ally Handout" in Appendix 3N. Ask them to review the handout in preparation for participation in the curriculum designs to follow.

## 4. Closing the Introductory Module and Preparing for Curriculum Designs (25 minutes)

Remind participants that the next part of the course will focus on one specific form of oppression. Make sure all participants know when and where the next class will meet. Tell them what reading assignments they must complete in preparation for the course and that a written reflective reaction to the readings will be their "ticket" into the course. End the introductory module by asking each participant to identify (a) something they learned from the introductory modules that will stay with them, and (b) one thing they are looking forward to in the social justice curriculum designs to come.

## Note

1. The author acknowledges the work and influence of Alison George and Andrianna Foiles, graduate students at the University of Massachusetts Amherst, in developing a matrix of oppression that includes border social groups.

# 4

# Designing Social Justice Education Courses

## LEE ANNE BELL AND PAT GRIFFIN

If we are to be intentional about social justice education, we need a clear and well-thought-out blueprint for enacting our goals. We want to focus our courses in ways that will join our participants where they enter and build upon the questions and concerns they bring. We also need to understand the challenges to self that emerge when confronting oppressive assumptions, beliefs, and behaviors (Arnold, Burke, James, D'Arcy, & Thomas, 1991). Finally, we need to set goals for learning that make sense educationally and are reachable within the time constraints of our courses. To address these and other issues, we discuss in this chapter the elements that scaffold our approach to designing social justice education courses.

- Identify relevant characteristics of participants, and develop goals appropriate to the learning needs of the group.
- Matching the environment to student social-emotional learning processes: Attend to the experiential phases learners often go through in a social justice education class, and structure an environment that supports them appropriately at different points in the course.
- Structuring content and learning activities: Select specific class activities to address key concepts in social justice education, and match these to student learning needs.
- Sequencing learning activities: Develop an appropriate progression of activities to attend to both content and process as these evolve during the class.
- Accommodating a variety of learning styles: Build in a variety of ways to accommodate different student learning styles.

- Making adjustments as the class unfolds: Be flexible and ready to make design changes as needed while a class is in progress.
- Evaluating the course and grading student performance: Identify different components of evaluation as a key part of course design.

We have developed these design considerations over many years of teaching social justice education courses and integrating a variety of models and sequences. We encourage readers who are new to teaching social justice education courses to focus on one or two design issues at a time, develop facility in applying them to find out how they work in your courses, and then gradually add others, rather than feeling you must apply all of these sequences at once.

## Pre-assessment

As we anticipate and prepare to teach a new course three interrelated pre-assessment questions are relevant: What is the course focus? What are the characteristics of the participants who are taking the course? Given the answers to the first two questions, what should be the goals of the course? The answers to these questions help us match both overall goals and specific class activities to the particular needs of a group. We discuss each of these questions below.

### On What Issues or Topics Will the Course Focus?

Social justice courses can have a single-issue focus (racism or classism, for example) or a multiple-issue focus (sexism, heterosexism, and ableism). Single-issue courses, although examining one form of oppression in depth, also notice how different issues intersect in order to help participants understand the many parallels and connections among different forms of oppression. For example, a course may have a single-issue focus on sexism but also examine how women from different social classes, racial groups, religions, abilities, or sexual orientations experience sexism. Courses that focus on multiple issues can address each sequentially, for example, beginning with sexism, then racism, then heterosexism, while also noting similarities and interconnections among these topics as each is introduced thus bringing in connections throughout the class. A multiple-issue focus enables participants to revisit key conceptual organizers (social identity or levels of oppression, for example) with reference to different course topics (racism or classism, for example).

Another approach to social justice education is to analyze current events or controversial topics using either a single-issue or an integrated focus. For example, a course could focus on such topics as affirmative action or a campus visit by an antigay speaker and construct class activities around the event. Participants in a course using an integrated focus could, for example, analyze the event or issue through the lens of race, gender, sexual orientation, or socioeconomic class, or through a combination of these factors.

### What Are the Characteristics of the Participants Who Are Taking the Course?

Important factors to consider are the heterogeneity of the group, the multiple identities and interests represented in the class, and the prior experiences and motivations participants have for taking a social justice course. In most social justice education courses, participants are a mixed group of advantaged and targeted group members in relation to the topic of the course. For example, in a racism course one would typically anticipate a diverse mix of participants of color, white participants, and biracial participants. In a sexism course, we would expect both women and men. Where there is not an approximately equal number of advantaged and targeted group members enrolled, we would avoid planning activities that place the smaller number (either targeted or advantaged) in a vulnerable position in a class environment where they might already feel on the spot. As a general guideline, we try to ensure that at least one third of a mixed class is either advantaged or targeted group members.

## Multiple Identities and Interests

Participants who have multiple targeted identities bring a different worldview and different needs to the course than participants with a single or no targeted identity. In a sexism course that includes gay men and lesbians or people of color, for example, we can anticipate and provide ways to explore how participants encounter sexism differently through their experiences with heterosexism and racism. The presence of international participants, those for whom English is not a first language, or participants with disabilities may also require that we make modifications to ensure that readings and other class activities are accessible to all.

Participant professional interests are also relevant for planning. If the course includes a variety of majors and career orientations, a more generic approach to the course topic or the use of professional caucuses might be necessary to apply the material to participants' majors or professions. If participants are preparing to be teachers, we can emphasize the role of educators and schools in perpetuating and/or addressing oppression. Finally, it is useful to know whether participants are graduate or undergraduate, traditional or nontraditional, or a mixture. Each group brings to the course a different combination of work and life experiences that we can consider in planning classes to meet their needs and interests.

## What Prior Experiences With and Motivations for Taking Social Justice Education Courses Do Participants Bring?

For participants with no prior experience in a social justice education course, we anticipate less familiarity with an experiential approach that includes personal exploration and the expression of feelings. We therefore might need to spend more time with introductory activities, reviewing participation guidelines, providing a rationale for our interactive experiential approach, and establishing a safe and supportive environment. Participants with no prior experience in social justice education might be less open to challenges to their understanding of social justice than participants who have already had some experience interacting with these issues in a classroom.

It is also worthwhile to know what motivates participants to take the course. Some participants select social justice education courses because they are genuinely interested in the content and are excited about learning. Others take the course because they are required to (as a degree requirement for their major field, for example) or because it is expedient (simply because they need another credit or the class fits their schedule). With a group of "volunteers" who have chosen the course because of interest in the topic, we can usually assume a higher level of commitment to exploring issues and engaging classmates in discussion. With a group of "hostages" whose presence in the course is not a choice, but is simply to meet a requirement, there is more potential for hostility and resentment at being asked to actively participate in discussions that challenge their understanding of issues they might not even perceive to be connected to their personal or professional lives. With such participants, we might need to spend more time exploring the nature of the topic and its relevance to their lives to set a foundation for further learning.

## Stages of Social Identity Development Likely to Be Represented in the Class

The social identity development model described in Chapter 2 can be helpful for anticipating how different participants may respond to learning about oppression and interacting with others in the course. We often find that undergraduate participants who are in the advantaged group exhibit acceptance or resistance stages, whereas participants from targeted groups often demonstrate a broader range. Social identity development models can help us plan activities and promote discussions to engage participants and pose appropriate challenges that will make sense to their frame of reference and help them build upon current knowledge and awareness (see Hardiman, 1994; Hardiman & Jackson, 1992, 1997; Wijeyesinghe & Jackson, 2001).

Though participants will most often present a variety of social identities and developmental stages, as well as a range of prior experiences with social justice education, what we learn about our participants beforehand can help us plan more effectively to meet participants where they are and engage them in activities that reflect their felt concerns and questions. At the same time, we need always to treat this information tentatively, as a place from which to begin rather than pigeonhole participants as definitive types. Further discussion of the different developmental models we draw upon can be found in Chapters 2 ("Pedagogical Frameworks for Social Justice Education") and 17 ("Knowing Our Students").

## Preassessment Options

One way to obtain relevant information is to ask participants to fill out a preassessment personal profile worksheet in which they identify their social group memberships and prior experiences in social justice education courses (use Appendix 4A). Other methods include interviewing participants informally beforehand or talking with other teachers who are familiar with the participants who will be taking the course. Often informal preassessment activities can be completed during the initial class session, and curriculum adjustments made based on information about student identity, experience, and interests gleaned from these activities. Regardless of how this information is obtained, it is an important component of design that should not be overlooked.

## Given the Course Focus and Student Characteristics, What Should Be the Goals of the Course?

Three broad goals for social justice education courses are to increase personal awareness, expand knowledge, and encourage action. The relative emphasis we place on each of these goals will vary with the prior knowledge and experience of the group, with focus on the personal awareness end of the continuum for novice groups and more focus on the action end of the continuum with experienced groups.

### Increase Personal Awareness

Increasing personal awareness includes helping participants learn more about their own socialization and social identities, and their conscious and unconscious assumptions and prejudices. Through examining personal awareness, participants can develop greater clarity about the differential treatment they receive as a result of their own social group memberships. They can learn to identify and challenge what are often unexamined beliefs about themselves and others and understand how these beliefs have been established through an unequal system based on hierarchies of privilege and power. Here, course content helps participants recognize the ways in which specific forms of oppression are manifested in their everyday lives through interpersonal interactions, institutional practices, and cultural norms that influence their behavior as individuals.

For example, white participants as advantaged in relation to racism often enter a racism course thinking of "difference" as belonging to the cultural "Other." They may be fairly oblivious to their own role as culture bearers, and may downplay or deny the experiences of participants of color. Likewise, male participants in a sexism course may question the prevalence or seriousness of issues that affect women as a group such as sexual harassment or date rape. We would first focus on helping such participants increase their personal awareness of these issues since, in our experience, this happens more readily when examples are drawn from their immediate environment and daily interactions. We would focus activities and discussion on highlighting instances of individual prejudice or institutional discrimination that are readily identifiable to undergraduates in their college communities, so as to connect local "data" to more abstract historical or sociological information and concepts presented in the course. For example, participants might begin by looking at incidents of homophobic harassment in residence halls, baiting of mixed-race couples on campus, institutional patterns such as scheduling exams on Jewish or Muslim holidays, or holding public gatherings that are not accessible to participants with disabilities. Our goal is for participants to begin to connect seemingly individual incidents to broader structural and social patterns discussed in class and in the readings.

Throughout the course, we try to offer participants multiple opportunities to explore both advantaged and targeted aspects of their own identities. For instance, a Latina student may initially focus on her experiences in relation to targeted racial or linguistic status, then proceed to examine her advantaged identities as able-bodied, heterosexual, or Christian. Through shifting the focus of attention at various points in the course, she may be able to grasp the complexity of coexisting, multiple identities and thus be able to empathize with others who struggle to understand issues of racism or sexism that seem self-evident to her, just as she struggles to understand issues of ableism or antisemitism that are challenging for her but more easily recognizable to others who are targeted by those issues.

## Expand Knowledge

To expand knowledge, we ask participants to examine historical, economic, and social information that defines and reflects oppression. We provide data in the form of statistics about access to social resources such as health care, housing, employment, education, and government resources; examine incidences of violence and harassment; and identify patterns of institutional discrimination experienced by targeted groups in the United States. We discuss the history of disenfranchised groups so that participants have an understanding of forces beyond themselves that shape individual and group behavior. Reading, videos, lectures, and discussion engage participants in learning about the structural and institutional features of oppression and provide tools for them to analyze current examples of oppression in our society as well as identify ways people have struggled to resist oppression in every historical period.

In a course that explores multiple social justice issues, participants can begin to look at the commonalities and differences among different "isms," the historically situated particulars of each, and the parallels and interconnections among them. For example, participants who have studied racial, then gender, then class stereotypes can begin to see how stereotyping operates as a feature of many forms of oppression, and then be able to analyze the function of stereotyping in supporting prejudice and discrimination of all types.

## Encourage Action

We hope that participants will create meaningful ways to apply their new awareness and knowledge rather than feel overwhelmed by it. To this end, we provide models for identifying possible action steps, assessing the level of risk involved, practicing self-chosen interventions, evaluating the outcomes of their actions, and planning ways they can continue to act and get support for taking action beyond the course. We encourage participants to develop and draw upon the relationships they build with each other in class to support each other's analysis and development of action steps. They help each other identify various spheres of influence in their families, intimate relationships, friends or peers at work, school, places of worship, student activities, and campus or classroom interactions (see Appendix B). Our goal is for participants to see themselves as agents of change, capable of acting on their convictions and in concert with others against the injustices they see.

We try to touch upon all of these goals in every course, but the relative emphasis depends on a number of factors such as who the participants are, what the course topic is, and how long the course will last. For example, with participants who have never thought much about racism and are taking a course to fulfill a requirement, we place more emphasis on increasing awareness and knowledge. With participants who have a basic understanding of racism and are already committed to addressing it, we would spend more time on developing further knowledge and planning action strategies and interventions.

## Attention to the Social-Emotional Learning Process

One very important consideration in our design for social justice education is attending to the disequilibrium people experience as they begin to see the reality and pervasiveness of social oppression. Confrontation with the effects of oppression invariably calls into question deeply held assumptions about the social world and can literally throw participants off balance. This instability can be frightening as participants experience contradictions and begin to realize that previous ways of making sense of the world no longer seem adequate. However, in a supportive learning environment, disequilibrium can also be exhilarating as participants grapple with contradictions and seek more satisfactory ways to make sense of social reality.

Kegan (1982) provides a sequence for understanding this process of disequilibrium that we find useful as we plan our courses. He identifies three positions that learners take in a progressive sequence as they confront, engage, and eventually incorporate new learning. He calls these positions defending, surrendering, and reintegration (described below). This sequence provides a framework for making sense of the various psychological reactions or positions participants may experience at different stages in their learning and helps us to be empathic with their internal struggles for meaning making at each stage.

For each position, Kegan (1982) identifies a corresponding facilitating or classroom environment. Kegan calls these facilitating environments confirmation, contradiction, and continuity (pp. 118–120). The progression of facilitating environments offers a framework for creating appropriately supportive conditions in which participants can first open up to and engage with new ideas (as they are defending), next grapple with contradictions and challenges to previous knowing (surrendering), and finally incorporate new information and ways of making sense of the social world (reintegration). The following description is our adaptation of Kegan's sequence to the social justice classroom.

## Phase 1

### Psychological Position of Defending (embeddedness)

From a social-psychological perspective, people, consciously or unconsciously, develop and internalize a set of beliefs about social justice issues through living in this society. Each of us could be said to be embedded in a particular way of making sense of the world. Left unchallenged, this embeddedness leads us to take for granted our worldview as given, natural, and true, as simply "the way things are." In the social justice education classroom, these beliefs will be exposed to examination and questioning, unsettling the "taken-for-granted" worldview. Such challenge inevitably disturbs a person's equilibrium, can be experienced as threatening, and will often raise a person's defenses.

### Corresponding Facilitating Environment: Confirmation (holding on)

The way participants experience the environment of the classroom has a powerful effect on whether or not they will be willing to entertain conflicting information and internal disequilibrium. If the environment is perceived as threatening, a person's defenses may become fairly rigid. They will tend to ignore challenges to their worldview and rationalize conflicting information to fit their present belief system. In other words, they may cling to their "comfort zone" and be unwilling to test out any new knowledge or information.

However, if the environment is perceived as supportive, a person's defenses can be more permeable. In this case, despite the experience of internal conflict, the person may be willing to consider new information and grapple with the contradictions and discrepancies they perceive.

For these reasons, the initial phase of a social justice education course is very important. Our goals in this phase are to create an environment in which participants feel confirmed and validated as persons even as they experience challenges to their belief system. We want to construct an environment that is supportive and trustworthy, one in which uncomfortable and challenging issues may be raised and explored, where participants can express discomfort, confusion, anger, and fear and know they will be treated with dignity and respect. We call this finding their *learning edge*.

An example from a heterosexism course may be illustrative. Many participants, especially heterosexual participants, enter the course with little or no awareness of heterosexism and homophobia. Because of the unconscious homophobia endemic in our society, they may feel uncomfortable with the topic, apprehensive about what they might learn about their own feelings, and insecure with having a lesbian or gay instructor. Homosexual and bisexual participants, on the other hand, may be quite aware of heterosexism and homophobia but fearful that they will be exposed or unfairly treated in the course. To create a confirming environment, we want to help people break the ice and identify some commonalities they share. We also want to establish and model ground rules of listening respectfully and speaking truthfully from one's own experience. We identify stereotypes and assumptions that the culture fosters about homosexuality and bisexuality, and acknowledge that we all receive misinformation, in order to make it possible to openly examine taboo topics. Once participants experience support and realize it is safe to not have all the answers, to be confused or uninformed, and to make mistakes despite their best intentions, they may be able to relax their defenses enough to engage with classroom activities and information that question their assumptions about social reality.

## Phase 2

### Psychological Position of Surrendering (differentiation)

If we have succeeded in creating a supportive environment, participants may now feel secure enough to open up to contradictions to their old belief system and begin a process of exploration, to find their "learning edge" and live the inevitable discomfort there. They become willing to examine and differentiate ideas and feelings and try on different ways of making sense of the world. This process can be confusing, disorienting, and, at times, frightening. Participants might feel out of control, without known boundaries or familiar ground, and may experience a sense of loss or surrender as they literally "excavate the ground they stand on" (Barker, 1993, p. 48). As they learn new information, they may also experience strong emotions such as anger, resentment, and a sense of betrayal that they have not been informed by those who were supposed to tell them the truth about the social world. At the same time, they may feel a sense of freedom as they consider, discard, and eventually construct new ways of making sense of the world they encounter.

### Corresponding Facilitating Environment: Contradiction (letting go)

The supportive environment for this second position is one that allows participants to immerse themselves fully in whatever contradictions and conflicts arise as a consequence of engaging previously unknown ideas and exploring their own and others' feelings and experiences. The course content and process deliberately pose and explore contradictions and encourage participants to seek new ways to make sense of the material they encounter. This process is akin to Freire's notion of education for critical consciousness (1970/1994, 1973).

At this point, the environment shifts. It does not overprotect or enable participants to avoid feelings of discomfort, confusion, fear, and anger. Such feelings are an inevitable and ultimately helpful part of the learning process. Through engaging with challenging information and participating in experiential activities, participants are encouraged to let go of the comfortable and familiar and explore new territory.

To continue with the example from the heterosexism course, the environment now shifts to encourage exploration of feelings and identification of contradictions and discontinuities between what we are taught and what is hidden from us. A representative activity for this phase is one in which participants engage in guided imagery focusing on close same-sex friendships from childhood. One male student remembered his best boyhood friend and a time when the two little boys were playing in the bathtub, splashing each other, and began exuberantly flipping each other's penises. He recalled the spontaneity and sheer abandon of free play until his mother came into the bathroom and froze in horror. Not a word was said, but the game abruptly ended. As he recalled this long forgotten episode, the student realized that an unspoken barrier had arisen between him and his friend that affected their closeness, as well as his ability to be physically close to other men. He could then bring in other associations and learning that reinforced the lessons of homophobia and begin to examine the high price he pays as a heterosexual in limiting his ability to express intimacy and caring toward male friends.

## Phase 3

### Psychological Position of Reintegration (Transforming)

Once participants have left familiar ground and explored new territory, both affectively and intellectually, they are in a position to integrate what they have learned and establish a new foundation. This balance is gradually achieved as a new set of beliefs becomes "home base" for interpreting experience and creating meaning. The past is not wholly rejected, but is reinterpreted and reconstructed into a new frame of reference as participants come into a new "self-possession" (Harris, 1988).

## Facilitating Environment: Continuity (staying put)

The environment once again shifts to encourage the development of stability and continuity based on new insights and knowledge. Activities are designed to help participants articulate and confirm what they have learned and think about what this might mean for their actions beyond the course. Opportunities are provided to imagine taking new actions, the likely consequences of such actions, and types of support that could be called upon to sustain these changes. As they consider the future, we encourage them to develop ongoing systems of support for sustaining themselves beyond the course so they can continue a process of learning about social justice issues and acting on their convictions.

To conclude the heterosexism course example, participants were asked to imagine typical interactions with friends, family, and coworkers and reflect upon new insights about homophobia as these informed how they wished to behave in the future. The man in the previous example decided he wanted to develop more closeness and intimacy with his male friends and openly discuss with them the homophobic feelings that blocked such intimacy. He also wanted to look closer at the messages he might be communicating to his own sons and make sure he was allowing them full expression of feelings. We emphasize and affirm the importance of each student choosing and developing her or his own action plan, suited to his/her particular learning and comfort level.

In our experience, the process described above approximates fairly closely the psychological processes most participants seem to move through in social justice education courses. However useful as a guide though, we recognize that the map is not the territory. We can't always know whether participants are engaged in these ways, or whether the exploration they take up in class will continue beyond the course. Occasionally, some participants choose not to engage in the ways we hope they will. They may hold on to their frame of reference and refuse to explore contradictory information. We hope this process allows respect for them as well.

Below, we provide examples of the specific kinds of activities that structure content in each phase of the course to provide the appropriate facilitating environments as the course unfolds.

## Design Features of the Confirmation Phase

*Post an agenda and class objectives.* This step provides an explicit structure that participants can rely upon and, if desired, adjust to meet their own needs. It helps participants anticipate what the focus of the course will be and have some sense of the order in which activities will occur. This process also enables participants to share responsibility for following the agenda, identify ways the agenda does not meet their needs and adjust it accordingly.

*Begin with introductions and expectations.* This step recognizes the unique identity of each participant and lets people know they will not be treated as anonymous, but are indeed central to the course. They begin to understand that they will be asked to learn about and listen to each other. This step also helps participants begin to identify and develop their own goals for learning. Facilitators can then clarify ways the course will and will not meet the expressed expectations, and adjust the design accordingly. This step also supports the notion of an explicit agenda that can be adapted to meet student needs and expectations where possible.

*Acknowledge feelings.* During a social justice education course, many different feelings arise as participants grapple with perspectives and information that challenge their previous understanding. It is essential to acknowledge that these feelings are a natural and appropriate part of the learning process. Providing participants with some guidance for how to recognize, listen to, and learn from feelings encourages their expression in ways that help rather than hinder learning. The introduction of concepts such as *learning edge, comfort zone*, and *triggers*, for example, provides participants with a language and a process to use in examining and making sense of feelings that arise (see Chapter 3).

*Use low-risk self-disclosure and interaction in the early stages of the course.* Introducing activities early in the course where participants can comfortably interact with each other and discuss their own thoughts and feelings at a low-risk level establishes a norm of interaction and self-disclosure at the outset. This initial interaction should be low risk so that participants can comfortably practice what for many might be a novel experience of sharing feelings and personal experiences in the context of a classroom.

*Establish group norms for respectful interactions.* Creating a list of guidelines for interaction and asking the class to agree to abide by these guidelines provide clear boundaries for appropriate interactions. Mutually agreed upon guidelines create a climate of safety in which participants can feel responsible for themselves and each other and trust that they will be supported during the course.

## Design Features of the Contradiction Phase

Once the confirmation phase of the course is established, we move into the contradiction phase in which activities encourage participants to face the challenges posed by new information and different perspectives. Learning activities in the contradiction phase can focus on any of the several key concepts identified in Chapter 5 and exemplified in the course designs in this volume: (a) personal socialization and experience; (b) historical context; (c) manifestations at the individual, institutional, and societal/cultural levels; (d) power and privilege; (e) collusion and internalization; (f) horizontal oppression; and (g) advantaged group members as allies, and targeted group members as empowered.

*Validate personal risk taking.* Support and encourage participants to take risks in exploring perspectives, feelings, and awareness that contradict their prior understanding. Validate participants who express confusion or ask questions that reflect their personal struggle with issues discussed in the course.

*Encourage full discussion.* Encourage everyone to participate in class discussions, and elicit a variety of perspectives so that differences can be openly aired and explored. Inviting divergent perspectives enables participants to work with contradictions and have their own thinking challenged and extended.

*Allow contradictions and tensions to emerge.* Resist the tendency to smooth over tensions, resolve contradictions, or relieve uncomfortable moments in class. These experiences are an essential part of the learning process in a social justice education course. As long as participants use participation guidelines and treat each other with respect, discomfort with new perspectives and tension among different perspectives can help them engage with ideas and information in more critical and thoughtful ways.

## Design Features of the Continuity Phase

During the continuity phase of the course, participants turn their attention to how to integrate new awareness and knowledge into their lives and bring their experience in the course to a close. We focus on helping participants identify actions they want to take to further their learning and concretize their new perspectives in actions. Our intention is to help participants feel optimistic about social change rather than feel overwhelmed by the enormity of social oppression. Participants need to think about how to nurture and sustain their developing understanding of and commitment to acting against social injustice. The following guidelines help in planning this phase of the course.

*Identify a wide variety of action possibilities.* Encourage participants to identify actions that match their personal level of comfort. This means acknowledging and valuing actions at all levels of risk, from reading about racism, to objecting to racist jokes or comments in their classes or at the family dinner table, to joining a Third World caucus or white ally group on campus.

*Identify ways that participants can get support for their actions against social injustice.* Developing support for new awareness of and commitment to addressing social justice issues that extends beyond the course boundaries is an essential part of helping participants bridge the gap between class and their school, work, and personal lives. Helping participants develop support groups from class or learn about existing community or campus groups to join provides a way for participants to nurture relationships with others who share their developing commitments.

*Bring the class experience to a close.* Help participants achieve a sense of closure by providing a way for them to summarize what they learned, appreciate classmates, and identify next steps in continuing their learning.

Table 4.1 includes the phases in the facilitating environment and examples of the methods or structure in each phase. Each method or structure is intended to address

**Table 4.1**   Facilitating Environment and Method/Structure

| Facilitating Environment | Method/Structure |
| --- | --- |
| Confirmation (establishing the climate) | Post agenda and objectives. |
| | Begin with introductions and expectations. |
| | Acknowledge feelings. |
| | Use low-risk self-disclosure. |
| | Establish norms for group communication. |
| Contradiction (initiating the encounter) | Validate personal risk taking. |
| | Encourage full discussion. |
| | Allow contradictions to emerge. |
| Continuity (closure/transition out of course) | Summarize. |
| | Plan action/applications. |
| | Develop ongoing support. |
| | Evaluate the course. |
| | Close the course. |

the psychological concerns participants have as they move through the different learning phases of the course.

## Structuring Learning Content and Activities

With the model in Table 4.1 as a broad framework, we then plan content and activities for each class. In general, the internal structure of activities follows a basic progression, each of which is discussed in more detail below:

- Establish learning objectives and evaluation criteria.
- Identify key concepts.
- Allot time for each activity.
- Organize procedures for each activity.
- Gather equipment and materials needed.
- Develop processing format and questions.
- Agree upon leadership responsibilities (if co-facilitating).
- Plan for transition to next activity.

*Establish learning objectives and evaluation criteria.* We believe that it is important for social justice educators to have clear learning objectives for the activities we use and to establish explicit criteria for determining whether or not we have been successful in meeting our goals. These goals should guide the development of all learning activities.

*Identify key concepts.* Key concepts introduce new information or conceptual frames for participants to use in examining course content, issues raised in discussion, and their own experiences. Key concepts include, for example, stereotyping, the cycle of socialization, and the multiple levels of oppression. In an ableism class, participants may be introduced to the concept of stereotyping by exploring stereotypes of people with disabilities and examining the roots of these stereotypes historically and in their own learning.

*Allot time for each activity.* With experience, it becomes easier to anticipate how much time each activity will take. It is important to build in time for the experience itself, discussion following the experience, and questions and issues that arise from the group. General time guidelines and the flexibility to adapt time frames as needed are important. Posting time on the public agenda for the class also encourages the class to help in following the schedule as posted.

*Organize procedures for each activity.* The learning activity is a structured interaction or confrontation with one or more key concepts. Examples of activities include role plays, case studies, a brainstorming session, an interactive lecture, a video, a discussion, or a worksheet. The activity is designed to engage participants with the issues experientially and cognitively so that they can interact with the material and each other. In the ableism class introduced previously, participants might be asked to brainstorm a list of words and images they have learned or heard about people with disabilities. As they see the list of typically negative words and images emerge, they learn how pervasive these images are in the culture and can then use this information to examine the systemic nature of ableism.

The first step in designing the activity is to identify procedures and directions that will guide participants through the activity in a clearly defined and logical sequence. Nothing can spoil a learning opportunity like confusing or incomplete directions or a sequence that doesn't make sense. It is important to plan how to introduce the activity so that participants understand the objectives and how these fit into the overall curriculum. Often, it is necessary to prepare participants for potentially difficult aspects of an activity and remind them of course participation guidelines.

*Gather equipment and materials needed.* It is extremely important to organize all equipment and materials needed to complete an activity beforehand. This may include written information or handouts, newsprint, videos, scissors, masking tape, and whatever else is needed in quantities required for the group. Make sure to set up and test technology beforehand so as not to lose precious class time getting the equipment to work properly.

*Develop processing format and questions.* Processing is a critical step in learning because it gives participants time to reflect and make personal meaning, identify questions and contradictions, and draw new learning from the activity. During processing, facilitators pose questions to help participants discuss what happened, how they felt about it, and what they learned, and provide time for them to listen to the similar and different ways that others in the class experienced the activity. Reflection and discussion are important opportunities for participants to express confusion, ask questions, make observations, and challenge their own and others' thinking. In our hypothetical ableism class, after completing the brainstorm activity, participants might reflect upon and discuss the following questions: "What feelings do you have as you look at the list we have created?" "What surprises you about the list?" "What questions do you have about any of the terms on the list?" and "What themes do you notice when you look at this list of images?"

*Agree upon leadership responsibilities (if co-teaching).* Instructors who teach alone have to take care of all aspects of planning and implementation. If a course is co-facilitated, divide up preparation and leadership tasks so that both instructors have an equitable share of responsibilities. This is particularly important in terms of in-class leadership. Participants can learn unintended lessons from how instructors share leadership and relate to each other during the course. For example, if the nondisabled member of a facilitation team is patronizing or uncomfortable interacting with a co-facilitator who has a disability, this message can override any positive learning that the leaders hope for in the design.

*Plan for transition to next activity.* The transition to the next activity need not necessarily wait until resolution occurs. Participants can be left with questions and contradictions that are carried into the next activity. If learning activities are sequenced in a way that flows naturally from one theme to the next, summarizing the main points while processing one activity and introducing the next one will make sense. Encourage participants to stay with contradictions and questions as they move into the next activity. After discussing the questions posed during the processing phase of the activity, facilitators can help participants make a bridge to the next activity by saying, "Now that we have identified some of the stereotypes we have learned about people with disabilities, let's look closer at where these messages come from." The class could then move into an experiential activity or short lecture focused on socialization.

## Sequencing Learning Activities

Another important consideration in designing social justice education courses is the overall progression of learning activities within any one curriculum design. We consider several factors in selecting and sequencing activities so that the overall flow of the course makes sense to participants. This careful sequencing also enables us to introduce concepts and activities in an incremental way that builds upon student awareness and learning at different phases of the course (Brooks-Harris & Stock-Ward, 1999).

*Lower to higher risk sequencing.* Learners need to feel safe in order to be willing to express and examine deeply held feelings, confusions, and assumptions. Lower risk activities in the beginning of a social justice education course are designed to help participants get acquainted, understand interaction guidelines, and engage in superficial discussions before moving to activities that require more risky disclosure of feelings and perspectives. Moving from individual reflection to discussions in pairs or small groups before engaging in whole-group discussions is also a way to progressively increase the level of risk and to build in support as discussions proceed.

*Concrete to abstract sequencing.* This sequencing principle reflects our belief that participants learn best when their understanding of oppression is firmly rooted in concrete experiences and examples that provide a foundation for analysis of abstract concepts and the multiple levels on which oppression operates. Participants can then examine material in the context of concrete examples that illustrate the theoretical ideas being discussed.

*Personal to institutional sequencing.* In most of our courses, we begin with personal content, then introduce an institutional and cultural focus. We start with a personal focus because this level is more accessible to participants for initial exploration of the topic. After examining their own experience and socialization, and gathering information from many sources including readings, lectures, and discussions, participants are usually better prepared to explore how oppression operates on institutional and cultural levels.

*Difference to dominance (or diversity to justice) sequencing.* This sequence first focuses on helping participants describe and understand their own experiences as members of diverse social groups and listen to others in the course talk about their experiences and perspectives. The focus is on respecting, understanding, and acknowledging difference. After this, the concepts of dominance, social power, and privilege are introduced to help participants understand that difference is not neutral, and that different social groups have greater or lesser access to social and personal resources and power.

*Psychological and logical sequencing.* The structure of the course should make both psychological and logical sense to both facilitators and participants. *Logical sequence* refers to beginning with what people already know and presenting information that can be gradually integrated into expanding levels of analysis. *Psychological sequence* refers to how participants negotiate the course at the psychological and emotional levels. The low-risk to higher risk sequence supports effective psychological sequencing.

*What? So what? Now what? sequencing.* This is a handy shorthand sequence to use as a guide for organizing process as well as content by increasing awareness (What?), thinking and analysis (So what?), and experimenting with new behavior (Now what?) (Borton, 1970, p. 93). It begins by asking "what" participants currently know and feel in order to identify the information and

**Table 4.2**    Facilitating Environment, Methods/Structure, and Sequences

| Facilitating Environment | Methods/Structure | Sequences |
|---|---|---|
| | | What? So what? Now what? |
| Confirmation | Agenda/objectives | Psychological and logical difference (diversity) to dominance (justice) |
| | Introductions | Personal to institutional |
| | Warm-up | Concrete to abstract |
| | Fears/expectations | Low to higher risk |
| Contradiction | Advance organizers | |
| | Definitions | |
| | Activity (simulation, discussion, video, lecture, panel presentation, etc.) | |
| | Transition | |
| Continuity | Action planning | |
| | Support | |
| | Closure | |

supportive climate needed for initiating an activity or the course as a whole. The question "So what?" refers to how participants process an activity or activities to draw meaning that expands their awareness and knowledge. The question "Now what?" addresses the implications of what participants have learned and the next steps to be taken given new knowledge and awareness.

Table 4.2 summarizes the three previous sections to combine facilitating environments, methods and structures, and sequencing. This table can be helpful as a planning guide when designing a course.

## Accommodating Student Learning Styles and Needs

Facilitators, like participants, have their own learning style preferences, and we often teach in ways that favor our own preferred learning style. To resist this tendency and to consciously accommodate a variety of student learning styles and needs in our instructional designs, we find a useful guide in the experiential learning model developed by Kolb (Anderson & Adams, 1992; Brooks-Harris & Stock-Ward, 1999; Kolb, 1984; Smith & Kolb, 1986). This model provides guidance for selecting and sequencing learning activities to meet a range of learning style preferences, as shown in Figures 4.1 and 4.2. We also find Universal Instructional Design useful as a planning model for making social justice education courses accessible to a broad spectrum of participants with and without disabilities (Ouellett, 2000; Pliner, 2004).

The Kolb model identifies four learning modes: concrete experience, reflective observation, abstract conceptualization, and active experimentation. For each learning mode, the model lists instructional activities that are appropriate to that style. The model can be used as a checklist to plan a range of activities so that all four learning modes are engaged during a course. For example, using the model as a guide to evaluate whether the course designs in this volume include a variety of learning preferences, we note that simulations such as *Star Power* in the classism course curruciulum design and the *crossing the room* activity in several curriculum designs in this volume, engage participants in a direct and concrete manner (concrete experience). The processing

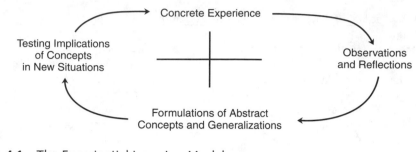

**Figure 4.1**    The Experiential Learning Model

**Figure 4.2**    Instructional Activities That Support Different Aspects of the Learning Cycle

questions that follow each activity, film, or lecture illustrate reflective observation. We note that the conceptual model of individual, institutional, and cultural levels of oppression is explained and used in several curriculum design chapters to analyze the dynamics of the "isms" explored in each course (abstract conceptualization). Finally, we see that participants develop action projects to apply learnings about racism, sexism, ableism, and other forms of oppression to at-home situations (active experimentation). This sequence is evident in the general flow of the modules in each design in this volume as well as within the flow of specific activities.

Kolb's (1984) model illustrates the learning strengths of each style and the preferred learning situations of participants with those particular strengths. Most courses include participants with a range of learning style preferences, and the Kolb model enables us to be deliberate in our planning and include a variety of learning activities in each class so that all students can both access their preferred style and stretch to accommodate other learning styles as well.

Universal Instructional Design is an adaptation of the Universal Design model used to enhance architectural accessibility in the physical environment (Pliner, 2004; Silver, Bourke, & Strehorn, 1998). Just as ramps and automatic doors for building entrances, books on tape, and auditory signals at traffic lights are useful to everyone, Universal

Instructional Design is intended to serve as a guide for curriculum planning to serve the needs of all participants. Rather than focus on accommodating "special needs," Universal Instructional Design principles are integrated into the planning process for all courses (Ouellett, 2000).

For example, facilitators using Universal Instructional Design principles would routinely ensure the following in their course planning:

1. Classrooms are in wheelchair-accessible spaces with accessible toilet facilities.
2. The classroom itself is wheelchair accessible.
3. The classroom has good ventilation and fresh air.
4. Instructional materials, including reading assignments and books, are available on computer disks, on audiotape, and in large print.
5. Lecture notes are available in print.
6. Video presentations are closed-captioned.
7. Instructional material posted on chalkboards or newsprints is available in print and also read aloud to the class.
8. Appropriate breaks are scheduled during class meetings.
9. If tests or papers are assigned, reasonable flexibility in time is made for student completion.

The range of potential disabilities make it impossible to preplan for all of them, but Universal Instructional Design principles call on facilitators to plan for as many as are reasonable. When a student requires additional accommodation, such as a sign language interpreter, these needs should be addressed on an individual basis. As a routine aspect of, facilitators should ask participants in each class about their specific learning needs either before the course begins or at the first class meeting. By incorporating these principles in course planning, the instructor can integrate accommodation of student learning styles and needs into the classroom routine rather than treating these as an add-on or extra task.

## Design Format Alternatives

*Four-module format.* The curriculum designs in this book are organized into four 3–4-hour modules. These modules can be taught in weekly segments spread over 4 weeks. Another option is to teach all four modules in a more concentrated format over a 2-day period in which Modules 1 and 2 are planned for day 1, and Modules 3 and 4 are taught on day 2.

*Multi-issue semester course format.* Another instructional format conforms to a more traditional structure in which courses meet weekly throughout a semester. In this semester format, a course can be designed so that a number of specific forms of oppression such as racism, classism, antisemitism and religious oppression, sexism, heterosexism, and/or transgender oppression are interwoven with key concepts taught as curriculum organizers (see Chapter 3 for key concepts).

The curriculum might, for example, consist of five forms of oppression, each examined in 2-week segments over a 10-week period (see Table 4.3). The remaining 4 weeks can be used to begin and conclude the course, present and illustrate conceptual organizers, consider parallels and interconnections among the five "isms," and examine the interaction of socioeconomic class with other issues, especially with race, gender, and antisemitism.

**Table 4.3**    Sample Sequence of Course Topics

| | |
|---|---|
| Week 1 | Course introductions |
| Week 2 | Sexism, part 1 |
| Week 3 | Sexism, part 2 |
| Week 4 | Heterosexism, part 1 |
| Week 5 | Heterosexism, part 2 (interconnections with sexism) |
| Week 6 | Racism, part 1 |
| Week 7 | Racism, part 2 |
| Week 8 | Parallels and interconnections (classism) |
| Week 9 | Antisemitism, part 1 |
| Week 10 | Antisemitism, part 2 (parallels with racism and classism) |
| Week 11 | Ableism, part 1 |
| Week 12 | Ableism, part 2 |
| Week 13 | Parallels and interconnections, classism, student projects |
| Week 14 | Closure, student projects |

A multiple-issues course, like the single-issue courses described in Chapters 6–15, has basic learning goals of raising awareness, knowledge, conceptual understanding, and action. These learning goals can be addressed sequentially. The first three goals of awareness, knowledge, and conceptual understanding can organize the approach to the initial course topics. By midsemester, the design pays more attention to goals such as recognizing critical incidents in everyday life and developing action plans and appropriate intervention skills. The interplay of learning goals with course topics or "isms" is shown in Table 4.4.

Design for the multiple-issues course also considers the emphasis upon the various key conceptual organizers in relation to the specific course topics. In this way, conceptual organizers play out throughout the course, and their repetition with a difference is one of the ways in which parallels and intersections among social justice issues become evident to participants. The interplay of key concepts with course topics or "isms" is shown in Table 4.5.

**Table 4.4**    Learning Goals in Relation to Course Topics

| | Sample: Learning Goals in Relation to Course Topics | | | | |
|---|---|---|---|---|---|
| Topics | Awareness | Information | Concepts | Recognition | Action |
| Sexism | xxx | xxx | xxx | x | O |
| Heterosexism | xxx | xxx | xxx | x | X |
| Racism | xx | xxx | xxx | xx | xx |
| Antisemitism | x | xxx | xx | xxx | xx |
| Ableism | x | Xxx | xx | xxx | xxx |

Note: X's indicate relative weight and emphasis.

**Table 4.5**    Key Concepts in Relation to Course Topics

| | Sample: Key Concepts in Relation to Course Topic Areas | | | | |
|---|---|---|---|---|---|
| Topics | Cycle | Identity | Agent/Target | Levels and Types | History |
| Sexism | xxx | Xxx | xxx | Xx | o |
| Heterosexism | xx | Xx | xxx | Xx | x |
| Racism | o | Xx | xx | Xxx | xx |
| Antisemitism | o | Xx | xx | Xx | xxx |
| Ableism | o | Xx | xx | Xx | xxx |

The conceptual (as distinct from topical) dimension of this sample semester-long course format involves a backward and forward recycling of key concepts across the designated subject areas. For example, an exploration of historical context provides multiple instances of the levels and types of antisemitism in medieval and modern European laws, media, and bureaucracy. Although introduced with reference to anti-semitism, this also suggests new ways to reframe and understand the historical dimension of other forms of oppression. In racism, for example, the historical background of slavery and forced segregation for African Americans, the World War II internment camps for Japanese Americans, the expropriation of Mexican American wealth and property in the early 19th century, and the extermination of entire villages and cultures of Native Americans by colonists and westward settlers offer startling glimpses into an unacknowledged, often unknown, dimension of our shared American history. These often shock participants to want to know more.

From the parallels and interconnections that emerge through the conceptual intersections of the course topics, participants can also explore agent and target identities and experience directly the compounding effect of multiple social identities. For example, linkages and interconnections may emerge for participants who experience multiple oppressions (an African American lesbian, a hearing-impaired Jewish woman, participants from mixed racial parentage), who experience multiple privileges (a heterosexual white Christian woman, a gay white Christian man, a heterosexual white Jewish man), and who focus exclusively on both target and privileged status (a Jewish woman in relation to race, an African American Christian man in relation to antisemitism). Participants begin to understand how their multiple social identities have internally reinforcing as well as complicating effects.

Sustained contact with students during a 14-week semester enables instructors to structure, facilitate, and follow up on students' efforts to transfer insights back and forth between the classroom and their home communities. Examples taken from campus experience can be used in lectures or discussions, and then examined in class so that students learn from each other's views on different racial, ethnic, or gender issues.

Homework, journal assignments, reflective papers, simulations, and role plays help students sharpen their analytic skills. Participants become adept over time in their ability to recognize and record instances of oppression in their daily lives. (For other dimensions of multiple-issue course formats, see Adams & Marchesani, 1997; Marchesani & Adams, 1992.)

## Making Adjustments as the Class Unfolds

More times than not, the design that facilitators have prepared prior to the start of the course requires adjustment once the course begins. The flexibility to make needed design adjustments based on what is happening in the moment is an essential design skill. Many factors can necessitate redesigning a course. information about participants may be incomplete or inaccurate. Incidents in a class may require a change in design to capitalize on a spontaneous learning opportunity or "teachable moment" that presents itself unexpectedly during the class. Participant expectations for the course may not match the design. Activities may take longer than the time allotted for them in the original design, and facilitators need to change plans as a result. Informal participant evaluations in the midst of the course may signal the need to make design adjustments (see Chapter 17 for further discussion). In all of these cases, it is necessary to reevaluate the design and decide how to make adjustments that will maintain the flow of the course while addressing the essential key concepts.

## Evaluating the Course, Facilitator, and Participant Performance

Our social justice education designs interweave social science theory with personal experience. They combine traditional aspects of academic work (papers, reading, homework assignments, and final exams) with active, experiential pedagogy. They also use participant writing as a tool for self-exploration and reflection. Thus, social justice education courses meet general education emphases upon critical thinking, writing and grounding in theory.

Course evaluation can include several components: evaluation of the curriculum, the facilitator, and participant performance. Evaluation can occur during the course (formative) or at the end of the course (summative). Planning evaluation procedures as part of course design enables facilitators to be intentional about selecting evaluation procedures that match the specific learning goals and objectives for each activity planned. Below are some considerations we have found useful for the evaluation of our courses.

## Differentiate Grades and Evaluation From Partcipant Personal Opinions and Perspectives

In social justice education courses, when we assign letter grades to our evaluation of student work, we need to differentiate grading or evaluation from the equally important feedback we give to participants to challenge their thinking or point out disparities and inconsistencies. We carefully avoid grading participants on the content of their perspectives to avoid the perception or the reality that participants must adhere to a "politically correct" party line to receive a passing grade.

Our goal is to invite participants to challenge their thinking, listen to different perspectives, deepen their awareness of social justice issues, and take action on their new perspectives. These goals can only be reached when participants know that they can freely express themselves without fear of receiving poor grades based on their failure to express the "correct" perspective.

We also want to be able to challenge the more dualistic thinking of some participants who reduce complex issues to simpler dichotomies of right/wrong, true/false, or good/bad, without lowering their grades for reasons they do not yet understand. Further, some participants expect at the beginning of the semester that we will enforce political correctness in a course dealing with social justice. Our intention in differentiating between grades and student expression of perspectives is to enable participants to freely express their beliefs, especially when they disagree with the facilitator or other participants in class.

Grades and evaluation should always be based upon assigned work, such as questions about assigned texts and other readings, preparation of homework assignments, and completion of in-class activities; written papers that follow a sequence of reflective questions or structured guidelines; and a final essay exam, based on broad conceptual questions prepared in advance that test participants' utilization of concepts and knowledge (see example of reading assignments in Appendix 4C).

We may disagree, and sometimes even dislike and disavow, some of the views expressed by participants in these assignments, and we will always ask questions or give feedback (see Appendix 4D), but the actual course grades derive from grade points and grade percentages set in advance for each assignment and for various questions inside each assignment.

This rigorous, demonstrable differentiation of qualitative or personal teacher-to-student feedback from the quantifiable and basically "fair" grading of performance turns around this initial and understandable distrust, and protects the integrity of our open-ended dialogue-and-discussion teaching approach. We have confidence that participants who do the assigned coursework will, by the end of the course, have had to examine and interrogate their prior beliefs and assumptions, increase their knowledge base, grapple with theoretical and conceptual interconnections, and recognize course concepts in real-world examples. As a result of engaging in this learning process, we believe that many participants will consider and try out new perspectives and actions in their everyday lives.

## Evaluating Course Curricula

We value participant feedback about the course and invite such feedback both during and at the end of the semester. Formative evaluation can be informal: for example, asking open-ended questions such as "What learning activities have been most effective in helping you to learn more about sexism?" or "What made these activities effective?" Formative evaluation can also be formal: Instructors develop specific questions about learning activities, sequencing, reading assignments, and grading criteria, and ask participants to rate them on a Likert scale. Formative evaluation has the advantage of enabling instructors to make midcourse changes based on feedback from the class. Nonetheless, summative evaluation is equally important in determining how an entire curriculum works after it is completed. Summative evaluation can make use of institutionally designed forms or those created by the instructor to evaluate the course as a whole.

## Evaluating Facilitators

Many schools require faculty to conduct evaluations at the end of a course and provide standardized computer forms for this purpose. Often, faculty are able to add their own questions to these forms to tailor them to the needs of the course. These evaluations can be helpful for social justice educators, and we also recommend developing additional questions to supplement the standardized forms when possible. Because social justice education courses incorporate experiential learning and rely heavily on participant interaction as central to the learning process, standardized forms can miss important opportunities for improving teaching based on feedback. Hearing how participants respond to a facilitator's ability to lead discussions, negotiate difficult interactions, ensure that all perspectives are aired, and ask questions that challenge thinking without invalidating the speaker are all examples of specific leadership skills that might be included on a supplement to standardized forms.

We offer the design tools in this chapter as a guide to help facilitators have confidence that what they have planned will enable participants to explore difficult social justice issues in the most supportive learning environment possible. We provide sequencing ideas we use to help participants understand the dynamics of oppression in their own lives and in the larger society. We hope these principles will also be useful and adaptable for developing new designs for social justice education classes that meet the particular needs of the groups you teach. With practice, these principles can become a routine part of planning and a basis from which to create and explore new activities and approaches to social justice education.

# 5

# Facilitating Social Justice Education Courses

## PAT GRIFFIN AND
## MATHEW L. OUELLETT

In a traditional learning environment, the focus is primarily on cognitive learning via content or information delivery and is most often one-way—teacher as expert, and students as learners. Facilitation, however, focuses on active engagement, cognitive, affective, and kinesthetic, in multiple learning domains (Bloom, 1956), and assumes that participants have valuable knowledge and expertise from which both peers and teachers can learn (Brooks-Harris & Stock-Ward, 1999). In this perspective, learning is a complex and interactive engagement that might include receiving information via lectures, but also involves participants' thinking and talking about their experiences and feelings in relationship to the topic as they explore different perspectives and challenge their own understandings and attitudes. *Facilitation* thus refers to the leadership strategies and skills instructors use with participants across a complex array of learning domains and outcome goals. *Curriculum design* includes all of the planning, assessing, and evaluating activities instructors engage in prior to and after class meeting with participants. Though facilitation and curriculum design are interrelated and overlapping, we find this differentiation useful in preparing to teach social justice education (see Chapter 4 on curriculum design).

For faculty who are more comfortable and experienced in traditional lecture methods of teaching, facilitating social justice education classes can be an exciting way to expand their teaching repertoire, though some might also experience disequilibrium and uncertainty. Facilitation requires sharing control and inviting participants to take an active part in class activities. Facilitation also calls for faculty to trust that active engagement can effectively lead to deeper understanding of and commitment to social justice learning goals. It requires that instructors be willing to incorporate pedagogical strategies that shift the classroom focus away from facilitator expertise to participant-centered learning.

Social justice education requires awareness of content and process, and an ability to simultaneously participate in the process and step outside of it to assess and mediate interactions in the group. Such skills are learned through experience, trial and error, and ongoing experimentation. In fact, much of facilitating social justice education requires thinking on one's feet. In this chapter, we will address a range of leadership issues to which facilitators must attend, and will describe some common participant reactions and suggest strategies to address them. We encourage faculty to adopt a "learn-as-you-go" mind-set and to *not* wait until feeling completely "expert" before beginning to adopt innovations. Even seasoned facilitators continue to learn from new situations. We have found that experience is often the best teacher in identifying what works and in getting comfortable with the challenges and satisfactions of facilitation. We hope this chapter provides helpful guidelines that will encourage educators to experiment in developing an effective facilitation style that works for them.

## Assessing Initial Readiness to Facilitate Social Justice Education

The first task is to assess the personal resources facilitators bring to the task (Phillips, 1987; Schwarz, 1994; Weinstein & Obear, 1992). Parker Palmer (1998) posits that the best teaching flows from congruity in the identity and integrity of the facilitator—that, in essence, we teach who we are. This can be especially true in the context of social justice education. The following questions serve as guides for helping prospective social justice educators determine readiness in five critical areas: support, passion, awareness, knowledge, and skills (Bailey Jackson, personal communication, 1992).

### Support

*Support* refers to the availability of professional and personal support for teaching about social justice issues. Teaching social justice education courses is more rewarding if you have colleagues and friends with whom you can discuss issues, challenge your awareness, receive help, and commiserate when things don't go as planned.

- What is the climate in your program, department, and school for addressing social justice issues? How are these issues addressed in other courses? Are there significant events on campus or in other courses that may "spill over" into your course?
- What kind of administrative support do you have? Will administration back you up if there is parental or community concern? Do the personnel committee and/or chairperson of your department understand that there is commonly an initial drop in participant end-of-semester evaluations when implementing new pedagogical methods?
- What kind of personal support do you have from colleagues and friends? Do you know other teachers who are addressing these issues with participants with whom you can share resources, exercises, materials, or readings?
- Is there institutional support for you to team teach social justice education courses?
- Do you have someone you can talk with who will help you plan and evaluate lessons?

### Passion

Social justice education requires substantial commitment and passion to sustain facilitators when the challenges become temporarily overwhelming. Belief in the importance of social justice education and the possibility of social change provides facilitators with visions to work toward.

- How important is it to you to address social justice issues with participants?
- Can you articulate a clear rationale to yourself and others for why these issues need to be addressed?
- Are you willing to risk being the center of controversy if there is community or parental objection?
- Social justice education courses often discomfort participants emotionally in ways that other courses do not. Have you considered how addressing these issues will affect participants' perceptions of you (positively and negatively)?
- How comfortable are you with discussing social justice issues? For example, do you prefer to avoid emotional or conflictual encounters? Do you assume that learning happens only when participants "enjoy" the class or feel good about it?

### Awareness

Learning about social justice issues is a lifelong process. Excitement and humility about continuing to learn about one's own social group memberships, one's access to privilege, and ways to empower one's self not only make for better social justice education but also keep one in touch with the learning process in which participants are engaged. Awareness about one's feelings in difficult or challenging discussions is important, as is gauging one's ability to listen to multiple perspectives and emotions.

- How much thought have you given to your own beliefs and feelings about social justice issues? For example, how have you become more aware of your own privilege and prejudice?
- What strategies do you use to stay alert to how a range of social justice issues are manifested in your school?
- How aware are you of the interrelationships among different forms of social oppression, and what are your strategies for continuing to deepen such learning?

### Knowledge

The more information facilitators bring into the classroom, the richer the experience for participants. When social justice educators keep up with research, writing, and current events about different manifestations of social oppression, they are better prepared to integrate this information into their teaching. Also, participants find it very helpful when instructors draw examples and analogies of important concepts and models in class from daily life.

- What information about different forms of social oppression are you most comfortable with and know the most about (e.g., qualitative information like narratives and personal stories that illuminate individual experiences of oppression, or empirical research like statistics or large data sets that help illuminate the experiences of groups)?
- How prepared do you feel to provide a range of types of information about different forms of social oppression to participants?
- Do you have access to resources you can use to increase your knowledge (people, books, workshops, courses, videos)?

## Skills

Because of the participatory and interactive nature of social justice education, facilitators use an array of process and leadership skills to create a learning environment in which participants can engage with the topic and each other productively.

- What skills do you have for leading discussions?
- How comfortable are you with participants expressing a variety of emotions? How comfortable are you with participants expressing conflicting beliefs?
- Can you listen to prejudiced comments in class discussions without becoming emotionally "triggered" or expressing anger? How comfortable do you feel in addressing anger or other emotions that participants direct at peers?
- Can you plan questions to help participants challenge and confront their own stereotypes and fears about different social groups? How easily do you identify with and draw connections between participants' comments and the core content?
- Are you comfortable disclosing your own fears, uncertainties, and openness to learning as a way to model this behavior for participants?

## Solo Facilitation or Co-Facilitation

One of the first decisions when planning a social justice education course is whether to teach alone or with a co-facilitator. By *co-facilitation*, we mean two facilitators who collaboratively develop, teach, and evaluate every session of the course. This is different from models of team teaching where a series of instructors take individual responsibility for segments of a course but may not attend each other's sessions. We strongly recommend co-facilitation in two-person teams for a number of reasons. Two facilitators who, between them, bring a multiplicity of social identities to the leadership team provide greater opportunities to explore the intersections of identities in relationship to the topic of the course. This configuration enables the leadership team to better connect with participants in the course from both advantaged and targeted groups. Two different leadership perspectives also enrich planning, teaching, and evaluating the course. Moreover, co-facilitators can support each other during difficult and challenging class incidents in ways a solo facilitator cannot. Ouellett and Fraser (2005) describe many of the positive attributes of co-teaching as well as guidelines for avoiding common pitfalls.

We believe that co-facilitation by an advantaged and a targeted group member in relation to the focus of the course is most effective (for example, in a sexism class a teaching team that includes a woman and a man). Some parts of the content and process of the course are more appropriately addressed by a facilitator from the advantaged group, and others are best dealt with by a facilitator from the targeted group. This leadership configuration also provides participants with role models from both the advantaged and targeted groups as they grapple with challenging issues. Leaders from the targeted group model empowerment and affirmation. Advantaged leaders model how to be a self-affirming and effective ally. Both facilitators enrich the variety of experiences and perspectives participants hear when they integrate their own experiences into the class discussions. Such a co-teaching relationship can be the first time that some participants will see respect, collegiality, and open communication across different identities such as race, gender, and sexual orientation. Also, facilitators benefit enormously through the ready feedback on their teaching and exposure to alternative pedagogical strategies and styles.

As in any co-facilitation experience, it is important to discuss compatibility prior to planning the course curriculum. Co-facilitators must agree on how best to teach about the nature and dynamics of oppression. They need to discuss teaching goals, teaching philosophies, facilitation strengths and challenges, preferred teaching styles, and content strengths. Co-facilitators must also discuss their interactions with each other as members of advantaged and targeted groups, and be alert to how their interactions are an integral part of the curriculum that must be attended to intentionally and consciously. When a male co-facilitator in a sexism course takes on primary responsibility for lectures, takes lots of air time, or interrupts his female co-facilitator, these interactions send contradictory messages to participants that undermine educating about sexism. Co-facilitators need to maintain open communication before, during, and after each class. Successful teams learn how to provide each other with constructive feedback, share feelings or concerns, and collaboratively redesign classes and activities as the need arises. Co-facilitators need to identify an ongoing process for debriefing the leadership experience in class as well as during class planning and evaluation sessions. For example, some co-facilitators make it a practice to tell participants at the outset of the course that they will respectfully share the facilitation process. This means that there will be times during class when the teaching team expects to turn to each other and discuss what is transpiring in the class, compare what each sees as available options, and decide together what is most important and how to go forward (Ouellett & Fraser, 2005).

Co-facilitation is unfortunately not a practical option for all teachers. Solo teaching social justice education can also be successful and rewarding when individual facilitators can identify ways to create out-of-class support and assistance. Although an instructor cannot presume to speak for a different group, in such a situation she may want to acknowledge and note at the outset (and thereafter as appropriate) the absence of other perspectives. Meeting with an outside support group of colleagues who are interested in social justice education or who are solo teaching their own social justice education courses is one way to create support. Providing an in-class perspective different from the facilitator's can be accomplished by bringing in outside speakers, choosing readings, and selecting videos and other activities that present perspectives from different social groups and positions. Solo facilitators must also develop a flexible set of leadership skills and confidence in their ability to manage challenging discussions in the course.

## Facilitator Responsibilities

We define *facilitation responsibilities* as leadership during the class, as distinguished from *design responsibilities* that include course preparation prior to meeting participants and evaluation after the course is completed. Design and facilitation skills do, however, overlap as facilitators adjust design during the course.

After deciding whether a solo or team facilitation format will be used, facilitators need to attend to a wide array of responsibilities for planning and teaching social justice education courses. These responsibilities include (a) establishing an effective learning environment, (b) choosing appropriate process leadership roles, and (c) attending to a variety of leadership tasks.

### Establishing an Effective Learning Environment

Four broad areas are important to establish an effective learning environment: time, teaching aids, task, and climate. These are discussed below.

## Time

From the facilitator's perspective, there never seems to be enough time in a social justice education course. Because institutionally determined course-ending times rarely match the natural ebb and flow of learning, especially in a social justice education class, facilitators are constantly monitoring time and making decisions about how to best use the time available. Managing time includes planning activities that are appropriate for the available time, monitoring class time to ensure that all participants have time to speak in small and large groups, and knowing when to cut short or extend an activity depending on how engaged participants are and on the time remaining in the class period.

When planning time allotments for an activity, facilitators must consider how much time participants need to complete an activity and how much time they need to discuss the activity once it is completed. Much of the important learning from an activity comes from the discussion or processing time after an activity. Most novice facilitators either plan too many activities for a class period or underestimate how long it will take to complete an activity. As a result, there is often insufficient time for processing activities, and participants are left to make sense of activities on their own without the benefit of facilitator guidance or other participant perspectives. Typically, we recommend allotting at least as much time to discuss an activity as it takes to do the activity. Activities that are particularly rich or emotionally engaging may need twice the amount of time for discussion. Leading these discussions is at the heart of facilitation in social justice education courses and can distinguish high-quality learning from an engaging activity from superficial learning without adequate discussion.

## Teaching Aids

Using all available teaching aids enhances participant learning by meeting the needs of different learning styles, abilities, and preferences. Using a variety of visual, audio, Internet-based, and other computer technology learning also avoids boring routines and keeps the class fresh and lively. Many professionally produced videos and audiotapes on social justice topics are available for use in class or assigned as homework. Many such resources are listed in the appendices on the accompanying CD.

## Task

Learners can participate most fully when they have a solid sense of the learning objectives, outcome goals, and facilitators' expectations before each class to provide them with a sense of control over the nature and direction of their learning experience. Receiving the agenda ahead of time can address participants' expectations and create shared ownership and responsibility for the learning environment. During the first class meeting, participants should be given a class syllabus with explicit evaluation criteria included.

Managing individual activities is another task responsibility for facilitators. This requires that facilitators choose activities appropriate to specific learning goals for the course, describing and setting up activities with clear directions, preparing materials ahead of time, and identifying a range of stimulating discussion or processing questions to maximize meaningful learning from the activity. In addition, facilitators also help to keep participants on task, invite everyone to speak, and encourage the expression of a variety of perspectives.

## Climate

One of the most important facilitation skills is developing an effective learning environment. How the facilitator designs the course is the platform for a powerful learning experience, but attention to the climate during class meetings is the most crucial factor in sustaining an environment that invites and supports critical examination of their own experiences as raced, gendered, sexed, classed people. Listening to new and challenging perspectives, questioning beliefs, and identifying new actions and attitudes are at the heart of the social justice education process. The better able the facilitator is in allaying participants' fears and self-consciousness, the more likely participants who feel vulnerable will be to express and explore unexamined or unpopular beliefs and values. Addressing climate can be enhanced by (a) identifying participation guidelines, (b) attending to personal comfort, (c) setting the tone, (d) evaluating the physical space, (e) ensuring access, (f) differentiating between safety and comfort, and (g) attending to group development in multicultural classes.

## Identifying Participation Guidelines

Establishing a safe environment in which participants can discuss ideas, share feelings and experiences, and challenge themselves and each other to reevaluate opinions and beliefs is one of the primary facilitation responsibilities. Identifying a set of interaction guidelines at the beginning of the course is one way to meet this responsibility (see the introductory modules in Chapter 3 for more information about participation guidelines). Once identified and agreed upon by participants and facilitators, it is the responsibility of the facilitator(s) to insure that the guidelines are used and to remind participants to use them as needed during the course.

## Attending to Personal Comfort

Within the context of any class structure, it is important to attend to attention span and personal comfort. Providing participants with periodic breaks is essential to an effective learning environment. As a guide, we encourage a 10–15-minute break every 60–90 minutes, even if participants are engaged in experiential activities.

With daylong classes, meal breaks are physically as well as mentally important. As part of an introduction to the course, we tell participants when breaks will occur and the locations of the closest bathrooms and snack or drink machines. Asking participants at the beginning of the class to either write down or talk for a minute with a classmate about something they are missing or escaping in their lives in order to be in class and then to put it aside for the duration of the class can be effective way to help participants focus and avoid distractions. Attending to these comfort issues in advance allows participants to concentrate more fully on class activities and to pace themselves as the class unfolds.

## Setting the Tone

Creating an atmosphere that is both serious and light works well in setting a tone for the class. This means treating social justice content as the serious issue it is, but incorporating activities that include humor and playfulness along with those that can stimulate sadness, anger, or confusion. Planning activities so that participants can experience serious feelings without becoming enmeshed in them is an intentional process of deciding when participants need a break, a chance to sit with feelings of discomfort, time to reflect, or a complete change of focus. Light activities refresh participants, relieve tension, and enable everyone to focus more effectively on the desired learning goals. Such activities inspire joy and hopefulness, which help contradict and dispel preconceptions that social justice change efforts are necessarily doomed to fail. "Icebreaker" games, singing, or physical activities like group stretches can facilitate transitions between activities and introduce kinesthetic aspects to the learning climate. Other activities such as role plays can be simultaneously light and serious as participants create humorous ways to illustrate or address serious issues.

## Evaluating the Physical Space

A social justice education facilitator must consider aspects of the physical environment that affect learning. Lighting, room temperature, ventilation, acoustics, room color, distracting noise, seating comfort and placement, access to audiovisual technology, and room cleanliness can all affect how inviting a classroom is and how well participants can concentrate. We have found that teaching in classrooms with movable chairs allows participants to arrange themselves in a variety of group configurations depending on the class activity. We prefer variations on circles and semicircles because participants can see and hear each other better than they can in a traditional audience-style classroom in which all participants face the facilitator. Circles and semicircles also encourage participants to talk with each other and be active participants in the class.

## Ensuring Access

Making sure that all aspects of the learning environment are accessible to all participants is essential. Facilitators can assess the physical space such as the classroom, bathrooms, and eating areas to determine whether or not it is accessible to participants with a range of disabilities. Facilitators should also check to see if there is a gender-neutral bathroom available. At the beginning of the course, facilitators can ask participants to identify documented learning needs to the instructor so that accommodations can be made to class activities, assignments, and experiences (see Chapters 4 and 14 for more information about universal instructional design).

## Differentiating Between Safety and Comfort

We want all participants to feel they can actively engage in class activities and discussions, regardless of their point of view. Feeling safe doesn't mean they will never be challenged or uncomfortable, but facilitators must maintain an environment in which participants can describe their feelings and perspectives without being overly criticized or silenced for using "incorrect" language or expressing "unpopular" attitudes. Such a climate enables participants to be more open to critically examine their worldviews.

We express directly to participants that we want them to feel safe, but not always comfortable. We believe that feeling uncomfortable at times is a valuable and an expected part of an effective social justice education class. Such feelings of discomfort can be experienced intellectually (e.g., encountering a challenging new perspective, new information, or experience), emotionally (getting feedback from other participants about how one's behavior or attitudes affect others in the class), or physically (experiencing shortness of breath, accelerated heartbeat, or perspiring), and are important learning opportunities for all participants in the class regardless of their social identities. This discomfort can be the basis for intellectual breakthroughs, increased personal insight, and changes in behaviors, awareness, and actions. We refer to these moments of discomfort as *learning edges* and invite participants to notice and explore when they are on a learning edge rather than retreat to their comfort zone of familiar beliefs and experiences. Differentiating safety and comfort and reframing discomfort as an essential aspect of learning in social justice education help participants understand their feelings better and see discomfort as an opportunity to learn. Learning to notice the signs of being on a learning edge is a useful mechanism for realizing when we care deeply about something or experience challenges to taken-for-granted assumptions.

In social justice education courses, such self-awareness is an explicit learning outcome goal (see Chapter 3 for a discussion of learning edges and comfort zones).

## Attending to Group Development in Multicultural Classes

Every group of participants, whether in a workshop that meets only once for 2 hours or multiple classes over the course of a semester, will go through stages of development that affect the group's performance as well as that of individuals in the group. Astin (2003) reports that students succeed best in college when they are able to create significant relationships with peers and faculty. For this reason, a basic understanding of group theory can help make sense of group dynamics in the class (Carew, Carew, & Blanchard, 1990; Moosbruker, 1987). Information discussed in the group development and group dynamics literature offers useful guides for facilitation of social justice education classes (Johnson & Johnson, 1987; Walter & Stephan, 1996).

As facilitators, we strive to make pedagogical decisions that reflect and model our values and assumptions. We work to create classrooms that are centered on student learning, have high levels of positive interdependence between participants and the facilitator, and create relationships between the facilitator and participants that underscore high expectations of success for all, and where members are expected to learn the collaborative skills necessary to promote each others' learning and success (McKeachie & Svinicki, 2006).

## Choosing Appropriate Process Leadership Roles

Facilitators take on several different process leadership roles that are distinct from postures associated with traditional teaching modes. Brooks-Harris and Stock-Ward (1999) describe this as a paradigm shift from a unidirectional, content-focused model where the teacher is the source of all information to a model where the facilitator intentionally encourages "learning between and among participants ... valuing and promoting experience and growth as much as knowledge," and elevating the process of learning to equal importance with acquisition of content (p. 7). Facilitators do this by simultaneously monitoring individual, group, and intergroup interactions as participants engage with the class content and develop as a group.

In a social justice education course, it is essential that the facilitator get to know participants well, help them get to know each other, and enable them to develop a secure enough sense of themselves as a group that they can relax into the learning opportunity. To this end, roles a facilitator can play include participant, guide, teacher, role model, and change agent. Each facilitator will likely be more comfortable in some roles than others. The challenge is to develop the ability to comfortably move between different roles and to know which is most appropriate during different aspects of a class.

## Participant Role

Social justice education is enriched when the facilitator can comfortably share with participants her own experiences, feelings, and struggles with social justice topics. Disclosing some of our own journey with participants can deepen their understanding of these complex issues. Personal disclosure also models for participants how to make personal connections themselves. Such efforts also help to break down an "all or nothing" mind-set (i.e., "Either I am a racist or I'm not a racist"). For example, when a white facilitator tells about his own confusion and fear as a participant in his first racism course, he helps white participants experiencing similar feelings to acknowledge and work through them. When a lesbian facilitator discusses her experience of coming out to her family, she helps heterosexual participants understand the fear and isolation many lesbian, gay, and bisexual people feel among their loved ones.

### Guide Role

A social justice education facilitator must also develop the ability to pose questions, raise contradictions, encourage and model self-reflection, and summarize group discussions. These skills lead participants to more sophisticated self-understanding and elaborated awareness of the dynamics of social oppression in their lives. The challenge here is to provide appropriate guidance and encourage participants to reevaluate for themselves "commonsense" understandings they have developed through their own socialization, without dictating what to believe.

### Teacher Role

Facilitators need to be able to present information (such as statistics, research, and conceptual models) accurately, clearly, and concisely. These data or "public knowledge" comprise an important part of understanding social injustice and an essential complement to analysis of personal experiences, feelings, and beliefs. Participants benefit from facilitators who help them learn and practice how to find, critically evaluate, and use effectively a variety of sources of information, data, and resource materials.

### Role Model Role

Facilitators are important role models for participants. By selective sharing of personal experiences, facilitators model their own journeys as "works in progress," always learning more about their own identities in relationship to the focus of the class. Co-facilitators are also role models in their interactions with each other, demonstrating respectful dialogue and an effective collaborative relationship. Advantaged group facilitators are important role models for being an ally, and targeted group facilitators model empowered behaviors. Co-facilitators representing different social identities convey consistent and powerful messages about addressing social injustice and the roles everyone, regardless of their social identities, can play to address injustice.

### Change Agent Role

At times, it is appropriate to encourage participants to act on their beliefs. By providing a range of options, from low to high risk, and encouraging participants to take action appropriate for their readiness level, the facilitator helps them understand how to transform a concern for social justice into concrete actions toward social change.

### Organizing Discussions

Leading discussions in social justice education classes is one of the most important and difficult responsibilities a facilitator undertakes. Because the activities in a social justice education course are designed to raise contradictions and challenge participants to rethink their understanding of social power relationships, discussions can be intense as conflicting perspectives are expressed. Structured activities must include the opportunity to collectively reflect on and discuss reactions to the activities, or participant learning will be limited. We call discussion of class activities *processing*. Processing is an intentional and systematic guided discussion of a class activity that encourages the expression of divergent perspectives and enables participants to derive cognitive as well as experiential understanding from the activity. Leading these discussions requires facilitators to trust the process that participants need to go through to deepen their understanding of social justice issues. Effective facilitators guide and monitor discussions, but do not dominate or become dogmatic (Dillon, 1994).

After each class activity, we lead participants through a processing progression that begins with their own *individual reactions* to the activity, then guides them through more *abstract analysis* of the oppression issues raised in the activity, and finally focuses on how they can *apply* this new information.

### Individual Reflection

Immediately after an activity is finished, we ask participants to identify personal thoughts and feelings about the activity by thinking about their reactions for a few minutes or writing them down. For example, after a panel presentation by a group of people with disabilities in an ableism course, we might ask participants to think about or write down their feelings as they heard different panelists talk about obstacles in gaining access to public buildings. Questions for participants could include "What feelings did you have as you listened to the panelists' stories?" and "What did the panelists say about their experiences as people with disabilities attending this school that you had never thought about before?"

### Descriptions of Reactions

We next invite participants to talk about thoughts and feelings stimulated by the activity that they identified during their individual reflection. This phase of processing can be accomplished in pairs, small groups, or the whole group. The focus of this phase is to listen and understand, not challenge, differing reactions. During this discussion, participants often notice the variety of reactions to the same activity.

### Analysis

Next, we ask participants to shift their focus to a discussion of how the activity illustrates particular dynamics of oppression. We invite them to identify questions, contradictions, or insights raised by the activity, and to discuss parallels and connections among different forms of oppression that the activity helped them to see. For example, following a role play about sexual harassment, we might ask participants, "How did the actions of men and women in this role play reflect gender socialization?" "In what ways are the power dynamics in this situation similar to other forms of oppression?" or "How might the experiences of women from different racial groups compare in this situation?"

### Summary

It is important for facilitators to draw the discussion to a close to help participants achieve some degree of closure, not to create agreement among all participants or to answer all questions, but to help participants pull thoughts together so that they are ready to make a transition to the next activity or to end the class session. In summarizing a discussion, facilitators and participants identify themes that emerged, unresolved questions, divergent perspectives, and other important points raised. Time to reflect enables participants to step back, summarize learning, and develop cognitive as well as experiential understanding of the issues raised in the activity. For example, during a classism course, the facilitators might say, "From this discussion, it appears that we have several different understandings of how to define social class in this group. Can we name those differences?" or "I notice a conflict in this discussion between what many of us have believed about equal opportunity in the past and what we are beginning to see about the effects of class differences on economic opportunity." We do not expect participants to end a processing discussion feeling that they have completely resolved their discomfort with different ideas and perspectives. Some disorientation is a sign that participants are grappling with new awareness and knowledge. We encourage them to notice discomfort, challenge themselves to stay on their learning edge, and consider new ideas rather than retreat to the comfort of more familiar perspectives.

### Application

The intention in the application phase is to help participants begin to identify how they might apply new understanding and information. We might ask participants to reflect on how the information they learned in the activity might affect their future attitudes, beliefs, and actions. To help participants apply what they have learned in an activity during an antisemitism class, for example, we might ask, "How might this activity affect your feelings about scheduling group activities on Jewish holidays?" or "What will your response be the next time someone tells a joke that relies for its humor on Jewish stereotypes that you find offensive?" Because Module 4 of most of our curriculum designs includes more extensive activities to help participants develop action plans, we typically do not spend as much time focusing on behavioral change in earlier parts of the curriculum, and we focus more on action goals toward the end of the course.

### Alternative Discussion Formats

We use a variety of discussion formats, including whole class, small groups, triads, and pairs. Whole-class discussions are a staple in all classes. In this format, facilitators have the most control over discussion and can effectively assume a variety of leadership roles to facilitate thoughtful exploration of a range of perspectives and information and invite involvement from of all members of the class. Two disadvantages of whole-class discussions are that some participants are reluctant to speak in front of the whole group, and other participants dominate or get locked into face-to-face debate. Therefore, we also use small-group discussions (four to six people) to provide a more comfortable discussion environment for participants who do not like talking in whole-group discussions and to ensure that all participants have the opportunity to speak. We also use triads when we want to provide participants with even more opportunities to talk. In groups of three, participants can have an extended conversation that is not possible in the large- or small-group discussions. Pair discussions are also useful, especially if the topic is potentially more sensitive for participants or to help participants gather their thoughts before participating in a larger group discussion. Pair discussions allow participants to express themselves in greater completeness than may be possible in large-group discussions. They are also helpful after conflict or a particularly emotional exchange in the large group, and enable participants to reflect upon and articulate their reactions in a more protected environment. Individual reflection time is used to enable participants to identify and organize their feelings and thoughts before talking in either small or large groups. We encourage participants to keep a class journal in which they write their reactions, questions, and thoughts during individual reflection times.

### Attending to a Variety of Leadership Tasks

Facilitators can take different roles during small-group discussions. They can let the class know they are available if anyone has questions and then allow the groups to work independently unless invited to join them. Facilitators can also "float" among different groups, stopping to listen or even participate in the discussions of several groups. We take on both roles at different times during a class, depending on the group task, participant preferences, and our own energy level.

## Leading Discussions

During class discussions, the facilitator has a number of possible leadership tasks depending on the needs of the group and the purpose of the discussion. Deciding when each task is appropriate requires experience and careful attention to the discussion process as it unfolds, guided by the question "What is the best leadership task for me to fill right now?" Tasks include giving information, conceptualizing, reflecting, using silence, monitoring and redistributing, questioning, challenging, observing and reporting, accepting the expression of feelings, disclosing personal information, and addressing conflict.

## Giving Information

Sometimes, providing factual information in the form of statistics or descriptions of current events is useful. Participants may request information, or the facilitator may decide that providing facts will address misconceptions or fill a gap in the information participants use to support a particular position. The following examples illustrate the information-giver role.

- A participant states that most people are middle class. The facilitator responds, "Though most people tend to think of themselves as middle class, U.S. Census statistics show that most of the wealth in the United States is controlled by less than 5% of the people."
- A participant states that gay men are child molesters. The facilitator responds, "Police records show that well over 90% of child sexual abuse involves heterosexual men molesting female children."

## Conceptualizing

Sometimes, feelings overwhelm participants and cause them to shut down or a discussion to lose its focus. The introduction of a conceptual model can provide participants with a way to understand feelings in a broader theoretical context or can focus the discussion to proceed more productively. For example, facilitators can refer to the oppression model, cycle of socialization, identity development theory, or learning edge/comfort zone models discussed in the introductory modules to help participants understand their experience (see Chapter 3).

- A heated argument ensues about whether or not it is reasonable to ask people to avoid wearing perfume in the workplace when someone with an environmental illness is aggravated by scents. The facilitator responds, "I think several of us might be on a learning edge here. Check and see if that is true for you. How can we decide what we each need to do to stay with that edge to see what we can learn?"
- A white participant is ashamed because she could not identify any African American historical figures on a short quiz. The facilitator responds, "How does the cycle of socialization we talked about earlier help us to understand how we have been kept from knowing about cultures different from our own?"

## Reflecting

One of the most effective ways to encourage participants to think more deeply and critically when they seem reflexively locked into a position is to reflect back what they say.

Hearing their own words reflected back to them can enable participants to understand the impact of their statements and to identify underlying assumptions.

- The facilitator repeats a participant's statement, "So, what you are saying is that poor and homeless people have the same opportunity for advancement as people who have more financial resources. They are just too lazy."
- The facilitator repeats a participant's statement, "You believe that Jews are not really discriminated against because they are mostly financially secure."

### Using Silence

Many, facilitators and participants alike, are uncomfortable with silence in a classroom. Facilitators need to learn to wait after asking a question, rather than either answering their own question or posing questions in quick succession to fill a silence. In the social justice education classroom, silence can have many different meanings. Participants often need silence to think about new information or to articulate perspectives on an issue. For example, a brief period of silence is useful to provide participants time to think through their perspectives, experiences, feelings, and ideas before launching group discussions.

Differentiating productive silence from bored or fearful silence is an important facilitator skill. Signs of a fearful or uncomfortable silence include lack of eye contact among participants, yawning, physical shifting and movement in seats, or tense expressions on faces. However, facilitators should not assume that a period of silence necessarily reflects fear, discomfort, or unwillingness to continue pursing a topic under discussion. Silence can often be a learning opportunity and deepen the discussion. Strategies helpful for bridging these moments include brief writing assignments, which involve asking participants to write down their feelings at that moment or turning to a neighbor to share their thoughts, and provide a way to acknowledge and clarify reactions before moving on. Another strategy is to do a quick "whip" around the circle in which each participant in turn says one word that describes his or her feelings at that moment. Sometimes simply commenting on silence opens the discussion, enabling it to restart and potentially deepen individual understanding.

- In response to a processing question, the group is silent and no one is making eye contact. The facilitator says, "I'm not sure what this silence means. Can anyone say what you are thinking or feeling right now?" or "Let's just sit with this silence and give all of us time to sort out our feelings. When someone feels ready to answer one of the processing questions, please do."
- An emotional exchange between a Jew and a Gentile about the prevalence of antisemitism on campus leads to a long period of silence. The facilitator says, "Why don't we each take a few minutes to jot down what we are feeling right now? Then we can talk with a partner before we come back to the whole group." Or, the facilitator could say, "Wow! We have really strong feelings about this topic, don't we?" This normalizes an emotional, as well as intellectual, response to the topic.

### Monitoring/Redistributing

Several cues help facilitators assess how a discussion is progressing. Participant engagement is reflected through body posture, side conversations, the number of participants actively participating in a conversation, the attention given to whoever is speaking, and the animation with which participants talk with each other. Another important cue is whether participants listen to each others' comments and build on them versus "leapfrogging" over each others' comments to make their own point. Monitoring the process provides the facilitator with information about what role to take in the discussion. For example, when one participant or a small group of participants dominates discussions or when some participants are always silent, the facilitator can help to make a space for others to participate in a number of ways.

- One participant has taken an active role in class discussions, contributing to every conversation. The facilitator says, "Before we hear from you again, Steve, I'd like to see if some of the people who have not spoken up would like to say something."
- The facilitator notices that a quiet participant has been trying to say something, but keeps getting cut off by other, more active participants. The facilitator says, "Maria, it looks like you've been trying to get into this discussion. What would you like to say?"
- The facilitator notices that five participants have not said anything during large-group discussions. He says, "Let's do a quick pass around the circle. Each person share a short sentence that describes your reaction to this activity. Choose to pass if you wish."

The facilitator may also revert to dyads for a brief amount of time to simultaneously get at least half the class talking or ask participants to respond to a brief writing prompt as a way to help them organize their thoughts and prepare to offer comments aloud.

## Questioning

Asking questions is often an effective way to challenge assumptions, solicit factual information, and redirect discussion. Rather than directly challenge participant perspectives through statements, questions can encourage participants to examine their own assumptions and values in a respectful way and to differentiate between anecdotal, individual experience and the experiences that are generally true of a group. Questions can also help participants understand when they are repeating an unexamined belief or perspective. One question we use is "Can you say how you came to this position?"

- "What kinds of portrayals of Latino/a people do you see in the movies and on television? How do these portrayals affect your perception of what Latino/a people are like?"
- "What image of people with disabilities do you get when you watch the Jerry Lewis Telethon?"

## Challenging

Sometimes it is useful, even essential, to directly intervene and challenge what a participant says: for example, if she or he is personally attacking a classmate or if a participant is saying something that is clearly inaccurate. When needed, such corrections can help to refocus a constructive direction for the discussion or activity and help ensure that all participants feel able to participate.

- A participant rolls her eyes and looks away when a man tries to challenge her belief in the fairness of affirmative action programs. The facilitator says to her, "There needs to be room for all of us to express our beliefs here. We may not all agree, but we need to be able to disagree respectfully. We need to express our disagreement in ways that are consistent with our discussion guidelines."
- A participant states his belief that gay men want to be women. The facilitator says, "People who choose another gender are called *transgender*. Transgender people can be gay, lesbian, heterosexual, and bisexual, or may identify their

sexuality in an entirely different way. Most gay men are as comfortable as heterosexual men with identifying themselves as men."

## Observing/Reporting

Naming what is happening in a group discussion helps participants understand how the dynamics of oppression are operating within the group. This requires the facilitator to be conscious of intergroup and interpersonal dynamics (Gudykunst, 1994; Porter, 1982).

- In a small-group discussion of institutional racism, only the two men in the group are talking, and they direct all their comments to each other. The facilitator says, "I notice that even though there are more women in this group, the men are talking more and seem to be looking to each other as they talk. Has anyone else noticed this? How can we be sure everyone has a chance to talk and be listened to?"
- In a racism class, white participants are directing questions to the participants of color as if their role in the class is to teach white participants about racism. The white facilitator says, "I notice that we white folks sometimes tend to ask questions of the black, Asian, Latino/a, and Native American participants about racism. Has anyone else noticed this, and what do you think of it?"

## Accepting the Expression of Feelings

For some facilitators and participants, expression of feelings in a classroom is an unusual experience that takes getting used to (Auvine, Densmore, Extrom, Poole, & Shanklin, 1978). This is because traditionally, education environments have discouraged the public expression of emotions as inappropriate. Some participants (e.g., women and some ethnic and racial groups) may have experienced penalties for showing emotions in the classroom and criticized as less rigorous thinkers, less analytical, or unable to be frame an impartial argument. In social justice education classes, participants get angry at each other, themselves, and the facilitators. Sometimes, participants cry while remembering painful experiences or hearing a classmate recount a painful story. Participants feel frustrated by the pervasiveness of social injustice. Other participants feel deceived because they didn't learn about oppression before. Although no one should feel that intense emotion is required for effective learning, all should be prepared for the expression of honest feelings that may arise at different times in the course and be reminded of the important learning outcomes that can come from staying open to listening closely to the experiences, and feelings, of others.

- A participant begins to cry as she recalls how a younger brother with a developmental disability was teased by classmates at school. The facilitator says, "It seems like that is still a painful memory for you. Thanks for telling us about this experience. It is a powerful reminder of how deeply name-calling can affect us. Do other people have similar memories?"
- Asking participants to go around the circle and give a one-word description of what they are feeling in reaction to an intense video about the Holocaust, the facilitator says, "Please pass if you want to keep your feelings private right now."
- Sometimes, participants say things that are factually incorrect and perhaps inflammatory, but also reflect a commonly held misconception, prejudice, or stereotype. A facilitator can address such a comment directly and sensitively by first depersonalizing the comment and then focusing on the correct answer. "John says he believes, as do many people, that people of color

commit more crimes than do Whites. However, as statistics from the Department of Justice show us ..."

## Disclosing Personal Information

When facilitators express their own feelings in reaction to discussions about social injustice, they model what is acceptable in class and can help participants feel more comfortable expressing their own feelings. Emotional reactions to social justice education are a natural and human response for facilitators as well as participants. Facilitators can be triggered by statements that participants make, just as participants can trigger emotional reactions in each other. A facilitator who feels emotionally triggered needs to stay in the facilitator role and attend to group needs, but can also respond honestly. A co-facilitator can be helpful in these situations because rarely are both facilitators triggered at the same time, and the one who is not triggered can think more clearly about what leadership role to take (refer to Chapter 3 for more information about triggers).

Facilitators need to choose carefully when to disclose their personal reactions or stories and be clear about the purpose of this disclosure. It is never appropriate for facilitators to work out their own issues during a class. This important work is better attended to at some other time. If facilitators tell too many personal stories or talk about their experiences too much, participants might begin to discount the course as the facilitator's "personal agenda," and it can subvert the focus from a participant-centered to a facilitator-centered environment. All personal disclosure by facilitators should be for the purpose of helping participants achieve a better understanding of the topic. For example, a facilitator may tell participants at the beginning of a racism course: "I remember the first racism course I attended. I was so afraid of saying something that might be interpreted as racist that I never said a word and never got to ask the questions I needed to." The facilitator in this situation uses personal disclosure to help participants understand that reactions they might be having at the beginning of the course are not bad or unusual (further discussion is in Chapters 16 and 17).

Participants depend on facilitators to provide a safe and stable class environment. Ultimately, facilitators may disclose personal stories and reactions but need to keep in mind that they are not participants and are responsible for insuring a productive learning environment for all.

## Addressing Conflict as Learning Opportunity

Faculty often cite lack of preparation or skills for knowing how to effectively address conflict and a concomitant fear of losing control of class discussions as a primary obstacle to initiating a social justice education. Inviting conflict and emotional dissonance other than in the most traditional forms of argumentation and debate seems counterintuitive to maintaining "proper" classroom decorum. The initial response of many faculty members to potential conflict in the classroom is to shut down any disagreement, ignore the emotional and affective tone in a class, and keep a tight focus on intellectual and informational content. In the social justice education classroom, conflict and dissonance are valued, even necessary, parts of the process that enable values, beliefs, and ideas to emerge so that different perspectives can be explored. Our goal is to work through immediate conflicts and emotions so as to understand the individual, institutional, and cultural implications of the topic at hand. We do so by encouraging participants to consider and analyze multiple perspectives on any given topic. Important learning opportunities are missed if participants do not have the opportunity to honestly express feelings, concerns, questions, and disagreements.

Conflict in a social justice education class may arise in several ways. Conflict can arise at the intrapersonal level as participants are confronted with internal conflicts between unexamined perspectives and information, and experiences they encounter in class that challenge these perspectives (Tatum, 1994). At the interpersonal and intergroup levels, participants encounter conflicting beliefs and experiences among themselves as they interact in class activities. Sometimes, an individual participant or a group of participants is in conflict with facilitators. It is important for participants to be able to challenge ideas and behaviors without personally attacking individuals or groups within the class. Our goal is to encourage the expression of conflicting ideas and help participants practice the skills necessary to successfully sustain honest and respectful dialogues in ways beneficial to learning for all. Productive conflict means that all participants have a voice, their right to express differing perspectives is assured, and all participants listen to and challenge each other and the facilitators respectfully.

One of the most important strategies for ensuring productive conflict is to prepare participants for it and to help them understand that conflict and dissonant feelings are expected and helpful parts of the learning process. Clearly stated participation guidelines and skillful facilitation of interactions within the group provide participants with a process for expressing conflicting ideas, experiences, and feelings. We use such concepts as *comfort zone, learning edges, I statements,* and *triggers* to help participants develop a vocabulary and process for recognizing and dealing with conflict (see Chapter 3).

## Common Themes of Response in Social Justice Education

Class discussions provide rich opportunities for examining dynamics of social injustice and exploring socially learned behaviors and attitudes as these play out in class. We can use these interactions to help participants reflect on their socialization as advantaged and targeted, and invite them to challenge "commonsense" understandings of social justice issues.

Participants' reactions to class activities and discussions range from excitement about gaining new perspectives on social justice issues to anger at having some of their perceptions and perspectives challenged (Tatum, 1994). In our experience, most participants enjoy the challenge to their understanding of these complex issues and appreciate the opportunity to engage others in discussions about social justice. It is not realistic, however, to expect participants to immediately embrace all, or even most, of the new perspectives they encounter. Not all participants appreciate or are initially receptive to the new perspectives they are introduced to in social justice courses. For some, these new perspectives may counter long-standing attitudes and perspectives held by their families and communities. Likewise, not all participants are patient or compassionate with other classmates who struggle with understanding advantages of their social group membership or who resist the idea that achieving equality of opportunity is a more complex and difficult goal than they have been taught to believe.

Below, we identify some common reactions to having one's worldview questioned. The identity development model presented in Chapter 2 and applied in Chapters 3 and 17 is a valuable conceptual tool for putting participant reactions into a context that can guide facilitator responses to these reactions. Strategies for responding to participant reactions are also discussed in Chapters 6–15 in the context of curriculum designs. The participant reactions we describe here are dissonance, anger, immobilization, disassociation, and conversion.

## Dissonance

Raising social justice issues in a classroom unsettles both unconscious and deeply held beliefs about society, self, and social relations. This disequilibrium can be uncomfortable, as familiar ground shifts and participants encounter uncertainty, doubt, and self-questioning as they attempt to regain their balance (see Chapter 4). We understand dissonance as an integral and valuable part of the social justice educational process and believe we should not dismiss such reactions as intransigence or participant refusal to "get it." Respectfully working with participants who experience dissonance is crucial to a establishing a safe class environment. Some participants may experience feelings of "too much, too soon." For example, if a heterosexual participant is completely unwilling to explore issues of homophobia and heterosexism, it may first be necessary for that participant to "back up" and spend time learning more about how gender role stereotypes and sexism play out in heterosexual relationships. Our goal as facilitators is to help participants build resilience and internal resources that enable them to think critically and tolerate ambiguity and complexity so that they can choose behaviors and attitudes that are congruent with their commitments to social justice.

Dissonance can be expressed in many ways and can be experienced by members of both advantaged and targeted groups. Having one's worldview challenged, and being asked to acknowledge unasked for privilege or understand how one is discriminated against, are painful and uncomfortable experiences. Helping participants understand dissonant feelings and learn from them is a vital part of social justice education. Unless participants feel comfortable to express honest reactions, class discussions are likely to be shallow and forced. The following participant reactions illustrate different responses to dissonance. (These are selected examples and not all-inclusive.)

### Claim That the Status Quo Is Part of a "Natural Order"

In a heterosexism class, some heterosexual participants might claim that physical anatomy "proves" that homosexual relationships are unnatural and therefore lesbians, gay men, and bisexual people should be discriminated against. In a racism class, some white participants might use their belief in the innate intellectual superiority of Whites to explain statistics on crime, educational achievement, or welfare.

### Invalidation of Targeted Group Members' Experience

When advantaged group members are confronted with a description of social reality that contradicts their own experience, they may question the credibility of the targeted group's experience. They may suggest that targeted group members are oversensitive or exaggerating their experiences, or that targeted group members are dwelling too much on past injustice, that the situation has changed, and that the issues being raised have already been addressed. Gentile participants might claim that the Holocaust happened over 50 years ago and that Jews are no longer oppressed, or they might even question whether or not the Holocaust occurred. Middle-class participants might claim that most people on welfare are taking advantage of the system rather than finding a job and working like everyone else.

### Protection of Advantaged Group Members by Targeted Group Members

Sometimes in a sexism class, women will join with men who claim that women no longer experience sexism or that men are victims of "reverse sexism." Occasionally, women will protest that men in the course are being criticized unfairly when issues of male privilege are raised.

### Advantaged Group Members' Need to Have Own Pain and Hurt Recognized

Sometimes, advantaged group members do not differentiate between the hurt they experience and the oppression that targeted group members experience. In a sexism course, some men might claim that they, too, are targeted by sexism because of rigid gender roles and the social sanctions applied to men who violate gender stereotypes. Although it is important for advantaged group members to understand the ways in which their lives are limited or diminished by oppression and for facilitators to provide opportunities for them to explore how they are hurt by oppression, we believe it is essential for advantaged group members to explore and understand the differences between their experience of hurt and targeted group members' experience of oppression.

### Advantaged Group Members Focus on an Identity in Which They Are Members of the Targeted Group

Some participants have difficulty thinking about themselves from the perspective of their advantaged identities. Participants who are angry about one or more of their targeted identities and "live" in these identities find it difficult to shift that part of their identity to the background in order to foreground an advantaged aspect for scrutiny. For example, in a heterosexism class, an African American heterosexual man focuses exclusively on his experience of racial discrimination and will not consider the privilege he receives as a heterosexual. Because participants bring all of their identities, both advantaged and targeted, to every class, it is essential to integrate this complexity into the course to help participants draw connections across oppressions. A participant's experience of oppression as a targeted group member in one area can provide a bridge of understanding to other issues in which she or he is an advantaged group member, if participants are encouraged to see parallels and connections among different forms of oppression.

### Invalidation of the Facilitator

Sometimes, participants claim that the facilitator is biased, especially if she is a member of the targeted group. For example, in an antisemitism course, a Jewish facilitator might be criticized by Gentile participants as too personally involved to be "objective." On the other hand, facilitators who are members of the advantaged group are sometimes invalidated by both advantaged and targeted group participants because participants do not believe that an advantaged group member can understand oppression they have not personally experienced as a target.

### Invalidation of the Class

Sometimes, participants criticize class assignments and activities in order to avoid perspectives with which they do not agree. Participants might also claim that the class is a form of indoctrination and that they are not free to express a range of beliefs or experiences, and they attribute all attempts to challenge the status quo to "political correctness." This stance allows them to dismiss the entire course without critically examining the issues raised in class.

### Anecdote Raised to the Status of Generalized Fact

A participant, most often a member of the advantaged group, will relate a story they heard on the news or from a friend in which an advantaged group member is victimized in some way by the targeted group, either directly or as the result of a program or policy intended to prevent discrimination against targeted group members. The participant uses this anecdote to invalidate targeted group members' experience and/or even the oppression model. For example, a participant might tell of an instance where a man of color beat up a white man or how a white person was denied a promotion because of affirmative action as "proof" that racism goes both ways.

## Domination of Class Discussion

Occasionally, participants will resist by arguing every point made in class with which they do not agree, taking more than their share of air time in class, challenging the legitimacy of information presented or the validity of others' experiences, and presenting their own perspectives as "truth."

## Hostile Silence

Sometimes, participants express resistance by refusing to participate in small- or large-group discussions. Their silence can be accentuated by such defensive postures as arms folded across the chest, caps pulled down over eyes, or focusing on non-class-related reading or other activities.

We try to maintain the perspective that all participants are engaged in a learning process, and that a journey through resistance is not the final destination. The struggles we see in class often lead to learning that emerges later on, sometimes long after the course has ended. Facilitators need to trust the process of the course to encourage participants to consider new information and perspectives, and have faith in the potential for even the most resistant participants to change.

Several strategies are useful in addressing participant dissonance so as to promote learning. Foremost is the imperative that participants are not graded on their opinions and beliefs (see Chapter 4). In addition, facilitators need to make sure to invite all perspectives and listen respectfully, even to those that challenge the very existence of oppression. Adhering to the participation guidelines established at the beginning of class can ensure that divergent beliefs can be expressed. In addition, the inclusion of films, research, statistics, guest speakers, and outside readings provides participants with sources of information about oppression other than that provided by the facilitator and members of the class. Journals in which participants write reactions to class discussions and activities can provide a way for them to articulate their perspectives and feelings. Journals that are shared with facilitators can provide an especially important point of entry for connecting with and understanding the nature and dynamics of individual experiences. Inviting participants to make appointments for private discussions can also help facilitators ask more direct questions and better explore and understand participant dissonance than may be possible in front of the entire class. Such meetings also offer an opportunity for the facilitator to encourage individual participants to critically explore issues and information they find challenging.

## Anger

Some participants react with anger to what they are learning in a social justice education class. Our goal is to acknowledge anger and provide a constructive way for participants to express feelings. Participants who are members of advantaged groups sometimes are angry that rights they assumed were available to everyone, or achievements they have always accepted as earned by their own hard work or merits, may be unearned privileges not equally available to everyone. Targeted group members feel anger at the injustice they and other members of their social group have experienced. Targeted members may also feel angry and impatient with other classmates' resistance and lack of awareness. Both advantaged and targeted group members may be angry that uncritical beliefs in basic equality and fairness in the United States are being contested.

Strategies to address anger include normalizing such feelings and providing ways to express anger that do not target other participants or the facilitator. Journal writing, pair discussions, conferences with facilitators, individual written assignments, and time spent in caucus groups are all ways to address anger. Teaching as part of a team is an effective way for facilitators to maintain their own balance and perspective when dealing with angry participants. If the teaching team is mixed, then it is particularly useful for the member of the team who shares the angry participant's social group membership to speak with her or him. Sometimes, it is not necessary for facilitators to address participant anger in the moment; instead, they may thank the participant for expressing honest and heartfelt feelings, letting the discomfort stand for the time being and checking with the participant later.

### Immobilization

Participants who feel overwhelmed by new feelings and information in reaction to what they are learning in social justice education courses often feel immobilized. In response to challenges to familiar ways of experiencing the world and social differences, some participants shut down. Some participants feel that embracing new perspectives may mean losing friends or distancing themselves from family members. They feel overloaded and hypersensitive to issues that they may never have been aware of before, begin noticing oppression "everywhere," and are overwhelmed by this flood of awareness. Such feelings are uncomfortable, and shutting down is an attempt to regain a sense of equilibrium. This response can take several different forms, as discussed below.

### Withdrawal From Participation

Some participants might actually physically withdraw from the class or return late from breaks. More typically, they remain in the class, but do not participate in class discussions.

### Sense of Powerlessness to Change Oppressive Conditions

Sometimes participants, both advantaged and targeted group members, get stuck in feelings of helplessness. They feel powerless to do anything to change the oppression they now acknowledge exists. To think further about issues raised in the class is painful because they believe they cannot make a real difference. The problems related to oppression feel too pervasive and deeply rooted for them to believe they can effect change.

### Fear of Being Perceived as a Bigot

Most participants come to a social justice education course with a desire to learn and grow, but also fear unintentionally saying or doing something in class that will lead others to see them as prejudiced. Because there is so much new information and awareness for some participants, they do not fully trust themselves to decide what behavior is appropriate. This fear can stifle discussion and lead to shallow and safe participation as participants engage in self-protection rather than self-exploration.

### Advantaged Group Members' Guilt About Their Advantaged Status

Some participants respond to learning about social oppression by feeling guilt and shame about their advantaged status. They have difficulty taking pride in their identities and moving beyond feelings of shame and guilt. White participants often enter racism courses with an enormous burden of guilt about being white in a world they acknowledge as racist (Tatum, 1994). Being immobilized by guilt can prevent feeling a sense of agency and capacity to act against racism.

### Fear of Conflict and Disagreement

Participants with prior relationships outside of the course can be reluctant to disagree with each other or to express dissenting perspectives. Sometimes, participants who do not see social oppression as an issue in their lives are afraid to say so when they perceive that the rest of the group does. They may not feel safe enough to disclose their thoughts and feelings. For example, a Latina participant might not speak out about her experience of racism on campus if her white friends in class do not seem to recognize racism or understand how they benefit from racism on campus.

An effective way to address immobilization is to help participants identify the people and groups in their lives with whom they have influence or to remember individual people who have had an influence on their lives. Providing historical and contemporary models of advantaged group members acting as allies against social injustice helps participants see how social change can occur. Identifying specific actions from low to high risk, rehearsing new behaviors in small groups, or setting up support groups out of class enables participants to believe they can make a difference. Finally, insuring that mixed classes include enough members of both advantaged and targeted groups helps to encourage divergent perspectives, challenges to dominant understandings, and fuller participation.

### The Need to See Only the Most Extreme Bigots as Agents of Oppression

In a racism course, white participants will sometimes spend time differentiating themselves from the "real" racists who join white supremacist groups or who actively and intentionally discriminate against people of color. By only focusing on the most extreme or overt forms of racism, white participants avoid examining their own subtle racism.

### Willingness to Focus on the Oppression of Targeted Groups, but Not on the Privilege of Advantaged Groups

Advantaged group members may expect that the course is about understanding how targeted group members are oppressed. They believe that discrimination is wrong and see their role in fighting oppression as "helping" targeted group members. For example, nondisabled participants sometimes come to an ableism class feeling pity or empathy for the "plight" of people with disabilities. They are unprepared to have their own attitudes about disability challenged or to explore how their status as temporarily able people provides them with privilege. Such participants may be angry or confused to find that an important part of the oppression equation is understanding that they benefit from oppression and that eliminating oppression requires that they acknowledge and give up their self-perceptions as neutral bystanders who can choose to help others or not.

We try to help participants avoid distancing themselves from these issues by planning activities that enable them to see the personal costs of social injustice. We also spend part of every course focusing on privilege and helping advantaged group members understand that they benefit from oppression even if they do not actively promote it. By exploring how they can recognize privilege, decline to take advantage of it, or use it in the service of eliminating oppression, advantaged group members can take a proactive stand against social injustice.

### Conversion

Conversion occurs when participants embrace perspectives presented in class without critical examination or adequate self-reflection. Rather than resisting or feeling angry or immobilized, they become "born-again" converts to the struggle against social injustice with little tolerance for anyone with a different perspective. For example, a man may challenge everyone in the class who uses language he thinks is demeaning to women or present himself as superior to other men in the class because of his sensitivity to women's issues, all the while taking far more than his share of "air time" in class discussions and speaking for women in the class as well. Another example is a lesbian who is critical of other lesbians, gay men, and bisexual people in the class who do not come out.

### The "Good" Advantaged Group Member

These participants assume that they have done the work and that they understand the targeted group's experience. They often want to leap to action without exploring the complexities of being an ally. They want to separate themselves from other advantaged group members who they perceive as less enlightened. These participants are eager for the targeted group members of the class to see them as allies and want to align themselves with targeted group members in the class.

### Correcting Others

Participants who have experienced a conversion often express newfound awareness by taking responsibility for monitoring and correcting the language and behaviors of others and generally show little or no tolerance for dissenting views. They might express impatience with facilitators who do not "correct" classmates for expressing "incorrect" attitudes or using "incorrect" language. This reaction can inhibit authentic participation and keep the participant from developing a deeper understanding of his or her own role in perpetuating social injustice.

It would be disingenuous to pretend that a social justice education course is neutral or objective any more than are any other courses. Participants are correct in perceiving that there is a particular perspective represented in a social justice education course. It is essential, however, that there is room for all perspectives to be heard and challenged respectfully. When facilitators or participants squelch the expression of views or experiences that are counter to the underlying beliefs guiding the course, social justice education courses are vulnerable to charges of political correctness. We assure participants that we all have prejudices and encourage them to see the course as an opportunity to consciously examine prejudices and choose beliefs based on new information and understanding, rather than allowing our unexamined prejudices to guide our thinking.

### Romanticizing Targeted Groups

Occasionally, advantaged group members who have had conversion experiences in class, or who enter the class as converts, develop an idealized, unrealistic, and ultimately dehumanizing image of targeted group members. They defer to targeted group members in class and are reluctant to disagree with them. They sometimes identify more with targeted group members and their culture and express discomfort with their own advantaged identity. They also distance themselves from other advantaged group members in an attempt to gain favor with targeted group members and may become angry or confused when targeted group members express a need or preference for time within their own group.

### Reversing Power Dynamics

Targeted group members sometimes use their status as "victims" to intimidate advantaged group members in class. In this "tyranny of the targets," they play on advantaged members' guilt and confusion and misinterpret the course as an opportunity to tell advantaged group members how they should act and what they should believe, or to vent anger at them. These targeted group members set themselves up as experts who are the final arbiters of acceptable and unacceptable attitudes and behaviors from advantaged group members.

### Demonizing Advantaged Groups

Targeted group members sometimes direct their anger about oppression at all members of the advantaged group. They are critical of everything that advantaged group members say or do, and can refuse to participate in small groups with classmates who are members of advantaged groups.

Strategies include reminding participants that stereotyping groups of people based on their group memberships is counterproductive, no matter who is doing the stereotyping, whether or not the stereotypes are blatantly negative or appear benign on the surface (i.e., all Asians are smart in math). Modeling ways that participants can express their own perspective without correcting classmates or presenting their perspective as the only acceptable one is useful. Activities that help participants see each others as human beings rather than merely as members of social groups with unequal power can also prevent participants from objectifying each other on the basis of social group membership. If caucus groups based on social group membership are used, it is helpful to prepare participants ahead of time and facilitate a way to become a whole group again afterwards.

The primary purpose of facilitation in social justice education is to create an environment in which participants are invited to discuss and raise questions about common understandings and choose new beliefs and actions based on a critical examination of their own values, skills, and knowledge base. Consideration of the facilitation issues discussed in this chapter can assist social justice education facilitators in planning and conducting classes in which all participants, advantaged and targeted group members, are engaged in a positive and productive learning experience for all.

# PART II

# Curriculum Designs for Diversity and Social Justice

# Overview

## Twenty-First Century Racism

### LEE ANNE BELL

How is it that a nation legally committed to equal opportunity for all—regardless of race, creed, national origin, or gender—continually reproduces patterns of racial inequality?

**Lawrence, Sutton, Kubisch, Susi, and Fulbright-Anderson (2004, p. 2)**

The next two chapters explore racism in the 21st century as it affects both white people and people of color, including new immigrants to the United States who are incorporated into the racial structure they encounter when they arrive. Together, these chapters are intended to help readers understand the institutions and patterns that evolved historically to become the system of racism we see today. Chapter 6 updates the racism design from the first edition of *Teaching for Diversity and Social Justice* to focus more explicitly on the construction of race and the role of institutionalized advantage for Whites in perpetuating racism. Chapter 7 is new to this edition and extends our analysis of racism to look at the experiences of immigrants as they enter the United States and the roles they take up as they are incorporated in and respond to this racialized system. We decided to add this chapter to take account of current debates about immigration and citizenship, terrorism and racial profiling, and the role of race in how these debates play out in the media and public discourse. We also look at the role of globalization and U.S. economic and military dominance in shaping immigrant experiences and racial formations in the United States.

This overview discusses the historical context and unifying themes that are developed further in the curriculum designs in Chapters 6 and 7, where lessons and materials for teaching about racism and white privilege (Chapter 6) and racism, immigration, and globalization (Chapter 7) are provided. We hope the overview is a helpful resource and orienting frame for instructors as they prepare to use these designs in their courses. A historical timeline of key events that relate to and exemplify features of racism explored in these connected chapters is provided in Appendix 6C on the accompanying CD.

## The Construction of Race and the Reality of Racism

*Race* is not a biological category but an idea, a social construction—created to interpret human differences and used to justify socioeconomic arrangements in ways that accrue to the benefit of the dominant social group. The term *racial formation* refers to the process by which social, economic, and political forces construct racial categories and meanings (Omi & Winant, 1986). Although we know from genetics that race has no biological significance and that we are all part of the same human family, race is a powerful idea that affects our lives in psychologically and materially consequential ways.

Despite prevailing views that we have become a "color-blind" society and have moved "beyond race," constructed racial categories determine to a large degree where we live, who we marry, how much we earn, with whom we worship, the quality of health care we receive, how long we will live, who represents us in the government, how we are portrayed in the media, how much wealth we accumulate and pass on to our children, and other factors that affect life opportunities and well-being in significant and enduring ways (Bonilla-Silva, 2003; Feagin, 2001; Lipsitz, 1998; Marabel, 2002;Oliver & Shapiro, 1997). How did this come to be so, and, more importantly, why does it continue to be the case despite advances in civil rights and purportedly more tolerant racial attitudes in our time? This central question is explored in the curriculum designs that follow.

## The Evolving but Persistent Nature of Racism

In this book, we define *racism* as a system of advantage based on race and supported by institutional structures, policies, and practices that create and sustain benefits for the dominant white group, and structure discrimination, oppression, and disadvantage for people from targeted racial groups (Chapter 6). Racism is a social expression of power and privilege, the consequence of discriminatory policies in the past that endure, always adapting to new circumstances but ultimately prevailing through practices of inequality that continue and sometimes manifest in new but persistent ways (Marabel, 2002; Omi & Winant, 1986; Winant, 2004).

Taking the long view of history is crucial for understanding the resilience of racism as a system and its capacity for regeneration in new forms (Winant, 2004). History provides the stories about how racism persists over time and, despite incursions against it at various periods in our history (see, for example, Foner, 2005), how it has "shape-shifted" and returned in modified, though often as virulent, forms. Understanding the historical development, formation, and evolution of racism is important for critical social analysis, for contesting racial formations, and for developing antiracist visions and strategies. Thus, we highlight the importance of history as an analytic frame in the curriculum designs that follow.

We also think it important to learn about the unacknowledged contributions of people of color in the making of America as a way to counteract Eurocentric notions of superiority that saturate and sustain racial beliefs and stereotypes. The American nation that came to be called the United States was from its very origins built on expropriated Native American land (Stannard, 1992; Wright, 1992). It was further enriched by the enslavement of African peoples and the free labor they provided in building the country's agricultural economy (Berlin, 1998; Franklin & Moss, 2000), and it owes much of its early prosperity to the exploitation of Japanese, Chinese, Filipino, and Mexican laborers who constructed the infrastructure in railroads, agriculture and irrigation, mining, and other areas that made possible U.S. economic and political dominance in the world (Gonzalez, 2000; Takaki, 1993). Indeed, as Marabel (2002) argues, structural racism and the exploited labor of people of color laid the foundation for American capitalism and this nation's prosperity and dominance in the world.

From the beginning, a racial ideology that assumed white supremacy enabled European conquerors and settlers to define Natives, Blacks, Mexicans, Chinese, Filipinos, and others as less than fully human and to codify these beliefs into law and public policy (Haney Lopez, 1996). Assumptions about white superiority became the taken-for-granted national "common sense," one that after time needed no repeating (Almaguer, 1994; Blum, 2005; Marabel, 2002; Roediger, 2005; Winant, 2004). White advantage or privilege became normative in law, politics, property, economic rights, and immigration policy, indeed threading through all of American institutional and social life (Foner & Frederickson, 2004; Haney Lopez, 1996; Katznelson, 2005; Winant, 2004).

Today, the relative position of Whites as a group is taken as natural, deserved, and the result of merit and hard work, erasing the quite systematic ways in which Whites have reaped the benefits of a privileged status for over 400 years. Those who do not know this history tend to assume continuous progress in race relations, view racism as mostly a thing of the past, and argue for a color-blind ideology that ignores the impact of racial status in contemporary life (Bell, 2003; Bonilla-Silva, 2003). Current white hostility to affirmative action, for example, ignores the relationship between affirmative action and the effects of inequitable government and social policies that compound white advantage and black disadvantage far into the future (Brown, 2003; Katznelson, 2005; Lipsitz, 1998; Shapiro, 2004). Without understanding this history and its consequences, we cannot address racial inequality, sustained and committed enough to level a playing field that has been so unevenly paved.

## Exported Racism Abroad and Immigration at Home

From almost our beginning as a nation, the United States has also been involved in colonial adventures justified by racial ideas about Manifest Destiny and U.S. (i.e., European, white) superiority. Whenever the United States expropriated natural resources and labor from other nations to build up our economy or support foreign policy objectives, the negative effects on the home economic and political systems of those countries simultaneously impelled streams of migration to the United States (Gonzalez, 2000; Takaki, 1990). The contemporary slogan among immigration activists, "We are here because you were there," is in fact grounded in truth (Rumbaut, 1996).

Because of the racialized society they enter, the experiences of migrants from Latin America, Asia, Africa, and the Caribbean differ substantially from those of their European predecessors. Just as with the descendants of Native Americans and enslaved Africans, immigrants of color have not been allowed to fully join the mainstream and instead often remain in a "linguistic/racial caste" limbo (Gonzalez, 2000), defined by a racial system, that despite actual skin hue in many cases, defines them as non-white. The typically negative comparison with European immigrants ignores the very different economic circumstances during which racialized immigrants of color often entered. Unlike their European counterparts, for example, many immigrants of color have been brought in as temporary laborers intended to return to their home countries after filling our needs. They also enter now during a postindustrial phase in which unionized factory jobs that enabled European immigrants to advance are no longer available.

U.S. (and European) racism and Eurocentrism have also left their mark on the home countries from which immigrants of color come, so that today we see a global system of racial stratification and inequality that closely follows North–South lines drawn by the previous colonial system (Winant, 2004). The International Monetary Fund, for example, now structures debt peonage on a global scale, creating a color-coded division of the world into a white and advantaged northern hemisphere with economic, political, and military dominance over a colored and disadvantaged southern hemisphere and its representatives within U.S. borders (Macedo & Gounari, 2006).

The two chapters that follow examine the ways that groups of color, both native born and immigrant, are targeted and disadvantaged by structural racism. In each curriculum design, critical analysis of the historical and contemporary patterns that shape racial experience is an important objective. Each chapter looks at how white racial advantage is perpetuated through individual, cultural, and institutional patterns, both locally and globally.

## The "New" Racism: Meritocracy, Color Blindness, and Unearned White Advantage

Many Americans, particularly white Americans, believe the playing field has been leveled and our society now operates as a meritocracy in which, despite race or station, anyone willing to work hard enough can get ahead. Yet segregated schools and neighborhoods, job discrimination and pay inequity, and the enduring legacies of past discrimination continue to sustain a hierarchy of racial privilege and disadvantage in all areas of life—employment, health care, housing, media, education, and politics (Oliver & Shapiro, 1997). In other words,

> Race has been and continues to be a valuable social, political and economic resource for white Americans. It grants them easier access to power and resources and provides them better insulation from negative pre-judgments based on physical features, language, and other cultural factors than their non-white counterparts. (Lawrence, Sutton, Kubish, & Susi, 2004, p. 17)

By masking these ongoing advantages, color blindness maintains structural racism and ultimately undermines democratic potential.

Racism is not only a Black-White issue but also affects everyone in our society—White, Black, Latino, Asian, Native American, biracial, and multiracial people—in its allocation of social advantage and disadvantage. Although racial group status can and has changed over the course of American history, it has not done so voluntarily, and it has always done so in ways that redraw the color line to the continuing advantage of Whites. For example, Irish, Italian, and Jewish immigrants were able to become "white" over time and accrue the benefits of white privilege by giving into Anglo-conformity (Brodkin, 1998; Ignatiev, 1995; Jacobson, 1998; Roediger, 2005; Steinberg, 1981). More recently, the "model minority" status assigned to Asian Americans extends some of the privileges of whiteness to them but also leaves them as a group in a precarious position where their status as "perpetual foreigner" or "other" can always be reinvoked (see, for example, Lee, 2001).

In the curriculum designs that follow, we look at the relationships among individuals and groups within the system of racism to emphasize the structural power dynamics that target people of color while maintaining white advantage. By focusing on these dynamics, we hope to stay open to the ways in which racial practices can shift for the better in response to current struggles as well as regroup and continue in force. "New" racism in the United States, for example, may follow South African and Brazilian models by including certain elite members of minority groups as "honorary whites." Marabel argues that "a select elite among African Americans may still encounter personal discrimination, but their class status and economic affluence provide the space to create 'white lives'" (2002, p. 327).

Racism may also reform through adjustment of the color line to include certain ethnic groups such as Asians and light-skinned Latinos while continuing to exclude African Americans, Native Americans, and darker-skinned Latino and Asian people (Gregory & Sanjek, 1994; Haney-Lopez, 2006). The color line can also adjust to racialize Arab Americans, dark-skinned or otherwise, as "Other" and thus beyond citizenship (Ladson-Billings, 2004). In either case, determinations of position and mobility remain under white control. Members of subordinated groups may adopt mainstream habits and values, change their names, and drop their native language or religious affiliation in order to be accepted into the dominant group, but it is always the dominant group that determines who will be allowed access. Thus, positions along the color line may shift but are always dependent on the dominant (white) group's "exclusionary or inclusionary exercise of political, economic, and cultural power" (Lawrence, Sutton, Kubish, & Susi, 2004, p. 11).

## Antiracist Challenges

Fortunately, the inherent contradictions and hypocrisy of racial discrimination that undermine the democratic principles this country espouses, have motivated people in each generation to critique, resist, and struggle to change them (Takaki, 1998a; Zinn, 1980/1995). We can learn a great deal from studying previous activism and the backlashes to it so as to build organizations, coalitions, and movements that may be more flexible and durable in countering or thwarting regressive policies of the future (see Chapter 1).

During World War II, for example, Asians, Native Americans, African Americans, Mexican Americans, Arab Americans, and other people of color, though not often acknowledged in the history most students learn in high school, joined Whites in the war effort to protect democracy (Orfalea, 2006; Takaki, 1993). Yet, African Americans, many of whom had family members in the armed forces, were subjected to racism in the military and segregation and lynching back home (McGuire, 1993). Some Japanese Americans, even as they were categorized as suspect aliens and imprisoned in camps, enlisted to serve (Asahina, 2006). Soldiers of color who fought against fascism returned home to encounter discrimination restricting their ability to utilize GI housing and education benefits that white soldiers could freely use. Unearthing this history is an important part of anti-racist struggle.

The stark contrast between defending democracy abroad while subjecting our own citizens to discrimination, segregation, and violence at home exposed American racial hypocrisy and laid the seeds for a Civil Rights movement that came to fruition 25 years later. Civil rights agitation through the courts (*Brown v. Board of Education*, 1954) and in the streets (the 1955 Montgomery Bus Boycott) led ultimately to the 1965 Immigration Reform Act, the 1968 Voting Rights Act, and other legislation to remedy racist practices and policies.

However, state-based racial reform, while resulting in civil rights laws, more inclusive immigration policies, the extension of citizenship, and widespread official professions of commitment to racial equality (all very real and important advances), ultimately failed to achieve more far-reaching changes that would have ended race-based advantage–disadvantage (Winant, 2001, 2004). Class divisions that have been successfully exploited throughout our history to prevent people from organizing across race lines were again used to create a white backlash to these reform efforts. Similarly, today we see attempts to pit one immigrant group against another and against African Americans as a strategy to prevent organizing for change across ethnic, racial, and class lines. One valuable lesson from this history is the need to understand the links among forms of oppression and to create a broad vision for change that includes people from all groups. The racism curriculum designs presented here try to create the conditions for cross-group dialogue that might make sustained coalition building and joint action possible.

## Building an Inclusive Vision for the Future

We hope this overview and the two racism curriculum designs in Chapters 6 and 7 will help people understand the roots and effects of racism, at home and abroad, and the very real threat to democracy they pose. Ultimately, change will come when common people demand that our government live up to the promise of democracy codified in our Constitution and Bill of Rights. This promise has inspired, and continues to draw, people from all over the world; people whose belief in these principles strengthens our commitment to them (Marabel, 2002; West, 2004). Each design that follows includes a module addressed to ongoing education, involvement, and antiracist activism. Following Guinier and Torres (2002), we affirm the need to dream of and enact together an antiracist agenda that can "complete our democracy" through living these principles in our daily lives.

# 6

# Racism and White Privilege Curriculum Design

## LEE ANNE BELL, BARBARA J. LOVE, ROSEMARIE A. ROBERTS*

Teaching about racism in the United States is an intellectually, emotionally, and politically challenging project, complicated by the shortage of supportive spaces to think and talk about racism in diverse groups. It is made even more difficult because of the racial divide in knowledge about and experience with racism (Bell, 2003b). Participants bring to a course on racism a wide range of feelings and experiences, and often misinformation, confusion, and bias. White participants may sincerely want to learn about racism and figure out how to play a role in making their communities, schools, and workplaces welcoming places for all, but fail to see the role white skin privilege and accumulated white advantage play in perpetuating racial inequality. Participants of color may want to figure out how to break through the silence about racism as a historic and contemporary force that differentially shapes their lives, but fear having their concerns dismissed, being viewed as too sensitive or as troublemakers, or being misunderstood by white peers and teachers. Participants from all racial groups may be reluctant to explore racism, especially in mixed groups, given the complex and often painful web of emotions that discussions about racism inevitably raise.

Careful planning and facilitation can create a safe enough space to talk about racism in ways that encourage participation and learning, enable people from all groups to develop a more sophisticated understanding of racism and foster the development of a knowledge base to support effective strategies for working in coalition with others to do antiracist work. Creating a space where issues of racism and social justice

* We ask that those who cite this work always acknowledge by name all of the authors listed rather than either only citing the first author or using "et al." to indicate coauthors. All collaborated on the conceptualization, development, and writing of this chapter.

can be aired and honestly discussed can enhance participation even in courses where the subject is not specifically racism or issues of social justice. We find that the most generative way to teach about racism is to create opportunities for participants to talk about their life experiences in the context of information that helps them understand how these experiences are shaped by systemic patterns of institutional and cultural racism and its corollary, white privilege/advantage.

## Racialized Differences in Opportunities and Outcomes

Although racism impacts all institutions, we explore racial dynamics in five mutually reinforcing areas: education, the labor market, housing, the media, and the criminal justice system. Racial differences in opportunities and outcomes in these institutions are particularly critical to a person's (and group's) social, economic, and political standing in American society. Despite civil rights advances and purportedly more liberal attitudes toward race today, we can see that race serves as a reliable predictor of racially unequal levels of participation and success in these institutions.

## Education

The American public education system has historically been considered a social equalizer, presumed to provide equal access to education for all and the means for social advancement regardless of class, race, or national origin (Hochschild & Scovronick, 2003). While this has to a large extent been true for white immigrants to this country, the 1954 *Brown v. Board of Education* decision, and other court cases in Texas and California, show this not to be the case for African Americans, Mexican Americans, Native Americans, and Puerto Ricans. Despite decades of efforts to integrate the schools and provide equal education for all, schooling inequalities and segregation by race continue and deepen (Bell, 2004; Kozol, 1992, 2005; Orfield & Eaton, 1996; Whitlock & Adams, 2004).

Disparities in access to equal education by race are greater than ever and closely parallel disparities in school funding (Carey, 2004; Orfield & Lee, 2006). Nationally, school districts with the highest enrollment of white students have on average $902 more to spend per student than school districts with the highest enrollment of students of color (Lawrence, Sutton, Kubisch, Susi, & Fulbright-Anderson, 2004). Based on an average classroom size of 25 students, this adds up to a difference of $22,500 more per classroom in schools with the highest enrollment of white students. Despite the success of recent court cases in New York and California requiring redress of gross funding inequities, remedies have not been forthcoming (see Campaign for Fiscal Equity, n.d.; Decent Schools for California, n.d.).

In addition to being denied adequate funding, minority students in racially segregated schools encounter a less rigorous curriculum, face lower expectations from their teachers, and receive inadequate, if any, information about financial aid, college opportunities, and other avenues to well-paying careers (Lipton & Oakes, 2003). Research shows, for example, that public schools where white students are the majority are more than twice as likely to offer advanced placement (AP) classes as schools where black and Latino students are the majority (Lawrence, Sutton, Kubisch, Susi, & Fulbright-Anderson, 2004). Even in desegregated suburban public schools, 58% of Asian/Pacific Islander students and 56% of white students are in AP/honors classes compared to only 33% of black students and 27% of Latino students in such classes (Fine, Roberts, & Torres, 2004; see Noguera, 2003 for similar findings). Because many colleges give extra admission points to students who have participated in honors and

AP classes, students of color, who are more likely to attend schools that do not offer AP, end up losing twice.

At the same time that resources for public education are shrinking, demands for performance by teachers and students are going up. Underresourced schools have to deal with overcrowding, aging school facilities, and much smaller per pupil expenditures than white suburban schools (Kozol, 1992; Kozol, 2005). They are also less likely to be able to hire teachers who are certified or hold master's degrees than their suburban counterparts (Lankford, Loeb, & Wyckoff, 2002). And although the population of students in public schools is increasingly more racially and linguistically diverse, the teaching force remains overwhelmingly white and monolingual (Nieto, 1999), less likely to be knowledgeable about families and communities of students of color (Irvine, 2003; Ladson-Billings, 1994) and less aware of the challenges of racism their students face (Bell, 2003a; Marx, 2006; McIntyre, 1997).

Racial disparities are also evident in higher education (Orfield, Marin, & Horn, 2005). In 2003, 42% of white students, 32% of black students, and 23% of Latino students aged 18 to 24 years old were enrolled in college (U.S. Department of Education, National Center for Education Statistics, 2004). College graduation rates also show the same racial patterns, with a larger percentage of white students graduating in 5 years than black and Latino students graduate from predominantly white institutions in 5 years (U.S. Department of Education, National Center for Education Statistics, 2000).

In sum, 50 years after *Brown v. Board of Education* outlawed segregated schools, we see regressive resegregation to a dual and grossly unequal system of education based on race and class (Kozol, 2005), "recording the tenacity of America's commitment to racial inequality" (Darling-Hammond, 2006, p. 13). This is occurring in a context where options for economic mobility are tightly constricted and racially biased.

## Labor Market

Not only are there widely varying differences in academic achievement by race, but income and life chances for people with the same educational attainment are also widely disproportionate across racial groups (Lui, 2005; Shapiro, 2004). Within the context of the U.S. economic system of supply and demand, access to jobs is theoretically race neutral. However, labor market participation rates indicate that race plays a significant role in determining access to employment. Over the past 30 years, the unemployment rate for black people has consistently been twice that of white people (National Urban League, 2006). Furthermore, people of color and women are overrepresented in the lowest paying and least desirable jobs, and occupational segregation is most pronounced among black male youth (Lawrence, Sutton, Kubisch, Susi, & Fulbright-Anderson,, 2004).

Although 25 to 33% of the gap between the earnings of Whites and African Americans, Native Americans, and Latinos can be explained by educational differences (Harris, 2004), labor practices add to these disparities. A recent study revealed that employers were 50% less likely to call for an interview applicants with common black names on their résumés than applicants with common white names, even though all job applicants in the study had exactly the same résumé (Lawrence et al., 2004). During the recession of the early 2000s, black workers lost jobs at twice the rate of white and Latino workers. Almost 90% of lost jobs were decent-paying jobs in the manufacturing sector, jobs that are unlikely to return (Lawrence, Sutton, Kubisch, Susi, & Fulbright-Anderson,, 2004). In the same period, government jobs, the sector that previously offered the most opportunity to people of color, had also declined (National Urban League, 2006). Access to decent jobs determines to a large degree whether or not one can buy a home, accumulate assets, and use these assets to improve life chances for one's offspring.

## Housing

Home ownership is one of the means by which wealth can be accumulated and passed on to the next generation. Significantly, redlining, a practice initiated by the U.S. government, and mortgage lending practices over the past 60 years have largely excluded people of color from significant home ownership while benefiting and advantaging white people by comparison (Katznelson, 2005; Lipsitz, 1998). For example, one study showed that banks are less likely to offer a mortgage to a black applicant than to a white applicant with the same earnings, the same educational level, and a comparable job (Sickinger, 1999). Research also reveals that people of color pay more in interest rates than white people pay for similar mortgages (Perez, 2002). Gentrification often opens opportunities for housing for white people and displaces families of color and the poor through eliminating affordable housing in the face of escalating rents and housing prices (Freeman, 2006). Meanwhile, housing segregation maintains racial separation in schools, friendship, work, and other areas that in turn insures continuing white ignorance about people of color and the stereotyping and discrimination that ignorance feeds (Bonilla-Silva, 2003; Cashin, 2005). The media both reflect and perpetuate these stereotypes.

## Media

Historically, the media have served as a key socializing agency, informing and shaping as well as helping to change beliefs, attitudes, opinions, and understandings about different groups of people in our society. In its many forms (newspapers, magazines, books, radio, television, and movies), the media can inflame and propagate racism as well as provide information with which to counteract it. The media paint landscape themes that serve as the backdrop for how society views and responds to people from different racial groups (Cortes, 2000). These themes shape public opinion and public policy, the responses of bureaucracies and individual public officials, as well as the attitudes and behavior of the public at large.

Media ownership and control of the images portrayed of people of color are overwhelmingly in white hands. For example, only 4.2% of media outlets are minority owned, yet they employ more than half of all people of color in radio and television (Gonzalez & Torres, 2006). For example, UPN had the highest concentration of writers of color employing sixty-three percent of writers of color in 2005–2006 (Themba-Nixon, 2006).

The images that mostly white mainstream media portray of people of color tend to be selective and biased in ways that support stereotyping. Cortes (2000) argues that by selecting and continually repeating news stories of a particular type about a social group, the media increase the likelihood that consumers will develop stereotypes about that group. For example, showing black and Latino men as criminals but ignoring other activities in which they engage perpetuates stereotypes, normalizes racially defined characteristics attached to particular groups, and ultimately legitimizes racial hierarchy (Bogle, 2001; Wilson, Gutierrez, & Chao, 2003). This occurs whether the stereotypes are of African Americans (Entman & Rojecki, 2001), Asian Americans (Lee, 1999), or Arab Americans (Shaheen, 2001).

The lack of minority perspectives in the media has very real consequences for the way news is reported. For example, during the Hurricane Katrina disaster of 2005, the mainstream media portrayed white victims trying to survive as "finding bread and soda from a local grocery store," whereas black victims in exactly the same circumstance were portrayed as "looting a grocery store" (Snopes.com, n.d.). This marked contrast in descriptors for white and black people engaged in the same activity illustrates one of the key ways that the media both mirror and perpetuate the racism of the larger society. This is also evident in the way crime is portrayed both in news reporting and in television and movie characters that stereotype men of color, particularly black and Latino men, as criminals (Entman & Rojecki, 2001).

### Criminal Justice

Racial discrimination and prejudice deeply affect the criminal justice system in areas such as profiling, sentencing, access to adequate legal representation, incarceration, and parole, culminating in dramatic racial differences. These discrepancies begin in adolescence. For example, African American youth are six times and Latino youth three times more likely than white youth to be incarcerated for the same offenses. Although African Americans make up only 12% of the U.S. population, they represent a shockingly disproportionate 46% of the prison population. Racial disparities are most dramatic in states where people of color are concentrated in urban areas, where there tend to be higher crimes rates, and where there are higher levels of law enforcement activity (Human Rights Watch, 2002).

Incarceration rates for men are higher than for women, yet the rate at which women (disproportionately women of color) are incarcerated has grown faster than the rate for men in recent years, particularly since welfare reform and harsher penalties for drug crimes have been implemented. The number of incarcerated women has increased by 118% since 1990 (U.S. Department of Health and Human Services, Health Resources and Services Administration, 2005).

Juvenile detention rates reveal similarly deep racial inequities. In New York City, African American and Latino youth comprise 95% of those entering juvenile detention centers, even though they represent only two thirds of all youth in New York City (Correctional Association of New York, 2004). In 2002, of youth in the custody of the New York State Office of Children and Family Services, a state agency responsible for incarcerating and placing youth in detention, 63% were African American, 23% were Latino, and 16% were white (Correctional Association of New York, 2004). Significantly, half of youth who enter detention come from only a quarter of New York City neighborhoods, those with the highest levels of poverty, poor housing, and underperforming schools (Correctional Association of New York, 2004).

Quality education is one of the most effective forms of crime prevention (Center on Crime, Communities and Culture, 1997). Yet the State of New York, in a trend similar to many other states, reduced spending for higher education by $10 million during a 10-year period in the early 1990s while simultaneously increasing prison spending by roughly the same amount (Ziedenberg & Schiraldi, 2002). Notably, during this period, the average annual cost to incarcerate one youth in detention was $141,000, whereas the average annual cost per pupil in a New York City public school was $9,998 (Correctional Association of New York, 2004). In this curriculum design, we explore the interconnections among these and other institutions to help participants see and analyze the effects of interconnected institutional patterns within the web of racism (see Figure 6.1).

Taken together, these systems interact to create a web of interlocking systems that create racially different opportunities and outcomes that reflect and sustain institutional racism.

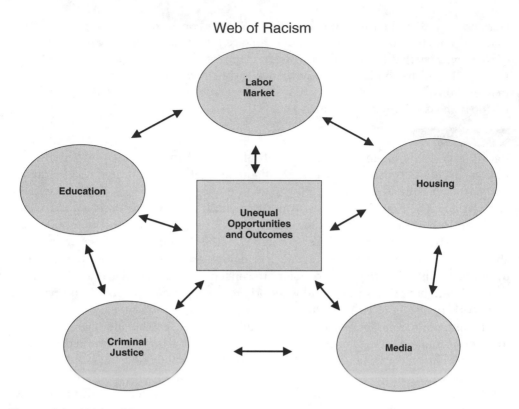

**Figure 6.1**    Web of Racism

## Campus Context

The current campus context both replicates the racism in the larger society as well as provides spaces within which students can develop knowledge and skills to understand and challenge racism. Many of the incidents that have arisen on campuses in the past few years, such as "affirmative action bake sales," white fraternity parties with "ethnic themes," and racial harassment, are rooted in racial stereotyping and hostility toward race-conscious campus policies. At the same time, colleges have historically been places that inspire agitation for social change, and provide the opportunity to form cross-racial student coalitions to work for common goals of equality and inclusion. A course on racism can offer a framework for examining such incidents, helping participants understand their historical context, and identifying ways they contribute to racism on campus. Education about racism provides participants with a vehicle for civic engagement and social responsibility and the opportunity to translate awareness into action that can enable them to take their learning beyond the course and into their daily lives.

## Racism and White Privilege Curriculum Design

## Overall Goals

At the conclusion of the course, we hope that participants will have achieved the following goals:

- Have a greater understanding of how we in the United States are socialized into a system of racism and white privilege/advantage.

- Understand how individuals internalize and respond to racism and white privilege/advantage on both conscious and unconscious levels.
- Learn definitions of *race*, *racism*, and *white privilege/advantage*.
- Increase awareness and understanding of individual, institutional, and societal manifestations of racism.
- Have a greater understanding of the role people from all racial groups can play in working for racial equality and justice.
- Feel capable and motivated to work with others to organize antiracist action at multiple levels (personal, social, and institutional).

## Overview of Racism and White Privilege Modules

Note to readers: The curriculum design in this chapter is based on the assumption that participants have completed the introductory module(s) described in Chapter 3 prior to beginning this design and have a basic understanding of the conceptual framework of oppression described in Chapter 3.

**Table 6.1**   Overview of Modules: Racism and White Privilege

| Module 1: What Is Race? What Is Racism? (4 hours) | Module 2: Social Construction of Race and Institutional Racism (4 hours) |
|---|---|
| 1. Welcome, Introductions, Hopes, and Fears (50 min.) | 1. Sculpting Power Dynamics (15 min.) |
| 2. Prevalence of Race Continuum (30 min.) | 2. The Stories We Tell About Race (50 min.) |
| 3. The Illusion of Race, the Reality of Racism (70 min.) | 3. Conversation Café (65 min.) |
| Break (10 min.) | Break (10 min.) |
| 4. Personal Timeline (35 min.) | 4. History of Racism Timeline (60 min.) |
| 5. Cycle of Socialization (35 min.) | 5. Institutional Racism (30 min.) |
| 6. Closing (10 min.) | 6. Closing (10 min.) |
| **Module 3: Unearned White Advantage (3 hours, 20 minutes—4 hours)** | **Module 4: Taking It With You (3 hours, 20 minutes)** |
| 1. Check-In and Review of the Agenda for the Day (15 min.) | 1. Emotional Timeline (30 min.) |
| 2. Crossing the Room (30 min.) | 2. Characteristics of an Ally (25 min.) |
| 3. The Construction of White Privilege/ Advantage (60 min.) | 3. Costs and Benefits of Interrupting Racism (15 min.) |
| Break (10 min.) | 4. Action Continuum (25 min.) |
| 4. Fishbowl or Caucus Groups (90 min.) | Break (10 min.) |
| 5. Pairs/Journals (20 min.) | 5. Spheres of Influence (20 min.) |
| 6. Closing (15 min.) | 6. Action Planning and Taking It With You (45 min.) |
| | 7. Closing (30 min.) |

## Module 1: What Is Race? What Is Racism?

Time needed: 4 hours

### Objectives

- Create a positive learning environment through developing group guidelines for support and risk taking.

- Explore the personal experience of learning about race and racism, and develop an understanding of the ways that racism is communicated and reinforced.
- Develop a shared understanding of key terms and ideas, including racial formation, race, racism, socialization, and social construction.
- Begin exploration of institutional and cultural forms of racism.

**Key concepts**: race, racial formation, racism, individual racism, active racism, passive racism

## 1. Welcome, Introductions, Hopes, and Fears (50 minutes)

As participants enter the room, give them a copy of any readings that you have assigned (if you have not done so ahead of time), a name tag, a blank index card, and a pen or pencil. Welcome participants, introduce yourselves as facilitators, and give a brief summary of your background. Thank participants for their willingness to explore issues of race and racism and to embark on this learning journey. Let them know that you are aware that the exploration of so weighty a subject as racism can evoke anxiety and that the class will begin with an explicit examination of the hopes and fears people bring as a way to establish guidelines for the class.

To assess the hopes and concerns of participants, ask them to write an expectation that they have for the course on one side of the index card, and on the other side of the card a fear or concern that they have about the course. Participants should not put their names on their cards. Collect the cards, reshuffle, and pass them out again so that each person receives someone else's card. Participants then introduce themselves, by name, describing something about themselves, and reading the hope and fear card that they received. If they receive their own card, they should simply read it anonymously. Once the cards have been read, introduce the concepts of *comfort zone* and *learning edge* (see Chapter 3). Use these concepts to facilitate a discussion of ways that the class can support each other in realizing their hopes for the class and mitigating their fears. Develop a list of class guidelines together.

Review the outline of the agenda, and note your planned starting and ending time, breaks, the location of restrooms, and any other details related to general personal comfort. Invite participants to tell you of any particular comfort, access, or learning needs they may have so that you can make appropriate accommodations. Participants should have let you know about any of their specific learning needs, such as large print, assistive listening devices, or interpreters, prior to the class.

## 2. Prevalence of Race Continuum (30 minutes)

This activity draws out some of the differential experiences participants have with race and racism. It asks participants to reflect on their own experiences and surfaces questions they have on the topic. Set up the room ahead of time by placing a "True for me" sign at one end of the room, a "Not true for me" sign at the other end, and a "Don't know" sign in the middle.

Ask participants to stand, moving chairs against the wall so there is room to move around. Tell them you will read a series of statements for them to think about and then move to the sign that most closely reflects their response to the statement (use statements in Appendix 6A). After each statement is read and participants have placed themselves near the appropriate sign, they should turn to someone nearby and talk about why they placed themselves as they did. After a few minutes, ask for volunteers to share with the whole group why they chose their current location, to get a range of experiences from those clustered around each sign. Note that people may have very different reasons for making the same selection. Then read the next prompt and continue in the same way until all statements have been read, responded to, and discussed.

Afterward, ask participants to write in their journals about where and why they placed themselves in relation to each question and any insights or questions from listening to other's choices and experiences. Ask them to note any questions this activity raises for them about racism and to keep these questions in mind as the course progresses.

## 3. The Illusion of Race, the Reality of Racism (70 minutes)

Show Episode I of *Race: The Power of an Illusion: The Difference Between Us* (available from www.californianewsreel.com; California Newsreel, 2003b). This excellent film provides historical information about the development of racism and white privilege in the United States and lays a foundation for understanding the systemic features of racism. Ask participants to take notes as they watch the film, jotting down questions, reactions, and feelings as they watch.

Following the film, ask participants to form groups with three other people, being sure to learn each other's names, and then respond to the following questions through discussion. Post the questions on chart paper or on the board. Ask for one volunteer in each group to take notes and report out key points at the end of the discussion.

1. What in the film surprised you?
2. How did the film challenge or change any of your assumptions? What challenged your previous ideas the most in watching this film? What feelings did the film stimulate in you?
3. What were you confused about or need to know more about?
4. Having seen the film, how would you define race? Racism?

Bring the groups together, and ask for groups reports of key points from their discussions, keeping track of questions for further exploration as the course proceeds. As part of the discussion, review the definitions of *race*, *racism*, *racial formation*, *individual racism*, *active racism*, and *passive racism* on the handout in Appendix 6B.

### Facilitation Issues

The film begins to raise questions about the meaning of race and its validity as a category for dividing human beings. Participants are often surprised to learn how arbitrary racial categories are, yet how tenacious their hold on our thinking remains. At this point, encourage participants to raise questions without seeking closure and to stay open to learning more about concepts we so often take for granted. The DVD is divided into three segments. For each segment, there is both a 1-hour-long version and an excerpted version. You can use whichever version time allows in your classroom. The Web site of California Newsreel (2003a; www.californianewsreel.org) also has many additional resources you may draw upon to further develop the activities in this module.

## Break (10 minutes)

## 4. Personal Timeline (35 minutes)

This activity structures an opportunity for participants to examine early memories related to race in order to explore how they learned (consciously and unconsciously) messages about race, their own racial group, and other racial groups. The activity enables participants to begin to analyze the multiple levels on which racism has affected their lives.

Begin the exercise by acknowledging that the attitudes, values, and beliefs we have internalized regarding race and racial groups are shaped by societal norms and patterns. You might say something like the following: *To a larger extent than we would like to believe, we do not have the opportunity to choose what we have learned about different racial groups, including our own. The beliefs and attitudes that we hold are a cultural and historical legacy from a society characterized by racial domination and subordination. For the most part, we do not think about when, where, or from whom we acquired a specific attitude or belief about race and racial groups. This exercise is designed to help uncover the experiences and processes through which we acquired our understandings, beliefs, and attitudes about race and racial groups in order to help us gain the flexibility to think outside the socialization that has been instilled in each of us. In this exercise, we will respond to a series of questions designed to help us think about our early memories related to race and racial groups.*

At this point, review the confidentiality guidelines and the characteristics of active listening. Remind participants that this is a "speak and listen" exercise, not a conversation or dialogue. Organize into trios and ask participants to assign each member of the trio the letter *A*, *B*, or *C*. Tell them you will read a series of questions and then each person in turn, beginning with A, will have the opportunity to respond to the question for 1 full minute, while the other two members of the group practice supportive listening without talking or adding to what the speaker is saying. Note that you will keep time and call out when they should switch to the next speaker (B), who will also speak uninterrupted for a full minute. Switch to person C in the same manner.

Some potential questions are listed here. You should choose the actual number of questions depending on the amount of time you have for the activity and the makeup of the group.

The following questions ask participants to reflect in each of their examples, on "What happened?" and "What do you remember doing, thinking, and feeling?"

1. When were you first aware of yourself as a member of a particular racial group?
2. When were you first aware of people from other races? Which races?
3. When did you first witness or experience someone being treated differently because of his or her racial group?
4. When was a time that you were proud of your racial identity?
5. When was a time you realized that you would be treated differently because of your race?
6. What are some times when you had (have) friends from different racial groups?
7. What is one other significant event in your life related to race or racism?

### Processing

After participants have completed responding to these questions, ask them to appreciate the other members of their group before returning to the large circle. Request examples of what people learned from answering the questions and listening to the answers of others. Ask participants to focus on their own stories and not the stories of others. If a story told by someone else resonates strongly with them, then they should focus on how their own experience seems to be similar to the other person's story. The point is to stay focused on their own socialization rather than the experiences of others. This guideline also helps to protect the confidentiality of other's stories. If a participant starts to describe another person's experience, remind them of the guideline and ask them to refocus on their own experience.

As the discussion continues, begin to call attention to the sources of early learning about race and racism. Highlight messages, both subtle and blatant, that people received about race and racial groups from family members and others. Often, white participants note examples such as seeing their parents lock car doors when driving through certain neighborhoods, hearing family members tell jokes about members of other racial groups, and seeing family members disapprove of interracial couples or avoid in-depth socializing with people from other racial groups; including being told they could not play or eat at certain people's houses or invite them over to your house. Participants of color may note messages about racial profiling by the police, store clerks, or others; being told to be careful around white people or not to trust them; or stereotyping or telling jokes about other racial groups.

### Facilitation Issues

This is a relatively high-risk activity, so it is important to review course guidelines especially related to active listening and confidentiality for work in the small groups. White students are likely to have very different memories and experiences from students of color. This is a good time to reinforce the concepts of comfort zone and learning edge and to underscore that these will vary for different people so that each individual should monitor their own internal reactions accordingly.

### 5. Cycle of Socialization (35 minutes)

Move the discussion to the "Cycle of Socialization," posting the diagram in Appendix 3E and providing individual copies to participants. Explain that this model illustrates how systematic socialization through individual, cultural, and institutional interactions and norms teaches us to accept a system of racism and white privilege/advantage. Tell participants you will walk them through the model with examples to illustrate and ask them to note on their copies of the model any examples from their own experiences that are pertinent. Use the following text as a guide for describing the Cycle of Socialization: *We are born without awareness of race and without racist attitudes, values, or beliefs. We acquire attitudes, values, and beliefs that support racism through a socialization process that is often more subtle than overt. From our earliest experiences, we learn lessons about our own and other racial groups through listening to and observing our parents and family. As we move out into the wider world, we take in lessons from our society and its institutions that socialize us to internalize and take for granted racialized norms, values, and assumptions.*

*Family, peers, and community are among the most powerful of these early socializing influences. White parents, peers, and community may reinforce fear or avoidance of people of color and instill beliefs that white values and standards are the correct norm to follow and by which to judge others. Parents, peers, and communities of color may teach children to avoid interactions with white people, to adjust to the standards of white society for their own protection, or to contain their feelings in situations deemed racially dangerous.*

Stop briefly to allow participants time to note examples from their own early experiences that illustrate socialization by family and peers. Then continue turning to the institutional level as follows:

*These early messages about race and racism are reinforced through contact with institutions, including the media, schools, religious institutions, the judicial system, and economic and political systems, among others. We learn that powerful people are mostly white (such as the president, Congress, police officers and judges, teachers, doctors, news commentators and television personalities, and historical figures studied in school). We internalize assumptions that white people are the ones who make history, and are those "naturally" in positions of power and influence. Whiteness unconsciously becomes the standard of normality.*

*Linguistic conventions teach us to unconsciously assign positive virtues to "Whiteness" and negative values to "Blackness," such as in "The heroes wear white hats and villains wear black hats"; "A pure heart is white, but an evil heart is black"; and "white lies are small, but black lies are evil." It is taken as an unquestioned matter of course that "flesh" as a color for crayons, or "nude" as a color for women's hosiery, matches the pigmentation of white people.*

*The educational system promotes through a curriculum that is mostly based on white (and male) achievements the notion that white people are naturally leaders, capable, and meritorious. We learn to accept differential resources and access to education as the norm. We come to assume that Whites who gain acceptance to colleges or other opportunities do so purely through merit.*

*The media exert a major socializing influence on us through the differential portrayal of people of color and white people. The majority of actors, commentators, writers, and producers are white. People of color are often relegated to stereotypical or minor roles that frequently depict them engaged in criminal activity or violent behavior. This association is combined with limited portrayals of people of color engaged in positive roles.*

*Religious institutions contribute to racist socialization through, for example, portraying Christian religious figures as light skinned, whereas "villains" such as Judas and Cain are portrayed as dark skinned. The story of Noah is construed to provide a religious justification for slavery, as when Ham is told that he and his children would be servants.*

*The combination of messages that we receive from our families, our communities, the surrounding culture, and the institutions of society creates a social system based on the "Rightness of Whiteness," the systematic oppression of people of color, and the collusion by individuals in the cycle of racism.*

Stop and ask participants to note further examples on their individual sheets. Invite them to share these examples with the larger group. Note that although socialization is powerful, new information can enable us to become conscious of socialized messages about other groups based on race and enable us to choose different attitudes, assumptions, and behaviors that challenge racism.

### 6. Closing (10 minutes)

To draw this section to a close, ask each participant to briefly share a thought, feeling, or question in response to the previous activity. Allow individuals to pass if they wish to do so.

### Facilitation Issues

This section of the course is important because it sets the foundation and tone for the modules that follow. Issues of trust and safety are usually paramount in the minds of participants. Working together to develop and *practice* the guidelines is very important. You can be an active role model from the start by describing your own thoughts and feelings, sharing examples from your own socialization, and acknowledging attitudes and assumptions about other racial groups that you later learned to question.

Participants may feel embarrassed by examples of their own early experiences and internalized racism, and as a result, they may be very cautious. White participants may be hesitant because they are afraid of offending participants of color, and participants of color because they may not feel safe enough to trust white facilitators and/or participants. White people may sit back and wait for people of color to teach them about racism, assuming that they themselves know little about racism and will need to hear about it from the "people who have it done to them." Some people of color may assume that they know everything there is to know about racism from their own experiences, and may be skeptical that they will hear or learn anything new. Others may assume the role of "expert" to teach white participants about racism. Be particularly attentive to such issues, so that participants of color are not asked to be educators or spokespeople for their entire racial group. Assign readings that can provide information for all participants to draw upon and elaborate.

Activities that examine participants' early experiences often have an emotional weight that facilitators should acknowledge and be prepared to address. For some people of color, recounting early experiences with racism can stimulate reliving situations where they or members of their family were targets of prejudice, discrimination, or violence, bringing up the emotions felt at that earlier time. For some white people, realizing that parents and others whom they love and trust have taught them stereotypes about other racial groups may cause discomfort, anger, or sadness. It is helpful to note that one of the costs of racism is the emotional pain and dehumanization that it causes all people living in a racist system. It is important to create a safe enough space that people can express some of those painful emotions while maintaining a productive learning environment. It may be useful to remind participants that feelings are neither right nor wrong, but simply feelings. Acknowledging feelings is an important step in distinguishing feelings from thoughts and in determining actions based on choice rather than unconscious socialization.

## Module 2: Social Construction of Race and Institutional Racism

Time needed: 4 hours

### Objectives

At the end of this module, participants will be able to do the following:

- Identify and analyze the material consequences of racial construction for people defined as people of color.
- Describe the cultural and institutional privileges/advantages attached to "Whiteness" in the United States.

**Key concepts**: social power, resistance, dominance, collusion, institutional racism

### 1. Sculpting the Dynamics of Power (15 minutes)

In this activity, participants begin to explore concepts central to understanding institutional racism through using their bodies in physical movement, without relying on the use of words. Form groups of three to five participants, and assign each group one of the following terms: *social power*, *domination*, *resistance*, and *collusion*. Ask each group to use their bodies to sculpt a tableau of their term by creating a still image or frozen moment that communicates the meaning of that term. Give each group 5 minutes to create their image, and then have each group enact their tableaux for the whole group. Ask participants to silently observe the tableaux for a few seconds, and then describe what they are seeing. Pull out as many observations as possible, even if they are conflicting or contradictory. Note where the tension points are in each tableau and both active and passive stances that participants might take. In what ways do the parts work together to create a whole? Finally, ask participants to guess what term is being sculpted. Applaud each group for their performance.

## 2. The Stories We Tell About Race (50 minutes)

Show Episode 2 of *Race: The Power of an Illusion: The Story We Tell*; either the full or excerpted form, depending on time available. After viewing the segment together, ask participants to respond to the following questions in their journals:

1. What in the film surprised you?
2. How did the film challenge or change any of your previous ideas and assumptions?
3. What feelings did the film stimulate in you?
4. What were you confused about or need to know more about?
5. Having seen the film, how would you now define race? Racism?

## 3. Conversation Café* (65 minutes)

This activity enables participants to engage in a series of conversations about race and racism that begin to tease out systemic features of racism, its history in our nation, and current challenges to eradicating racism today. Ahead of time, set up three to five circles with five chairs in each, and place one of the written questions for discussion in the middle of each circle. You might also provide cookies and soda to convey a café atmosphere.

Introduce and explain the activity. Ask participants to walk around and read the questions, decide where they would like to sit for a discussion, and go sit there. Let participants know they will have a chance to rotate three times to discuss different questions, or they can remain with a discussion circle in any round if they do not want to rotate. Once they have selected their first question, they should take a seat in that circle.

Review the guidelines, and encourage people to use them in the discussion. They will have 20 minutes for the first discussion. You should circulate around the room to spend time with each group and note points to raise in a later whole-group discussion. After 20 minutes, stop the conversations. Participants can then decide to move to a different group/question location, or remain where they are and continue the discussion with whomever joins that group. Have another 20-minute discussion, stopping to allow people to change groups or remain and continue. Rotate once more.

### Questions for the Conversation Café Circles:

1. Discuss the difference between a biological and a social view of race. How might you challenge biological assumptions about race?
2. How has "Whiteness" been defined historically? What purposes have changing definitions of Whiteness served in American society?

---

* This activity is adapted from the Storytelling Project: Teaching About Race and Racism Through Storytelling and the Arts, Barnard College (see www.barnard.edu/education). The original idea for Conversation Cafés came from the Conversation Café project of the New Road Map Foundation. See their Web site, www.conversationcafe.org (Road Map Foundation, 2002–2003), for more information.

3. If race is a fallacy biologically, how do you make sense of the reality of race (and racism) in people's lives?

4. Why is color-blindness problematic in addressing racism? Is it possible to address racism without taking account of race?

5. How could you communicate what you have learned about racial formation through a performance or visual presentation?

Bring the group together for a discussion of key points raised in each conversation circle. Then post and discuss the definitions in Appendix 6B, drawing on the previous discussion when possible and supplementing with responses to other questions and input participants may have.

**Break (10 minutes)**

**4. History of Racism Timeline (60 minutes)**

This section focuses on patterns in U.S. history that help to illustrate the systematic and enduring features of racism, as well as highlight moments in history when racism was challenged or altered by collective human action.

Review key points in the history of racism and the experiences of different racial groups in the United States using the timeline provided in Appendix 6C. Review the information included on the timeline in any of the formats described below.

*Format 1:* Present a brief lecture based on timeline in Appendix 6C. Post the timeline on newsprint, as overheads, or as a PowerPoint presentation so that it is visible to all participants. Also provide a copy of Appendix 6C for each participant. Ask participants to follow the lecture by making notes on the timeline as you go.

*Format 2:* Ahead of time, put historical events from the Appendix 6C timeline on cards or sheets of paper and the dates on another set of cards or sheets of paper. Give some participants the sheets with dates printed on them, and other participants the sheets on which the events are printed. Then ask participants to work together to match dates and events. At the end of the activity, participants will have matched dates with events, and in a few cases, there may be several people clustered to represent two or more events that occurred in the same year or same time period.

*Format 3:* Post dates in sequence around the room. Give participants 3.5" × 5" cards on which events are described. Ask participants to tape their cards on the posters (stand in the space) with the appropriate date.

*Format 4:* In advance, construct a racism history quiz. Participants complete the quiz, then discuss the answers to the quiz. Participants can score their quiz, give themselves a grade, and discuss how much or little they knew about the history of racism and why.

*Format 5:* Construct in advance a racism history Jeopardy game, using the format of the *Jeopardy* television show.

## Processing

After participants have completed examining key points in the history of racism through one of the formats above, discuss the following questions as a group:

1. What is one thing that you learned in this activity?

2. What surprised you about this activity?

3. What do you want to find out more about as a result of this activity?
4. What events described in this activity did you learn about in school?

## Facilitation Issues

The timeline offered in Appendix 6C is fairly extensive, and it is not likely facilitators will have time to go over every item listed. Be selective and encourage participants to note and follow up on other events that interest them. You can also assign this as homework.

Historical understanding points out the systemic and enduring features of racism that underlie ongoing racial problems. Because many people do not know this history, they are likely to assume that the United States has made steady progress in eliminating racism and that racism as a problem of individual bigotry or discrimination has mostly been ameliorated. Knowledge of history can help participants understand the structural and cultural bases for racial problems we still face today. Such knowledge makes it possible to imagine solutions that address these underlying problems.

## 5. Institutional Racism (30 minutes)

### Option A: Building a Web of Institutional Racism

The objective of this activity is to build an actual web in the classroom to illustrate how various institutions work together to systematically limit the full participation of people of color in society. The actual web created in the activity symbolizes the "web" of institutionalized racism that, like the spider's web, "catches" targets and limits their mobility and life chances.

Review the social institutions that perpetuate racism through policies, practices, and norms (see the introduction to this chapter). Ask participants to think of examples of ways that racism in one institution supports or reinforces racism in another institution.

The following is an example of how various institutions are connected to perpetuate racism: financial institutions are connected to housing in that a bank manager may see people of color as a greater financial risk than white people and thus be less likely to offer mortgages to them. Without a mortgage, people cannot afford to buy a home. People who cannot buy homes are more likely to live in neighborhoods that have less funding for schools. People who attend inadequately funded schools receive a lower level education. People who receive a lower level education get lower paying jobs.

Ask participants to stand in a circle, assigning an institution to each participant and yourself (such as schools, local businesses, the military, places of worship, the media, banks, criminal justice system, etc.). As facilitator, begin by giving an example of how your assigned institution perpetuates racism, then, holding one end of a roll of masking tape, toss the roll to another participant, naming a connection to that person's institution. That person should then give an example of how their institution perpetuates racism and, holding their spot on the tape, toss the roll to someone else in the circle, naming a connection to that person's institution. Other participants can help name a connection if the person is stumped. Continue until as many connections as people can think of have been made.

If participants have trouble thinking on their own of examples of institutionalized racism and how various institutions are connected, then ask the group to provide some examples. With a less advanced group, this activity can be framed from the start as more of a group activity, broadening the sources of data, taking the pressure off of individuals, and incorporating information covered in readings or other information sources.

At the end of the exercise, participants will find they are attached through a web of tape. You can ask them to gently place their tape on the floor and step away. What is left is a web of tape showing connections among institutions in our society that support racism. You can make the point that these connections continue whether we are standing in the web or standing apart from it. This helps make the point that systemic racism continues with or without the active, conscious participation of individuals, and that we are implicated in this web whether we wish to be or not.

Summarize some of the connections that participants have named in the ways that institutions perpetuate racism. Emphasize the importance of understanding racism as consisting of interrelated, institutionalized practices and the need for collective social change efforts if we are to address these various aspects in powerful and sustaining ways.

*Facilitation Issues*    As an alternative to using tape in this activity, the web can be created on paper by writing the various institutions in a circle when they are first generated by the larger group, and then drawing lines to symbolize the connections the group makes among these institutions.

## Option B: Designing a Nonracist Institution

The goal of designing a nonracist institution is to have participants increase their awareness of racism by identifying attitudes, behaviors, policies, and practices that would have to be changed if an institution were to become nonracist. After brainstorming a list of societal institutions in the large group, divide participants into small working groups, each group assigned a particular institution. Ask them to create a nonracist institution on large sheets of newsprint, using words and symbols. Participants should explore questions such as the following:

1. What is the underlying philosophy of this institution toward race?
2. How does this institution acknowledge race, if it does so at all?
3. What racial groups are represented in this institution, and what positions and roles do they fill?
4. What are some of the norms and values of this institution?

Add other questions that tap into how the institution might address racism on the individual, cultural, and institutional levels. Provide time for each group to present and describe their non-racist institution to the rest of the class. Note common patterns across institutions that define them as non-racist. Applaud each group's creativity and effort.

### 6. Closing (10 minutes)

As a way to bring closure to this module, invite participants to offer a thought, feeling, question, or insight based on the previous activities that they wish to share with the class. Go around the circle, and give participants the option to pass if they wish.

## Facilitation Issues

We have encountered participants, especially white people, who discount examples of cultural or institutional racism as atypical. Some participants may argue that there is reverse racism in education and employment as a result of affirmative action or non-discrimination policies. Still others may feel that the slight increase in the number of people of color in positions in government, the media, or other professions is an indication of the end of racism.

In responding to these statements, encourage participants to say more about what *they* understand the issue to be, so that they are pushed to go beyond a surface analysis to think of the issues underlying their position. It is our experience that participants often base their positions on traditional societal norms and beliefs that they take for granted without deeper reflection. Feeling comfortable with these challenges to "commonsense" understandings of social inequity is difficult for participants who have never considered these issues before. Helping them to analyze their own statements rather than arguing with them is usually more likely to encourage openness to considering alternative information and analysis.

## Module 3: Unearned White Advantage

Time needed: 4 hours

### Objectives

- Encourage whites to explore the concept of white privilege/advantage and the costs and benefits of colluding with the system of racism.
- Encourage people of color to explore the concepts of internalized subordination and empowerment.
- Listen to the experiences of people from different racial groups, and create the opportunity for dialogue.

**Key concepts**: White privilege/advantage, collusion, ally, internalized racism, horizontal racism, empowerment

### 1. Check-In and Review of the Agenda for the Day (15 minutes)

Ask participants what differences in their own perceptions they have noticed in light of previous discussions. For example, have any found themselves noticing examples of racism in the media? Often, participants will be sensitized to see examples in institutions that they may have overlooked before and will state that they are now seeing racism everywhere. Note that such heightened awareness is good preparation for developing action plans to address racist patterns and practices.

### 2. Crossing the Room: White Privilege Activity (30 minutes)

Create an open space in the room by moving chairs to the side.[1] Ask participants to line up at one end of the open space and hold hands. Tell them you will read a series of statements and ask them to move one step forward if the statement is true for them. Ask them to remain silent throughout the activity and to try to keep holding hands as long as possible.

**Statements**

Use the list of statements in Appendix 6D. Once all statements have been read, ask participants to freeze where they are and look around the room. Ask them what title they would give this image. Then discuss the following questions as a group:

1. How did people feel at different points in the exercise?
2. What happens when some people move forward and others cannot?
3. Did anyone question why they should move forward? Did anyone think of resisting or refusing? Why not?

Ask participants to turn to the person next to them and briefly discuss their responses to the activity. As a whole group, take a few minutes to discuss what happens to community (holding hands) when people have different levels of privilege or advantage. Then move on to the next activity where they will continue examining white privilege/advantage and its consequences.

### 3. The Construction of White Privilege/Advantage (60 minutes)

Show Episode 3 of *Race: The Power of an Illusion: The House We Live In*. Ask participants to take notes on new information or surprises in this segment.

### Break (10 minutes)

### 4. Fishbowl or Caucus Groups (90 minutes)

Select one of the following options for discussing the film.

### Option 1: Fishbowl Discussion

After the film, ask participants to form three groups, and have the first group sit in a circle in the center of the room with the other participants sitting around the outside of the circle in fishbowl fashion. Begin with going around the fish bowl and asking each person to give an initial, brief response to the topics listed below. Then open up for discussion of the topic provided.[2]

Allow 10 minutes for each fishbowl, then rotate to the next group until all three groups have had a round in the center, and each of the 3 topics has been addressed..

*Topic 1:*   The American Dream suggests that anyone who works hard enough will be rewarded. How has this been made more difficult for people not defined as White? What has been the long-term impact of that denial? What difference does access to financial resources make in terms of one's life opportunities?

*Topic 2:*   U.S. Supreme Court Justice Harry Blackmun said, "To get beyond racism we must first take account of race. There is no other way." Do you agree? Contrast Blackmun's statement with people who strive to be "color-blind." Who benefits if we adopt a color-blind approach to society? How is color-blindness different from equality?

*Topic 3:*   Discuss legal scholar John A. Powell's observation that in a racist system, privilege is often conveyed, not earned: "Most of the benefits can be obtained without ever doing anything personally. For Whites, they are getting the spoils of a racist system, even if they are not personally racist."[3]

Process this discussion by responding to any questions or comments at the end of the third round. Introduce the key concepts of *white privilege/advantage, collusion, horizontal racism, internalized racism, ally,* and *empowered person of color* listed in Appendix 6E. Review the definitions of each term and provide examples, making connections to the previous exercise where appropriate. Emphasize that each of us has an important role to play in dismantling racism, using the resources available to us from our various social locations, and working collaboratively with others from different groups.

### Option 2: Caucus Groups

See directions in Appendix 6F.

### 5. Closing (15 minutes)

Integrate everyone back into the large circle and go around the circle, providing the opportunity for each participant to use one word to describe how they are feeling about the topic of racism in the present moment. Express appreciation to the group for staying on their learning edge, taking risks and being willing to live with the discomfort of new knowledge and awareness that may challenge our assumptions about how the world is organized.

## Module 4: Taking Action

Time needed: 3 hours, 20 minutes

### Objectives

- Identify ways to take action against racism in personal, work, and community settings.
- Provide a framework for developing a personal agenda for action (next steps).
- Explore ways of empowering ourselves to eliminate racism in various areas of everyday life.
- Explore challenges faced in implementing action strategies.

**Key concepts**: ally, costs and benefits, spheres of influence, action continuum

### 1. Emotional Timeline (30 minutes)

Give each participant construction paper and a magic marker, and ask them to draw a timeline or graph noting the emotional high and low points that they experienced within the course so far. After 5 minutes, invite participants to share their timeline/graphs with the rest of the group. Then review the goals, concepts, and agenda for this module.

### Facilitation Issues

This activity often helps participants acknowledge and reflect on the roller coaster of emotions they may have experienced as they moved through the course, and take stock of their learning thus far. Sharing the charts enables them to appreciate their own and others' process of understanding racism and its manifestations. This can be empowering as participants acknowledge ways they have stayed on a learning edge and contributed to learning for others in the class. Frequently, participants identify the same activities or moments in the course as highs and lows thus reflecting a shared group experience as well.

### 2. Characteristics of an Ally (25 minutes)

Begin this activity by reviewing the definition of an ally ("Characteristics of an Ally" in Appendix 6G). In this series of activities, encourage white people to think of themselves as allies both to people of color and to other white people who are interrupting racism. Encourage participants of color to think about how to support members of their own racial group, members of other targeted racial groups, and white people who are interrupting racism.

To build on this definition and make it more concrete, ask participants to form pairs, and discuss a time when each of them experienced someone acting as an ally. This example may or may not be related to issues of race. Their discussion should focus on what the other person did that made him or her a good ally, how others responded to the actions of the ally, and what participants can learn from this example that can apply to being an ally against racism.

After the pairs have been together for 10 minutes, ask participants to report out some of the characteristics of good allies. Record these characteristics on newsprint, and post them on the wall for reference during the following activities.

### 3. Costs and Benefits of Interrupting Racism (15 minutes)

Ask participants to brainstorm some of the costs and benefits of interrupting racism. Examples include risking the loss of friends who choose to collude with racism, or giving up access to goods or services by refusing to do business with companies that are found to have racist practices. Benefits can include knowing others more fully without the fear, prejudice, or mistrust that racism engenders and having more accurate information about the contributions to society that are made by all racial groups. Note examples of costs and benefits on newsprint, and post this list next to the characteristics of good allies.

## 4. Action Continuum (25 minutes)

To prepare participants for developing their own personal action plan, present the "Action Continuum" (Appendix 6H). Give examples of strategies for taking action against racism, such as reading books and articles to find out more about racism, attending cultural or political events focused on concerns of different racial groups, confronting someone making a racist remark, or boycotting a company with racist business practices. Ask participants to form pairs or trios to brainstorm as many actions as they can think of for each stage of the action continuum, and write these on newsprint to post on the wall. These lists then provide ideas for the next steps, when participants develop their own specific action plans.

## Break (10 minutes)
## 5. Spheres of Influence (20 minutes)

Present the "Spheres of Influence" (Appendix 4B), and ask participants to brainstorm strategies for combating racism in each sphere. Participants can refer to the action continuum for ideas. For example, in the sphere of the self, a person could read a book, explore the concept of white privilege/advantage or internalized subordination, or attend a cultural or educational event that will push his or her learning edge a little further. In the sphere of work, a person could examine the environment and culture of his or her workplace to see how inclusive it is of the values, contributions, and experiences of people of color. During this activity, discuss how each action carries a level of risk that may vary in light of each person's circumstances. Interrupting a racist joke may seem easier with friends, but riskier with parents or a boss. Record ideas generated by the group on newsprint, and post them on the walls so that they can be used as references during the next activity.

## 6. Action Planning and Taking It With You (45 minutes)

Give each participant an "Action Planning Worksheet" (Appendix 6I). Ask each participant to identify at least three areas in which he or she can interrupt racism in the future, using any of the strategies in any of the spheres of influence. The action should be realistic in terms of that person's willingness and ability to carry out the particular strategy. For example, a college-age participant who is planning to confront her parents about racism should be encouraged to identify the costs and benefits of different ways of dealing with her parents, and to identify realistic goals for this intervention, given what she knows about them and her relationship to them. Similar issues relate to a participant who is going to confront a boss or institutional policy that perpetuates racism in his or her workplace.

Give participants 10 to 15 minutes to create a change contract for themselves and to discuss it with a partner. Instruct the partner to ask questions about the timeline for completing the action strategy, possible outcomes of the strategy, the support needed in order to carry out the strategy, and sources of encouragement and support that can be called upon during the implementation of the strategy.

Remind participants to develop realistic action plans, while also stretching a bit beyond their comfort zone. A person's place on the action continuum will be a function of her or his awareness of racism, readiness, and willingness to take action, and where he or she is in terms of personal comfort zone (see Chapter 3). For some participants at the beginning stages of awareness of racism, reading a book may be most appropriate. This action will give them needed information to prepare for more informed action and does not require them to confront someone else. Other participants who have more awareness of racism but who have not confronted racism in interpersonal interactions may be interested in strategies for interrupting racist or stereotypical comments or jokes. Participants who have worked to interrupt racism at the individual level can be encouraged to do antiracist work at a community or organizational level, such as joining a local or national organization working for change, or participating in letter-writing campaigns or boycotts against companies that discriminate based on race.

The more fully participants can develop their action plan (timelines for taking action, potential obstacles, potential factors that might facilitate change, and potential support systems), the more they can use others in the class for feedback and support. Encourage participants to commit at least one strategy to paper.

Action plans encourage participants to carry their new awareness into their life outside of the class. To help participants make the transition from their experience in class to doing antiracist work outside the class, ask each group to discuss implementation issues. Encourage participants to consider the level of risk for each of the activities in their contract; how they can minimize this risk; and what tools, skills and information, they will need to effectively carry out their strategies. Some participants may want to get more feedback on their action plans. Others may want to role-play how they might interrupt someone making a racist remark or having a conversation with a relative about a previous incident of racism. Facilitators can serve as consultants to help individuals or groups use this time as effectively as possible.

## 7. Closing (30 minutes)

End the course by having facilitators and participants appreciate each other for the level of attention, risk taking, care, and commitment that group members demonstrated throughout the course. As a closing activity, invite participants to talk about one of the following:

- A new learning that they have had while in the class
- A feeling that they have about the class
- Something that they are taking away from the class
- An appreciation for someone in the group from whom they have learned

Go around the circle, allowing each participant to briefly respond to one of the items. Allow anyone who wishes to pass to do so. Facilitators can go last; using your statement(s) to pull the group together and say goodbye.

## Notes

1. Adapted from McIntosh (1989).
2. Adapted from California Newsreel (2003a).
3. Questions adapted from California Newsreel (2003a).

# 7

# Racism, Immigration, and Globalization Curriculum Design

## LEE ANNE BELL, KHYATI Y. JOSHI, XIMENA ZÚÑIGA*

This chapter builds on the previous chapter by extending the analysis developed there to an examination of the connections among racism, immigration, and globalization. It presents a curriculum design to help participants understand how migrants to the United States have been received at different points in our history, and the role that race and racism have played in U.S. immigration policy and the immigrant experience, both historically and in the present. Here, we note the influence of globalization and the impact of American economic and foreign policy, on migration and racial formations in the United States. Ideally, the Overview: Twenty-First Century Racism, Chapter 6, and this chapter should be used together in sequence because they build upon and reinforce each other.

## A Nation of Immigrants: But Not All Equal

Although the United States has been a country of immigrants since its inception, not all have been equally welcome. From the beginning, naturalization and immigration law "reflected, reinforced and reproduced racial hierarchy" (Lee, 2004), creating racial distinctions that excluded or restricted immigration and citizenship of any group not considered White (Foner, 2005; Roediger, 2005). In 1790, Congress declared that only "free white" persons could become naturalized citizens, and naturalization of "persons of African descent" was not extended until almost a century later, after the Civil War. Between 1878 and 1952, 52 racial prerequisite cases, including 2 heard by the U.S. Supreme Court,

---

* We ask that those who cite this work always acknowledge by name all of the authors listed rather than either only citing the first author or using "et al." to indicate coauthors. All collaborated on the conceptualization, development, and writing of this chapter.

were argued to determine who would be considered White, thereby setting racial parameters for naturalization (Haney Lopez, 1996). The progression of these cases provides a fascinating look into the social construction of race, as court decisions about who would be deemed White ricocheted between "scientific" definitions of race popular at the time and, when these did not serve for excluding Japanese Americans or South Asians, definitions based on "what the common man thinks" (Gaultieri, 2001; Haney Lopez, 1996). In truth, both definitions were created by and reinforced white prejudices.

Entrance into a racially coded U.S. society has meant that the economic and social experiences of immigrants considered White have been quite different from those considered non-White. European immigrants, such as the Irish, Italians, Greeks, Poles, and Jews, faced considerable hostility and discrimination upon their arrival and were initially considered inferior by the Anglo-Saxons who preceded them (Brodkin, 1998; Foner, 2005; Guglielmo & Salerno, 2003; Jacobson, 1998). However, by the second and third generation, immigrants from Europe gained social and economic mobility and gradually "became" White, though this change in racial status came at the price of giving up their native languages, cultural traditions, and ethnic identities (Brodkin, 1998; Ignatiev, 1995).

This has not been the case for the descendants of non-European immigrants, who have often been perceived as outsiders, no matter how long their families have been in the United States. Pedraza (1996) describes the designation of certain immigrant groups as "perpetual foreigners" "a form of racial caste subordination held in place by law, custom, and violence" (p. 16). This idea has contributed to a racialized view by which non-European immigrants constitute a "threat" to the country, putting entire communities under suspicion, as in the case of the ongoing "illegalization" of Mexicans (Chacon & Davis, 2006) and the harsh treatment of citizens of Middle Eastern and South Asian descent since September 11, 2001 (Orfalea, 2006; see also Chapter 11).

Throughout U.S. history, xenophobic, nativist, and white supremacist sentiments interacted to fuel policies aimed at excluding immigrants of color from citizenship, and during recurring periods have led to vigilantism, mob violence, incarceration, and mass deportation (Chacon & Davis, 2006; Feagin, 1997). For example, the Asiatic Exclusion League worked rabidly to prevent Chinese immigration to the United States (Takaki, 1998b). Mexicans, who had been residents of the Southwest before it was annexed by the United States, at first traveled freely back and forth across a permeable border to work and visit family. However, beginning in 1924, they were increasingly categorized as "illegal," whether citizens or not (Chacon & Davis, 2006; Foner & Frederickson, 2004). During recurring waves of nativism, the Chinese in California and Mexicans in the Southwest experienced frequent vigilante violence in the 1900s, thousands of Filipinos and Mexicans were deported during the Depression, and Japanese Americans were forced into camps and their land appropriated by Whites during the 1940s (Chacon & Davis, 2006; Foner & Frederickson, 2004).

Immigration law and policy paralleled nativist sentiment. The Chinese Exclusion Act of 1882 denied entry and citizenship to Chinese laborers, and the National Origins Acts of 1921 and 1924 established a quota system explicitly favoring immigration from northern and western Europe while limiting immigration from other parts of the world (Cho, Paz y Puente, Ching Yoon Louie, & Khokha, 2004). As a result, between 1924 and 1950, 90% of immigrants to the United States were (white) European or Canadian (M. Suarez-Orozco, 2005). Even with the 1965 opening of immigration from other parts of the world, fears about diminishing white dominance dictated priorities that continued to privilege immigration from Europe (Lee, 2004; further discussion in chapter 11).

Despite continuing exclusionary efforts, however, the 1965 act did open the doors to people from other parts of the world so that by the 21st century the top sending countries are Mexico, China, the Philippines, India, Cuba, Vietnam, El Salvador, Korea, the Dominican Republic, and Canada (Portes & Rumbaut, 2001). The majority come from Latin America and the Caribbean (52%), and from Asia (29%), creating a dramatic shift in our population and in many ways stimulating a resurgence of the anti-immigrant nativism of previous eras.

## Push/Pull Factors Influencing Migration to the United States

Most immigrants to the United States are pushed by one set of conditions and pulled by another. Pull factors may be more salient for some immigrants, such as workers who have been actively recruited by U.S. employers, and push factors may be more salient for others, such as political refugees and asylees who have been forced to leave by oppressive or dangerous conditions at home. The United States in recurring cycles has invited workers from other countries to fulfill labor demands here, followed by later exclusion of these workers once their labor was no longer needed. For example, Chinese workers who built the railroads in the 1800s and Mexican braceros who developed our agricultural programs and filled labor shortages during World War II were later sent back to their home countries once these demands had been filled.

Many highly skilled immigrants who have been pushed to leave their native lands by lack of resources or opportunities have also been pulled by incentives of better jobs or pay in the United States. Middle-class and educated Koreans who emigrated in the 1970s and 1980s, for example, were pulled by the possibility of obtaining a higher standard of living and a college education for their children, and pushed by the lack of opportunity to attend highly selective institutions of higher learning in Korea (Min, 1996). On the other hand, many small farmers who emigrated from Central America were forced off their lands by commercial agriculture, a problem exacerbated by "free trade" agreements, such as the North American Free Trade Agreement (NAFTA), that caused the displacement of over 6 million Mexican farmers (Schepers, 2005).

Many Americans blame failure to eradicate poverty in the home country as causing the influx of poor and unskilled immigrants to the U.S. However, not all poor countries send immigrants to the United States and those that do so tend to have an extensive local history with U.S. military, political, cultural, and economic involvement (Rumbaut, 1995). For example, immigration from El Salvador and Haiti increased substantially as a result of U.S. military and political intervention in these nations. Furthermore, although many immigrants are poor, others are both highly skilled and affluent. For example, immigration from Vietnam, triggered by U.S. military involvement in the affairs of that nation, initially included many affluent Vietnamese.

Political and economic conditions in Central America, the Caribbean, and Southeast Asia have been exploited by U.S. corporations which actively recruit people for low-wage work that cannot be exported to other countries, such as cleaning hotel rooms and working in the meat-packing industry (Cooper, 2000). The dependence of U.S. businesses, such as produce growers, the hotel and restaurant industries, and the construction industry, on immigrant labor (whether legal or illegal) creates a magnet for people who can earn far more at very low wages in the United States than they could in their own nations.

## Economic Interests and Intersections of Race and Class

Cycles of xenophobia, violence, and perceived threat have tended to coincide with economic cycles (Chacon & Davis, 2006). Since slavery, U.S. business interests have relied on cheap or coerced labor, in large part from immigrants of color, to build the economy and maintain economic dominance in the world (Winant, 2001). Such immigrants have been both expendable when the economy shrinks and irreplaceable when the economy expands and their labor is once more needed (Martinez, 2004).

Immigrants today, 80% of whom are of immigrants of color, encounter a highly segmented labor market, shrinking middle class, and increasingly large gap between "the haves and the have-nots" (Portes & Zhou, 1993). They enter a postindustrial "hourglass" economy characterized by a bottom portion of low-skilled, low-wage, nonunion jobs and a top portion of high-paying jobs that require an elite education. Whereas those with education may be able to move into middle-class neighborhoods and mainstream venues, the majority encounter economic restructuring and corporate downsizing that have eliminated the types of jobs that enabled economic mobility for earlier immigrants. As manufacturing jobs have been replaced with low-paying service jobs (Barlow, 2003; Rumbaut, 1995), these groups and their heirs face the likelihood of no or downward mobility unless the economy changes dramatically (M. Suarez-Orozco, 2005; Waldinger & Feliciano, 2004).

## Negotiating Immigrant Status in a Racist Society

Although all immigrants must contend with the racial structure and normative assumptions they encounter on arrival, the racialized experiences of people from different immigrant groups also vary in important ways. Factors such as gender, class background, English speaking ability, educational level, religion, and generational status, generally helpful to mobility, are in many instances mitigated by the way immigrants are constructed racially (Portes & Rumbaut, 2001). Race affects the degree of assimilation or mobility, most notably in the areas of residential segregation, intermarriage, and second-generation patterns of survival and adaptation (Foner, 2005; M. Suarez-Orozco, 2005).

There is some debate about whether or not, for some groups of color who have economic and educational status, the color line will shift to include them as "honorary" Whites while continuing to lock out others (Gregory & Sanjek, 1994; Marabel, 2002; Tuan, 2001; Warren & Twine, 1997). Foner (2005) reflects that the current "White–non-White frame" seems to be giving way to a new "Black–non-Black frame" that will sort new immigrants accordingly. Some groups of color, like Puerto Ricans, Mexican Chicanos, and African Americans, remain relatively segregated generation after generation in ethnic enclaves separated from the white mainstream that excludes them. Foner and Frederickson (2004) note that "people of African ancestry, immigrant and native alike, continue to be highly segregated from the white majority—much more so than Asians and Asian Americans and lighter skinned Latinos" (p. 15). Socioeconomic status, for both Asians and Asian Americans and Latinos, is the most powerful determinant of residential location. The higher their income and education, the more likely they are to live in neighborhoods with non-Hispanic Whites (Foner & Frederickson, 2004). In such cases, class seems to trump race, as in the case of dark-skinned South Asian immigrants with education and economic resources who move into white, suburban communities (Portes & Zhou, 1993). In the case of African Americans with similarly high education and economic resources, however, race seems to continue to trump class, though this may be changing (see Foner, 2005). Rates of out-marriage with Whites show the same trend, with Black–White intermarriage rates remaining low, whereas significant numbers of second-generation Asian Americans and Hispanics have non-Hispanic White spouses or partners (Foner & Frederickson, 2004).

The influence of race on the experiences of the 1.5- and second-generation children of immigrants is also profound.[1] In many cases, these children hold dual citizenship in the United States and their country of origin and lead transnational lives, calling multiple places home (Joshi, 2006; Levitt & Waters, 2002). Yet here, despite economic status or success, they and their parents often have to cope with racism and ethnocentrism from Whites in their schools, neighborhoods, and communities, as well as in the mainstream media (Martinez, 2004; for the conflation of racism with religious oppression, see chapter 11). Juggling multiple realities may reinforce a strong sense of self and identity for many who see the world and their experiences from a dual frame of reference (Falicov, 2005; Kao & Tienda, 2005). For some, however, the effects of this negative "social mirroring" can have cumulative and long-lasting negative effects on their sense of identity, group identification, and achievement (C. Suarez-Orozco, 2005).

As a result of the economic squeeze, "large numbers of immigrants of color are settling into highly segregated neighborhoods where deep poverty, violence and substandard schools are the norm" (C. Suarez-Orozco, 2005, p. 143). Among the children of these immigrants, researchers note declining returns to education, in effect replicating the ways that enduring racism has dampened expectations for educational and economic success among long-standing minorities such as African Americans, Native Americans, Puerto Ricans, and Mexican Chicano/as (Foner, 2005; Spring, 2003).

Some immigrants of color are compared to others in ways that may seem flattering but ultimately serve the purpose of maintaining a white racial norm. The double-edged term *model minority*, first coined in the mid-1960s, describes Asian Americans as examples of a formerly marginalized group that, through hard work and determination, rise above the ranks of "problem minorities" (Lee, 1994; Tuan, 2001; Winnick, 1990). Although perceived as "positive," the stereotype of Asian Americans as quiet, well-behaved, studious, and naturally intelligent is harmful in many ways. It not only ignores the experiences of a broad range of Asian immigrants by lumping groups from many different national origins and economic situations into one group, but also fails to account for the stratification that occurs when various Asian groups enter the racialized U.S. system. For example, well-educated Indian and Pakistani immigrants have had more opportunities for mobility and social integration than Vietnamese and Cambodian refugees. Along with obscuring serious problems in Asian American communities, the "model minority" myth has been used to justify omitting Asian Americans from some federal funding, university admissions, and opportunity programs. Imposing a categorical label on all Asian Americans silences their multiple voices and erases "ethnic, cultural, social-class, gender, language, sexual, generational, achievement, and other differences" (Lee, 1996, p. 6).

The model minority myth minimizes the effects of racism as a determining factor in achieving success in the United States and is often used to set standards for how other minorities should behave, serving to discredit claims of injustice by African Americans and others who demand social equality (Lee, 1996). It also justifies requiring Asian Pacific Americans to perform at significantly higher levels than their white counterparts to qualify for the same rewards, often fanning resentment of their success by other groups (Martinez, 2004).

Language interacts with race as well to affect status in the United States. Here, we use the term *linguicism* (Nieto, 2003) or *language domination* (Dardar, 1991), to describe prejudice and discrimination based on language. The intersection of linguicism and racism can be seen in "backlash practices" that "use race as a screening device to categorize and marginalize sectors of the population ... creating surrogates, such as language and ability, for the larger category race" (Gutiérrez, Asato, Santos, & Gotanda , 2002, p. 343). Current efforts to legislate "English-only" signs and public information and to ban bilingual education from schools target immigrants of color and reinforce ethnocentrism and linguicism (Alamillo, Palmer, Viramontes, & Garcia, 2005; Valenzuela, 1999).

## Contemporary Manifestations of Racism

Once again, as in repeated cycles throughout history, we see a resurgence of nativism and anti-immigrant backlash in the United States (Feagin, 1997; Perea, 1997). This backlash has taken a number of forms: individual acts of violence toward immigrants or those perceived to be immigrants, vigilante efforts by hate groups such as voluntary "border patrols" like the Minutemen, and the militarization of the U.S. border with Mexico and to some extent Canada (Lovato, 2005; *The Nation*, 2006; Southern Poverty Law Center, 2001a, 2001b). Since the early 1990s, nativist and white supremacist groups have sponsored anti-immigrant referenda, organized boycotts and demonstrations, and attempted to change state and local policies to limit immigration and/or expel those who are already here. The best known of these, California's Proposition 187, promoted by an organization called Save Our State (SOS), was ratified in 1994 by a margin of 59 to 41 percent. Though it was later found to be unconstitutional by the U.S. Supreme Court, it has spurred continuing efforts to deny access to social service and public education for undocumented immigrants, even though their wages pay taxes that support these benefits (Brugge, 2006).

Hate crimes committed on the basis of race/ethnicity, national origin, and religion also impact immigrant communities of color; these have been steadily increasing since the mid-1980s and spiked after the attacks of September 11, 2001 (Abdelkarim, 2003; Moser, 2005; National Asian Pacific Legal Consortium, 2002; Prejudice Institute, 2005). For instance, in the year following the attacks on the World Trade Center and Pentagon, hate crimes against Arab American and South Asians Muslims and Sikhs (and those presumed to be) were 17 times higher than in the previous year (Orfalea, 2006).

Immigration issues post 9/11 have become increasingly linked to national security concerns, creating a whole host of new and complex issues for many immigrants of color. For example, federal and state efforts have aimed at passing legislation that would require a national social identification card for air travel, opening a bank account, collecting Social Security, and accessing most government services. Protect Arizona Now, the organization that launched Proposition 200 in Arizona in an effort to stop undocumented immigrants from getting driver's licenses, is now trying to expand nationally. Seventy-one members of the House of Representatives, almost all Republicans, have formed a caucus to promote anti-immigrant legislation and block a proposed guest worker program (Schepers, 2005).

Racial profiling is on the rise both at the Mexican border and in interactions with those perceived to be potential terrorists because they are presumed to be Muslim. The USA PATRIOT Act has enabled indefinite detention, wiretapping without warrants, search and seizure, and deportation without due process (Orfalea, 2006). Recent reports of large-scale government surveillance of the American public, justified in the name of fighting terror, have affected not only immigrants but also potentially the larger public and the constitutional principles upon which our democracy was founded (Risen, 2006).

Immigration, especially immigration by undocumented Mexican people, represents a conundrum for politicians because anti-immigrant sentiments among many voters are in direct conflict with the interests of U.S. corporations and the military. Many employers rely upon undocumented and low-skilled immigrant workers who they can pay less, prevent from unionizing, and let go during economic downturns (Barlow, 2003; Cooper, 2000; Schepers, 2005). The military, at a time when they are having great difficulty recruiting U.S. citizens to serve in the armed services, relies heavily on immigrants who enlist in exchange for the opportunity to become legal residents. Twenty thousand military servicemen and -women have become citizens since July

2002, in many instances without completing the years of residency typically required for getting citizenship (Wong, 2005).

Immigrants do not merely respond to their environments, however; they actively engage in efforts to influence and transform them. Some, for example, cope with linguistic and cultural barriers by using the universal languages of mathematics and the sciences as a way "to excel in a new land" (Portes & Rumbaut, 2001; Winerip, 2005). Ethnic communities play an important role in helping newcomers gain access to resources and build kinship networks. Dominican and Colombian communities in New York City, for example, have organized cultural, recreational, and professional associations that assist in the transition process (Sassen-Koob, 1987; for the role of ethnic religious communities, see Warner & Wurthnow, 1998; Yoo, 1999; chapter 11, this volume). Some ethnic communities, such as New York City's West Indian community, also provide financial assistance through rotating credit associations that provide an important source of capital for business ventures (Foner, 2005). Other immigrant groups, such as Mexicans who helped organize the United Farm Workers and, more recently, the Union of Needletrades, Industrial and Textile Employees (UNITE), have significantly changed their economic and political circumstances, and, to the ultimate benefit of all workers, helped to strengthen a union movement that has been in decline (Chacon & Davis, 2006). On May Day 2006, 10 million immigrants and their allies in over 200 cities across the country mobilized to demand legalization of undocumented people (Hin, 2006).

## Globalization, Racism, and Immigrant Vulnerability

Globalization increases the vulnerability of populations, especially those of color, who exist on the bottom of the global economy. Forced by harsh economic conditions at home, in large part spurred by globalization as well as famine and war, many thousands of people must move simply to survive. Current "deadly" border and immigration policies in the United States both create and profit from this vulnerability (Martinez, 2004). Undocumented workers often work long hours for extremely low pay under very poor working conditions and receive no health benefits or workers' compensation for on-the-job accidents or work-induced illnesses. They are also vulnerable to all kinds of abuse and exploitation because fear of deportation prevents them from seeking social services and/or legal recourse for harm done to them. Nor are they likely to call for protection by police, who are often (correctly) assumed to work with the INS and Border Patrol. Often, adults and their children are subjected to weekly roundups, held in jails, and deported, wreaking havoc on their families, especially children (Southern Poverty Law Center, 2003).

Women make up more than half of all new immigrants, working as the new "braceras" as maids, nannies, and cooks, under harsh conditions, with little protection, and separated from their own children and families for extended periods of time (Ching Yoon Louie, 2001; Cho, y Puente, Ching Yoon Louie,, & Khokha., 2004; Hondagneu-Sotelo, 1994). Involuntary immigrants, such as Eastern European, Asian, and Latin American women and children who have been forced into sweatshops or human and sex trafficking, are even more vulnerable and powerless.

One in five children in the United States today is the child of an immigrant; 75% of these children are born in the United States and are citizens (Foundation for Child Development, 2004). If current trends continue, immigrant children will represent at least a quarter of all U.S. children by 2010 (Urban Institute, 2006). Because of the high poverty rate, this is a group that is particularly vulnerable when social services in education and health care are cut back or denied (van Hook, 2003). There is evidence, for example, that the children of Mexican immigrants become less healthy the longer they live in the United States (National Research Council, 1998). Educational account-ability mandates also negatively affect immigrant children of color, as they do children of color in general in the United States (McNeil, 2005), through high-stakes tests that ignore level of English speaking ability, the poor quality of schooling and teachers, and the challenges of adapting to new cultural and social norms. For example, the drop-out rate of immigrant youth in New York State alone since the implementation of No Child Left Behind has almost doubled from 17% in 1998 to 31 % in 2001. Increasing numbers of immigrant children of color are pushed out or drop out of school at a time when there are virtually no meaningful jobs for those without formal schooling (Orfield, 1998). This does not bode well for their future political and economic integration or participation in American society.

## Rationale for Educating about Racism, Immigration, and Globalization

Throughout U.S. history, both conflict and cooperation have marked intergroup rela-tions across racial and ethnic lines. All too often, groups have been pitted against each other in ways that maintain the racial status quo in favor of white elites. At other times, however, common problems and interests have united groups along and across the color line. Such is the case today.

For example, strained relationships among different immigrant groups of color, such as between Koreans and African Americans, do exist. As poor immigrants of color are squeezed into urban communities, they compete with African Americans and Puerto Ricans for political influence, housing, and other scarce resources. How-ever, they also develop mutual dependence, friendships, political alliances to address school and community concerns, and coalitions to fight for their rights and against racism (Foner & Frederickson, 2004).

As in the past, constricting economic circumstances lead poor, working-class, and, increasingly, middle-class Whites, and recently African Americans (Swarns, 2006), to scapegoat immigrants as the source of their problems, rather than inter-rogating economic policies that harm all workers and pit them against each other for the benefit of employers and others who rely on immigrant labor to keep wages low. Cross-class and cross-race alliances have been and are possible (Hin, 2006; Zinn, 1990/1995), but require historical and current information about how racism sub-verts such alliances.

Knowledge of our racial history as a country is also important in order for people to make sense of current immigration debates and to identify and support policies that honor our immigrant roots as a nation and the democratic ideals that define our country at its best. Understanding the history of racialization and treatment of immigrant groups is needed as an antidote to nativist and xenophobic move-ments today (*The Nation*, 2006). Such knowledge is crucial if we are to genuinely address current economic frustrations over stagnating wages and disappearing benefits that have led to a shrinking middle class and reduced economic mobility. A combination of factors including economic restructuring, corporate outsourcing and other neoliberal economic policies that work against the best interests of the majority of Americans of all races is to blame, not immigrants. Finally, we cannot separate the problems of the color line without also addressing the problems of the border line(s) and our responsibilities as world citizens in an interconnected and increasingly fragile globe.

## Racism, Immigration, and Globalization Curriculum Design

### Overall Goals

At the conclusion of this curriculum, we hope that participants will achieve the following goals:

- Understand how xenophobia and racism impact American views of immigration and immigrants of color both historically and contemporarily.
- Increase awareness of individual, institutional, and societal manifestations of anti-immigrant racism.
- Have a greater understanding of the role all of us can play in working for equality and justice for immigrant people.
- Feel capable and motivated to organize at multiple levels (personal, social, and institutional) and work collaboratively with others to promote democratic, egalitarian, and inclusive immigration policies and practices.

### Overview of Modules

**Note to readers**: The curriculum design in this chapter is based on the assumption that participants have completed the introductory module(s) described in Chapter 3 prior to beginning this design and have a basic understanding of the conceptual framework of oppression described in Chapter 3. This curriculum design on Racism, Immigration, and Globalization should be preceded by the curriculum design in Chapter 6: Racism and White Privilege.

See Table 7.1 for an overview of this chapter's modules.

### Module 1: Personal Connections

Time needed: 3 hours, 25 minutes

**Table 7.1**  Overview of Modules: Racism, Immigration, and Globalization

| Module 1: Personal Connections (3 hours, 25 minutes) | Module 2: Forces Shaping Immigrant Experiences in the United States (3 hours, 40 minutes) |
|---|---|
| 1. Welcome and Introduction: What's in a Name? (30 min.)<br>2. Journeys to the United States (25 min.)<br>3. Where I'm From Poems (60 min.)<br>4. Analyzing Images of Immigrants and Immigration (30 min.)<br>5. Quiz: What Do We Know? (40 min.)<br>6. Closing Whip (10 min.) | 1. Tracing Patterns in U.S. Immigration History (30 min.)<br>2. Immigration Timeline Activity (90 min.)<br>3. Global Patterns and Interests That Drive Migration Today (90 min.)<br>4. Closing (10 min.) |
| **Module 3: Personal to Institutional Connections—Racialization and Linguicism (3 hours, 5 minutes)** | **Module 4: Taking Action/Becoming Allies (2 hours, 50 minutes)** |
| 1. Exploring Differences and Common Ground (45 min.)<br>2. Key Definitions, Levels, and Types of Racism and Linguicism (45 min.)<br>3. Gallery Walk and Discussion (75 min.)<br>4. Closing (20 min.) | 1. The Local Is Global: Learning About Your Local Community (40 min.)<br>2. Spheres of Influence and Personal Action Planning (90 min.)<br>3. Closing and Wrap-Up (40 min.) |

### Objectives

- To listen respectfully to each other's stories and make personal connections between U.S. history and immigration policy and how it affects peoples' lives
- To see patterns in stories across generations and different countries of origin, and have participants understand both the commonalities and differences in the immigration experience
- To identify stereotypes about immigrants in popular culture and to understand their origins and connections to racism
- To understand the role of race in immigration policy and in U.S. political, economy, and military history

**Key concepts**: assimilation, Anglo-conformity, nativism, xenophobia

### 1. Welcome and Introduction: What's In a Name? (30 minutes)[2]

Welcome participants and ask them to introduce themselves by saying their name and the meaning or derivation of all or any part of their name. Begin with your own name and derivations/meaning to model what you are asking of them. Once all have introduced themselves, note some of the associations or derivations that are made with names. Possibilities include connections to relatives or ancestors, to geographic places, to religious icons or spiritual meanings, to famous people, to particular languages, or to future expectations.

Explain that our names often connect us to the past and to the places from which our ancestors came and/or to the hopes and aspirations of our parents and forebears. Note that if you roll back the migration clock far enough, everyone's ancestors "originally" came from somewhere else.

Review the objectives for the course, and take care of any other logistics (see Chapter 3). Then introduce the next activity as one that will allow further exploration of family origins and journeys.

### Facilitation Issues

If you have not already done so, you should establish guidelines for the class following the methods suggested in the Racism and White Privilege Curriculum Design in Chapter 6. This activity may feel emotionally risky if you are meeting a group for the first time. If, however, you have already taught the Racism and white Privilege curriculum (Chapter 6) as we recommend, this activity will deepen engagement for participants who already know each other while expanding their analysis of racism to include the immigrants of color.

This activity allows participants to make personal connections to the idea of immigration and may help them begin thinking about what they know and don't know about the immigration experiences of their own ancestors as a basis for exploring the topic of the course. Be aware, however, that the issue of names and origins can be loaded for many. Participants who are African American or Native American heritage may have painful connections to a history of oppression in which names were forcibly changed. Other participants had ethnically-identified names changed at Ellis Island or other ports of arrival. Also, participants who are adopted may have had to change names, or may not know about their ancestry for a variety of reasons. Acknowledge the power of naming and knowing one's roots, and affirm the range of experiences that participants bring to this topic.

### 2. Journeys to the United States (25 minutes)

Provide each participant with a copy of the handout "Personal/Familial Journey to the United States" (Appendix 7A). Give the class 10 minutes to go through the list on their own, and jot down responses to as many questions as possible.

Poll the class using the following questions:

1. How many people were able to respond to the majority of questions?
2. Who had difficulty responding? What factors made that so?

Discuss as a whole group why, for many, it is difficult to answer these questions. For example, African American ancestors were brought here against their will, and their names were changed when they arrived, so that much familial or generational information has been lost or destroyed. Participants of European background may have lost information about their specific national or ethnic origins as a result of these group's assimilation to an Anglo-European norm that required them to lose or mute customs and language in order to fit in to the Anglo-American mainsteam (Anglo-conformity). Other participants may have direct and immediate connections to their countries of origin and recent memories about the journey here. Affirm the variety of ways and conditions that govern arrival to these shores, and acknowledge that there is no one "immigrant story" that defines us all, despite the iconic stock story of immigration and the melting pot.

As a group, notice the variety of stories and common themes and distinctions that differentiate the stories. As homework, ask participants to take the handout home with them and use it to interview other family members to fill in blanks whenever possible. Ask them to bring the handout, with whatever new information they are able to glean, to the next class. You could also ask participants to bring a family photo or artifact that represents family roots for them.

## 3. Where I'm From Poems (60 minutes)

Introduce "where I'm from" poems using the examples provided in Appendix 7B or drawing examples from Christensen (2000).. Ask participants to analyze the structure of these poems. Invite participants to write their own "Where I'm From" poems. To prime the pump, ask them to jot down, in whatever language feels most at home for them, visual images that describe the place that they or their families identify as their "home," smells that remind them of home, feelings that suggest home, and sounds they would hear there. Ask them to draw on these images, smells, sounds, and feelings as they construct their own poems using the format "I am from ..." and filling in as many lines as they like.

Let participants know they can write their poem in any language and that the poem does not need to rhyme or be a particular length. Some participants may express hesitation about composing a poem. Assure them there is no "correct" way to do this, and encourage them to play with the "I am from ...'" format to see what emerges. Most participants become very engaged with the activity and sometimes even have a hard time cutting things out when they edit their poems. Ideally, you as facilitator will also write and share your own poem.

### Sharing Poems

Explain that each person will read her or his poem, and then continue to the next person until all poems have been read. Encourage participants to listen supportively and think about commonalities and differences in the poems. For groups of 20 people or fewer, all poems should be read aloud to the entire group. For groups of more than 20 people, divide the group in half and ask group members to read to each other. Each poem should take about 90 seconds to read.

Once everyone has read, invite a round of applause. Then ask participants to discuss the following questions as a group:

1. What was it like to write the poem?
2. What was it like to read your poem aloud?
3. What did you learn from the other poems you heard?

## Facilitation Issues

It is important that participants give their undivided attention while poems are being read. Readers should not provide any explanations before reading their poem. They should simply read—even if this is difficult. Acknowledge that the poems can be emotionally powerful both for the reader and for the listeners. Encourage participants to listen quietly and supportively as each poem is read, noticing their own emotional responses to the poem. Affirm the value of having one's personal story acknowledged in a supportive group and the power of the activity for acknowledging the range of experiences evoked in these stories. This activity provides a personal ground from which to examine the way we learn societal images of immigrants in the next activity.

## 4. Analyzing Images of Immigrants and Immigration (20-25 minutes)

Introduce the activity as one where participants will compare and contrast images of immigrants and immigration at different points in time. If possible, provide material for them to read ahead of time. See Appendix 7I for suggestions.

Start the activity by asking participants to think about what they have read and learned in their schooling about different groups of immigrants to the United States.. Who were these earlier immigrants? What images do they have about these immigrants based on textbooks, stories they have heard, what they have read, family stories, and so on? Conduct a group brainstorm of all the information, images, and knowledge participants have about different generations of immigrants to the United States. Examples might include *European*, *Italian*, *Potato Famine*, *Jewish*, *escaping poverty*, *fleeing persecution*, *industrious*, and *melting pot*. Make a list of the images on the board or chart paper.

Next, make a second list of images of immigrants today. Who are the "new" immigrants? What images do we have about them based on textbooks, newspaper articles, and television reports? Add this list next to the previous one. Examples might include *predominantly Mexican*, *poor*, *illegal*, *escaping poverty*, *hardworking*, *high-tech*, and *Asian*. Add this list next to the previous one.

As a whole group or in small groups of four to five per group, ask participants to examine and compare the two lists. What similarities do they notice? What differences? What do they think accounts for differences noted? What role might race play in these differences?

Bring the class together, and discuss their responses to the questions above. Pay particular attention to the role of race in the differences noted. Tell participants to check the veracity of these points as the course proceeds. Note that we will be looking more closely at the role of race and racialization in the differing experiences of immigrants from different national/ethnic groups as the class proceeds.

## Facilitation Issues

Use this as an opportunity to find out gaps in knowledge about immigration that people bring into the class, and begin to offer more accurate information as needed. Note issues to come back to later once participants have had the opportunity to read more on the topic. For example, you might hear them say that earlier immigrants learned English quickly. If so, you can note that in fact there were projects to open – and later to close -- schools in German, French, and other languages for these immigrants. Or someone might have listed that immigrants today are "illegal," and you can point out that there was no such category during earlier waves of immigration. Ask them to consider why these differences are emphasized today and think about the role that race and racism could play in underscoring these differences.

## 5. Quiz: What Do We Know? (40 minutes)

This activity draws upon what participants already know and highlights areas of misinformation or lack of knowledge about immigrants and their contributions to the United States. Provide participants with a copy of the quiz (Appendix 7C). Allow 10 minutes to complete it individually. Once they have finished, inform them that all of the statements on the quiz are true.

Poll participants to find out which questions were most difficult or confusing as a point of departure for analysis of the reasons for the lack of information or misinformation we tend to have about this issue. Take a poll to find out which question was answered incorrectly by most participants. Use that statement first as a starting point for the discussion. Ask participants to explain why they thought the particular statement was false. Discuss as many of the questions as time allows, using the information provided in the answer section of Appendix 7C and drawing out participant assumptions and misconceptions for further exploration. Wrap up the discussion, and say that the next modules will explore these issues further in historical and contemporary context.

### Facilitation Issues

Keep track of the assumptions and misconceptions raised by participants in this discussion, and refer back to them as you proceed through the modules. They provide an important focal point for connecting with the knowledge and questions participants bring to the course.

## 6. Closing Whip (10 minutes)

Ask participants to stand and form a circle. Go around the circle, asking each participant to state one question raised for them in the session that they would like to explore further. Note these questions to follow up on during the next module.

## Module 2: Forces Shaping Immigrant Experiences in the United States

Time needed: 3 hours, 40 minutes

## Objectives

- To begin to understand historical, economic, and other forces that shape racialized immigrant experiences in the United States
- To examine the patterns in how immigrants of color are treated once they arrive in the United States, and differences in experiences from those considered White
- To look at the connections between U.S. government, economic, and military policies at home and abroad and immigration patterns and experiences
- To compare and contrast how immigrants from different groups have been treated in U.S. history and law, and to explore the role that race has played and continues to play in this differential treatment

**Key concepts**: naturalization, immigration law, historical cycles, xenophobia and nativism, globalism, globalization

## 1. Tracing Patterns in U.S. Immigration History (30 minutes)

Introduce the activity by explaining that historical patterns, though often invisible today, are crucial for understanding the underlying causes of present-day issues and challenges. Today, we will be exploring these patterns in relation to immigration policies, practices, and the racialized experiences of different groups in this country. Ask participants to form groups of four and jot down their responses to the following questions (10 minutes):

1. Why do people migrate to the United States from other countries? List as many reasons as you can.
2. List immigrant groups with which you are familiar. For each group, what was their experience when they arrived? How were they treated by the people already here?

Ask someone from each group to come up and list the reasons for migration discussed in their group until you have a complete list. Then list the immigrant groups and experiences on arrival, combining information from all of the groups. List responses in three columns of newsprint with the headings "Group," "Reasons for Migration," and Treatment Upon Arrival" (15 minutes). Possible responses might be the following:

*Reasons for migration*:
- economic hardship in home country,
- political repression,
- human rights violations,
- better life opportunities,
- reconnection with family,
- war,
- invitation by U.S. businesses,
- political asylum

*Groups and treatment*:
- Africans—enslaved;
- French Huguenots—given land;
- Mexicans—land stolen, forced out, brought in, and then forced out again;
- Chinese—invited, then expelled;
- anti-Castro Cubans (first wave)—welcomed;
- Japanese—interned;
- Haitians—turned back at the border

Tell participants we will use this information as a starting point for exploring the history of immigration in the United States in the next activity.

## 2. Immigration Timeline Activity (90 minutes)

Introduce this activity as a way to understand recurring patterns in U.S. immigration history. Ahead of time, make note cards or photocopies of the timeline dates and events listed in Appendix 6C. Distribute the timeline dates and descriptions randomly to class participants. Ask participants to identify the earliest date and read the event aloud, placing it on one end of a wall. Then ask for the next date and proceed in order until all cards have been read and placed on the timeline on the wall. (Facilitators may want to have a master list from Appendix 6C to anticipate the next date and prompt as needed.)

Once all cards have been posted, ask participants to walk along the timeline, noting patterns as they proceed through it. Then reconvene for a whole-group discussion, using the following questions as a guide:

1. What patterns do you see recurring? What might be the reasons for these recurring patterns?
2. What roles might race and racism play in the events listed?
3. Note that one pattern that can be identified shows restrictive or discriminatory policies, whereas another pattern shows openings in policy and/or resistance to discrimination. What do you think accounts for these different patterns?
4. How has the definition of *citizenship* changed over the course of U.S. history? What factors contributed to this? How is citizenship defined by race? What effect does this have for different immigrant groups to this country?
5. How does Emma Lazarus's poem on the Statue of Liberty, "The New Colossus" ("Give me your tired, your poor / Your huddled masses yearning to breathe free ..."), compare and/or contrast with reasons for cycles of immigration discussed previously?
6. How do current debates about immigration repeat patterns of the past?
7. What would a nonracist immigration policy look like?

Ask participants to identify places in the history timeline where backlash against immigrants (xenophobia and nativism) appear to be operating. What circumstances (economic, political, military) surrounded these times? What tentative conclusions do participants draw from looking at these questions? Note that the next activity will work with these ideas further.

### Facilitation Issues

Some patterns that should be noted include the following: Migration is affected by larger economic, social, and political factors; immigration policy controls who is included or excluded on the basis of race (and also class, gender, national origin, political affiliation, sexual orientation, and disability); migration is both forced and voluntary, often corresponding to the demand for cheap labor; U.S. political and military intervention displaces people; patterns of xenophobia and nativism have occurred throughout our history; there is a tendency to blame immigrants for problems such as unemployment, crime, overburdened social services, and other issues; and social justice movements have successfully organized to fight against racism and anti-immigration xenophobia throughout U.S. history.

### 3. Global Patterns and Interests That Drive Migration Today[3] (90 minutes)

Play the song "Are My Hands Clean?" by Sweet Honey in the Rock. (This is available on *Sweet Honey in the Rock: Live at Carnegie Hall*, lyrics and music by Bernice Johnson, ReagonSongtalk Publishing Co., 1985; information to access the lyrics is given in Appendix 7E.)

In preparation for this activity, prepare the lyrics from the website, and ask participants to discuss what the song is about. Then ask them to pair up and look at the labels on an item of clothing they are wearing and identify where it was made. Use a world map to note where each piece of clothing was manufactured. Typically, the majority of labels will be from Third World countries outside the United States, although increasingly items are made in a "free trade zone" in a Third World country, then shipped to the United States for final touches where the "Made in U.S.A." label is added. Ask participants to suggest reasons why this might be so. Ask them to imagine the workers who made their clothing—where do they live? What are their working conditions? What do you know about their culture, families, and communities? Are members of the group represented among immigrant populations in this country? What prompted them to move? (See introduction to this chapter.)

This discussion will likely raise issues about labor costs, cheap labor, trade deficits, and less expensive products for U.S. consumers. Note that NAFTA allows corporations and capital to travel freely across national borders, but restricts any such movement of people. Ask participants to consider the economic, political, and cultural impact on Third World countries of "free trade".

Next show the film *Uprooted: Refugees of the Global Economy* (available from www. nnir.org or www.teachingforchange.org for about $20). This 28-minute video follows the lives of three immigrants to the United States from Bolivia, Haiti, and the Philippines. Their stories illustrate how global institutions like the World Bank and the International Monetary Fund, as well as multinational corporations, drive immigration by making it difficult for people to survive in their home countries.

Before showing the video, ask participants to count off by three and write their number at the top of a piece of paper. Each number will be assigned a character in the movie to focus on closely as they watch the video. For example, participants with the number 1 will pay particular attention to and take careful notes on Maricel's story, those with the number 2 will follow Jessy and Jaime in the same way, and those with the number 3 should do so for Luckner.

After participants have viewed the video, ask them to get into groups with others who have the same number, that is, all the 1's in a group, 2's in a group, and 3's in a group. Facilitators can form more than one group for each number to keep groups small enough for good conversation; there should be no more than four or five participants in a group. Ask groups to discuss for 15 minutes the following questions, with one person responsible for taking notes of key points in the discussion:

1. What are the conditions faced by your character in their home country? In the United States?
2. Why did your character migrate? What factors in the sending country forced your character to migrate?
3. What policies in the United States made it difficult for them to migrate?
4. Why do you think your character became involved in community activism?

As participants to rejoin the full classroom group, and ask each small group reporter to briefly read out the key points from the discussion. Then facilitate a general discussion emphasizing the factors affecting migration and the effects of globalization on the migration of people around the world. Ask participants to discuss how migration for these characters and people like them is similar to and different from earlier European migration. What do they think race/racism have to do with their experiences? Allocate 30 minutes for this discussion.

## Option 2: Alternative Activity: The Transnational Capital Auction[4]

This role play is another way to bring out the reasons why people migrate, the corporate and governmental factors that drive migration, and the role of globalization in promoting racism and discrimination in the United States toward people who migrate.

*Facilitation Issues*    Participants are likely to share the ignorance and misinformation our general population has about how consumer goods are produced and the suffering that enables the discounted prices we pay for commodities. Looking at the human face of this suffering can be challenging. Also, participants may find it difficult to focus on macroeconomic policies that seem complicated and far away. The activities provided here are intended to make these policies clear by connecting them to real people at the local level where commodities are produced and consumed. Encourage participants to keep making connections and to realize that all policies have local impacts.

**4    Closing (10 minutes)**

Go around the class and ask participants to share one new idea or fact they have learned today that surprised them.

## Module 3: Personal to Institutional Connections—Racialization and Linguicism

Time needed: 3 hours, 5 minutes

**Objectives**

- To explore our common and different experiences based on race, ethnicity, ethnicities, immigrant experience, and language in society
- To identify and examine some of the patterns of individual, institutional, and cultural discrimination based on citizenship status and language

**Key concepts**: race, ethnicity, racialized ethnicity, racism, linguicism, individual racism and linguicism (active versus passive), institutional and cultural racism and linguicism

**1    Exploring Differences and Common Ground[5] (45 minutes)**

This activity is a variation of an activity commonly used in experiential learning to provide participants with the opportunity to explore differences and commonalties, and helps to surface some of the ways people are differentially impacted by racism, immigration, and globalization. Provide the participants with copies of the list of statements in Appendix 7F, and select 10 to 20 statements to read based on your knowledge of the group in making the statement selection.

Ask participants to form a large circle. Inform the group that the activity will allow them to explore how racism, immigration, and globalization issues may impact them in similar and different ways. Tell the participants that you will read a series of statements. If the statement is true for them, they should walk to the center of the circle in silence and notice "who is in" and "who is out." Then, silently step back to their previous place. This activity works best when the facilitators ask participants to move in and out in silence, and repeat "Step in" for each statement, asking the group to notice "who is in" and "who is out" each time participants move into the center of the circle. Modeling with a few examples that apply to the facilitator and a few members of the group can be a helpful way to begin.

Once you have read all of the statements, ask the group to comment on the following questions:

1. What stood out about doing this activity?
2. What statements were more challenging and why?
3. What patterns, if any, did they notice? Personally? In the group?
4. What might be some reasons for some of these patterns?
5. What questions do you have?

Ask participants to turn to the person next to them and share their feelings about the activity. Either in dyads or back as a large group, some helpful processing questions are as follows: What did you notice as you and others were going in and out of the circle? What surprised you? What was uncomfortable for you? What was comfortable for you? What do you think made this so?

In wrapping up the activity, note that it is usually uncomfortable to become aware of the ways in which our experiences differ from those of others, especially when we realize the ways in which our privileged status can blind us to prejudice or discrimination faced by others. Highlight the value of exploring commonalties and differences as a way to broaden our understanding of the world and our capacity to see others' experiences. Note that this capacity is a basis for developing the kind of empathy that enables one to see others on their own terms and not unconsciously filtered through one's own values and experiences. This is essential for developing the capacity to work effectively with others as an ally.

## Facilitation Issues

This activity can be set up in many different ways depending on the size of the room, the amount of open space, and the mobility of the participants. Participants can make a large circle, or simply raise their hand or stand up from their desks or chairs. Select a range of statements that surface issues of social identity as well as issues of both advantaged/privileged and targeted status. Facilitators may want to conduct the activity in silence, asking participants to simply notice who enters the circle and who does not as you go through the statements. Allowing sufficient time to debrief and dialogue is important. After debriefing participant reactions and feelings, link the discussion to the levels and types of oppression represented in the next activity.

### 2. Key Definitions, Levels, and Types of Racism and Linguicism (45 minutes)

This activity enables participants to understand racism and linguicism, and identify and discuss examples of racial and language prejudice, discrimination, and oppression toward immigrants at the individual, institutional, and cultural levels and at conscious and unconscious levels. Use Appendix 7G, which draws on Katz's (1978) "Levels and Types of Oppression" as a visual organizer to help frame this discussion; or organizers in chapter 3 and Appendix 11A.

On newsprint or an overhead transparency, post the terms and definitions of levels and types of racism and linguicism in Appendix 7D. Discuss each term, and provide two or three examples to illustrate each type. Documented examples that you can prepare related to immigration status, language, and race may be found on the Web sites listed in Appendix 7H. Invite questions and clear up any confusion before proceeding to the gallery walk activity. Once you are sure that participants understand these definitions, move on to the next activity.

## Facilitation Issues

You could ask participants to research these Web sites as homework individually or in small groups prior to this session, and you should prepare several examples yourself ahead of time. You could also ask participants to bring copies of the Web pages researched as well as artifacts to visually illustrate some of their examples.

### 3. Gallery Walk and Discussion (75 minutes)

Prior to the activity, hang newsprint in three areas of the room labeled "Individual," "Institutional," and "Cultural." Ask participants to form three groups, and assign each group to one of the posted areas. Give them 15 minutes in their small groups to generate examples of how both conscious and unconscious racism and linguicism are manifested at the individual, cultural, and institutional levels through conscious and unconscious attitudes, beliefs, and behaviors. Next, ask participants to quietly write their examples in the appropriate newsprint. Add your own examples if participants have trouble getting started (see Appendix 7H for resources related to this activity). Some examples you might offer include the following:

At the *individual* level: individual attitudes, beliefs and behaviors that privilege whiteness and English usage and proficiency. For example, individuals who assume speakers of Spanish or Arabic are uneducated or backward; coworkers who make fun of someone's accent; high school or college students who avoid study groups that include immigrant students who are not English proficient or who are of color; teachers who assume that Asian and Asian American students will be good at math; supervisors who express negative or xenophobic attitudes toward "foreign" or immigrant workers of color; individuals who attack day workers waiting for jobs on a street corner; a landlord who refuses to rent an apartment to an immigrant family from Africa, Latin America or Asia; and a salesperson who doesn't wait on customers who don't speak "good" English.

At the *cultural* level: cultural attitudes, beliefs, and behaviors that value and privilege the norms and standards of the dominant racial (white) and linguistic (English language) groups. For example, when values and standards espoused by white culture are considered the norm by which other cultural norms, traditions, and practices are judged (e.g., holidays and celebrations, standards of dress and beauty, and cultural values that emphasize individualism, direct communication, time and action orientation, materialism, and efficiency). Similarly, when values and standards emphasize and privilege the usage and importance of English proficiency and "good" English as a normative expectation in everyday interaction regardless of the population being served in schools, hospitals, businesses, governmental agencies, and legal institutions. For example, the assumption that English fluency and "good" English signify intelligence and professionalism; the assumption that when people talk in their native language at school or work they are being rude or talking about people behind their backs; the assumption that adult immigrants can learn English easily even though most English-speaking adults find learning a new language difficult; and the expectation that everyone can read prescriptions and other medical instructions or financial aid applications and government forms that are only in English.

At the *institutional* level: institutional attitudes, beliefs, and behaviors that inform policies and practices that privilege the dominant racial and linguistic group. For example:

- *Education*: policies that prevent appropriate bilingual or English Second Language (ESL) instruction to students who need it; and refusing to enroll children of "illegal" immigrants.
- *Economic*: paying immigrants less than the minimum wage paid other workers, threatening immigrant workers who attempt to unionize with deportation; and denying Social Security, disability, or unemployment benefits to immigrant workers even though they pay taxes that support such benefits.
- *Health Care*: denying care to those without health insurance.
- *Transportation*: racial profiling of people who are or appear to be Muslim or Middle Eastern.
- Government: denying driver's licenses or identification cards to those who request them.
- *Political*: requiring identification cards, preventing people from voting even in local municipal elections, threatening those who demonstrate for their rights, and not prosecuting perpetrators of hate crimes.

Once examples have been posted, ask participants to circle the gallery in silence, reading everyone's examples. After all participants have looked at the entire gallery, ask them to pair up with another person to share their reactions and write these on self-stick notes that they place next to the appropriate examples or categories. Participants then recircle the gallery and read everyone's responses.

Bring the group back together, and debrief the activity. Emphasize the notion that racism and linguicism toward immigrants are more than individual actions and beliefs; they are part of the fabric of our cultural and institutional life. Also point out that these levels of oppression happen simultaneously and reinforce each other continuously. We need to be aware of these levels when we begin to think about how to take action in support of immigrant rights and against racism and other systems of oppression that affect immigrants of color.

### Facilitation Issues

Participants are often overwhelmed by the pervasiveness of racism and linguicism toward immigrants that this activity illustrates. Encourage people to focus on the value of being able to identify the different levels in order to think about the causes and effects of these inequalities and consider more equitable alternatives. Inviting people to ponder what might be some of the reasons underlying some of these dynamics locally, regionally, nationally, and globally may help frame the discussion in more complex ways. To help process participants' affective and cognitive reactions to activity, you could ask them to free-write on a blank piece of paper, and then ask them to share highlights using a round-robin format. Remind people that systems can be changed to help participants begin to identify places or areas in which they can consider taking actions for change.

### 4. Closing (20 minutes)

Ask participants to pair up and share their personal responses and feelings about the lessons in this module. What next steps might they want to take to learn more about a particular issue that has been raised for them? Tell them you will pick up here when the group reconvenes.

### Module 4: Taking Action/Becoming Allies

Time needed: 2 hours, 50 minutes

### Objectives

- To appreciate the activism within immigrant communities and what we can gain from their contributions
- To learn about ways to support their work as allies (look at spheres of influence, etc.), develop action commitments, and closure

**Key concepts**: allies, action continuum, spheres of influence

### 1. The Local Is Global: Learning About Your Local Community (40 minutes)

Ask participants to form trios and tell each other about a person they know or have read about who works on issues affecting immigrant people and/or policy. This could be a person they actually know or someone they have read about in their community. After they have come up with a few persons, people, or groups, ask them to brainstorm arenas or actions that constitute working to challenge anti-immigrant racism. Write these responses on newsprint.

Next, ask participants to count off and form groups of five people each, then sit together in a circle. Tell them their task will be to "create an interview protocol for immigration rights and antiracism work in their community." Ask each group to come up with three ways they would go about finding a person, people, or group in their community to interview. Then, together, they should construct and post on newsprint 10 questions they would ask this person, people, or group in order to find out about the work they do, its purpose and goals, the features that they find most successful in doing their work, and the obstacles they encounter. Give participants 15–20 minutes for this task.

Call the groups back together, and ask one group at a time to present how they would go about finding their person, people, or group and their 10 interview questions. The composite list of questions provide a way to summarize learning from the course through applying it to a real world context. The questions should reflect awareness of the conditions immigrants from different groups face in coming to the U.S. today and the issues that are of most concern to them, including policy issues affecting them.

### Facilitation Issues

If this is an ongoing course, you might ask participants to actually identify resources in their community (or on the Web), carry out their interviews, and report back to the class before moving to the next step. For suggested resources, videos and reading assignments, see Appendix 7I.

### 2. Spheres of Influence and Personal Action Planning (90 minutes)

Note that participants who are interested in acting as allies on immigration and racism issues have many opportunities to get involved. These include working directly with immigrant groups in their community and/or becoming involved in areas that affect immigrants such as antiglobalization, environmental, human rights, and social justice movements. Churches, temples, and mosques; labor unions; antipoverty, housing, and welfare reform groups; university-based groups; and others are involved in immigrant rights education and activism. In this activity, participants begin to focus on their own commitments and areas of interest and to think about how they might expand their learning about immigration issues. Participants may also choose to focus on acquiring further information on these topics through reading relevant books, articles and journals. Affirm how different action strategies may each be valuable, depending on the participant and his/her sphere of influence.

Introduce the concept of "Spheres of Influence" (Appendix 4B). Note that each of us has several spheres of influence where we can extend our own learning and that of others, as well as take action against institutional policies that discriminate against others. Ask participants to think about their own lives, interests, and spheres of influence. Given the list of people and organizations generated in the previous activity, ask them to identify an area that most closely matches their interests. They should write this at the top of a piece of paper. Then ask each person to think about what they might do to further learn about and support this person, people, or group's work and/or the issues with which it is concerned.

Next, ask participants to think about their own spheres of influence, such as educating self; educating others among one's family, friends, and coworkers; and/or joining community or action groups that work on this issue. Then, note the actions they might take in their various spheres of influence to try to have an impact on their issue of concern. Actions might include educating oneself further about the group by volunteering or joining the organization, educating others by creating an ally group to support the group's work, and working toward institutional or social change by targeting anti-immigration policies, leafleting, or fundraising to block discriminatory legislation. For example, education is an arena that participants who are teachers might want to explore in greater detail.

Participants might decide to read about globalization, immigration, and racism alone or create a reading group with others to learn more. They might find out about a group in their community that is challenging proposed laws requiring teachers to report undocumented students and join in actions with that group such as creating public service announcements, leafleting, and writing letters to the editor. They might join with other educators in their school to analyze whether their school is providing culturally relevant curriculum materials, working supportively with English language learners, supporting parents with information and legal support, and the like.

Ask participants to pair up with another person to help each other flesh out their action plans. Take 10 minutes for this sharing.

Bring the whole group together again, and ask participants to share their action plans. Ask whether they have a broader sense of possible ways to take action as an ally to immigrants, particularly immigrants of color. Ask them to note who else is planning to work in the same area. After all have finished, give people 5 minutes to link up with others who share their interests. The learning experience could end here if they choose. If they wish to continue beyond the class, they can exchange e-mail and phone numbers if they wish to actually engage in the action identified and then make a date to get together to plan after the class ends.

### 3. Closing and Wrap-Up (60 minutes)

Ask participants to form new groups of three and together create a poem titled "We Are From ..." Using the same method as in Module 1, invite participants to complete the sentence stem with thoughts, ideas, and images that represent an embracing image of "we the people"—one that acknowledges our diverse experiences, contributions, interests, and perspectives. Provide 15–20 minutes for the brainstorming and creation of the poems.

Close by having each group read their poem. Note that we can work together to build the future we imagine in these poems. Thank participants for engaging in this process, and close the class.

### Notes

1. The term *second generation* refers to the American-born children of immigrants. Immigrants in the first generation are those who arrived to the United States from another country as adults. The *1.5 generation* refers to those born in another country and arriving in the United States before adolescence (Zhou, 1997).
2. From *Reading, Writing and Rising Up* by Linda Christensen (2000).
3. Adapted from Cho et al. (2004).
4. From Bigelow (2006).
5. Adapted from Susie Mitton (2000), Social Justice Education Program, School of Education, University of Massachusetts Amherst (mimeo).

# Overview

## Sexism, Heterosexism, and Transgender Oppression

### PAT GRIFFIN

Sexism, heterosexism, and transgender oppression are distinct yet overlapping manifestations of oppression. Because of their interrelationship and the identity concepts associated with them, sex, gender, and sexuality are often confused or conflated. This lack of understanding is accentuated because the language associated with sexism, heterosexism, and transgender oppression is continually evolving as our understanding of these manifestations of oppression becomes more sophisticated, differentiated, and nuanced.

The emergence of a transgender rights movement separate from the lesbian, gay, and bisexual rights movements highlights the limitations of binary understandings of sex, gender, and sexuality and challenges social justice educators to sharpen our awareness and understanding of these interrelated identity concepts and forms of oppression.

With this in mind, this new edition of *Teaching for Diversity and Social Justice* adds a chapter on transgender oppression. The sexism, heterosexism, and transgender oppression chapters are grouped together in this section of the book because of the interrelationships among sex, gender, and sexuality and the manifestations of oppression that are associated with each of these identity categories.

### Historical Intersections of Feminism: Lesbian, Gay, Bisexual, and Transgender Rights Movements

The history of the social justice movements that challenge sexism, heterosexism, and transgender oppression reveals the ways in which these movements are interwoven and how they developed and built on other earlier social movements. The homophile movement of the late 1940s and 1950s focused on political reform to decriminalize homosexuality by providing educational programs for medical experts. The goal was to increase tolerance of homosexuality and win the support of "experts" who could be allies in efforts to stop the widespread persecution of homosexuals in the 1950s (Jagose, 1996).

Secret organizations like the Mattachine Society and Daughters of Bilitis played key roles in these educational and political campaigns as well as providing support for a largely closeted membership. Though open to women, the Mattachine Society was primarily a male organization and focused on issues of concern to homosexual men. The Daughters of Bilitis developed out of a need for an organization that focused on the needs of lesbians (D'Emilio, 1983).

Though the Mattachine Society's original goals were much more in tune with later liberationist elements of the gay and lesbian rights movement, by the late 1950s, they became much more conservative, focusing on increasing tolerance for homosexuals by transforming public attitudes (Jagose, 1996).

Homophile organizations of this era often are characterized as "assimilationist" because of their efforts to encourage lesbians and gay men to adopt dress and mannerisms that conformed to traditional gender expectations of the time. These organizations rejected anyone who transgressed these gender norms such as drag queens or butch lesbians, who were associated with the primarily working-class bar culture (Jagose, 1996).

Neither the Mattachine Society nor the Daughters of Bilitis achieved widespread public recognition of or appeal to lesbians and gay men. Cultural perceptions of homosexuals during the 1950s and early 1960s as sick, perverted criminals were so deeply entrenched that public acknowledgment of one's homosexuality (often in news accounts of police raids on gay bars) almost always resulted in loss of employment and rejection by family.

In the 1960s, however, the emergence of the second wave of feminism, anti–Vietnam War protests, and a youth-based counterculture sparked challenges to prevailing gender and sexual norms (D'Emilio & Freedman, 1997). A shift toward a more liberationist focus characterized campus gay organizations and community activism as the emerging lesbian and gay rights movement adopted some of the political strategies of the Black Civil Rights movement of the 1960s.

In 1969, during a routine police raid on a gay bar in Greenwich Village, an angry crowd of primarily working-class lesbians and gay men of color, including drag queens and butch lesbians, fought back. In an explosion of rage and pride, bar patrons held police at bay for 3 days. The Stonewall rebellion is accepted as the event that triggered the birth of the modern lesbian and gay liberationist movement. The liberationist movement, in contrast to the homophile movement, challenged the status quo, celebrated difference, and encouraged pride in a distinct "gay" identity rather than assimilation into the mainstream and tolerance from heterosexuals (D'Emilio, 1983; Jagose, 1996).

The second wave of feminism, also emerging in the 1960s and 1970s, presented another challenge to traditional gender and sexual norms. Though decidedly middle-class and white, the feminist movement's early leaders encouraged women to demand equality in the home and at work. Betty Friedan's book *The Feminine Mystique* (1965) awakened the consciousness of women all across the United States and spurred the organization of informal consciousness-raising groups, where (mostly white heterosexual) women met and reconceptualized their subordinate relationship to men and supported each other in challenging the sexist status quo (Morgan, 1970).

The emergence of the feminist movement also provided lesbians in the gay rights movement an alternative to sexism they experienced in male-dominated gay organizations. Unfortunately, lesbians who participated in the early feminist movement were not welcomed with open arms by their heterosexual sisters (Abbott & Love, 1973). Lesbian feminists found their voices silenced and their needs subordinated to those of heterosexual feminists who were afraid that an association with lesbianism would hurt the cause and damage the reputation of feminist organizations.

By the early 1970s, fractures in the feminist movement and the gay rights movement developed as subgroups within each movement demanded that their voices be heard. Many lesbians formed separatist communities in which both heterosexual women and all men were excluded and members of the community worked to support and nurture each other in the face of homophobia from heterosexual feminists, sexism from gay men, and heterosexism in the larger culture (Faderman, 1991). Likewise, lesbians and gay men of color, working-class gay and lesbian people, transgender people, and bisexual people demanded recognition of their needs in lesbian and gay organizations just as women of color and working-class women expressed their dissatisfaction with the middle-class white focus of mainstream feminist organizations (Lorde, 1984; Moraga & Anzaldúa, 1981/1983).

Some early gay, lesbian, and feminist writers understood the connections between gender and sexuality and how rigid gender norms reinforced heterosexism (Altman, 1973; Jay & Young, 1992). They called for challenging gender norms as well as sexuality norms in the service of liberation from sexism and heterosexism, and called into question the categories of *heterosexual*, *homosexual*, *masculine*, and *feminine* as constructions that enforce oppression.

Just as the needs of lesbians and women of color were not part of the agenda for the early feminist movement, the gay and lesbian rights movement of the 1970s did not address the needs of bisexual people. Many lesbians regarded bisexual women as "traitors" or "fence-sitters" who took advantage of heterosexual privilege. For other lesbians and gay men, bisexuality was a phase rather than an "authentic" identity (Hutchins & Kaahumanu, 1991). In response to this rejection, a bisexual rights movement related to but separate from the lesbian and gay rights movement emerged in the 1980s. Evidenced by this increasing visibility and voice, the names for many lesbian and gay organizations and pride marches were changed to incorporate "bisexual" as recognized members of sexual minority communities.

In a similar transition, the transgender rights movement gained visibility as separate from the lesbian, gay, and bisexual rights movement in the early 1990s (Feinberg, 1999). Just as lesbians were often unacknowledged active participants in the early gay and feminist movements, transgender people were active in the early lesbian and gay rights movement, but were often seen by lesbian and gay people as part of an unacceptable fringe group that made acceptance by the general public more difficult. Transgender people raised uncomfortable questions about gender and sexuality that challenged long-held "truths" among not only the general population but also the feminist, lesbian, gay, and bisexual movements (Bornstein, 1994; Green, 2004). Sex, gender, gender identity, sexual orientation, and gender expression all interact in nonbinary ways that both inform and "trouble" the categories upon which sexism, heterosexism, and transgender oppression depend.

Because the feminist movement, the lesbian and gay rights movement, the bisexual rights movement, and the transgender rights movement are fairly recent developments (emerging over the last 45 years), each one continues to evolve in complexity and analytic sophistication as the dynamics of oppression that affect each group are clarified. As in all social movements, language develops and changes along with deepening understanding and analysis. Terms come into and go out of favor with different segments of each of the diverse communities comprising the targeted groups. Any attempt to hold fast to particular terms as "correct" or most "appropriate" is doomed to fail as younger generations take on the struggles of older generations.

## Introductory Definitions of Terms

The curriculum designs presented in Chapters 8, 9, and 10 explore differences among these identity concepts and forms of oppression. Because of the interconnections among sexism, heterosexism, and transgender oppression, it is important to delineate how these forms of oppression are both different and interrelated.

Conflation and misuse of key identity concepts associated with each of these three manifestations of oppression can confuse and mislead participants. Unless facilitators understand the complicated interconnections and are intentional in their choice of language, they can perpetuate misunderstanding rather than help participants better understand sexism, heterosexism, and transgender oppression. Among the key concepts needing clarification are (a) biological or birth sex, (b) gender identity, (c) gender role, (d) gender expression, and (e) sexual orientation.

*Biological sex* or *birth sex* refers to the physical, hormonal, genetic characteristics we are born with that are the basis for categories of female and male. Not all infants are born with a clearly differentiated biological makeup. *Intersex* (formerly hermaphrodite) refers to babies born with some combination of male and female biological sex characteristics (Preves, 2003). Some medical experts estimate that 1 in 4,000 babies born each year is intersex (Fausto-Sterling, 2000). Though these babies most often are healthy, binary cultural assumptions and expectations often lead physicians and parents to immediately assign these children as either male or female through surgery and subsequent hormone therapy and social reinforcement of the assigned sex (Kessler, 1998).

*Gender identity* refers to how we identify ourselves and is typically based on our biological or birth sex. *Woman, man, girl*, and *boy* are the typical gender identities. However, for some people gender identity is incongruent with the sex they are assigned at birth. Biological males can identify as girls or women, and biological women can identify as boys or men. People who choose to change their bodies through surgery and/or hormone treatment to better match their gender identity often claim a transsexual identity. Moreover, the spectrum of gender identities is much broader than the simple western-based woman–man binary (Fausto-Sterling, 2000). Once the expected woman–man binary is challenged, as it is in non-western cultures, such as some Native American cultures, other gender identities emerge. *Genderqueer* (gender expression or identity that challenges what is considered "normal") or *transgender* are examples of these emerging identities (Nestle, Howell, & Wilchins, 2000).

*Gender role* is the socially constructed, historically and culturally grounded group of behavioral and psychological characteristics expected of women (femininity) and men (masculinity). Gender roles are assumed to be a "natural" expression of gender identity. Over the last 30 years, terms like *androgynous* and, more recently, *genderqueer* have emerged as challenges to the masculine-feminine binary and to uncouple gender expression from biological sex.

*Gender expression* challenges the gender role binary and refers to a spectrum of possibilities for behavioral and psychological expressions of gender that challenge the gender–sex binary and uncouple gender from biological sex (Butler, 1990). *Gender expression* is a newer term that challenges the naturalness of binary gender roles as the only expressions of gender identity.

*Sexual orientation* refers to one's predominant sexual and romantic attractions toward someone of the same sex (lesbian or gay), another sex (heterosexual), or any sex (bisexual). Historically, sexual orientation has been described variously as an innate and unchangeable characteristic, a fluid behavioral choice, and an identity that must be viewed in historical and cultural context (Katz, 1995). No matter what perspective is taken, however, the dominant perspective is that heterosexuality is the normal, superior, natural sexual orientation. Sexual orientation is often linked with stereotypical assumptions about gender identity and expression. For example, gay men are often assumed to have a feminine gender expression, or lesbians are often assumed to want to be men.

Confusion and conflation of these concepts are based on two assumptions. One assumption is that a consistent and "normalized" relationship among these concepts exists and is based on biological sex (see Appendix A). Once biological sex is determined, a specific gender identity, gender expression, and sexual orientation are assumed to follow. For example, a biological male is expected to identify as a boy or man (gender identity), appear and act in masculine ways (gender expression), and have a heterosexual sexual orientation. A biological female is expected to identify as a girl or woman, appear and act in feminine ways, and have a heterosexual orientation. Biological sex, gender identity, gender expression, and sexual orientation are assumed to be binary concepts, and a person is either male or female, man or woman, masculine or feminine, and gay/lesbian or heterosexual. Diversity of biological sex, gender identity, gender expression, and sexual orientation outside the expected binaries and discontinuities among these identity categories are perceived as abnormal, inferior, or disruptive to social and cultural norms.

When a person does not conform to these binaries, the potential for stereotyping, discrimination, and oppression on the basis of sex, gender, and sexuality arises. Many of the stereotypes associated with one or more of these different social identity groups are based on assumptions of congruence among them. For example, the stereotypes that gay men (sexual orientation) are effeminate (gender expression) and that transgender people (gender identity or expression) are lesbian or gay (sexual orientation) are examples of this assumed congruence. Understanding and differentiating the relationships among these identity concepts will help to dispel stereotypes and increase appreciation for the range of sex, gender, and sexual orientation diversity concealed by assumptions about what is normal (see Appendix B).

Heterosexism addresses the oppression of people who are (or are perceived to be) lesbian, gay, or bisexual. Sexism addresses the oppression of biological females, intersex people, and transgender women. Transgender oppression is directed at people whose gender identity and/or gender expression is not congruent with their biological sex and the social expectations placed on them based on their biological sex. Heterosexism, sexism, and transgender oppression are systems of advantage or privilege afforded to heterosexuals (heterosexism), men (sexism), and gender-congruent people (transgender oppression) in institutional practices and policies and cultural norms.

How these three forms of social oppression overlap also complicates addressing each as a separate manifestation of oppression. For example, sexism focuses primarily on ways that males are advantaged and females are disadvantaged individually, institutionally, and culturally. Yet a central component of sexism is the way that gender roles are imposed and how they help to support an imbalance of power based on assumptions about females and males. Moreover, transgender people and intersex people are also victimized by sexism.

In similar ways, heterosexism is supported by gender expression assumptions associated with gay men and lesbians so that nontraditional gender expression is often the basis for assuming that someone is lesbian or gay. Transgender people, whose gender identities and expression challenge binary assumptions about gender, also call into question traditional sexuality labels such as *heterosexual*, *lesbian*, and *gay*.

These examples demonstrate how sexism, heterosexism, and transgender oppression, though based on power imbalances among different identities, are also overlapping systems that are best understood in relation to each other (see Appendix C).

Transgender oppression needs to be examined within the contexts of both sexism and heterosexism. Because transgender identities challenge the gender binaries that support both sexism and heterosexism, sexism and heterosexism curricula must be attentive to assumptions about sexuality and gender that perpetuate binary thinking. For example, forming groups by gender or sexuality should avoid forcing participants to choose groups based on binary assumptions about gender identity and sexual orientation that will exclude people whose identities challenge these binaries. Similarly, heterosexism must be addressed in sexism and transgender oppression, and sexism must be addressed in transgender oppression and heterosexism. For example, in a sexism course, it is important not to assume that all participants have intimate relationships with someone of another gender or sex when discussing relationship violence and to understand that transgender and intersex people are also targeted by sexist violence. Likewise, in a transgender oppression course, facilitators should be alert to the interactions of sexism and heterosexism that affect the experiences of transgender women and men in ways that differ from those of participants who have more traditional gender identities and expression.

The sexism, heterosexism, and transgender oppression curriculum designs described in the next three chapters describe and explore the complex and evolving interrelationships among these three forms of oppression. We encourage facilitators to read and explore all three chapters before planning a course or workshop focused on any one of them.

# 8

# Sexism Curriculum Design

## STEVEN BOTKIN,
## JOANNE JONES,
## TANYA KACHWAHA*

In addressing the issue of sexism, we take our place among thinkers, activists, theologians, and extraordinary ordinary women and men who have, for centuries, spoken and taken action against the debilitating effects of gender-based inequality in public and private life. What we now call the feminist movement and struggle to end sexism has linkages to many events of the past. The first Women's Rights Convention in Seneca Falls, New York (1848); the Suffragette movements in Australia, Great Britain, and the United States (early 1900s); the second wave of feminism linked often with the publication of Betty Friedan's *The Feminine Mystique* (1963); and the third wave of feminism reflected in the work of Rebecca Walker (1995), among others, are cornerstones of our contemporary efforts to include women as full partners in all spheres of life and to combat all forms of gender-based, power-fueled violence.

Gains have been made. There are active, organized, global efforts aimed at providing girls and women safety and opportunity and engaging men as allies. Much work remains. As we embark on *this* educational effort, we acknowledge that we stand on the shoulders of many sung and unsung s/heroes including Emma Goldman, Sojourner Truth, Margaret Sanger, Emmeline Pankhurst, Gloria Anzaldúa, Elizabeth Blackman, Betty Friedan, and June Jordan.

The tendency, however, to heighten the power of men as a group continues to evolve as a global phenomenon that uses and abuses women, those deemed "womanlike," and children under the rubric of "progress and democratic development."

---

\* We ask that those who cite this work always acknowledge by name all of the authors listed rather than either only citing the first author or using "et al." to indicate coauthors. All collaborated on the conceptualization, development, and writing of this chapter.

Furthermore, this informs all of our attitudes and behaviors toward our own gender and those of other genders. Today we see the effects of this all around us, such as the increased incarceration of women (of color), the abuse of women and child workers through global trade agreements that keep women and their families in poverty, the growth of the sex slave trade of young girls, the dramatic spread of HIV/AIDS to women in developing countries, the rightward shift in perspectives on abortion and contraception, the backlash against feminism and antisexist organizing, and the growth of conservatism and "traditional family" values.

The system that allows for the existence of this patriarchal tendency is usually described as sexism. We define *sexism* as a system of advantages that serves to privilege men, subordinate women, denigrate women-identified values and practices, enforce male dominance and control, and reinforce forms of masculinity that are dehumanizing and damaging to men. Sexism functions through individual beliefs and practices, institutions, images, and ideas, and is enforced by economic structures, violence, and homophobia (Blood, Tuttle, & Lakey, 1983; Griffin & Harro, 1997; Johnson, 1997; Pharr, 1988).

Although sexism impacts all women and men, it does so differentially through access to financial resources with white/European ancestry as a significant factor cushioning the impact. World Bank and United Nations data indicate that 70% of people living in extreme poverty worldwide are women, primarily in Africa, the Middle East, Southeast Asia, and South and Central America (Briggs, 1995). The Internet, e-mail, cell phones, and television news media give us a window on the world unprecedented in its ability to describe and explain all manner of gendered inequalities, ranging from bride kidnapping in Kyrgyzstan, rapes committed by United Nations peacekeepers, and violence against women being linked with the spread of HIV/AIDS. The increasing global interconnectedness is both a cause for alarm and a call to action. This proliferation of information catalogues abuses in every corner of the world, demanding that we see the catastrophic costs of the subjugation of women for all of us.

## Feminism

Along with the global patriarchal ideology and practices that oppress women, we also see the development of countermovements that work to inform people of their rights and choices, contradict cultural norms in attitudes and behaviors, and support equality and social justice for all. The women's movement of the 1960s and 1970s in the United States, an outgrowth of the Civil Rights movement, is one recent historical example of a countermovement. It was not only a call for action against sexism, but also the development of the second wave of feminism. Today, countermovements manifest as men's organizations working against violence; coalitions working toward global justice; lesbian, gay, bisexual, transgender, queer, and questioning (LGBTQQ) groups organizing against homophobia, gender oppression, and heterosexism; and communities of color organizing to gain racial, class, and transgender justice, to name just a few examples.

The international information highway transports knowledge to us about how women across the globe are also continuing to take action to improve their lives and the lives of their families and communities. Examples include a microlending program in Springfield, Massachusetts; a school in Lagos, Nigeria; and health clinics for women in Rwanda. Various local efforts then quickly become part of larger global efforts that serve to stop the destructive force of sexism. True gender justice means understanding that violence perpetrated against women in the name of U.S. economic growth or war and the continuing impoverishment of indigenous and Third World women have serious consequences for everyone.

Feminism, described as a movement to end sexism, sexist exploitation, and oppression (hooks, 2000) and the conceptual lens with which we fight sexism, requires us to care about the violence and abuse of power that oppress girls and women and distort and damage men and boys in the most intimate areas of their lives, in every corner of the world.

## Men and Sexism

Men are both privileged and damaged by sexism. In many cultures around the world, norms about leadership and power position men to control resources and decision making in relationships, the family, economics, and politics, and position women to serve men physically, emotionally, and sexually.

Men are socialized to be masculine in a way that confuses self-esteem and intimacy with emotional repression and domination. This socialization is reinforced by the benefits of privilege and the threats of isolation, marginalization, and violence for those who do not comply, and is made invisible by the dominant culture's assumptions about what is natural and normal.

Men have much to gain from and much to contribute to the work of undoing sexism. Domination and emotional repression are not inherent parts of male nature, but rather damaging effects of patriarchy on men. Men play a unique and important role in challenging sexism personally, institutionally, and culturally. In families, organizations, and communities around the world, men are learning to be proud and powerful allies with women, and women are welcoming men as partners in the struggle for gender equality and nonviolence.

## This Design

This book can also be defined as part of a countermovement toward justice, with this sexism curriculum specifically designed to contextualize the individual as a member of multiple social groups within national and global movements of both oppression and liberation.

The main intention of this chapter is to present a design that communicates our best practices for teaching about sexism that can be adapted to a variety of settings and constituencies. Through the implementation of this curriculum design, we aspire to enable educators to provide a clearer conceptual understanding of the concept of sexism and its linkage to heterosexism, gender oppression, and other forms of oppression both nationally and globally. We also seek to instill a sense of hope that change is possible and provide some tools for taking action against sexism and other forms of oppression.

## Our Assumptions

The curriculum design that follows rests on four primary assumptions. Our first assumption is that we need to be conscious of the limitations of a binary conceptual framework that fails to see beyond the constructs of men and women and ignores the complexity of a range of gender expressions and gender identities. The idea that there are only two very distinctly defined genders is the basis for our sexist system that privileges and provides power to one gender (men) over the other (women). Much of anti-sexist theory and practice has also been based on similar assumptions. This design supports a more inclusive exploration of sexism and its impact on all people. It also integrates an understanding of sexism with parallel understandings of heterosexism and transgender oppression with the assumption that these and other forms of oppression are inextricably connected and do not stand alone (see *Overview: Sexism, Heterosexism, and Transgender Oppression* for clarification).

Our second assumption is that *sexism is often experienced in the most intimate parts of our lives*. Restrictions ranging from open and safe self-expression, physical safety, clothing preferences, control over one's own body, physical movement, relationship choices, and sexuality are limitations imposed by cultural standards and enforced in private spaces. The combination of the privacy of enforcement and intimacy of socialization are significant challenges in making this form of oppression visible and in excavating its emotional landscape. A central goal of this curriculum, then, is to make more visible what is too often hidden and identified as simply "personal" and provide the opportunity and skills for addressing these issues in an educational context. A third assumption is that *violence is a key thread that weaves through all manifestations of sexism*. We assume, in fact, that violence is essential in maintaining male hegemony. Evidence of how violence is inextricably linked to sexism includes escalating rates, globally and nationally, of domestic assault, rape, murder, sexual harassment, date rape, emotional degradation, as well as the perpetuation of stereotypes of female capabilities that limit aspirations and possibilities.

The fourth assumption underlying this curriculum is that *sexism, like other forms of oppression, relies on a form of power based in domination and control*. Because of both its intimate and violent nature, sexism reinforces our acceptance of this "power over," and the discounting and devaluing of other healthier forms of power available to us. Challenging sexism requires all of us, women, men, and transgender people, to understand and practice forms of empowerment within ourselves, our personal relationships, and our social engagements.

As the curriculum design progresses, facilitators move participants through a process of examining sexism and its interconnectedness with other forms of oppression through exploring gender socialization and gender-role conformity, intimacy and relationships, objectification and violence, and power and empowerment.

## Overall Objectives

At the conclusion of the course, participants will

- have a greater understanding of conceptual levels of sexism and the emotional price everyone pays as a result of rigid gender roles, patriarchy, and the oppression of women.
- have a greater understanding of the personal and societal impact of gender-based violence.
- more fully understand the connectedness of sexism to heterosexism and transgender oppression and to other forms of oppression, such as racism and classism.
- have a greater understanding of the role all of us can play in creating gender equality.
- feel capable and motivated to organize action at multiple levels (individual, institutional, and cultural) and work collaboratively with others in order to do so.

**Table 8.1**  Overview of Modules: Sexism

| Module 1: Understanding Gender (3.5 hours) | Module 2: Intimacy and Gender Differences (3 hours) |
|---|---|
| 1. Welcome and Introduction (30 min.)<br>2. Guidelines (20 min.)<br>3. Agenda and Overview of Sexism Workshop (10 min.)<br>4. Making Connections (20 min.)<br>5. Considering Herstory (30 min.)<br>6. Learning Gender (70 min.)<br>7. Definitions (15 min.)<br>8. Closing (15 min.) | 1. Overview (10 min.)<br>2. Rules for Intimacy: Paired Questions (20 min.)<br>3. Gender Rules for Intimacy (60 min.)<br>4. Differences in Gender Experience (60 min.)<br>5. Cycles of Male and Female Socialization (20 min.)<br>6. Closing (10 min.) |
| **Module 3: Understanding Violence (3.5 hours)** | **Module 4; Understanding Power (3 hours, 10 minutes)** |
| 1. Welcome and Reflection on Module 2—if Appropriate (15 min.)<br>2. The Normalcy of Violence in Our Lives (40 min.)<br>3. The Normalcy of Violence in Our Lives Revisited (140 min.)<br>4. Closing (15 min.) | 1. Introduction to This Module and Reflections From Module 3 (20 min.)<br>2. Taxonomy of Power (20 min.)<br>3. The Power Grid (30 min.)<br>4. Historical Perspective on Power and Empowerment (30 min.)<br>5. Power in a Global Context (30 min.)<br>6. Empowerment (40 min.)<br>7. Closing (20 min.) |

## Sexism Curriculum Design

Note to readers: The curriculum design in this chapter is based on the assumption that participants have completed the introductory module(s) described in Chapter 3 prior to beginning this design and have a basic understanding of the conceptual framework of oppression described in Chapter 3. See Table 8.1 for an overview of this chapter's modules.

## Module 1: Understanding Gender

Time needed: 3.5 hours

### Goals

- Create a positive learning environment through developing group guidelines and personal sharing.
- Explore the personal experience of learning gender, and increase understanding of the ways gender messages are communicated and reinforced.
- Develop shared understanding of key terms and ideas, including sexism, feminism, binary, patriarchy, and gender roles.
- Begin exploration of the themes of intimacy, power, and violence.

**Key concepts**: binary, sexism, feminism, gender roles, gender-role socialization, sex, gender, masculinity, femininity

### 1. Welcome and Introduction (30 minutes)

As participants arrive, hand out index cards. Ask each person on one side to write one expectation or hope they have for the course. On the other side, ask them to write one concern or fear. Ask them not to put their name on the card, but to make a note for themselves stating their own expectation and concern. Collect the cards.

Begin with introducing the facilitators. Say your name, why you are delighted to be with this group, something about yourself, and the importance of time to think collectively about *sexism*. State clearly that the intention of the course is for extending understanding and exploring ideas and feelings, not assigning blame. Ask each participant to say her or his name and whatever else he or she chooses to share at this time.

Tell the group that there is an agenda of goals and activities for the module and for the course, and it is also important that the course, as much as possible, meets participants' needs. Before proceeding to share the goals for the first module and the overview of the sexism curriculum, shuffle the cards and hand out one to each person. This is the time to start learning as a group about expectations, as well as concerns, for the workshop.

After hearing the concerns and expectations, ask if there are additional thoughts about what would make the course successful and additional worries about what might make the course more difficult.

Collect all of the index cards, and after the module ends, type the comments made to serve as a reference during the entire course. Tell participants that they will each receive a copy of what was just discussed.

### 2. Guidelines (20 minutes)

Discussing sexism can generate many feelings and reactions. The next part of the agenda involves collecting and deciding on what the guidelines will be for talking and interacting. This will help make the time together productive.

Follow the process for discussing and developing guidelines described in the introductory modules in Chapter 3.

### 3. Agenda and Overview of Sexism Workshop (10 minutes)

Present an overview of the curriculum in general and the goals for the first module. Note that the course will focus on how sexism is personally experienced and how it functions and is maintained. Explain that in addition to providing a general picture, the course looks at the themes of intimacy, violence, and power as central to the understanding and perpetuation of sexism.

### 4. Making Connections (20 minutes)

Ask participants to take out a piece of paper and pen or pencil. Ask them to think about the sentence stem "In order to know me, you need to know that ..." and write three different endings to the sentence. Use a personal example to model the activity. For example, in order to know me you need to know that I am shy; I love to dance; I hate being interrupted.

Next, ask all participants to stand. Tell them that they will be finding three different partners during this exercise and sharing a different sentence completion answer with each partner. Each person will have 1 minute to identify their personal comment and make any other clarifying remarks in relation to that comment.

Ask them to begin with someone they do not know well. One person speaks for 1 minute. Then, the partner speaks for 1 minute. After 2 minutes, signal that it is time to change partners. This time, they must respond with a different answer. They cannot give the same response to a new partner. Do three rounds of this exercise.

Ask people to remain standing, and call out what they noticed: about them, the process of partnering, and observations about those they spoke to. Make a list on newsprint of the kinds of responses given.

Refer now to the definition of gender roles in the overview of sexism, heterosexism, sexism, and transgender oppression chapters.

**Gender roles**: the socially constructed and culturally grounded group of behavioral and psychological characteristics expected of women (associated with the idea of femininity) and men (associated with the idea of masculinity). Gender roles are assumed to be a "natural" expression of gender identity.

Explain that this definition refers to the constellation of roles, the things we do or don't do, the ways in which we act, and what we say or don't say in relation to what we have learned is "correct" for females and "correct" for males. *Social construction* means that these behaviors aren't innate, like being left-handed, but are learned. The ideas about what is "correct" vary greatly, including within and between cultures and across generations.

Now that the idea of gender has been introduced, go back to the previous exercise and ask participants if there were any behaviors or attitudes that might reflect gender-role socialization. For example, in selecting a partner, did that bring up issues of being asked or having to be the asker in a social situation (like a dance)? Who did you select? Who did you decide not to approach? What did you screen?

## 5  Considering Herstory (30 minutes)

This activity is intended as a quick energizer and as a way to introduce some historical information. It is also intended to underscore the importance of learning history and recognizing those people in one's own life and community who have and continue to fight for gender justice.

Hand out worksheets (see Appendix 8A). Tell participants that they have 5 minutes to identify the correct answers and that prizes will be given to the winners. After 5 minutes or so, go over the answer key: 1 = 5; 2 = 6; 3 = 1; 4 = 2; 5 = 10; 6 = 3; 7 = 4; 8 = 9; 9 = 8; 10 = 7.

Give all participants a prize, such as candy or a sticker. Explain that it is not their fault if they do not know much about women's history, but rather this is how a patriarchal educational system works by keeping men at the center of history. Ask the group why they think learning women's history is important for them, and take a few comments. Then ask each person to also identify people in their lives who are examples of fighting against the power of patriarchy (this can include mothers, grandmothers, uncles, and grandfathers). List all the names up on newsprint. Keep this newsprint up throughout the workshop.

## 6  Learning Gender (70 minutes)

This activity extends the conversation about what is gender? How do we learn about ourselves as gendered people? How do we learn about what it means to be a man or a woman?

Divide into groups of three to five people. Each group will have newsprint, colored markers, glue, sparkles, feathers, and any other artistic materials available. The group task is to depict the process of learning gender. Make sure to state that there are no wrong answers and that this is not a test of drawing ability. Have the questions below posted on newsprint in front of the room. Tell the participants that this activity asks them to pool their creativity and draw on their own experiences to understand how gender gets learned and absorbed in our lives.

The questions are as follows:

- What were the gendered messages in your home? For example, girls could … , boys could … , girls couldn't … , boys couldn't …
- What roles and behaviors were expected of you in your home because of your gender?
- Were there consequences for not following gendered expectations?
- What did you see as models of women's roles/work/place? What did you see as models of men's roles/work/place?
- What were the lessons of your early years in school? What models of maleness and femaleness did you see?
- What were the lessons of your teenage years? How did you see yourself in relation to maleness and femaleness? What did you notice around you?

Ask each group to capture their collective experiences in a way that describes how gender is learned. Tell them to do their best and find a way to capture their collective responses on paper. Each group then presents their picture to the whole group.

In processing the activity, ask for observations. Then ask students, "What can you say about how gender is learned?"

## Facilitation Issues

It is likely that some participants will have experienced significant gender restrictions in their home. Talk about how learning gender and the sanctions against defying gendered expectations are carried out in the home, in the most intimate corners of one's life. Note that gender socialization and the practice of sexism take place in intimate settings.

It is likely that some participants will have experienced some form of violence, either in terms of sexual exploitation or sanctions for not fulfilling expected gendered roles, or will have witnessed violence toward others. Note that violence is central to maintaining gendered boundaries and perpetuating sexism.

It is likely that some participants will have experienced the power of maleness, male hegemony, in their early years. This may have occurred in the form of control over their actions and decisions based on gendered expectations or by having primarily models of men wielding position and authority outside of the home. Note that power and control are essential to maintaining sexism.

## 7. Definitions (15 minutes)

Acknowledge the hard work and honesty that have been demonstrated so far in the course, and point out that many of the concepts that are key to understanding sexism and how it works have been experienced in their lives and demonstrated in the "Making Connections" and "Learning Gender" activities.

Hand out and refer to definitions in the overview of sexism, heterosexism, and transgender oppression chapters. As each definition is described, try to connect the definition with a comment, behavior, or conversation that has taken place in the course so far.

- Binary: (There are only two choices: femininity if you are seen as female; masculinity if you are seen as male.)
- Sexism: (Identify any experiences of inequality, or restrictions because of gender.)

- Feminism: (Identify views that contradicted stereotypes of male and female.)
- Patriarchy: (Note any conversations that spoke to learning that men were "supposed" to be in charge, that men are the bosses.)

## 8. Closing (15 minutes)

Ask each person to reflect for a moment about her or his expectations and fears as noted in the beginning of the course, and then invite students to say if their expectations are being met and their fears minimized. Ask each person to identify what was most useful from the experiences in Module 1. Offer a preview of the next modules.

## Module 2: Intimacy and Gender Differences

Time needed: 3 hours

### Goals

- Explore the effects of gender socialization on relationships and our experiences of intimacy.
- Expand our ability to listen, empathize, and communicate across gender differences.
- Develop the ability to engage in critical gender analysis of personal experiences.
- Identify some of the differences in our individual gendered experiences.

**Key concepts**: intimacy, gender rules, cycles of male and female socialization, costs and benefits of gender conformity

## 1. Overview (10 minutes)

### Objective

- To introduce the concept of intimacy as one frame of reference for understanding sexism

After welcoming participants back, ask if anyone has any questions or comments about the course so far. Review the goals for this module.

Present the following definition of *intimacy*: our natural ability to experience close connection with others in ways that feel safe, authentic, and mutually satisfying. Describe intimacy as our "birthright" that we experience initially without shame or gendered restrictions (e.g., our first reflex is rooting, to turn our face toward touch). Explain that in this section of the course, we will explore how gender socialization affects our experiences of relationship and intimacy.

## 2. Rules for Intimacy: Paired Questions (20 minutes)

### Objective

- To identify childhood lessons about gender relationships and how these lessons were taught

Have participants organize into two lines facing each other. Ask participants to pair up with someone opposite them in the other line. Explain that they will each have 2 minutes to talk while the other person listens without interrupting. After they decide who will go first, ask them to respond to the following questions:

- When you were a child, what is one message you were taught about relationships between girls and boys?
- How were you taught this lesson?

After 2 minutes, ask everyone to change speaker and listener roles, so the other person has 2 minutes to answer the same questions. After another 2 minutes, ask everyone to change partners. Use the same instructions for answering the next questions:

- When you were a child, what is one lesson you were taught about how males were supposed to relate to each other?
- How were you taught this lesson?

After each person has had 2 minutes to respond, change partners one more time for the following questions:

- When you were a child, what is one lesson you were taught about how females were supposed to relate to each other?
- How were you taught this lesson?

## 3. Gender Rules for Intimacy (60 minutes)

### Objectives

- To explore the advantages and disadvantages of gendered rules about relationship and intimacy
- To identify costs and benefits for gender-role conformity
- To practice respectful discussion between women and men about gender relationships

After bringing everyone back to the large group, write two headings on newsprint or chalkboard: "Rules for Females" and "Rules for Males" (see Table 8.2). Draw a vertical line under each heading, dividing the area below into two sections. Label one subsection under each heading "With Females," and the other subsection under each heading "With Males."

First, ask the group to identify lessons they were taught about how girls and women were supposed to behave in relationships. Write these under appropriate subcategories (or in the middle, if nonspecific). Then, do the same with rules for boys and men. When this is complete, invite observations, questions, or comments from the whole group.

Ask the people who were raised female to discuss first the advantages and then the disadvantages of following the rules for females, while the people raised male listen without interrupting. After 5 minutes, ask the people who were raised male to express appreciations about what they just heard. Then, repeat the process with the people who were raised male discussing the advantages and then the disadvantages of following the rules for males. After listening without interrupting for 5 minutes, ask the people

**Table 8.2**  Rules for Females, Rules for Males

| Rules for Females | | Rules for Males | |
|---|---|---|---|
| With Females | With Males | With Females | With Males |
| | | | |
| | | | |
| | | | |
| | | | |

raised female to express appreciations about what they just heard. When this is complete, invite observations, questions, or comments from the whole group.

Draw a box around the rules for females and one around the rules for males. Facilitate a whole-group discussion using the following questions:

- What happens to those of us who do not fit in the box of gender rules for relationships?
- What happens to the part of you that doesn't fit in the box?
- Why would someone step out of the box of gender rules?
- What would be helpful to encourage more people in getting free of the gender rules?

## 4. Differences in Gender Experience (60 minutes)
### Objective

- To practice critical analysis of gender experiences

Describe the next activity as continuing to identify ways that sexism affects women and men similarly and differently. Ask participants to form mixed-gender discussion groups of three to five people. Post the following questions to guide the next 20 minutes of small-group discussion. Hand out two pieces of newsprint and markers to each group.

- Describe a time when you noticed yourself or someone else being treated differently based on gender. What happened? How did you feel? What did you do? What assumptions about males and females were being expressed in this experience?
- In what ways are socialization experiences of females and males the same, and in what ways are they different? Record responses on two lists on newsprint.

Bring the groups back together again, and tape the lists on the walls. Ask for several people to describe a time when they noticed themselves or someone else being treated differently based on gender (What happened? How did you feel? What did you do?). Ask the whole group to identify assumptions about males and females that were being expressed in this experience.

Ask someone from each group to review their lists of similarities and differences. Facilitate a whole-group discussion using the following questions:

- Did you notice any gender differences in how people in the small groups interacted?
- Were there any disagreements about similarities and differences of gender experience?
- In what ways do the differences in gender socialization prepare males for achievement and success? In what ways do the differences in gender socialization prepare females for achievement and success?

## 5. Cycles of Male and Female Socialization (20 minutes)
### Objective

- To review the ideas discussed in this module through the use of a cognitive organizer

Hand out and review the "Cycles of Male and Female Conditioning" handout (see Appendix 8B), making the following points:

- Females and males share the need for connection, and experiences of violation and powerlessness as children.
- Sexism provides us with social definitions of femininity and masculinity that we are trained to accept with rewards and punishments. Our desire for connection and to avoid victimization and powerlessness drives us to gender conformity.
- We are then trapped in a self-perpetuating cycle that gives males access to some forms of institutional and interpersonal power, and leaves us all isolated and damaged.

### 6. Closing (10 minutes)

Ask each person to describe something they learned from this module.

### Module 3: Understanding Violence

Time needed: 3.5 hours

### Goals

- To explore personal experiences with violence specific to gender
- To tell personal stories within gender-specific groups and across gender groups
- To listen for understanding and without judgment

**Key concepts**: violence, emotional abuse, physical abuse, sexual abuse, financial abuse, bullying, sexual harassment, molestation, domestic violence, sexism, patriarchy

### 1. Welcome and Reflection on Module 2—if Appropriate (15 minutes)

**Objective**

- To welcome the group and share thoughts, feelings, and reflections about the last module

Welcome the group back. Take a few minutes to go over the agenda for this module before beginning the reflection exercise.

Reflection in pairs: Ask participants to consider what they learned in the last module by saying, "Take a few minutes to reflect on what was talked about in Module 2 and how it affected you personally, then we will share some of your thoughts with the large group."

After giving participants a few minutes to silently reflect, ask them to pair up with someone else in the room, preferably someone they do not know very well, and take turns to share their thoughts and reflections. Ask them to practice attentive listening by just listening when it is their turn to listen and talking freely when it is their turn to speak. The focus should be on listening and speaking freely, not on having a conversation. You may want to time this pair-share so each person has 2 or 3 minutes to talk about their reflections. Be sure to let participants know when to switch over from one person to the other (from being the speaker to the listener).

Gather back in a large group, and ask for some people to share their reflections. If you feel that some important pieces of information need to be recapped, make sure you or your co-facilitator brings up these points after the group has shared.

Begin this module by discussing why and how the topic of violence connects to intimacy and gender differences discussed in Module 2. You can do this by saying something like the following: *Just as you all have said, the way we are all treated by each other based on our gender identity and gender expression impacts our daily lives, including our most intimate relationships. We are expected to dress and behave in certain ways, and if we don't conform we often get punished by being called names, being harassed, or being ostracized. Even when we do conform, we often get harassed, such as when a woman dresses sexily or acts flirtatious, she may be called a slut or a whore. One of the ways we punish each other and keep each other conforming is through acts of violence. Violence and abuse take many forms and are rampant in our everyday lives. In the next few hours, we are going to explore our experiences with violence and how they help to shape our relationships with each other.*

## 2. The Normalcy of Violence in Our Lives (40 minutes)

### Objective

- To explore the prevalence and normalization of violence in our lives within the context of sexism and patriarchy

### Part 1: Common Ground (see statements below) (10 minutes)

Ask participants to stand (if they are able to) in a large circle. Explain that you will read 10 to 12 statements. When each statement is read, they should take one step into the circle in silence if the statement is true for them, look around, and notice who is in the circle with them and who is not. Then you will thank participants and ask them to step back. You will then read the next statement, and so on. Inform the group that this activity is done in silence. Ask them to be observant and self-reflective. Explain that they are to be as honest as possible during this activity but to also care for themselves. This means that they do not have to divulge any information about themselves that they are not comfortable sharing. This also means that people need to keep information of others in the group to themselves and not push someone to step in if they choose not to. Participants decide for themselves when they will step in. Once you have finished reading all of the statements, ask the group to comment on their experience of this activity with these prompts:

- What was it like for you to do this activity? What was easy or hard about it?
- What did you notice?
- What surprised you?
- Why do you think we do this activity?

Wrap up this activity by summarizing the learning that participants have expressed in the debriefing conversation. Also make a point to mention the prevalence of violence in each of our everyday lives. *Note*: Add or subtract statements to suit the needs of your group. For example, more specific statements relating to domestic abuse could be added.

### Common Ground Statements (choose only 10 to 12 statements)

Step in if ...

- you have ever seen a violent movie that has made you uncomfortable.
- you have ever heard music or seen videos that degrade or sexually objectify girls or women.
- you or someone you know has called a woman a slut, bitch, or whore.
- you or someone you know has been picked on, bullied, or harassed.

- you have ever bullied or harassed someone.
- you have ever seen someone be bullied, picked on, or harassed and done nothing.
- you have ever seen someone be bullied, picked on, or harassed and done something.
- you or someone you know has ever been abused in a dating relationship.
- you or someone you know has ever feared an ex-boyfriend or girlfriend.
- you or someone you know has an abusive relative.
- you have ever seen or played a video game that shows men hitting, slapping, or punching women.
- you or someone you know dated someone who is jealous or possessive.
- you have heard someone say, "She asked for it" or "She really meant yes" or "She shouldn't have led me on."
- you have ever heard derogatory language used toward women.
- you or someone you know has ever been touched in a way that was embarrassing and unwanted.
- you or someone you know has ever been sexual with another person when they didn't want to be.
- you or someone you know has ever laughed at an inappropriate joke about women.
- you or someone you know has ever commented on someone else's body parts.
- you or someone you know has used sexual orientation as an insult, like "You're so gay" or "He's a fag."
- you have ever seen someone grab or touch someone when it was unwanted.
- you or someone you know has ever been yelled at, commented upon, whistled at, or harassed by someone in a public place.
- you or someone you know has ever said, "Yes" to someone because of being afraid to say "No."
- you have ever heard someone say, "She [or he] made me do it."
- you have ever heard someone say, "He's a wimp."
- you or someone you know has ever been hit by a man.
- you or someone you know has ever been hit by a woman.
- you or someone you know has been told, "If you love me, you will . . "
- you or someone you know has been in a relationship with a person who uses their to frighten people.
- you or someone you know has felt stupid or ugly because of what a partner has said.
- you have ever felt powerless in a relationship.
- you have ever felt afraid of someone and not known what to do.

## Part 2: Naming Violence Brainstorm (20 minutes)

After the "Common Ground" activity, facilitate a brainstorm to identify different forms of violence by saying, "When you hear the words *violence* and *abuse*, what comes to mind?" Be as broad as possible in this brainstorm. During the brainstorm, you can prompt the group by asking, "What other kinds of violence have you heard of or experienced?" If the group does not do so, you may want to help them categorize violence and abuse into groupings such as *sexual abuse, emotional abuse, physical abuse, financial/economic abuse*, and so on (see key concepts, above).

After the brainstorm, ask the group to help you place their brainstormed list into themes based on individual, social/cultural, and institutional. You will find that many forms of violence fall into multiple categories. Try to point out that violence is happening at all levels in society from the most intimate places like the home and in intimate relationships (as talked about in Module 1) to institutions like government (through social programs, etc.), schools, religious organizations, and so on.

Sample list:

Hitting, slapping, shouting, grabbing, pulling, pushing, punching, squeezing or pinching skin, name-calling, putting down verbally, isolating someone from friends and family, making fun of someone in a mean-spirited way, taking money away or not giving money, manipulating, possessiveness, jealousy, controlling behavior, racial slurs, discrimination, racism, war, shooting, sexism, homophobia, derogatory graffiti, ostracizing somebody intentionally, bullying, harassment, sexually harassing, child abuse, torture, and so on

This is just a sample list. Allow your group to brainstorm their own list.

Define *sexism* and *patriarchy*, and post these definitions on newsprint (10 minutes). Ask the group how these definitions relate to their brainstormed lists. With the group's help, contextualize some of the brainstormed categories into these definitions.

*Sexism*: a system of advantages that serves to privilege men, subordinate women, denigrate women-identified values and practices, enforce male dominance and control, and reinforce forms of masculinity that are dehumanizing and damaging to men. Sexism functions through individual beliefs and practices, institutions, images, and ideas, and is enforced by economic structures, violence, and homophobia (Blood et al., 1983; Griffin & Harro, 1997; Johnson, 1997; Pharr, 1988).

*Patriarchy*: a society in which men have more social power and are more highly valued than women. Or, the attitude that it is right for men to have the most authority and power in society (*Cambridge Dictionary of American English*, 2003; Grey, 1982; Johnson, 1997).

## 3. The Normalcy of Violence in Our Lives Revisited (140 minutes)

### Objective

- To express, share, and dialogue about our experiences with violence

### Caucus Groups and Fishbowls

Set up the next 2-hour session by saying something like: *In the next 2 hours, we will be asking you to separate by self-identified gender to discuss experiences with violence, then get together in a fishbowl format to share your caucus group experience with other groups. Three groups will be offered: men, women, and transgender people. For some people, it can seem useless or unproductive to go into gender-specific groups to discuss issues related to sexism; however, we ask that you trust us and trust the process. We find that most people have not had the opportunity to discuss issues related to violence and sexism in gender-specific groups. We ask that you try it, and we can discuss what the experience was like afterwards. We will return from caucus groups after about an hour, then gather one group at a time in fishbowls. A fishbowl is when one group (men, women, or transgender people) sits in a circle facing each other and talking to each other about their caucus group experience, while the other two groups form an outside circle and listen attentively to the inner circle's conversation. We will have fishbowl questions for you to consider. After the fishbowls are finished, we will gather back as a large group to talk over the whole experience.*

## Caucus Groups (60 minutes)

*Objective*

- To identify and share thoughts and feelings about times when we have been both victims and perpetrators of violence

Get into caucus groups by gender for 60 minutes. Keep in mind you may need to have two or three gender caucus groups depending on how participants identify their gender (men, women, or transgender). Explain that we will be separating by self-identified gender, offer three groups, and let people choose where to go. Be sure to have a skilled facilitator available for each group and breakout rooms so each group has a space to work in. Also have newsprint for each group with the following questions for them to take with them to breakout rooms.

Begin the caucus group experience by asking people to reintroduce themselves briefly. Then post the questions on the wall and take a few minutes of silent writing and reflection time for people to consider the questions and what they would like to share.

Encourage personal storytelling by asking questions of individuals telling their stories (such as "Can you talk a little bit about how you ended up in that situation?") and to the rest of the group to affirm shared experiences (such as "Has anyone else experienced anything like this?"). Be sure to manage time well so all participants can talk about their experiences as victims and as perpetrators of violent or abusive behavior.

Ask all groups to discuss the following questions:

- Have you ever been a victim of violence or abuse of any kind (e.g., bullying; harassment; domestic violence in your home growing up; relationship abuse; violence on the streets; or racial, homophobic, or class-based discrimination)?
    - How did it make you feel?
    - How do these experiences affect you now?
    - What did these experiences have to do with your gender?
- Have you ever been violent or abusive toward someone else (e.g., bullying; harassment; domestic violence in your home growing up; relationship abuse; violence on the streets; or racial, homophobic, or class-based discrimination)?
    - How did it make you feel?
    - Why did you do it?
    - How have these experiences affected who you have become?
    - What did these experiences have to do with your gender?

## Fishbowls (60 minutes)

*Objective*

- To share experiences of violence across gendered groups

Post the following questions for the fishbowls to consider:

- What was it like to get into caucus (gendered) groups?
- What experiences came up in your group about being a victim of violence or abuse?
- How have these experiences affected your behaviors, and what did they have to do with gender?
- What experiences came up in your group about being violent or abusive toward others?

- How have these experiences affected who you are, and what did they have to do with gender?

After all groups have reentered the main room, ask everyone to sit in a large circle. Briefly explain again how the fishbowl exercise will work, then point out the list of questions on the wall and read them aloud. Attend to any questions, then invite your first group to move their chairs into the middle to form an inner circle (you may want to have the transgender group go first if you have one). Let everyone know that each group will have about 15 minutes in the fishbowl. Remind the group that they will just have a conversation with one another based on the questions. Ask them to also help draw each other into the conversation. The facilitator for each caucus group needs to join their group in the inner circle and help facilitate the conversation by asking the first question, "What was it like to get into caucus (gendered) groups?" The other facilitators need to write up what each group says on newsprint (maybe organized in two categories: experiences as a victim of violence and abuse, and experiences as a violent or abusive person). These pieces of newsprint can help to provide context for Module 4.

## 4. Final Group Process (20 minutes)
### Objective

- To debrief the caucus group and fishbowl activities

After all caucus groups have had a turn in the inner circle, gather back as a large group, and thank everyone for their honest participation and hard work. Ask how people are doing. Remind the group of some of the crosscutting themes that arose and of some of the very different perspectives that were expressed (refer to newsprint). Also go over how people saw these experiences as gendered. Relate all to sexism and patriarchy definitions described earlier. Ask for any questions or comments, then facilitate a closing round: "Say one sentence describing what you are thinking about or feeling based on your caucus group and fishbowl experience today."

## 5. Closing (15 minutes)
### Objective

- To provide closure to the group experience and check in on the group process

Pass out index cards. Ask participants to write a few words about how well the group process is working for them, how they feel about the content of the course, and how well the guidelines are working for them. Collect index cards to look over and discuss with the group in the next module.

## Module 4: Understanding Power

Time needed: 3 hours, 10 minutes

### Goals

- To understand various definitions and kinds of power
- To explore own experience with power
- To develop new empowering strategies for addressing sexism

**Key concepts**: social power, personal power, power over, power within, power with, empowerment

## 1. Introduction to This Module and Reflections From Module 3 (20 minutes)

Ask if anyone has questions or reflections following the caucus groups that concluded Module 3. Present a summary of participants' course assessments so far from index cards filled out at the end of Module 3. Acknowledge that this is the final module of the sexism curriculum, although the work of understanding and acting continues.

## 2. Taxonomy of Power (20 minutes)

### Objective

- To develop an understanding of the different forms of power

Ask for a quick brainstorm of what participants think *power* means. Write on newsprint. Post the following definitions:

- *Power*: ability to act or produce an effect
- *Power over*: the use of domination to act or produce an effect; also called *false power* because it does not get us what we really want
- *Power with*: the use of connection and cooperation to act or produce an effect
- *Power within*: the use of inner wisdom to act or produce an effect
- *Personal power*: the use of individually unique characteristics and resources to act or produce an effect
- *Social power*: the use of social identity to access resources and to produce an effect
- *Empowerment*: increasing individual or collective power by exposing the fallacies of power over and increasing our abilities to use power with and power within

## 3. The Power Grid (30 minutes)

### Objective

- To use personal experiences with gender to further clarify different forms of power

Ask participants to reflect on their personal experiences with power and write an example in each box of the Power Grid (i.e., personal and social power over, power with, and power within; see Table 8.3): for example, a woman being coerced by a man's use of physical intimidation to do what he wants (personal power over), a woman building the self-confidence to become a leader in her work (personal power within), and men joining together to challenge sexism (social power with).

Form triads and have participants share some of their examples with each other. In the large group, list examples of each form of power on newsprint.

### Processing

Ask participants to respond to the following questions:

**Table 8.3**   The Power Grid

|  | Personal Power | Social Power |
|---|---|---|
| Power over |  |  |
| Power within |  |  |
| Power with |  |  |

- What new information did you learn about power in these activities?
- How does what you learn affect your thinking about sexism?

## 4. Historical Perspective on Power and Empowerment (30 minutes)

### Objectives

- To explore key events in history that helped women gain power, equality, access, and choice in the United States
- To discuss the impact of this history on the lives of young people today

It is ideal to reproduce the timeline (see Appendix 8C) so it can be hung around the room. You may want to write up or copy each year onto a separate page, enlarge it, and then hang on the wall in chronological order. If this is not possible, the timeline may be photocopied and handed out to each person.

Begin this activity by providing about 10 minutes for participants to walk around the room and read some of the timeline. Then, place people in groups of four and provide them with 10 minutes to discuss the following questions:

- What surprised you the most, and why?
- Why do you think you have little knowledge about women's history?

Gather back as a large group, and ask small groups to share some of what they discussed (10 minutes).

Talk about how women have struggled and worked hard to gain power throughout American history. Mention how many women and their male allies have never been docile, subservient, or inactive in their pursuit of power, equality, access, and choice for women.

Ask, "How do you think this history impacts all of our lives today?" Discuss some responses, and support the group in recognizing that women have fought to achieve equal rights and the fight for equal rights continues today. For example, women still earn less than men for doing the same work. The gap has been widening in recent years and not closing due to a backlash against affirmative action and feminism.

Transition into the next activity by noting that we lack knowledge about women's history in the United States and we are also extremely limited in our knowledge about women's struggles for power around the world.

## 5. Power in a Global Context (30 minutes)

### Objective

- To understand issues of sexism and power in a global context

Begin this section by talking about why it is important to think about and learn about women, men, and power within a global perspective. The more we are disconnected from ourselves; from the reality of those around us; from the social, political, and economic forces in which we live; and from the global interconnections of our lives, the more the ground of sexism is seeded. We need to know about our sisters and brothers around the globe in part because they suffer as a result of U.S. foreign policy, in part because they labor to produce many of the goods we buy, and in part because they provide profound examples of strength and resilience.

What do you know? Ask participants to call out what they know about issues confronting women in other countries. Ask participants to call out names of women who are leaders and role models from other countries. What is our responsibility to women and men around the globe? (This is another brainstorming activity designed to identify ideas without judgment.)

Using the framework for understanding power just discussed, take a look at women globally using these constructs. (Offer current examples, depending on when this activity is done.)

## Power Over

Examples include sex trafficking, and rape that occurs during military conflicts, for example Darfur and Iraq; point out that women are the victims of rape by all sides, including those serving as "Peace Keepers"; stoning as a punishment in some Islamic cultures from bearing a child "out of wedlock" or for having extramarital sex; the rise of AIDS in sub-Saharan Africa; U.S. policies that limit prenatal services and contraceptive information to international organizations that also provide information about abortion; female genital mutilation, which, even though outlawed by many governments, is still a common practice; and "honor" killings of women thought to have engaged in extramarital sex.

## Power With

Examples include women working together to start microbusinesses; the V-Day observances and actions, using Eve Ensler's work from the *Vagina Monologues* (V-Day, n.d.); and the development of a women's rights movement in South Africa.

## Power Within

Share the story of Mukhtaran Bibi, a Pakistani woman who was raped by judicial order by several men as punishment for an offense attributed to her teenaged brother. She took the men to court, risked her own life, stood up to the customs of the day while maintaining her pride and love for her village, and became an international symbol of resistance and courage. Use this last example of a woman of courage who found power within herself to both maintain her cultural pride and stand up to injustice. Then, lead into the discussion on empowerment.

## 6. Empowerment (40 minutes)

### Objective

- To expand participants' ability to identify characteristics and examples of empowerment

Write the words *expressions of empowerment* on the chalkboard or newsprint, saying the following: *All too often, we focus on how disempowerment is experienced and expressed. It is also true that in every moment, each of us is reaching to express our empowerment. Please take a few minutes in silence right now to reflect on how this has been true in this course. [Pause.] Look around the room. [Pause.] As you look at each person, think of one way you that you have seen them express their empowerment. When you have done this for everyone else, think about one way that you have expressed your own empowerment in this class. You may wish to write notes to remember these examples.*

After 5 to 10 minutes, ask for examples of expressions of empowerment, and write them on the chalkboard or newsprint. These could be examples of others and/or oneself. Continue soliciting examples until everyone has an expression of empowerment identified about them.

Write the words *characteristics of empowerment*. Ask the group to identify some general qualities or characteristics of empowerment based on the specific examples from this course. Write these on the chalkboard or newsprint.

Form groups of three or four. Ask participants to take turns, first naming how they have expressed empowerment in the class (as identified by themselves and/or others), and then describing how they could further develop one or more of the qualities of empowerment. Request that a different group member serve as note taker for the person who is speaking. Group members are encouraged to ask clarifying questions. Cue them every 3 minutes to switch to another person.

Make sure all note takers have given their notes to the person who was speaking. Invite observations and comments when the whole group has reconvened.

## 7. Closing (20 minutes)

Ask each person to say

- something you appreciate about this group.
- something you learned from this course.
- something you still have a question about.

Use your turn as an opportunity to make closing comments.

# 9

# Heterosexism Curriculum Design

PAT GRIFFIN, KATJA HAHN
D'ERRICO, BOBBIE HARRO,
TOM SCHIFF*

The focus of this chapter is the oppression of lesbian, gay, and bisexual people. Though the oppression of transgender people is often linked with the lesbian, gay, and bisexual rights movements and there are important interconnections between these two oppressions, oppression based on gender identity and expression will be addressed in Chapter 10.

The Stonewall riots in 1969 were a pivotal event in the history of struggle for lesbian, gay, bisexual, and transgender rights in the United States. Often represented as a rebellion of lesbian and gay people, the Stonewall riots were initiated by a diverse group of people including drag queens and kings, butch lesbians, and transsexuals, many of whom were working-class people of color. Angered by persistent police harassment and societal condemnation, participants in the Stonewall riots fought back in an eruption of outrage and pride that many activists accept as the beginning of the lesbian, gay, bisexual, and transgender rights movements.

Since 1969, societal perspectives on sexuality, gender, and sexual orientation have entered a period of immense change and upheaval in which the previous social consensus that lesbian, gay, bisexual, and transgender people are sick, sinful, and criminal has shifted. The medical and religious models that, until the early 1970s, dominated thinking about lesbian, gay, bisexual, and transgender people, now compete with a civil rights model in which lesbian, gay, bisexual, and transgender people are an oppressed minority denied access to the full spectrum of institutional rights and protections afforded heterosexuals and gender-conforming people. A more radical model has also emerged in which the focus is shifted from achieving civil rights to changing social

---

* We ask that those who cite this work always acknowledge by name all of the authors listed rather than either only citing the first author or using "et al." to indicate coauthors. All collaborated on the conceptualization, development. and writing of this chapter.

institutions and sexuality and gender norms that stigmatize and exclude people on the basis of their sexual and gender identities and choices. In this changing social context, lesbian, gay, and bisexual people are living openly in greater numbers, demanding recognition as a minority group unjustly subjected to prejudice and discrimination, and challenging the social institutions that support heterosexuality as the only normal expression of sexuality (Jagose, 1996).

In opposition, many conservative religious and political groups view the acceptance of lesbian, gay, and bisexual people as evidence of the moral breakdown of western civilization and work against efforts to provide lesbian, gay, and bisexual people with civil rights protection; to portray positive media images; or to include educational programs about them in schools (Herman, 1998). Many people lie between these two extremes and experience discomfort or uncertainty with openly lesbian, gay, and bisexual people. This discomfort or uncertainty reflects socialization into a society where lesbian, gay, and bisexual people have been stigmatized and rendered invisible.

## Defining Terms

Over the last 20 years, the term *homophobia* has gained increasing use among the general population. Coined by psychologist George Weinberg in the late 1960s, homophobia was originally defined as a clinical condition of irrational fear of homosexuals (Weinberg, 1973). Educators and activists expanded the use of this term to focus on fear, discomfort, or hatred of lesbian and gay people caused by internalizing negative societal perspectives on homosexuality. As the bisexual rights movement emerged in the early 1980s, the term *biphobia* was coined to describe fear and discomfort with bisexual people (Hutchins & Kaahumanu, 1991).

The roots of the term *homophobia* (and its cousin, *biphobia*) in psychology and its association with individual pathology limit its usefulness for understanding and challenging institutional and cultural policies and norms that stigmatize and discriminate against lesbian, gay, and bisexual people. Similarly, the term *homosexual* has roots in the late 19th- and early 20th-century search for a medical cure for homosexuality (Katz, 1976). For this reason, many lesbian and gay people do not use *homosexual* to refer to themselves.

To address the limitations of the term *homophobia*, many educators and activists use *heterosexism* to describe the system of advantage or privilege afforded to heterosexuals in institutional practices and policies and cultural norms that assume heterosexuality as the only natural sexual identity or expression (Herek, 2004). Some theorists use the term *heteronormativity* to describe the assumption that heterosexuality is the only normal or natural sexual identity or expression (Warner, 1993).

## Conceptualizing Sexual Identity

Sexual identity is historically and culturally specific. The identification of people as gay, lesbian, bisexual, or heterosexual is a 20th-century phenomenon. Prior to the late 19th century, sexual behavior did not define a person's identity (Katz, 1995). Knowledge of these important historical shifts forms an important foundation for heterosexism education in the 21st century. Similarly, sexuality and sexual expression are culturally specific. The focus of this chapter is on understanding heterosexism and dominant assumptions about sexuality and sexual expression in the United States.

## Increasing Visibility

The increasing visibility of lesbian, gay, and bisexual people in the public sphere has raised awareness and increased the numbers of heterosexual people who knowingly have daily personal contact with gay and bisexual people in families, the workplace, and friendship circles. Media coverage of voter referenda on civil rights laws outlawing employment discrimination on the basis of sexual orientation, inclusion of sexual orientation in hate crimes laws, the U.S. Supreme Court ruling sodomy laws unconstitutional, the right of same-sex couples to marry, the right of lesbians and gay men to adopt children, and the harassment of lesbian, gay, and bisexual students in schools have forced heterosexual people to confront their feelings and beliefs about these issues. Lesbian, gay, and bisexual characters are included in television shows and movies, and advertisers are beginning to court the lesbian, gay, and bisexual market. These developments over the last 20 years have brought gay, lesbian, and bisexual issues into the homes, schools, and workplaces of Americans in an unprecedented way.

## Backlash

As with any social justice movement, increasing visibility and expanded civil rights for minority groups provoke backlash from those determined to maintain the status quo. Leaders of the religious right have led this backlash movement in the United States (Martin, 2005). Capitalizing on fear, stereotypes, and hatred of lesbians and gay men, these groups mount formidable opposition to institutional, legislative, or judicial action that challenges the dominance of heterosexuality or enhances the rights of lesbian, gay, and bisexual people. Examples of backlash are the passage of "defense of (heterosexual) marriage" laws at the federal and state levels; legal challenges to school activities or policies that promote inclusion and acceptance of lesbian, bisexual, and gay students and teachers or curriculum addressing lesbian, gay, and bisexual issues; and attempts to repeal civil rights laws that include sexual orientation as a protected category.

High schools and elementary schools are particularly emotional battlegrounds for conflict about addressing lesbian, gay, and bisexual issues. Many schools are ill-prepared to address the needs of lesbian, gay, and bisexual students, teachers, or parents. Fears about inappropriately influencing the sexual orientation of young people, addressing sexuality issues in general, and being perceived as advocating or promoting homosexuality make school officials reluctant to address heterosexism or homophobia. Well-organized right-wing religious groups actively monitor and oppose any efforts by schools to address issues related to homosexuality. This intense scrutiny causes many school administrators to avoid addressing the needs of lesbian, gay, bisexual, and transgender students rather than risk controversy and conflict.

## Diversity and Conflict Within the Lesbian, Gay, and Bisexual Communities

There is no monolithic lesbian, gay, and bisexual community, and the increasing complexity of issues inevitably surfaces tensions and prejudices among the diverse groups who all demand inclusion in the sexual minorities community. Over the last few years, bisexual women and men; transgender people; lesbians and gay men of color; working-class and poor lesbians, gays, and bisexuals; lesbian, gay, and bisexual people with disabilities; queer-identified youth and older gay- and lesbian-identified people; and others have stretched the boundaries of issues and identities that need to be addressed when we discuss homophobia and heterosexism (Boykin, 1996; Brandt, 1999; Geller,

1990; Jacobs, 1997; Kumashiro, 2001, 2003; Leong, 1996; Ramos, 1994; Ratti, 1993; Smith, 1998). Even the profusion of self-chosen labels reflects the range of diversity under the broad umbrella of "queer" identities: lesbian, gay woman, gay man, same-gender loving, two-spirit, queer, dyke, genderqueer, butch, fem, lesbian-feminist, lesbian-identified bi woman, faggot, fairy, drag queen, intersex, transgenderist, male-to-female transsexual, dyke, Chicana lesbian, and womanist bisexual are examples of this proliferation.

In particular, over the last few years the long ignored demands of transgender people for explicit inclusion among the groups under the umbrella of identity groups that defy traditional gender or sexuality norms have expanded the borders of the struggle for social justice (Bornstein, 1994; Feinberg, 1997; Nestle, Howell, & Wilchins, 2002; Stryker, 2006). Because of the complicated interplay among gender identity, gender roles, and sexual identity, transgender people are often assumed to be lesbian or gay (See *Overview: Sexism, Heterosexism, and Transgender Oppression*). Though a transgender person might identify as lesbian or gay, he or she might also identify as heterosexual or as something else entirely. Because transgender identity challenges a binary conception of sexuality and gender, educators must clarify their own understanding of these concepts. The intersections of multiple identities and the effects that these identities have on experience require an understanding of how racism, sexism, classism, ageism, and other social justice issues interact to privilege and disadvantage lesbian, gay, and bisexual people.

This chapter explores the ways that lesbian, gay, and bisexual people are targeted by heterosexism because of the common thread of nonheterosexual identity they share. This chapter also looks at the interconnections among sexism, heterosexism, homophobia, and transgender oppression that interact to oppress lesbian, gay, bisexual, and transgender people.

## Facilitation Issues

Teaching about heterosexism in such a complex and dynamic social context presents facilitators with both challenges and opportunities. Some of these are as follows:

- *Understanding the connections among sexism, heterosexism, and transgender oppression*: Facilitators must be able to help participants understand the connections among sexism, heterosexism, and transgender oppression and the ways in which gender roles are maintained, in part, through homophobia. The hierarchical relationship among genders in which men have more access to social power than do women, intersex, or trans people is maintained by labeling as lesbian or gay anyone who steps out of expected gender roles. For these labels to be effective markers of gender boundaries, homosexuality must be strictly stigmatized and silenced. This synergistic relationship among sexism, transgender oppression, and heterosexism is dependent on the cultural functions of homophobia in maintaining the status quo (Pharr, 1988).
- *Coming-out issues for facilitators and participants*: Whether to disclose your sexual orientation, when, and to whom are questions that many heterosexuals have never considered, whereas most lesbian, gay, and bisexual people face these decisions multiple times each day. Because heterosexuality is the presumed sexual orientation in our society, it is the norm for heterosexuals to "come out" frequently, blatantly, and safely in all contexts without even realizing that they are doing so. The decision is

much more conscious and deliberate for many lesbian, gay, and bisexual people. The climate is not always safe, and tangible repercussions of discrimination or violence are possible. In addition, because coming out as a lesbian, gay man, or bisexual person is a developmental process, people can be in different stages of acknowledging their own identities. Some people may be quite open about being gay or bisexual; others may be cautious and private; others may have never told anyone; still others may be questioning and unsure about themselves. Participants should not be required to identify their sexual orientation. If the facilitators are effective at creating a climate of trust and openness, people will make their own decisions about whether or not to come out.

Facilitators have several responsibilities related to the questions of coming out. It is useful for facilitators to disclose their own sexual orientations so that participants know the perspective from which each facilitator speaks and to model pride and comfort in one's identity. Course guidelines should include confidentiality agreements, create a safe climate for people who choose to come out, and protect those who choose not to come out. No one should "out" another participant. Facilitators also should point out that it isn't necessary for heterosexual participants to "credential" themselves each time they speak. Encourage heterosexual participants to be aware of how often they unconsciously proclaim their heterosexuality, and to experiment with refraining from doing so for some part of the course. In addition to helping heterosexual participants recognize the privilege of visibility and safety they enjoy, this can relieve the discomfort that closeted gay, lesbian, bisexual, or questioning participants might feel about not disclosing their sexual orientation until they feel ready.

- *Religious issues*: We respect people's religious beliefs as private, and it is not the intention of these courses to change what someone believes. Course goals are to understand how heterosexism hurts, limits, mistreats, and even kills people of all sexual orientations, and learn how we can work toward fair treatment and respect for each other regardless of our personal religious perspectives. Facilitators should discourage religious and moral debates based on conflicting religious perspectives on homosexuality because they can be divisive and rarely resolved successfully. Instead, invite respectful discussion, and encourage participants to challenge themselves to consider differing points of view.

- *Terminology*: Because of our ever evolving understanding of the diversity within lesbian, gay, and bisexual communities, no terminology is completely inclusive of all people targeted because of their sexual orientation. We use *lesbian, gay, and bisexual* in this course design because these terms are commonly accepted and recognized among people of all sexual orientations. These terms include the three major sexual identity groups targeted by heterosexism. By naming each group, we are reminded that the experiences of lesbians and bisexual women and the experiences of gay or bisexual men are different because of interactions of sexism and heterosexism. Lesbians and bisexual women are doubly targeted as women and as sexual minorities, whereas gay and bisexual men are privileged as men and targeted as a sexual minority. We also believe it is important to differentiate the experiences of bisexual men and women from those of lesbians and gay men. Stereotypes of and discrimination against bisexuals among heterosexuals and within lesbian and gay communities can isolate bisexuals and prevent coalitions among lesbian, gay, and bisexual people.

Some lesbian, gay, bisexual, and transgender people and heterosexual allies have reclaimed the term *queer* over the past 10–15 years. Once a derogatory term for homosexuals, *queer* is often used, particularly but not exclusively, among young people as a self-chosen label of pride and challenge to heteronormative expectations. In this spirit, *queer* is an inclusive term referencing broad communities of sexuality and gender minorities. Some black gay and lesbian people of color prefer *same-gender loving* over *lesbian* or *gay* to highlight the difference that racism makes in their experiences. Likewise, some Native Americans refer to themselves as *two-spirit* to differentiate their gender and sexuality identities from those of white lesbian, bisexual. and gay people.

We encourage lesbian, gay, and bisexual participants in the course to name themselves in ways that best reflect their self-understanding, and we incorporate these self-chosen labels during the course. This is an excellent opportunity to acknowledge and affirm the diversity among lesbian, gay, and bisexual people.

## Heterosexism Curriculum Design

### Overall Goals

- To understand socialization into sexuality and gender expectations
- To understand the complexities of sexuality and gender
- To understand historical roots of contemporary heterosexism
- To understand institutional aspects of heterosexism
- To understand heterosexual privilege
- To identify personal action plans to counteract heterosexism

### Overview of Modules

Note to readers: The curriculum design in this chapter is based on the assumption that participants have completed the introductory module(s) described in Chapter 3 prior to beginning this design and have a basic understanding of the conceptual framework of oppression described in Chapter 3. See Table 9.1 for an overview of this chapter's modules.

### Module 1: Understanding Sexuality and Gender

Time needed: 3 hours, 10 minutes

### Objectives

- To begin to create safety and boundaries for group learning
- To describe course goals and agenda
- To reflect on gender and sexuality socialization
- To understand gender and sexuality vocabulary
- To explore the complexities of gender and sexuality
- To clarify understanding of the concept of heterosexual privilege

**Key concepts**: socialization, birth sex, gender identity, gender expression, sexual orientation, heterosexism, homophobia, biphobia, heterosexual privilege

**Table 9.1**  Overview of Modules: Heterosexism

| Module 1: Understanding Sexuality and Gender (3 hours, 10 minutes) | Module 2: Historical and Religious Perspectives (3.5 hours) |
|---|---|
| 1. Introductions (15 min.) | 1. Check-In (20 min.) |
| 2. Agenda, Goals, Guidelines, and Introduction to Check-Ins (20 min.) | 2. Historical Foundations for Contemporary Heterosexism (65 min.) |
| 3. Introduction to the Journal Writing Assignment (5 min.) | Break (10 min.) |
| 4. Telling Our Sexuality and Gender Stories (75 min.) | 3. Religious Perspectives on Lesbian, Gay, and Bisexual Rights (95 min.) |
| Break (10 min.) | 4. Journal Writing and Check-Out (15 min.) |
| 5. Defining Sexuality and Gender Terms (30 min.) | 5. Homework (5 min.) |
| 6. Understanding the Complexity of Sexuality and Gender (20 min.) | |
| 7. Journal Writing (5 min.) | |
| 8. Check-Out (5 min.) | |
| 9. Homework (5 min.) | |

| Module 3: Institutional Heterosexism (3 hours, 5 minutes) | Module 4: Heterosexual Privilege and Choosing Action (3.5 hours) |
|---|---|
| 1. Check-In and Homework Review (30 min.) | 1. Check-In (20 min.) |
| 2. Exploring Institutional Heterosexism (45 min.) | 2. Exploring Heterosexual Privilege (75 min.) |
| Break (10 min.) | Break (10 min.) |
| 3. Understanding Intersections of Sexual Orientation and Other Social Identities (75 min.) | 3. Planning Actions (75 min.) |
| | 4. Closure (20 min.) |
| 4. Journal Writing (10 min.) | 5. Course Evaluation (10 min.) |
| 5. Check-Out (10 min.) | |
| 6. Homework (5 min.) | |

## 1. Introductions (15 minutes)

Introduce yourself to the class and give some background information about yourself, including what motivates you to teach this class. Identify how your other social group memberships (class, race, ethnicity, religion, ability status) affect your experience of heterosexism.

Ask participants one by one to give their names and mention one issue related to heterosexism that they want to see addressed in the class. Record these issues on newsprint. If there are any items that will not be covered in the course, invite participants to talk with you outside of class to identify resources they want.

## 2. Agenda, Goals, Guidelines, and Introduction to Check-Ins (20 minutes)

After introductions, post on newsprint and review the agenda and goals. Keep them visible for the duration of the course so that everyone can refer to them.

Establishing guidelines is critical to setting a proper tone for the course because an atmosphere of trust and safety is important. Prior to the beginning of class, create a list of guidelines for class participation (see introductory modules in Chapter 3 for an alternative method to identify guidelines). Post the guidelines, then review them, taking time to make sure that participants understand them. Invite questions, additions, and revisions, and then ask for agreement on the guidelines from the whole group with a show of hands.

### Check-Ins

At this point, introduce the concept of checking in. Point out that check-ins are part of the agenda at the beginning of each of the modules. The purpose of checking in is to allow participants to express any thoughts, questions, insights, or concerns that they have from the previous session. Tell the class that everyone might experience some loose ends at the end of each module as well as at the end of the course and that the course is intended to raise some questions and well as answer others. Check-ins may be open ended or more focused on a particular activity or topic. Suggestions for check-in questions are included later in this design.

### 3. Introduction to the Journal Writing Assignment (5 minutes)

Introduce the journal writing assignment using the following instructions: *Reflecting on your experience in this course is an important part of grappling with, digesting, and clarifying information and feelings. Because the course generates new information, feelings, questions, conflicts, and thoughts, we suggest that you keep a two-sided journal notebook for the course. A spiral-bound notebook works well, but any notebook that allows you to write on the back side of the pages as well as the front side will suffice. Use the right side for note-taking during the course. Use the left side (back of the previous page) for reflecting on your experiences in the course. It may be helpful to label the right side "Notes" and the left side "Reflections" on the notes.*

Make it clear that this is a personal journal for recording feelings, ideas, questions, or reflections that participants want to think about. Participants will not be required to share this journal with the facilitators or other participants. During a module or at the end of a module, facilitators will pose a question or assignment for reflection and allow time for participants to jot down thoughts. Participants should record the question or assignment, and then write their responses. Participants may be invited to share something from their journals, but the decision to share should be completely voluntary.

There are no requirements for the journal. Participants can use whatever format and writing style work for them. Participants should bring their journals to all course sessions.

### 4. Telling Our Sexuality and Gender Stories (75 minutes)

The objective of this activity is to provide participants with an opportunity to reflect on and talk about their own gender and sexuality socialization. This storytelling encourages everyone to understand how social and cultural expectations are communicated through parents and family, peer groups in school, religion, popular media, and other individuals and institutions in our lives. Storytelling also is a way for participants to understand that, regardless of our individual sexual orientations, we are all affected by our socialization and by homophobia and heterosexism. Encourage participants to think about the following topics as they reflect on their gender and sexuality stories:

1. Describe an early memory when you understood that there were particular behavioral or attitudinal expectations of you because of your gender.
2. Describe how your parents or other family members influenced your beliefs about sexual orientation.
3. Describe how your school classmates influenced your perceptions about your sexual orientation or sexual orientation in general.

4. Describe how you learned that heterosexuality was the "normal" sexual orientation
5. What stereotypes about lesbian, gay, and bisexual people did you learn while you were growing up? Where did this information come from?
6. Describe an early memory when you realized that lesbian, gay, and bisexual people are stigmatized or discriminated against.

Model the activity by telling your own gender and sexuality stories in front of the class before participants reflect on their stories.

After facilitator modeling, ask participants to think about their own stories. Provide 2 minutes for participants to write down some notes on what parts of their stories they would like to tell. Tell them that they will choose a group of three and each person will have 12 minutes to tell their story—10 minutes to tell their story and 2 minutes to talk about what it was like to tell their story. Listeners will not comment on individual stories. Their role is to listen supportively and attentively. When the groups return to the large group, everyone will be asked to identify commonalities and differences they noted in their three stories without breaking the confidentiality of specific personal details shared in the groups. Break into storytelling triads. Keep time for all groups to ensure that everyone has the same time to share.

When the triads are finished, gather the whole group together and ask the following questions:

1. What was it like to tell your gender and sexuality story?
2. How was your story affected by social expectations about gender and sexuality?
3. What did you learn about gender and sexuality socialization by listening to other stories?
4. What were some commonalities and differences among the three stories in your group (remind everyone about confidentiality agreements)?

## Facilitation Issues

This activity asks for personal sharing early in the course. Remind everyone about participation guidelines, and make sure individual participants only talk about aspects of their gender and sexuality stories they are comfortable sharing. No one should be pressured into sharing more than is comfortable for them. Letting participants choose their own groups can provide more safety for personal sharing. With these provisions, this is an excellent early activity because it sets the tone for interaction and lets participants get to know more about two others in the course early on.

Facilitator modeling before participants tell their stories is an important aspect of making this activity a success. This makes the expectations for storytelling clear and enables the facilitators to introduce themselves and their gender and sexuality stories to the participants. Facilitators should plan what they want to say as part of the modeling activity and share this with their co-facilitator ahead of time.

## Transition to Next Activity

Use the following as a transition to the next activity: *During storytelling, everyone used the terms or vocabulary they are familiar with for discussing gender and sexuality. In the next activity, we will have an opportunity to develop some common understandings of terms related to heterosexism that may be misunderstood or new to you. We will also discuss the relationships among heterosexism, sexism, homophobia, and gender oppression.*

Break (10 minutes)

## 5. Defining Sexuality and Gender Terms (30 minutes)

The objectives of this activity are to introduce several terms that will be used in the course, acknowledge the fluidity of terminology, and encourage participants to understand the value of developing a common vocabulary.

Divide participants into groups of three to five. Give each participant a copy of the gender and sexuality vocabulary quiz (Appendix 9A). Invite each group to work together to match each of the terms on the left side of the sheet with the descriptions on the right side. Encourage discussion in the groups by emphasizing that completing the quiz is a group, not an individual, activity. After the groups have had 10–15 minutes to work on the definitions, call them back to the whole group. Post a list of "correct" answers on newsprint (see Appendix 9B). Reveal and read aloud the answers to each item on the quiz. After the answers are revealed, ask participants the following questions:

1. Which definitions were easiest for you?
2. Which terms were unfamiliar?
3. What definitions would you like to discuss further?

Lead any discussion of the terms initiated by participants. At the end of the discussion, remind participants that the purpose of the quiz is to establish some common understanding of terms often used interchangeably and that understanding these terms will enhance learning in the course.

### Facilitation Issues

One of the challenges in defining terminology in a social justice course is the fluidity of language. Rarely are universal definitions or terminology agreed upon among members of targeted social groups. Invite participants to share and listen to different perspectives on the terms and definitions on the quiz.

## 6. Understanding the Complexity of Sexuality and Gender (20 minutes)

The objective of this activity is to understand the complexity of gender and sexuality and to understand the roles of homophobia, biphobia, and transphobia in maintaining what we accept as "normal" sexuality and gender. Note that gender and sexuality are far more complex than the either/or categories most of us have learned to accept. Present the following lecture/discussion to clarify the relationship of the terms defined in the previous activity.

### Lecture (refer to "Overview: Sexism, Heterosexism, and Transgender Oppression" for more information)

*We are each born into a physical body, and, depending on the physical attributes and genetic makeup of our bodies, we are assigned a biological sex category at birth, either male or female. We are expected to develop a gender identity (our sense of ourselves as man or woman) that is consistent with the physical body we are born into. We are then socialized into specific gender roles (socially constructed behavioral expectations of masculinity and femininity) that are consistent with our physical bodies and gender identities. For example, boys are expected to be aggressive, rough, and physical. Girls are expected to be quiet, diffident, and pleasant. Both girls and boys are expected to develop heterosexual attractions and relationships (sexual and emotional feelings for the other sex). In our society, these routes to gender and sexuality identity are the only acceptable options for men and women. (Use Appendix A in the "Overview: Sexism, Heterosexism, and Transgender Oppression" to illustrate these expectations.) There is, however, far more variability in the relationships among our biological sex, gender identity, gender expression, and sexual orientation (use Appendix B in "Overview: Sexism, Heterosexism, and Transgender Oppression" to illustrate this variability). Some people do not have a gender identity that matches the sex they were assigned at birth (transsexuals/transgender people, intersex people). Many people whose gender identity is consistent with their biological/birth sex do not adopt traditional gender roles. They may adopt behaviors and interests that are more associated with another sex or are gender-neutral. Some people enjoy dressing in clothes not typically associated with "appropriate" gender role expectations (cross-dressers). Finally, there is a wide range of ways that people can express their sexuality. Heterosexuality is only one option. (The Klein Grid is a way to help participants acknowledge the complexity of sexual orientation. See Appendix 9C.) Lesbian, gay, and bisexual identities are also ways in which people express their sexual desires.*

*How we identify and express ourselves sexually is far more complex and fluid than we are taught to believe. We are socialized to believe that the possibilities for how we identify ourselves are narrow and fixed. In actuality, there are many possibilities for the relationship among our biological/birth sex, gender identity, gender roles, and sexual orientation.*

*Homophobia plays an important role in maintaining the boundaries around what our society considers "normal" gender and sexual identity and expression. When people violate these gender and sexuality norms, homophobia is one of the primary tools that is used to let people know they are "out of bounds." The narrow construction of gender and sexuality we have learned to accept as normal and natural depends in part for its maintenance on stigmatizing lesbians, gay men, bisexual people, and transgender people. Homophobia, biphobia, and transphobia are the glue that holds traditional gender roles and power imbalances between women and men in place. (Use Appendix C in "Overview: Sexism, Heterosexism, and Transgender Oppression" to illustrate this relationship. Also, see the "Walk Like a Man/Walk Like a Woman" activity in Chapter 10.)*

After giving this short lecture, invite participants to ask questions. Welcome their perspectives, and encourage them to remain open to new perspectives as the course continues. Some questions to ask participants include the following:

- Can you think of times when you or someone you know felt pressure to conform to gender and sexuality norms out of fear of being called lesbian or gay?
- How does this information confirm or contradict what you have learned about the relationship among biological/birth sex, gender identity and expression, and sexual orientation?
- How does confusion among biological/birth sex, gender identity and expression, and sexual orientation support stereotypes of lesbians, gay men, or bisexual people?

Make the following points to conclude the lecture/discussion:

- These models describe the complexity of gender and sexuality.
- Sexual orientation is not an either/or issue. It is a highly complex identity, some aspects of which may change over time.

## Transition to the Next Module

Prepare participants for the activities in the next module by telling them that now that we have explored definitions and have identified some of the ways we are socialized into our beliefs about gender and sexuality, we will examine how lesbian, gay, and bisexual people are treated in this culture.

## Facilitation Issues

These conceptual organizers will challenge how some participants understand gender and sexuality. Encourage participants to think about their beliefs and remain open to new information as we progress through the course. Encourage participants to express reservations and questions about the definitions. Remind them that there will be several opportunities to revisit these questions during the course.

## 7. Journal Writing (5 minutes)

Before closing the module, ask participants to open their journals to the "Reflections" page opposite their notes on this module. Offer the following four prompts, and suggest that they choose one of the four or simply record their reflections on today's session:

- What new understanding have you gained from some part of today's module?
- What "Yes, but ..." reactions are you experiencing?
- What aspects of this material are confusing? Write some questions that you have now.
- What are your thoughts on what we discussed today?

## 8. Check-Out (5 minutes)

### Introduce the Concept of Checking Out

The purpose of checking out is to "complete the circle of the day." It should be done in the large group rather than in pairs or small groups. It is ideal if there is time for everyone in the class to speak. The activity should be relatively short, and participants may need to be given some guidelines like "Keep your comments to one sentence, two ideas, or three words" and "Please reflect back rather than opening up new ideas." Checking out gives facilitators a read on how participants are responding to the course and can aid in making adjustments to the next module.

Checking out can have several goals: to help people synthesize learning, to identify questions for addressing in the next module, to solicit reactions to the module to provide a bridge to the next module, or to get a read on participants' levels of understanding and reactions.

Checking out can take several *forms*: It could be "Write something and then share what you choose from it." It could be "Say whatever comes to your mind when I ask this question ..." It could be "Summarize your feelings right now in one word." It could be "What is something that you appreciated about today?" or "What is one suggestion you would make for the next session?"

After introducing the concept of "checking out," pose one check-out question or direction for Module 1: "Capture how you are feeling right now with just one word." Participants might share responses such as "Enlightened," "Confused," "Still thinking," or "Looking forward to the next class."

Go around the group so that each participant speaks in turn, or invite everyone to speak as they are moved to do so. Make sure that everyone gets a turn. Participants may pass, but return to them with a second opportunity. If someone passes a second time, don't push, but check in with them after the session. You should also share your response to the check-out prompt.

## Close the Module

After each person has had a turn, make a closing remark to end the module.

### 9. Homework (5 minutes)

Ask participants to read over the sexuality historical timeline (see Appendix 9D). Invite them to write reactions to the following prompts:

- Name some events on the timeline that were new for you.
- Name some events on the timeline you remember from your own life experience.
- List 2–3 questions you would like to discuss about the events on the history timeline.

## Module 2: Historical and Religious Perspectives

Time needed: 3.5 hours

### Objectives

- To understand some of the historical roots of contemporary heterosexism
- To explore heterosexism and religion

**Key concepts**: historical context, social construction, institutional heterosexism in religion

### 1. Check-In (20 minutes)

## Objective

To clear up confusion over core concepts and definitions presented in the previous module

Following the break, take time to "check in." The purpose of this first check-in is to answer questions about the material presented in Module 1 before we look at some historical aspects of heterosexism.

What new understanding have you gained from Module 1?
Are there any concepts introduced in Module 1 that are still confusing?
Are there new connections or insights you have made since Module 1?

## Facilitation Issues

There are many factors to consider in deciding how much time to devote to checking in, such as size of the group, how much time you have, and whether the focus is on content versus process check-ins (to clarify content or to address emotional state of the group).

Size and time considerations typically can be addressed by breaking the group into pairs or small groups and giving them structured questions to answer. This allows for all participants to speak and address points for clarification or to share an emotional response to the material being presented. This can be followed by a brief whole-group check in which a few participants volunteer to share closing thoughts.

Complex issues are sometimes raised in check-ins. These issues may quickly take the group away from the planned agenda. Moving away from the agenda can be an incredible opportunity for learning for experienced facilitators who feel comfortable "going with the flow." Considerations for deciding whether to move away from the agenda include the following:

> The group is excited and interested in staying with the discussion.
> There is confusion or heated disagreement on key concepts.
> If taking more time will enable the group to work together more productively.

If you decide to take more time with the check-in, set a limit for discussion and then move on to the next activity, adjusting the time allotments as needed.

## 2. Historical Foundations for Contemporary Heterosexism (65 minutes)

### Preparation

Assign participants to read the "History Timeline: Transitions in Western Perspectives on Same-Sex Sexuality" (Appendix 9D). We also recommend creating a timeline on newsprint sheets to display in the classroom, highlighting some of the events described in the reading.

The objective of this activity is to describe some of the historical roots of contemporary heterosexism. Prepare participants for the activity by describing how we can deepen our understanding of social justice issues by learning how societal, institutional, and individual perspectives have changed over time. Exploring historical perspectives on same-sex sexuality will enable us to better understand the complexities of contemporary heterosexism.

1. Divide participants into five groups. Assign each group one section of the time-line to focus on. Ask them to discuss the following questions in the small group and be prepared to report on highlights of their discussion with the whole group.
   - What information was new for you?
   - What information did you know beforehand?
   - How did you learn of the information that was already familiar to you?
   - What did you learn about this section of the timeline that helps you to better understand contemporary dynamics of heterosexism?
   - What questions were raised for you about contemporary heterosexism as a result of discussing this part of the timeline?
2. Bring the small groups back to the whole group. Invite each small group in turn to describe some of the highlights of their discussion after briefly summarizing some of the important events described during the era they focused on.
3. Ask the following questions of the whole group:
   - How does the information presented in this timeline relate to the treatment of other stigmatized or oppressed groups during this time period?
   - How do these historical foundations help to explain contemporary institutional manifestations of heterosexism in law, medicine, religion, and education?
   - Who is missing in this timeline? Women? People of color?
4. Summarize the activity by making the following points:
   - Heterosexism must be understood in historical as well as cultural contexts. Sexual orientation also must be understood in historical and cultural contexts. This activity helps us to appreciate this.
   - The history also shows us how heterosexism intersects with racism, ableism, antisemitism, transgender oppression, and sexism during different historical eras.

## Transition to the Next Activity

These historical foundations set the stage for exploring contemporary manifestations of heterosexism and contemporary perspectives on lesbian, gay, and bisexual people that are rooted in this history.

**Break (10 minutes)**

**3. Religious Perspectives on Lesbian, Gay, and Bisexual Rights (95 minutes)**

*Sacred Lies, Civil Truths*: a film examining Christian right-wing efforts to oppose lesbian, gay, and bisexual civil rights (35 minutes) (Saalfield & Phipps, 1993)

### Objectives

- To explore how right-wing Christian perspectives on lesbian, bisexual, and gay people and their place in society have influenced a powerful political movement in opposition to any recognition of the rights of nonheterosexual people
- To examine some of the strategies used by right-wing Christian groups to demonize lesbian, gay, and bisexual people and perpetuate damaging false stereotypes of them
- To identify alternative religious perspectives that support civil rights and respect for lesbian, gay, and bisexual people and families

### Introduce the Film

Tell participants that the film is called *Sacred Lies, Civil Truths* and describes how a network of right-wing Christian political groups organize to oppose any acknowledgment of lesbian, gay, or bisexual people as deserving of civil rights or recognition of any kind. Remind participants that the perspectives presented in the film do not represent the perspectives of all religious groups. In fact, religious perspectives on lesbian, gay, and bisexual people range from affirmation to condemnation. Not all conservative Christians share the views of the right-wing Christian political organizations represented in the film. However, the political power and influence of these groups in the United States privilege their perspective in the making of public policy and can affect the lives of lesbian, gay, and bisexual people in the workplace, their schools, and their families, and can even affect their safety on the street. Invite participants to note parts of the film they want to discuss. Encourage them to challenge the perspectives presented in the film as well as explore different points of view. Tell participants that the film is 30 minutes long and that they will have a chance to discuss the film after viewing it. Post the following discussion questions:

- What are your feelings and reactions to this film?
- Which part of this film had the most impact on you?
- According to the film, what is the goal of the religious right?
- What does the film say about coalitions among different groups working toward social justice?
- This film was made in 1993. What relevance do you think the film has for the present?

At the end of the film, ask participants to write down some of their initial reactions. After this free-write, have participants move into groups of three to five to discuss the questions, which you post on newsprint.

After the small-group discussions, reconvene the whole class. Invite participants to share questions or comments about the film that arose during the small-group discussion. Ask participants which of the discussion questions they found most challenging and why.

Call participants' attention to Suzanne Pharr, one of the speakers featured in the film. Tell them that she wrote a book entitled *In the Time of the Right* (1996), in which she outlines some of the strategies the religious right uses to oppose lesbian, gay, and bisexual rights. Give participants a handout outlining these strategies (Appendix 9E). Briefly describe the strategies. Ask participants to work in pairs to cite examples in the film that illustrate these strategies. Ask them to identify other examples from their experience and current events.

Invite participants to talk about the challenges of protecting the civil rights of lesbian, gay, and bisexual people and, at the same time, ensuring freedom of religion when these perspectives are in conflict. Invite participants to talk about the concept of the separation of religion and state and how this principle applies to the conflicts.

## Facilitation Issues

This film can provoke powerful participant responses. For participants who are unaware of the political power amassed by the religious right, it can be a frightening eye-opener. For participants who perceive the film as an attack on religion, it might provoke anger or discomfort. If you are uncomfortable with these participant reactions, you might choose to use the *All God's Children* film instead (see Appendix 9F). *All God's Children* is not as confrontational about the religious right as *Sacred Lies, Civil Truths*, and, as a result, it might be a more acceptable choice for some groups.

Place the discussion in the context of tensions between private and public, religion and state, and democracy and theocracy, and the challenges of living in a diverse society in which perspectives on the civil rights of lesbian, gay, and bisexual people are changing and challenging.

This discussion will require strict adherence to discussion guidelines established for the class to maintain a climate in which civil dialogue can occur. Ask participants to focus on understanding and sharing different perspectives and not on debating the merits of different perspectives.

Remind them that if these issues were easily resolved, they would not raise as much passion, fear, and anger as they do.

### 4. Journal Writing and Check-Out (15 minutes)

The purpose of this activity is to provide an opportunity for participants to reflect on the history discussion, film, and analysis by Suzanne Pharr. Give the following instructions to the participants: *Take a few minutes to write some initial reflections on today's material (history, film, Suzanne Pharr). Include new information, a theme that was particularly powerful to you, something that you disagree with, a question you have, a reaction you had during the session, or something about which you need to think more.*

Provide 5 to 10 minutes, and then, as a check-out activity, ask if any volunteers would like to share one of their reflections. Remind participants that there should be no discussion of anyone's reflections. Participants should focus on listening to each other. After any volunteers have spoken, assign the following homework for the next module.

### 5. Homework (5 minutes)

Ask participants to identify an incident related to gay, lesbian, or bisexual issues they have read about or seen in the media or from their personal experiences. Ask them to describe the news item or experience. Next, ask participants to write about how the news item or experience is related to heterosexism. For example, a news article reported that a local restaurant refused to hire servers who "looked gay." This is an example or either individual heterosexism (if the manager made the decision only for his or her own restaurant) or institutional heterosexism (if it is the policy of a restaurant chain). Ask participants to be prepared to share their homework during the Module 3 check-in.

Close the module.

## Module 3: Institutional Heterosexism

Time needed: 3 hours, 5 minutes

### Objectives

- To identify and discuss *institutional heterosexism*
- To define and discuss *heterosexual privilege*
- To explore the effects of multiple identities on experiences of heterosexism

**Key concepts**: institutional heterosexism, heterosexual privilege, multiple identities

### 1. Check-in and Homework Review (30 minutes)

**Objectives**

- To provide opportunities for participants to share what they noticed since the last session
- To create a lead-in to the exploration of institutional heterosexism and privilege
- To welcome participants back to class and reestablish a safe learning environment

Have participants talk with two classmates about their homework. After about 10 minutes, invite several participants to share their homework with the whole class. Respond to any questions about the homework. Then tell the group that this is a great lead-in to this module's theme, which is institutional heterosexism and heterosexual privilege.

### 2. Exploring Institutional Heterosexism (45 minutes)

**Objectives**

- To introduce the concept of institutional heterosexism
- To give participants the opportunities to identify examples of institutional heterosexism
- To explore ways in which heterosexism is rooted in systemic structures
- To begin to discuss the concept of heterosexual privilege

**Introduction**

Prior to beginning this activity, post six newsprints around the room. Write one of the following institutions on the top of each newsprint:

- Family
- Education
- Health care
- Workplace
- Legal systems
- Media

Explain that the next activity will focus on institutional heterosexism or how institutional policies, practices, and norms reinforce heterosexism. Remind the participants that institutional heterosexism can be conscious or unconscious. Institutional heterosexism advantages heterosexual people and disadvantages lesbian, gay, and bisexual people. Define the advantages that heterosexuals receive as *heterosexual privilege*. Give a few specific examples from your local community or from the homework assignments just completed. Other examples of heterosexual privilege are in Appendix 9G.

Divide the class into groups of three to five people. Smaller groups may encourage participation by quieter members of the group. Give each group a marker. Assign one group to each of the institutions on the newsprints. Ask participants to list as many examples of institutional heterosexism for this institution as they can in 2 minutes. You can write one example on the newsprint for each institution before beginning the activity. After 2 minutes, all groups rotate clockwise to the next institution. Give them 2 minutes to work on the new institution. Keep rotating until all groups have worked on all institutions posted around the room.

As groups rotate, they should first read what previous groups have written and then add only new examples. After all groups have worked on all newsprints, invite participants to take a gallery walk around the room reading all of the examples for each institution (see Appendix 9H for a list of "Examples of Institutional Heterosexism").

After the gallery walk, ask the participants to return to the circle to share observations.

## Processing

Ask if anyone needs clarification on the examples of institutional heterosexism posted on the newsprints. If so, ask the group who wrote the item to explain what they meant. Focus on one institution at a time. This affords the opportunity to discuss the ways in which these institutions work in concert to create a web of heterosexism. Some questions include the following:

- For which institutions was it easy or difficult to identify examples of institutional heterosexism? Why?
- What was new or surprising to you?
- How do these institutional factors advantage heterosexual people?
- How do these institutional factors disadvantage lesbian, gay, and bisexual people?
- How do the institutional manifestations we have listed reflect and reinforce prejudices about gay, lesbian, and bisexual people?
- What connections can you make to what we have discussed earlier in this course?

Reintroduce the concept of heterosexual privilege and define it (see definitions in Appendix 9G). Make the point that these "exclusive rights" are the result of cultural and institutional heterosexism. It is not necessary for heterosexuals to give up rights to dismantle privilege, only to give up the exclusivity of those rights. Give some examples of dismantling privilege by giving up exclusivity, such as the following:

Instituting domestic partnership benefits or marriage rights for same-sex couples
Legalizing adoptions by gay families
Passing national, state, or local legislation protecting lesbian, gay, and bisexual
people from employment discrimination based on sexual orientation

## Facilitation Issues

Lesbian, gay, and bisexual participants in the class may have experienced the examples of institutional heterosexism in this activity. If anyone chooses to share a personal story or a story of a friend or relative who was discriminated against, this adds an important element of credibility to these hypothetical examples. Any such sharing should be strictly voluntary. It is important to be sure that everyone remembers the participation guidelines.

Examining privilege may bring up feelings of defensiveness, guilt, anger, or detachment among heterosexual participants. Acknowledge these feelings as part of the learning process, and invite all participants to reflect on this process as part of the ongoing challenge of being an ally (see Appendix 3N).

## Break (10 minutes)

## 3. Understanding Intersections of Sexual Orientation and Other Social Identities (75 minutes)

**Key concepts**: multiple identities, privilege, targeted identities, advantaged identities
The objective of this activity is to raise awareness about how the intersections of multiple identities intensify the challenges experienced by gay, lesbian, and bisexual people in institutional settings.

## Introduction

The previous activity explored institutional heterosexism. This exercise explores how multiple identities further complicate a gay, lesbian, or bisexual person's experience of institutional heterosexism.

## Preparation

Using colorful 8" × 11" construction paper, create cut-out outlines of people (similar to cookie-cutter gingerbread people). Using self-stick notes, label each cut-out "person" with multiple identities (religion, ethnicity, gender, age, sexual orientation, and class). Include several different combinations of identities:

   Lesbian, White, Uses a Wheelchair, Poor
   Gay Man, Latino (English is a second language), Working Class
   Bisexual Man (in a relationship with a woman), Jewish, Middle Class
   Transgender Man, Black, Christian
   Genderqueer Heterosexual Woman, Asian, Working Class

## Activity

*Part 1*    Divide participants into groups of three to five. Invite each group to choose one of the cut-out cookie people, and spend 15 minutes discussing the multiple identities of their cookie person, including the implications of the various intersections of identity.

*Part 2*    Give each group scenarios in which to imagine their cookie person (samples below). Give all the groups the same scenario, give different scenarios to each group, or give each group all four scenarios. Invite each group to spend 20 minutes reading their scenario(s) and discussing the implications of their person's multiple identities on their experience in the scenarios. In what ways would their person experience the disadvantages of targeted identities and the privileges of advantaged identities in each scenario? Have each group record the disadvantages and privileges they identify to share with the class.

1. You are a high school junior in a small city. No other gay, lesbian, or bisexual students or staff have publicly identified themselves in your school.
2. You have been harassed and called antigay slurs while walking on a street in your town.
3. You and your longtime same-sex partner have decided to have a ceremony celebrating your commitment.
4. You just got a call at work that your longtime same-sex partner was in a car accident and is in serious condition, unconscious, and in the emergency room at the local hospital.

*Part 3*    Invite each group to share the multiple identities of their cookie person. Next, ask each group to share, in turn, the privileges and disadvantages their person might experience in one of the scenarios. Repeat this process for all four groups. Spend 30 minutes discussing as a whole group the following questions:

- What did you notice about how the intersections of multiple identities might affect the experience of people in these scenarios?
- How do these scenarios and experiences of the cookie people help you to better understand the complexities of heterosexism when we think about having multiple targeted identities? Multiple advantaged identities?

### 4. Journal Writing (10 minutes)

Ask participants to reflect in their journals on the following question: How does heterosexual privilege affect your life? Note that people of any sexual orientation can answer this question, but from different points of view.

### 5. Check-Out (10 minutes)

Invite participants to share one sentence that summarizes something they learned about institutionalized heterosexual, heterosexual privilege, or how multiple identities affect experiences of privilege and disadvantage.

### 6. Homework (5 minutes)

Read the list of "Examples of Heterosexual Privileges" (see Appendix 9G). Reflect on them in your own life in preparation for Module 4 activities.

## Module 4: Heterosexual Privilege and Choosing Action

Time needed: 3.5 hours

### Objectives

- To examine heterosexual privilege
- To explore actions participants can take to challenge heterosexism in their personal and professional lives
- To bring some closure to the course
- To provide participants with an opportunity to give feedback on the course, facilitators, and their participation in the course.

**Key concepts**: heterosexual privilege, individual and collective action

## 1. Check-In (20 minutes)

Inform the class that the purpose of this check-in is to see what questions participants have about heterosexual privilege. Tell them that the first activity in this module will help everyone clarify their understanding and apply this understanding to their personal lives.

Using the "Examples of Heterosexual Privilege" (see Appendix 9G), ask participants if they have questions about any of the examples listed. Invite participants to respond to the questions raised. After 20 minutes, end the discussion and tell participants that the next activity will provide an opportunity to further explore heterosexual privilege on a personal level.

## 2. Exploring Heterosexual Privilege (75 minutes)

The purpose of this activity is to raise awareness of heterosexual privilege in participants' lives using a fishbowl format. Describe how a fishbowl works: One subgroup of the class sits in a circle in the middle of the room (the "fish") and has a discussion among themselves. The other participants sit in a larger circle around them and listen without participating (the "bowl"). In this case, the heterosexual participants and facilitator are going to be the "fish" and discuss heterosexual privilege and strategies to dismantle heterosexism. The lesbian, gay, and bisexual participants and facilitator will be in the outside circle listening to the discussion.

Invite the participants who identify as heterosexual to join a heterosexual facilitator in the inner circle. The heterosexual facilitator should remind everyone of the definition of heterosexual privilege and model talking about personal experiences with heterosexual privilege. Invite each heterosexual participant to describe a situation in which they experienced heterosexual privilege. Use the questions below to guide the discussion. This is an opportunity for heterosexual participants to identify how heterosexual privilege affects them personally. After everyone has had a chance to speak, the heterosexual facilitator should invite the heterosexual participants to share what it was like to participate in the fishbowl.

After all heterosexual participants have had an opportunity to speak, invite everyone to spend a few minutes in silence reflecting on the discussion using the processing questions below. After a few minutes, the lesbian, gay, and bisexual facilitator should invite the people in the outer circle to reflect on what they heard people in the inner circle say using the processing questions provided.

### Sample Heterosexual Fishbowl Questions

- Given what you have learned so far in this course, describe a situation where you experienced heterosexual privilege. Were you aware at the time of your privilege? When did you become aware of your privilege?
- In a similar situation, would you behave differently given your current understanding of heterosexual privilege? How?
- How has your awareness of heterosexual privilege changed based on what you learned from this course?
- How can you challenge heterosexual privilege in your personal and work/school life?

### Sample Processing Questions

Questions for heterosexual participants:

- How did it feel being in the fishbowl?
- What did you learn about your experience of heterosexual privilege?
- What surprised you about your experience?
- What appreciations would you like to give to lesbian, gay, and bisexual participants?

Questions for lesbian, gay, and bisexual participants:

What did you learn about heterosexuals' experience of privilege?
What appreciations would you like to give to heterosexual participants?

### Facilitation Issues

Often fishbowl exercises have all participants spend time in the inner and outer circles. Because this exercise is focused on issues of privilege, only the heterosexual participants are asked to go into the inner circle. This is a difficult, high-risk activity, and heterosexuals are in a vulnerable spot in the fishbowl. We place the activity three quarters of the way through the curriculum when participants are better prepared to engage in an activity that calls for greater risk taking. Even so, heterosexual participants may feel some anxiety about this activity.

It is essential that participants have the option of not self-identifying as any particular sexual orientation. Encourage participants to push their learning edges and participate in the activity; however, if any participants need to opt out of the activity for this reason, they should be allowed to do so without question.

The heterosexual facilitator must be able to push with compassion when appropriate as well as lend support to heterosexual participants if they are struggling with identifying their heterosexual privilege. One of the roles of the heterosexual facilitator is to encourage everyone in the inner circle to participate.

It is equally important to make sure that lesbian, gay, and bisexual participants do not use the fishbowl activity as an opportunity to criticize the heterosexual participants. Most lesbian, gay, and bisexual participants appreciate that the focus is on the heterosexual participants discussing privilege and embrace their role as witnesses. Stress the importance of compassion and support in this process. If lesbian, gay, and bisexual participants are uncomfortable with this one-way fishbowl, the activity can be adapted to have the lesbian, gay, and bisexual participants also take a turn in the fishbowl to discuss how heterosexism has affected their lives.

### Break (10 minutes)
### 3. Planning Actions (75 minutes)

**Objective**: To help participants identify actions to take that challenge heterosexism

### Introduction

To prepare for thinking about action plans, tell participants the following:

- Taking action means engaging in specific behaviors to challenge heterosexism and heterosexual privilege.
- We are all in different stages of readiness to take action.
- There are many ways and opportunities to take action.
- Although we each need to decide what our personal next step might be, it is important that we do take steps to confront heterosexism and homophobia.
- Taking action often requires us to move out of our comfort zones.

**Option 1: Role Plays (see Appendix 9I for Options 2 and 3)**

Ask participants to think about situations in which they will find themselves in the next few weeks where they will have the opportunity to challenge heterosexism. For example, these situations could be at work, with family or friends, or at a meeting. Give some examples. Have participants write down some of their situations. Ask for volunteers to describe one of their situations to the class. Ask for other volunteers to act out the situation with an action to challenge heterosexism. Have the person who posed the situation watch the role play so he or she can see different action options acted out by other participants. Give the following directions:

- Role plays should go quickly because that is how situations happen in "real life."
- Try to be real rather than exaggerate the situation.
- Anyone can stop the action by yelling "Freeze!" and then taking the place of the person making the intervention in the role play.
- Feel free to "rewind" the action to any specific point and replay the situation with a new action response.

After three to five interventions for one situation, stop the action and ask the person who posed the situation if any of the role plays included actions they could see themselves taking. Use the following questions:

- What seemed useful to you?
- What do you think would work for you? Why?
- What do you think would not work for you? Why?
- What are plusses and minuses for each intervention option?

Repeat the process with other situations as time allows. This activity can also be used in small groups, with each group role-playing different situations posed by group members.

### 4. Closure (20 minutes)

The objectives of this activity are to conclude the course and to share participants' action plans. Ask participants to sit in a circle. Remind them that every action, no matter how small or on what level, makes a difference in the world. Invite participants to make one closing statement about the course and share one action they are committed to taking in their personal or professional lives that will challenge heterosexism. Give participants a few moments to think about their answers. Participants can use any of the following sentence stems:

One action plan I commit to completing is ...
An appreciation I'd like to give someone in the class is ...
A question the course raised for me is ...
Something I learned in the course is ...
The one thing I know I will remember is ...
The most important thing I learned about myself is ...
One major concern that I have about this information is ...
One way that I have been changed by this course is ...
Someone that I will share my learning with is ...
My next step is ...

- After a minute or two, tell participants that each person in turn will have an opportunity to share one (or more, if time permits) of their responses to the sentence stems. Ask participants to be brief so everyone has time to speak. No reactions, responses, or questions from the group are permitted. If any participant wants to pass, they will have an opportunity to speak after everyone else has spoken.
- Ask who would like to begin the go-around. After this participant speaks, invite him or her to indicate which way the go-around will proceed around the circle. Begin the go-around. Facilitators should also share a response to the sentence stems.

After everyone has had a chance to speak, thank everyone for participating together. Finish up any administrative details, and pass out the course evaluation forms.

### Facilitation Issues

Remember which participants choose to pass, and return to them at the end of the go-around. If someone takes too much time, gently remind them to be brief. If someone responds to a comment, remind them that our role in this activity is to listen, not respond. Occasionally, a participant might make a comment in the closing go-around that is provocative or opens up the possibility for an extended discussion. If this happens, remind participants that the closing is meant to bring the course to a close, but the complexity of the issues addressed calls for continued thought and discussion that you hope participants will have after the course is over. Do not let the closing activity become an extended discussion.

### 5. Course Evaluation (10 minutes)

The objective of this activity is to provide participants with an opportunity to evaluate the course, the facilitators, and their own participation in the course. Post the course agenda and learning goals, or pass out copies of the course outline. Ask participants to use this information as a reminder of class activities, assignments, and readings as they complete the course evaluation. Ask a participant to distribute the evaluation forms (see Appendix 9J) to the class and collect the completed forms in a large envelope at the end of the evaluation. Tell participants that they do not need to put their names on the evaluation. Tell them that the information on the evaluation form is important to you as you revise the course design and that their honest opinions are most helpful. Finally, ask participants who finish quickly to remain quiet after they have completed their evaluations so that others who are still writing can concentrate without distractions. If there is time following the collection of the forms, invite participants to share responses, discuss which goals were most useful, and discuss how well they were met. Be sure that all participants have completed and turned in the form before the discussion begins. Tell participants who would like to discuss the course further to contact you after grades are submitted and give them your contact information. Thank participants for taking time to complete the evaluation.

# 10

# Transgender Oppression Curriculum Design

CHASE CATALANO,
LINDA MCCARTHY,
DAVEY SHLASKO*

To our knowledge, this is one of the first curriculum designs for teaching about transgender oppression to be published. Therefore, we have designed this chapter with the aim of providing a broad, basic framework for understanding transgender oppression.

## What is Transgender?

We use *transgender* to refer to individuals who transgress the gender norms of the dominant culture and/or their specific culture, in ways that significantly impact their everyday life and/or are central to their understanding of themselves. For example, people who describe themselves as *transsexual, transgender, genderqueer, gender non-conforming, gender-variant, cross-dressing, tomboy, butch, femme, drag king,* and *drag queen* might all fit under the broad rubric of transgender (definitions of specific identities may be found in Appendix 10A). Yet, it is important to distinguish between transgender as a descriptive term and transgender as an identity. Many people who fit into our broad definition of *transgender* may not claim a transgender identity. We affirm the right of all individuals to describe and label their own gender identities in whatever ways feel most appropriate to them. At the same time, in this chapter we employ *transgender* descriptively to include all people who fit this definition, whether or not they might call themselves transgender.

---

\* We ask that those who cite this work always acknowledge by name all of the authors listed rather than either only citing the first author or using "et al." to indicate coauthors. All collaborated on the conceptualization, development, and writing of this chapter.

Although transgender identity is often included with gay and lesbian identity in the familiar acronym *GLBT*, transgender, unlike gay, lesbian, or bisexual, is not a sexual orientation. Transgender experiences are unique and distinct from the experiences of nontransgender gay, lesbian, and bisexual people. As indicated in Griffin's overview of the sexism, heterosexism, and transgender chapters, gender and sexual orientation are conceptually distinct, though interrelated. Some transgender people may identify as gay, lesbian, or bisexual; some transgender people are heterosexual; and some may find that none of these categories adequately describe their sexuality.

People often conflate transgender with intersex. *Intersex* refers to people who are born with bodies that are not easily classified as male or female, either from birth or as a result of hormonal changes at puberty or later. Transgender and intersex communities overlap (i.e., some transgender people are intersexed, and vice versa), but they are not the same. Likewise, the political interests of these groups intersect in some areas, and diverge in other areas. This chapter focuses on transgender oppression. To learn more about intersex issues, we refer readers to the Intersex Society of North America (1993–2005; www.isna.org).

## Our Perspective on Transgender Identity

Among transgender communities and theorists, there are myriad ways of understanding the relationship of gender identity to the physical body, and of gender transition to physical procedures. As authors, we share similar understandings on many of these issues, yet we approach them from different perspectives. We are a female-bodied woman, a transgender man (female to male, or FtM), and a transgender/genderqueer person (female-bodied). Our work on transgender issues has included basic transgender education, transgender community building and political organizing, and health education and advocacy. In this chapter, our different perspectives inform and balance each other as we strive to create a basic introduction to transgender issues and transgender oppression.

Despite our different identities and backgrounds, we agree that gender is socially constructed rather than essential. In taking a social constructionist approach, we take issue with the medical model, which has been the primary framework for making sense of sex transition for over 50 years. The medical model frames transsexuality as a disease, with the cure being physical transition from one sex to another, via sexual reassignment surgery. It defines a dichotomous approach to sex transition, and relies on a gender binary. From our perspective, pathologizing transsexuality and transgender expression is problematic, not only in its maintenance of the gender binary but also because any "medical condition" will require "treatment" and, ultimately, a "cure." People find many ways to be and identify as transgender, some drawing upon medical approaches to gender transition, and others finding alternative ways to enact gender transgression.

Our work and perspective are informed by queer theorists such as Michel Foucault, Judith Butler, and Judith Halberstam. In particular, Foucault (1995) and Butler (1990) assert that gender is a social construction, rooted in culture rather than biology. Halberstam (1998) advances these concepts in *Female Masculinity*, which explores the dynamics of sexuality, masculinity, masculine women, and transgender identity. The work of these and other postmodern academics extends discussions of sex and gender beyond the realm of biology, medicine, and psychology. Taking the theory out of the abstract, transgender theorists such as Aaron (Holly) Devor (1989), Jason Cromwell (1999), and Pat Califia (1997) offer a merging of theory and lived experience.

Our perspective is also informed by the more accessible and equally valuable innovative work we call *pop queer theory*, which includes the writing of transgender activists such as Kate Bornstein (1994), Riki Wilchins (1997), Patrick Califia (1997), Leslie Feinberg (1997), and Ki Namaste (2000). The writings anthologized in *Gender-queer: Voices From Beyond the Binary* (Nestle, Howell, & Wilchins, 2004) also provide a contemporary approach to gender identity, and present a diverse range of voices from within gender-transgressing communities. Additionally, the emergence of transgender narratives that diverge from the medical model gives new voice to the experiences and lives transgender people. For example, transgender-identified scholars such as Jamison Green (2004) and Dhillon Khosla (2006) have depicted their experiences with sex transition, but have also complicated and challenged the idea of a binary transition from one sex to another. Given that the majority of transgender writing has been by white people, we look forward to reading more work by transgender people of color.

## What is Transgender Oppression?

*Transgender oppression* is the oppression of people whose gender expression, gender identity, and/or sex identity does not match the expectations of the dominant norm of society. *Transphobia* is a fear or hatred of atypical gender expression or identity, or of people embodying or expressing an atypical gender identity. Those who are targeted by transgender oppression and transphobia include people whose gender transgression is conscious or unconscious, deliberate or not deliberate, and/or intentionally political or apolitical in intent. They include people who identify with terms such as *transgender*, *transsexual*, *genderqueer*, and the others listed above, as well as others who do not identify with any of those terms, but whose gender expression nevertheless transgresses gender norms. Someone need not be connected with a transgender community or movement in order to experience transgender oppression. In fact, one need not even necessarily appear to transgress gender at any given moment. For example, some transsexuals who present as the gender they identify with (rather than the sex they were assigned at birth) may not appear to transgress gender at all. The fact that many transsexuals need to conceal their pasts in order to be accepted as the sex and gender they are is itself a manifestation of transgender oppression.

Transgender people and those who transgress gender norms face oppression and transphobia on the individual, cultural, and institutional levels. Like any form of oppression, transgender oppression works in conjunction with other manifestations of oppression such as racism, ableism, and classism. Whether people are reinforcing gender norms through everyday words or actions or through more overt policing behaviors such as harassment or violence, transgender oppression is experienced in many contexts. On an institutional level, transgender people may face job discrimination in hiring and promotion, have little or no protection from being fired, and can, in most places, legally be evicted from public housing or denied services because of their transgender status or gender nonconformity. Cultural images of people who transgress gender norms are rarely positive and affirming. Perhaps most damaging, on an individual level, some transgender people may feel as though they must hide their gender identity. For those whose gender identity is visibly out of the norm, negotiating and managing other people's assumptions, interpretations, and questions about their gender are parts of daily life. Many transgender people experience violence and harassment, and may lack institutional protection and support from law enforcement and the legal system. (The film *The Brandon Teena Story* [Muska and Olafsdóttir, 1998] presents a compelling illustration.)

Enforced gender roles are limiting and sometimes harmful, not only to transgender people but to everybody. Gender roles (or rules) instruct us as to how we should look and act, form our expectations for relationships and career possibilities, and even influence how we are supposed to think and what we are supposed to be good at. Men and women who transgress gender even slightly may experience disapproval and other social consequences as a result, regardless of their relative positions in a system of sexism. Yet just as we use *sexism* to talk about the specific ways in which women are targeted and men are privileged by a system of oppression, *transgender oppression* refers to the system that targets transgender people (in the broad sense defined above) and privileges those whose gender identity and expression generally align with social norms. As with all forms of oppression, those who are privileged may not feel advantaged. Indeed, they may feel limited by gender norms and resent the pressures to conform. Nevertheless, the oppression experienced by transgender people is different from the constrictions and privileges faced by nontransgender men and women within the context of a patriarchal society.

## Historical Context

Perspectives on gender transgressions have varied throughout history. In recent U.S. history, the prevailing view has progressed from an essentialist viewpoint that individualized and pathologized gender nonconforming people to one that conceptualizes gender as a social construct that dictates gender roles, presentation, identity, and sexual orientation.

In the late 19th and early 20th centuries, gender transgression was viewed through a moral lens, congruent with the dominance of religiosity at that time. Corresponding with the rise in popularity of Freud, psychoanalytical and psychological interpretations of gender identity gained prominence in the early to middle part of the 20th century. Biological theories that centralized physiological conditions as causative grew popular in the 1960s and 1970s. Both psychological and physiological theories have remained prevalent in the medical and psychiatric fields.

The clinical view employed by the medical model depends on physiological and psychodynamic explanations for gender "deviance." Perceiving atypical gender behavior, expression, or identity as a "condition" invokes both treatment and a cure, and relies on a binary view of gender and sex. The name Harry Benjamin is synonymous with the medical model, as it was he who developed the "Standards of Care" (Benjamin, 1966/1977). For many years, Benjamin's Standards of Care dictated the requirements necessary for a person to be considered transsexual and to qualify for medical transition, as well as the scope of therapies, treatments, and surgeries that a transition would include. Although Benjamin helped many transgender people by creating a medical and legal process whereby they could "prove" their transsexual status and gain access to medical transition care, he also imposed a definition of transsexuality and an obligatory course of medical and surgical treatment. Many therapists and medical providers still rely on the Standards of Care, though the guidelines are often adhered to less rigidly than in the past. Currently, few health insurance companies cover costs related to sex/gender transition, despite the medical model's validation of transition as an appropriate "cure" for transsexuals. The medicalization of transgender expression, unfortunately, still results in many transgender people receiving care that is inappropriate and even abusive (see Burke, 1997). For example, Scholinski (1998) details an experience of being hospitalized for, among other things, atypical gender expression.

A profound paradigm shift occurred in the 1990s—in the expression, acceptance, and acknowledgment of transgender identity on the social, interpersonal, and individual levels (see Bockting, 1997). Some call the 1990s the decade of emergence of the role of the transgender (Bolin, 1997), and many would agree that the years 1990–2000 were pivotal for the movement. Transgender issues and identity gained mainstream exposure through popular culture in films, books, the Internet, and television. A growing social movement, increasingly distinct from the gay, lesbian, and bisexual movement, began to coalesce. Transgender communities have mobilized to create political action groups (Gender Public Advocacy Coalition , n.d.; www.genderpac.org), have pushed for civil rights protections (www.transgenderlaw.org), and have instigated a growing awareness of the complexities of gender identity. More recently, mainstream films such as *Boys Don't Cry* and *TransAmerica* have brought sympathetic support from the general public for the violence and stress that transgender people may face. As a result, a 2002 poll conducted by the Human Rights Campaign showed that 70% of those surveyed have heard the word *transgender*, and 61% believe that legal protections are needed to protect transgender people from discrimination.

## Transgender People in Gay and Lesbian Communities and Movements

Transgender people have long been integral members of GLB communities in the United States and of the lesbian, gay, and bisexual civil rights movement. Though they were at the margins, drag queens, transvestites, and transsexuals were a part of the gay liberation movement that began in the United States in the late 1960s (Jagose, 1996). Ironically, the Stonewall riots of 1969, which are widely viewed as the event that launched the gay rights movement, were instigated by drag queens and other gender transgressors, alongside gays and lesbians. Communities such as those described in *Boots of Leather, Slippers of Gold: The History of a Lesbian Community* (Kennedy & Davis, 1994); *Stone Butch Blues: A Novel* (Feinberg, 1993); and *Mother Camp: Female Impersonators in America* (Newton, 1972) articulate the complex interconnections between sexual orientation and gender identities, and demonstrate the importance of community among gender transgressors.

The relationship between transgender-identified people and gay, lesbian, and bisexual people in the movement was sometimes difficult. The visibility of transgender people within the movement worried some gays and lesbians, who feared that including transgender people and their concerns would make it more difficult to acquire acceptance and support for gays from the heterosexual majority. This conflict has continued and is evident in decisions to set aside the concerns of transgender people in order to pursue civil rights for lesbian, gay, and bisexual people.

The publication of Janice Raymond's (1979) *The Transsexual Empire* represented one stream of second wave feminism's response to transsexualism—that transsexuality reflects and perpetuates our culture's strict adherence to gender roles and that transsexual women cannot also be feminists. An important outcome of the second wave of feminism in the 1970s was the creation of women-only spaces. With the emergence of the transgender rights movement, tension developed between female-born women and transgender women about who is welcome in women-only space.

## Contemporary Transgender Organizing

The liberation movement, in which transgender people pursue the right for everyone to express their gender as they experience it internally, strengthened significantly during the 1990s. The release of Kate Bornstein's *Gender Outlaw: Men, Women, and the Rest of Us* (1994) launched the most recent wave of transgender activism as a movement of empowerment. Leslie Feinberg's (1999) *Trans Liberation: Beyond Pink and Blue* put forth the proposition that "each person has the right to express their gender in any way that feels most comfortable, masculine, feminine, androgynous, bi or tri gender expression, gender fluidity, gender complexity, and gender contradiction" (p. 53). More recently, transgender communities have united around specific social change goals such as hate crime laws, nondiscrimination policies, and preventing violence against transgender people despite differences and conflicts within these communities across gender and other social identities.

Currently, people are realizing that they can explore a variety of ways of expressing their gender; through complete medical transition, through selecting certain medical procedures but rejecting others, or through altering their bodies through nonprescription hormone supplements, body modifications such as piercings and tattoos, or temporary devices like chest binders. Rather than requiring transgender people to fit themselves into a specific mold that may or may not work for them, transgender activists seek to shift the onus to society to change so that all gender identities and expressions are respected and affirmed.

## Transgender Youth

Transgender youth are among the most vulnerable members of our communities. If they are not lucky enough to have the support of their family of origin, they have few places to turn. Many trans or queer youth become homeless or enter the foster care system. Navigating the network of service providers can be a formidable challenge, especially when transgender youth end up educating those who are supposed to help them.

In 2001, Human Rights Watch released a report indicating that transgender youth experienced discrimination and mistreatment in schools (Bochenek & Brown, 2001). Later, the Gay, Lesbian and Straight Education Network (GLSEN) released findings in a report entitled "The National School Climate Survey: The Experiences of Gay, Lesbian, Bisexual and Transgender Youth in Our Nation's Schools" (Kosciw & Diaz, 2006). GLSEN's report was notable for its attention to, and separation of, sexual orientation and gender expression. These recent findings reflect the fact that gender-transgressing youth are now more likely to identify openly as transgender, and at younger ages. Even so, in most studies, transgender youth are lumped in with LGB youth (or are misidentified as LGB), so there is limited empirical data to describe their experiences. However, from the statistics on LGBT youth, we can infer that transgender youth are far more likely than nontrans, heterosexual peers to be threatened with a weapon at school, experience unwanted sexual contact, have unprotected sex, smoke cigarettes, drink alcohol, and attempt suicide (Kosciw, 2002; Massachusetts Department of Education, 2004). Service providers in cities across the United States estimate that up to 40% of homeless young people self-identify as lesbian, gay, bisexual, or transgender (Truong, 2004). Among transgender youth who are enrolled in school, almost 90% report feeling unsafe in school, more than half report being physically harassed, and 35% report being physically assaulted in school because of their gender expression (Kosciw, 2002). GLSEN's report found that more than 60% of students frequently or often heard negative remarks about someone's gender expression.

Transgender communities and movements have always included young people. Sylvia Rivera, one of the drag queens who led the Stonewall Riots, was herself not quite 18 years old at the time. She continued to organize and advocate for the rights of homeless queer and transgender youth, especially youth of color, until her death in 2002 (Shepard, 2004). In recent years, young people have contributed an added dimension to the transgender movement, especially in terms of activism and social change. Transgender youth inside and outside of academia are challenging and redefining gender every day, creating new terms to describe their lives faster than theorists can keep track of them. Youth provide a vital and dynamic force that pushes the boundaries not only of normative gender but also of transgender communities and movements themselves.

Because individuals are identifying as transgender at younger ages, some are transitioning or already living in their new sex while attending college. This presents new challenges to college administrators in health care, housing, and registration. For example, campus health care centers are rarely trained in, or sensitized to, the medical concerns of transgender students. Residence halls generally assign rooms based on someone's birth sex, which presents a problem for transgender students, who may feel uncomfortable living in a building or hallway based on sex. Some colleges are addressing this by creating gender-neutral floors, or by including transgender students in special-interest floors with gay, lesbian, and bisexual students. Campus bathrooms are particularly difficult spaces for transgender students, due to their own or others' discomfort. They face possible harassment in women's rooms because women fear that a man is in the bathroom, and they face harassment in men's rooms because men might perceive them as "not a man," and therefore suspect. Lastly, students who have changed their sex, or who change their sex while at college, may need to change their name and/or sex on all college documents, and perhaps to obtain a new identity photo. Forms that restrict gender options to male or female invalidate students' identities.

## Legal Protection

Although there is no federal protection against discrimination based on gender identity or gender expression, as there is for race, religion, gender, national origin, and disability, some individual states and municipalities have taken this initiative. As of 2006, eight states (CA, IL, HI, ME, MN, NM, RI, and WA) plus the District of Columbia provide protection against discrimination for both sexual orientation and gender identity (Human Rights Campaign, 2006; www.hrc.org). Three other states (IN, KY, PA) provide protection, but only for public employees. Further, eight states (CT, FL, IL, HI, MA, NJ, NY, VT) have interpreted existing laws to include some protection against discrimination against transgender people (Human Rights Campaign, 2006). These laws generally provide protection against discrimination in employment, housing, education, public accommodations, and the right to file a lawsuit.

Like members of other targeted groups, transgender people are at high risk for violence and harassment. In September 2005, Congress voted to add "actual or perceived sexual orientation, gender, gender identity and disability" to federal hate crimes laws. (Hate crimes laws increase penalties for violent crimes and hate speech, but do not prohibit discrimination.) As of May 2005, 10 states specifically include gender identity in hate crimes laws (Human Rights Campaign, 2006). Besides individual states, counties, cities, and transnational corporations such as Raytheon have changed their nondiscrimination policies to include gender expression. Indeed, 71 of the Fortune 500 firms include gender identity and expression in their policies (Human Rights Campaign, 2006).

## Facilitation Issues

There are some considerations that need special attention when teaching about transgender oppression. For example, one issue especially important to recognize is the inherent limitation of language. Even while new terms, expressions, and identities constantly evolve, we are at the same time limited by the existing language available at this moment. Further, despite the rapid evolution of terms among transgender communities, their adoption and recognition outside those communities are much slower.

It is important to value and recognize individuals' identities, regardless of whether or not they correspond with facilitators' or participants' understanding of "male," "female," "masculine," "feminine," or "transgender." For example, an individual may identify as "masculine," and at the same time reject the qualities we culturally associate with masculinity. Questioning how someone constructs their sense of self is disrespectful. Facilitators should provide opportunities for participants to ask questions, but not allow participants to challenge an individual's right to self-definition. Questions about an individual's identity should always be asked with the intent of understanding, not challenging. Respecting a transgender-identified person's freedom to explore an identity is one way that communities can support gender freedom for all people.

As a corollary, it is vital to respect and use individuals' preferred pronouns. Doing so demonstrates respect for the individual's experience and sense of self. Facilitators can model this behavior by identifying themselves and their preferred pronouns at the beginning of the workshop. Facilitators can also model the respectful use of participants' preferred names and pronouns.

## Guiding Assumptions

We believe it is important to provide participants with some guiding assumptions about how the facilitators are approaching the material. We recommend relaying the following assumptions as a start.

1. Sex, gender, and sexual orientation are separate though interconnected identities.
2. The binary gender system is limiting to all people (not just transgender-identified and intersex individuals).
3. Transgender experience exists in relation to cultural constructions of gender. In other words, we cannot understand transgender without also understanding the sex/gender system.
4. Although gender is socially constructed, the experiences of it are very real.
5. Language is limiting, but we are nevertheless dependent on it.
6. Everyone is an expert on hir, his, or her own identity, and has the right to self-definition.
7. There is a diversity of transgender identities, and those identities are always evolving and changing.
8. All transgender identities are valid transgender identities. No transgender identity (e.g., transsexual, transgender, or genderqueer) is "more transgender" or more "really transgender" than other identities, and no transgender expression is "more authentic" than another. Rather, they are different ways of transgressing gender.
9. Not everyone who identifies as transgender wants or intends to transition physically to a different sex.

10. Not every transgender person is an expert on gender theory or gender oppression; not every transgender person is a gender radical or activist.
11. The problem with gender oppression is the *oppression*, not the transgender people.
12. There is no end to learning about transgender experiences.

## Cautions about Common Forms of Resistance

There are particular reactions that commonly arise in transgender oppression courses. We articulate these below so that facilitators can consider them and be prepared to respond.

1. Disgust: Some participants may react to the idea of transgender as offensive or as a personal affront. They may express a view that transgender is grotesque or disgusting, or may reject information about bodies, sex, or other aspects of transgender experience that they see as "personal." Establishing respectful norms and guidelines at the beginning of the course will help facilitators enforce respectful attitudes and open minds.
2. Fetishizing: Participants who fetishize transgender people may overly sexualize transgender people, ask inappropriate questions, and unduly focus on gender expression or sexuality even when it is peripheral to the topic at hand. Encourage transgender participants to set boundaries about what they are willing to discuss. Set ground rules about discussions of sexuality in the course.
3. Sensationalizing/objectifying: Because of the corporeal nature of transsexuality, some participants may objectify transgender bodies. Do not let participants treat transgender experience like a specimen under a glass. Participants can get caught up in the details of transgender experiences (which may not necessarily illustrate the experience of oppression). Draw their attention back to the topic at hand: oppression.
4. Romanticizing/pitying: Some participants may romanticize the experience of being transgender by focusing on their stereotype of transgender people as being radical, embattled, spiritual, or liberated. Most transgender-identified people want agents of transgender oppression to recognize both the privilege that accompanies conforming to gender norms and the institutional and cultural oppression of transgender oppression, and not to feel bad for them because of their difference. Remind participants that people who experience transgender oppression are not victims, or "special," but whole human beings. Transgender oppression is one part of their experience.
5. Dismissal/postmodern dismissal: Some participants may embrace the concept of the social construction of gender and therefore conclude that "everyone is transgender." For example, a woman who wears baggy jeans may claim that doing so is transgressing gender and that she therefore experiences transgender oppression. Or, one might say, "If gender is a social construction, then why do you need to change your body?" These responses overapply the idea that everyone is impacted by transgender oppression, and uses queer theory and gender theory against transgender people, disregarding the difficult choices that transgender people face in trying to express a transgender identity in a social system that does not acknowledge

that possibility. Remind participants that oppression is systematic and cultural, not merely individual.

## Transgender Oppression Curriculum Design

### Overall Goals

- To increase understanding of gender as a social construction and as learned behavior
- To explore the diversity of gender identities and expressions
- To identify ways in which transgender oppression affects people on the personal, cultural, and institutional levels
- To draw conceptual and practical connections among transgender oppression, heterosexism, and sexism, and also other forms of oppression
- To envision a world without transgender oppression and to develop skills to work for gender liberation in our personal, academic, and professional lives

### Overview of Modules

Note to readers: The curriculum design in this chapter is based on the assumption that participants have completed the introductory module(s) described in Chapter 3 prior to beginning this design and have a basic understanding of the conceptual framework of oppression described in Chapter 3. See Table 10.1 for an overview of this chapter's modules.

**Table 10.1**   Overview of Modules: Transgender Oppression

| Module 1: Personal Gender Reflection Theme (2 hours, 40 minutes) | Module 2: Language and Transgender Experience Themes (4 hours, 15 minutes) |
|---|---|
| 1. Introductions (15 min.) | 1. Opening (10 min.) |
| 2. Agenda, Goals (10 min.) | 2. Genderbread Cookie (30 min.) |
| 3. Developing Group Guidelines (15 min.) | 3. Terminology (45 min.) |
| 4. Icebreaker: Five Things You Did This Morning (15 min.) | 4. History Presentation (30 min.) |
| 5. Early Learnings About Gender Conformity (60 min.) | 5. Bringing Transgender Voices Into the Room (105 min.) |
| 6. "Walk Like a Man/Walk Like a Woman" (45 min.) | 6. Closing, Feedback, and Homework (15 min.) |

| Module 3: Transgender Oppression Theme (3 hours) | Module 4: Transgender Liberation Theme (3 hours, 55 minutes) |
|---|---|
| 1. Attending Activity (10 min.) | 1. Welcome Back, Agenda Review (10 min.) |
| 2. Welcome, Review Agenda (10 min.) | 2. Check-In (10 min.) |
| 3. Go Over Homework (30 min.) | 3. Envisioning: Free-Write (10 min.) |
| 4. Levels and Types of Transgender Oppression (40 min.) | 4. Envisioning: Collage Activity (60 min.) |
| 5. Drawing Connections (50 min.) | 5. Sharing Our Visions (30 min.) |
| 6. Some Privileges of Being Gender Conforming (30 min.) | 6. Action Planning: Individual Level (40 min.) |
| 7. Closing (10 min.) | 7. Action Planning: Broader Levels (40 min.) |
| | 8. Closing Activity (20 min.) |
| | 9. Feedback (15 min.) |

## Facilitation Issues

### Preparing for the Seminar: Creating a Welcoming Environment

It is always important to take stock of the physical environment before a seminar begins. Specifically, when teaching about transgender oppression, make sure there is a gender-neutral restroom nearby. (Ideally, it will be a single-stall restroom with no specific gender designation.) If there are no gender-neutral restrooms in the building, look into the possibility of relabeling one for the duration of the seminar. This accomplishes two purposes. First, if you have one or more participants who are transgender or otherwise gender nonconforming, they will have the option of using a restroom where they are unlikely to experience gender harassment. Second, it models for all participants one simple way to alleviate the effects of transgender oppression.

Decorating classrooms gives the room a cozy, informal feeling and may help to put participants at ease. One possibility is to put up art pieces that celebrate transgender people. (Print, video, and internet resources are listed in Appendix 10M.) During breaks, participants can congregate around pieces that interest them and discuss issues evoked by the art and/or the seminar.

It is also helpful to bring in books, videos, and other media resources. Set them up on a table or windowsill so that they are a visible presence throughout the seminar. Like the artwork, they can serve as conversation foci for participants during breaks. They also give participants an idea of the range of resources available to them.

## Module 1: Personal Gender Reflection Theme

Time needed: 2 hours, 40 minutes

### Objectives

- To get to know each other
- To begin thinking about gender as something we do
- To identify and think reflectively about our own genders
- To learn how gender is socially constructed
- To explore how gender is performative
- To generate in-depth, specific discussion about one example of a learned gendered behavior
- To explore how gender oppression hurts transgender and nontransgender people
- To identify some stereotypes about gender-variant people
- To reflect on our own socialization around gender and gender variance
- To notice how socialization minimizes the amount of gender variance that is expressed

**Key concepts:** gender role socialization (institutional, cultural, and individual), reinforcement of norms

### 1. Introductions (15 minutes)

As participants arrive for the first session, have a station set up for them to create nametags. The nametags should be preformatted with a space for the person's name and another space for the gendered pronoun they prefer to use for themselves.

Welcome participants and introduce yourselves by giving some background information about yourselves, including what motivates you to do social justice–oriented work generally, and transgender issues in particular.

Ask participants to share their names, pronouns, any other identifier that are helpful for facilitators and participants to know (e.g., class year, department, and job title), and what brings them to this class.

## Facilitation Issues

If you are transgender or otherwise gender nonconforming, consider carefully whether you will want to "come out" during your own personal introduction. By disclosing your gender identity and history casually and early on, you demonstrate that a transgender identity is simply a part of who you are, and not a cause for shame or secrecy. You also save yourself and the participants the potential embarrassment of having a participant misread your gender later on. On the other hand, deliberately leaving your gender expression open to participants' interpretation may help to make a point about the flexibility of gendered meaning, as well as to encourage participants to focus reflectively on their own gender, rather than yours, during this first module. In deciding whether and how to come out in your introduction, consider the purpose of your coming out both in terms of participants' learning and in terms of your own comfort and needs as a facilitator.

Whether or not you are transgender, use your own personal introduction to explain how you came to be involved in education around transgender issues, and your relationship, if any, to transgender communities. If there are transgender participants, it will be important for them to get a sense of you as a knowledgeable ally, so that they can feel comfortable participating fully and revealing their identities if they choose.

During introductions, you will be asking participants to indicate which gendered pronouns they prefer to be called during the seminar. Gendered pronouns are words like *he*, *she*, *him*, *her*, *his*, and *hers* that identify a person's gender even though gender is not necessarily central to the communication. In general, we use pronouns for people that "match" their gender identities—*he*, *him*, and *his* for men, and *she*, *her* and *hers* for women. Many transgender and other gender-nonconforming people have had the painful experience of being called a pronoun that doesn't match their gender identity, either because people mistakenly don't recognize their gender identity, or because people deliberately call them by the wrong pronoun. Additionally, some gender-nonconforming people use other pronouns, sometimes called *third-gender* or *gender-neutral* pronouns. There are several sets of third-gender pronouns currently in use in transgender communities. The most widely used are *ze* and *hir*, where *ze* sounds like "zee" and is analogous to *he/she*, and *hir* sounds like "hear" and is analogous to *him/her* and *his/hers*. Other people choose to use no pronouns at all, so when talking about such a person you would repeat that person's name several times throughout a sentence rather than using a pronoun.

Pronoun preference is something that many transgender people have to explain about themselves often (especially if they don't "pass" as their self-identified gender or if they use pronouns other than *he* or *she*), but most people who are not transgender have probably never been asked. We ask everyone to share their pronouns to normalize the process, and also to minimize the possibility of a participant "misgendering" another participant or the facilitator. Asking participants to explicitly state their preferred gender may trigger mild confusion and even embarrassment for some. One likely response is that participants who are not transgender may joke about it or say, "Isn't it obvious?" By insisting that it is not obvious, facilitators can begin to help participants rethink their assumptions about the links between internal identity and external gender expression. It is also useful to point out that participants are asked to identify their preferred pronoun for that day only. They are free to change their minds about all aspects of their gender expression, including their pronoun.

## 2. Agenda and Goals (10 minutes)

Briefly review the agenda for this module and for the course as a whole. Present the overall goals for the course. Inform participants that they will have an opportunity to share their own personal goals for the group and for themselves.

Pass out two self-stick notes to each participant, one in each of two colors. Ask them to write a goal they have for themselves for this course (e.g., a topic they want to learn more about, a skill they want to develop, or a question they want to have answered) on the first sticky note. On the other color, ask them to write a goal they have for the group as a whole. When everyone has finished, invite them to arrange their sticky notes together under the headings "Individual Goals" and "Group Goals" on a large sheet of paper posted on the wall. After they have taken their seats, ask a volunteer to read aloud all of the goals that have been posted. Wrap up this segment by connecting the participants' goals back to the overall goals and the agenda, and explaining how you hope to meet some of the goals throughout the course.

## 3. Developing Group Guidelines (15 minutes)

Ask the group to generate guidelines that will help them feel comfortable sharing and learning together. Record the guidelines on a sheet of newsprint that will remain visible throughout the course so that facilitators and participants may refer back to them as needed. Ask participants to clarify any guidelines as needed. (Refer to the introductory module in Chapter 3 for more information about specific guidelines.)

There are also some guidelines that are specifically useful when discussing issues related to transgender oppression. For example, it is important that everyone in the room make every effort to use individuals' preferred pronouns. In addition, if there are only one or two transgender people in the room, it will be important for facilitators and participants to be aware of not pigeonholing those transgender people into the role of resident experts, and to avoid asking inappropriate personal questions. If participants do not suggest guidelines to address these issues, facilitators should add them.

## 4. Icebreaker: Five Things You Did This Morning (15 minutes)

Inform participants that we will be doing a short, engaging activity to get us started.

Ask each participant to write on a piece of scrap paper five things they did to gender themselves before they left the house that morning. Give them 2 or 3 minutes to complete the task. Model the activity by saying something like the following: *When I got up this morning, I put on my fluffy bathroom slippers. I went into the bathroom and looked in the mirror and noticed how messy I look when I first wake up. Then I took a shower and I used shampoo that is marketed to women. When I got out of the shower, I wrapped a towel around my waist (not around my chest). I did not comb my hair because it's so short it does not need combing. I thought about putting on some eyeliner, but decided against it. Then I put on my deodorant, which is marketed to men. All this before I even got dressed!*

After participants have recorded their responses, ask them to form groups of three by joining with two other participants whom they do not know well. Ask them to introduce themselves and then share their lists. Give the groups about 5 minutes to share and discuss.

Ask for volunteers to report out any immediate thoughts or reactions in the large group.

Wrap up by pointing out that everyone carries out multiple gender-specific behaviors every day without even realizing it. These behaviors are learned (e.g., we are not born preferring men's shampoo to women's shampoo), and they take up a lot of our time.

At this point, participants have begun to think about the way that gender, both consciously and subconsciously, impacts their current lives. The next activity will continue their reflective thinking about how gender has previously shaped their self-understanding.

## 5. Early Learnings About Gender Conformity (60 minutes)

Inform participants that we are going to explore some of our early learnings about gender roles and gender conformity. Encourage them to consider gendered messages in the broadest terms. In addition to thinking about what it means to be a girl or a boy, they might reflect on messages they received about what it is to be feminine/masculine, ladylike/manly, weak/strong, and a mother/a father, as well as what it means to be well behaved, attractive, mature, or popular as a boy/girl.

Remind participants that although we all learn about gender and gender conformity as children, the specific messages that we receive will vary according to our cultural background, family situation, geographic context, and many other factors. For example, what it means to be a girl in a white, middle-class suburban family with a mom and a dad may be very different from what it means to be a girl in an African American community, or on a farm, or in a family headed by a single parent, by same-sex parents, or by more than two adults. By noticing and sharing these differences as well as experiences we may have in common, we can enrich our understanding of our own gendered experiences and of gender in general. At the same time, as we each learn about gender in our own particular contexts, we are also affected by the gender norms of the dominant culture as transmitted through media, schools, toys and games, and other people's assumptions about us. For some of us, the messages we received about gender from the dominant culture may have seemed to contradict the messages we received at home or in our own communities.

Ask participants to pair up with someone they do not know well. Give them about 20 minutes in these pairs to discuss the following prompts. (Some participants may benefit from having a few minutes to think or write before speaking.)

1. Describe the earliest time you remember being aware of your gender.
2. Describe a time as a child when you were told (explicitly or implicitly) that you should or should not do something because of your gender.
3. Describe the first time you remember being aware that someone else was doing something that stretched the boundaries of what was acceptable for them as a boy/man or girl/woman to do. What were they doing? What did you think or feel about it? How did you and others respond?
4. Describe a time when your own understanding of your gender or of what you should do as a boy/girl was in conflict with someone else's expectation. How did it feel to be in that situation? How do you make meaning of this situation in retrospect? Was the conflict related to other social identities such as race, class, sexual orientation, or age?

Bring participants back to the large group, and lead a discussion drawing on the conversations they had in pairs. Use these processing questions:

- What emotions came up as you identified early gendered memories?
- What came up that was new or surprising?
- Did any themes emerge within your pair?
- What did you learn from these early experiences about your own gender? About people who did not conform to gender expectations?
- Where do these messages come from?
- How have these early experiences affected how you do gender now? Is there anything that you do or do not do, because of your gender? Is there anything that you do, or do not do, in spite of your gender?
- Think back to the icebreaker. If you had been socialized as a boy rather than a girl, or as a girl rather than a boy, what might have been different about your morning behaviors? If you think your behaviors would be the same, how would it have been easier or more difficult for you to do that as a member of "the other" gender?

The previous two activities allow all participants to reflect on gender-role socialization. The next activity helps participants further understand how we express or perform our gender through an ordinary activity for many people: walking.

## 6. Walk Like a Man/Walk Like a Woman (45 minutes)

Divide the participants into groups of 8 to 10. The groups should disperse to separate rooms if possible, and each group will conduct the activity with its own facilitator. Depending on the demographics, mix the groups in terms of sex and gender to allow for differing perspectives.

In each group, ask for two volunteers to walk for the class. One volunteer should be female-bodied and woman-identified, and the other should be male-bodied and man-identified. Explain that the woman is going to walk "like a man" and the man is going to walk "like a woman." (They will walk one at a time.) The remaining participants in the group will "coach" the person walking. As coaches, they should call out instructions or suggestions to help the walkers improve their performance and be more believable in their gendered walk. For example, people might say, "Take smaller steps!" or "Hold your shoulders back more!" After about 5 minutes, or when the group is satisfied with the walker's performance, the first volunteer can rejoin the group and help to coach the second volunteer.

After the second volunteer has finished walking, give both "walkers" the opportunity to process their experience before continuing to the discussion of the activity. Ask the walkers:

- What was that experience like?
- What did you think and feel while you were walking?
- What were your reactions to some of the suggestions about how to change your gait?
- Is there anything else you want to share with the group?

Thank the walkers for their contributions. Then, lead a 30-minute discussion of the activity based on the following prompts:

- What were some of the coaching tips that were called out? How did it feel to coach someone with those suggestions?
- Do you think the person was initially believable in their gender walk? What about by the end? In what ways did the walker significantly change their style of walking?
- What does this activity tell you about how men and women are taught to walk?

- What, if anything, is the difference between a woman learning how to walk "like a man" and a boy learning how to walk "like a man"? Or, between a man learning how to walk "like a woman" and a girl learning to walk "like a woman"?
- How did you learn to walk? Were you ever made fun of or chastised for walking the "wrong" way? What did you think and feel about it at the time? What happened? What do you think and feel about it now?
- How did you learn these messages about how men and women are "supposed to" walk?
- What does this activity tell us about gender?

If you have divided the group, save a few minutes to come back to the large group and share a little about the groups' experiences with this activity before closing Module 1.

## Facilitation Issues

For this activity, it is especially important for the facilitator to explain the entire sequence of events before beginnng. Participants may be worried about expressing or reinforcing stereotypes. Assure them that the facilitators are aware that the coaching will be based largely on stereotypes. Even though we know that not all women walk "like a woman" and not all men walk "like a man," it is also true that many women and men do fit the norms about how men and women are "supposed to" walk. This activity will help us to investigate this particular example of a gendered behavior in order to explore how gender norms impact all of us.

If there are any transgender or gender-nonconforming participants in your group, we suggest you speak with them prior to the activity and encourage them not to volunteer, as the walker will be in the vulnerable position of having their gender performance under the direct, unapologetic scrutiny of the group. This may be a distressingly familiar dynamic for some transgender and gender-nonconforming people, and it is important to give them permission not to volunteer to subject themselves to this. Additionally, keep in mind that much of the data for the discussion of this activity come from what the coaches find themselves saying. Because many transgender people have practice at expressing gender in more than one way, they may not need much coaching, and so having a walker who already knows how to walk "like a man" or "like a woman" may lead to a less rich discussion. For the same reason, transgender people make excellent "coaches," especially if they have had to learn a specific gendered way of walking as part of a gender transition. Explain the purpose of the activity to transgender and gender-nonconforming participants, and tell them that you value their unique perspectives as coaches for this activity.

Processing the activity allows participants the opportunity to reflect on how they have learned and express their gender. It also allows them to think about how they "coach" other people on their gender. The focus of the activities has been to allow those participants who more closely conform to gender norms to realize that they too have constructed their gender. Remember, the point of reflection is meant to raise awareness, not guilt, and to realize that we are all affected by gender stereotypes and gender expectations/assumptions. At this point, the participants should be able to move toward learning about transgender identity, language, and experience.

To accommodate those with physical disabilities, this activity may be adapted to "Sit Like a Man/Sit Like a Woman." Just as we are taught to walk within particular gendered parameters, we are also taught to sit in particular ways, based on our assigned sex. Aside from sitting rather than walking, the activity is the same.

## Module 2: Language and Transgender Experience Themes

Time needed: 4 hours, 15 minutes

### Objectives

- To establish some common vocabulary with which to discuss transgender identities, experiences, and oppression
- To establish a conceptual separation among assigned sex, gender identity, gender expression, and sexual orientation
- To explore and understand how transgender people define themselves and experience being in the world
- To offer a framework for understanding a broad range of gender/sexuality experiences
- To provide some historical U.S. context for discussing contemporary transgender issues
- To identify the impact of transgender oppression on the everyday lives of a diverse group of transgender people

**Key concepts**: definitions, historical context

### 1. Opening (10 minutes)

Welcome participants back to the class. Summarize activities in Module 1. Invite participants to share with the large group any new thoughts or insights they have had. Briefly review the agenda for Module 2.

### 2. Genderbread Cookie (30 minutes)*

Materials required:

- Genderbread cookie handouts (Appendices 10B and 10C)
- Genderbread cookie graphic on newsprint

On newsprint, prepare a "genderbread cookie" similar to the one on the handout (Appendix 10B). This will serve as a visual focus for a short lecture based on the outline below. As the lecture proceeds, you will add additional terms and information to the diagram (Appendix 10C). The four lines on the diagram represent four dimensions of sexual/gender identity: biological sex/assigned sex, gender identity, gender expression, and sexual orientation.

For the first half of the lecture, define each of the four dimensions on the diagram, beginning at the top. For each term, explain the *usual* definition and how it is *usually* measured. Add the words for how it is usually quantified at the dots, as in Appendix 10C. Check for understanding. Note that the usual assumption is that we each fall into one column of terms or the other—either male/man/masculine/attracted to women, or female/woman/feminine/attracted to men. This represents the binary gender system. For detailed definitions and "scripts" for certain terms, use Appendix 10D.

Starting at the bottom, go back up the chart and complicate the binary gender system by noting the additional possibilities of (a) more than two categories on each dimension; (b) flexibility, or change in category over time; and (c) a person falling in different horizontal locations for different dimensions. Also note some of the ways in which the binary gender system is culturally specific. For example, some cultures understand there to be more

---

* The Genderbread Cookie is adapted from an activity by T.A. Hans & T. Sangrey (2001), in the Trans Activists Network Facilitators' Guide, as self-published material. Available as pdf on *www.riseconsulting.org*

than two genders, some cultures do not define sexual orientation in terms of gender at all, and cultures have varying definitions of masculinity and femininity. As you move up the diagram, for each axis ask participants to help you generate terms that might belong on that axis in between (or on either side of) the two "usual" possibilities. Examples of such terms are italicized in Appendix 10D. Add these to the diagram as in Appendix 10C. If participants request it, you can ask the group to define these additional terms. However, the main point here is to put all of the terms into a context of binary and nonbinary gender. There will be an opportunity later in Module 2 to further explore the terminology.

When you have finished these explanations, you can use the genderbread cookie as a graph to chart particular individuals' sexual/gender identities. You might chart the two facilitators as examples, and then ask for volunteers from among the participants. To chart a person, simply draw a dot (or more than one dot) on each dimension representing where that person falls on the scale. Then connect the dots.

## Facilitation Issues

The genderbread cookie presents a great deal of information all at once. It also contradicts the everyday assumptions about gender that most people unconsciously accept. For both reasons, it may be cognitively and emotionally difficult for participants to absorb all of the information. Assure participants that they need not immediately understand every term or idea in this model. Part of the point of this activity is to question what we think we know about gender, and so to feel confused is normal and even encouraged. The main point is that gender is much more complicated than we usually acknowledge, and many more possibilities exist than we usually account for.

If participants get caught up in details and want a complete explanation of every term that someone offers, the genderbread activity can easily run over time. If a term is totally unfamiliar to the majority of participants, you might give a brief explanation and move on. However, do not try to define everything. Instead, reassure participants that the purpose of this activity is to get an idea of the *range* of possibilities of sex, gender, gender identity, gender presentation, and sexual orientation. The next activity will focus on understanding specific terms in greater depth.

In particular, the idea of intersexuality may be new for most participants, and they might be very eager to know more. Because intersex issues are not the focus of this course, present some basic information such as that provided in the genderbread cookie outline, and then refer participants to additional sources (listed in Appendix 10M).

## 3. Terminology (45 minutes)

Materials needed:

- A set of posters or sheets of paper, each printed with some or all of the following terms: gender, genderqueer, transgender, transsexual, biological sex, medical model, passing, masculinity and femininity, Benjamin Standards, butch, femme, sexual orientation, intersex, queer, FtM, MtF, and any other terms you want to provide (see Appendix 10A for terms)
- A set of posters or pieces of paper, each printed with the definition of one of those terms
- Markers

In preparation for this activity, post the terms (without the definitions) around the room. Organize participants into groups of three or four, and distribute the definitions among the groups. Instruct participants to match their definitions to the terms. Each group should work together to agree on where the definitions go. When they find a match, have them post the definition on the wall next to the appropriate term. Give the groups about 20 minutes to complete this task.

When all the groups are finished, bring everyone back into one large group. Have a volunteer read each term aloud along with the definition that is matched to it. Check for understanding. If there is a question or disagreement about any of the matches or the definitions themselves, put it to the group for discussion. Correct any factual misunderstandings, while keeping in mind that the language of transgender identity and experience is constantly evolving and culturally specific. There may be more than one correct definition for a given term depending on participants' ages, geographic context, and the particular transgender communities or understandings of transgender identity they may be familiar with. Amend or elaborate on definitions as necessary.

## Processing Questions

Lead a discussion using the following processing questions:

1. Are there any terms or concepts that are still unclear?
2. Are there any terms or definitions that are missing?
3. There are many terms and concepts here. How does it feel to realize that sex and gender are much more complicated that you thought?

## Facilitation Issues

Depending on the knowledge level of the participants, you may wish to select fewer terms from our list, or you may wish to add your own. Because the vocabulary of transgender identities varies significantly by culture and context, it may be particularly useful to add culturally specific terms of relevance to the community in which the course is taking place. Keep blank paper on hand to put up terms that participants bring to the course.

## 4. History Presentation (30 minutes)

Materials needed:

- Timeline handout (Appendix 10E)
- Posted timeline (We recommend you create a large paper timeline based on the handout, and post it around the room. The visual impact of the length of transgender history, posted in the room, is much more effective than only reading the handout.)

Before this activity, post the timeline on the wall(s) in the room (based on Appendix 10E). Introduce the activity by explaining the importance of having a historical context for understanding transgender oppression. Ask the participants to form small groups and to walk their way through the timeline. Have one person in each group make notes of questions raised, suggested additions to the timeline, and common themes.

## Facilitation Issues

Participants may be particularly interested to learn about notable regional history. We recommend that you identify local transgender groups and local resources available to transgender people.

## Processing Questions

Have each group discuss the following questions, and then facilitate a large group discussion on their answers.

1. What are some common themes among the events listed in the timeline?
2. What events seem particularly significant or momentous?
3. In what ways do you think individual transgender people might have been affected by these events?
4. How did this information corroborate or contradict your previous knowledge of transgender history?
5. What are questions that you are left with after this activity?

The timeline presents historical information about the significance of transgender identity within U.S. culture. The following activity provides the participants a glimpse into the contemporary lives of transgender people.

## 5. Bringing Transgender Voices Into the Room (105 minutes)

### Option A: Panel

(If convening a panel is not feasible, consider Option B presented in Appendix 10F.)

Invite a panel of transgender people and allies of the transgender community to share how they understand their own gender identity and expression, and talk about their experiences. You might locate speakers through a local LGBT speakers' bureau or transgender organization. Remuneration is appropriate, if available.

Try to get a diverse range of experiences on the panel. For example, a panel with diversity of race, culture, class background, ability, sexual orientation, and religious background is ideal. Age is another important factor, because there have been significant generational shifts in transgender peoples' experiences and self-understanding. It is also vital to have a wide range of gender diversity. If some of your panelists are female to male (FtM), make sure that others are male to female (MtF). If some of your panelists are undergoing medical transition, make sure to have other panelists who choose not to (or who are not able to). If some of your panelists identify as cross-dressers, make sure to invite others who identify as transsexual, transgender, or genderqueer. Consider inviting people who do not identify as transgender, but who do transgress gender norms significantly in their everyday lives. Partners, family members, and other close allies of transgender people can also make valuable contributions to such panels.

Give panelists information about the participants and the course prior to the panel. Offer guidelines ahead of time, including information about how long you want them to speak and the topics they might address. Inform them about who else will be on the panel. Ask them to focus on their personal experiences, with specific emphasis on the everyday realities of living as a transgender person (or however they identify), or as an ally. Assure panelists that they can choose what to share or not share and that their stories will be kept confidential. Plan for the panelists to speak for about 30 minutes total. Depending on the size of the panel, each panelist will have about 5 to 10 minutes.

### Introducing the Panel

Greet the panelists and thank them for their participation. Explain to participants that the panelists have been asked to speak about their personal experiences. Let them know that the panelists will speak for about 30 minutes total, and then take questions for about 30 minutes. Take a moment to remind participants about the guidelines established during Module 1, especially the policy about confidentiality. Inform them that participants are welcome to ask any question, but that panelists will decide whether or not to answer.

To encourage participants to ask thoughtful questions, hand out index cards before the panel begins. Have them write down any questions that may arise during the panel. When the panelists are finished speaking, collect the index cards. Encourage participants to ask their questions verbally. If the group seems reluctant to ask questions, or if you notice that there are questions on the cards that are not being asked aloud, read aloud some of the questions from the cards. After about 30 to 45 minutes, bring the question-and-answer session to a close.

After the panel, take a break. This gives you time to thank the panelists, and offers an opportunity for participants who were too shy to ask a question in the large group to approach panelists one-on-one.

### Processing

Take 30 minutes to process the panel with the participants after the panelists have left. You may choose to process in a large group or in smaller groups. If many participants seem to be having a strong emotional reaction to the panel, consider starting the discussion in small groups. If they have many factual questions, consider staying in the large group so that you can clarify any misunderstandings. If you do use small groups, be sure to bring the large group together for a few minutes at the end of the processing time. Use the following processing questions to start the conversation:

- What thoughts and feelings came up for you during the panel?
- What surprised you about the panelists' stories? About your own reactions?
- Was there anything that the panelists said that made you uncomfortable?
- Were there any questions that you wanted to ask but didn't? Why?
- How were the experiences the panel described similar to each other? How were they different?
- What voices or perspectives were missing from the panel? (For example, think of transition status and direction, different identities within the transgender spectrum, sexuality, age, race, ethnicity, class background and current class status, educational background, religion, ability, and so on.)

### 6. Closing, Feedback, and Homework (15 minutes)

Do a 5-minute closing round in which participants share their response to the following: What is one new piece of information or new idea that you learned today? What is one thing you are still thinking about?

On index cards, ask participants to write down feedback to hand in to you anonymously: What is one activity that worked well for you? Why? What is one aspect of this module that could be improved? How?

Appendix 10G lists several possible homework assignments. Select one option, or create your own. Distribute the homework assignment. Ask participants to think about their new awareness about transgender identities as they complete the homework.

### Module 3: Transgender Oppression Theme

Time needed: 3 hours

### Objectives

- To help participants link their observations with examples of transgender oppression
- To identify specific examples of transgender oppression
- To organize these examples into levels and types of oppression

- To identify how individuals, institutions, and cultures perpetrate forms of oppression against transgender people(s)
- To explore how gender-conforming individuals identify and acknowledge their privilege
- To describe how transgender oppression may interact with other forms of oppression in the lives of transgender or gender-conforming people

**Key concepts**: oppression, privilege, collusion, internalization

### 1. Attending Activity (10 minutes)

Choose an activity to bring the group's attention back to the topic of transgender oppression. (See Appendix 10H for one example.)

### 2. Welcome, Review Agenda (10 minutes)

Welcome participants back to the class, and review the agenda for the module.

Summarize the information from the feedback participants provided at the end of Module 2, and explain how you took it into account in preparing for Module 3.

### 3. Go Over Homework (30 minutes)

Post the homework assignment where everyone can see it. Have participants gather in groups of three to four. Explain that they will have 15 minutes to discuss their experiences of completing the homework. Urge participants to focus specifically on what actually happened and what they felt and thought at the time. Inform them that they will have an opportunity afterward to reflect on their experiences.

After 15 minutes, explain that the group will begin to make sense of their experiences in terms of three levels of transgender oppression: individual, cultural, and institutional. Distribute worksheets to each group with columns labeled "Individual," "Cultural," "Institutional," and "?" (Appendix 10I). Based on what they have shared with each other about their homework, have participants fill in examples of transgender oppression for each of the three levels. In the fourth column, they can record any aspects of their experience about which they have questions.

### Processing Questions

- What was challenging about this assignment?
- What information did you find that was unexpected/surprising? How so?
- Did you discuss this assignment with anyone outside of the class? If so, what was the reaction?

The participants have begun to share out their information in smaller groups, and the next activity will bring the learning to the larger group to help enhance everyone's knowledge of transgender oppression.

### 4. Levels and Types of Transgender Oppression (40 minutes)

Bring participants' attention back to the large group. Post a chart that is similar to the one in Appendix 10I. Ask for volunteers from each of the small groups from the previous activity to report out some of their examples for each level, and record those examples on the chart. Invite participants to add other examples from their homework, from previous modules, or from their own experience or imagination. For items that participants recorded in their "?" columns, ask the group to help decide how to categorize them.

Use Appendix 10J to have some examples of levels and types of transgender oppression, to help start the discussion. Depending on the knowledge base among your participants, you also may decide to distinguish between conscious and unconscious types of oppression, as well as individual, institutional, and cultural (see Chapter 3).

### Processing Questions

1. How did it feel to organize the information into the "Types of Oppression" categories?
2. How do these forms of oppression make clear the forms of privilege that gender-conforming people benefit from?
3. What are some ways in which you have been unconsciously colluding with privilege or internalized oppression based on this information?

### 5. Drawing Connections (50 minutes)

In groups of five or six, ask participants to discuss the connections they see among transgender oppression and other forms of oppression. If the participants have completed readings (such as books or internet resources cited in Appendix 10M), urge them to utilize the readings during this discussion, and provide them with some quotations from what they have read that may highlight interconnections. Otherwise, provide specific situations or contexts to prompt discussion. See Appendix 10K for examples of situations to provoke discussion.

### Processing Questions

1. How do multiple identities impact transgender oppression?
2. What are the ways in which transgender oppression impacts other social identities?
3. What are some connections among different forms of oppression?
4. What are some distinctions among different forms of oppression?

At this point, participants have identified many ways that transgender oppression manifests itself in the lives of transgender people. The next activity will focus on the ways in which nontransgender participants collude with and receive gender privilege.

### 6. Some Privileges of Being Gender Conforming (30 minutes)

Based on their experiences in Modules 1–3, ask participants who identify as gender conforming to write down at least two ways in which they experience privilege because of gender identity and expression. (Possibilities for gender nonconforming participants are noted below.) Then ask gender conforming participants to gather in groups of four to share their examples and record their collective lists on newsprint. After about 15 minutes, bring participants' attention back to the large group and have them report out their lists. Some examples of privilege are as follows:

- I can use the restroom in public spaces without fear that I will be asked if I am in the right location or responses of violence.
- I can apply for jobs without having to worry about my gender identity.
- I can adopt a child without worry that my gender identity will make me ineligible.
- I can use my driver's license or other forms of identification because the gender listed on my license matches my current gender.
- I can feel confident that I will be addressed by my preferred pronoun by sales clerks or strangers.

- I can refer to my past without changing my pronouns.

## Processing Questions

- Was it difficult to come up with privileges? Why or why not?
- What were some privileges that you had not considered as such prior to this activity?
- What were some privileges that you had realized and may have worked toward challenging?

## Facilitation Issues

If you have one or more participants who are transgender, they may choose to use this time in various ways. They might want to help the gender-conforming groups come up with examples of gender privilege. Or, they might want to gather in a different space to generate their own list of privileges, or to continue processing the earlier activities. They might choose to generate a list of things they love about being transgender, which they can share with the large group.

The process of examining privilege and oppression is often difficult for participants. Participants' feelings of guilt or denial may make it difficult for them to identify gender privilege, and it is important to remind them that awareness is the first step toward liberation. The next module will allow them to begin to take steps to change how oppression and privilege impact their lives.

## 7. Closing (10 minutes)

Acknowledge participants' efforts to stay engaged through the module. Thank them for their attention, and remind them that the next module will focus on liberation/action for social change.

Ask participants to jot down their responses to the following prompts:

1. What feelings came up for you during this activity?
2. What is one idea that is sticking with you or one question you still have from this module?
3. What is one idea, thought, or hope that you want to carry with you into the last module?

After a few minutes, ask for volunteers to share their responses with the large group.

## Module 4: Transgender Liberation Theme

Time needed: 3 hours, 55 minutes

### Objectives

- To engage our imagination and creativity in envisioning a world without transgender oppression
- To help participants move toward liberation
- To help participants move toward taking action against transgender oppression
- To develop specific and realistic action plans for working against transgender oppression on the individual level
- To help participants focus on individual learning goals and to continue their education on transgender identity and oppression

- To help participants focus on group work that will help challenge transgender oppression

**Key concepts**: liberation, activism, social change, individual learning goals, collective action

### 1. Welcome Back, Agenda Review (10 minutes)

Welcome participants back for the last module of the course. Briefly review the agenda for Module 4.

### 2. Check-In (10 minutes)

Invite each participant to comment on their thoughts and feelings moving into this last module. For example, they might talk about thoughts, feelings, or questions left over from Module 3; something that came up outside of class; or what they are looking forward to in Module 4.

### 3. Envisioning: Free-Write (10 minutes)

Explain that we will spend time in this module thinking about our visions of a world free of transgender oppression. To start, invite participants to take 10 minutes to write a description of their ideal world without transgender oppression. Emphasize that it is okay if they do not have a clear vision. Inform participants that this writing is private; they will not be asked to share it.

### 4. Envisioning: Collage Activity (60 minutes)

Materials required:

- Collage materials: construction paper, scissors, glue, diverse magazines to cut up, glitter, string, markers, crayons, any other available art supplies
- Stickers

Invite participants to gather in small groups of their choosing. Give each small group a set of collage materials. Explain that each participant will make a collage individually, based on their own personal vision of a world free of transgender oppression. However, urge them to interact with each other while working on their collages, noticing the similarities and differences, and discussing any part of their visioning free-write that they might want to share.

Because participants are often reluctant to finish their collages, give several time-checks after 30 minutes, 45 minutes, and 55 minutes. Remind participants that they may continue working on their collages after they go home. It is acceptable to share a work that is still "in progress."

### 5. Sharing Our Visions (30 minutes)

Have participants post their collages around the room. Make sure that every collage is labeled with a participant's name. Provide participants with stickers (e.g., gold stars) that they may choose to affix to their collage to indicate that they are willing to answer questions from others about their collage and their vision. Give participants 30 minutes to mingle, view others' collages, and ask willing participants questions about their vision.

**Processing Questions**

1. What images did you look for to create your collage?
2. What ideas did you feel were important to put on your collage?
3. What did you feel were the limitations in creating this collage?

4. What do you feel are the goals that you would like to highlight for the group?

The next activity will allow participants to write out goals that go beyond the broad notion of liberation into attainable actions that are suited to each participant's desired outcome(s).

## 6. Action Planning: Individual Level (40 minutes)

Remind participants about the levels and types of transgender oppression. Inform them that this activity focuses on the individual level. Provide a worksheet (Appendix 10L – Part 1) for each participant with the following prompts:

1. What have I learned about transgender oppression during this course? (New learnings might include information, ideas, feelings, skills and behaviors.)
2. What questions do I still have about transgender oppression?
3. What specific steps can I take to continue to educate myself?
4. What, specifically, would I like to do to work against transgender oppression on an individual level?
5. What barriers (internal, external) prevent me from doing those things?
6. What can I do to overcome these barriers?

Give participants 10 minutes to fill out the worksheets individually. Then invite them to partner with someone and share their responses. Pairs can help each other develop ideas for questions 3, 4, and 6.

For the last 15 minutes, invite anyone who wishes to share their action plans (including how they will overcome any barriers).

## 7. Action Planning: Broader Levels (40 minutes)

In preparation for this activity, prepare a list of relevant contexts for participants (for example, "in this school," "in my dorm," "in my workplace," "in this organization," or "in my family").

Explain that participants will gather in groups of four to think about how to address transgender oppression in a specific context. Present the list of contexts you have prepared, and invite participants to add any additional contexts. Take a quick poll by asking for a show of hands of people who would be interested in working on each context on the extended list. Then allow participants to form groups based on the context they want to discuss.

Provide a worksheet ( Appendix 10L – Part 2) with the following prompts:

1. What would we like to do to work against transgender oppression on individual, cultural, and institutional levels in _____ (a specific context)?
2. What barriers may prevent us from achieving what we want to achieve? Consider individual barriers (e.g., individuals' attitudes, beliefs, and skills), cultural barriers (e.g., broadly accepted stereotypes, norms about how change happens in this context), and institutional barriers (e.g., policies, power structure).
3. What specific steps can we take to overcome these barriers?

Give small groups about 20 minutes to fill in the worksheet as a group. Encourage them to be very specific. Then invite each small group to present their ideas to the large group.

Provide participants with a copy of Appendix 10M for additional print, Internet, and film resources addressing transgender oppression, for further learning.

## 8. Closing Activity (20 minutes)

Gather in a large circle. Encourage every participant to share a thought or feeling that they are taking with them from the course. Then, ask participants to express an appreciation of another participant or of the group as a whole. For example, people might appreciate something someone said that helped them to understand an issue better, or a risk that someone took, or a positive impact that someone had on the group's dynamic. The facilitators should also participate in this process.

## 9. Feedback (15 minutes)

Collect written feedback about the course (see Appendix 9J for a model).

# Overview

*Religious Oppression*

MAURIANNE ADAMS

It may seem counterintuitive to use the term *oppression* in conjunction with the role of *religion* in society, given that *religion* is generally understood to be a basis for social morality and the opposite of what is implied by *oppression*. Discussions of religion evoke deeply held and publicly sanctioned beliefs and experiences, including matters of doctrinal faith that transcend the mundane concerns of the political domain. But *oppression* is precisely the word we need for the inquiry pursued in the next two chapters, where we explore how religion can be and has been used to maintain cultural and political domination and subordination.

Throughout this volume, the term *oppression* is used to refer to social structures, policies, and practices that maintain systemic domination and subordination, "the everyday practices of a well-intentioned liberal society" (Young, 1990a, p. 41). We do not use traditional or popular meanings of oppression (such as a ruler's tyrannical rule or a nation's conquest and colonial domination of other peoples), although "oppression" as conquest or domination does convey the erasure of Native American Indian and African religious traditions under U.S. federal or state jurisdictions (Spring, 2007). Oppression is "structural" and "systemic," and usually operates under the radar because it is part of an unequal society's "unquestioned norms, habits, and symbols"; its "normal processes of everyday life"; and its "assumptions underlying institutional rules and the collective consequences of following those rules" (Young, 1990a, p. 41).

The discussions of various historical and contemporary manifestations of religious oppression in Chapters 11 and 12 focus upon what religion "does" rather than what religion "is." We take a sociological and historical approach to the dynamics of domination and subordination, power and powerlessness, and advantage and disadvantage within social systems that are interwoven with religious beliefs and practices. Because of the special challenges intrinsic to this topic, it is useful to start by describing this sociological approach to religion before moving on with an inquiry into how religious institutions and culture interact with other social systems in the maintenance of power and privilege, domination and subordination.

## Historical and Sociological Approach to Religion

The role of religion in society—and thus in domestic as well as international conflicts—is a subject for historical and sociological inquiry that is completely separate from questions of theology or religious belief (see Dillon, 2003; Ebaugh & Chafetz, 2000; Fox, 2002; Johnstone, 2004; Warner & Wittner, 1998). The approach taken in these next two chapters is historical and sociological, not theological. We present numerous historical examples of religion being used to establish and maintain political, social, and cultural dominance, and use historical legacies to analyze contemporary religious oppression. We thus analyze the *social* role of religion, its position of relative persuasive power in *social institutions and systems*, and the *historical* reproduction of dominant national religious identity through hegemonic religious culture. We do not discuss or compare religious or theological beliefs or affiliations.

The sociological approach to religion (Fox, 2002; Johnstone, 2004) suggests that religion serves several social purposes, such as (a) a framework for understanding the meaning and direction of human existence, (b) rules and standards of behavior that link individual and social behaviors to this framework, (c) authority from an external source that is believed to be divine and/or universal, (d) connections among individuals or groups of individuals and a greater whole, (e) formal institutional structures that claim to represent the greater whole, and (f) legitimacy for actions taken by individuals, groups, or nations. These six frameworks (Fox, 2002, pp. 11–21) help illuminate our analyses of the histories and social dynamics of religious oppression in Chapters 11 and 12.

## Role of Religion in Global and Domestic Conflicts

Global, international, nationalist, and domestic U.S. conflicts are often posed in religious terms as theological clashes of good versus evil, such as the World War II struggle between democracy and fascism, the Cold War struggle between capitalism and the forces of so-called godless Communism, and the post-9/11 political, cultural, and theological "war against terrorism" waged by the United States and Europe (along with allied Middle Eastern and South Asian states) against "Islamic militants," "radical Islam," and "Islamic terrorists." "Clash of civilizations" is a popular phrase that simplifies the political, cultural, and ideological sources of the current conflict between militants who claim extreme Islamic ideologies and global, financial networks affiliated with the West (Huntington, 1993, 1996).

The recent popular and journalistic conflation of terrorism with Islam makes it especially urgent to disentangle the *religious* dimensions of these conflicts and hostilities from dimensions that are largely political, ideological, or cultural. We need to understand how religious motives and justifications are used in the service of cultural, ethnic, racial, and class antagonisms. This point has been captured in the aphorism "It is not so much that religion has become politicized, but that politics have been religionized" (Juergensmeyer, 2004, p. 2).

Our decision to examine *religious oppression* in this way grows out of our efforts, during the past 10 years, to understand the many domestic as well as international conflicts that draw upon explicit religious justifications for popular support. At the same time, it has become clear during the past decade that religion interacts in important ways with ethnicity, class, gender, and nationalism, and that we must consider the interactions of various dimensions of social identity (religion, ethnicity and ethnocentrism, racial formation and racism, and class positions and conflicts) that had previously been considered in an either/or analysis that isolated one at the expense of the other. Our approach requires us to complicate our understanding of the intersections among *race*, *ethnicity*, *class*, and *religion* rather than analyze them as separate social categories.

Current examples of "religionized" domestic U.S. politics abound. They include bitter conflicts over competing end-of-life and beginning-of-life issues (such as euthanasia and stem cell research), competing rights such as "the right to decide" versus "the right to life," and the authority of local school boards to substitute creationism or intelligent design for evolution in science curricula. "Religionized" U.S. political issues also include legal and constitutional struggles to extend or prohibit gay marriage, or to extend or prohibit school prayer. Domestic struggles such as these can be seen as manifestations of historical political debates concerning the authority of religion in public life. This recurrent source of contention flares up into public view when citizens contest civic religious displays (at Christmas or Easter), the use of tax-funded vouchers for private religious schools, or the funding of faith-based initiatives as a substitute for increased public services.

These struggles, often played out in political arenas, can be understood as efforts to enshrine (as well as resist) explicit denominational views of the dominant religion as a template for public policy. Rather than "culture wars" merely, these political conflicts also enact conflicts among religious perspectives (in some cases, between religious fundamentalisms)[1] that are opposed not only to each other but also to the alternatives of religious pluralism or secularism in civic life (Grew, 1997; Wuthnow, 2005). These conflicts are often carried out in the name of a single religious group's commitment to its own universal, unitary, and religiously "correct" understanding of morality and conduct, as against the interdenominational or nonsectarian assumption that a religiously diverse citizenship is better served by religious pluralism or by secularism in the civic arena. According to these two alternative viewpoints—the one endorsing religious pluralism, and the other preferring a secular political consensus—the political or cultural domination by any one religious perspective at the expense of others, or over the right of others to not claim a religious affiliation, threatens the civil rights and democratic aspirations of all citizens. No single religious or nonreligious belief or observance can be more or less free than the others. This view raises complex as well as contentious political issues, and scholars and historians have tended to shy away from them, except in examination of the First Amendment or civil rights constitutional questions that we discuss in Chapter 11.

## A Social Justice Approach to Religious Oppression

In light of the frameworks and conflicts noted above, it is important to consider some of the ways religion has been used to maintain, justify, and reproduce patterns of domination and subordination—as well as the role of religion on behalf of antioppression and social justice movements. This approach examines the ideological use of religious rationales to enforce (or contest) the maintenance of social and institutional power. It also explores the interaction of religion with national identity and the ways in which religious groups are admitted to or denied access to the benefits of public life (such as citizenship, housing, health care, schooling, political representation, and the protection of law).

Chapter 11 examines the ways in which Christian sectarianism combined with U.S. military and political power to restrict Native American Indian and African religious practices in the colonial period, and the practices of Hindus and Muslims in the modern period. These interactions on American soil were rooted in older religious conflicts imported from Europe, Asia, and Africa. What became the dominant form of Protestant Christianity was derived from belief systems that colonists, settlers, and immigrants from Europe took to be superior to the oral religious traditions of the Americas or Africa and, later, to the Buddhist, Hindu, Jewish, and Muslim religious traditions brought into the United States by non-Christian immigrants (Carroll, 2000; Min & Kim, 2002; Wills, 2002; Wuthnow, 2005).

Chapter 12 explores the oppression of Jews in the historical context of medieval and modern Christian Europe, with global ramifications extending to North African and Arab Islamic countries as well as the United States. Chapters 11 and 12 address the conflation of religion with racial difference as a way of isolating and delegitimating the "Other" (Jews among Aryan Europeans, and Native American Indians, African Blacks, Asians, and Arabs living within the white-dominated United States). The conflation of race and racism with religious oppression builds upon concepts of *racialization* and *racial formation* to convey "the extension of racial meaning to a previously racially unclassified relationship, social practice or group" (Omi & Winant, 1986, p. 64). In other words, the extension of *racial* (for example, Arab or South Asian) meanings affects communities who identify themselves primarily as *religious* (for example, Christian or Muslim, Hindu or Sikh).

Chapters 11 and 12 are linked not only by the antioppression conceptual frameworks and the interactions of religion with ethnicity and culture, race and class. They are also linked by similar historical experiences of forced conversion, territorial expulsion, and physical and cultural extermination. These patterns can be mapped onto the phenomenon of antisemitism in Christian Europe and the experiences of Native American Indians, Buddhist and Confucian Japanese, and South Asian or Arab Muslims in the Christian United States.

## Ethnocentrism and Ethnoreligious Oppression

The phenomena identified above as *racialization* and *racial formation* are closely linked to *ethnocentrism,* a term used to convey the cultural domination of a specific ethnic (often majority) group in a larger national context (see discussion in Chapters 3 and 7). The literature associated with ethnocentrism and racism sheds light on our analysis here of religious oppression (Fox, 2002; Fredrickson, 2002; Goldschmidt & McAlister, 2004). This literature also uses the term *ethnoreligious* to suggest the "intertwined and mutually reinforcing" symbiosis between racial and ethnic attributions and religion, whereby religion is used to justify and mobilize ethnic aspirations, and ethnicity is seen as a "birthplace of religions" (Fox, 2002, p. 26; MacDonald-Dennis, 2006). In this sense, the term *ethnoreligious* conveys the coexistence of multiple identity categories—religion, ethnicity, race, and culture.

However, in Chapters 11 and 12, we take the position that the term *ethnoreligious* conceals rather than illuminates the *religious* dimensions of global and domestic religious oppression. The term *ethnoreligious* emphasizes the ethnic and cultural dimensions of adherence to Buddhism, Hinduism, Islam, and Judaism within a U.S. context and, in our view, diminishes their self-identity as *religious* communities as well as obscures their specific experiences of religious oppression. Minority religious communities in the United States, such as Catholics, Jews, or Muslims, are represented in contradictory ways by the majority culture—sometimes as religious, sometimes as ethnic, and sometimes in terms of national origins or assumed divided loyalties as "Papists," "Zionists," or "terrorists." The tendency to grossly oversimplify the religious as well as the ethnic or racial Other is reinforced by the practice of the U.S. Census, and some workplace and educational bureaucracies, that list mutually exclusive or check-one "boxes" for race, ethnic, and linguistic self-identification.

## Theorizing Religious Oppression

The systemic approach to religious oppression taken in the next two chapters sheds light on the historical legacies as well as the contemporary manifestations of religious oppression as it operates throughout the "normal processes of everyday life." We draw upon Young's "five faces of oppression"—exploitation, marginalization, powerlessness, cultural imperialism, and violence (1990a, p. 40)—to establish clear analytic frameworks for everyday injustices experienced by religious minorities in the United States. These "faces" or dimensions of oppression identify the obstacles that prevent minority religious communities from partaking fully in the opportunities of American life unless they deny or hide the visible symbols of their religious affiliations.

Another conceptual framework used throughout this volume and in the next two chapters derives from Hardiman and Jackson's account of the dynamics of oppression at various levels of social interaction—the individual/interpersonal, the institutional, and the cultural/societal (Chapter 3). In the curriculum designs in Chapters 11 and 12, we incorporate examples of individual, institutional, and cultural religious oppression in the U.S. legal system, in public schools and universities, and in the workplace.

## Integration And Interactions Of Religion With Other Social Categories

Religious difference suffuses some of the most intractable global, regional, ethnic, national, and domestic conflicts and generates intensity, partisanship, and sectarian solidarity, often sanctified by a particularistic view of a group's divine election. It is challenging to try to disentangle religion from other dimensions of a group's social identity and cohesion, or in its conflicts with other groups, in order to ask, How much is religion? How much is culture or ethnicity or race or economic class or national aspiration? In these chapters, we focus upon religion as one among several core ingredients in group identity and group conflict, and note that although its role in international or nationalist conflicts such as in the Middle East, the Balkans, and Kashmir is generally acknowledged, its significance within distinctive U.S. regional identities, historical periods, social movements, and conflicts is often underestimated.

This approach to religious oppression appreciates the "co-constitutive relationships" that link religion to the other social categories considered elsewhere in this volume—religion *and* race *and* ethnicity *and* economic class—*and* nationalism, this last a phenomenon that has had severe consequences for the religiously identified "Other" and national "outsider" (Marty & Appleby, 1997). This approach juxtaposes as figure and ground, foreground and background, "the coarticulation of race, nation and religion ... the complex ways such categories intersect in the construction of collective identity, difference, and hierarchy" (Goldschmidt & McAlister, 2004, p. 5). For example, Chapter 11 examines the oppression of Native American Indians in the United States as a complex and cumulative interaction of religion (Christian versus heathen), race (White versus Red), culture (civilized versus barbarian), and economic competition over land. Chapter 12 examines the oppression of Jews in Christian Europe as a similarly complex and cumulative braiding of religious hatred, economic resentment, and racial stereotyping. In both cases, it is daunting to try to hold in place the one strand—*religion*—while also understanding that it is not truly a single strand but involves a "simultaneity of systems" in which the solo issues we call *race* and/or *ethnicity* and/or *culture* and/or *religion* are interactive rather than unitary, "constructed in and through each other, and through other categories of difference" (Goldschmidt & McAlister, 2004, p. 7).

The integrative approach we are taking here also poses certain challenges. Adding *religion* as yet another category of analysis within systems of domination and oppression makes for a slippery slope if one attempts merely to differentiate, isolate, or freeze the religious justifications from a complex that includes cultural, ethnic, and also racial rationales for oppression. The primary reason for attempting this disentanglement is to better understand the previously underexamined religious justifications used in tandem with racism or classism to dehumanize the Other, dismiss minority religions, relocate or restrict their living spaces, and eradicate their cultures. "Land acquisition and missionary work always went hand in hand in American history" (Deloria, 1969/1999, p. 22).

## Historical Framework

It is impossible to grasp the complexity of global or local political or ideological conflicts without considering the historical backgrounds of religious conflicts. For example, the continuing conflicts in the Middle East, the Balkans, the Sudan, northern Ireland, and the United States are rooted in long-standing religious, ethnic, and economic struggles, and competing historical narratives, between dominant and subordinated peoples (Cohen, 1994; Fox, 2002; Juergensmeyer, 2000, 2004; Said, 1979, 1993). These conflicts seem baffling without an understanding of their historical origins, historically unique contexts, and symbolic meanings for the participants. For example, European antisemitism is integrally related to the emergence of Christian-identified European nation-states, whereby Jews were forcibly converted, expelled, or exterminated as the non-Christian "Other." Moreover, Jews were the non-Christian "Other" in part because Islam had already been forcibly expelled from Christian Spain, with a legacy of conflict that resurfaces today in international power politics as well as in the vulnerability and mistreatment of Muslims (or those thought to be Muslims, such as Sikhs) in present day Christian-identified countries.

The historical legacy of religious-nationalistic global power struggles shaped the United States as well. Religious conflict within the early colonies reflected international power struggles among Catholic- and Protestant-affiliated France, Spain, England, Holland, and Germany, and these distrusts and loyalties remained at issue in subsequent U.S. history. Who won had direct consequences for who lived or died. These virulent and politically sanctioned religious struggles within and between European nation-states, reenacted in the Americas, became the crucible for the founding myth of the "New World," by which the American colonies established freedom of religion as a way of preempting state-sponsored religious domination by one or another of the founding Protestant sects (Fraser, 1999; Wills, 2002).

The freedom within the colonies from religious domination by the Church of England, or by each others' religious establishments, did not extend to free religious exercise for all within any one colony. Religious conflicts within specific colonies were treated as dangerous heresy and resolved by expulsion and flight to another colony or by the execution of the heretic. Colonial American history has many examples of religious persecution in the name of Protestant sectarianism: the persecution of Quakers in Plymouth Colony, the tradition of anti-Catholicism and the exclusion of Jews from political life throughout the 18th and 19th centuries, and the violence against Mormons and Jehovah's Witnesses (Ahlstrom, 2004; Albanese, 1999; Butler, Wacker, & Balmer, 2003; Wills, 2002; Wuthnow, 2005).

Hostility toward the "Other," whether based on sectarian religious affiliations or on stereotypes of ethnic and racialized ancestry, has been a foundational dimension of the history of the Americas, as Chapters 6 and 7 make clear. Examples include cycles of discrimination and mob violence by (mainly white) Christian settlers and organized militias against Native American "heathens" or by Christian communities against their "Mahometan" (meaning Muslim) and "Hindoo" (often mistakenly referring to Sikh) neighbors. Examples also include discrimination and mob violence against (mainly white) Mormons or against Chinese or Japanese communities (Chapter 11) and against Jews (Chapter 12).

## Christian Hegemony in the United States

The term *Christian hegemony* may startle readers who are not aware of the pervasive cultural position of *normative Christianity* in everyday life within U.S. schools, neighborhoods, and the workplace. *Hegemony* is another way of describing the cultural and societal level of oppression or "cultural imperialism" as a form of oppression (Young, 1990a). *Hegemony* refers to a society's unacknowledged adherence to a dominant worldview (Chapter 1). In this case, we refer to a religious worldview that publicly affirms Christian observances, holy days, and sacred spaces at the expense of those who are not Christian and within a culture that normalizes Christian values as intrinsic to an explicitly American public and political way of life. Christian norms are termed *hegemonic* in that they depend only on "business as usual." This normative Christianity is generally more noticeable to immigrants who have not been born or socialized within Christianity, or to observers from abroad who may be surprised, for example, by Christian prayer at public events.

Christian hegemony has roots in the formative role of Protestant sectarianism in the American colonies and early Republic, yet it remains largely invisible to Americans born and socialized into these traditions, assumptions, and values, whether or not they themselves are observant Christians. Christian hegemony, also referred to as *normative Christianity*, results in Christian *privileges* that are unearned cultural and social assets or advantages that come to members of the dominant religious group by virtue of their status in the United States (see Chapters 1 and 3). There are many examples of hegemonic Christianity (also discussed as Christian privilege) in Chapter 11: school and workplace holidays are keyed to the Christian calendar, politicians make frequent references to the Christian bible, the weekend supports Christian worship, and Christian proselytizing is difficult to challenge.

The emphasis thus far has been upon exploring our approach to *religious oppression* in U.S. and global contexts. It is critical to acknowledge, however, the important historical and contemporary role of religion in contesting oppression and working to create social change. There are many notable cases in which organized religion has supported movements for social justice and social change, such as the role of Protestant churches in the antislavery and abolition movements, the importance of Christian and Jewish ecumenical coalitions in the Civil Rights movement in the United States, and the influence of Catholic Liberation Theology on liberation movements throughout the Americas. There are important examples in which religion has provided and continues to afford community support, organized resistance to oppression, and group solidarity, as in the Black Church, the community supports provided by Buddhism and Christianity during the Japanese internment in concentration camps, and the exponential growth of Hindu temples, Sikh *gurdwaras*, and Muslim mosques to support religious, ethnic, and linguistic-identified communities (Eck, 2001; Hondagneu-Sotelo, 2007; Iwamura & Spickard, 2003; Min & Kim, 2002; Orfield & Lobowitz, 1999). These are inspiring instances that offer a vision of religion that encourages and supports social justice movements rather than religion used to sanctify reactionary political and social movements or to divide peoples from each other (See Hondagneu-Sotelo, 2007). In this spirit, the following two chapters present opportunities for participants to identify openings for change and to develop thoughtful and appropriate action plans that are based on real-world situations that participants can implement following the completion of the course.

## Note

1. *Fundamentalism* refers to "any claim to exclusive authenticity within a religious tradition" (Barkun, 2004, p. 60). Initial use of the term derives from internal conflicts within U.S. Protestantism, in which those "traditionialists" who were opposed to liberal Protestants articulated their views as *The Fundamentals* in a series of 1909–1915 pamphlets by that name. See Barkun (2004), Dinges (2004), Marty and Appleby (1997), Odell-Scott (2004), Phillips (2006), and Saha (2004).

# 11

# Religious Oppression Curriculum Design

## MAURIANNE ADAMS
## AND KHYATI Y. JOSHI

In this chapter, we explore some of the ways that religion has shaped the cultural, social, and political life of the United States, and has been used to justify the actions and policies of the dominant religious majority.[1] This exploration challenges deeply held American assumptions about religious freedom and First Amendment constitutional protections. It leads to a reassessment of the roles of racism, ethnocentrism, and classism in supporting systems of religious domination and subordination. For example, we pose questions about the religious rhetoric used historically to justify race-based slavery in the United States, the tribal and cultural genocide of Native American Indians, and the expulsions and incarceration of Japanese Americans. Turning to the present day, we note the religious profiling and detention of Muslims and Sikhs and instances of local community resistance to the building of mosques, temples, and *gurdwaras* in "our" neighborhoods and backyards (Eck, 2001; Joshi, 2006a; Singh, 2003). We note the religious basis of opposition to gay marriage, stem cell research, and school board conflicts over evolution versus creationism and intelligent design in K–12 science curricula. Some of these issues are discussed as themes in this introductory segment, and others appear in the curriculum design, the chapter endnotes, or the chapter appendices in the accompanying CD.

## Sociological Frameworks for Religious Domination and Subordination

This approach to *religious oppression* draws upon a sociological analysis of the roles and functions of religion in the larger society. In this chapter, we draw upon three specific conceptual frameworks also used elsewhere in this volume. The first conceptual framework calls attention to the "levels and types" of social organization within which religious oppression plays out at interpersonal, organizational and cultural/social levels, along with conscious and unconscious types (see Chapter 3 and Appendix 11A). The second uses the organizers of exploitation, marginalization, powerlessness, cultural imperialism, and violence (Young, 1990a) to bring dimensions of U.S. religious oppression into focus (see Appendix 11B).

The third framework illuminates the historical construction and contemporary reproduction of a *Christian hegemonic culture* in the United States to maintain and justify patterns of religious (and racial, ethnic, and economic) domination and subordination (Harvey, 2003; Martin, 2003; Wills, 2002). This intersectional framework highlights connections among religion, race, and ethnicity in U.S. history (Goldschmidt & McAlister, 2004; Prentiss, 2003; Wills, 2002). For example, this intersectional analysis examines the oppression of Native American Indian peoples in the United States by coordinating *religious oppression* (Native Americans constructed as "heathens") with *racism* (Native Americans understood by Europeans to be an inferior "race" of peoples) and *classism* (the pressure of economic factors, especially settler land acquisition). In such an analysis, each factor is necessary but by itself not sufficient to account for historical examples such as the allocation of generous federal land grants to Christian missionary organizations in exchange for their "'religious or educational work among the Indians'" (quoted in Echo-Hawk, 1993, p. 35). In order to comprehend the full picture, it is necessary to focus on the specifically religious (in this case, Christian) rationale for instances of oppression and to differentiate it from economic and racist justifications and motives. A similar intertwining of factors occurs in religious, economic, and race-based rationales for enslaving African peoples and, more than 2 centuries later, the internment of Japanese Americans (See Fredrickson, 2002, and Chapter 12 of this volume, for the intertwining of religious, economic, and race-based ingredients within antisemitism). In this chapter, we use these conceptual frameworks to illuminate Christian and white domination over groups whose religious difference becomes conflated with their presumed racial inferiority.

## Role of Religious Oppression in U.S. History

It is especially important in discussing religious oppression in the United States to present a view of U.S history that foregrounds religious domination and subordination. An examination of U.S history through this lens provides a foundation for understanding the religious advantage and disadvantage that are experienced by contemporary majority and minority religious groups, and shows the contradiction to traditions of U.S. religious freedom. Religion has been integral to U.S. national identity and group conflict from colonial origins on, and it remains important today (for recent discussions, see Phillips, 2006; Polk, 2006; Taylor, 2006).

Religion has justified economic advantage in the United States from the early colonial period on, and provides a context for understanding 350 years of U.S. territorial and national expansion, conquest, and settlement, as these play out in a perpetual legacy of *religious* struggle for domination. These struggles can be seen in denominational conflicts among Protestant sects, between Protestant and Catholic colonists and immigrants (English, German, Irish, Italian) and also between Christians and Buddhists, Hindus, Jews, Muslims, Native Americans, and Sikhs (Butler, Wacker, & Balmer, 2003; Haddad, 2002).[2]

## Religious Oppression and Racialization

The preceding *Overview* identifies the interaction of religion with race and ethnicity in the historical processes of sociopolitical domination and subordination. This account of the interaction of religion with race and ethnicity—that is, racialization—draws upon the concept of *racial formation*, by which we mean "the extension of racial meaning to a previously racially unclassified relationship, social practice or group" (Omi & Winant, 1986, p. 64). When religion is racialized, a particular set of phenotypical features, understood in a specific social and historical context, comes to be associated in the popular mind with a given religion and/or with other social traits. The racialization of religion results in or exacerbates the religious oppression of the minority group. For example, the foundational religious colonies along the eastern seaboard saw themselves as *white* religious communities, and their conflicts with Native American Indians as well as the policies that shaped African race-based slavery were justified in religious as well as race-based terms (Harvey, 2003; Johnson, 2004; Loewen, 1995; Wills, 2002). Settler incursions into Native American territories and the brutality and profits of slavery and the slave trade set in motion a specifically white *racial* and Christian *religious* national identity that advantaged free, white Christian men as citizens in the new republic, and subordinated religious and racial others (Harvey, 2003). Religion played a role in "making and preserving those very social boundaries that we call 'races' and ethnicities'" (Prentiss, 2003, p. 1) that, with national origins, became indistinguishable strands in a xenophobic religious discourse used to justify the expulsion of Native American peoples from their ancestral lands, the westward expansion by white American settlers and white European immigrants, and the 19th-century absorption of Spanish and Mexican lands into the new states of the American Southwest and California (Almaguer, 1994; Takaki, 1993).

The juxtaposed terms *Christian*, *English*, *free*, and *white* suggest how deeply religion, race, and national origins have been co-constructed within U.S. history (Jacobson, 1998; Wills, 2002). The religious sanctioning of military, racial, and cultural domination enabled devout colonists to perceive divine purposes behind their appropriation of Native American lands, villages, and farmlands by conflating *religion* (Christian versus barbarous and heathen) with *civilization* (civilized versus primitive and savage), and both with *race* (see Jacobson, 1998; Loewen, 1995; Prentiss, 2003). In later periods of U.S. history, religious beliefs interacted with political, cultural, and racial discourses to rationalize race-based segregation between white and black congregations within the same Protestant denominations (Baptists, Methodists, Pentecostals; Emerson & Smith, 2000; Wills, 2002) and justify rigid social boundaries that excluded Asians and Middle Easterners as the threatening and racial/religious Other (Harvey, 2003; Johnson, 2004; Lee, 2004). This discourse made no distinctions between Asian and "Hindoo," Arabs and North Africans, and "Mahomedans" and Muslim (Said, 1978; Snow, 2004).

Stereotypes about the religion, race, civilization, and character of the Other shaped white, U.S.-born nativist illogic, and immigration and naturalization policy, from the 18th and 19th centuries through to the present day (Goldschmidt & McAlister, 2004; Haney Lopez, 1996; Jacobson, 1998; Lee, 2004).

Although these and other examples of religious marginalization and violence have been typically framed in terms of ethnocentrism and racism, we argue in this chapter that *religious oppression* should be differentiated from ethnocentrism or racism in order to better understand the specific dimensions of discrimination, marginalization, and exclusion based on religious beliefs and identity (Goldschmidt & McAlister, 2004; Joshi, 2006a, 2006b).

## The Emergence of Protestant Domination and Minority Religious Subordination

Two fundamental and interrelated themes help us to understand the enormously complex interactions of Protestants with other religious-identified groups in U.S. history.

One centers on the emergence of the Christian domination of U.S. political, economic, and culture institutions, and the other centers on its opposite, the relative disadvantage experienced by religious minorities. The first of these focuses on the historical bases for Christian hegemony, with examples such as colonial sectarianism, Christian denominational missions and schools established for Native American Indians and Blacks, military and political conquest over the Catholic Mexicans of Texas and California, and the exploitation of Punjabi "Hindoo" farm laborers and Chinese "heathen" indentured laborers who built America's transatlantic railroads and worked in mines and on plantations (Almaguer, 1994; Jacobson, 1998; Lee, 2004; Min & Kim, 2002; Snow, 2004; Takaki, 1998b). In every case, *Christian* meant superior, was associated with whiteness, and conveyed moral and cultural attributes considered necessary to the benefits of citizenship, democracy, self-rule, and naturalization as American.

The second theme, the disadvantage experienced by religious minorities, suggests a photographic negative or mirror image to the first by focusing on the exclusion from citizenship of those many Native, enslaved, colonized, or immigrant peoples identified as the religious and racially inferior Other. Historical examples of the mutual reinforcement of these two themes include the doctrine of Manifest Destiny, which tied a belief in *racial* Anglo-Saxon superiority to the *religious* conviction of a providential, divinely sanctioned struggle of Protestants against heathenism, barbarism, and primitivism (Axtell, 1985; Cherry, 1971; Johnson, 2004; Tuveson, 1968). Further examples appear in 19th-century Protestant nativist[3] xenophobia against Catholic and Jewish immigrants, and in 20th- and 21st-century harassment of Hindu, Muslim, and Sikh immigrants (Ahlstrom, 2004; Eck, 2001; Jacobson, 1998).

From a historical perspective, the current resurgence of Christian fundamentalism and the vulnerability and harassment experienced by minority religions are not at all new. Although the founding U.S. historical narrative portrays the early colonies as havens for religious groups persecuted elsewhere, we now know that most early U.S. religious communities were homogeneous and theocratic, and that they persecuted members of other faiths as well as dissenters from their own sectarian beliefs (Ahlstrom, 2004; Fraser, 1999). The early religious theocracies, such as the "holy commonwealth" in New England and the established church in the Virginia colony, combined religion with economic imperatives—for example, extending Christian missions to Native American Indians as one way of securing land, goods, and settlements in the Americas (Axtell, 1985; Echo-Hawk, 1993; Philbrick, 2006; Spring, 2007).

Christian hegemony was historically rooted in political, economic, legal, and military subjection, by (primarily) Protestant armies, politicians, missionaries, and settlers, upon ethnic and religious minorities whose land or labor was needed—Native American Indians; Mexican landowners and rancher-workers; Chinese agricultural, railroad, and mine workers; and Japanese and Sikh farmers in California and Washington.[4] In all cases, the religious identity of the Native and the foreign-born Other has been compounded by negative stereotypes of race, civilization, and/or language, justifying atrocities such as the massacre of Native American Indian Ghost Dance worshippers at Wounded Knee, South Dakota (1890). For the children of religious and racialized minorities, Christian hegemony was established through the forced Christian education of Native children at Protestant and Catholic residential schools, the involuntary segregation of Chinese and Japanese children in Protestant denominational and mission schools, and explicit efforts to "assimilate" Catholic children through Protestant public or "common" schools (Fraser, 1999; Perlmutter, 1991; Spring, 2007; Takaki, 1998b).

Although in many cases the groups who experienced religious oppression were racially subjugated in the United States, minority white religious sects also experienced religious subjugation (Mazur, 1999). For example, violent hostility was directed against U.S.-born Christians who broke from denominational Protestantism to form the Church of Jesus Christ of Latter-Day Saints (the Mormons), the Seventh-Day Adventists, and the Jehovah's Witnesses, each of them critical of Protestant orthodoxy and denominational organization, and resistant to the religious hegemony in established state or federal political jurisdictions (Albanese, 1999; Butler, Wachar, & Balmer, 2003; Mathisen, 2001; Prentiss, 2003; Wilson & Drakeman, 2003). The clashes that pitted police and armed mobs against Mormons or Jehovah's Witnesses ended only with their withdrawal into relatively autonomous geographical spaces and/or the relinquishment of their own sectarian claims to political autonomy (Mazur, 1999).

## Nativist Backlash to Maintain Christian National Identity

During the first part of the nineteenth century and prior to the Civil War, it is estimated that over half of the U.S population and 85% of Protestants were evangelical (Emerson & Smith, 2000). Given this history and these early demographics, the linkage between Protestantism and American national identity is not surprising. In the decades between 1840 and the early 20th century, significant increases in immigration challenged this homogeneous, albeit racialized, mainly Protestant understanding of American national identity.

The demographics hint at the challenge to religious, cultural, linguistic, and political hegemony. Total immigration rose from 143,000 for the decade of the 1820s to 8,800,000 for the first decade in the 20th century (Office of Immigration Statistics, 2004). By 1860, the foreign-born American population was over 4 million, with more than 1.5 from Catholic Ireland (Jacobson, 1998). By 1920, more than a third of the total population of 105 million Americans included immigrants and their children (36 million), the majority of them Roman Catholic, Greek Orthodox, and Jewish, with smaller numbers of Buddhists and Sikhs from China and India (Daniels, 2002).

During this period, Irish Catholics, driven by the potato famine of the 1840s, migrated to east coast and midwestern cities, and Italian Catholics and Jews in flight from European revolution, poverty, and pogroms settled mainly but not exclusively in urban communities. Asian immigration (first Filipino and Chinese, followed by Japanese and South Asian) and Middle Eastern immigration (initially, Syrian or Lebanese Maronite Christian) brought Buddhist, Confucian, Hindu, and Sikh as well as Orthodox religious adherents to the United States (Ahlstrom, 2004; Albanese, 1999). The immigrant newcomers were largely Catholic and Jewish, with smaller immigrant Buddhist, Confucian, Dao, Hindu, Muslim, and Sikh populations. Immigrants from Europe (Catholics and Jews among them) and Syrian Christians were able to become naturalized as "white men," whereas Asian and non-Christian Arab immigrants were denied naturalization (Gaultieri, 2001; Haney Lopez, 1996; Snow, 2004).

Also during this period, southern and rural Blacks (mainly Protestant) moved into northern and midwestern cities for jobs, carrying forms of Christian worship that were not welcome in white Protestant congregations. Before, during, and after legalized race-based slavery, mainstream white Protestant congregations had split over the religious justification for slavery and developed contradictory biblical interpretations and theological arguments rationalizing or excoriating race-based segregation. These bitter denominational and sectional disputes over slavery and segregation stimulated the growth of a separate Black Church, with congregations organized in local homes and communities as well as on plantation missions. Black Protestant denominations provided refuge, community solidarity, and support for ex-slaves and for black sharecroppers in the Jim Crow South, fostering political leadership, economic development, education, and protest during the 19th and 20th centuries, including and beyond the Civil Rights movement (Ahlstrom, 2004; Fulop & Raboteau, 1997; Lincoln & Mamiya, 1990; Raboteau, 2001). Similar community support and cultural, ethnic, and linguistic solidarity as well as resistance can be seen in the more recent emergence of Chinese, Korean, and Latino/a Evangelical or Catholic religious communities (Carnes & Yang, 2004; Ebaugh & Chafetz, 2000; Min & Kim, 2002; Orfield & Lebowitz, 1999).

From the post–Civil War period through the turn of the 20th century, Native American Indians were massacred, relocated, and resettled into areas not wanted by white farmers and settlers. As noted above, religious motives (as in the denomination-run residential schools) interacted with white economic expansion and cultural imperialism.

In this volatile context of national expansion, immigrant religious outsiders poked large holes in the already-stretched fabric of Protestant national identity. The demographic challenge posed by waves of immigrants to an American identity based on religion (Protestantism), culture (Western European heritage), and race (whiteness) led to violent xenophobic backlash and restrictive anti-immigrant policy. The first expression of nativism was anti-Catholic, aimed at Irish and German Catholics (1830s–1850s) and sustained in part by a Protestant-dominated system of public schooling. Anti-Catholicism continued into the 20th century, directed increasingly against Italians (Guglielmo, 2003; Merithew, 2003). The second wave of nativism was largely anti-Asian and led to the Chinese Exclusion Act of 1882 and the Immigration Act of 1917 (known as the "Barred Zone" Act). The anti-immigrant nativist sentiment culminated in the Johnson-Reed Immigration Act of 1924, also know as the National Origins Act. The act set a percentage for immigrants entering the United States at 2% of the total of any nation's residents in the United States as reported in the 1890 U.S. Census. The intent of this law was to restrict immigration from southern and eastern Europe and Asia while welcoming newcomers from Britain, Ireland, and northern Europe.

These targeted legislative restrictions on immigration were part of the nativist opposition to non-Anglo-Saxon and non-Protestant immigrants, within a longer national tradition of identity-based protests against non-English-speaking, darker-skinned, working-class or farming Catholics and Jews, Buddhists, Confucians, Hindus, Muslims, and Sikhs (Feagin, 1997; Perea, 1997). This is also the period during which a revived Ku Klux Klan and new Christian identity groups added anti-Catholicism and antisemitism to their racist agendas (Cowan, 2003; Daniels, 2002; Lee, 2004).

One obvious consequence of this restrictive immigration legislation was to severely limit non-Protestant immigration (Daniels, 1997; Prewitt, 2004). Immigration restriction (including severe limits on the immigration of Jews from European antisemitism in the 1930s and the Holocaust of the 1940s) was maintained until the United States reopened its doors with the Immigration and Naturalization Act of 1965.

Another consequence of the larger xenophobic and nativist backlash to immigration described above can be found in restrictions to the naturalization of non-Christian immigrants of color. For example, in the 1920s government officials considered Hinduism to be "an alienating and barbaric social and religious system, one that rendered 'Hindus' utterly unfit for membership in the 'civilization of White men'" (Snow, 2004, p. 268). The decision against Bhagat Singh Thind's citizenship claims turned on whether a "Hindu, of full Indian blood" (in fact, Thind was Sikh) could be considered white by naturalization law. Similarly, the dark-skinned Yemeni Arab Muslim Ahmed Hassan was denied citizenship through an argument that conflated religion with race: "'a wide gulf separates [Mohammedan] culture from that of the predominately Christian peoples of Europe'" (Gaultieri, 2001, p. 81), and in contrast to earlier Syrian Christians whom the courts ruled to be white (Gaultieri, 2001; Haney Lopez, 1996; Odell-Scott, 2004; Snow, 2004).

During the years between the 1924 (anti-) Immigration Act and the reopening of immigration after 1965, educational, residential, and professional barriers were slowly dismantled for white Ashkenazi Jews and for white Catholics (Italians and Irish), but not for black or brown Catholics or Protestants (African Americans, Afro-Caribbeans, Puerto Ricans, Chicanos/as and Mexican Americans, and South or Central Americans) (see Brodkin Sacks, 1994; Guglielmo, 2003; Ignatiev, 1995; Roediger, 1991). This was a period during which most Jews and Catholics became white, or at least "almost" if "not always quite" white, at the same time that religious observance became increasingly private, either through separate parochial, Jewish, or home schooling, or weekend Protestant, Catholic, or Jewish religious education (so-called Sunday schools).

The Immigration and Naturalization Act of 1965 reopened the door to immigration and permanently altered the racial, ethnic, and religious makeup of the United States, continuing into the present day. By 2000, immigrant and second-generation Americans numbered nearly 55 million people, more than 32.5 million of them immigrants and many of them migrating as family units within strong religious community networks (Portes & Rumbaut, 2001). One outcome of the family unit of immigration following the 1965 Immigration Act is the growing Hindu, Muslim, and Sikh religious, cultural, and ethnic communities in the United States (Eck, 2001; Joshi, 2006a; Kurien, 1998; Mann, 2000; Min & Kim, 2002).

## The Constitutional Guarantees of Religious Freedom

The background briefly summarized thus far in this chapter emphasizes the history behind Christian domination and the subordination of minority religions in the United States. Knowing this history provides an explanatory context for the dramatically different experiences of Christians and non-Christians in contemporary U.S. culture. Knowing this history also challenges the core myth of national religious freedom and equality, taught to most American schoolchildren in the early grades. Only by questioning the assumptions about freedom of religion and equality of opportunity can the specific role of *religion* in American social and cultural life become clear.

There is a second core myth, also taught in schools and largely unexamined, that requires clarification in this chapter, namely, the assumption that free religious exercise is assured by the First Amendment to the U.S. Constitution. However, this article of national faith is difficult to maintain, for example, in light of the constitutional rulings against the protection of Native American Indian sacred sites and rituals, or failed legal efforts to gain constitutional redress for restrictions on minority religious *practices* as distinct from religious beliefs (see Echo-Hawk, 1993; Feldman, 1997; Long, 2000; Mazur, 1999; see Appendices 11C and 11D).

Although the history of religious protective litigation is complicated, at times contradictory, and daunting to summarize, the topic is important for anyone hoping to understand U.S. religious oppression historically as well as the constitutional conflicts that continue to the present day. What follows is a brief introduction to the constitutional issues at stake, to clarify the importance of the curriculum segment focused on constitutional protections and to provoke awareness of the role of the Supreme Court as final arbiter of U.S. religious freedom.

The religion clauses of the First Amendment to the U.S. Constitution (1791) stipulate that "Congress shall make no law respecting an establishment of religion, or prohibiting the free exercise thereof" (Amendment 1 to the U.S. Constitution, 1791; see

Appendix 11C for more background, with cases incorporated into the history timeline of Appendix 11E). The First Amendment provides, in effect, a religious mutual assurance pact, agreed upon by the major Protestant denominations within the original 13 colonies to prevent any one of them from becoming a federally established church supported by public taxes (Fraser, 1999; Mazur, 1999).

The first clause of the First Amendment, known as the *Establishment Clause* ("Congress shall make no law respecting an establishment of religion"), prohibits the federal government from establishing or supporting any single religion or religious denomination or sect, and is generally known as the *separation of church and state.*[5] The second part of this constitutional guarantee, known as the *Free Exercise Clause* ("Congress shall make no law prohibiting the free exercise thereof"), has been variously interpreted to include freedom of religious belief and practice, although the latter (that is, religious practice) has been hedged by extensive case law (see Appendix 11C for discussion). In the curriculum design that follows, we provide further discussion with examples of First Amendment litigation to illustrate both the successes and the limitations to constitutional protection for minority religions that are outside Christian cultural hegemony.

## Civil Religion in U.S. Public Life

Although the First Amendment was designed to safeguard minority religious beliefs and practices from those of any majority religious sect, the Supreme Court has affirmed governmentally sanctioned religious speech, ritual, and symbols, generally referred to as "civil religion" (Bellah, 1967, 1970; Richie & Jones, 1974) but derived nonetheless from Christian texts and traditions. Examples include the motto "In God We Trust" on U.S. currency, the pledge that the United States is one nation "under God," and the customary presidential benediction "God Bless America" (see Albanese, 1999; Henry, 1981; Maddigan, 1993; Mirsky, 1986). Sectarian religious themes can be traced in presidential addresses from George Washington to George W. Bush (Goldberg, 2006; Kaplan, 2004), alongside religious justifications for 19th-century national expansion (the doctrine of Manifest Destiny, noted earlier) and for 20th- and 21st-century military and imperial interventions abroad (Kaplan, 2004; Phillips, 2006). Supreme Court decisions between 1890 and 1930 had affirmed that the United States "is one of the 'Christian countries'" and a "Christian nation," and that "We are a Christian people," although in 1952 the phasing became more ecumenical: "We are a religious people whose institutions presuppose a Supreme Being" (quoted in Feldman, 1997, p. 231, see also pp. 231–232 and n. 52).

Arguments on behalf of a "civil religion" also suggest the use of hegemonic but nondenominational Christianity as a moral "glue" or compass for a religiously diverse American people. The hegemonic use of civil religion also reflects the increased cooperation between mainstream Protestantism and Catholicism toward a normative and ecumenical national Christian identity (Albanese, 1999; Wuthnow, 2005). It is also a reaction to the genocidal massacre of Jews in Christian Europe during World War II, which shocked ecumenical religious leaders into forging stronger relationships between Judaism and Christianity, even going so far as arguing for a "Judeo-Christian" tradition in the West.

The Supreme Court has generally accepted the view that civil religion does represent a shared American identity that is constitutionally acceptable as "typically nonsectarian, symbolic, and without specific theological content" (Davis, 2004, p. 41). Yet it can also be argued that naming the deity in a way familiar primarily for Christians in effect excludes others such as Orthodox Jews (who must not write or utter the divine name) and Muslims (who invoke Allah). From this perspective, even if American civil religion is "a distinctive form of religion that is different from creedal [sectarian or denominational] religions ... it is religion just the same" (Davis, p. 43).

## Christian Hegemony and Privilege

In the *Overview: Religious Oppression* that precedes this chapter, we defined Christian *hegemony* as an "unacknowledged adherence to a dominant worldview ... a religious worldview that publicly affirms Christian observances, holy days, and sacred spaces, at the expense of those who are not Christian and within a culture that normalizes Christian values as intrinsic to an explicitly American public and political way of life" (see p. 253; see Blumenfeld, 2006). This concept of "hegemony" or "business as usual" enables us to analyze the normative role of Christianity in U.S. history, law, policy, and culture.

Although the First Amendment requires the government to allow and in some cases accommodate different religious practices, and forbids the government from negatively impacting any particular religion, it is important in this chapter to ask, "Which religions are accommodated, and which religions experience negative impacts?" Examples are so deeply ingrained in U.S. national culture as to seem invisible. The school and workplace calendar of "holy days" ("holidays") is structured around a Christian calendar, particularly Christmas and Easter, but not Diwali, Ramadan, or Rosh Hashanah. School prayer or prayer at school athletic events and public assemblies is unquestioned in many states and school districts (see Feldman, 1997) and presents a stark contrast to the difficulties that obstruct the observant Muslim *salat* (daily prayer) obligation (Nimer, 2001). Similar contradictions between mainstream and minority religious acceptance can be seen in the state and municipality "Sunday laws" that regulate the conduct of business and the selling of alcohol on Sundays, a normative Christian practice that favors Sunday over Friday, the Islamic day of prayer and the evening that begins the Jewish Sabbath.[6] The U.S. calendar is a Christian calendar, looking backward and forward from the birth of Christ, whether noted as B.C. ("before Christ," sometimes termed BCE for "Before the Common Era") or A.D. ("anno Domini," or "year of our lord," sometimes termed CE for "Common Era"). Christianity's normative nature is reflected in the many references to Christian scripture by U.S. presidents and other public officials of both major political parties, even when their speeches are unrelated to the subject of religion, and the increasingly visible and single-issue role of conservative Protestant congregations in local and national politics (Feldman, 1997; Goldberg, 2006; Kaplan, 2004; Mazur, 1999; Phillips, 2006).

Christian hegemony can also be referred to as the exercise of *Christian privilege*. Having *privilege* with respect to normative Christianity means that people need not question "the assumptions underlying institutional rules and the collective consequences of following those rules" (Young, 1990a, p. 41). Christian privilege is a phenomenon maintained through the cultural power of *normative* religious practices that, by affirming the norm, exclude and disqualify what is outside the norm (Beaman, 2003; Blumenfeld, 2006; Clark, Brimhall-Vargas, Schlosser, & Alimo, 2002; Schlosser, 2003).

Discussing the parallel concept of white privilege, McIntosh (1998) writes that privilege is "an invisible package of unearned assets," a "weightless knapsack of special provisions, maps, passports, codebooks, visas, clothes, tools, and blank checks" (p. 79). *Privilege* means having and using these "unearned assets" every day and yet remaining oblivious to them—it suggests that *rights* assumed to belong to all citizens equally are not equally accessible to members of socially targeted groups. In this sense, "rights" may be experienced only by advantaged groups and thus more accurately described as "privileges."

The U.S. linguistic and symbolic vocabulary of faith, practice, prayer, and belief largely ignores the existence of non-Christian religions among its citizenry, despite the fact that many of the religions that seem "new" on the American religious landscape are in some cases older than Christianity—Hinduism and Judaism, for example. Because Christianity is normative, non-Christians are asked, "What is 'your Bible'?" and "When is 'your Christmas'?" Similarly, Christian myths such as the virgin birth or the Assumption are accepted as believable, in contrast to "unbelievable" myths such as Mohammed's midnight flight to heaven (Islam) or Vishnu's periodic visitation of the Earth under different guises (Hinduism). American religious images include a white man with a flowing beard or the Virgin Mary, not Krishna with his blue skin or the four-armed Saraswati, goddess of knowledge, wisdom, and learning. This distinction cannot be characterized as anything but normative: the Christian stories of the Immaculate Conception and the bodily resurrection of Jesus are accepted as plausible, whereas the idea of a half-elephant and half-man protector god—Ganesh—is considered an impossible fantasy (Sethi, 1994). Finally, the Christian norm is associated by the Christian majority with the idea of "goodness" or righteousness, and these other faiths appear illegitimate by comparison.

## Current Religious Diversity and Examples of Current Religious Oppression

It is difficult to get an accurate reading of specific *religious* demographics in the United States, because the national census does not provide the demographic information on religion that it offers for ethnic and racial self-identification. Nongovernmental surveys that collect data on religion are often voluntary, based on organized religious congregations or affiliations, and thus unlikely to yield reliable data. Buddhist, Hindu, Muslim, Sikh, and Native American religious practice is not necessarily congregational or documented by official listings, thereby compounding the difficulty of gathering demographic data on the numbers of adherents. The following numbers (Table 11.1) are gathered from composite sources to provide an estimate of religious demographics (Pluralism Project, 2006).

These approximate numbers include converts of all races as well as immigrant first-generation and second-generation Americans. Buddhists have come primarily from Japan, China, Tibet, Thailand, Cambodia, and other Asian nations. Approximately 75–80% of American Buddhists are of Asian ancestry. The 1.7 million Indians in the United States are mainly Hindu (Gupta, 2003, p. 194). Most Sikhs are of Indian origin, from Punjab. Islam is a pan-ethnic religion, with adherents in the United States from East, Southeast, Central, and South Asia; Africa; and the Middle East. There are also African American and European American (mainly Albanian) Muslims. Currently, the ethnic origin of the Muslim community in the United States is approximately 26.2% Middle Eastern (Arab), 24.7% South Asian, 23.8% African American, 10.3% Middle Eastern (non-Arab), and 6.4% East Asian (Islam for Today, 2006; McCloud, 2003).

For members of these religious communities, who also are members of visible

**Table 11.1**  Estimate of U.S. Religious Demographics

| | |
|---|---|
| Buddhist | 2.5–4 million |
| Christian | 162 million |
| Hindu | 1.2–1.7 million |
| Jewish | 5–6 million |
| Muslim | 2.5–6 million |
| Sikh | 250,000–500,000 |

*Source:* Pluralism Project (2006).

racialized groups, the burdens of outsiderness are compounded. For example, South Asian Americans encounter discrimination simultaneously on religious *and* racial levels in neighborhoods, schools, and workplace (Joshi, 2006a, 2006b). At the societal and institutional levels, these groups are subject to oppression and face conflict on the basis of attire, rituals, and practices that mark their outsider *religious* status, a status that is confounded with and multiplied by outsider *racial*, *ethnic*, and *linguistic* status.

Hinduism, Islam, and Sikhism especially have been *racialized* (Omi & Winant, 1986, p. 64), so that racial phenotype becomes proxy for religious identity, that is, a visible attribute (race) generates a presumption about religious identity (Joshi, 2006a, 2006b; Singh, 2003). By exaggerating and stereotyping the identification of religious with racial Otherness, the racialization of religion compounds the delegitimization of these faiths (Joshi, 2006a).

The conflation of religion with race experienced by South Asian Americans, Hindus, Muslims, and Sikhs leads also to stereotyped views of religion that confuse one group's religion with another's. For example, Hindus, Sikhs, and Muslims are sometimes presumed to be theologically similar because they appear to be phenotypically and racially similar, a misconception that is further reinforced by their geographic proximity of national origins. Conflation and racial lumping affect the lives of South Asian Americans in many ways, such as the frustration of being misidentified and the lack of services or provision of inappropriate services in the public school system or in commercial transactions. The mistaken identification of Sikhs with Islam, particularly since the events of 9/11, has resulted in physical attacks on Sikh Americans targeted for hate crimes by misguided racists who found them to be convenient scapegoats for the dehumanized, non-white, turban-wearing "Others" whom they wanted to strike down (Iyer, 2003; National Asian Pacific American Legal Consortium, 2002). Hate crimes and harassment directed against minority religious symbols put extreme pressure on those religions' adherents to visibly assimilate and shed obvious markers of their faith. The impact of harassment due to religious attire or associations is experienced by these communities as *religious* discrimination and harassment.

Islamophobia[7] in the United States is not a post-9/11 phenomenon, but the religious and racial stereotyping of Muslims as if all were Islamic militants has accelerated in response to the oil crisis of 1973; the first Gulf War of the 1980s and 1990s; the attacks of September 11, 2001; and the bus, train, and subway bombings in London and Madrid. Uncritical conflation of theology and ideology with race and national origins leads to the essentializing of all Arabs and Asians with "Muslims" and all Muslims with "Islamic terrorists" and fanatics. Stereotypes in the media and statements by government officials paint Islam and Muslims as intrinsically violent, destructive, and incapable of self-regulation or democracy, whether on the basis of theology or genetics (Afridi, 2001; Mamdani, 2004; Nimer, 2002). Remarks from political leaders and by the news media, with caricatures that are the filmmakers' or cartoonists' stock-in-trade, lead incrementally to the stereotyping of all brown-skinned Muslims as the enemy of a democratic West (Shaheen, 1984, 2001).

There are many other ways in which minority religions are affected by the ignorance, obliviousness, misguided intentions, and harassment by a hegemonic majority. One form is the experience by non-Christians of Christian evangelism—that is, the assumption by some Christians that it is their responsibility to bring their truth to so-called nonbelievers (Joshi, 2006a; Wuthnow, 2005). Proselytizing shades into religious oppression when the person being proselytized experiences it as an act of harassment and as an assault on the legitimacy of their own religion.

## Imagining a Pluralistic Religious Future

This account of Christian hegemony and advantage in present-day U.S. culture and institutions traces an interwoven group of braided strands in an even more complex tapestry. The race-based stereotypes that historically separated mainstream Christianity from a number of non-Christian religions are today less viable, given the dramatic growth of Latino/a and Asian Christian communities whose identity and forms of worship are firmly rooted in their own culturally and linguistically homogeneous ethnic communities of origin (Carnes & Yang, 2004; Eck, 2001; Min & Kim, 2002; Warner & Witner, 1998; Yoo, 1999). Historians of religion in the United States note the shifts and transformations within Christian denominations (Eck, 2001; Warner & Witner, 1998; Wuthnow, 1996) and the strengthening as well as increased visibility of Buddhist, Hindu, Jewish, and Muslim adherents and communities (Carroll, 2000; see also Pluralism Project, 2006).

In the fall of 2006, some 55 million children are enrolling in the nation's schools (Dillon, 2006) and presenting the most diverse group of students in many decades, with new challenges to the hegemonic status quo. The status quo in many cases has involved the avoidance of religion, whether through fear of violating the Establishment Clause, discomfort when faced with religious differences, or lack of teacher preparedness. The National Council for the Social Studies (1998) has urged, "Knowledge about religions is not only a characteristic of an educated person but is absolutely necessary for understanding and living in a world of diversity" (p. 2).

Teachers will need to understand the religious dimensions of intergroup communication and conflict, and administrators will need to scrutinize language usage and calendars from perspectives other than the Christian norm (Anti-Defamation League, 2004; First Amendment Center, 1999; Greenawalt, 2002). As with any change, this increased diversity of religious background and affiliation offers challenges as well as opportunities.

The challenges have already been noted in this overview. The opportunities must be noted as well. There is a hopeful interreligious as well as ecumenical tradition in the United States of peoples motivated by diverse faith and religious traditions to work for social change. Historical examples date back to the abolition movement, worker and liberation theology movements, various settlement and social reform movements, and the Civil Rights movement. Today, peace activists and interfaith communities work at the local level to provide support for the needs of different faith communities, and Hindu, Muslim, and Sikh political organizations speak out to protect the religious and civil rights for community members, with the active support of mainstream Christian and Jewish organizations (see Appendix 11F; Hondagneu-Sotelo, 2007).

## Religious Oppression Curriculum Design

### Overall Goals

- Understand religious oppression in U.S. history and contemporary life.
- Understand the historical background for U.S. Christian hegemony, the advantages for Christians, and the disadvantages for subordinate religious groups such as Buddhists, Hindus, Jews, Muslims, Sikhs, and members of Native American Indian religions.
- Understand the roles and functions of religion in relationship to social institutions, political/national identity, and culture.

- Understand stereotypes and experiences of subordinate religious communities in U.S. history and contemporary life.
- Use theories and models of social oppression to analyze historical and contemporary examples of religious oppression.
- Understand interconnections and interactions between religious oppression and other forms of social oppression, such as classism, ethnocentrism, and racism.
- Recognize examples of religious oppression in everyday interpersonal interactions and in institutional, social, and cultural life.
- Plan ways of taking action against different types of religious oppression.

(See Appendices 11G through 11J for participant reading assignments, resources for facilitator preparation on curricular content, and facilitation issues specific to the religious oppression curriculum design.)

### Overview of Modules

Note to readers: The curriculum design in this chapter is based on the assumption that participants have completed the introductory module(s) described in Chapter 3 prior to beginning this design and have a basic understanding of the conceptual framework of oppression described in Chapter 3. See Table 11.2 for an overview of this chapter's modules.

### Module 1: Personal Awareness of Religious Identity and Religious Difference in the United States

Time needed: 4 hours

### Objectives

- Build a supportive learning community.
- Identify elements of effective, respectful, culturally appropriate communication while discussing religious oppression.
- Name and acknowledge difficulties of discussing religion and religious oppression in a classroom setting with people from different religious backgrounds and experiences.
- Acknowledge the different religious backgrounds and legacies of participants in the class.
- Clarify the historical and sociological approach to religious oppression to be taken in this class.
- Understand interactions of religion with ethnic, national, and other social group identities.
- Understand conceptual frameworks such as "Levels of Oppression" or "Five Faces of Oppression."

**Key concepts**: religion, religious belief, religious institutions, culture, stereotypes, oppression, domination and subordination, social systems, levels and types of oppression, "faces" of oppression, historical legacy, religious identity and ethnic identity

### 1. Introductions, Agenda, Goals, and Guidelines (60 minutes)

Introduce yourselves to the class and offer your perspective on why it is important to discuss and understand religious oppression in the United States. Mention your own religious background, and how your other social identities (race and ethnic-

**Table 11.2**    Overview of Modules: Religious Oppression

| Module 1: Personal Awareness of Religious Identity and Religious Difference in the United States (4 hours) | Module 2: Historical and Conceptual Understanding of Religious Oppression in the United States (3.5 hours) |
|---|---|
| 1. Introductions, Agenda, Goals, and Guidelines (60 min.)<br>2. Religious and Ethnic Family Backgrounds (35 min.)<br>3. Common Ground Activity (20 min.)<br>Break (15 min.)<br>4. Knapsack of Christian Privilege (45 min.)<br>5. Model of Oppression (levels and types): Options A or B (30 min.)<br>6. Closing Questions and Issues (10 min.) | 1. Opening (10 min.)<br>2. Interfaith Four Squares (25 min.)<br>3. Stereotypes (40 min.)<br>Break (15 min.)<br>4. Roots and Development of Christian Privilege and Minority Religious Oppression in U.S. History: Options A or B (60 min.)<br>Break (15 min.)<br>5. U.S. Constitutional Safeguards for Freedom of Religious Belief and Observance (20 min.)<br>6. Homework Assignments and Closure (15 min.) |
| **Module 3: Institutional Examples for an Oppression Perspective (3.5 hours)** | **Module 4: Next Steps and Action Plans (3 hours, 45 minutes)** |
| 1. Opening (10 min.)<br>2. Institutional and Cultural "Web" of Religious Oppression (20 min.)<br>3. How Schools or Workplaces Maintain Christian Hegemony (70 min.)<br>Break (15 min.)<br>4. Scenarios Concerning Protection for Religious Minorities (75 min.)<br>5. Reactions, Responses, and Closing (10 min.) | 1. Opening (10 min.)<br>2. Framework for Change: Cycles of Liberation (40 min.)<br>3. Reopen Knapsack and Scenarios for Action Planning: Options A or B (40 min.)<br>Break (15 min.)<br>4. Ingredients of a Personal "Action Plan" (85 min.)<br>5. Closing and Evaluations (15 min.) |

ity, class, gender) affect your experience of religious identity. Ask participants to give their names and to identify one question or issue related to religion and religious oppression they would like addressed in this class. Provide self-stick notes on which they can write the issues or questions, and post them all together in one section of the room. As issues or questions are addressed, participants may move their self-stick notes to another location to acknowledge the learning that is taking place in the class.

If participants have completed assigned readings in advance (see Appendix 11G) and written a short reflective paper, ask them to turn in their papers.

## Goals and Agenda

Provide a handout of the goals and agenda (or write them on newsprint). Allow for participants to add goals that facilitators agree can be included. The agenda should also be sufficiently flexible to allow for additional goals identified during the class.

## Participant Hopes and Concerns

Distribute 3 × 5 cards, and ask participants to write one hope and one concern about participating in this seminar. Collect, shuffle, and redistribute the cards. Ask each participant to read first a concern, then a hope. Write the hopes and concerns on a chalkboard or newsprint.

## Guidelines

Invite active student participation in identifying respectful communication guidelines for discussing religious oppression. These guidelines will shape how people talk with each other and can be invoked if there are difficulties in class discussions. Assure participants that they can add guidelines if the need arises later in the class. Facilitators include their own norms and guidelines in this process. (See Chapter 3 and Appendix 11I for sample guidelines.)

## Facilitation Issues

Participants might be uneasy talking about religion in public, and facilitators can model effectively discussing this topic by talking briefly about their own religious identity, family religious legacies, and personal experiences. Call attention to experiences within multireligious families, prior to participant introductions, to help open up discussion of this issue.

Participants may comment on their personal religious beliefs, as distinct from their religious heritage or background. Welcome these remarks, and say that having this information can help us acknowledge each other's viewpoints but also remind the group that this class focuses on the historical and sociological dimensions of religion, not religious or theological beliefs (see Appendix 11J for additional comments).

As a transition to the next activity, facilitators should clarify the following: *This course on religious oppression uses a historical and a sociological lens. It is sociological in that it focuses on the role of religious status and religious institutions in the United States. It is historical in that it examines the historical role of sectarian Christianity (specific Protestant sects such as Congregationalists or Methodists, or Protestants in relation to Catholics) in shaping dominant U.S. social systems and cultural values, while simultaneously using religion—Christianity—to maintain advantage within a Christian culture and subordinate religious status for groups such as Hindus, Jews, Muslims, Mormons, and Seventh-Day Adventists.*

Be explicit about distinguishing between

1. the historical role of religion in the United States—and of religious institutions in shaping early and contemporary U.S. social institutions, law, policies, and practices—from discussions of personal religious belief or affiliation; and
2. the sociological perspective on the social role of religion (as distinct from personal belief or theology) and on the role of religion in intergroup conflict. This is often an especially difficult concept for participants to understand, namely, that the curriculum is not looking at personal beliefs or comparing or assessing theologies, or the rightness or wrongness of specific religious practices.

If the confusion between personal religious beliefs and the historical role of religious systems emerges more than twice during the class, it can be added to the "guidelines for communication" as an issue to track and notice.

## 2. Religious and Ethnic Family Backgrounds (35 minutes)

The purpose of this activity is to build a learning community by enabling participants to see themselves and each other in a shared historical context, based on what they know or can guess about their family religious and ethnic legacies.

You have already modeled this group-building activity by talking about your own family's religious and ethnic backgrounds. Now ask participants to discuss their family's religious heritage, their family's ethnic or national heritage, whether their names reflect religious traditions, whether their family surnames changed during immigration or reflect slavery or colonization, or whether their families had multiple-religious backgrounds or -sectarian backgrounds (e.g., Christian and Jewish, Methodist and Baptist, and Protestant and Catholic). Participants might want to talk about religious rituals or traditions in their families, or their experience of sameness or difference in their home neighborhoods.

## Facilitation Issues

This activity enables participants to share their own religious background information with each other. It is important to model the tone and content you want to elicit from participants. It may be challenging to strike a balance between getting enough information from the participants and having an activity that takes too long. Decide whether to do this as a whole-group or small-group activity, and estimate how long each participant can take for the introduction, depending on the number of participants in the class.

### 3. Common Ground Activity (20 minutes)

The purpose of this activity is to gain awareness of the different religious experiences and traditions that are present in the room, or that are notable by their absence. It builds on the connections among family histories discussed in the preceding activity and begins to establish a more personal framework for discussions of advantaged and targeted religious groups in the United States.

Instructions for this activity also appear in Chapters 7, 8, 13, and 17. Ask participants to form a circle. As identifying statements are called out, participants for whom the statement is true enter the circle, stand there for a moment, and look at who has joined them in the inner circle and who remains in the outer circle before returning to the full group. Prepare in advance statements from the examples in Appendix 11K to emphasize various family and intergenerational religious affiliations held by group members. Also, provide statements that identify experiences not represented in the group. Invite participants to add their own sentence stems.

When all of the statements have been called out, and participants have had time to offer their own statements, ask the group to remain standing in the circle, to talk about what stand out as "privileges" experienced by Christians as an advantaged religious group, and as "challenges" or "exclusions" experienced by non-Christians as targeted religious groups. Ask participants to "hold" their substantive questions until they return to their seats.

After discussion of privileges and challenges, have participants briefly write questions and personal feelings about this activity. After a few minutes, place them into groups of three to four (or in pairs) to discuss issues that arose. If time permits, ask volunteers from the small groups to offer to the whole group some of the insights, issues, or questions that came up for them in this activity and the discussions.

### Break (15 minutes)

### 4. Knapsack of Christian Privilege (45 minutes)

This purpose of this knapsack activity is to generate from the participants a composite list of religious privileges that they themselves have experienced or can imagine experiencing.

Initiate this activity by explaining the idea of a "knapsack" of privilege that provides guides and roadmaps for daily life (definitions of key terms are in Appendix 11L; specific knapsack examples are in Appendix 11M). After explaining the concept of a "religious privilege knapsack" and providing specific examples, ask participants to write at least five examples of privilege that they have experienced, observed, or heard about. Ask participants to read aloud their examples. Write the examples on chalkboard or newsprint, with checks next to items that are repeated.

Questions for the whole group:

- What common themes do you notice among the items in your knapsacks?
- Who carries this "religious privilege" knapsack?
- What is the experience of people who do not have a religious privilege knapsack available to them?
- What are some religious groups that do not have a religious privilege knapsack within the United States?

### Facilitation Issues

It is helpful if participants have already read the list of privileges from McIntosh (1998), Schlosser (2003), or the examples listed in Appendix 11M. These lists work to "prime the pump" and help participants begin to see the difference between the experiences of those advantaged and those targeted by religion.

### 5. Models of Oppression (levels and types): Options A or B (30 minutes)

This activity enables participants to explore a conceptual framework that helps to organize ways in which religion can advantage some while targeting others. It draws upon two conceptual frameworks presented in this volume.

### Option A: Levels and Types of Oppression

(Note: Option B, using the "Five Faces of Oppression," appears in Appendix 11B.)

Review the concept of oppression, and the interpersonal, institutional, and cultural/societal "levels" and the conscious and unconscious "types" of its societal manifestations, using the information presented in Chapter 3, in *Overview: Religious Oppression*, and this chapter introduction.

After explaining the conceptual framework, post or hand out copies of the matrix in Appendix 11A, and ask for several examples to clarify the distinctions among the various levels and types. Ask participants to work in pairs or in small groups to come up with examples that fill in each of the matrix cells in Appendix 11A. After participants complete the matrix, ask them to provide their examples, which can be posted on the chalkboard or on newsprint. As participants offer examples, lead a discussion of how these examples play out in everyday life and how they may interact—for example, an interpersonal interaction between a teacher and a student, or two coworkers, may also be an example of an institutional policy.

Bring closure to this activity by asking participants to keep these levels and types of oppression in mind as a way to make sense of new information and insights about religious oppression.

### 6. Closing Questions and Issues (10 minutes)

Distribute three 3 × 5 cards or self-stick notes to each participant. Use one to write any new questions that have emerged for them during this first module. Use the second to note any insights or new learning from this module. The third is for concerns or challenges that have come up for participants.

Call participants' attention to the lists of questions posted on the wall earlier in the class. Ask participants to add the new questions they have to this list and move questions that have been answered to another section of the room. Establish a third section for concerns or challenges that have come up for participants, and a fourth section for insights, new learnings, or a-ha's.

Ask participants to move around the room to read each other's cards. If time permits, ask participants to comment on any themes they may have noticed in the questions, challenges, or new learnings and insights.

## Module 2: Historical and Conceptual Understanding of Religious Oppression in the United States

Time needed: 3.5 hours

### Objectives

- Become aware of the stereotypes and subordination of ethnically diverse religious minorities in U.S. history, with particular focus upon Native American Indian religions, Buddhists, Hindus, Jews, Muslims, and Sikhs.
- Understand the visibility and benefits of Christian identity for some U.S. citizens ("Christian hegemony") with the concomitant invisibility and disadvantage for the religious Other.
- Understand the historical backgrounds for religious domination and subordination in U.S. history and the interactions of race with religion in U.S. citizenship, naturalization, and immigration laws and policies.
- Analyze examples of religious oppression in the United States, drawing upon theories and models of social oppression.

**Key concepts**: religious majorities and minorities, religious domination and subordination, hegemony, Christianity, Protestantism, Catholicism, Native American Indian religions, Buddhism, Hinduism, Islam, Judaism, Sikhism

### 1. Opening (10 minutes)

As participants enter the room, ask them to write and to post any new issues or questions that have come up for them, move those that have been answered or addressed, and read what has been posted. Welcome participants back to the class, and ask whether there are group norms and guidelines participants wish to add or clarify.

### 2. Interfaith Four Squares (25 minutes)

The purpose of this activity is to increase participants' basic knowledge of religions that may be unfamiliar to them. This activity enables participants to identify missing information and suggests ways that they can learn about different religions.

Distribute Appendix 11N (question sheets), "Interfaith Four Squares," and ask participants to fill in as many squares by themselves as possible (5 minutes). Then, allow participants 10 minutes to go around the room reintroducing themselves to each other and provide each other with assistance in finding answers to the questions that remain unanswered on their own copies of the "Interfaith Four Squares."

Ask the participants to take their seats, distribute Appendix 11O (answer sheets), and review the answers one by one. Facilitators can raise questions such as the following:

- How challenging was this activity?
- How many squares were you able to fill out in the 5 minutes allotted?
- How does it feel to know the answers or not know the answers?
- Why do you think you were or were not able to answer these questions?

Ask where or how this information could be learned, with questions such as *Did you have neighbors, friends, or school peers of different religions? Did you ever talk about religion with your friends, peers, or neighbors? Did your family ever discuss religious differences? Did you ever feel "inside" or "outside" the religious mainstream of your neighborhood? Of your school? Of the culture represented on television?*

This last series of questions provides a transition to the next activity about sources of stereotypes and misinformation about religious differences.

### Facilitation Issues

During the interactive part of this activity, make sure that everyone is not congregating around one person to get all the answers. Encourage participants to interact with as many different people as possible.

If you are able to identify the specific religious backgrounds of participants in advance, it is helpful to adapt questions in the squares (see Appendix 11N) to ensure that all participants, especially those of minority religious faiths, are reflected in the activity.

Explain to participants that knowing this basic information is part of being informed, engaged citizens in a pluralistic democracy. Inform them that knowing "the basics" such as the names of sacred texts or scripture, holy cities, deities and religious leaders, and major holidays is an excellent place to start.

### 3. Stereotypes (40 minutes)

The purpose of this activity is to acknowledge and discuss the stereotypes and misinformation participants have heard about members of targeted religious groups.

Draw on the definitions and functions of stereotypes in the introductory module (Chapter 3) and in Appendix 11P to develop a brief clarification (10 minutes) of what stereotypes are and how we learn them.

Following this brief clarification, ask participants to form five small workgroups, and ask each workgroup to spend 15 minutes writing a list of stereotypes they have heard or read about a specific targeted religious community (each workgroup is assigned one of the following): (a) Native American Indian religions, (b) Buddhists, (c) Hindus, (d) Jews, and (e) Muslims. These lists will be posted in the room for a "gallery walk."

### Gallery Walk

Ask the workgroups to post their newsprint in a gallery around the room, and ask participants to walk around and read the newsprint gallery. When participants have finished reviewing the newsprint, ask them to brainstorm and then discuss the commonalities and the differences identified among the stereotypes for different religious groups. Call attention to the role of racialization in the stereotypes applied to the Buddhist, Hindu, Jewish, and Muslim communities with African, Asian. or Middle Eastern immigrant heritage.

To facilitate this discussion, provide the following two questions in advance:

- What stereotypes are used to name the members and the religious rituals or practices of targeted religious communities?
- What connections do you see among the religious, ethnic, racial, and cultural stereotypes attributed to members of privileged or targeted religious groups?

### Facilitation Issues

Remind participants that their ability to generate lists of stereotypes does not mean that they believe those stereotypes. Once these lists are posted, they should be kept in place for the duration of the class. The closing activity for this module returns to the lists of stereotypes.

Depending on the religious backgrounds or interests of a specific group of participants, you might want to add other targeted religious groups, such as atheists, Buddhists, Pagans, Rastafarians, Sikhs, or Wiccans (Albanese, 1999; Carroll, 2000; Ebaugh & Chafetz, 2000; Eck, 2001).

### Break (15 minutes)

### 4. Roots and Development of Christian Privilege and Minority Religious Oppression in U.S. History: Options A or B (60 minutes)

#### Option A: Lecture

(Note: Option B in Appendix 11Q offers three interactive alternatives to the formal lecture format.)

The objective of this segment is to explain and illustrate the hegemonic role of Christianity throughout the course of U.S. history. *Christian hegemony* refers to the "unacknowledged adherence to a dominant worldview ... a religious worldview that publicly affirms Christian observances, holy days, and sacred spaces, at the expense of those that who are not Christian and within a culture that normalizes Christian values as intrinsic to an explicitly American public and political way of life" (p. 253; see also Appendix 11L).

Prepare in advance a brief, focused lecture (20 minutes) that presents key themes or issues in the emergence of Christian privilege and religious oppression in the history of the United States. This lecture should be designed to help participants understand the role of Christianity in shaping political power, economic advantage, and social and cultural identity in the history of the United States. The lecture explains how Christian privilege has been historically intertwined with the religious oppression of subordinate peoples in U.S. history. Reading materials, maps and illustrations, and video or other resources to help facilitators to prepare this lecture are suggested in Appendix 11H; an extended chronological guide to key events and an overview for use in preparing the lecture appear in Appendix 11E and Appendix 11R (see also introduction to this chapter and *Overview: Religious Oppression*). (Interactive alternatives to the lecture are described in Appendix 11Q.)

Introduce this segment by explaining to participants that we all need to become more aware of the role of Christianity in shaping U.S. politics and culture, if we are to understand the social and cultural restrictions on religious minorities or the different experiences of advantaged and targeted religious groups in the contemporary United States.

Write the following questions on newsprint or chalkboard, and ask participants to write (2 to 3 minutes) some personal notes about the first things that come to mind in response to them:

- What is the role of Christianity in the founding and development of the United States?
- What is the present-day role of Christianity in the United States?

Ask several volunteers to share their "first thoughts" as a brainstorm with no discussion. The opportunity for discussion comes in the next segment of this module.

Present a brief (20-minute) lecture on key historical themes (Appendix 11R) that clarify the role of Christianity in shaping a majority religious culture, and maintaining political, economic, social, and cultural power and advantage in the United States. Use PowerPoint or overhead transparencies to present a lecture outline and also to illustrate your lecture with maps or other visuals.

Following the lecture, ask participants to form small groups to explore one or more of these questions:

- Has this new information challenged or reinforced your "first thoughts" about the historical or contemporary privilege attached to Christianity?
- Are there any connections between your own family's religious and ethnic history and the history presented in the lecture, or in the readings?

For example, ask participants to discuss the following:

- Where do you see your own family fitting into the history presented earlier?
- Where do you see other families you know of fitting in?
- Are there religious groups you know about that are not represented here in the room or in this discussion so far?

### Facilitation Issues

Both options, whether lecture or interactive group alternative formats, cover a considerable historical and political time span and multiethnic, multiracial, and multi-religious thematic range of issues. The facilitators should be focused on providing the big picture with some examples to illuminate major themes. It is likely that questions will be raised for which there are no easy or immediate answers. These questions can be deferred to later discussion, with the facilitators and participants sharing responsibility for seeking information to share with the class. It is also likely that there will be no one "correct" answer to questions that involve distinctive perspectives. Questions are likely to be raised about the entry of different religious groups into the colonies or the United States as voluntary or involuntary migrants, and these questions can be deferred for later discussions also.

### Break (15 Minutes)
### 5. U.S. Constitutional Safeguards for Freedom of Religious Belief and Observance (20 minutes)

This segment will enable participants to examine their assumptions about the role of the First Amendment to the U.S. Constitution in maintaining religious freedoms. Its purpose is to clarify the actual content of constitutional protections of religion and to provoke awareness of the role of the Supreme Court as final arbiter of U.S. religious freedom.

Introduce this topic by posting a copy of the two clauses commonly known as the Establishment Clause and Free Exercise Clause in the First Amendment (quoted above, and also in Appendix 11C). Ask participants the following:

- What specific aspects of religious belief does the First Amendment actually protect?
- What specific aspects of religious behavior does the First Amendment actually protect?
- What are examples of the kinds of government establishment of religion that are prohibited by the First Amendment?
- What minority religious practices would not be protected by the First Amendment?

Lead this discussion as a brainstorm (with no discussion of participant ideas). Post participant responses on newsprint or chalkboard for reference during the next segments of this module.

Prepare in advance some clarifying comments to enable participants to understand the basic religious protections of the First Amendment and also to consider what might be involved for a religious group in carrying a First Amendment lawsuit all the way through the federal or state legal systems in order to exercise their constitutional right to religious freedom. Provide examples of some of the cases involving school prayer, tax support for religious education, and Amish and Mormon religious practices. Explain that some Supreme Court litigation reflects conflicts between specific religious practices of minority groups that challenge local, state, or national laws or policies—fire and building codes, zoning regulations, and medical and public health regulations—which are generally reflective of Christian norms. Examples include the traditions of fire in Hindu or Native American Indian religious ceremonies, public animal and fowl sacrifices in Santería, building a *gurdwara* in a residentially zoned neighborhood, and wearing a *kippah* (yarmulke) underneath a military helmet. (See Appendix 11C for sample cases, Appendix 11D for the legal findings, and Appendix 11S for examples of accommodation and inclusion.)

### Facilitation Issues

Assure participants that this topic is complicated, and the cases are sometimes contradictory, but the constitutional protections for religious freedom and the role of the Supreme Court in creating legal precedent for religious freedom in the current day are important for them to know about.

### 6. Homework Assignment and Closure (15 minutes)

Remind the class of readings on the two conceptual organizers for religious oppression, "the level and types of oppression" and the "Five Faces of Oppression," in Appendices 11A and 11B. Ask participants to apply one of these two frameworks to assigned readings on religious oppression (Appendix 11G) as their homework assignment for the next module. In closing, ask participants to say one word or a few words about one thing that stood out for them from this module, or one thing they want to continue thinking about for the next class.

### Module 3: Institutional Examples for an Oppression Perspective

Time needed: 3.5 hours

## Objectives

- Recognize the interconnections between religious oppression and other forms of social oppression, such as racism, sexism, and classism.
- Recognize examples of religious oppression in contemporary everyday life.
- Understand constitutional safeguards for freedom of religion as well as the current limits in case law.

**Key concepts**: institutional oppression, cultural/societal oppression, workplace, school, constitutional safeguards, case law

## 1. Opening (10 minutes)

Welcome participants, and summarize what the group has experienced together at this midpoint of the class. Take stock of the questions that have been answered and the new questions or concerns that have arisen. Reconfirm or add to the group's list of norms and guidelines.

## 2. Institutional and Cultural "Web" of Religious Oppression (20 minutes)

The purpose of this activity is to provide a physical representation of the weblike interrelationships among institutional forms of religious oppression in the present-day United States.

Open this activity by asking participants to name the many social institutions involved in everyday society, such as law enforcement, the courts and justice system (state and federal), advocacy groups, schools, businesses, human service agencies, health care systems, newspapers and TV stations, town and city officials, and state and federal park and forestry bureaus. Ask participants to think about how religious advantage and disadvantage might play out in these various social institutions.

Prepare this activity by having several examples ready to use (see Appendix 11T) and a ball of yarn. All of the specific setup instructions for this activity, examples to use as prompts, and facilitation notes are presented in Appendix 11T.

While this human "web" is in process, be prepared to write on a chalkboard or newsprint (in two columns) the institutions or aspects of culture (column 1) and the specific examples (column 2) that participants are naming (examples for facilitator prompts appear in Appendix 11T).

## 3. How Schools or Workplaces Maintain Christian Hegemony (70 minutes)

### Option A: Small-Group Scenario Resolution

(Options B, C, and D for this activity are described in Appendix 11S.)

This activity is intended to build on the specific examples of religious advantage and disadvantage generated in earlier activities. Whereas they asked participants to name instances of religious advantage and disadvantage that play out in various social institutions, this activity asks participants to discuss scenarios of religious disadvantage and subordination in schools and in the workplace.

Distribute copies of four school and workplace scenarios selected or adapted from those presented in Appendix 11U. Ask participants to join one of four workgroups, and assign each group one scenario selected or adapted from Appendix 11U. Ask groups to respond to the questions listed with the scenarios and prepare a newsprint with their ideas to display in a gallery.

After 30 minutes, ask groups to post their galleries and walk around to review each other's recommendations. Reconvene the whole group, and ask participants (or, based on class size, several small groups) to brainstorm about how to prevent religious preju-dice, exclusion, or disadvantage. Ask them to begin to imagine how institutions and cultural practices might change to remove religious advantage and disadvantage. As prompts for the whole group or small-group discussion, facilitators should ask ques-tions such as the following:

- What are the religious advantages that can be made more inclusive?
- What are the disadvantages that can be eliminated?
- If you were in charge of creating a religiously inclusive school or workplace, what would you want to change?
- How would you go about making this change? Whom would you ask to work with you in the change process?

### Facilitation Issues

There are other "scenarios activities" that will challenge participants to think specifi-cally about Christian hegemony and discuss effective change strategies. Assure par-ticipants that there will be other opportunities in this module and the next module to reflect on effective change strategies. In this first effort to grapple with real-world sce-narios, make sure to hear from all groups and keep time to assure that all groups have equal time to share. Help participants differentiate between broad institutional visions and narrowly tailored specific strategies, as a segue to creating their action plans in Module 4.

### Break (15 minutes)

### 4. Scenarios Concerning Protection for Religious Minorities (75 minutes)

The purpose of this activity is to involve participants in working with actual case law dealing with First Amendment protections of religion. The litigation and case law under the First Amendment are both complex and contested. Participants will get a sense of the issues involved by trying to "decide" difficult First Amendment religious freedom cases on which courts have already rendered judgment.

Open this activity by reminding participants of the earlier discussion of the First Amendment protections of religious freedoms. Remind them that the judicial system is an important social institution in determining religious privilege and disadvantage.

Ask participants to work in small groups (three to four participants). Distribute one or two First Amendment cases to each workgroup. (Select these cases from Appendix 11D1.) Each small group will "decide" one or two cases as if they were judges. Their "decisions" should be based on their understandings of what the Constitution guar-antees through its First Amendment rights. Ask the groups to prepare brief newsprint reports, and post them in a gallery. (All participants need to have copies of all scenarios for reference during the subsequent discussion.)

After 20 minutes, ask the workgroups to post their newsprint "decisions" in a gallery. Ask participants to review each group's "finding" in the case by visiting each station in the gallery (10 minutes). Give participants self-stick notes to use for any comments they might want to add to the cases in the gallery. Reconvene for a whole-class discussion of different views among participants about the groups' decisions (15 minutes).

### First Amendment Case Legal Decisions

The purpose of this phase of the activity is to expose participants to some of the com-plexity and legal constraints surrounding the constitutional First Amendment reli-gious guarantees.

Distribute Appendix 11D2, which presents the actual court findings on the cases that had been "decided" by the participants. Appendix 11D2 includes background explanations quoted from legal scholars who argue for and against these decisions. Give participants several minutes to compare the actual court findings with their own decisions. The remaining discussion time (20 minutes) should be devoted to their reactions, their rationale for agreement or disagreement with the court decisions, and the arguments they might want to make to reargue any of these decisions.

### Facilitation Issues

Full reports from each of the small groups may not be possible, given the complexity of thinking surrounding some of these provocative cases. Each of the cases provides food for further thought and reflection. It is not the purpose of this segment to resolve these difficult and challenging questions, but rather to frame them in ways that will motivate further study. Conclude this discussion with a list of resources for further study selected from Appendices 11H, 11C , and 11D.

### 5. Reactions, Responses, and Closing (10 minutes)

Invite participants to share one-word or one-sentence reactions, learnings, a-ha's, or things to think about. Make sure everyone in the group has a chance to say a single word or sentence.

## Module 4: Next Steps and Action Plans

Time needed: 3 hours, 45 minutes

### Objectives

- Consider why people accept "business as usual" with Christian hegemony and religious oppression.
- Understand how people can begin to question and to change "business as usual."
- Identify ways to interrupt instances of religious exclusion and prejudice, and to create change.
- Create an action plan.

**Key concepts**: liberation, action planning, ally

### 1. Opening (10 minutes)

As participants return for this fourth module, ask them to move cards or self-stick note questions that have been answered to the section of the room where answered questions have been posted. Raise the possibility that participant change strategies can answer questions that were not addressed in the preceding modules.

### 2. Framework for Change: Cycles of Liberation (40 minutes)

The purpose of this activity is to provide one of several organizers that will help participants to be systematic and thoughtful in their approach to change.

Post or distribute copies of the "Cycle of Socialization" and the "Cycle of Liberation" (use Appendices 3E and F). Spend 15 minutes asking participants for specific examples for each part of the Cycle of Liberation, and write the examples into the posted cycle. Emphasize the many opportunities that the Cycle of Liberation offers to transform "business as usual" to create a more religiously inclusive environment.

## 3. Reopen Knapsack and Scenarios for Action Planning: Options A or B (40 minutes)

(Option B in Appendix 11S offers "Inclusion and Accommodation Scenarios.")

This activity reminds participants of the privileges they identified earlier in the religious privilege knapsacks and of the religious advantages and disadvantages they noted in the school and workplace scenarios. Refer participants back to the written materials from these earlier activities. Ask participants to return to the workgroups they participated in for the school and workplace scenarios.

After the participants have had a chance to review the Christian privileges they noted in these activities, and to reexamine any religious advantages and disadvantages they may have as individuals, ask them to prepare to design a personal action plan by focusing on one specific area of privilege or disadvantage—or one particular individual or institutional context—for which they want to take action.

## Break (15 Minutes)

## 4. Ingredients of a Personal "Action Plan" (85 minutes)

Remind participants that they have already identified many opportunities for taking action to create change. Explain that for change to be effective, it is important to develop a plan that takes into account a number of factors.

The first of these factors involves an understanding of personal risk levels. Distribute Appendix 11V, and ask participants to note whether various actions would be high risk or low risk for them. Invite participants to come up with other examples and note whether they are high risk or low risk:

- Attending a religious service that is different from your own with a friend or acquaintance
- Making sure that your school or workplace acknowledges different religious holidays and schedules public events not to occur on religious holidays
- Creating and participating in a religiously diverse study group to extend your understanding of different religious beliefs, texts, and traditions
- Creating and participating in a religious environment task force that identifies and recommends changes in your school or workplace
- Other: ...
- Other: ...

Ask volunteers to share what was high risk and what was low risk for them. Ask participants to think about their own personal risk levels when planning change strategies.

The second of these factors is understanding one's sphere of influence. Post and also distribute copies of Appendix 4B, which shows personal, familial, institutional, and public spheres of influence. Ask participants to spend several minutes quietly filling in examples of their various spheres of influence. Then ask volunteers to provide specific examples—and add comments to link those specific examples about whether acting in specific spheres of influence would constitute high risk or low risk for them personally.

The third of these factors is understanding that there is an action continuum, involving lesser or greater challenge in the action taken. Post and distribute copies of Appendix 6H, which presents a sample action continuum. Ask participants to talk in pairs about the places on the action continuum that look most likely for them and to offer several examples of what that specific action might be.

Distribute Appendices 11W and 11X, which provide a matrix that coordinates various elements for specific action plans, and a worksheet for action planning. Give participants 5 to 10 minutes of quiet writing time to use the frameworks that seem most useful and prepare notes on an intended action plan.

After 5–10 minutes, ask participants to stand up, stretch, and meet with a partner to talk about their action plan notes. Ask them to take 5 minutes each to present their action plans to each other, referring to whatever handouts and planning materials seem most useful to them. Encourage partners to ask clarifying questions to help each other develop a well-thought-out plan. Remind participants that everyone may choose different actions and that all are important steps toward addressing religious oppression. Emphasize that the action plans need to be realistic so that they will be implemented. Depending on the size of the group, ask volunteers briefly to describe their action plans to conclude this activity.

## 5. Closure and Evaluations (15 minutes)

This closing activity is designed to hear a concluding thought from each of the participants, while taking symbolic action on the lists of stereotypes that are still posted around the room.

Remind participants that the posted stereotypes (Module 2, Activity 3) still remain on the wall and are still active in the broader social environment. Although they cannot be fully removed from everyday life, it is possible to tear them up now as a visible symbol of everyone's intention to take action to create positive change.

Ask participants to form a circle while you remove the stereotype lists from around the room. Post the following sentence stems on chalkboard or newsprint:

- One thing I'm willing to do is ...
- One thing I've learned is ...
- One thing I want to tell you is ...

Ask participants to take turns tearing up and throwing away a segment of the stereotype newsprints after completing one of the sentence stems. Continue around the circle until all of the participants have spoken and all of the stereotypes have been torn up and thrown away.

## Notes

1. Our primary examples focus on the domination of mainstream Protestant denominations in the United States over the religions of subjugated peoples. These subjugated religions include the spiritual beliefs and practices of Native American Indians and African peoples, and the religious beliefs and practices of Catholics, Hindus, Jews, Mormons, Muslims, and Sikhs. It is not possible in this brief introductory overview to provide illustrative examples for other groups who are important among U.S. religions, such as atheists, Buddhists, Confucians, Daoists, Jehovah's Witnesses, Mennonites, Pagans, Rastafarians, Santeríans, Seventh-Day Adventists, or Wiccans, although some examples for a few of these religious minorities appear in the curriculum design that follows and the appendices in the accompanying CD. For further information, see Ahlstrom (2004); Albanese (1999); Coward, Hinnells, and Williams (2000); Haddad (2002); Iwamura and Spickard (2003); Wuthnow (2005); and Yoo (1999).
2. Recent developments within U.S. Christianity greatly complicate an already complex understanding of the relations between dominant Christianity and subordinated non-Christian and typically non-white religious communities. First, the dramatic growth of Protestant Evangelical "fundamentalism" has emerged

as a political anchor for the right wing of the Republican Party, conflating religious ideology with bruising political wedge issues and upon occasion linking the apocalyptic expectations of Evangelicals with the interests of Zionists in the Middle East (Goldberg, 2006; Kaplan, 2004; Phillips, 2006). Provocative and helpful discussion of a number of religious "fundamentalisms"—Hindu, Islamic, and Jewish as well as Christian—can be found in Fox (2002), Juergensmeyer (2004), Marty and Appleby (1997), Odell-Scott (2004), Saha (2004), and Weinberg and Pedahzur (2004). The absence of a historical perspective on the recurrent cycles of American Evangelicalism exacerbates the political intensity of these debates. A second and far more extreme development on the fringes of Christianity is the resurgence of Christian Identity militant movements that have added virulent anti-Muslim hate speech and harassment to their antisemitic and racist agendas (Cowan, 2003). Third, as mentioned in the *Overview*, both mainstream and Evangelical Protestantism have been transformed by the dramatic growth among Latino/a and Asian Christians whose worship remains firmly rooted in culturally and linguistically homogeneous ethnic communities (Carnes & Yang, 2004; Eck, 2001; Min & Kim, 2002; Warner & Witner, 1998; Yoo, 1999).

3. *Nativism* is used in this chapter to refer to historical cycles of race- and religion-based political reactions to religious, racial, and linguistic immigrants in the United States (Feagin, 1997; Higham, 2004; Jacobson, 1998), going as far back as political reactions to perceptions of overinclusivity in the category *white persons* in the 1790 naturalization law. Most discussions of nativism focus on anti-immigration, racism, and eugenics mainly in the period 1840–1920 (that is, from the immigration of Irish during the potato famine until the restrictive legislation of 1924). However, as Jacobson (1998) points out, "[T]he loudest voices in the organized nativism of the 1840s and 1850s harped upon matters of Catholicism and economics, not race" (p. 69), although in the stereotypes, for example of "Papists," "religion was sometimes seen as a function of race" (p. 70). Whereas *nativism* is a recurrent (or continuous) phenomenon in U.S. history, the express hatred of others can be termed *xenophobia,* and the preferences for one's own can be termed *ethnocentrism. Nativism*, as used with these historical meanings, is an appropriation of the notion of native birth, that is, of U.S. birth among Anglo- or white Americans as distinct from foreign-born immigrants. In this sense, it must not be confused with the notion of "Native" as in Native American Indians.

4. Almaguer (1994) details the popular stereotype of the "Heathen Chinese" as "superstitious" "pagan idolaters" (pp. 158–159) and quotes this telling passage of a speech delivered (1877) to the General Association of Congregational Churches in California:

Slavery compelled the heathen [Blacks] to give up idolatry, and they did. The Chinese have no such compulsion and they do not. ... Slavery compelled the adoption of Christian forms of worship, resulting in universal Christianization. The Chinese have no such influence tending to their conversion. ... Slavery took the heathens and by force made them Americans in feeling, tastes, habits, language, sympathy and spirit; first fitting them for citizenship, and then giving them the vote. The Chinese [remain] ... the same as they were in old China, unprepared for citizenship, and adverse in spirit to our institutions. (Quoted in Almaguer, 1994, p. 159)

5. See Fraser (1999) for historical context of the phrase "separation of church and state" used by Thomas Jefferson in a letter (1802) to assure the Baptists of Danbury, Connecticut, that the language of the First Amendment had built "'a wall of

separation between Church and State'" (p. 19). The phrase has come into general usage, although *church* no longer represents the forms of religious worship (as in cathedral, church, *gurdwara*, mosque, synagogue, or temple) that are "walled off" from government.

6. Despite their religious origin, the U.S. Supreme Court has upheld Sunday blue laws, concluding that although the laws had roots in the Christian religion, it is within the powers and rights of a state to set aside a day of rest for the well-being of its citizens. See Feldman (1997, pp. 232–234, 252, and n. 53) on the four relevant 1961 Supreme Court cases, one of which instances numerous exceptions such as charity, sale of drugs or tobacco, and running of trains and boats, but no exception for Orthodox Jews who observed the Sabbath on Saturday (Feldman, p. 232).

7. *Islamophobia* is used to emphasize the phobic dimensions of the "fear or hatred of Islam and its adherents that translates into individual, ideological and systemic forms of oppression and discrimination" (see Zine, 2003, p. 40).

# 12

# Antisemitism and Anti-Jewish Oppression Curriculum Design

MAURIANNE ADAMS AND
KATJA HAHN D'ERRICO

This chapter assumes familiarity with the preceding *Overview* and Chapter 11, "Religious Oppression," by presenting an extended example of the religious oppression experienced over many centuries by the Jewish people. This form of religious oppression is generally known as *antisemitism*, alternatively termed *anti-Jewish oppression* in this chapter.

*Antisemitism* has been called "the longest hatred" (Wistrich, 1991) to describe the millennia during which the Jews maintained a collective identity as a people in diaspora (Greek for "dispersion"), first as a monotheist people subjected or colonized by polytheistic empires (Egypt, Assyria, Babylonia, Greece, and Rome) and later as marginalized, separate, sometimes ghettoized religious and ethnic communities within Christian and Islamic countries (Boonstra, Jansen, & Kniesmeyer, 1993; Cohn-Sherbok, 2002; Perry & Schweitzer, 2002).

Jewish identity, religion, law, and custom were forged during 2 millennia bookended on one side by a Hebrew monarchy in Palestine (1200-900 BCE) destroyed by Assyria's conquest of northern Israel (800 BCE) and Babylonia's deportation of Jews from southern Judah (600–500 BCE), and, on the other side, by the establishment of an Israeli democratic state in 1948. During this diaspora, Jewish communities located in European, Arab, and North African countries experienced periods of relative acceptance, assimilation, and prosperity interacting with violent cycles of enslavement, expulsion, massacres, pogroms, and state-organized genocide.

This chapter builds on the *Antisemitism* chapter (Weinstein & Mellen, 1997) in the first edition of *TDSJ*, and includes historical materials from that chapter on the CD that accompanies this edition (Appendices 12A, 12B, and 12C). During the intervening decade, we have taken an approach that considers multiple forms of religious oppression, presented in the *Overview* and in Chapter 11. This revised "Antisemitism and Anti-Jewish Oppression" chapter should be read in that larger context, while also standing alone as testimony to an extraordinarily complex and richly documented historical and present-day instance of religious oppression intersecting with racism, ethnocentrism, classism, and nationalism.

Jews have been oppressed as a religious people, an ethnically distinct people, and a racialized people, vilified and hated regardless of the reasons given, stereotypically associated with class (money) and class ideology (capitalism as well as communism). The conflations and challenges of the intersecting social identity categories within the designations *Jewish* or *Jew*—ethnic, racial, and religious—are as confusing today as they are to the historian who tries to disentangle the interconnected religious, economic, ethnic, and racial dimensions of antisemitism in earlier periods and contexts (Fredrickson, 2002; Prager & Telushkin, 2003). Studied from a social justice and antioppression perspective, antisemitism and anti-Jewish oppression offer a fascinating and complicated story of oppression coexisting with survival and liberation.

## Terminology: Antisemitism and/or Anti-Jewish Oppression?

The word *antisemitism* derives etymologically from the biblical name Shem ("Semitic"), a son of Noah identified in several religious traditions as ancestor to both Jews and Arabs (as well as ancient Babylonians, Assyrians, Phoenicians, and other ancient inhabitants of the eastern Mediterranean). *Semitic* has been used to designate a language group that includes Arabic, Amharic, Aramaic, Ethiopic, and Hebrew. The term *antisemitism*, however, attributed to the Austrian journalist Wilhelm Marr, founder of the Anti-Semitic League (1871), is used explicitly to convey hatred toward Jews but not toward other "Semitic" language speakers. Because Jews were the only so-called Semites remaining in Christian Europe after the expulsion of Arabs from Spain in the 15th century, *antisemitism* connotes the fanatical and racialized vehemence of self-termed "Anti-Semites" in the oppression of Europe's (and the United States') Jews. In this sense, the term *antisemitism* acknowledges the specific form of race-based oppression directed against Jewish victims by European Christian perpetrators. The term becomes more problematic when used to describe the subordination of Jews in medieval Islamic countries or to discuss their exclusion and expulsion from modern Arab and North African Muslim countries (Cohen, 1994; Sacher, 2005) because of their shared Semitic origins. *Antisemitism* in this chapter will be used mainly to refer to the racial formation of Jews as Europe's racialized "Other" from the fifteenth century (Fredrickson, 2002; Mosse, 1985) into the twenty-first century.

The ethnic and linguistic associations with the term *antisemitism* have made it a magnet for Jewish–Arab tensions in the context of contemporary Middle East politics and also within European Arab and Jewish immigrant communities. This contestation has led to challenging discussions among Arab- and Jewish-affiliated participants in our courses, concerning what constitutes an accurate and appropriate terminology to describe historical and contemporary oppression experienced by Jewish people in the United States and worldwide. Used uncritically and ahistorically, the term *antisemitism* can fuel the sense of invisibility experienced by other Semitic peoples, mainly Muslim Arabs. An alternative term, *anti-Jewish oppression*, parallels the usage for other forms of oppression described in this volume, but fails to evoke the virulent fanaticism, the history, or the racialized phases of this specific oppression. One can go around and around on these more than "merely semantic" discussions whose fraught meanings suggest the challenges in speaking about this specific oppression, identity, and history.

In this chapter, we use each of these two terms intentionally within specific historical and geographical contexts. We use *anti-Jewish oppression* to refer, first, to the early and preracialized Christian roots of this religion-based oppression in Christian and non-Christian countries (sometimes also termed *Jew hatred, anti-Judaism*, or *Judeophobia*) and, second, to manifestations of this oppression currently in Arab and African countries and in the United States. We intentionally use the historical term *antisemitism* to convey the explicitly racist European meanings in general usage up through the mid-20th century, and still in use by white Christian identity groups in Europe and the United States . The term *antisemitism* is also widely used in scholarship that explores the full history and global manifestations of antisemitism (Bronner, 2000; Dinnerstein, 1994; Langmuir, 1990; Michael, 2005; Weinberg, 1986; Wistrich, 1991).

The complicated religious, ethnic, linguistic, and cultural strands of contemporary anti-Jewish oppression are not easy to disentangle from the racist meanings attached to antisemitism—or both from recent, politically oriented critiques of the policies of Israel toward the Palestinians. At times, though certainly not in every case, these critiques intentionally or unconsciously conflate political anti-Zionism with echoes of earlier European antisemitism. This presents one of the more daunting challenges in teaching about this issue of oppression in the current political climate.[1]

## Importance of History

Participants need to become familiar with the social and historical roots of *anti-Jewish oppression* and *antisemitism* in order to understand the Holocaust within its Christian European context rather than misinterpret it as a unique historical event (Cohen, 1994; Hilberg, 1992; Mosse, 1985). The oppression of Jews is both a "historical" and contemporary phenomenon, deeply rooted in the history of Christian Europe. For example, Mel Gibson's film *The Passion of the Christ* portrays a sectarian understanding of the Crucifixion derived from provocative passages in the Christian Gospels that were over many centuries used to whip up anti-Jewish fervor and justify anti-Jewish violence.[2] Another recent example: The conspiracy theory, accepted by many, that several thousand Jews were warned to stay away from their offices in the World Trade Center on September 11, 2001, is one of many modern reincarnations of the idea of Jewish world control, first propagated in *The Protocols of the Elders of Zion* (Bronner, 2000; see also Sacher, 2005). The ancient accusation of "blood libel" that Jews ritually murder Christian babies for Passover rituals, a libel that dates back to the 12th century, was played out in the United States less than a century ago in Messina, upper New York State, in 1928 (Perry & Schweitzer, 2002; Prager & Telushkin, 2003).

The story of the Jews' struggle for survival as a diaspora people in European, Middle Eastern, and North African countries and the Americas is a key dimension of this curriculum. During the 2 millennia that Jews lived throughout Christian Europe, religious hatred of Jews and destruction of Jewish temples, holy books, and communities took many forms: restrictive canonical law from the third century on, massacres of entire Jewish communities during the Crusades, forced conversions in Catholic Spain followed by Inquisition and expulsion, state-sponsored pogroms in Poland and Russia, and genocide during the Nazi Holocaust. The repeated cycles of expulsion of Jews from England, France, and Spain (1290–1492) were also political outcomes of religious and ethnic conflict during periods of national unification, a relationship repeated in modern European pogroms, genocide, and ethnic cleanings (see Appendices 12A, 12B, and 12D).

Jews who lived for centuries in Muslim-dominated Arab and North African countries were not viewed as aliens there—partly because they were not the only ethnic or religious minority, partly because they looked more like their Arab-Muslim neighbors, and partly because they joined preestablished Jewish communities in Palestine, Egypt, North Africa, and (Muslim) Spain (Cohen, 1994; Lewis, 1984; O'Shea, 2006). Under Islam, Jews shared with Christians the subordinate legal category *dhimmī*, which designated non-Muslim "People of the Book" who were recognized recipients of earlier revelation. *Dhimmīs* held lower status than Muslims, and their subordinate status was regulated by requirements governing distinctive clothing, restrictions on religious and domestic architecture, choice of personal names, exclusion from public office, and payment of the *jizya*, or poll tax. This last guaranteed physical and religious protection and residential rights according to Islamic law, "a surer guarantee of protection from non-Jewish hostility than their distant brethren had in the Latin West ... a recognized, fixed, safeguarded niche within the hierarchy of the Islamic social order" (Cohen, pp. 72, 112). These Jewish communities did not survive the 20th-century national liberation movements in Arab or North African Islamic countries, or the reach of the Holocaust or the violence that followed the establishment of Israel (see Appendix 12E).

Jews in Islamic countries, during the years that parallel Europe's Middle Ages and modern era (up through the 1930s),[3] did not stand out as the sole religious and ethnic "Other" as they did in Christian Europe (Cohen, 1994; Lewis, 1984). Ethnicities in Muslim countries included Arabs, Berbers, Europeans, Iranians, Jews, Kurds, Turks, and Persians, so that subordinate religious and ethnic status was more ethnically diverse than in Europe. Although discrimination against *dhimmīs* was structural and systemic in Islamic countries, as it also was in Christian Europe, Jews, when persecuted by Muslims, were "treated as *dhimmīs* [along with Christians], not as Jews," and this differs "from European persecutions, which, by definition, were anti-Jewish and from the time of the First Crusade, were widespread and characteristic" (Cohen, p. 164).

The discussion in this chapter of the cyclical recurrence of anti-Jewish oppression and antisemitism focuses on Christian Europe because Europe was the progenitor for the oppression experienced by Jews historically in the United States. Our discussion is organized around three major themes: specifically, *religious* anti-Jewish oppression (from the ancient up to the modern world, but most pronounced in Christian Europe, where Jews were blamed as Christ killers); *economic and political factors* that grew out of the religious exclusions in polytheistic, Christian, or Muslim countries; and the development of *racialized antisemitism* in the context of 18th-century biological science (Frederickson, 2002; Hilberg, 1961; Mosse, 1985; see also Appendix 12B).[4]

For U.S. Jews with family members who lived through or perished in the Holocaust or with memories of East European pogroms in their extended family backgrounds, present-day incidents of anti-Jewish oppression on college campuses, in U.S. cities, and in European schools and neighborhoods are experienced as evidence of the here-and-now reality of anti-Jewish oppression and antisemitism. For those who know little or nothing of the cyclical history of antisemitism, graffiti on a campus building and offensive remarks by Russian politicians, French Muslim youth, or Christian identity groups may seem to be isolated acts, not worth worrying about, and Jewish expressions of anxiety shrugged off as hypersensitivity and overreaction (for incidents and audits, see U.S. Department of State, 2005; and Appendix 12F).

People who do not acknowledge the multiple, cyclical, and interconnected repetitions of patterns within antisemitism or anti-Jewish oppression may dismiss them as merely the echo of an outmoded Eurocentric past, less pressing than other forms of oppression in today's globalized world. Such tendencies not to take seriously anti-Jewish oppression or antisemitism within social justice or multicultural curricula perpetuate this mistaken view (Biale, Galchinsky, & Heschel, 1998; Brettschneider, 1996; Langman, 1995; MacDonald-Dennis, 2005, 2006; Schultz, 2001).

## Palestinian Rights and Criticism of Israel

The escalating political and military conflicts over territories claimed both by Israelis and Palestinians have been protested and challenged by both Palestinian and Israeli (as well as other) writers.[5] These challenges are directed at specific Israeli policies in Palestine, and more recently Lebanon, as well as the killing of Israeli citizens by Islamic groups opposed to the presence or the encroachments of Israel. These critiques of Israeli military force and U.S. financial support, whose effect is to displace and oppress another group of people, must not be confused with *antisemitic* discourse that blames "the Jews" for actions taken by Israel as an autonomous nation-state. Implicit in such indiscriminate blame is an essentializing double standard that implies all Jews everywhere are responsible for Israel's current nationalistic policies, or that Jews are the only people with no right to national sovereignty (see analysis in Finkelstein, 2005; Kushner & Solomon, 2003; Lerner, 1992).[6] One cannot make sense of contemporary Israeli-Palestinian liberatory and national aspirations, compounded by their religious and territorial conflicts, without first understanding their competing histories. The mutually destructive violence of these two religiously identified peoples to secure the same piece of land has been sanctified by Jewish and Islamic sacred texts that have been encoded upon the same geographical territories.

The difficulties inherent in helping participants in our courses to understand these complicated historical, religious, and territorial challenges, without indiscriminately blaming whole peoples or perpetuating anti-Jewish and/or anti-Arab anti-Muslim stereotypes, are also taken up in the curriculum that follows. In order to enable participants from different religious, political, and ideological perspectives to talk meaningfully with each other, we urge facilitators to require reading of common texts to ground discussion and dialogue (see Appendix 12G).

## U.S. Jewish Identity and Self-definition

Jewish identity, religion, law, and custom were forged in Jewish communities as far-flung as Afghanistan, Brazil, China, Ethiopia (Beta Israel), India (Bene Israel and Cochin), Jamaica, and Yemen—as well as throughout the Americas, Europe, the Middle East, and North Africa. Today, there are 120 countries with a Jewish community (Tobin, Tobin, & Rubin, 2005; see also World Jewish Congress, 2004–2005).

Sephardic Jews reached the Americas following expulsion from Spain and Portugal in the late 15th century, and Ashkenazi Jews migrated to the Americas from Central Europe (1840s onward) and in much greater numbers from Eastern Europe (1870s onward) (Diner, 2004; Michael, 2005; Sacher 1992). Jews from older, more established communities in Ethiopia, Egypt, Morocco, or Iran have immigrated to the United States more recently and in relatively small numbers (Tobin, Tobin, & Rubin, 2005). The fact that most U.S. Jews are ethnically Ashkenazi has led to racial stereotypes of Jews as white, a designation that makes obvious sense in the U.S. racial context (Brodkin Sacks, 1994; Higham, 2004; Kaye-Kantrowitz, 2001; MacDonald-Dennis, 2005), but does not make sense for Jews who immigrate to the United States from communities in North African or Arab countries or their descendants, or American Jews of racially mixed parentage, or African Americans who are members of Hebrew Israelite congregations that go back in the United States more than a century (Adams & Bracey, 1999; Khanga, 1992; Khazzoum, 2003; Tobin, Tobin, & Rubin, 2005; Walker, 2001; see also Shohat, 1988/1997).

Thus, the question "Who (or what) is a Jew?" defies the established ethnic and racial social identities and categories in the United States (Adams, 2001; Kaye-Kantrowitz, 1996). If Jews constitute a *religious* category only, how does one account for nonobservant or nonpracticing secular Jews, Jewish atheists, Jewish Buddhists, or Evangelical Christian Jews, or the range of religious beliefs and practices that differentiate Hasidic or Orthodox Jews from Jews who are Reform or Reconstructionist? If Jews in the United States are understood to belong to an *ethnic* group (parallel to Irish or Italian Americans), how does one understand the ethnic differences among Sephardic, Ashkenazi, and Mizrachi Jews? If Jews are identified by *national origins*, what meaningful distinctions should be made among Jews from Cuba, Morocco, France, or the Ukraine, or American Jews and Israeli Jews? And if Jews are identified as a *race*, what does it mean to say that Jews are "white" within U.S. racial categories, when a half-century ago Jews were officially designated non-Aryan throughout Nazi-occupied Europe, and non-Anglo-Saxon in former British colonies (including the United States)? Jews who emigrated from European countries where they had been legally labeled an inferior ("Semitic") racial group, and came to the United States where racial designations separated Whites from peoples of color (the "one drop" rule), experienced a radical reversal from earlier race-based subordination to a new, sometimes puzzling, status of race-based domination.

Thus, binary social designations that oversimplify complex and interactive components of identity in the United States—religious, racial, ethnic, cultural, gender, and class—do not account for the complicated intersecting social positions and identities of Jews as a diaspora people who have crossed and recrossed racial, ethnic, and national boundaries numerous times; maintained separate or affiliated community identities across thousands of years in many lands; and intermarried with Europeans, Africans, and Arabs. Their offspring look like other Europeans or Africans or Arabs, and yet are nonetheless known to themselves and to others as Jews. Jews are thus linked as a people through shared history, cultural heritage, language, traditions, and religious observance and rituals that date back 4,000 years to the Hebrew tribes of Canaan (Dever, 2003). Their numerous migrations have led to adaptations of religion and culture that reflect the various stopping places along the way (Tobin, Tobin, & Rubin, 2005).

Jewish participants in our classes not surprisingly vary in the ways they construct their identities as Jews. Some have strong and clear identities, both religious and cultural; some identify culturally but do not follow religious beliefs and practices; some come from families who have assimilated into Christian culture; some come from racially, ethnically, and/or nationally mixed parentage, or construct their Jewish identity through intersections with their gender, sexuality, disability, and/or class.[7] Some participants come to our courses with questions about what being Jewish means for them, with family "secrets" of hidden Jewish ancestry, biracial parentage, and intersecting salient identities (gender, sexuality, class). These issues are confusing for non-Jewish participants who expect that all Jews are—well, you know—Jews.

For participants who are not Jewish, the notion of being a *Gentile* may be new and surprising. It is also painful to acknowledge an identity often tied to the oppression of the Jewish "Other." For Christian Gentiles, feelings of guilt, anger, or denial may accompany their learning about the role of institutional and state-sponsored

Christianity in recurrent cycles of persecution of Jews. And those from mixed Jewish–Christian parentage may experience confusion in trying to coordinate their combined inherited legacies.

Whereas for Gentiles this course offers a perspective on Jews as the oppressed Other and their role in that oppression, for many Jewish participants this course stimulates a renewal, or in some cases the discovery, of their identities as Jews.[8] Because the denial and trivializing of historical antisemitism by both Gentiles and Jews are obstacles to be overcome, and because the most poignant evidence of anti-Jewish oppression often lies in the personal pain and struggles that individual Jews experience in their daily lives, personal stories help to bring the issues alive. We thus advocate an experiential and mixed-group approach to this issue, in which historical overview and personal experience are brought into dialogue. At the same time, we avoid temptations to simplify our historical analysis of a narrative almost as old as recorded history, or to present only one perspective on the enormously complicated forces that are in conflict in the Middle East. We believe that only by knowing the history can we move beyond it, and only by honoring the multiple perspectives in present-day religious conflicts can we imagine new ways to transform them.

## Antisemitism and Anti-Jewish Oppression Curriculum Design

### Overall Goals

At the conclusion of this curriculum, we hope that participants will have achieved an awareness and understanding of

- the thematic and cyclical nature of anti-Jewish oppression throughout the history of the Christian West, and its emergence in the Middle East.
- the historical roots, contexts, and recurrence of antisemitic stereotyping, and the roles of classism, ethnocentrism, sexism, racism, and religious oppression in shaping these stereotypes.
- the roles of European powers and the United States in the founding of Israel, and the role of multiple international powers on both sides of the Middle East conflict.
- the perspectives of Jews and Palestinians as two historically oppressed and exiled peoples, and of the Middle East conflict within an antioppression and liberation perspective.
- strategies and action plans to interrupt antisemitism and anti-Jewish oppression in everyday life on an individual, institutional, cultural, religious, and societal level.

### Overview of Modules

Note to readers: The curriculum design in this chapter is based on the assumption that participants have completed the introductory module(s) described in Chapter 3 prior to beginning this design and have a basic understanding of the conceptual framework of oppression described in Chapter 3. See Table 12.1 for an overview of this chapter's modules.

### Module 1: Building a Learning Community and Developing Awareness

Time needed: 3 hours, 15 minutes

**Table 12.1**   Overview of Modules: Antisemitism

| Module 1: Building a Learning Community and Developing Awareness (3 hours, 15 minutes) | Module 2: Understanding the History of Antisemitism (3.5 hours) |
|---|---|
| 1. Introductions, "What's in a Name?" (40 min.)<br>2. Agenda, Goals, and Assumptions (15 min.)<br>3. Group Norms and Guidelines (15 min.)<br>4. Stereotypes of Jews (30 min.)<br>5. "Who Is a Jew?" (20 min.)<br>Break (15 min.)<br>6. Examples of Anti-Jewish Oppression in Everyday Life (60 min) | 1. Check-In (15 min.)<br>2. History of Antisemitism, Part 1 (60 min.)<br>3. Review of Stereotypes (20 min.)<br>Break (15 min.)<br>4. History of Antisemitism, Part 2 (60 min.)<br>5. Themes and Connections Among Forms of Antisemitism (20 min.)<br>6. Closing: Personal Reflections (10 min.)<br>7. Reading Assignments for Module 3 (10 min.) |
| **Module 3: Framing Discussion of Middle East Conflicts (3.5 hours)** | **Module 4: Planning Strategies and Taking Action (3.5 hours)** |
| 1. Check-In (15 min.)<br>2. Middle East Conflicts: 1945 to Current Day (50 min.)<br>3. Middle East Conflict: Dialogues and Discussion (60 min.)<br>Break (15 min.)<br>4. Middle East Conflict: Full-Class Discussion (60 min.)<br>5. Closure (10 min.) | 1. Check-In (10 min.)<br>2. Taking Action to Create Change (40 min.)<br>3. Everyday Contexts for Practical Change (40 min.)<br>Break (15 min.)<br>4. Frameworks for Change: Cycle of Liberation and Liberatory Consciousness (20 min.)<br>5. Developing Effective Action Plans (30 min.)<br>6. Paired Sharing of Action Plans (20 min.)<br>7. Written Evaluations and Group Closure (35 min.) |

## Overview of Goals

- Develop a sense of personal safety and community within a seminar learning setting while staying open to one's "learning edges."
- Increase awareness of individual, institutional, and societal manifestations of historical and contemporary antisemitism.
- Have greater understanding of the importance of stereotyping in maintaining anti-Jewish oppression.

**Key concepts**: antisemitism and anti-Jewish oppression, Jews, Jewish, Gentiles, social construction, racial formation, stereotypes

## 1. Introductions, "What's in a Name?" (40 minutes)

Welcome participants and talk briefly about why we are committed to teaching about antisemitism and anti-Jewish oppression. Give participants note cards or self-stick notes to write questions about antisemitism and anti-Jewish oppression they bring with them into the seminar. Participants will post these questions on one side of the room and move them to other locations during the seminar as they are answered.

Note that each of our names conveys ethnic, religious, cultural, and/or generational family meanings and history. This activity explores the religious, historical, and ethnic meanings for our names (see Appendix 12H for examples) by introducing ourselves and talking about our names and what we know about our family's ethnic, national, and religious history. These name introductions offer opportunities to forge historical, geographical, and personal interconnections among participants and help us to recognize our complex family linkages to periods and places we will be talking about in the seminar. Model the introductory go-around by talking about the history of your own family name.

### Facilitation Issues

In this first set of introductions, it is helpful for Jewish facilitators to identify themselves as a *Jew* rather than as *Jewish*. Participants sometimes are aware that, historically, the noun *Jew* has been associated with fear, anxiety, and dangerous, life-threatening exposure. This introduction can be used to explore why publicly identifying oneself as a *Jew* can feel intimidating for some Jewish participants. Sometimes, Jewish identity has been a carefully guarded family "secret." By acknowledging the fact that public labeling can be a source of anxiety, participants' attention can be drawn to an identity issue that is one of the consequences of antisemitism. Non-Jews may admit to feeling uneasy about identifying someone as a *Jew* (noun) rather than describing them as being Jew-*ish* (adjective), and this discussion can lead to valuable insights about the role of language.

Allow processing time after this activity so that trust can develop early on and help establish a sense of safety for all participants.

### 2. Agenda, Goals, and Assumptions (15 minutes)

Move directly from the "What's in a Name?" introductory go-around to a review of the planned agenda, curricular goals, and shared assumptions (guidelines are in Chapter 3, and curricular goals are in Appendix 12I). These materials can be prepared and posted in advance, with copies handed out as participants enter the room. Participants can follow along with the handouts as you review the posted agenda, goals (see Appendix 12I), and assumptions (see Appendix 12J) posted on the wall. Affirm group inclusion by asking each participant to share in a read-around of each of the guidelines, goals, and assumptions, and assure participants that they will have opportunity to revisit these items later in the course if necessary.

### 3. Group Norms and Guidelines (15 minutes)

This discussion of group process guidelines provides a cornerstone for the group dynamics expectations throughout the course (see Chapter 3) and serves as a reference point for resolving potential later conflicts.

Post and distribute copies of Appendix 12K. Ask participants to "read-around" the list of group norms and guidelines. Ask for clarifications, additions, and revisions. This process will generate discussion, and it is important to provide opportunities for participants to personalize the guidelines. Conclude by asking whether participants agree with these norms and guidelines, and to affirm their agreement by saying "Yes" or nodding their heads.

### Facilitation Issues

This conversation should be carefully monitored and requires careful listening. If discussion of norms and guidelines is too brief, participants may not feel safe, but if it takes too long or repeats earlier discussions of norms and guidelines, participants may tune out.

## 4. Stereotypes of Jews (30 minutes)

The purpose of this activity is to illustrate the pervasiveness of antisemitic and anti-Jewish stereotypes in the present day, and to prepare for discussion of their historical roots in a later module. The materials for a brief presentation (or review, if discussed in an earlier introductory module based on Chapter 3) of the definition and characteristics of stereotypes can be displayed as overheads or posted on newsprint where all can see, and included in participant handout materials (see Appendix 12C).

Introduce this activity by acknowledging that participants will work together to identify stereotypes about Jews that are familiar to most of us often without realizing that they are stereotypes. Explain that in a subsequent module, the group will explore the historical roots for many of the stereotypes they identify in this activity.

As further introduction to this activity, explain the purpose of brainstorming stereotypes: Brainstorming includes everyone's contribution without explanation or judgment. A brainstorm is a free-flowing collection of ideas, not a judgment or open for debate. In order to encourage participation in the brainstorming activity, note that participants' ability to name a stereotype does not mean that they believe the stereotype.

Allow participants to form groups of three to four (so that Jewish students can decide whether to work together or work in mixed groups), and give each small group newsprint and markers. Ask the groups

- to brainstorm stereotypes they've heard about Jews (10 minutes) and write these stereotypes on newsprint.
- to post their newsprint as a gallery and silently walk around the room to read each group's newsprints.

When the groups have posted their newsprint and reviewed the gallery, and participants have returned to their seats, ask them to respond to the following questions as a whole group. These questions focus on understanding the functions of stereotypes:

- What do you notice about the stereotypes? (Example: Most are negative.)
- What stereotypes appear most frequently? (Examples: Jews are cheap, pushy, J.A.P., or clannish.)
- Are there common themes among the stereotypes? (Examples: assumptions about socioeconomic status, about money, about gender, and about appearance)
- What are the intersections of other forms of oppression with these stereotypes? (Examples: Jewish American Princess or Jewish mother stereotypes show intersection with gender. All of the issues of status and money show intersection with class.)
- Are there contradictions between various stereotypes? (Examples: Jews are capitalists, Jews are communists; Jews are cheap, and Jews are showy.)
- Why do you think we were able to generate this large list so quickly?

To help participants understand some of the characteristics of stereotypes, refer to these commonalities (posted and as handouts from Appendix 12C):

- The advantaged religious group usually projects self-denied attributes (usually negative but sometimes positive) onto the targeted religious group. (Examples are in the "They are"/"We are" box list in Table 12.2 below.)
- Stereotypes sometimes may contain a grain of truth, but have been generalized beyond their historical or social contexts.
- Group attributions are depicted as unchanging, and considered to be "essential" group characteristics.

**Table 12.2** *"They Are"/"We Are"*

| Targeted: "They Are" | Advantaged: "We Are" |
|---|---|
| Aggressive | Ambitious |
| Stingy | Frugal |
| Money-hungry | Entrepreneurial |
| Exclusive | Discriminating |
| Clannish | Loyal |
| Different, strange | Unique, individual |
| Clever, shrewd | Intelligent |
| Unethical, cheats | Doing business |
| Stiff-necked, stubborn | Independent |

*Source:* From Weinstein & Mellen, 1997.

- Group attributions are experienced as hurtful and limiting by the targeted group, and the same attributions may be renamed in a positive way by the advantaged group when alluding to themselves.

To further illustrate these points, post and distribute copies of Table 12.2. Discuss the implications of the "They are"/"We are" chart.

Bring closure to this activity by helping participants to understand how stereotypes can function to maintain oppression:

- Stereotypes provide a rationalization for oppression. They place blame on the target group, implying that because of these attributes they ask for and deserve what they get. (Example: "If Jews weren't so pushy and aggressive, they wouldn't be mistreated.")
- Stereotypes dehumanize the targeted group in the eyes of the advantaged group, making it easier for the advantaged group to deny or rationalize any pain they might inflict on the targeted group. (Example: "The Jews are the cause of our problems, so don't trust them.")
- The perpetuation of stereotypes is based on two important omissions: (a) They neglect to take into account the historical context within which culture and behaviors were created; and (b) they apply a generalization to arrive at conclusions about all individuals within the social group.
- Because stereotypes are applied to a whole group of people, individuals become invisible.

## Facilitation Issues

Draw upon Chapter 3 for discussion of the "Cycle of Socialization" (Appendix 3E) to provide information on the formation and maintenance of stereotypes. Assure participants that the history presented in Module 2 will provide a context for understanding the roots of the stereotypes identified during this activity.

This activity is likely to be painful for Jews, who are the targets of these stereotypes and who are usually all too familiar with them. Gentiles may be shocked at the ease with which they find they can generate these stereotypes. Help Gentiles understand how prevalent these stereotypes are, even for participants who feel they know nothing about Jews.

### 5. "Who Is a Jew?" (20 minutes)

This activity explores some of the challenges presented by terminology, language, and U.S. social identity categories in talking about this topic. Post and distribute copies of the bullet questions in Appendix 12L, "Who Is a Jew?" These question draw on clarifying readings (Appendix 12L) that explain how Jews have become a single people who are also in some cases multidenominational, multiethnic, multinational, and/or multiracial.

## Facilitation Issues

Participants may feel confused that Jews do not "fit" into single, binary, either/or ethnic or national or racial categories. Remind participants that the history to be presented in Module 2 will clarify how Jews, as a diaspora people, cut across simplistic and unitary social categories. In some cases, participants may tie this discussion to their own more complex ethnic, national, racial, and religious backgrounds.

The strong feelings that often are triggered by the noun *Jew* as distinct from the adjective *Jewish* should be noted, as well as the meanings associated with the word *antisemitism* as distinct from *anti-Jewish oppression*, described in the introduction to this chapter.

### Break (15 minutes)
### 6. Examples of Anti-Jewish Oppression in Everyday Life (60 minutes)

### Option A: Peer Panel

### Option B: Unpacking the Knapsack of Christian Privilege
### (see Appendices 12N and 11M)

This activity enables participants to hear personal stories of cultural, personal, and institutional antisemitism and anti-Jewish oppression.

This activity needs to be set up in advance, either with members of the class who identify as Jews and are willing to discuss their experience openly, or with others who agree to join the class for the panel and talk about their experiences. Suggestions for how to select and prepare the peer panel appear in Appendix 12N.

The questions addressed by the panelists (see below) are designed to problematize the binary either/or U.S. constructions of race, ethnicity, national origins, religion, language, and culture, which fail to capture the range, complexity, and diversity of Jewish identities (as well as the interaction of Jewish identity with other social identities). The panel provides opportunities to describe concrete examples of the interpersonal, institutional, and/or cultural forms of oppression experienced in everyday life, as well as the feelings that remain long after any individual incident. This activity carries forward some of the insights from the earlier discussion of our names as well as the previous question, "Who is a Jew?"

The peer panel addresses these questions:

- What is our own personal or familial understanding of Jews as a social identity group (historically, culturally, ethnically, religiously, politically)?
- How do we experience ourselves as Jews in our daily lives (religious, secular; visible, invisible; Jewish-identified, not identified, or hidden)?
- What is our experience as Jews of anti-Jewish oppression in everyday life, on this campus, in the media, and in neighborhood, school, or work settings?

### Facilitation Issues

The dynamics of discussion following the panel presentation depend upon the religious identities of participants. For example, if Jewish participants in the class constitute the peer panel, then the discussion will be mainly between them and the Gentile observers. In that case, observers are asked to hold all questions until after the panel. Then ask observers to first identify something they have learned from the panel before they ask clarifying questions. (We ask that observers frame clarifying questions, not reactive comments.)

Help observers listen carefully to panelists and process what they hear in a respectful way. Comment on unexpected displays of feeling (anger, defensiveness, fear), and also intervene if Gentiles respond by defending their religious faith rather than focusing upon the institutional and cultural sources of religious and ethnic oppression described by the panelists.

## Module 2: Understanding the History of Antisemitism

Time needed: 3.5 hours

### Overview of Goals

- Understand the history of antisemitism and anti-Jewish oppression in Christian Europe and the Middle East.
- Learn about emergent themes and their connections to present-day antisemitic and anti-Jewish stereotypes.

**Key concepts**: historical overview of anti-Jewish oppression and antisemitism, domination, hegemony, privilege

### 1. Check-In (15 minutes)

Welcome participants, and ask for challenges and insights that may have surfaced in Module 1. Refer to the questions posted during Module 1, and have participants move questions that have been answered to another wall designated for answered questions.

### 2. History of Antisemitism, Part 1 (60 minutes)

This presentation introduces the long history of antisemitism and anti-Jewish oppression, its connectedness to stereotypes of Jews, and cyclical themes that will continue to be developed in Module 3.

The entirety of this module is devoted to a thematically organized overview of the history of (mainly European) antisemitism. This can be presented in several ways, depending on facilitator readiness and the opportunities for prior readings by the participants. Each of these alternatives focuses upon the emergent and accumulating themes of antisemitism described in Appendix 12B, with chronologically organized examples. Historical readings and resources for facilitator preparation are cited in the introduction to this chapter, in the paragraphs below, and in readings listed in Appendix 12M. Appendix 12A provides a chronological guide to the history of anti-Jewish oppression and antisemitism. Participant readings to prepare for the history presentation and discussion are listed in Appendix 12G.

Option 1: historical presentations and emergent themes (two 60-minute illustrated presentations, followed by two 20–30-minute small-group reflections)
Option 2: vignettes, case studies, jigsaw group study (see Appendix 12D2 & 3)

The history lecture (Option 1) is divided into two major chronological segments, each of which is organized thematically, and processed by small-group discussion. The focus is on the themes that characterize the emergence and evolution of antisemitism in the West with some brief reference to anti-Jewish oppression in North Africa or the Middle East. This material focuses on the history of antisemitism and anti-Jewish oppression, rather than on Jewish history and culture.

Prepare for this lecture by reading several of the histories described in a resource list (see Appendix 12M) and using the various historical summaries presented in this chapter and in Appendix D. The first author of this chapter dramatizes the thematic presentation using illustrative photographs, drawings, cartoons, and other visual materials collected from the historical resources listed in Appendix 12M. Historical and contemporary maps can be used to illustrate the global range of Jewish diasporas from early nomadic movements between Palestine and Egypt up into the expulsions in the Middle Ages and the migrations of current times. These materials can be organized as transparencies, slides, or PowerPoint illustrations to pace the thematically organized historical material, and focus student attention and interest. A long scroll with key dates (based on Appendix 12A) can be posted around the room to list the major events in the history of Jewish oppression and help participants track the presentation through this complicated and global history of anti-Jewish oppression and antisemitism. Charts or a timeline drawing upon Appendix 12A can be handed out so that participants will not need to keep informational notes, but only note their questions.

Note the many ways in which medieval "canonical" laws provided a basis for the religious subjugation of Jews within Europe and also a precedent for the racialization that became explicit in the Nazi anti-Jewish laws of the 1930s leading up to the Holocaust (Hilberg, 1961). For example, an early form of this racialization can be seen in the Spanish obsession with "blood purity" (*limpieza de sangre*, which designated non-Jewish ancestry) that justified the rooting out and expulsion of Crypto (hidden) Jews (see Appendix 12D). This obsession represents an early "essentializing" of Jews that is related to later 19th-century pseudo-scientific racism, views of unalterable Jewish racial inferiority, and justifications for "racial hatred" (Fredrickson, 2002; Hilberg, 1961, Jacobs, 2002; Rosenbaum, 2004).

Antisemitism within Christian Europe started as competition between the small, vulnerable communities of early Christians against their older and more established Jewish rivals (many early Christians were Jews). After Christianity became state religion in the Holy Roman Empire, and Catholicism became institutionalized, antisemitism developed into bitter and deadly hatred of Jews, fueled by a myriad of religious and economic justifications, and supported by the power of organized European Christianity and the resources of modern Christian-identified nation-states. Thus, while it is important to note the early precedents that anchor 19th-century antisemitism and 20th-century Nazism, we also need to acknowledge that the Nazi Holocaust differs from this earlier European history mainly because of its genocidal ambition and the scientific, technological, and industrial resources of a powerful Nazi nation-state used to plan, coordinate, and carry it out. Sample lecture appears in Appendix D.

## Facilitation Issues

Anticipate dramatically different levels of historical knowledge and understanding among participants. This information challenges uncritical, received views of European history and the institutional role of Christianity (see discussions in Chapter 11). Participants may have questions or need time for note taking or paired sharing. This also provides a short break before returning to the lecture.

Make choices on the content of the lecture based upon what material you feel confident in presenting. The broad brush strokes of cumulative themes of antisemitism are far more important than the details of specific historical periods. Connect the emergent stereotypes to the historical content.

Leave enough space during the lecture for participants to ask questions throughout, preparing yourself for the possibility of switching your visuals back and forth while responding. The maps, timeline, and other visuals enliven the thematic repetition.

To maintain a trusting learning environment, remain focused on the institutional and cultural forms of antisemitism and anti-Jewish oppression. Keep in mind that learning about these historical facts, about the political and economic dimensions of institutional, state-based Christianity, does not negate anyone's personal religious or spiritual beliefs, or the beliefs of peoples in the past.

### 3. Review of Stereotypes (20 minutes)

Ask participants to spend a few minutes writing their thoughts about the history, then turn to the person next to them to note new insights and personal reactions to this history. Next, ask participants to walk over to the gallery of stereotypes they created earlier, and identify the historical contexts for some of stereotypes that have religious and economic roots. (It is important that participants not try to identify roots as either/or but realize that stereotypes can have multiple, cumulative, and intersecting sources.) Ask participants also to move earlier posted questions if they have been answered.

### Break (15 minutes)

### 4. History of Antisemitism, Part 2 (60 minutes)

The break can be followed by Part 2 of Option 1, or a continuation of Option 2 (both in Appendix 12D).

### 5. Themes and Connections Among Forms of Antisemitism (20 minutes)

This second processing time is an opportunity to draw interconnections among antisemitism and racism, classism, and other social justice issues. Ask participants questions such as these:

- Why is "class" so important in the anti-Jewish and antisemitic stereotypes?
- Are there parallels between antisemitism in 19th-century Europe, and anti-Black or anti–Native American Indian racism in the United States, or between German "concentration camps" for Jews and U.S. "reservations" for Native Peoples and "concentration camps" for Japanese?
- Can antisemitism be seen as an example of "racial formation" (refer to Chapter 11), or "racism" in its European context? How is it similar to, or different from, U.S. racism?

### 6. Closing (10 minutes)

Invite participants to engage in individual silent reflection and journal writing followed by a short conversation about their reflections with a partner. Go around the circle and ask participants to share a few thoughts for the module.

### 7. Reading Assignments for Module 3 (10 minutes)

The reading assignment (in Appendix 12G) provides a transition from Module 2 to Module 3. While establishing closure for the thematic and historical insights of Module 2, it is important to also establish historical and thematic continuity to the current conflict in the Middle East presented in Module 3. Module 3 will frame the conflict in the Middle East as one of competing religious, economic, and ethnic identity liberation movements, as well as competing nationalisms, for differently oppressed peoples—the Jewish people and the Palestinian people. It will be necessary to establish the groundwork with carefully selected reading assignments that provide different perspectives on Israel and Palestine.

## Module 3: Framing Discussion of Middle East Conflicts

Time needed: 3.5 hours

### Goals

- To learn about the history of Palestine prior to the founding of Israel as a nation-state
- To understand the historical role of European powers and the United States in the founding of Israel, and the present-day role of global international powers on both sides of the conflict
- To acknowledge the perspectives of Jews and Palestinians as two historically oppressed and exiled peoples
- To view the contemporary conflicts in the Middle East within an anti-oppression and liberatory perspective

**Key concepts**: nation-state, colonialism, national liberation, national politics, international power

### 1. Check-In (15 minutes)

This check-in provides an opportunity for participants to express further insights and responses to the history presented in Module 2, or to the reading assigned for Module 3. Invite participants to move questions posted from the preceding modules that have now been answered, and post any new questions.

### 2. Middle East Conflicts: 1945 to Current Day (50 minutes)

This activity provides a transition from the Module 2 history segment, which ends with 1945, and an understanding of the Middle East, which reaches back historically to examine the relations of Jews and Arabs in the Middle East, and then moves forward from 1945 to the establishment of Israel in 1948 and subsequent Middle East conflicts.

Prepare in advance some informative overview comments on the history of Jews and Arabs in the Middle East, and the post-Holocaust momentum behind the establishment of Israel (see Appendix 12E). Visual aids such as maps of the Middle East and historical timelines help participants follow what may be new information for them, especially the shifting borders of a two-state territorial division (see Appendix 12E). The maps make visual allusion to places seen in maps presented during Module 2 in the history of Jewish diasporas.

### Facilitation Issues

It is extraordinarily difficult, within a single module, to develop a nuanced, multiply viewed perspective that is adequate to the religious, nationalistic, ethnic, cultural, economic, and international complexities of the Israeli-Palestinian conflict. It is especially challenging to coordinate an understanding of the successive Jewish expulsions from European, North African, and Arab countries (presented in Modules 2 and 3) with the present-day situation of Palestinians in Israeli-held territories (presented in this module). We continue to struggle to adequately acknowledge the competing claims of two differently victimized and oppressed peoples struggling with unmatched resources over the same pieces of homeland (discussion in Appendix 12E). For inspiration, we draw on these sentences from Memmi's *The Colonizer and the Colonized* (1967/1991), which we post in the room before the start of Module 3 as a reminder of the challenge: "Must the just cause of a people include its deceptions and errors?... Furthermore, can one justify the historical misfortune of a people by the difficulties of another?" (pp. 37, 113).

### 3. Middle East Conflict: Dialogues and Discussion (60 minutes)

This activity enables participants to process their insights and reactions to the readings and lecture, in order to communicate respectfully across different perspectives.

> Option 1: discussion groups on selected topics and/or selected readings.
> Options 2–4 appear in Appendix 12O: These options include a write-around activity (Option 2), a discussion based on the Memmi quote (Option 3), and a fishbowl activity (Option 4).

### For Option 1

Following overview comments (as described in Appendix 12E), ask participants to organize themselves into discussion groups of four. Ask the small groups to discuss the questions listed below. Distribute the list of questions to the groups. The questions are based on the assigned reading for Module 3 (see Appendix 12G). Explore with the whole class whether the discussion groups should be organized around several different themes or focused on different readings.

Distribute or adapt the questions listed below. Ask the groups to prepare newsprint listing the questions or issues they discussed.

Sample questions for small-group discussion:

1. How did the readings contribute to your understanding of the historical background and competing perspectives on the Middle East conflict?
2. How does the knowledge of the history of antisemitism help Gentiles as well as Jews understand the vulnerability experienced by many Jews during discussions of Israel and Palestine?
3. How can we understand the competing sense of Homeland and Exile, experienced by both the Israelis and Palestinians, in a way that does not stereotype or dismiss the claims of either group?
4. What do you see as the major themes, challenges, and opportunities in multiparty discussions or dialogues on the Israeli-Palestinian conflict?

When they have completed their discussion, have the groups post their major discussion points in a gallery, and ask participants to walk around the gallery to read the points noted by the other groups. After the gallery walk, have the whole group identify the themes or issues they most want to consider in the whole-class discussion that follows.

### Facilitation Issues

Each group member has a group-facilitation role as well as a responsibility to discuss the themes and/or readings. Have a timekeeper identified for each group, as well as someone responsible for assuring that everyone has a chance to speak. Another participant can manage the agenda of agreed-upon themes or questions, and a recorder can prepare the newsprint for the walk-around gallery.

**Break (15 minutes)**

**4. Middle East Conflict: Full-Class Discussion (60 minutes)**

This activity brings the whole group back together, for an intentional approach to conducting difficult dialogues while remaining open to new viewpoints.

This whole-group discussion builds on the options laid out in the preceding activity. For example, in the preceding activity, *Option 1* had participants post the newsprint from their discussion groups in a gallery, walk around to read the newsprint gallery, and brainstorm what they want to discuss as a whole group. *Option 2* (see Appendix 12O) uses a write-around format to generate themes and topics that are noted on a chalkboard or on newsprints. *Option 3* (see Appendix 12O) uses a single-quotation format to raise themes and questions. *Option 4* (see Appendix 12O) is a fishbowl discussion activity.

## Facilitation Issues

It is important not to rush this whole-group discussion of themes and questions and to pay close attention to agreed-upon guidelines for conversation. Although participants are talking about emergent themes and asking questions of each other, pay careful attention to who is talking and who remains silent, and who may appear to be triggered by this discussion (i.e., Jewish, Muslim and/or Arab participants, or participants with political commitments to a "position" on the Middle East). It may be necessary to comment on the difficulties of talking respectfully about highly charged political, religious, and national liberation issues. This conversation focuses upon "how" to have such a multilayered conversation across different religious and ideological commitments or family-ethnic histories, rather than any attempt to "resolve" a complex international situation such as the Middle East conflict. It may prove more important to offer an intentional format of "phenomenological listening"—that is, how to "speak and listen" (see Appendix 15C)—than to try to resolve the content within the discussion. Participants may need to be reminded that this discussion cannot be "completed" until the conflicting parties in Israel and Palestine themselves are able to converse with each other and can come to a mutually satisfactory resolution.

Ask participants at key points in the discussion, *What questions remain unanswered, or concerns not addressed? How might you facilitate your own further learning on these issues? Where might you go to learn more? What other perspectives might be needed on this topic?* Note that certain perspectives appear to be missing from the discussion, depending on who the participants are, and the specific knowledge and awareness they bring.

It is important for participants to understand the difference between the actions of a nation-state (such as Israel) taken as a political entity, and its inhabitants or advocates or co-religionists taken as individuals (individual Israeli or U.S. Jews).

Whatever combination of activity options chosen, close with a short discussion that brings participants together again, despite their differing opinions, experiences, and solutions for peace in the Middle East. It is important to be able to keep open hearts and minds toward each other's perspectives and experiences, as a key precondition for actions or coalitions toward peace.

## 5. Closure (10 minutes)

This activity provides an important formal closure to the conversation before ending the module. Ask each participant to reflect on the discussion using one of the following sentence stems:

- One new insight that I have is ...
- One continuing question that I have is ...
- One way that I will continue to learn about this topic is ...

## Module 4: Planning Strategies and Taking Action

Time needed: 3.5 hours

### Goals

- To be aware of various targeted and advantaged identities and their impact on participants' experience with antisemitism.
- To reflect on what it means to be an ally to Jews as a Gentile, or how to be aware of internalized antisemitism as a Jew.
- To develop strategies and action plans to interrupt antisemitism and anti-Jewish oppression in everyday life on an individual, institutional, cultural/ religious, and societal level.

**Key concepts:** ally, internalized antisemitism, cycle of socialization, cycle of liberation, liberatory consciousness, action plan, sphere of influence

### 1  Check-In (10 minutes)

This final welcome-back for participants offers a last opportunity to tie up loose ends from the preceding three modules. Invite participants to identify questions and issues raised earlier in the class that they are still thinking about. Participants also can move posted questions that have been answered and offer a final round of new questions that have emerged.

### Facilitation Issues

Be aware that this is the final check-in, notice who is speaking and who is not, and make room for emerging or unheard voices to speak. As the course moves toward closure, participants often feel freer to speak in the large group and silent group members can be encouraged to speak in the whole group.

Help participants acknowledge that not all questions can be quickly or easily answered. Some participants may want to address their own ongoing questions as part of their action plans. Inform the class that there are naturally many loose ends, which reflect the state of the current political global situation.

### 2  Taking Action to Create Change (40 minutes)

This activity introduces the ways that members of advantaged religious groups can serve as allies to Jews, and presents real-life examples of courageous people who have worked against antisemitism and anti-Jewish oppression.

This segment starts with showing the film *Courage to Care* (see Appendix 12M), a documentary that highlights people who took personal initiative during the 1940s to save Jews from being deported and murdered, or who themselves were saved by such actions (Block & Drucker, 1987; Gilbert, 2003; Satloff, 2006). What is most striking in this short documentary is the acknowledgment by the speakers that they did not have time to make careful plans or contemplate the level of risk or difficulty before taking action. Instead, they emphasize how their actions were guided by basic assumptions about what it means to be human and the resources immediately at hand, while sometimes putting their lives on the line to help others. They also illustrate the courage people draw upon in small everyday actions that have significant consequences.

Participants are likely to want a few minutes of silence after viewing the film before turning to each other (in pairs) to share their reactions and feelings.

After the film and short silence, the following questions can help generate thoughtful discussion or responses from a few volunteers:

- What does courage mean for you in your own life?
- What nurtures your ability to have courage?

## 3. Everyday Contexts for Practical Change (40 minutes)

This activity encourages participants to begin thinking about change strategies. It starts this process by referring them back to introductory discussions of the "Cycle of Socialization" (see Chapter 3, Appendix 3E) and/or "Levels and Types of Oppression" (see Figure 3.1 and Appendices 10I, 10J, 11A, and 12P) as frameworks for developing action plans. Post the "Cycle of Socialization" (see Appendix 3E) and "Levels and Types of Oppression: Antisemitism" (see Appendix 12P), and ask participants to fill in examples of antisemitism and anti-Jewish oppression for both the "cycle" and the "levels and types."

### Facilitation Issues

The two conceptual frameworks reinforce each other, in that examples generated during the "Levels and Types of Oppression: Antisemitism" activity reexamine examples of institutional and cultural/societal socializing forces presented as part of the "Cycle of Socialization."

Reintroducing these two conceptual frameworks (if they have been introduced during an introductory module as in Chapter 3) in this activity enables participants to review what they have learned about anti-Jewish oppression and antisemitism from a "macro" or systemic perspective. Clear examples of antisemitism and anti-Jewish oppression noted during this review, from whatever personal, societal, or historical contexts, will help participants to have specific examples in mind when they begin to design action plans. This review also enables participants to notice intersections of anti-Jewish oppression with other forms of oppression that may have come up during the Module 1 stereotype activity (such as Jewish American Princess and Jewish mother stereotypes, and stereotypes of social class, status, and money).

## Break (15 minutes)

## 4. Frameworks for Change: Cycle of Liberation and Liberatory Consciousness (20 minutes)

The "Cycle of Liberation" (see Appendix 3F) enables participants to revisit the everyday examples of antisemitism and anti-Jewish oppression named during the cycle of socialization from a liberatory perspective.

Participants should have read the short essays that present the conceptual frameworks for this segment of Module 4 (Appendix 12M), or you will need to design brief lectures to present the concepts.

Post and distribute copies of the "Cycle of Liberation" (see Appendix 3F) and the worksheet for "Liberatory Consciousness" (see Appendices 12Q or 15W). Ask participants to provide examples of actions they can imagine themselves or others taking to transform anti-Jewish oppression, utilizing both frameworks. Having identified examples of actions that they or others might take within the "cycle of liberation" and as examples of "liberatory consciousness," participants are now prepared to develop action plans.

## 5. Developing Effective Action Plans (30 minutes)

The purpose of this sequence of steps is to explore and make use of a framework for action planning that takes into consideration a number of criteria. The activity enables participants to identify the challenges and supports they can anticipate in interrupting everyday examples of anti-Jewish oppression. They can then develop a personally appropriate and effective action plan against anti-Jewish oppression.

### Criteria for Personal Effectiveness

Depending on the time available and the readiness of participants, a number of criteria for effective action plans can be presented and explored by participants. These include the following:

- Privileged or targeted religious status (see Chapters 3 and 11)
- Intersections of other identities with religious status (see Appendix 3J)
- Assessments of relative level of risks (see Appendix 11V)
- Considerations of challenges and supports (see Appendix 12R)
- Spheres of influence (see Appendix 4B)

Decide which of these selected criteria will be most useful for participants in helping them assess what action plans might be most personally appropriate (status, identities, relative risk levels, spheres of influence) and effective (considerations of challenges and supports). Ask participants to work for several minutes filling in the selected worksheet, and then turn to a person next to them to explain their selections. Then ask volunteers to offer examples to the whole group.

Initiate the process for putting together an action plan, by posting and distributing copies of "Matrix of Considerations for Action Plans" (see Appendix 11W). (The "Action Continuum," if adapted from Appendix 6H, presents another option.) Review the considerations with the whole group, and ask participants to brainstorm a range of different personal examples for each one of the considerations. (Examples of actions taken against antisemitism and anti-Jewish oppression by groups, towns, and communities appear in the Resource List of Appendix 12S.)

Have participants spend 5 to 10 minutes writing up a specific action plan using the "Worksheet for Action Plans" (see Appendix 11X).

### Facilitation Issues

The group activity enables participants to hear that one person's challenge or risk (saying something in the presence of a family elder, for example) may not be as challenging for another person. Participants are likely to anticipate different opportunities posed by different spheres of influence. They may need to acknowledge that their wish to live in accordance with their personal values of decency and humanity (modeled in the film *Courage to Care* or resources in Appendix 12S) may be challenged by various fears, real or imagined risks, and real-life obstacles. In these cases, thinking about them in advance and coming up with a realistic plan may empower them to take action in the future.

## 6. Paired Sharing of Action Plans (20 minutes)

Ask participants to share personal action plans with each other to gain another perspective on the steps and resources noted in the action plan and to develop accountability for following through on the plan.

Point out that, unlike the allies in the film *Courage to Care* who did not have time or opportunity to evaluate the risks of their actions or the needed supports, the participants have this opportunity to help each other evaluate potential risks or obstacles, and to identify supports and resources that will help them carry out their action plans successfully. Paired sharing enables participants to draw upon each other's ideas, questions, or perspectives, while having greater air time and more privacy than in a small group. For example, it might be a high-risk action for a participant to interrupt the antisemitic jokes or comments in his or her workplace or in a team's locker room, and it might be important for these participants to anticipate how they can find support to carry out the planned intervention. Actions on an institutional level often call for support from colleagues, and it is helpful to understand the hierarchical power structure of one's own organization. Collaborations and coalitions may be needed to interrupt cultural, societal, and/or religious anti-Jewish incidents or policies.

After sharing the main elements of their action plans, have paired participants ask each other questions such as these:

- What are your specific risks in this plan?
- Are there ways you can minimize your sense of risk?
- What obstacles do you anticipate within yourself and from others?
- What opportunities do you anticipate?
- What resources can you draw upon?
- What supports do you need?
- Are there people you can count on to support you in this action?

## 7. Written Evaluations and Group Closure (35 minutes)

Feedback on the effectiveness of the content, design, and facilitation of this course is important for future planning (see Appendix 9J). Providing a process for participants to give anonymous feedback about the course and facilitators is important before intentionally closing the course. Prepare in advance evaluations that will address the course content and leadership.

While participants fill out the evaluation forms, take down the newsprints with stereotypes (from Module 1) to prepare for the final activity, and also post the following sentence stems on chalkboard or newsprint:

- One thing I learned ...
- One thing I appreciated (will remember) about this group ...
- One thing I promise I will do . .
- One thing I want you to know ...

Place a wastepaper basket on the floor in the middle of the room, and ask participants to form a circle around it. Model the closure process by completing one of the sentence stems, while ripping up a piece of the stereotype list and dropping it in the wastebasket. Explain that this symbolic action recognizes that although stereotypes still exist, the work of this learning community, combined with the participant action plans, will help to destroy them.

Going around the circle, ask each participant to tear a piece off the stereotype sheets, toss it into the waste basket, and share a personal statement based on one of the sentence stems.

## Notes

1. For discussion of the tendency to conflate antisemitism with criticism of specific consequences of Israeli expansionism and also with anti-Zionism, see Finkelstein (2005), Pensler (2005), and Rosenbaum (2004). To argue that hostility to Israel and hostility to Jews are one and the same thing is to conflate the Jewish state with the Jewish people. In fact, Israel is one entity, and Jewry another (Klug, 2004; also Remba & Klug, 2004).

2. The key texts are in the Gospels of Matthew and Luke (King James Version): The chief priests and elders said to Pilate, "Let him be crucified. ... His blood be on us and on our children" (Matthew 27:22, 25). The cry "Crucify him, crucify him" is from Luke 23:31. See Boys (2004) and Prager & Telushkin (2003).

3. Historians carefully differentiate between the situation of Jewish communities in Islamic countries prior to World War II and in the aftermath of the establishment of Israel in 1948 with greatly increased Jewish immigration. See Sachar (2005), Weinberg (1986), and Wistrich (1991). For personal accounts, see Khazzoum (2003), Memmi (1975), Shohat (1988/1997), and Tolan (2006). See also Cohn-Sherbok and El-Alami (2003), and Laquer and Rubin (1995).

4. Frederickson (2002) noted,

    Anti-Judaism became antisemitism whenever it turned into a consuming hatred that made getting rid of Jews seem preferable to trying to convert them, and antisemitism became racism when the belief took hold that Jews were intrinsically and organically evil rather than merely having false beliefs and wrong dispositions. (P. 19)

    For a clear, convincing account of the relationship between racist forms of antisemitism and racism(s) founded on white supremacy, read Frederickson (2002). See also Mosse (1985).

5. For example, Gilman (2005), Grossman (1998), Kaye/Kantrowitz (1992), Said (1992), Said and Hitchens (2001), Tobocman (2003), and Young (1992). Kushner and Solomon (2003) document the long tradition of Jewish American critique of Zionism (as an expression of expansionist nationalism) and of Israeli incursions into Palestinian territories.

6. Endelman (2005) proposes the following criteria for establishing when legitimate critique of Israeli policies become antisemitic: (a) when legitimacy of the Jewish state and Jewish nationalism, but not that of any other state or nationalism, is questioned; (b) when the character of the Jewish state is questioned but not that of any other state (French, Muslim); (c) when it demonizes the Jewish responsibility for the Arab–Israeli conflict as a problem for which Jews solely are responsible; and/or (d) when it expresses "an obsessive, exclusive, and disproportionate concern" with Israeli shortcomings in a conflict seen as between cosmic good and evil (p. 71).

7. Examples of some intersecting identities can be found in Balka and Rose (1989), Frommer and Frommer (1995), Goldberg and Krausz (1993), Kaye/Kantrowitz (1996), Khazzoum (2003), Shneer and Aviv (2000), Silberstein (2000), and Tessman and Bar On (2001). Also see McKinney (2001).

8. In some families, the Jewish legacy may have been obscured by intermarriage, or by assimilation. Jacobs (2002) tells the history and describes (concealed or transformed) Jewish observances and rituals in the surviving Crypto-Jewish culture of the U.S. Southwest and Latin America, where Sephardic Jews had settled during the Spanish and Portuguese colonial period following the expulsion of Jews from Spain. As current generations discover their hidden Jewish ancestry,

> [I]t is largely through a veil of secrecy and uncertainty that they come to understand and appreciate the extent to which danger and anxiety remain part of the legacy of crypto-Judaism ... [D]isclosures were frequently accompanied by a warning to keep this information inside the family. (Jacobs, 2002, p. 34)

# 13

# Classism Curriculum Design

## BETSY LEONDAR-WRIGHT AND FELICE YESKEL

The gap between rich and poor in the United States is the greatest it has been since 1929. In the United States, since the late 1970s, the wealthy have gained a bigger share of the nation's private wealth, so that now the richest 1% of the population owns a greater share of the wealth than the bottom 90% combined. Income inequality has grown as well. Average Americans were actually making less, on an hourly basis, at the end of the 1990s than they made in 1980 (Collins & Yeskel, 2005). Even billionaire investor Warren Buffett reflects, "It's class warfare. My class is winning" (in conversation with CNN's Lou Dobbs, June 2005).

Some results of this changing economic picture include more families with dual-wage earners, more part-time and overtime employment for working-class and middle-class families, significantly less leisure time, less access to health care, higher overall unemployment, and a greater burden of debt. The federal government now plays a smaller countervailing role in counteracting poverty than in the decades from the 1930s through 1970s. For example, President Ronald Reagan reduced spending on affordable housing and home ownership by 80%, saying he wanted to "get the government out of the housing business"; this spending has never been restored.

Some people believe that U.S. society is breaking down and that the economy is in decline. Many of today's social problems fit this pattern of decline, including urban decay, increased homelessness and hunger, increasing numbers of youth not in school or unemployed, and an increase in stress-related illnesses. For many Americans, this situation has led to increasing anxiety about the future and a growing disillusionment with government and corporations.

## The Global Context

With the rise of multinational business and global markets, class issues in the United States have become ever more complex. The same multinational corporations that increased U.S. prosperity in the 1950s and 1960s by manufacturing here and selling their products around the globe are now draining the United States and other economies by moving jobs to wherever wages are lowest and environmental standards lax, or taxes can be avoided (Derber, 2002; Pizzigati, 2004). The status of average American workers is ever more closely tied to the economic and working conditions of laborers in Third World countries, and class politics in the United States often center on international trade issues, such as the debate over the Central America Free Trade Agreement, the World Trade Organization (WTO), and the International Monetary Fund (IMF) (Cavanagh, Mander, Anderson, & Barker, 2002).

The structural adjustment policies and austerity measures that are inflicted on developing countries, further impoverishing their citizenry, find their U.S. parallels in privatization, cuts in domestic social programs, and the weakening of the post–World War II safety net. For example, college scholarship grants have been reduced (Draut, 2006), and welfare is now a fixed block grant that doesn't expand when unemployment grows (Coven, 2006). Tax cuts targeted at the wealthiest Americans have resulted in massive federal debt that will burden future generations. To date, U.S. economic prominence has been held in place by wars over natural resources (such as the Iraq war and our dependence on oil) and by a fragile coalition among industrialized capitalist countries.

The overall decline in manufacturing jobs (a highly unionized sector), which once offered the possibility of attaining a middle-class lifestyle to blue-collar workers, has dramatically changed the class picture in the United States to resemble more that of Third World countries. Although an introductory course on classism cannot address this issue in any depth, and this curriculum design has been deliberately and artificially limited to U.S. issues, it is important for facilitators to be informed about these global changes and their effects on the American workforce. Useful resources are provided in Appendix 13M.

## Intersections of Class with Other Forms of Oppression

Issues of class clearly intersect with every other form of oppression. For example, although about half of all poor people are white, wealthy people are disproportionately white, and poor people are disproportionately black, Latino, and Native American. The racial wealth divide is even wider than the income gap: People of color own about 18 cents for every white dollar in assets (Lui, Robles, Leondar-Wright, Brewer, & Adamson, 2006). Racial divide-and-conquer tactics have historically been used to limit working people's demands; this dynamic has contributed to lower wages and a weaker safety net in the United States than in most other industrialized countries.

People living in poverty are more likely than others to be disabled, and disabled people are more likely than able-bodied people to be poor. A far higher percentage of people with disabilities live in households that are below the poverty level (29 versus 10% overall), and a similarly disproportionate number report not having adequate access to health care or transportation (National Organization on Disability, 2000).

The feminization of poverty in the last 30 years has increased the intersection of classism and sexism. Women still perform endless hours of unpaid work caring for children and the elderly (Folbre, 2001). Men are socialized to equate self-worth with what they produce, with their net worth. Women doing comparable work to men are still not paid an equal amount.

Class is also related to age. The changes in the economy over the last few decades mean that younger people today face a much more challenging economic environment than their parents and grandparents did. A college degree now is equivalent to the high school diploma of the past, and the cost of college has escalated dramatically, whereas the availability of scholarships has decreased. This means that today's college generation graduates with substantially greater debt than prior generations (Draut, 2006; Kamenetz, 2006). Sometimes, middle-aged people do not adequately understand the economic pressures facing today's youth. Seniors also have higher poverty rates than middle-aged people.

## Non-economic Aspects of Classism

The harm from classism extends far beyond economic hardships. Popular culture and the media in the United States are full of classist stereotypes. Working-class people are often portrayed as dumb buffoons, whereas poor people are depicted as criminals, tragic victims, or heartwarming givers of wisdom. Wealthy people are rendered as shallow and vain, or as evil villains. Portrayed as normal is an expensive upper-middle-class lifestyle that is in fact affordable to no more than 10% of American families. This combines with manipulative advertising to fuel consumerism, the overemphasis on buying more and better things as a component of happiness, which in turn fuels excessive consumer debt (Degraaf, Wann, & Naylor, 2001; Frank, 1999).

Prejudice exists in our language, in words such as *trailer trash, white trash, redneck, ghetto, low class,* and *classy.* The same prejudice is manifested in treatment of service workers, such as underpaying them, disregarding their humanity, and creating unnecessary messes for them to clean up.

Many working-class lives, especially those of people in poverty, are full of stress. The shortage of options and scarce resources take an emotional toll (Sennett & Cobb, 1972). Bad health outcomes, such as shorter life expectancy, higher infant mortality, and more preventable diseases, are prevalent among working-class and poor people. These stem not only from inferior health care, poor diet, and long hours and physical work that take a toll on workers' bodies, but also from the stress of living in a society that looks down on them. Disrespect is harmful (Lawrence-Lightfoot, 2000; Miller & Savoie, 2002).

Classism can be internalized, causing low expectations, discouragement, and self-doubt, in particular about one's intelligence. Internalized classism can also be manifested through disrespect toward other working-class people, in the form of harsh judgments, betrayal, violence, and other crimes. Upward mobility, far from bringing relief from classism, can bring culture shock and painfully divided loyalties (Jensen, 2004; Lubrano, 2003).

Middle-class people are harmed by isolation from working-class people, and by being taught they are superior to them and ought to be in charge. They are harmed by misinformation about how society works (they are sometimes less clued in to social and economic trends than working-class, poor, or rich people), and by conditioning that shapes their behavior to a narrow "proper" range, preparing many for dull middle-management jobs (Leondar-Wright, 2005).

Wealthy people find that others sometimes connect with them primarily in relation to their money, and may have trouble trusting others' motivations. Some learn a sense of entitlement and arrogance that makes them unable to connect across class differences. Some owning-class children, in particular those from multigenerational, superwealthy families, grow up in intense isolation uncommon in other families, such as being raised by nannies and seeing parents infrequently, going to boarding school at a young age, or spending a lot of time alone in a different wing of a house than other family members (O'Neil, 1996).

## The Social Reproduction of Class

In *The Forms of Capital* (1986), Bourdieu distinguishes three types of capital:

1. *Economic capital*: control over economic resources (cash, assets).
2. *Social capital*: access to resources based on group membership, relationships, and networks of influence and support.
3. *Cultural capital*: education, skill, forms of knowledge, any advantages a person has that give them a higher status in society, including high expectations. Parents provide children with cultural capital, the attitudes and knowledge that make the educational system a comfortable, familiar place in which they can succeed easily.

In *Reproduction in Education, Society and Culture* (1977), Bourdieu and Passeron introduced the idea of cultural reproduction to describe how existing disadvantages and inequalities are passed down from one generation to the next, partly due to the education system and other social institutions.

Many of the ways we "read" someone's class, or "size someone up" in terms of class (a process that can be quite unconscious), are based on their cultural capital. Cultural capital includes the internalization of certain "dispositions of the mind and body"—what an individual knows and utilizes from within (including normative behaviors such as language use, manner of dress, and the "proper" guidelines for conducting oneself, i.e., manners). Although these things can be learned, the process is not easy. Cultural capital also refers to familiarity with cultural objects such as books, fine art, and jewelry.

Students who have knowledge that allows them to navigate through the school system by displaying desired behavior and/or conforming to unspoken norms are more likely to succeed. The tracking system may track, among other things, the amount of cultural capital a student possesses. This is often masked through the ideology of meritocracy: Individuals who do not have the desired cultural capital are labeled as lacking in intelligence and the drive to succeed. In this manner, social classes are reproduced.

## Difficulties in Teaching about Class

The ability of average Americans to analyze and understand economic and social patterns is thwarted by prevailing myths about class and classism, compounded by lack of knowledge of global economic trends, global capitalism, and colonialism and imperialism, as well as by a mainstream version of history in which class and classism are largely invisible. "Class in America is a taboo subject because of the national reluctance to examine how the class system of the United States operates on a day-to-day basis" (Perrucci & Wysong, 2002, p. 4).

## The Myth of Meritocracy

The American Dream is that anyone in this country can attain enough income to own their own homes and provide comfortably for their families if they work hard enough. The fact that most Americans can point to at least one example where this is true reinforces the myth of class mobility and assumptions that those who don't move up lack a strong work ethic. Although it is true that there is some class fluidity, and that class status may change over the lifetime of many individuals, the reality is that class is much less fluid than most people think. A series on class in the United States, later compiled into a book called *Class Matters*, reviewed research on class mobility and concluded that the amount of upward mobility in the United States has either stopped increasing or has actually decreased (*New York Times* Correspondents, 2005).

This *New York Times* poll, conducted in 2005, demonstrated that the popular misconception that it is possible to start out poor, work hard, and become rich is actually more common now than it was 20 years ago (*New York Times* Correspondents, 2005). However, according to Princeton economist Alan Krueger (2002, p. C2), "if the United States stands out in comparison with other countries, it is in having a more static distribution of income across the generations with fewer opportunities for advancement." There is a particular cruelty to our situation in the United States, where people are more likely to believe that they can make it when in fact they are less able to succeed. People in this situation, without adequate understanding of how class works, often internalize classist attitudes, and blame themselves or each other. The psychological investment most Americans have in a meritocratic American Dream makes it difficult to challenge the obstacles to making the dream come true (McNamee & Miller, 2004).

During periods of social and economic crisis or frustration, in the absence of a framework for understanding the situation, people often turn to scapegoats and distractions. Thus, the underlying factors (imperialism, war, global trade policies, multinational corporate power, and domestic tax and spending policies, for example) that create vast inequalities in wealth, along with the beneficiaries of these policies, remain largely invisible (Collins & Yeskel, 2005; Kivel, 2004). Instead, people on welfare are blamed for causing our budget woes, urban young men of color are blamed for crime, immigrants are blamed for taking away jobs, working women and gays and lesbians are held responsible for the breakdown of the nuclear family and the moral decay of society, Jews are labeled as controlling the banks and the media, and other countries are blamed for taking our jobs. In the post-9/11 United States, Arabs and Muslims are presumed to be terrorists. The fears created by the corporate media provide the rationale for wars that funnel money to corporations and their wealthy stockholders, while poor and working-class American soldiers' families hold bake sales to pay for body armor, and spending on social programs is slashed.

Public policy debates center around fighting terrorism, criminalizing undocumented immigrants, welfare reform, or getting tough on crime, whereas proposals to increase capital gains taxes, make child health programs universal, ensure access to higher education, increase estate taxes on multimillion-dollar inheritances, or raise the top income tax bracket back to previous levels seldom enter the public debate.

The terms of public debate are set in large part by a small number of major media outlets, whose corporate owners and major advertisers have a vested interest in promoting policies favorable for corporate profits. The true beneficiaries of the redistribution of wealth are rarely visible or acknowledged (Collins & Yeskel, 2005; Pizzigati, 2004). Just as the beneficiaries remain hidden, so too does the existence of poverty and racial divides, except for rare moments such as the aftermath of Hurricane Katrina in 2005. However, as with Katrina, public acknowledgment of extreme inequality quickly fades from view.

As global citizens and voters, the participants in our social justice classes will find themselves needing to make judgments about proposals for political and economic change that differentially affect various groups in our society and abroad. Understanding how social and economic class operates in the United States, as well as globally, is important for them to be able to participate in these debates in an informed way. Although not replacing macroeconomic and political science courses, this curriculum is designed to introduce participants to a framework for understanding the broad outlines of economic class structures, as well as dealing with social and cultural classism in the United States and considering steps toward a more equitable and respectful society.

## Taboo about Class

In the United States, discussions involving issues of class and money are often more taboo than those involving sexuality. Deep-seated prohibitions about disclosing the facts of one's class identity are learned quite early in our lives. Most parents or caregivers do not tell children how much money they have or earn; if they do, children learn not to discuss these topics with others. Shame at being poorer or richer than others leads to secrecy and silence. This silence powerfully maintains the invisibility of class.

## Differing Definitions of Class

Economists, sociologists, political scientists, anthropologists, and activists define *class*, *social class*, and *socioeconomic class* differently. For some sociologists, class is defined by *occupational* status: blue-collar, pink-collar, or white-collar, for example. For some economists, class is defined by *income* and *economic* strata, whereas for other economists, particularly Marxists and neo-Marxists, *ownership*, *power*, and *control* figure most prominently in defining class. These varying definitions can be confusing for participants who may be considering class for the first time.

Our working definition is that class is "a relative social ranking based on income, wealth, education, status, and/or power," indicators of class that tend to go together. If you have power, you tend to have wealth and status; if you have wealth, you typically have power and are given status; and so forth.

Participants may not have considered their own class identity prior to this course. When asked to do so, many conclude that they are more or less middle class. Even if some indicators would link participants with the working class or the owning class, most will tend to stress contradictory indicators that point instead to middle-class affiliation. For example, "Even though my parents had lots of investments, we lived in a small house and mowed our own lawn," or "We were always broke, but because my dad was a preacher, we got lots of respect from the community." Thus, we need to define class and classism, as well as discuss criteria for distinguishing different classes, before we can usefully examine this topic. We do this in the first module of the course.

## Higher Education: The Access Channel

Education is the class-sorting mechanism or access channel, setting up future vocational opportunities and thus income. Ostensibly, the sorting is by merit, but in fact it is heavily influenced by class background (see Brantlinger, 2003). Students arrive at college with beliefs about why they and their fellow students were admitted that are tinged with classism. Questioning the fairness of the system of sorting can feel personally threatening to some students, who may be invested in their self-image as smarter than others who didn't gain admission to the same type of school. Deconstructing test scores, the educational tracking system, the "halo" effect, the impact of role models and access to information, and legacy and other class-based admission policies, not to mention the cost of college and financial aid policies, could be a course in itself.

## Hidden History of Classism and Resistance to Classism

History is typically taught from the perspective of the privileged. Much of what we learn in public school, for example, is told from the perspective of political and military leaders and other famous personages who usually are members of the upper classes. The perceptions and realities of everyday working people are less commonly explored. For example, industrialization is typically taught as a positive transformation of society. From the perspective of the average worker at the time, the era brought loss of control over working conditions when factories and assembly lines replaced craft guilds. The economic "progress" of industrial development looks quite different from the perspective of slaves, indentured servants, and impoverished immigrants, whose perspectives are usually invisible in our history books (Jones, 1998; Takaki, 1993; Zinn, 1980/1995). Currently, increased productivity to make the United States "more competitive" is widely accepted as a positive goal, despite the fact that "productivity" is often a code word for replacing jobs with machines and thus displacing workers.

The history of resistance to classism also remains largely invisible. Strikes, boycotts, slowdowns, and labor organizing are all tactics that workers have used to fight class oppression (Zinn, 1995). The labor movement used New Deal labor laws to organize many industries, reaching a 35% unionization rate by 1954. But as of 2005, only 12% of workers were in unions, according to the Bureau of Labor Statistics (2006). Currently, the role of the media cannot be emphasized enough. The increased concentration of corporate media ownership by a few elites ensures that the information to which most of us have access is biased in favor of the media owners (Bagdikian, 2004; McChesney, 2004) or those in the upper classes. It is difficult to get multiple perspectives, especially those of the people on the receiving end of classism as systemic inequality.

## Conflation of Democracy and Capitalism

During the Cold War between the United States and the former Soviet Union from the 1950s to the 1980s, capitalism and communism became polarized. Capitalism was equated with democracy, whereas communism, by comparison, was equated with undemocratic and totalitarian political systems. Whenever the capitalist economic system in the United States has been challenged, the challenge has been framed as an attack on the political system of democracy. Raising issues of class inequality is often labeled as *antidemocratic, class warfare, communist, red,* or *unpatriotic,* with the effect of marginalizing or silencing criticism of the economic structure. This conflation of democracy and capitalism confuses political and economic critique, so that challenges to the economic order are cast as opposing democracy in favor of communism, thus preventing consideration of alternative economic policies and structures. The psychological investment most Americans have in the American Dream makes it difficult to challenge the problems of advanced capitalism and address these issues clearly.

In fact, true democracy in the United States is limited by the extraordinary influence of large multinational corporations and wealthy donors over our political process. Unfortunately, the influence of this concentrated economic power isn't understood by most Americans (Collins & Yeskel, 2005; Kivel, 2004; Pizzagati, 2004).

## Economic Mystification

Issues of class may be less familiar than other issues of oppression partly due to secrecy about the personal aspects of class identity and the confusion surrounding the societal aspects. Participants who are unfamiliar with even the economic basics (the difference between income and wealth or between salary and wages, or the meaning of terms like *gross national product* [GNP]) often feel overwhelmed while studying social class. Math anxiety and math phobia also contribute to a feeling of disempowerment toward or distrust of statistical information that documents class issues. Print resources that explain economic concepts in clear understandable language (such as Collins and Yeskel 2005; Anderson & Cavanagh 2005; Teller-Elsberg, Folbre, Heintz & the Center for Popular Economics 2006 and the other print and video resources listed in Appendix 13M), can be useful in demystifiying classism.

## Hopelessness and Helplessness

Interrupting classist slurs, changing classist language, and changing consumer behavior seem insignificant in comparison to the immensity and complexity of the problem. The need to work against classism on a systemic level is overwhelmingly evident, yet what to do is contested. This can lead to an enormous sense of helplessness, based on several factors: the seemingly intractable imbalances in the distribution of wealth, economic power's influence on political power, the complexities of economic theory, and the contradictory explanations of experts.

The fact that class inequality is getting worse rather than better, and the lack of a major visible economic alternative, can lead to overpowering hopelessness. The linchpin of the hopelessness is the limited scope of the organized social movement against classism. Meanwhile, other social movements have made visible progress over the last 50 years, starting with African American civil rights, women's liberation, and more recently lesbian, gay, bisexual, and transgender liberation and disability rights movements. If participants are unaware of organized efforts for economic justice, they may feel that classism is a fact of life, hopelessly entrenched and unchangeable, or a result of innate human nature or laws of the marketplace. However, recent successes in organizing service workers (including recent immigrants) and in the living wage campaign show promise of creating such a movement. The campus living wage movement and Students Against Sweatshops may be part of this upsurge in economic justice organizing that is most visible to students.

Because classism operates at many levels, an antidote to hopelessness is to focus on personal and organizational manifestations, about which participants can take action. Speaking up when classist jokes and comments are made, developing class-sensitive payment systems, and appreciating the range of skills necessary to get something done are all ways participants can take action about classism in their lives. Taking action is a good cure for hopelessness.

## Overall Issues for Facilitators

Classism is a huge topic ranging from daily experiences to the workings of global macroeconomic structures. The following modules represent an introduction to the topic of classism. Because of time constraints, we have focused on the experience of classism in the United States. We want to acknowledge that participants who are immigrants to the United States will have different experiences with classism based on their class standing in their country of origin, on whether or not their class standing changed in immigrating to the United States, and on their country of origin and its relative status (northern European countries like England or Scandinavian countries are viewed more favorably than Latin American or African countries due to racism).

Discussions of classism can often be challenging. For one, it is hard to name class identity. There is often confusion over, and may be differences between, class origins and current class standing. Participants' deficits in economic literacy result in confusion over the difference between income and wealth, and the political system (democracy) and the economic system (capitalism). There is a strong attachment to beliefs about meritocracy that is supported by anecdotes—everyone knows someone who made it against the odds. In an experiential teaching situation, this makes it difficult to intervene. Participants will wonder about the vision of changing the system—do we get rid of classism by getting rid of class? Does class only occur in capitalist systems? This may be a recurrent issue that you can't fully explore in this curriculum, but you can invite participants to follow up in other courses.

Therefore, it is especially important for the facilitator to develop her or his own understanding about classism. It is also necessary to prepare participants for the challenge of being respectful of individual experience while placing personal stories in the larger context of systemic classism. Facilitators should be calm and nondefensive, reminding the group of the discussion guidelines as necessary. For many participants, this will be a first exploration of class, and more time may need to be allocated to the first three modules before participants will be able to move to action.

## Classism Curriculum Design

### Overall Goals

- Begin to explore the impact of class on our personal lives, institutions, and culture.
- Develop an understanding of basic concepts about class and classism.
- Understand the systemic dynamics of classism.
- Understand the intersections between classism and other forms of oppression.

### Overview of Modules

Note to readers: The curriculum design in this chapter is based on the assumption that participants have completed the introductory module(s) described in Chapter 3 prior to beginning this design and have a basic understanding of the conceptual framework of oppression described in Chapter 3. See Table 13.1 for an overview of this chapter's modules.

**Table 13.1**  Overview of Modules: Classism

| Module 1: Defining Class (4 hours, 10 minutes) | Module 2: Individual, Institutional, and Cultural Classism (3.15 hours) |
|---|---|
| 1. Welcome and Introduction (10 min.) | 1. Individual, Cultural, and Institutional Classism (50 min.) |
| 2. Common Ground, Part 1 (20 min.) | |
| 3. Assumptions, Guidelines, and Agenda (20 min.) | 2. Brainstorm Stereotypes (20 min.) |
| | Break (15 minutes) |
| 4. First Memories and Class Indicators (40 min.) | 3. First-Person Accounts of Diverse Class Experiences (70 min.) |
| Break (15 min) | |
| 5. Class Background Inventory (50 min.) | 4. Income Distribution Activity (20 min.) |
| 6. Common Ground, Part II (15 min.) | 5. Wealth Distribution Activity (30 min.) |
| 7. Class Caucuses and Whole-Group Sharing (50 min.) | 6. Closing, Homework, Wrap-Up, and Feedback (20 min.) |
| 8. Key Definitions (30 min.) | |

| Module 3: Manifestations of Classism (3 hours, 10 minutes) | Module 4: Action Against Classism (3 hours, 20 minutes) |
|---|---|
| 1. Cultural Classism (30 min.) | 1. History of Classism and Anticlassism in the United States (45 min.) |
| 2. Institutional Classism (165 min. incl. break) | 2. Acting as Allies (30 min.) |
| 3. Closing (10 min.) | Break (15 min) |
| | 3. Classism in Your School (60 min.) |
| | 4. Actions Against Classism (45 min.) |
| | 5. Closing Circle: Personal Next Steps and Evaluation (20 min.) |

## Module 1: Defining Class

Time needed: 3 hours, 55 minutes

### Objectives

- Create a safe environment in which participants can discuss difficult issues.
- Reflect on class experience, and name class of origin.
- Understand working definitions and basic concepts about class and classism.

**Key concepts**: class indicators, social class, ruling class, owning class, middle class, working class, poverty class, classism, class continuum, cultural capital, class privilege

### 1. Welcome and Introduction (10 minutes)

Welcome participants to the course, introduce yourselves, and tell a bit about your background and experience with the issue of classism. Then ask participants to introduce themselves and state one reason they are taking this course.

### 2. Common Ground, Part I (20 minutes)

In order to help people begin to know one another, ask participants to stand in a circle. Explain that you will name a series of categories and those who fit the category should take a step into the center of the circle, look around, and note who else shares this common ground. Start with low-risk categories, such as "common ground for everyone who ..."

- got 5 or less hours of sleep last night.
- would rather be asleep now.
- is an oldest (youngest, middle, only, twin) child.
- grew up in a city (rural area, small town, suburbs).
- is first-generation American (a citizen of another country, grew up outside of the United States).

Make up other categories as you go, and invite participants to suggest categories. You may also want to include questions that will give you as the instructor some sense of participants' understanding of and/or comfort with economics, such as:

- who has ever taken a course on economics.
- whose eyes glaze over when reading a chart or talking about statistics.

### 3. Assumptions, Guidelines, and Agenda (20 minutes)

Print the goals listed at the beginning of this design on newsprint, and discuss them in light of the assumptions discussed in the introduction to this chapter. Review guidelines with the group. These can be brainstormed together, or you can post a list from those outlined in Chapter 3. Post the agenda on newsprint, and review it in a general way, highlighting major items.

### 4. First Memories and Class Indicators (40 minutes)

Ask participants to pair up and take turns listening and responding to the following questions:

- What is the first memory you have of someone you thought was of a more privileged or "higher" class than you? Why did you think so?
- What is the first memory you have of someone you thought was of a less privileged/"lower" class than you? Why did you think so?

First, one person will speak while the other listens; after 5 minutes, ask participants to switch speaker/listener roles. Then reconvene the group and ask for volunteers to share the memories they discussed in order to elicit a variety of examples. In particular, note factors that indicate different class positions, and write these on newsprint. The list should include indicators such as income, education, housing, occupation, need to work, neighborhood, language (accent, vocabulary, grammar), assets or wealth, appearance (dress, condition of teeth, posture), possessions (computers, TV, DVD/VCR, cell phones, iPods, types of cars), and leisure (types of activities, hobbies, travel).

### Facilitation Issues

Pay particular attention to nonmaterial examples of class privilege such as forms of knowledge, skills, values, expectations, and so on that are types of "cultural capital." It is often more difficult for participants to notice these types of class indicators than the material ones. You may also notice that there are examples of contradictory class indicators, such as someone who has a well-paying job but very little education. This is one of the reasons class is so complex and confusing.

### 5. Class Background Inventory (50 minutes)

Pass out the class background inventory (Appendix 13A). If you are co-facilitating, model interviewing each other while participants observe, using the inventory as a guide. (If you are teaching alone, you can play both roles—asking, then answering the question.) Ask each participant to note his or her own responses to the inventory, then pair up and take turns interviewing each other as the facilitator(s) did. After 5 minutes, tell them it's time to switch. Next, ask each pair to join another pair, creating small groups of four. Ask each person in the group to briefly share a few items from his or her background, still using the inventory as a guide.

Ask participants to take a 5 × 8½-inch index card and, based on the activities, write a short description of their class of origin. They will not be asked to share these cards but will periodically review them to add to what they've written. The card will serve as a record of their learning about their class identity as the course proceeds.

### Facilitation Issues

Facilitators should be able to provide information and model comfort and awareness in discussing their own class background(s) during this activity. Often, people at either end of the class spectrum experience feelings of shame. The more matter of fact the facilitator(s) can be about their own class of origin, the more at ease participants will be. Especially when co-facilitators are from different class backgrounds, this activity will help participants feel more at ease in sharing their stories. Encourage participants to jot a few notes rather than extensive responses to the inventory. If participants report confusion, or if their class situation changed as they were growing up, suggest that they focus on formative childhood experiences.

At times, participants' current class position is different than their class of origin or class background. We think it is still important to spend time focusing on class background. Many of our formative experiences happen in childhood. Although material situations may change later, many times our values, assumptions, expectations, and sense of place in the world stem from our childhood class experience. Sometimes, the lessons of our class of origin, our class culture, linger even though our class changes.

## 6. Common Ground, Part II (15 minutes)

Ask the group to stand in a circle, shoulder to shoulder, with one facilitator in the middle. Reintroduce the activity, this time asking people to step into the circle when the class category fits. "Common ground for anyone ..."

- who grew up in rented apartments
- who has owned a house
- whose family owns a summer home or other second house
- who has a credit card their parents pay for
- who has traveled internationally
- who is on a scholarship
- who has worked at a fast-food restaurant
- who has a trust fund or owns stocks and bonds in your name
- who shared a bedroom as a child
- who has shopped with food stamps

You can ask members of the group to make other common-ground statements as long as whatever they say is true for them and relevant to the topic of class. This gives participants a chance to learn about others with similar experiences.

Process the Common Ground activity with the following questions, while still standing in the circle. Ask participants, "What feelings came up for you as you took part in the common-ground activity?" "Did anyone choose not to step into the circle even though the common ground item was true for you?" "What new information does this give you about your own class background?"

## 7. Class Caucuses and Whole-Group Sharing (50 minutes)

This activity gives participants an opportunity to spend time with others who have similar class backgrounds, and to notice what similarities and differences might exist among class caucuses. Following are suggestions of ways to help participants form caucus groups.

Ask participants to pay attention to which people they saw most often in the "Common Ground: Part II" activity and join them. Once they are together in a small group, you might ask them to give their group a class name. (Other options for breaking into class caucuses are included in the supplemental materials on the CD; see Appendix 13B.)

Once participants form class caucuses, ask them to select a note taker who will report back to the whole group. Give them 30 minutes to focus on the following questions:

1. What positive (knowledge, skills, community support networks) did you gain from your class of origin? What was good about your class experience growing up? What did you gain from it?
2. What was challenging about your class experience growing up? What was limiting about it?
3. What do you not want others to say, do, or think about your group?
4. How did race, ethnicity, and/or immigration status impact your experience of class?

After 30 minutes, bring the whole group back together and give each group recorder 2 to 3 minutes to report back to the whole group on their group's responses to the questions. Ask which group would like to go first, and take each group in turn until all have shared with the whole group.

## Facilitation Issues

It is often difficult for class groups to form because participants are often confused on the subject. Encourage people to do their best, and tell them that they may later learn they are in a different group. You may also want to model naming your own group and sharing your responses to the questions. Tell participants that there are no hard-and-fast lines about class definitions and class identity. The process of coming to understand one's class identity (either background or current) may be one of trial and error.

### 8. Key Definitions (30 minutes)

Using newsprint or overhead transparencies, present the definitions of general concepts for classism in Appendix 13C and give examples. If necessary, review definitions of *oppression, prejudice, social power, stereotype, advantaged* and *targeted*, and *ally* (Chapter 3) before presenting and discussing the definitions.

Because our definition of class involves the concepts of income, wealth, education, occupational status, and power, make sure that participants understand these concepts. *Income* is the amount of money, from all sources, that comes into your household (could be a family or one person) in a 1-year period. *Wealth* is the same as assets, the amount that you have accumulated over time. *Education* refers to the highest level of educational attainment. Every job or *occupation* can be categorized according to where it fits in the status or prestige hierarchy of professions. There are a variety of scales or measures. *Power* can refer to the amount of control someone has at work or the amount of social and political influence they have in the wider society.

Ask participants to reflect on the definitions and consider what they might add or change in the description they wrote on their card earlier concerning their own class background. They can add changes to their card, but should not cross out anything written before, so as to keep a record of their evolving understanding of class as the course proceeds.

## Facilitation Issues

People are often reluctant to acknowledge the existence of classism, so it is important to start with participants' lived experience and with indisputable facts such as U.S. Census data rather than theories and definitions. Be aware of the political and ideological issues surrounding class and classism, and try to steer clear of ideological arguments. Share theories, definitions, and models as useful concepts and working models rather than as the truth. Acknowledge the diversity of thought on this subject, and explain your rationale for choices you've made, rather than argue for a single correct framing of the issue.

Participants may be more comfortable focusing on race and educational attainment rather than explicitly talking about class. Facilitators will need to keep the focus on class without denying its interconnections to race and ethnicity, education, or other factors. Either/or debates on which is the real underlying issue are not useful; instead, provide participants with language and ideas that can increase the complexity of their understanding.

### Module 2: Individual, Institutional, and Cultural Classism

Time needed: 3.5 hours

## Objectives

- Reflect on where participants' personal class experiences fit into the class spectrum in the United States.
- Increase awareness and understanding of individual, institutional, and cultural manifestations of classism in the United States.
- Learn about and understand the experiences of people from other class backgrounds.

**Key concepts**: income quintiles, stereotypes, internalized oppression, class continuum, individual classism, institutional classism, cultural classism

## 1. Individual, Cultural, and Institutional Classism (50 minutes)

Explain that so far we have been primarily focusing on the individual or personal level of class and classism and that we will continue to do so by looking at stereotypes and hearing first-person accounts. Briefly introduce the concepts of individual, institutional, and cultural classism (see Appendix 13D).

Ask the group to brainstorm a few examples of each type of classism, and be prepared with examples of your own. (For examples, see Appendix 13E.) Ask participants to form groups of four and come up with additional examples of individual, institutional, and cultural classism. Give them three different colored self-stick notes. Ask participants to write all their examples of individual classism on one color, using another color for institutional examples, and a third for cultural examples.

### Processing

After 10 minutes, bring the group back together to share examples and clarify distinctions among the different levels. Post newsprint for each level (individual, institutional, and cultural) on the wall. Ask each group to come up, and post and read out one example of each manifestation. Continue until all of the manifestations are posted. Discuss any disagreements or confusion about how an example was categorized. Poll the group about the type of manifestation that was easiest or most difficult to come up with. Discuss why that might be so. Then, move to a discussion of class stereotypes.

## 2. Brainstorm Stereotypes (20 minutes)

Have several sheets of newsprint posted on the wall ahead of time. At the top of each sheet, write one of the following: "Owning class," "Middle class," "Working class," and "Poor." Break the class into four small groups. Ask each group to gather next to one of the sheets; brainstorm as many images, words, or stereotypes as possible for their particular class group; and then record the stereotypes on the newsprint. Remind them to list all ideas that come to mind even if they are negative or false. Finally, ask one person from each group to share the group's list. Common examples are as follows:

- *Owning class*: effete snobs, incapable of anything physical, condescending, greedy, cultured
- *Middle class*: normal, regular, boring, wannabes, stodgy
- *Working class*: tacky, blue collar, bigoted, stupid, bad taste
- *Poor people*: trailer trash, irresponsible, can't delay gratification, lazy, stupid, disorganized, criminals

After each group has shared its list, ask for any additions. Then process the activity; first ask which of the stereotypes seems to hold some truth. For each of these, ask for any historical or structural underpinnings of the stereotype. Also, ask for examples of information they now have that contradicts or challenges any of the stereotypes listed.

## 3. First-Person Accounts of Diverse Class Experiences (70 minutes)

The purpose of this activity is to help participants learn about and understand the experiences of people from different classes and clarify their own class experiences. In some locations, it may be possible to organize a panel that includes people from diverse classes, or a fishbowl with participants that is representative of class diversity, whereas in other locations that are more homogeneous you will need to rely on other sources of information. It is often most powerful for participants to meet real people who have different class experiences from their own, but if this is too difficult to arrange, these other options provide exposure to a variety of class experiences. Two additional options are provided on the CD (see Appendix 13F).

### Panel of People From Diverse Classes

Ideally, the panel should include at least one person each raised as owning class and poor, and one or two others in between, such as working class and upper-middle class. To find an owning-class speaker, contact a local community foundation (call the Funding Exchange in New York City for local foundation names) and ask them to suggest one of their donors. To find raised-poor and working-class speakers, contact local antipoverty groups such as tenant groups, welfare rights groups, service workers' unions, or community action agencies, and ask for low-income speakers. Offer to pay for expenses such as transportation and child care, and an honorarium if possible. To find middle-class, lower-middle, and upper-middle speakers who are aware of classism may be harder. Try asking professors in sociology or social work departments, or call unions of professionals or semiprofessionals, such as nurses' or teachers' associations. Give the questions to the panelists ahead of time. (Directions for setting up panels are provided in Chapters 8 and 12.)

Questions for panel may include the following:

1. What have you gained from your class background? What advantages did you receive?
2. What has been difficult about your class background? What limitations did you experience?
3. Provide examples of memories/critical incidents in your awareness of your class.
4. What do you want others to know about people of your class?
5. How can others be your ally? How have you been an ally for others?
6. What strategies do you see for taking action against classism?

Once panelists have spoken and participants have had an opportunity to ask questions, thank the panel members for their participation and allow them to leave. Then, hold a discussion among participants using the following questions:

- What feelings did you have while you listened to the different panelists?
- How did the speakers challenge stereotypes we listed earlier?
- What similarities and differences of experience did you notice among the panelists?
- In what ways was classism manifested in the different panelists' experiences?

## 4. Income Distribution Activity (20 minutes)

Begin the activity* by posting a copy of the income distribution chart in Appendix 13G (cover it with newsprint until you are ready to reveal it) and the following definition: *Income Quintiles*: A method of comparing mean incomes of each one fifth of a country's families. If every family in the United States were lined up in order of income, and then divided into five groups with the same number of families in each group, and the incomes within the groups were averaged, the five resulting numbers could be compared as *income quintiles* for a measure of income inequality.

You can tell participants that this activity compares income distribution in two recent periods of economic growth in the United States, to demonstrate the growth and decline of incomes in these two periods. Ask five volunteer participants to come and stand in the front of the room. (For this activity to work well, volunteers need plenty of space to move forward and a little space to move back.)

### Props

It is helpful to make 8½" × 11" placards for each volunteer to hold, identifying the quintiles and showing the income range. Explain what is on the placards, and prepare them in advance (e.g., each placard will have one quintile, such as "Bottom 20%," with the income range for that quintile). Participants holding the placards will move to demonstrate changes in income growth during different periods.

### Instructions

1. State that you are going to look at the changes in *family* income during two recent periods of economic growth. Ask, "What are some examples of income?" Possible answers include wages, salary, savings account interest, social security checks, rent from owning real estate, capital gains from selling investments, dividends from stocks, and gifts. Ask the five volunteers to stand shoulder to shoulder. Give each volunteer a placard showing the income range—in pretax, year 2003 dollars—of the quintile they represent.
2. Review the definition of *income quintile* on wall chart. Economists often talk about the U.S. population in terms of "quintiles" or "fifths" of the population. They imagine the entire population of the United States lined up in order, from the lowest income to the highest. They then divide that line into five equal parts. This activity looks at what happened to the incomes of each quintile during two periods of economic growth: 1947–1979 and 1979–2003. Let's look at some of the folks who are in these quintiles. Ask participants to name what sorts of occupations or economic situations they imagine fall into each quintile. Remember, this is *family* income. (A family is two or more related individuals living together.)
3. The following demonstration may seem like the childhood game "Mother May I" (also known as "Giant Steps"). Each volunteer, representing a quintile or fifth of the U.S. population, will step forward or back according to whether their income gained or declined. Each step equals a 10% change, so, for example, two steps forward would indicate an income gain of 20%. Start with the lowest quintile, and have each person move the appropriate number of steps forward.

---

* This activity was developed by United for a Fair Economy, 29 Winter St., Boston, MA 02108, (617) 423–2148, www.FairEconomy.org.

**Table 13.2**    Percentage Change in Income Quintiles, 1979–2003

| Quintile | Steps | Percent Change | Yearly Income Range (2001) (family income before tax) |
|---|---|---|---|
| Lowest | 1/4 step back | –2% | $0–24,117 |
| Second | 3/4 step forward | +8% | $24,117–42,057 |
| Middle | 1 1/2 steps forward | +15% | $42,057–65,000 |
| Fourth | 2 1/2 steps forward | +26% | $65,000–98,200 |
| Highest | 5 steps forward | +51% | $98,200 and higher |

*Note:* Income ranges in 2003 dollars.
*Source:* U.S. Census Bureau (2004).

4. Between 1979 and 2003, here's what happened (see Table 13.2). Facilitators read from Table 13.2, while participants representing each quintile step backward or forward, as instructed by facilitator.

5. Tell the group you are now going to see what happens when we break down that top quintile even further and look at only the richest 5% of the population. Ask another volunteer to come forward to represent the top 5%—people with incomes of $170,082 and higher. From 1979 to 2003, the income of this group grew 75%. From the spot where the top quintile is standing, the sixth volunteer takes two and a half additional steps forward—seven and a half steps in total from the starting line.

    Top 5%      2 1/2 additional steps forward    +75%    $170,082 and higher

6. Processing: Ask participants what might have caused this widening income inequality. Some things to share:
   - From 1979 to 2003, there was much growth in income, but the distribution of that growth was very uneven. Although the top 20% as a whole did well, the ones who really made out were the top 5%. Some reasons for this skew of income from 1979 to 2003:
   - At the top, the biggest income growth source was income from assets (rental income; earnings from stocks, bonds, and other investments; and capital gains from sales of property and investments). Because asset ownership is heavily concentrated in the wealthiest 20%, it is not surprising that that's where the gains went.
   - There was explosive growth in CEO salaries.
   - At the bottom, the real value of the minimum wage has been allowed to fall since the 1980s.
   - A weakened labor movement was less able to prop up the wages of workers at the bottom of the scale.

7. Next, demonstrate what happened to the quintiles during the post–World War II years 1947–1979. Ask all volunteers to go back to the starting line. Ask the group how well they think the bottom quintile fared, or the top 5%. (See Table 13.3.) Facilitators read out the quintiles from Table 13.3, and participants step forward as directed by the facilitator.

8. Processing: Ask the group: What strikes you about these two periods in history? What are the reasons for the difference? How did women and people of color fare during these two economic periods? Some things to share include the following:
   - From 1947 to 1979, incomes for each quintile as a whole—from top to bottom—basically doubled. In fact, the greatest increase was experienced by

**Table 13.3**    Percentage Change in Income Quintiles, 1947–1979

| Quintile | Steps | Percent Change |
|---|---|---|
| Lowest | 12 steps forward | +116% |
| Second | 10 steps forward | +100% |
| Middle | 11 steps forward | +111% |
| Fourth | 11½ steps forward | +114% |
| Highest | 10 steps forward | +99% |
| Top 5% | 8½ steps forward | +86% |

*Source:* U.S. Census Bureau (2000).

the bottom 20%, and the smallest increase was experienced by the top 5%. In other words, the divide between top and bottom in the United States actually narrowed slightly during this period.

- However, although the rate of income growth during this period was generally the same for everyone within each quintile, the significant gap between the incomes of African Americans and white Americans remained wide.
- The point is not to glorify the 1950s but to point out that we achieved greater income equity across the quintiles, thanks to the positive impact of social programs from the 1950s through the 1970s.
- The period from 1947 to 1979 demonstrates that the great disparity in the distribution of income growth, as happened from 1979 to 2003, is not inevitable. Rather, it is, in part, the result of deliberate government policies.
- The goal of the government during the early postwar period was to build a middle class. Programs such as the GI Bill—which allowed hundreds of thousands of returned veterans to go to college and purchase homes—were funded by relatively high taxes on the wealthy (the top tax rate was 91%). It is important to acknowledge that these programs disproportionably favored white men. For example, the VA and FHA loan programs for housing, both of which utilized racially restrictive underwriting criteria, assured that hardly any of the $120 billion in housing equity loaned from the late 1940s to the early 1960s would go to veterans and families of color. These loans helped finance over half of all suburban housing construction in the country during this period, less than 2% of which ended up being lived in by people of color.

## 5. Wealth Distribution Activity (30 minutes)

Preparation:* Set up 10 chairs without armrests in front of the room.

1. Define wealth: One way to explain the difference between wealth and income is to think of income as the stream and wealth as the reservoir into which the stream empties. Wealth is what a person owns (assets), minus what they owe (debts). Ask participants to brainstorm examples of wealth. For people on the lower end of the continuum, wealth consists of things such as clothing, furniture, or a car (minus money owed). For those in the middle, it may be a house (minus mortgage) or a stake in a pension fund. For people on the upper end of the continuum, wealth consists of stocks, bonds, real estate, businesses, and artwork.

---

* This activity was developed by United for a Fair Economy, 29 Winter St., Boston, MA 02108, (617) 423-2148, *www.FairEconomy.org.*

2. To illustrate how wealth is distributed in this country, ask 10 volunteers to sit in each of the 10 chairs. Note that in this demonstration, *each person* represents one 10th of the U.S. *population*, and *each chair* represents one tenth of all the *private wealth* in the United States. (Try to select a person for the top 10% who is a bit of a ham.) Point out that if wealth were evenly distributed, this is what it would look like—*one person, one chair*. Make the point that this picture of equal wealth distribution has never existed and likely never will exist.

3. Currently (the most up-to-date data we have are for 2004), the top 10% (who average $831,600 in net worth) owns 70% of all private wealth, according to the Federal Reserve. The volunteer representing the top 10% takes over seven chairs, "evicting" the current occupants and making her or himself comfortable on this 7-chair expanded share of the wealth pie. The rest of the volunteers (representing 90% of the U.S. population) must now figure out how to share three chairs (or about 30% of the wealth pie).

4. Even within the top 10%, there is great disparity—a disparity that has increased significantly over the last 25 years. In 1976, the share of the top 1% was 22% (about two chairs). But by 2004, their share had increased to 33.4% of all wealth (more than three chairs)! That's a bigger piece of the wealth pie than the bottom 90% have combined! *To illustrate this, let the leg of the volunteer representing the top 10% represent the wealthiest 1% of the households, reaching across first two and then three chairs, "evicting" the rest of the person's body.*

## Facilitation Issues

It sometimes may require encouragement to get people to really get into this activity. Groups less familiar with one another will cluster sitting and standing around the chairs. Encourage folks to sit on each others' laps and the person representing the top 10% to sprawl across his or her chairs. In the discussion afterwards, make sure you ask participants to name the common themes in responses about the reasons for these distributions, rather than asserting their own individual opinions.

## Discussion to process this activity:

Ask the volunteers in the chairs:

- How are you feeling in the bottom 90%? Whom do you blame for being squished?
- How are you feeling at the top? How do you explain your greater amount of space?
- If you were going to push someone off the chairs to make room, who would it be?
- Where is the focus of public policy discussions—looking up the chairs at the top 10% or looking down the chairs at the people squished at the bottom?
- What information here on these chairs seems to contradict your prior assumptions about class?

Thank the volunteers, and ask the viewers to give them a round of applause. Then, post a copy of the Wealth Distribution Chart (Appendix 13H). Ask participants to pair up and discuss their reactions (thoughts, feelings, questions) with a partner. Ask participants the following questions:

- How did you feel when you saw the 10-chair activity?
- Is the distribution of wealth illustrated by the 10 chairs obvious in your life? In the media?
- What are some of the rationales people give for wealth being distributed the way it is?
- What questions did this demonstration bring up for you?

After 10 minutes, bring the group back together, ask for general reactions, and respond to questions. In closing, ask participants to revisit their card and consider how they would change their class description based on any of this new information.

## 6. Closing, Homework, Wrap-Up, and Feedback (20 minutes)

Review the definition of cultural classism, and assign for homework to look in the popular media (magazines, TV, radio, and newspapers) and find examples of cultural classism. Ask participants to think about the hidden messages or ideology contained in their examples in preparation for Module 3.

As a wrap-up to Module 2, ask participants to pull out the index card on which they described their social class at the end of Module 1, turn to their neighbor, and discuss: How would you change your self-description now? How do you feel about what's written there? Participants can make additions on the card to reflect any new thinking, but should not change what was written there earlier.

## Module 3: Manifestations of Classism

Time needed: 3 hours, 10 minutes

### Objectives

- Deepen participants' knowledge and understanding of the experiences of people of class backgrounds other than their own.
- Increase awareness and understanding of how a class-stratified system works and the power dynamics involved.
- Increase awareness and understanding of individual, institutional, and cultural manifestations of classism in the United States.

**Key concepts**: power, privilege, collusion

## 1. Cultural Classism (30 minutes)

Ask participants to form groups of four or five and share the examples of cultural classism they found for the homework assignment. Ask them to consider the following questions (15 minutes):

1. Is this example classist?
2. What messages does it give to people of different classes?
3. Does it reinforce stereotypes?
4. What values does it hold up as better or normative?

Next, ask each group to choose two clear examples to share with the whole group, noting the hidden (or not so hidden) messages conveyed. Make a list of these messages as each group reports. Discuss how the media communicate and enforce our culture's ideology about class.

## 2. Institutional Classism (150 minutes)

### *Star Power* **Simulation**

*Star Power* is a simulation game that illustrates the dynamics of power and privilege. The specific rules for playing the game are detailed in the instructor's manual that accompanies the game. *Star Power* may be ordered for $225 from Simulation Training Systems, P.O. Box 910, Del Mar, CA 92014, (800) 942-2900, (858) 755-0272, Fax: (858) 792-9743. The game cannot be played without the instructor's manual and simulation materials. (If you do not choose to use *Star Power*, see Appendix 13I for alternative activities on Institutional Classism.)

To prepare for this activity, ask participants to put chairs in three equal-sized circles, and invite everyone to take a seat in one of the circles. Tell them that *Star Power* is a game of trading and that the three individuals with the highest score at the end of the game will be declared the winners. Note that winners will receive a prize. (The prize can be anything that is divisible, such as a cake or other treat.) Go over the "Trading Rules" and "Scoring" sections detailed in the *Star Power* instructor's manual. Let participants know that the facilitators will be taking on specific roles for the duration of the simulation. Facilitators might even want to have a costume (or hat) to help participants differentiate between the facilitator and the "director" role she or he takes within the game. The rules can be confusing, so make sure before starting that the rules are clear. Let participants know that you will enforce the rules.

Play the actual game according to the rules for at least 1 hour. At the end of the time allotted, stop the game. Participants may still be immersed in the game, so ask them to remove their symbols and consciously get out of their roles. Make a display of taking off your costume and getting out of your role as well. Take a short break, and then regroup to talk about responses to the game.

### Facilitation Issues

It is sometimes hard to help participants let go of the simulation. You might want to do something physical for a few minutes, such as stretch and walk around, to help participants mentally remove themselves from the simulation. You should be aware that participants frequently get angry at the "director" in the game (usually the facilitator) for rigging the game, and you need to be prepared for that.

### Processing

Participants typically have very strong reactions to the *Star Power* simulation. Ask participants to pair up with someone for 5 minutes and talk about their reactions to the game with their partner. You might ask them the following questions:

- How did you feel when you first got your chips?
- How did you feel after each of the rounds?
- What did you feel and think when the "Squares" got the right to make the rules for the game?
- Did anything about your behavior surprise you? Someone else's behavior?

Then ask participants to come back together and discuss their experiences in the simulation with the whole group. Start with asking about how they felt at different points in the game and how they are feeling now. This will often involve discussing what happened in the game, who did what to whom, and how it felt to those involved. You may need to draw out particular people or groups; for instance, if only "Squares" are talking, invite the "Circles" or "Triangles" to join in. If one member of a group says something, such as "I realized after the first round that the rules were stacked," focus on this issue. Ask the other groups if and at what point they also realized it. Sometimes, "Squares" will be the most clueless about what happened, and others will want to tease them. Often, members of the "Squares" group will be defensive. Emphasize that one's *role* in the game often determines one's feelings, perceptions, and understanding.

Often, the facilitators will observe interactions that participants do not see. Share your perceptions also. Make sure people also process their feelings about the "director." Sometimes, people have the most intense feelings about this role. Discussing this can be a challenge if the facilitator is the same as the "director" in the game, because people may still act out toward the "director." If possible, let another person facilitate the processing so that feelings about the "director" can be aired freely.

When it seems that most issues have been aired and discussed, move the discussion to parallels between the game and the "real world." Help participants discuss similarities and differences. Encourage them to look at all levels—personal, institutional, and cultural. Go over the definitions of *power*, *class privilege*, and *collusion*, and consider how these were manifested in the game and in the "real world."

## Facilitation Issues

This segment completes the transition from individual experience to society-wide systems; if participants fail to make this transition, they will gain little from the remaining focus of the course. At no time is the possibility of going off-track into particular policy debates or tangential issues stronger than during the discussion of institutionalized classism. However, the sheer number of examples presented in the initial presentation and exercise should keep most participants from the misconception that the facilitators are equating classism with advocating a particular solution. Make sure you have a number of examples of each type of institutional classism, similar to the examples given above. Facilitators should point out the recurring themes in the examples and repeatedly restate the definition of institutional classism.

### 3. Closing (10 minutes)

Ask participants to pair up and talk about one thing they learned from this session and one thing they want to learn more about in the next session. When the groups come back together, have five or six participants share their responses. Have everyone write the thing they learned and what they still want to learn on a piece of paper and hand it in.

## Module 4: Action Against Classism

Time needed: 3 hours, 20 minutes

### Objectives

- Identify examples of opposition to classism in U.S. history.
- Identify ways of taking action against classism in everyday life, and make commitments to individual next steps.
- Increase understanding of the roles and importance of allies and cross-class alliances.

**Key concepts**: allies, cross-class alliances, economic justice, labor movement

## 1. History of Classism and Anti-classism in the United States (45 minutes)

Use the sample outline in Appendix 13J to emphasize that this is a very abbreviated version of a much more complex story. Encourage participants to read books and articles from the readings suggested in Appendix 13M. Talk in a lively, dramatic, storytelling way, using handouts and visual aids. A useful visual is a simple timeline with decades marked at intervals posted on the wall, to which the presenter can point. Emphasize historical examples of resistance to class inequality.

### Processing

Ask participants to pair up and share emotional responses, questions, and ideas. Ask them to take turns, and remind them when it's time to switch. Then, bring the whole group back together and facilitate a discussion using the following questions:

- What were your reactions to the history presentation?
- What themes or key ideas did you hear?
- What is still confusing or unclear?
- What aspects of this history have you heard before, and what, if anything, was new or surprising to you?
- Can you think of other social justice movements that connected with class movements? For example, sanitation workers striking in Memphis during the Civil Rights movement, the Poor People's Campaign, and women fighting for the right to vote.

### Facilitation Issues

Because most undergraduates don't know much history, the facilitators should expect varied nonhistorical issues to come up. This is a likely point in the course for participants to express disagreements with the course material. Further resources from Appendix 13M can be made available for future study by participants, perhaps as a self-education action plan.

## 2. Acting as Allies (30 minutes)

Introduce the concept of an ally as someone who speaks up or takes action against oppression of people from other groups. Ask participants to think about one time they had an ally and a time they acted as an ally; then have them pair up and take turns sharing their examples. In the whole group, ask for examples that relate to classism. For example, in one course, a participant talked about interrupting a store clerk who was disrespectfully treating a customer using food stamps. If necessary, share one or two of your own examples to prime the pump. Ideally, at least one interpersonal example (such as interrupting a "dumb hillbilly" joke) and at least one institutional example (such as not sending kids to private schools but working to make the public schools better) can be shared by participants or facilitators.

On a blank piece of newsprint or a chalkboard, write "Qualities of an Ally." Ask participants to draw out characteristics of an ally from the examples in their own pairs and in the whole group, then to think of others. Finally, give participants copies of the handout "Acting as an Ally" (Appendix 13K).

## 3. Classism in Your School (60 minutes)

Tell participants that we will be coming up with examples of how classism is manifested in their school so that we can later talk about taking action for change. Ask participants to brainstorm examples of classism they have observed at their school or college. Ask them, "What was a situation in which you wanted to be an ally or needed an ally against classism?" As they speak, write key words on newsprint or chalkboard. Allow clarifying questions and brief reactions, but enforce the rules of brainstorming (no discussions about what happened, whether it was really classist, who was to blame, or what to do about it). If the group is having trouble thinking of examples, prompt them with questions and examples. Examples can be found in Appendix 13L.

Ask participants to choose one example from the list that involves face-to-face interactions between people. If participants have trouble coming up with an interactive example of classism from their own school, have one of the examples from Appendix 13L ready for use. Ask for volunteers to play each role in the situation, or assign roles if there are no volunteers. Make sure at least one role is that of an ally against classism. Have the players stand up where the group can see them. Suggest an opening line for one actor, and ask the others to respond in their roles. At key moments, say, "Freeze!" and ask the rest of the group to suggest alternative responses. Stop the role play after a few minutes. Ask those playing anticlassist characters how they felt. "What did you feel worked? What didn't work?" Ask those playing classist characters how it felt to get different reactions to their behavior. If time allows, do another one or two additional role plays based on examples generated by participants, or examples in Appendix 13L.

## 4. Actions Against Classism (45 minutes)

Ask participants to pair up with someone in class with whom they feel they made a significant connection. Using the examples of classism at their school and using the action continuum in Appendix 6H as a guide (see also Chapter 14, Module 4 Activity 3), ask them to discuss ways they could be anticlassist, and then make at least one specific commitment to a particular action against classism. Pass out blank sheets of paper and envelopes. Ask participants to self-address the envelope and to write their future selves a letter reminding themselves of what they've learned in this course and what commitment(s) they made to an anticlassist action. Tell them you will mail the letters to them in a month.

## 5. Closing Circle: Personal Next Steps and Evaluation (20 minutes)

Have participants spend a few minutes on revisiting their index cards. Ask them to reflect on any new learnings that have impacted their understanding of their class of origin identity. Ask them what they would now say about their current class identity.

Next, ask the group to evaluate the sessions. There are a variety of ways to do this. It might be best to ask for participants to write their comments in response to the following questions:

1. What was the highlight of the course for you? What did you like best? What was most useful to you?
2. What I learned from this course was …
3. As a result of participation,
   • I will change my thinking by …
   • I will change my feelings by …
   • I will change the way I do things by …
4. As a follow-up to this experience, I would like to …
5. What aspects of the course would you have done differently? Please describe any changes that you feel would improve or enhance this course.
6. If future courses were offered on classism, what would you like to see covered?

7. I appreciated most that the facilitators ...
8. I might have had a better experience if the facilitators had ...

After collecting the written evaluations, lead a closing activity in which people go around a circle and share one thing they have learned about classism and one action they plan to take against classism in the future. Ask participants to respond to the following two sentence stems:

1. One thing I learned about classism was ...
2. One action I will take against classism is ...

# 14

# Ableism Curriculum Design

## PAT GRIFFIN, MADELINE L. PETERS, ROBIN M. SMITH*

Ableism, or disability oppression, is a pervasive system of discrimination and exclusion of people with disabilities. Like racism, sexism, and other forms of oppression, ableism operates on individual, institutional, and cultural levels to privilege temporarily able-bodied people and disadvantage people with disabilities. The systemic nature of this form of oppression is evidenced by patterns of treatment that discriminate against people with disabilities in such institutions as health care, education, housing, and employment. This phenomenon has been described by a variety of other terms, including *handicapism*, *disability discrimination*, *physicalism*, and *mentalism*. We prefer the term *ableism* to define the oppression of people with disabilities as a social justice issue.

### Language and Identity

Like other social justice movements, the disability rights movement has raised questions about language and identity as people with disabilities and their allies challenge terminology and assert their own definitions and identity claims. Terms once used to refer to people with disabilities in the 19th and early 20th centuries such as *defective*, *deformed*, *deaf and dumb*, *insane*, and *idiot* have been challenged as oppressive. More recent terms such as *retarded*, *handicapped*, and *mentally ill*, acceptable only a few years ago, have been largely replaced by terms such as *developmentally disabled* and *emotionally disabled*. More recently, a "people first" movement has emerged that encourages the use of *people with developmental disabilities* or *people with psychological disabilities* so as not to define people by a particular physical or mental condition.

---

* We ask that those who cite this work always acknowledge by name all of the authors listed rather than either only citing the first author or using "et al." to indicate coauthors. All collaborated on the conceptualization, development, and writing of this chapter.

Euphemistic terms, such as *physically or mentally challenged* and *differently abled*, despite their good intentions, have also been challenged by disability rights advocates who believe that they perpetuate ableism by trivializing the experiences of people with disabilities or minimizing the effects of disability oppression.

Many people with disabilities have redefined the term *disabled*, claiming it as a positive descriptor of a powerful and proud group of people with strengths and abilities, but "disabled" by unnecessary social, economic, and environmental barriers rather than by physical, psychological, or developmental conditions or impairments. Others reject the term *disabled* as a negative label forced on them by professionals who do not understand their needs or differences. In their view, they are not disabled but rather obstructed by negative interactions with controlling health and social service systems. Mental health system survivors, for example, reject psychiatric labels as part of their fight against forced "treatment" by the mental health system. Activist organizations such as MindFreedom: United Action for Human Rights in Mental Health (2003; www.mindfreedom.org) and Lunatic's Liberation Front (2006; http://walnet.org/llf/) advocate for awareness of and rights for psychiatric survivors, and share information on how to counteract the oppression of the psychiatric system, which includes forced outpatient drug treatment and mandatory mental health screening.

Some disability activists have reclaimed words that were demeaning in earlier times, such as *cripple* or *gimp*, as a way to challenge attitudes and reassert their ownership of the right to name themselves (Fleischer & Zames, 2001; Linton, 2005; Morris, 1991; Shaw, 1994). These differing uses of language reflect the variety of perspectives held by people with disabilities and the language used to discuss disabilities.

## Wide Range of Disabilities

People targeted by ableism include those with developmental, medical, neurological, physical, and psychological disabilities. The wide range of disabilities makes ableism a complex issue to address. For example, the experiences and needs of people with hearing or visual disabilities differ from those with mobility impairments or people with cancer, diabetes, or asthma. Some disabilities, like a variety of mobility impairments, are visible. Others, like learning disabilities or psychiatric disabilities, are not visible. The common thread that unites the experiences of people with diverse disabilities is having to contend with a culture that sees disability through fear, pity, or shame and teaches us to regard disability as a tragedy.

Anyone can become disabled through sickness, aging, accidents, or acts of violence or war, or even due to stresses from the increased pace of life. Thus, disability touches every one of us personally or through the lives of people about whom we care. For this reason, we refer to people who do not have disabilities as *temporarily able-bodied*. Temporarily able-bodied people often perceive people with disabilities to be less than fully human, unfortunate, or objects of charity. They often channel feelings of sympathy and pity by giving to charities rather than working to eliminate social and environmental barriers that limit access for people with disabilities. Such paternalistic attitudes, beliefs, and actions toward people with disabilities tend to prevent systemic change.

## Social and Physical Environment as Disabling

Perspectives on disability are shaped by cultural beliefs about the value of human life, health, productivity, independence, normality, and beauty. Such beliefs are reflected through institutional values and environments that are often hostile to people whose abilities fall outside of what is culturally defined as normal. The perspective presented in this chapter is that people have different kinds of impairments that limit their ability to function easily in a society where normality is too narrowly defined, and the social and physical environmental norms are disabling.

When the physical environment is constructed so that only a narrow range of abilities are accommodated, it is disabling for everyone whose abilities fall outside of this narrow range (Wendell, 1996). For example, a wheelchair user is disabled by buildings that require entrants to walk up stairs to enter or by bathrooms that are not designed to accommodate a wheelchair. People with visual or hearing impairments are disabled by a lack of access to computers or other services designed to accommodate their needs. People with asthma or environmental sensitivities are disabled by buildings that lack adequate ventilation systems or have molds in carpets.

The social environment is disabling when people fail to consider the barriers that their attitudes or the physical environment poses to people with disabilities and when they view accommodating a broader range of abilities as an unreasonable financial burden or as extra work. Paradoxically, meeting the needs and wants of people who do not have disabilities is rarely viewed as an accommodation. For example, most temporarily able-bodied people expect a wide range of choices in vehicles to purchase—large, small, and medium-sized cars or trucks with various options for color and accessories. Yet we have only recently begun to consider the transportation needs of people with disabilities and to pass laws requiring public transportation to be accessible to a wider range of abilities. Similarly, teachers who consider accommodating the needs of students with learning disabilities as an unreasonable burden or extra work often accept as integral their responsibilities to prepare different lesson plans for different classes. In these ways, we choose to create or allow barriers to access for people with disabilities.

## Universal Architectural Design

The social and physical environment can be changed to enable people with disabilities to function successfully. Universal design derives from architectural efforts to design buildings so that anyone can use them. Universal design features include ramps rather than steps for building entrances, lever door handles, Braille signage, wider door entries and hallways, raised electrical outlets, lower light switches, and flashing lights to call attention to a ringing phone. These and other accessibility features typically add little or no cost if included in the design stage of building construction.

Those advocating universal design in new homes and apartments also call for a standard of "visitability." If you don't live there, can you visit? For example, can you get in the door or enter the bathroom? Proponents of universal design argue that such accommodations benefit everyone, not just people with disabilities, by eliminating disabling characteristics of the physical environment (Grayson, 1995). For example, anyone carrying a heavy box or pulling a large wheeled suitcase benefits from doors that open automatically, entrance ramps, and elevators.

## Universal Instructional Design

Universal instructional design is an adaptation of universal architectural design applied to the learning environment in schools (Bourke, Strehorn, & Silver, 2000; Pliner, 2004; Silver, Bourke, & Strehorn, 1998). The core principle is to provide multiple ways to access curriculum and show understanding and learning (Ouellett, 2000). Technology, for example, can make reading accessible to students with processing or severe motor disabilities. Such assistive technology also helps temporarily able-bodied students who learn more easily through modes such as listening (tapes, computer-generated speech) or reading and listening simultaneously. Universal instructional design for classrooms also includes providing syllabi in alternate formats, making copies of notes, allowing extra time to complete exams for all students, and using alternative instructional options, such as illustration, speaking, or drama, to express understanding. As with universal architectural design, adaptations and accommodations for students with disabilities can benefit all members of the class, thus insuring that students who must have the accommodation are not singled out or stigmatized.

## Historical Treatment of People with Disabilities

Throughout history, people with disabilities have faced serious and persistent forms of discrimination, segregation, exclusion, and sometimes genocide (Covey, 1998; Longmore & Umanski, 2001). They have been viewed variously as menaces to society needing control, as children to be pitied and cared for, and as objects of charity (Morris, 1996).

In western societies before the 18th century, disability was considered an unchangeable condition that resulted from sin (Covey, 1998). People with disabilities were left to beg in the streets or were locked away. Beginning in the 18th century, people with disabilities were viewed as objects of curiosity or deranged monsters who were frequently displayed to the "normal" public in carnival freak shows or hidden in asylums where they were subjected to inhumane treatment. With the rise of science, medical doctors began to identify and classify the genetic deficiencies linked with disability. For example, in the 1880s and 1890s, "medical imbecility" was attributed to people with mental retardation, as well as to paupers, prostitutes, immigrants, and others struggling to assimilate into American society (Longmore & Umanski, 2001). Close links with the eugenics movement spurred policies to segregate and sterilize people considered to be hopelessly unredeemable due to their disabilities. Eugenics at its most extreme became the "scientific" rationale for Germany's extermination policies during World War II in which thousands of people with disabilities were gassed or starved to death (Gallagher, 1995).

Disabled veterans returning from World War II spurred doctors to focus on rehabilitation and the development of devices to help them return to work and live productive lives. This focus on rehabilitation marked a shift in the approach to working with people with disabilities. However, many continued to be segregated in special schools, sheltered workplaces, and medical institutions where they were treated as "patients" who needed supervision and care by others who knew best.

In the 1960s and 1970s, a social movement of people with disabilities began to emerge. Following the lead of other civil rights and justice movements like the Black Civil Rights movement, the feminist movement, and the gay rights movement, disabled activists began demanding their civil rights. The passage of Section 504 of the Rehabilitation Act of 1973 was a turning point. This act stated, "No otherwise qualified person may be discriminated against in any program receiving federal funds." The definition of disability set forth in the regulations of this act (34 C.F.R., 104) included impairments of major life activities (e.g., walking, seeing, hearing, and intellectual activity) and included temporarily able-bodied people perceived to be disabled even if they were not so. The language of Section 504 reflects the language of the Civil Rights Act of 1964, as does the Americans With Disabilities Act (ADA), a federal law passed in 1990 that requires public institutions to provide access to people with disabilities. The ADA asserts the full equality of people with disabilities and opens the door to the benefits and responsibilities of full participation in society.

## Contemporary Manifestations of Ableism

Ableism, like all other forms of social injustice, operates on multiple levels. Cultural beliefs about concepts such as beauty, normality, and independence affect social attitudes about disability and, consequently, how people with disabilities are treated in society. Institutional policies, beliefs, norms, and practices perpetuate ableism. For example, institutionalized religious beliefs that disability is punishment for sin or that disability can be "healed" through faith affect how some religious people respond to disability. Other major social institutions such as the law, housing, health care, the family, and government are part of the social web that reinforces ableism and erects barriers for people with disabilities and their allies.

Individual attitudes and actions are also an important part of how ableism is perpetuated. Individual paternalistic perspectives of sympathy or pity toward people with disabilities are part of the matrix of obstacles that help to create and aggravate barriers they face. Similarly, feelings of fatalism, fear, or dread about the possibility of becoming disabled influence many individuals to respond to disability issues and to people with disabilities in ways that are disempowering to them.

## Disability Rights Movement

Over the last 30–40 years, people with all types of disabilities have organized into an emerging political movement for disability rights and independent living, both in the United States and around the world (Charlton, 2000; Shapiro, 1993). People with disabilities who are part of this political movement reject the notion that being disabled is an inherently negative experience or in any way descriptive of something broken or abnormal. They see *disability* as a positive term. Proponents of this perspective take pride in the differences in their bodies and minds and strive to make others aware of their experiences and accomplishments. They see themselves as activists in the ongoing struggle against the oppressive social, economic, and environmental forces that limit opportunities for people with disabilities to achieve their full potential. Such activists see themselves as "disabled" by the social and environmental structures that were created without them in mind and that now prevent them from taking their rightful place in society. Perhaps most importantly, they recognize the connections and commonalities among people and strive to work in coalition across a broad range of disabilities as well as with other oppressed groups.

## Intersections of Ableism and Other Oppressions

People with disabilities represent all races, classes, ages, genders, sexual orientations, and religions, and their experience of ableism is mediated by oppression they experience through these other identities. For example, because of racism, children of African descent raised in a cultural milieu that values high-energy behaviors are often labeled as having discipline problems by white, middle-class teachers for engaging in behaviors valued in the child's home and community, but not in school (Franklin, 1992). Such children may be labeled with attention deficit or emotional disorders. Similarly, Latino/a children who have not mastered English as a second language may be labeled learning disabled or developmentally disabled despite laws mandating culturally sensitive testing (Duhaney, 2000). These forms of discrimination have led some scholars to highlight the necessity of teachers developing cultural competence or relevance if they are to be effective in educating children of color (Ladson-Billings, 1994).

Heterosexism, sexism, and classism also mediate one's experience of disability. People with disabilities who are gay, lesbian, bisexual, or transgender (GLBT) may not receive the same access to information and resources as temporarily able-bodied GLBT people in their community. GLBT people with disabilities may not have access to a partner's health insurance coverage if their relationship is not legally recognized. Women with physical or medical disabilities may be seen as unfit mothers, or as unattractive and asexual. The invisibility of women with disabilities carries over into the workforce, where they are not hired at the same rate and are not paid as much as men (Seabrook, 2002).

The interconnection among disability, employment, health care, and classism is particularly important. The costs of assistive technology that make it possible for people with disabilities to participate in many daily activities are prohibitive for poor or working-class people. Computers and software applications that enable people with disabilities to be employed, attend school, or socialize with friends are prohibitively expensive for many people. Although such devices as voice input and output for blind and mobility-impaired readers to read out loud, and digital hearing aids and cochlear implants for deaf or hearing-impaired people, are important advancements, these devices are beyond the financial resources for many people with disabilities.

For poor and working-class people, it is difficult to meet daily needs without social, medical, or technical support. People with medical or mobility disabilities find that expensive medications and appropriate orthopedic or physical therapies are out of reach for Social Security–based incomes, or insurance companies may make decisions that affect their ability to live independently. Persons with severe disabilities may have better access to needed resources when they have the financial resources and insurance needed to buy equipment, hire personal care attendants, or get expensive medical treatment.

## Ableism and Other Social Issues

Ableism has implications for other social issues such as assisted suicide and abortion. For example, arguments in favor of assisted suicide are complicated by attitudes about the value or viability of living with a disability. The belief that living with a disability is worse than dying consigns healthy people with disabilities to the same status as those who are terminally ill or living with chronic pain. Severely disabled people may be pressured to sign "Do Not Resuscitate" (DNR) orders even when in the hospital for minor procedures. The Human Genome Project—a project to map human genes—and the debate over euthanasia and end-of-life issues evoke heated debate over who decides the worth of an individual life. Opponents of legally assisted suicide argue that "legalized medical killing is about a deadly double standard for people with severe disabilities, including both conditions that are labeled terminal and those that are not" ("Not Dead Yet," 2006, ¶1).

Likewise, many disability rights advocates oppose abortion because of their objection to aborting fetuses with disabilities. They argue that pro-choice advocates have not considered the implications of their support for abortion for people with disabilities. Social policy on serious and controversial issues like euthanasia and abortion rights becomes even more complicated when dominant attitudes toward disability color the perspective of decision makers such as doctors who have power over others' lives.

School funding is another difficult area of public policy affected by ableism. The interests of temporarily able-bodied students are often pitted against the interests of students with disabilities in battles over dwindling school resources when programs to meet the needs of students with disabilities are considered an "extra" expense that places an unreasonable burden on taxpayers.

Finally, some groups of people defined by society as having disabilities do not see themselves as disabled at all. For example, many Deaf people see themselves as a cultural group separate from "the hearing" group. They take pride in and wish to preserve their own language and patterns of community. They capitalize the "D" in Deaf to signify their belief that the Deaf are a cultural group, not a disability. Such differing definitions and experiences complicate teaching about ableism and must be acknowledged in any comprehensive curriculum to address the oppression of people with disabilities.

## International Perspectives on Disability

There are an estimated 600 million people with disabilities in the world today, and this number is increasing due to aging populations, environmental contamination, ethnic and sectarian violence, war, and the increasing divide between the rich and the poor (Harrison, 2004). The United Nations is currently working on a treaty to protect the rights of people with disabilities. The goals of the international treaty are to raise public awareness about disability-related issues, highlight human rights abuses, develop knowledge about disability-related issues of governmental and nongovernmental groups, and offer capacity-building opportunities for disability groups through increased global focus on their issues (Harrison, 2004).

The rights of people with disabilities are being recognized in many countries. Great Britain passed the Disability Discrimination Act in 1995; Australia adopted the same law shortly after Great Britain. Statutes in countries such as Africa, Austria, Brazil, Germany, Finland, the Philippines, Malawi, South Africa, and Uganda have been amended to prohibit discrimination on the basis of disability (Harrison, 2004).

## Ableism Curriculum Design and Facilitation Issues

Without attention to the systemic nature of ableism, education about disability issues can reinforce existing stereotypes and beliefs. For example, "Disability Awareness" programs, a popular educational intervention in many schools and workplaces, often use disability simulation activities to educate participants. In such programs, participants are assigned a disability to "live" with for a period of time. After the simulation, participants discuss the difficulty of performing daily activities with their disability. Such simulations, unless very carefully designed and discussed afterwards, reinforce a view of disability as individual deficiency rather than fostering awareness of ableism as a form of oppression that operates on individual, institutional, and societal/cultural levels. In addition, these activities perpetuate negative notions about disability by focusing on what participants cannot do because of their "disability." This experience often reinforces participant fears of becoming disabled and condescending perceptions that people with disabilities should be pitied or helped. Having participants spend time using a wheelchair to understand mobility impairment may reinforce the idea that using a wheelchair is "tragic." People role-playing blindness may only remember their fear and incompetence and discount the training, adaptations, and accommodations they could use to ensure living fully should they lose their sight. A 1-hour experience being blindfolded or using a wheelchair obscures the fact that people live with these disabilities all their lives, know how to confidently get around, and are able to live their independent lives. Without attention to the systemic nature of ableism, education about disability issues can reinforce existing stereotypes and beliefs.

For these reasons, we believe that "disability awareness" activities should be designed to focus on ableism as a systemic phenomenon.

Facilitators should be aware of and sensitive to the range of awareness and knowledge about disability that participants bring so as to facilitate a meaningful experience for all, both temporarily able-bodied participants and participants with disabilities. For example, persons with disabilities may not be knowledgeable about or sensitive to people with disabilities different from theirs. Participants will also differ in their willingness to share their own experiences with disability. For example, those with hidden disabilities may or may not feel comfortable disclosing this information in class. Others may not think of themselves as disabled when they begin an ableism course but may come to identify as such as a result of participation in the course. All participants can benefit from an opportunity to explore their feelings about disability, including fears about their own fragility, loss of control, and death. In such discussions, participants may realize how fears cause them to avoid people with disabilities or feel anger toward people with disabilities for reminding them of these realities of life.

## Assumptions

Whatever specific activities we choose for a course on ableism, our teaching is guided by a set of assumptions we have about disability and oppression. These include the following:

- Having a disability is another interesting way to be alive.
- Becoming disabled involves major life changes including loss as well as gain, and is the continuation of a meaningful and productive existence.
- People with disabilities experience discrimination, segregation, and isolation as a result of other people's prejudice and institutional ableism, not because of the disability itself.
- Social beliefs, cultural norms, and media images about beauty, intelligence, physical ability, communication, and behavior often negatively influence the way people with disabilities are treated.
- Societal expectations about economic productivity and self-sufficiency devalue persons who are not able to work, regardless of other contributions they may make to family and community life.
- Without positive messages about who they are, persons with disabilities are vulnerable to internalizing society's negative messages about disability.
- Independence and dependence are relative concepts subject to personal definition, which every person experiences, and are neither inherently positive nor negative.
- Although laws now protect people with disabilities and their right to inclusion in the mainstream of our society, they are still not treated as full and equal citizens.

## Ableism Curriculum Design

### Overall Goals

- Participants will increase awareness of ableism and its manifestations at the individual, institutional, and cultural levels.
- Participants will learn how disability is constructed through social and environmental barriers.

**Table 14.1**  Overview of Modules: Ableism

| Module 1: Socialization and Definitions (3 hours) | Module 2: Historical, Institutional, and Cultural Perspectives (2 hours, 40 minutes) |
|---|---|
| 1. Introductions, Housekeeping, Guidelines for Participation, Goals, and Agenda (35 min.)<br>2. People Treasure Hunt (20 min.)<br>3. Early Learning About People With Disabilities (50 min.)<br>4. Journal Writing (10 min.)<br>Break (15 min.)<br>5. Types of Disabilities (30 min.)<br>6. Journal Writing (5 min.)<br>7. Homework Assignment (5 min.)<br>8. Closing Circle (10 min.) | 1. Check-In (10 min.)<br>2. Historical Perspectives on Disability (60 min.)<br>3. Disability as a Social Construct (30 min.)<br>4. Journal Writing (5 min.)<br>Break (15 min.)<br>5. Institutional Ableism (30 min.)<br>6. Closing (10 min.) |
| **Module 3: Voices of People With Disabilities (3 hours)** | **Module 4: Taking Action (2 hours, 55 minutes)** |
| 1. Check-In (15 min.)<br>2. Listening to the Voices of Disability: Panel of People With Disabilities (60 min.)<br>Break (15 min.)<br>3. Discussion of Panel Presentation (30 min.)<br>4. Journal Writing (5 min.)<br>5. Ableism and Controversial Social Issues (45 min.)<br>6. Closing Circle (10 min.) | 1. Check-In (15 min.)<br>2. Visioning an Accessible, Inclusive Society (60 min.)<br>3. Action Continuum (30 min.)<br>Break (15 min.)<br>4. Becoming an Ally (30 min.)<br>5. Journal Writing (5 min.)<br>6. Closing (20 min.) |

- Participants will increase understanding of the experience of living with disability in an ableist society.
- Participants will learn strategies for eliminating ableism.

## Overview of Modules

Note to readers: The curriculum design in this chapter is based on the assumption that participants have completed the introductory module(s) described in Chapter 3 prior to beginning this design and have a basic understanding of the conceptual framework of oppression described in Chapter 3. See Table 14.1 for an overview of this chapter's modules.

## Module 1: Socialization and Definitions

Time needed: 3 hours

## Overall Goals

- Increase awareness of early personal influences that shape perceptions of disability and people with disabilities.
- Identify and discuss common stereotypes and myths about people with disabilities.
- Identify the range of different kinds of disabilities.

**Key concepts:** socialization, stereotypes, targeted identities

## 1. Introductions, Housekeeping, Guidelines for Participation, Goals, and Agenda (35 minutes)

Introduce yourself to the class. Give the class some information about your background: Identify yourself as a temporarily able-bodied ally or as a person with a disability, describe how you became interested in teaching about ableism, and discuss other social identities that affect your experiences with ableism.

Ask participants to share (a) their name, (b) how disability touches their life, and (c) one thing they hope to learn in the course. Provide some examples of what you mean by "touching their life." For example, they have a disability, someone in their family or a close friend has a disability, they work with or teach people with disabilities, or they have had a short-term disability that affected their conduct of daily activities (on crutches, arm in a sling).

Inform the class where the wheelchair-accessible restrooms are located. Also, tell them about other accessibility features in the building, for example elevators, Braille door signs, audio signals to indicate elevator floors, and automatic doors. Tell participants where they can get food and drinks and when class breaks are scheduled. Ask participants who have learning needs you should know about to please let you know during a break in the class.

Tell the class that facilitators will read everything on newsprint so that everyone will be able to see or hear what is discussed. Identify participation guidelines that will be used in the course (see the introductory module in Chapter 3). Post and read the course goals and agenda.

## 2. People Treasure Hunt (20 minutes)

The purpose of this activity is to provide an opportunity for participants to meet others in the course and to help them to begin thinking about disability issues. Provide everyone with the People Treasure Hunt (Appendix 14A). Tell participants that they have 10 minutes to find other people in the class who can initial the boxes on the treasure hunt either because that experience is true for them or because they know the answer to the question posed. Participants cannot sign their own form. Try to encourage participants to get as many different initials as they can rather than asking one person to sign several boxes. Begin the activity.

After 10 minutes, ask everyone to return to their seats in the circle. Call off each item in the treasure hunt, and ask for a show of hands to indicate who was able to find someone in the class to initial that item. For items calling for knowledge, ask someone in the class to provide that information to the whole group. Be prepared to provide the information that no one else knows.

Conclude the activity by observing themes you noticed in the responses to the treasure hunt. For example, many people in the group know about the ADA or few people know about the independent living movement. Tell participants that this course is designed to provide more information and help participants to identify how they can address ableism in their lives.

### Facilitation Issues

Adapt the individual items on the People Treasure Hunt so that participants will learn about accessibility and resources in schools and communities where the course is being taught.

## 3. Early Learning About People With Disabilities (50 minutes)

**Key concepts**: stereotypes, socialization

The purpose of this activity is to identify how our early experiences and socialization influence our beliefs about disability and people with disabilities.

Tell participants that this activity will ask them to reflect on early memories about disability and how these memories inform their current thoughts, feelings, and actions in relationship to people with disabilities. Ask participants to take 10 minutes to briefly write answers to the following questions. Then ask participants to take 20 minutes to share their answers with a partner (10 minutes for each partner).

Choose two to five items from these suggested questions:

1. Describe the first time you can remember encountering a person with a disability. What were your reactions, feelings, and thoughts in this situation?
2. When were you first aware that people with disabilities were treated differently because of their disability?
3. Describe an early memory of a time you witnessed someone being hurt or discriminated against because they had a disability.
4. What were some of the assumptions you had about people with disabilities, or what it would be like to have a disability when you were in elementary school?
5. Recall what people (adults and peers) said about people with disabilities. Include labels and typical descriptions and attributes you heard.
6. Recall how people behaved toward people with disabilities. Describe a specific memory.

After the pair discussions, invite participants to return to the large group. Ask participants to share their responses to the following questions:

- What were some early messages you learned about disability?
- From whom did these messages come? Adults or peers? Media?
- How do these early messages about disability and people with disabilities affect you now?

As participants identify early messages about disability and people with disabilities, list them on newsprint or a chalkboard. Acknowledge participants' experiences, without judgment, and affirm that fear, discomfort, curiosity, and confusion about people with disabilities are typical experiences for children because we are often taught not to ask about disabilities and not to look at people with disabilities.

Next, invite participants to examine the list of messages: What do they notice about the list? Ask what themes can be identified in the list of messages. What feelings do they have as they examine the list? Ask participants to reflect on how these messages affect their perceptions now about disabilities and people with disabilities.

Some of the messages and associations participants may identify include those listed in Table 14.2.

Conclude the activity by describing the cycle of socialization, using specific examples related to ableism (see Appendix 3E). Reassure participants that although we all learn such messages innocently through the process of being socialized by our parents, teachers, and peers and by

**Table 14.2**  Messages and Associations About People With Disabilities

| Stereotypes/Myths | Names/Words |
|---|---|
| Eternal children | Crippled |
| Evil | Deformed |
| Depressed | Insane |
| Deranged | Drunk/druggie |
| Bitter | Deaf/mute |
| Dependent | Crazy |
| Burden | Physically challenged |
| God's children | Mentally ill |
| "Supercrip" | Survivor |
| Courageous | Retarded |
| Ugly | Differently able |
| Asexual | Patient |
| Tragic | Idiot |
| | Slow |
| | Dumb |

institutions such as education and the media, we also have an opportunity to learn new information and change our perspectives through discussion and learning.

### Facilitation Issues

Participants might feel uncomfortable hearing these stereotypes out loud. Some participants might laugh inappropriately as an expression of this discomfort. Remind participants that knowing about these stereotypes about people with disabilities is not surprising because we have grown up in cultures that taught us these messages. Remind them that many stereotypes we have of people with disabilities are rooted in historical perspectives on disability that will be explored later in the course. Although we take in all information from our cultures during our formative years, we now have an opportunity to question them and understand how we have come to learn them.

If people feel inhibited in generating the stereotypes list, you can ask them, "What do you wish people wouldn't ever say again?" You can also ask them if name calling in the playground included such terms as *moron* or *retard*. Ask what else they heard.

These stereotypes often influence the reactions of many temporarily able-bodied people toward people with disabilities. The word *tragic*, for example, is often used to describe a disability acquired as a result of accident or illness. Perceiving disability as a tragedy leads participants to fear disability or becoming disabled themselves. This reaction can prevent participants from understanding that, although the initial loss one experiences may be genuinely difficult, it is not accurate to assume that the lives of people who become disabled will be an ongoing tragedy. For many persons with disabilities, becoming disabled has profoundly changed their lives in positive ways that could not be imagined at the time of an accident or at the initial diagnosis of an illness. For increasing numbers of people with disabilities, becoming nondisabled, even through miraculous cures, is not what they desire. Sharing this perspective with participants can help them to reassess what they assumed to be true about people with disabilities.

In addition, the stereotypes keep us from forming authentic reciprocal relationships with people with disabilities. They also lead us to make decisions about people with disabilities based on what we think our experience would be instead of learning from them what their experience actually is. For example, Christopher Reeves became a quadriplegic after falling from a horse. Although his life was profoundly changed, he thrived on support from his friends and family, lived a full rich life, and advocated for research money for spinal injury cures. Although he advocated for a cure, he did not wait for one to get on with his personal and professional life. He also spoke out for the rights of people with disabilities. Yet reporters interviewing his wife continued to ask her questions about what it was like "to take care of him" and if she considered leaving him. Sharing examples like this can assist participants in identifying and challenging their own stereotypes of people with disabilities.

### 4. Journal Writing (10 minutes)

This is the first of a series of brief individual reflection times built into the course. It allows participants time to think about what they are learning in the course. Explain the purpose of journal writing, and tell participants that the journal is for their own use. Ask participants to spend 5 minutes thinking and writing about their reactions to either of the following questions:

- What have you learned that challenges what you previously thought about people with disabilities?
- What questions do you have about disability?

**Break (15 minutes)**

**5. Types of Disabilities (30 minutes)**

**Key concepts**: abilities and disabilities

This activity is designed to provide participants with an understanding of the range of impairments or conditions included under the large umbrella of disabilities. This activity will also introduce participants to some of the complexities of addressing ableism as a result of the wide range of different disabilities.

Post a newsprint sheet on the wall with the heading "Disabilities." Ask participants to brainstorm a list of types of disabilities. Write down each item without comment. When participants have identified as many disabilities as they can, ask them to look at the list and identify any disabilities with which they are not familiar. Briefly, answer questions about the disabilities with which participants are unfamiliar.

Distribute the "Definitions, Types, and Examples of Disabilities" handout to participants (see Appendix 14B). Ask participants to review the different kinds of disabilities on the list. Ask participants the following questions:

- What kinds of disabilities are listed on the handout that you did not name on your brainstormed list?
- Are there impairments or conditions on the kinds of disabilities handout that you did not previously think of as disabilities?
- How does this information change your answer to the question "How does disability touch your life?"

Bring attention back to the whole group. Invite comments on new information they learned about disabilities. Write down the Americans With Disabilities Act (ADA) definition of disability on the chalkboard or on newsprint: any impairment that substantially limits a major life activity. Major life activities are seeing, hearing, speaking, breathing, processing, caring for one's self, and working.

Note that many people have multiple disabilities. For example, a person with cerebral palsy might also use a wheelchair, or someone with asthma could also have a hearing or visual impairment. Call attention to the complexity of addressing ableism when there are so many different disabilities. These disabilities affect people from every race, gender, age, and class. Also note that this complexity makes the development of a disability rights movement that is inclusive of multiple disabilities more challenging.

### Facilitation Issues

Occasionally, a participant will ask if people who, for example, wear glasses are disabled. Refer them back to the ADA definition as a guide to determining when any impairment or condition constitutes a disability. If someone wears glasses or contact lens that correct their vision so that they can carry out their daily activities without substantial limitation, that level of vision impairment would not be included in a definition of disability.

**6. Journal Writing (5 minutes)**

Provide participants with time to write in their journals. Ask them to focus on what new information they have learned or questions they have about topics addressed in this module.

### 7. Homework Assignment (5 minutes)

Give participants the "Historical Timeline of Perspectives on the Treatment of People With Disabilities" (Appendix 14C). Ask them to read the timeline and be prepared to focus on the discussion questions at the end of the timeline.

### 8. Closing Circle (10 minutes)

Ask participants to identify something they learned from this module and something about which they still have questions.

## Module 2: Historical, Institutional, and Cultural Perspectives

Time needed: 2 hours, 40 minutes

### Goals

- Learn about the historical treatment of people with disabilities.
- Understand how disability is created by the social, cultural, and physical environments.
- Explore institutional and cultural ableism.

**Key concepts**: history, social construction, institutional and cultural ableism

### 1. Check-In (10 minutes)

Ask if there are questions left over from Module 1. After addressing questions, introduce Module 2 by identifying the goals of the module.

### 2. Historical Perspectives on Disability (60 minutes)

The purpose of this activity is to learn about the historical treatment of people with disabilities and to better understand the historical basis for contemporary ableism.

Divide participants into groups of 3 to 5, and ask them to discuss the history timeline (see Appendix 14C) and create a list of what they learned about ableism from the timeline. Write the discussion questions from the history timeline on newsprint or on the chalkboard, and ask each group to discuss the questions.

After 30 minutes, ask each group to share their list of important learnings about ableism.

Distribute copies of "Understanding Abilities and Disabilities: Toward Interdependency" (Appendix 14D). Discuss each of the different perspectives in the table, and ask participants to relate these perspectives to different historical eras in the timeline. Note that though the different perspectives can be associated with specific historical eras, different contemporary cultures and social groups within the United States continue to subscribe to many different perspectives. For example, some medical doctors or family members might take the medical or rehabilitative perspective, whereas disability activists take the interdependency perspective. Some people still believe that disabilities are the result of supernatural intervention or are punishment for sinful behavior. See Appendix 14E for a supplemental list of 20th-century legislation affecting the lives of people with disabilities.

### Facilitation Issues

As you present each perspective on disability, note changes in language that reflect differences in perspective. For example, ask participants to indicate which perspective is represented by the terms *sinner, idiot, patient, client,* and *consumer.*

## 3. Disability as a Social Construct (60 minutes)

**Key concepts**: social construction of disability, accommodation, independence, interdependence, ableism

The purpose of this activity is to provide participants with an opportunity to consider the impact that the social and physical environments have on living with a disability. This activity will help participants to explore how the social and physical environments create disability or make an impairment more disabling.

Ask participants to name elements of their physical and social environments that make their daily activities easier to perform. As they name these elements, write them on newsprint. Examples of these elements include the following:

- Computers
- Tutors
- Cell phones
- Traffic signs
- Lighting in homes, classrooms, and offices
- Microwave ovens
- Drive-through banks or food or beverage stores
- Restaurant home delivery services
- Eyeglasses or contact lens
- Alarm clocks
- Timers on coffee pots
- Books written in a language they can read
- Vacations, coffee breaks, weekends, and 9–5 work schedules
- Having a car to drive
- Child care or elder care
- Having friends and family who support and care for you
- Having a secretary, administrative assistant, or teaching assistant

Next, ask participants to imagine going through a day without these resources. How would their lives be different? What difficulties would they encounter in getting through their average day? Invite participants to think about these resources, which we often take for granted, as "accommodations" that enable us to get through our day successfully. If we did not have access to these resources, we would become "disabled" by our environment. We would not be able to carry out our daily activities as easily.

Introduce the concept of *social construction*: taken-for-granted assumptions about the world, knowledge, and ourselves assumed to be universal rather than historically and culturally specific ideas created through social processes and interactions. Invite participants to think about how disability can be created by the social and physical environment in the same way that temporarily able-bodied people would be disabled if they did not have access to the kinds of resources in the brainstormed list. People with disabilities are "disabled" when needed physical and social resources in their environment are absent. Define the social construction of disability as the interaction of the biological and the social. People with disabilities have impairments that place their ability to perform daily activities out of the norm for people who do not have disabilities. The impairments in and of themselves are not necessarily disabling. Disability is socially constructed through the failure or unwillingness to create social and physical environments that meet the needs of people who do not fit the physical and mental profile of "normal."

On newsprint or a chalkboard, list some of the following examples of how social and cultural factors contribute to the construction of disability: violent crime, poverty, war, stigmatization of people with disabilities. Invite participants to name others. Provide a more extensive list to participants, and discuss any examples about which they have questions (see Appendix 14F).

Ask participants to gather in groups of three to discuss the following questions:

1. What is your reaction to the idea that disability is socially constructed?
2. Are there any items on this list that are particularly interesting or surprising to you?
3. How does the idea that disability is a social construction change your thinking about disability?

Bring participants' attention back to the whole group. Invite them to think about disability from this new perspective: looking at the social and physical environments as the sources of the problem and the solution, rather than seeing the problem in the condition of individuals. Preventing disability requires providing the help necessary to create, wherever possible, the ability to participate in all major aspects of life in a society: work, social, political, cultural, personal, religious, and recreational.

### Facilitation Issues

Many participants think about having a disability as a "tragedy" or as a "fate worse than death." They are accustomed to feeling "pity" toward people who have disabilities. Refocusing attention on the social and physical environments as disabling is a way to help participants see disability in a different light and begin to identify ways that the environment can be changed to eliminate the obstacles that people with disabilities face in their everyday lives. This also helps some participants to understand how ableism is a social justice issue rather than an issue of charity or misfortune. They begin to understand how ableism is perpetuated through individual attitudes and actions as well as through institutional and cultural factors. The concept of the social construction of disability and this discussion come from Susan Wendell's (1996) book, *The Rejected Body: Feminist Philosophical Reflections on Disability*.

### 4. Journal Writing (5 minutes)

Ask participants to reflect in their journals on the following questions:

- What insights about ableism have you gained from this activity?
- How has your understanding of disability changed?
- What questions are raised for you?

(See Appendix 14G for an alternative activity to the Social Construction of Disability.)

### Break (15 minutes)

### 5. Institutional Ableism (30 minutes)

The purpose of this activity is to identify examples of institutional policies, practices, and norms that perpetuate ableism. The activity invites participants to think about how institutions create disability in the social and physical environments through their policies, practices, and norms.

On newsprint sheets, write the names of several major social institutions, for example education, health care, law, media, family, government, and sports. Write one institution at the top of each sheet, and post them on the walls around the room. Divide participants into groups of three to five, and ask each group to go to one of the newsprints. Tell participants that they will have 2 minutes to brainstorm examples of ableism in that institution and write their examples on the newsprint sheet. After 2 minutes, ask all groups to rotate one newsprint to their left and repeat the brainstorm process for that institution. Repeat this rotation until each group has visited all of the newsprints. Tell participants not to duplicate examples that are already on the list.

After these rotations are complete, invite participants to take a "gallery walk" to read the complete list of examples generated for each institution (see Appendix 14H for "Examples of Institutional Ableism").

Reconvene the whole group, and ask if there are questions or comments about the examples of institutional ableism on the newsprints. Add additional examples as needed.

### 6. Closing (10 minutes)

Ask participants to identify themes that stand out in this module. Ask them to identify what information is new or what questions are raised. Record this information on newsprint, and post for future reference. When the group reconvenes, use these themes to summarize what participants have learned before beginning the next module.

## Module 3: Voices of People With Disabilities

Time needed: 3 hours

### Goals

- To learn about the lives of people with disabilities from their perspectives
- To learn about institutional ableism from the perspectives of people with disabilities
- To increase knowledge of systematic consumer-driven social, political, and cultural approaches to eliminating the oppression of people with disabilities

**Key concepts**: lived experiences of people with disabilities, institutional ableism, independent living

### 1. Check-In (15 minutes)

Welcome participants to this module, and ask if there are questions or comments from previous modules that they would like to discuss before moving on. Preview the goals for Module 3.

### 2. Listening to the Voices of Disability: Panel of People With Disabilities (60 minutes)

The goal of this activity is for participants to listen to and talk with people with disabilities to better understand how ableism impacts their lives.

#### Preclass Preparation of Panelists

Prior to the class, identify up to five panel members with different disabilities. Panel members can come from a number of sources: university disability service offices, independent living centers, organizations that provide services for people with disabilities, as well as friends or colleagues. Select male and female panel members who represent a range of disabilities, ages, and ethnic, cultural, and economic backgrounds. The individuals selected should understand ableism and be able to present their personal experiences in the context of discrimination, oppression, empowerment, and liberation.

Prepare panelists by informing them about the range of participant knowledge and experience and the questions panelists might be asked. Assure panelists that they will have complete discretion as to how much personal information they share. Ask panelists to briefly describe their disability, but focus their remarks on personal experiences that illustrate ableism and provide insight into the disability rights movement and their own empowerment. Provide panelists with a set of questions in advance to help focus their remarks. These might include the following:

- What is your disability, and how long have you had this disability?
- As a person with a disability, what was your experience growing up and going to school?
- How did your family and friends react to your disability?
- As a person with a disability, how would you describe the environment in terms of accessibility and attitudes here at (name of college, university, or other setting)?
- As a person with a disability, what has been your experience with trying to find employment?
- How has your disability affected how you are treated in various social situations?
- What are some things you love about your disability?
- What has your disability taught you?
- What are some examples of ways that people can interact with you that feel most respectful?
- Can you name some physical, social, or cultural examples of ableism that you have encountered?
- What do you think the role of temporarily able-bodied people is in the disability rights/independent living movement?
- How can temporarily able-bodied persons be allies to people with disabilities? Give specific examples participants can use for reference.

## In-Class Preparation

Preparing the participants prior to the panel is as important as preparing the panelists. Before the panelists arrive, ask participants to write down questions they wish to ask the panel members. Encourage open-ended questions that allow them to learn about the panel members' experiences of discrimination, empowerment, isolation, segregation, and other effects of oppression.

Ask participants to identify hopes and fears they have regarding meeting the panel. Individuals who are uncomfortable asking questions aloud can give written questions to the facilitators to pass along to the panel members, though asking questions aloud is preferable. The process of asking questions and being an active participant in the panel rather than a passive listener makes the panel activity more interactive.

## Panel Presentation

Begin the activity by welcoming the panel and introducing each member. Give each panelist a name card or name tag so participants can refer to them by name when asking questions. Review guidelines for the panel presentation. Guidelines may include the following:

- Hold questions until all panelists introduce themselves.
- Respect panelists' right not to answer a question.
- Remember that panelists speak from their own experience, not for all people with disabilities.
- Remember that many people with disabilities are not represented on the panel. Not all disabilities and not all people from different racial, cultural, and economic backgrounds are represented on the panel.

Begin the panel by having each panelist give a 5- to 7-minute autobiographical sketch of his or her life. This can include brief descriptions of or reflections on their disability, family, friends, work, school, goals, and dreams.

Keep track of time, reminding each panelist when his or her time is up. When all panelists have finished their introductory remarks, invite questions from participants.

When the panel is over, thank panelists for taking time from their schedules to come to the class. After the departure of the panelists, ask participants to write their impressions, reactions, and unanswered questions in their journal.

### Facilitation Issues

Have some questions prepared in case the participants are slow to begin interacting with the panel. Generally, however, panels work best when facilitators assume a secondary role and panelists and participants interact directly with each other.

Participants' initial questions might focus on a person's disability rather than on their experiences related to oppression and discrimination. Encourage or interject questions that redirect the discussion toward the effects of oppression on the lives of people with disabilities (See Appendix 14I for a film alternative to the people with disabilities panel).

### Break (15 minutes)
### 3. Discussion of Panel Presentation (30 minutes)

Facilitate a discussion of participants' feelings, thoughts, or other reactions to the panelists' comments. Some questions to ask include the following:

- What information surprised you or contradicted something you believed?
- Refer to the list of myths and stereotypes from Module 1. Which ones were contradicted or confirmed by the panel?
- What questions were left unanswered?
- What examples of individual or institutional ableism did the panelists describe?
- What themes in the treatment of people with disabilities can we identify?
- How did other social group memberships—race, class, gender, and sexual orientation—affect the experiences of the panelists?

### Facilitation Issues

One of the goals of a panel presentation by people with disabilities is to put a human face on oppression issues. For participants who do not have friends or family members who have disabilities, interacting with the panel can challenge stereotypes of people with disabilities and misconceptions about what their lives are like. By hearing from and speaking with a group of people with disabilities, participants can more easily make connections between the information presented in the ableism course and real people's lives. Instead of an abstract notion such as "people with cerebral palsy," participants will be able to think of Joe or Linda whom they met on the panel.

Some participants are uncomfortable with panels of people with disabilities. This discomfort sometimes arises because the participants have not had much personal contact with people with disabilities. Occasionally, participants are uncomfortable with the necessity of having people with disabilities "on display" in front of the class. Invite them to discuss what makes them uncomfortable about this experience. Explore these feelings as part of how we are socialized to respond to people with disabilities. Remind participants that people who volunteer to be a part of panel like this do so because they feel good about who they are and want to help educate others about ableism.

### 4. Journal Writing (5 minutes)

Invite participants to reflect on what they learned and their reactions to either the panel or the video.

### 5. Ableism and Controversial Social Issues (45 minutes)

The purpose of this activity is to explore how perspectives on controversial social issues are complicated by an understanding of how ableism affects our attitudes and positions on these issues.

Introduce this activity as a way for participants to explore how an understanding of ableism can affect their perspectives on controversial social issues. Divide participants into five groups. Assign each group one of the following five questions:

1. What role do charities and telethons play in changing and/or perpetuating traditional social constructions of disability? Should we support them, change them, or eliminate them, and why?
2. How do the perspectives of disability rights activists conflict with the "right to die" movement and proponents of access to legal assisted suicide? How might these different perspectives affect life-and-death decision making by people with disabilities, their loved ones, and medical caretakers?
3. Many disability activists oppose abortion when fetuses are aborted because they would be born with disabilities. People who support abortion rights believe it is the mother's right to choose abortion if parents do not have the resources to care for a disabled child. How can conflicts between abortion rights and disability rights be reconciled?
4. Should financial, legal, and medical resources go to changing disabling environments and laws, assistive technology, and other resources for people with disabilities, or should resources focus on seeking cures for disabilities?
5. How can we provide excellent and appropriate public education for all students? How can we avoid pitting the educational needs of students with disabilities against the needs of other students? What political and social forces encourage this "us versus them" perspective?

Have each group address the following four questions in relation to its topic:

1. How would you define the controversy?
2. What different perspectives are there on this issue?
3. What have you learned in this course that informs your perspectives on this issue?
4. What do the course readings say about this issue?

After about 20 minutes, bring participants back to the whole group, and have each small group give a 2- to 3-minute summary of their discussion.

### Facilitation Issues

Emphasize that the purpose of the activity is to explore all the different perspectives on these issues through an ableism lens and to see how an awareness of ableism can complicate our understanding of other social issues. The purpose of the activity is not to identify a "correct" answer or to place any participant in an uncomfortable position because of their perspectives on these issues.

## 6. Closing Circle (10 minutes)

Ask participants to identify ways in which the activities in this module have raised questions or changed their thinking.

## Module 4: Taking Action

Time needed: 2 hours, 55 minutes

### Goals

- Create a vision for an accessible, inclusive society.
- Develop personal and group strategies for change.

**Key concepts**: institutional ableism, empowerment, liberation, equal access, inclusion, allies, taking action

## 1. Check-In (15 minutes)

Invite participants to share one thing they have learned that has changed their perspective on disability.

## 2. Visioning an Accessible, Inclusive Society (60 minutes)

The purpose of this activity is to enable participants to creatively explore a vision for the future.

Divide the class into groups of three to six people, and give each group newsprint and markers. Assign each group one of the following institutions: education, government, health care, employment, transportation, legal system, and housing.

Ask each group to do the following:

1. Envision the assigned institution as an accessible and inclusive community. Imagine the institution as one in which all physical and social barriers for people with disabilities are eliminated. Record on newsprint the characteristics of the institution that would make the institution accessible and inclusive. Identify inclusive policies, practices, social norms, resources, and physical changes that would accomplish this goal.
2. List some strategies or resources that would help to move from the present-day reality to their vision of an inclusive institution. It might be helpful to brainstorm a list of different resources that can enable people with different disabilities to gain full access to a range of opportunities. Examples include availability of personal care assistants, computer technology, books on tape, readers, sign language interpreters, ramps, large print, accessible restrooms, elevators, teletypewriters, TTYs, and personal help with information processing and self-expression.

Have each group write their lists on newsprint to share with the rest of the class. Small groups should work for 25 minutes.

Display the newsprint of each group on the wall for reporting back to the whole class. Reconvene the class, and ask each group to explain their vision and the strategies and resources necessary to achieve that vision. Instruct all groups to listen for key concepts during each presentation that overlap with other groups' presentations. Ask the class to reflect on the disability rights movement and legislation (see Appendix 14E) and to identify examples of strategies that are already being used to address ableism in the particular institutions they described.

## Facilitation Issues

If needed, be prepared to provide the small groups with specific information about barriers and access. For example, what would an accessible and inclusive medical system do to accommodate people with mobility impairments, visual impairments, cognitive impairments, and other forms of disabilities? Refer participants to the list of different kinds of disabilities from Module 1. Circulate among the groups to help them think of specific accessibility barriers and needed resources to make a change.

## 3. Action Continuum (30 minutes)

The purposes of this activity are to identify the range of possible actions one can take to address ableism, to identify where participants are on an action continuum, and to identify a next step for each participant on the action continuum.

Distribute the "Action Continuum" (Appendix 6H) to participants. Introduce the activity by explaining that both internal and external barriers discourage or encourage taking action against ableism: Internal barriers are our own attitudes and beliefs; and external barriers are institutional policy, norms, laws, and attitudes and beliefs of others.

Give the following lecture:

1. When we as individuals or when institutions *maintain the system of oppression*, it can be because we are
   A. *actively participating*: This means that the actions we take directly support the oppression of the people with disabilities. Can anyone give me an example of maintaining the system of oppression by actively participating in any "ism"? Examples include the following:
      - Making fun of people with disabilities
      - Engaging in verbal or physical harassment of a person with a disability
      - Opposing legislation that would benefit people with disabilities
      - Refusing to make an event accessible because it is too much trouble for not many people
   B. *denying or ignoring*: denying that ableism is a problem and/or ignoring discrimination against people with disabilities.
      - Failing to speak out when others make fun of, discriminate against, harass, or are rude to people with disabilities
      - Refusing to acknowledge the effects of ableism on the lives of people with disabilities
   C. *recognition, but no action*: recognizing that discrimination against people with disabilities is a problem, but failing to take any actions to address ableism.
      - Feeling uncomfortable when a friend tells an ableist joke, but not speaking up to object to it
      - A teacher realizes that her course materials are not accessible, but decides not to address this problem.
2. When we as individuals or as an institution begin *interrupting the system of oppression*, it can be because we are
   D. *recognizing and interrupting oppressive behaviors*: that is, we understand and take action against ableism.
      - Recognizing and responding to oppression against people with disabilities

- This is a transitional stage where one goes from maintaining the system of oppression to interrupting the system of oppression.
  E.  *educating self*: learn about the oppression of people with disabilities, and come to know the community of people with disabilities.
    - Reading a book, watching films, or researching on the Internet to learn more about people with disabilities and about ableism
    - Attending events and actively connecting to the community of people with disabilities
  F.  *questioning and dialoging*: research and understand all levels of the field of disabilities, and talk with others about the community and about discrimination against people with disabilities.
    - Educating others about ableism
    - Going beyond just interrupting oppressive behaviors to engaging people in dialogue about ableism
3.  When we work to change ourselves, other individuals, or institutions, it can be because we are
  G.  *supporting and encouraging*: we take action and support members of the community of people with disabilities and temporarily able-bodied allies.
    - Actions that support and encourage others in breaking of the cycle of oppression against people with disabilities
  H.  *initiating and preventing*: take the first step toward breaking the cycle of oppression and accommodating the needs of people with disabilities in order to create greater access and prevent discrimination.
    - Actions that actively anticipate and identify institutional practices or individual oppressive behaviors and interrupt them

Have participants identify where they tend to be on the ableism action continuum and where they would like to be. Solicit volunteers to describe where they are and give examples from their lives.

Have participants spend a few minutes discussing what benefits they experience when taking action against social injustice. Encourage participants to name benefits such as the following:

- I feel good making my workplace more accessible.
- It's the right thing to do.
- My sister has a disability, and I feel good about making her life better.
- Someday, I might be disabled and will need these changes.
- I have a disability now, and addressing ableism benefits me directly.
- I want to feel like I can make a change for the better.

Ask participants to work with a partner to discuss one barrier to taking action against ableism. Have one participant describe the barrier while their partner listens. During this time, listeners ask questions for clarification only. Ask the first partner to sit silently and listen as the other participant brainstorms ways to overcome the barrier. Finally, have the first partner choose one of the ways to overcome the barrier that feels best to them. Switch roles so that the second participant describes one barrier.

When partners are finished with this task, tell the participants that next we will look more closely at how to become effective allies addressing ableism.

### Break (15 minutes)

### 4. Becoming an Ally (30 minutes)

The purpose of this activity is to help participants understand the concept of becoming an ally to people with disabilities and to assist people with disabilities to work in coalition with people who have disabilities that are different from theirs.

Distribute handout on "Becoming an Ally" from Appendix 3N. Review the definition of an ally. Emphasize that, because there are so many different kinds of disabilities, it is important for participants with disabilities to see how they can work in coalition with people who have disabilities that are different from theirs. Ask participants to work with a partner to explore the examples of how to be an ally on the handout.

Ask participants to make a list of people in their lives and groups or organizations they are part of where they might be able to take action to address ableism. Invite them to think about people they work with, people they go to school with, or members of their family. Also, ask them to think about religious groups, social groups, clubs, work groups, and schools. Ask them to narrow down the list to one or two individuals or groups with which to begin. Then ask them to work with the same partner to identify what action they might take to address ableism with that individual or group. Let the pairs work together for about 10 minutes so that each participant can identify two actions they can commit to taking. Bring the group together, and ask each participant to share one of the actions they plan to take.

### 5. Journal Writing (5 minutes)

Ask participants to write down what motivates or encourages them to take the action they have identified. Also, ask them to write down barriers to taking their action.

### 6. Closing (20 minutes)

Going around the circle, ask each participant to take no more than 30 seconds to respond to one of the following sentence stems:

- The most important learning about ableism for me is …
- The action I plan to take to address ableism is …
- A question about ableism that I have now is …
- The next step I am going to take in learning more about ableism is …

After each participant has shared their sentence, conclude the course.

# 15

# Ageism and Adultism Curriculum Design

BARBARA J. LOVE AND
KATHLEEN J. PHILLIPS

"Remember, age is all in your mind ... the trick is to keep it from creeping down into your body," reads a greeting card from the supermarket shelf. "Turning 50 isn't so bad," quips another; "in fact, it beats the hell out of turning 60." Ironically, this blanket denunciation of aging is followed by the wish for a "Happy Birthday." The greeting card, cosmetics, and entertainment industries, along with other institutions of society, actively and sometimes aggressively portray negative assessments of "getting old." Another greeting card titled "The Top Ten Party Games for the Chronologically Challenged" brings socially approved negative attitudes about old people and young people together in one greeting card. Number 5 on the list, "Whack the Piñata Teenager," is accompanied by the following balloon captions: "Get 'em in the gizzards Edna," "Knock his block off," and "Kill, kill, kill."

These representations from the greeting card industry suggest some of the ways that normalize ridicule, stereotypes, and even violence toward young people and elders, and make them seem ordinary, acceptable, and even funny. In this chapter, we describe contemporary societal disparagement and mistreatment of young people and elders as a form of oppression. Although most people agree that differential access to power and institutional participation on the basis of social identity group memberships such as race or gender constitutes oppression, there is no broad consensus that similar mistreatment of people targeted because of their age-based identities also constitutes oppression.

## Defining Ageism and Adultism

Robert Butler, former director of the National Institute on Aging, is credited with being the first to use the term *ageism* (Butler, 1969). Writing in 1975, Butler argued, "Ageism can be seen as a process of systematic stereotyping of and discrimination against people because they are old... . Old people are categorized as senile, rigid in thought and manner, old fashioned in morality and skills" (Butler, 1975, p. 35). *Adultism*, a more recent term, refers to "behaviors and attitudes based on the assumption that adults are better than young people, and entitled to act upon young people without their agreement. This mistreatment is reinforced by social institutions, laws, customs, and attitudes" (Bell, 2000, ¶2).

We add a social justice framework to these earlier definitions of ageism and adultism, including both an analysis of the stereotypes, prejudices, individual beliefs, and acts of discrimination that characterize ageism and adultism, as well as an examination of everyday cultural practices and the underlying institutional policies and procedures that result in differential access to participation, resources, and power by young people and elders.

## Societal/Cultural and Institutional Manifestations of Ageism and Adultism as Oppression

Although the mistreatment of elders has been recognized by some experts as oppression (Butler, 1969; Nelson, 2002; Palmore, Branch, & Harris, 2005), the normalization of the subordination of young people is so extensive that very little of the research examining the experiences of young people characterizes that mistreatment as oppression. Seldom does the research examining child victimization, child neglect, child abuse, the mistreatment of young people in schools, abuses in the child welfare system, or infanticide describe that mistreatment as oppression. Though female genital mutilation in Africa is generally decried in the western world as oppressive, seldom is the widespread western practice of infant genital mutilation described as oppression. The writings of Memmi (2000), Young (1990a), Freire (1970), and other theorists provide useful conceptual frameworks for examining and characterizing the mistreatment of young people and elders. Here, we examine the mistreatment of young people and elders within the frameworks provided by Memmi and Young.

Memmi (2000, p. xvii) describes oppression as having four distinct criteria: (a) There is an "insistence on a difference, real or imaginary;" (b) a "negative valuation" is imposed upon members of the group judged to be different; (c) these negatively valued differences are generalized to the entire group; and (d) these generalized, negative valuations are then used to justify and legitimize hostility and aggression against that group. Ageism and adultism share each of these four aspects.

Memmi's first criterion, "an insistence on a difference," is revealed in the way that both elders and young people are set apart as different from the rest of the population. The work of developmental theorists describes this understanding of difference as well as the laws designed to protect young people, mandatory retirement laws, and restrictions placed on opportunities for young people and elders to participate in the ongoing life of the community.

Research showing widespread negative attitudes and values about elders and young people coincides with Memmi's second criterion. Many people hold negative assumptions and valuations about the physical and mental capacities of young people and elders (Palmore, Branch, & Harris, 2005), assumptions about their diminished intelligence (Calasanti & Slevin, 2001; Nelson, 2002), and assumptions about their capacity to make decisions regarding their own lives, about their capacity to participate effectively in the workforce, about their capacity to engage in acceptable social relationships, and about the sex lives of elders.

These negative assumptions and valuations about elders and young people are generalized to the entire group, consistent with Memmi's third criterion. These generalized negative valuations are then used to legitimize hostility and mistreatment toward the group as a whole. The rapid proliferation of "Must Be 18" (MB18) policies at shopping malls across the United States is one example. These policies restrict the entry and unsupervised participation of young people as a group because, according to the mall manager at Ingleside Mall in Holyoke, Massachusetts, "Just the fact that they're [young people] there is perceived by some people [adults] ... as intimidating. It might cause you [adults] to leave, or not shop in stores you [adults] want to shop in" (Russell, 2005, p. A1). In this real-life scenario, these institutions use the negative attitudes held by some adults toward young people (Males, 2004) to legitimize practices of exclusion based on age-group membership. Increases in age discrimination lawsuits provide evidence of widespread practices excluding workplace participation of elders based on negative assumptions about their mental capacities.

Young's "Five Faces of Oppression" (1990a) provides another framework for analysis and conceptualization of the mistreatment of young people and adults as oppression. Young describes five faces of oppression—exploitation, powerlessness, cultural imperialism, marginalization, and violence—which function as criteria, any one of which would determine the oppression of a social group. The policies and practices of institutions such as the health care system, educational system, legal and welfare systems, and workplace provide examples of the exploitation, powerlessness and marginalization of young people and elders, as well as age-based cultural imperialism and violence.

Child labor and financial abuse of elders through misappropriation of their assets are examples of exploitation. Youth and elders experience almost total powerlessness in most institutions set up to "care" for them. The state exercises absolute control over youth in its educational, child welfare, and juvenile justice systems. Nursing homes and schools resemble jails in their institutional structures. Cultural imperialism is manifested in the devaluing of the young and the old in the United States. They are seen as less capable or less productive. The music, language, and lifestyle of young people are deprecated by adults. Midlife adulthood is the standard against which young people and elders are measured and found wanting. Young people and elders are often marginalized and denied useful participation in economic or social life. Elders, for example, experience persistent discrimination in the workplace, and youth are allowed little meaningful involvement in decision making in almost all aspects of their lives. Violence in the form of physical abuse, although not socially approved, is still tolerated. Elders consistently experience inferior health care, often with life-threatening consequences.

## The Social Construction of Age-Based Identities

Our discussion of adultism and ageism is based on our understanding of elders and young people as members of age-based social identity groups. At the same time, we acknowledge and treat social identity groups not as fixed, biologically or genetically-based social categories, but rather as social constructions. This means that we assume that the social identity group status of elders and young people is rooted in social practice rather than in specific biological, genetic, or even anthropological phenomena. This view of social identity group formation challenges the notion that biological phenomena determine how people behave or ought to behave, and what roles should be available to them in society. Rather, we note that role assignments attached to varied age-based social identity groups have varied over time and across societies according to the particular values and social organization of a particular society during a given era. We also note that although the roles assigned to age-based social identity groups change over time and across societies, people still behave as though certain qualities are "essential" to specific age groups, and use that behavior to justify determinations about what roles can and "should" be played by young people and elders.

Childhood, according to many researchers, is a relatively new cultural invention (Postman, 1982). The social construction of childhood has been facilitated in the western world by a number of factors, three of which are discussed here: the invention of the printing press, the industrial revolution, and the advent of modern schooling (Rogoff, 2003). Similarly, the social construction of old age in the western world has been facilitated by the industrial revolution, the cultural value of productivity, and advances in modern medicine along with increases in life expectancy (Hendricks, 2004).

The invention of the printing press meant that the culture, tradition, and history of a society could be repeated innumerable times in exact detail through books (Branco & Williamson, 1982), thus eliminating a key educational role in cultural transmission previously played by elders. This supported the parallel trend toward the institutionalization of teaching and learning, the removal of young people from familial and community-based learning and the confinement of learning to the schoolhouse. Schools increased the "segregation of children from the full range of activities in their community" and spawned specialized child-focused institutions and practices, dedicated to preparing young people for later entry into the community from which they had been removed (Rogoff, 2003, pp. 8–9).

The industrial revolution (Nelson, 1982; Rogoff, 2003) demanded great mobility of families, making the extended family structure less adaptive and the nuclear family structure preferable. This resulted in the removal of grandparents and great grandparents from the home (Stearns, 1986) and a shift in their status as respected sources of wisdom and advice and keepers of the traditions, culture, and history of the group. It also resulted in the segregation of "work" from community life, accompanied by the institutionalization and specialization of jobs requiring long hours of difficult manual labor in factories. This was accompanied by the exclusion of elders and eventually of young people from the workplace. More recently, advances in medicine have dramatically extended life expectancy, resulting in a much larger population of elders. Poor societal preparation for this growing group of older people combined with lack of place for the group set the stage for further segregation of elders. This has been accompanied by the association of old age with negative qualities.

These intertwining social forces have led to the construction of commonly held negative views about what it means to be young or old, such as the perception of youth as a source of social disruption (Males, 2004), and of elders as noncontributing burdens on society (Krauss, 1987; Riley & Foner, 1968). These socially constructed beliefs support adultism and ageism and are reinforced through polices, practices, and institutions such as workplace discrimination, nursing homes, retirement communities, and education and juvenile justice systems, all of which segregate both young people and elders from mainstream society.

## Developmental Issues and Age-Based Oppression

Although we contend that age-based identities are social constructions, we recognize that adultism and ageism are complex concepts. People are born as babies needing total care, and proceed along an age continuum until death. It is not always easy to distinguish behaviors, policies, and procedures toward young people and elders that are oppressive from those that are respectful, protective, or developmentally appropriate.

Developmental theorists propose that human development and maturation proceed along predictable, age-based lines. In this view, young people are growing and developing physically and psychologically and need adults to provide safety, structure, and material and emotional support as well as to support and encourage the development of their thinking and maturation. Elders, in some cases, experience physical and/or mental health limitations that require specific attention. In this context, policies, programs, and institutional responses to these age-based developmental differences seem not only appropriate but also necessary.

Using developmental maturation or physical and/or mental disability as justification for providing differential treatment to the young or the old can be viewed by some as oppressive and by others as protective. The U.S. Supreme Court decision to grant due process to young people who commit crimes is "hailed by some as a great advancement in children's rights and by others as the criminalization of the juvenile court" (Ventrell, 1998, p. 21). Similarly, those who work with the elderly favor regulation of in-home service providers because of the threat of elder abuse, whereas people with disabilities want the freedom to hire in-home service providers without government regulation (M. Twomey, San Francisco Institute on Aging, personal communication, August 30, 2005).

Most people would agree that providing programs that expand learning opportunities for young people or enforcing laws against elder abuse is appropriate. Most would also agree that dismissing the ideas of a young person as unimportant or dismissing the physical complaints of an older woman as "hypochondria" demonstrates neither respect nor support. Although courts are increasingly inclined to seek the opinion of young people when making custodial decisions, there is less agreement about the extent to which young people should, for instance, be able to make decisions about their own learning, or the extent to which elders should be able to control their own finances.

Bell (2000, p. 2) suggests a way to assess individual actions to determine if they are oppressive to young people. His criteria are equally applicable to assessing behaviors toward the elderly. A behavior, policy, or practice "can be called adultist [or ageist] if it involves a consistent pattern of disrespect and mistreatment that has any or all of the following effects on young people" or elders:

- undermining of self-confidence and self-esteem
- increasing sense of worthlessness
- increasing feeling of powerlessness
- consistent experience of not being taken seriously
- diminishing ability to function well in the world
- increasing destructive acting out
- increasing self-destructive acting "in" (getting sick frequently, cutting, attempting suicide, depression, etc.)
- feeling unloved, unwanted, unwelcome, or invisible

## Interconnections Among Ageism, Adultism, and Other Forms of Oppression

All forms of oppression are interconnected. Other manifestations of oppression exacerbate and complicate the effects of ageism and adultism on the individual lives of young people and elders. Racism and classism, for example, intensify the disparities of power, privilege, resources, and status experienced by youth because of adultism (Fulbright-Anderson, Lawrence, Sutton, Susi, & Kubisch, 2005) and by elders because of ageism.

Gross disparities in access to health care, educational facilities, and quality of teacher training; disproportionate punishment (violating the law or school rules); and more limited job opportunities exist between white youth and youth of color and between middle- and upper-class youth and poor youth. White infants are nearly 2 1/2 times more likely than black infants to live past their first birthday. White youth receive more and better primary care, mental health, and asthma services than African American youth and, in some cases, Latino/a youth. This holds true even when family income and health insurance are taken into account. White youth attend schools that spend, on average, nearly $900 more per pupil than schools attended primarily by youth of color. African American students, according to data from the Advancement Project and the Civil Rights Project, Harvard University (2000), are suspended from public schools at rates that far exceed their proportion of public school enrollees, often for behaviors for which white students are not suspended. Although young people of all ages sell and use drugs at similar rates, African American youth represent 60–75% of drug arrests.

These race- and class-based inequities extend into old age, multiplying the negative impacts of ageism. Health care options are worse for people of color. African American elders have significantly fewer life-saving surgeries than white elders. Financial inequality actually increases with old age for women, poor and working-class people, and people of color (Calasanti & Slevin, 2001).

Age-based oppression is also impacted by sexism, heterosexism, and ableism. An extreme example of the interaction between sexism and adultism is female infanticide, the killing of female babies (Kohl, 1978). In societies characterized by male dominance and adult dominance, adults may prefer male children. When adults prefer male children and also exercise complete power and control over young people, unwanted female babies may be killed. Ethicists and physicians in Boston, Massachusetts, expressed concern that a test profiled by the *Boston Globe* in June 2005 "could lead to sex-selective abortion" (Goldberg, 2005). A California gynecologist has been asked to defend his practice of advertising a fetus sex determination procedure in certain communities where women have been known to seek an abortion after being told that they carried a female fetus (Schaefer, 1990). Girls experience sexist attitudes and behaviors regarding their appearance and their sexuality.

Sexism combined with ageism produces differential health care treatment for older women (Calasanti & Slevin, 2001). Although women of all races live longer than men, older women are perceived as less healthy than older men (Woolf, 2005) and more hypochondriacal than any other group of people, even through no differences have been found between them and older men or younger populations (Ross, Tait, Brandeberry, Grossberg, & Nakra, 1986). In addition, older women are more likely than older men to experience ageist attitudes and behaviors regarding employment, appearance, and sexuality (Duncan & Loretto, 2004). Men can be considered attractive ("distinguished") well into their 80s, whereas women are often viewed as unattractive on age-based characteristics as early as age 40. Men can marry women 20, 30, and 40 years their junior, whereas women who marry beneath their age are regarded negatively. Although older people are largely invisible in the media, older women are even less likely to be seen on television. Older people of color as well as older gay, lesbian, bisexual, and transgender people are largely nonexistent in the media. Heterosexism affects the economic security of same-sex partners who experience financial inequities in retirement because, in most cases, they cannot collect survivor benefits designated for "spouses" only. Homophobia also plays a major role in the high rate of suicides for young people who identify as lesbian, gay, bisexual, transgender, queer or questioning their sexual identity

(LGBTQQ) (Gibson, 2004). Age-based oppression and ableism intersect not only when older and younger people have disabilities but also for elders when they are *perceived* to be differently able.

## Liberation and Transformation: Eliminating Ageism and Adultism

In the end, our analysis of oppression is only significant insofar as it impels us toward liberation and the transformation of society. Our vision for a liberatory society is still in creation. Though we lack models for a liberatory society, we do have images of the kind of society that we want to inhabit. John Holt (1967) for instance, suggests that adults should be as respectful in their language and behaviors with young people as they are with adults. Simone de Beauvior (1972) suggests that our full humanity depends on our recognizing ourselves in all other humans, old people and young people alike. In his theory of justice, John Rawls (1971) offers a vision of a society in which any person would be happy to occupy any role or status. In Rawls' view, a society free of ageism and adultism would mean that whether we occupied the status of young person, elder or other, we could feel confident of a life experience free of oppression. Harvey Jackins (1997, p. 172) encourages that we "refuse to accept any oppressions" and "don't participate in oppressing anyone else."

Young people, elders, and their allies are actively challenging oppressive cultural attitudes and beliefs and individual and institutional policies and practices that maintain the oppression of young people and elders. They are developing policies, programs, and practices that enable young people and elders to contribute to their community and have real power in controlling their lives. They are working toward their vision of a liberatory society.

## Ageism and Adultism Curriculum Design

### Overall Goals

- Envision a society characterized by liberation and the elimination of ageism and adultism.
- Define and describe ageism and adultism as manifestations of age-based oppression, and understand the common elements in the treatment of young people and elders as oppression.
- Explore personal thoughts, beliefs, and feelings about ageism and adultism that contribute to the maintenance and perpetuation of ageism and adultism.
- Identify and describe manifestations of individual, institutional, societal, and cultural manifestations of ageism and adultism and ways in which they are internalized.
- Identify and develop action strategies to eliminate ageism and adultism and contribute to the transformation of society.

### Overview of Modules (see Appendix 15A)

**Note to readers:** The curriculum design in this chapter is based on the assumption that participants have completed the introductory module(s) described in Chapter 3 prior to beginning this design and have a basic understanding of the conceptual framework of oppression described in Chapter 3. See Table 15.1 for an overview of this chapter's modules.

**Table 15.1**   Overview of Modules: Ageism and Adultism

| Module 1: Understanding Ageism and Adultism (3.5 hours) | Module 2: Institutional Ageism and Adultism (3.5 hours) |
|---|---|
| 1. Envisioning a Liberatory Society (40 min.) | 1. Overview of the Module (15 min.) |
| 2. Welcome, Introductions, and Workshop Overview (40 min.) | 2. Video on Ageism (45 min.) |
| 3. Workshop Assumptions (10 min.) | 3. Institutional Manifestations of Ageism and Adultism (90–120 min.) |
| 4. Review of Foundational Definitions and Key Terms (25 min.) | 4. Brainstorm Guidelines for Assessing Ageism and Adultism in the Media (20 min.) |
| 5. Common Elements of Understanding Ageism and Adultism as Oppression (20 min.) | 5. Closing (5 min.) |
| 6. Beliefs, Attitudes, and Assumptions About Elders and Young People (30 min.) | |
| 7. Personal Experiences With Ageism and Adultism (25 min.) | |
| 8. Closing (5 min.) | |
| **Module 3: Cultural Ageism and Adultism (3–3.5 hours)** | **Module 4: Transformation and Change (3 hours)** |
| 1. Introduction (15 min.) | 1. Introduction and Manifestations of Internalized Ageism and Adultism (30 min.) |
| 2. Ageism and Adultism in the Media (45–60 min.) | 2. Developing a Liberatory Consciousness (15 min.) |
| 3. Ageism and Adultism in Language and Communications Patterns (20 min.) | 3. Envisioning a Society Free From Adultism and Ageism (40 min.) |
| 4. Ageism and Adultism in Humor (30 min.) | 4. Strategies for Interrupting and Eliminating Ageism and Adultism (60 min.) |
| 5. Ageism, Adultism, and Societal Standards of Beauty (45 min.) | 5. Summary and Closing (30 min.) |
| 6. Ageism, Adultism, and Violence: Child Abuse and Elder Abuse (40 min.) | |
| 7. Closing (15 min.) | |

## Module 1: Understanding Ageism and Adultism

Time needed: 3.5 hours

## Goals (distribute Appendix 15B)

- Explore participant conceptions of liberation, the characteristics of a liberatory society, and the strategies necessary to transform society toward liberation.
- Examine the notion that every human experiences adultism and faces the possibility of experiencing ageism.
- Examine individual beliefs, attitudes, and assumptions about liberation and the creation of a society free of ageism and adultism.
- Create a positive learning environment in which participants are empowered to explore issues of oppression.
- Identify and examine individual and organizational factors that will enable and inhibit the exploration of ageism and adultism as manifestations of oppression.
- Review and define key terms related to oppression, ageism, and adultism.
- Examine common beliefs, attitudes, and assumptions related to ageism and adultism.
- Examine personal experiences related to ageism and adultism.

**Key concepts**: ageism, adultism, liberatory society, age-based oppression, advantaged, agent, ageism, adultism, discrimination, oppression, prejudice, privilege, social power, stereotype, target, targeted (see Appendix 15B).

## 1. Envisioning a Liberatory Society (40 minutes)

Ask participants to form two circles, one inside the other, with those in the inner circle facing those in the outer circle. If the number of participants is uneven, have a facilitator join the circle so that everyone has a partner. (This activity can also be done in triads.) Describe this exercise as a "speak and listen." Review the guidelines for Phenomenological Listening (Appendix 15C), and stress the importance of listening. Explain that participants should speak of their ideas only and not respond to what their partner said or what they learned from their partner. Indicate that you will keep track of time and let participants know when to switch roles from speaker to listener.

Ask participants to exchange names and greetings. Begin by asking participants in the outer circle to respond to the first item on the "Envisioning a Liberatory Society: Questions" list (Appendix 15E). After 2 minutes, switch and ask participants in the inner circle to respond to item 1. Then ask the inner circle to move two people to the left and repeat this process with item 2. Continue alternating first speaker between inner circle and outer circle, rotating so that people have new partners for each item until all items are addressed.

At the end of the activity, thank participants for their participation and ask them to share with their current partner what it was like for them to experience this exercise, speaking and listening but without feedback or exchange. Debrief the exercise by asking, "What was easy or difficult about imagining such a society?" Ask two or three participants to share their responses. Often, participants will start to share what their partners said. Interrupt this tendency, and encourage participants to share their own thinking and not repeat what their partner(s) said. Conclude the debriefing by summarizing key points of the discussion, including the points listed in Appendix 15F, "Envisioning a Liberatory Society: Debriefing."

### Facilitation Issues

This is an introductory activity and helps to set the tone for the entire course. It is designed to capture the interest and enthusiasm of participants as they enter the room, and to engage their thinking with the issues of ageism, adultism, and liberation in a relatively low-threat manner. This activity helps to set a tone of thinking about possibility and liberation as a framework for the course, and helps to dispel notions that the study of oppression focuses on finding culprits and inducing shame and blame. This activity is an effective way for participants to quickly meet and hear the thinking of a number of other participants. In addition, this activity is a good way to start on time and reward those participants who are in the room on time, while allowing any latecomers to enter the room without disruption.

## 2. Welcome, Introductions, and Workshop Overview (40 minutes)

Welcome participants and thank them for choosing to examine issues of ageism and adultism. Let them know that you will encourage participants to stretch their thinking and imagination and provide opportunities to reexamine their own life experience as young people and as elders or elders to be. Give each participant two 3 × 5 cards. Review goals for this module (see Appendix 15B). Ask them to write one or more goals for themselves for this course on one card and one or more concerns or issues about the course on the other card. Collect the concern cards, shuffle, and reissue.

### Review Course Goals (see Appendix 15G) and Agenda (see Appendix 15A)

Ask participants to say their name and one goal from their card. Review goals for the course in Appendix 15G. Briefly describe how the course addresses the goals that are mentioned. Indicate where it is possible to flex the course design to meet participant goals that are not included in the prepared course design. Indicate which goals are unlikely to be met in this workshop. Refer to the list of resources (see Appendix 15H) that can assist participants in exploring issues and ideas that will not be covered in the workshop. Mention that there is a wide range of experience and knowledge about this issue among workshop participants. Encourage participants to talk with each other and to use each other as resources about ageism and adultism.

### Review Course Guidelines (see guidelines in Pre-module 1 from Chapter 3)

Distribute and review the confidentiality agreement (Appendix 15D), and indicate that you would like for all participants to agree to this guideline. Emphasize that this interpretation of confidentiality specifically prohibits reference to or repeating of personal stories of other participants, and to the attribution of comments to specific participants. Participants are free to discuss their own personal learning from the course, but not the contributions or learnings of others. Another person's story or comments may not be repeated. Emphasize that this confidentiality agreement provides a measure of safety for individual participants to share and learn from their own personal stories because they can safely assume that others will not repeat those stories. Distinguish between discussion of issues and individual personal stories.

### 3. Workshop Assumptions (10 minutes)

Discuss briefly the assumptions about ageism and adultism (Appendix 15I) that provide the foundation for this course. These include basic notions about oppression and liberation theory, and about the nature of personal, institutional, and societal change. Ask participants to reflect on these assumptions and to take a few minutes during the break to note which of these assumptions they also make, where they make different assumptions, the content of those differing assumptions, and probable implications of those differing assumptions.

### 4. Review of Foundational Definitions and Key Terms (25 minutes)

Begin with a review of key terms related to oppression if you have not already completed the introductory modules outlined in Chapter 3 (Appendix 15B). Ask participants to read each definition aloud. Ask if there are questions or requests for additional clarification. Post these definitions on newsprint so that they are visible throughout the course. Explain that they provide a foundation for this course. Indicate that although much of the research focuses on individual experiences, attitudes, and stereotypes, our definition includes an analysis of power differentials and institutional arrangements that result in differing treatment of individuals on the basis of their age status. (See Chapter 3 this volume, for more discussion.)

### 5. Common Elements of Understanding Ageism and Adultism as Oppression (20 minutes)

A foundation for the characterization of the treatment of elders and young people as oppression can be established through an examination of either Suzanne Pharr's (1988) "Common Elements of Oppression" (Appendix 15J) or Iris Marion Young's (1990a) "Five Faces of Oppression" (Appendix 15K). After your review, ask participants to reflect briefly on how the analysis fits with their assessment of young people and elders as members of an oppressed group.

> *Option 1*: Pharr's "Common Elements of Oppression" (Appendix 15J). Review the explanation for each element, then ask participants to give examples of each element for ageism and for adultism. Participants may be divided into groups of four, and each group asked to describe examples for three assigned elements of oppression. Give participants 5 minutes to identify their examples. Have each group share one example of ageism and one of adultism for one of the common elements of oppression assigned to their group.
>
> *Option 2*: Young's "Five Faces of Oppression" (1990a; see Appendix 15K). Review the description provided in Appendix 15K for each of the five faces. Divide participants into five groups. Ask each group to take one of the five faces and identify examples of ageism and adultism at the individual and institutional level. Share examples in the large group.

## 6. Beliefs, Attitudes, and Assumptions About Elders and Young People (30 minutes)

Ask participants to make a list of attitudes, assumptions, and commonly held beliefs about elders and young people. Individuals should pair up with another person and make a combined list. That pair should combine with another pair to make groups of four. The combined list of the group of four should be posted on newsprint. In their groups of four, ask participants to share their reactions to these questions:

1. Which of these attitudes, assumptions, or beliefs have you said, witnessed, experienced, believed to be true, or heard others express as true?
2. How are these attitudes, assumptions, or beliefs manifested in the social, cultural, or institutional treatment of young people and elders?
3. Which of these attitudes, assumptions, and beliefs would need to change in order to eliminate the mistreatment of elders and young people?

Ask each group to report out their responses to question 3. Ask a participant to write these social, cultural, and institutional implications for change on newsprint. Post the newsprint so that it is visible for the remainder of the course.

### Facilitation Issues

Discuss the role played by beliefs, attitudes, and assumptions in creating, maintaining, and perpetuating oppression against young people and elders.

Include the following points in this discussion:

1. Although we focus on institutional, societal, and cultural manifestations of ageism and adultism, we recognize that societal norms are enacted and enforced by individuals.
2. Change at the institutional and cultural levels will follow from increased awareness and personal responsibility at the individual level.
3. Elders and young people are marked as different because of their age.
4. Negative attitudes and stereotypes provide a basis for a negative valuation of young people and elders, and serve to rationalize, legitimize, and justify the oppression of elders and young people.

Conclude this exercise with a review of common beliefs and facts about aging (see Appendix 15L) and myths and facts about young people (see Appendix 15M).

## 7. Personal Experiences With Ageism and Adultism (25 minutes)

Introduce this activity by sharing the following points:

1. Every human has experienced the targeted status of youth and the oppression of adultism and, if they continue to live, will experience the targeted status of elder and the oppression of ageism.
2. Thus, every person will have the experience of moving from targeted status to advantaged status and has the potential to move back to targeted status again on the basis of an age-based identity.
3. For age-based identities, no action beyond continuing to live is required for movement from targeted to agent status.
4. Similarly, one only has to live long enough to return to targeted status.

Like other oppressions, ageism and adultism are complicated by other social identities such as class, race, gender, sexuality, ability and disability, religion, language, and nationality. Use either Option 1 or 2 to support participant exploration of personal experiences of ageism and adultism.

*Option 1*: Early Memories of Ageism/Adultism (see Appendix 15N)
*Option 2*: Experiencing Ageism and Adultism (see Appendix 15O)

## 8. Closing (5 minutes)

Close this module by having participants share one insight, one new learning, or one new question about ageism and adultism.

## Module 2: Institutional Ageism and Adultism

Time needed: 3.5 hours

## Goals (Distribute Appendix 15P)

- Examine levels and types of oppression.
- Distinguish between personal/individual and institutional manifestations of ageism and adultism.
- Identify and examine institutional manifestations of ageism and adultism.

**Key concepts**: level and types of oppression, institutional oppression, violence, institutional ageism, institutional adultism, institutional power, norms, policies.

## 1. Overview of Module (15 minutes)

Provide a brief overview of the agenda and the goals linking this module to the first. If necessary, review key terms and answer questions about those terms. Review the levels and types of oppression from the introductory module (Chapter 3). Indicate that in this module, we will focus on institutional manifestations of ageism and adultism while keeping the focus on liberation. Keep two "parking lot" sheets posted. Label one parking lot "Strategies for Change or Liberation Strategizing." Label the second parking lot "Interconnections." Encourage participants to write on the "Strategies" parking lot sheet their ideas about societal transformation as we move through this module. Also emphasize that although we focus on common manifestations of ageism and adultism, we hold awareness that both ageism and adultism are impacted by other social identities including race, gender, sexuality, and socioeconomic status. For instance, LGBT youth have one of the highest suicide rates, a combination of adultism, heterosexism, and homophobia. Elderly black women have the lowest standard of living, a combination of ageism, sexism, classism, and racism. Explain the importance of being specific and intentional in our acknowledgment of the ways that multiple identities combine with ageism and adultism to limit the life experience of young people and elders. Request that participants make notes on the "Interconnections" parking lot sheet when they notice a connection between ageism or adultism and other forms of oppression.

## 2. Video on Ageism (45 minutes)

Introduce the video, and ask participants to watch for examples of ageism.

> *Option 1*: Show *Old Like Me* (Canadian Broadcasting Corporation, 1987). This 28-minute video examines "how society treats older people ... and ... the terror that society can inflict on the young and old." Available from Filmmakers Library, Inc., 124 East 40th Street, Suite 901, New York, NY 10016, (212) 808-4980.

> *Option 2*: Show selected clips from *Still Doing It: The Intimate Lives of Women Over 65* by Deirdre Fishel (2003). This film "explores the lives of older women. Partnered, single, straight, gay, Black and White." Available from: New Day Films, 190 Route 17M, P.O. Box 1084, Harriman, NY 10926, (888) 367-9154, fax: (845) 774-2945, http://www.newday.com/films.
>
> Process video as follows:
>
> 1. Distribute and review Appendix 15C for description of "pair sharing," using phenomenological listening. Ask paired participants to share with each other any feelings that came up as they watched the video.
> 2. Ask participants what they noticed about the treatment of elders or about the treatment of young people.
> 3. Briefly highlight any institutional manifestations of ageism observed or presented.

> *Option 3*: Show the opening scene from the movie *Mystic River* up to the scene where one boy is driven away in a car. Ask participants to identify and discuss manifestations of adultism in this clip from the movie. As facilitator, be prepared to discuss the phenomena of adult supremacy and power over young people as evidenced by the fact that the boy felt obligated to obey the directions of an adult, even though the adult was a stranger. Discuss any links between this scenario and manifestations of adultism in the life experiences of course participants.

Transition from the processing of the video to a discussion of specific manifestations of institutional ageism and adultism.

## 3. Institutional Manifestations of Ageism and Adultism (90–120 minutes)

Review manifestations of institutional oppression through policies, laws, rules, norms, and customs that are enacted by organizations and social institutions and that disadvantage some groups and advantage other social groups (described in Chapter 3). Indicate that we will examine the ways that varied institutions of society create, maintain, and perpetuate ageism and adultism. Organize into six groups, one for each of six institutions: (a) the law, (b) health care, (c) education, (d) the welfare system, (e) faith-based organizations, and (f) the economic system. Have participants count off by sixes, and arbitrarily assign an institution to each group or post a sheet with each institution listed. Tell each group that they have about 50 minutes to examine the ways in which ageism and adultism are created, maintained, and perpetuated by the institution and to prepare a presentation for the class.

Each group should take 20 minutes to review and assemble data for their presentation using assigned readings and other materials, and 30 minutes to prepare a 6-minute presentation illustrating manifestations of ageism and adultism in the institution they have selected. They can share the results of their institutional analysis in one of the following formats:

1. A "documentary"
2. A curriculum design to teach others about ageism and adultism
3. A PowerPoint presentation for a conference presentation, a poster presentation, or a gallery walk
4. A "myths and facts" worksheet or a true-false "quiz"
5. Other format to be decided by their small group

Have groups present their 6-minute institutional analysis of ageism and Adultism in the format they have chosen. Provide time for questions and discussion.

## 4. Brainstorm Guidelines for Assessing Ageism and Adultism in the Media (20 minutes)

Let participants know that in Module 3, "Cultural Ageism and Adultism," they will examine the ways that the media foster and perpetuate cultural ageism and adultism. A homework assignment, which you will describe, will help them prepare for this examination. In the following exercise, the class will develop a set of guidelines for examining ageism and adultism in the media to assist in the completion of this homework assignment (use Appendix 15R).

*Homework assignment*: Tell participants to use the guidelines developed, along with the definitions of oppression, ageism, and adultism discussed earlier, to examine media portrayals of young people and elders in movies, television, or other forms of popular media, including curricular materials, literature, magazines, and music. For the next class, participants should bring three examples of ageism and adultism in the media and prepare to explain how their example illustrates how the media create, maintain, and perpetuate ageism and adultism.

## 5. Closing (5 minutes)

Ask participants in pairs to share one new learning that surprised them and one hope for the future that they had during this session.

## Module 3: Cultural Ageism and Adultism

Time needed: 3–3.5 hours

## Goals (distribute Appendix 15Q)

- Use an analysis of the media to examine ways that ageism and adultism are perpetuated through social and cultural institutions.
- Identify and examine manifestations of ageism and adultism in language and communication patterns.
- Identify and examine how humor is used in society to maintain and perpetuate negative and stereotypic attitudes and beliefs about young people and elders.
- Examine societal standards of beauty as manifestations of social and cultural ageism and adultism.

- Examine common societal manifestations of violence against young people and elders.

**Key concepts**: social oppression, cultural oppression, stereotypes (see Appendix 15S).

## 1. Introduction (15 minutes)

Review the goals for this module and the agenda. Refer to the discussion of levels and types of oppression and indicate that in this module, participants will focus on social and cultural ageism and adultism. Review definitions of social and cultural oppression (Appendix 15Q).

Explain that participants will explore several forms of social and cultural adultism and ageism manifested in the media, in humor, through societal standards of beauty, and through violence against youth and elders. The introduction to this module should include the following points:

1. Social and cultural adultism and ageism operate to make the subordination of young people and elders appear normal, natural, and inevitable.
2. Protectionism of young people and infantilization of elders both serve to "essentialize" characteristics of elders and young people that are used to "justify" the subordination of youth and elders.

## 2. Ageism and Adultism in the Media (45–60 minutes)

Ask participants to share their homework illustrating examples of ageism and adultism in the media

Review the guidelines for assessing ageism and adultism in the media (see Appendix 15R) and the definitions of oppression, ageism, and adultism discussed in Module 2. Give each person 1 minute to share his or her example of either ageism or adultism in the media. Use a timer to help manage equity of "air time." After all participants have shared, ask whether anyone has an additional example that they feel is particularly powerful. Post all examples on a "gallery wall" for participants to view. Allow 10 minutes for a gallery walk. Ask participants to check any item they wish to discuss further or about which they still have questions. If there are differing opinions about whether a particular item constitutes oppression, refer to the guidelines developed, to the definitions of ageism and adultism, as well as to the "common elements of oppression" (Appendix 15J) or to the "five faces of oppression" (Appendix 15K).

Summarize and conclude this activity by referring to the cycle of socialization (see Appendix 3E) and the role played by the media in conditioning all members of society to participate in the subordination of young people and elders and to consider such subordination as normal and natural.

## 3. Ageism and Adultism in Language and Communication Patterns (20 minutes)

Contemporary language and communication patterns support and reinforce patterns of ageism and adultism. In this activity, we will examine some ways in which ageism and adultism are expressed through language and communication patterns as examples of cultural oppression.

Be familiar with some examples of ageism and adultism in language. A few examples are listed in Appendix 15S. Ask participants to brainstorm a list of additional ways that ageism and adultism are manifested in language and communication patterns. Post the list. Ask participants to identify alternative language and communication patterns that interrupt ageism and adultism.

## 4. Ageism and Adultism in Humor (30 minutes)

Introduce this activity by sharing the following points:

1. Negative and stereotypic attitudes and beliefs about elders and young people are often shared through humor.
2. More than with any other target group, it is still acceptable and almost expected that people will poke fun at the elderly.
3. Internet humor, greeting card humor, cartoon humor, and after-dinner speakers all find jokes about old people with a negative punch line acceptable.
4. In this exercise, participants will examine the range of attitudes and stereotypes that are communicated and perpetuated through humor.

Ask participants to examine sets of greeting cards, cartoons, and other materials; identify the messages about young people and elders contained in the selections; and discuss the extent to which they foster positive and negative perceptions and attitudes toward young people and elders. Ask participants how these examples of humor might affect the life experience of young people and elders.

### Facilitation Issues

Bring to class a collection of materials for this activity, including greeting cards, cartoon clips, and Internet messages focused on the elderly and on young people.

## 5. Ageism, Adultism, and Societal Standards of Beauty (45 minutes)

Explain that people of many social identity groups are impacted by the advantaged culture's standards of beauty and the ways that these standards of beauty are created, maintained and perpetuated. Discuss some of the ways that standards of beauty are raced, gendered, classed, and affected by attitudes toward ability. For instance, advertisements offering age resistant serum and wrinkle defying creams target women. An old woman is considered an old woman, while an old man is a dignified gentleman. While standards of beauty are generally clear for both men and women, women are held to a very narrow range of standards, while men can be considered handsome across a much wider range of standards. Gendered standards of beauty include a range of homophobic elements so that men who possess features typically associated with women and women who possess features typically associated with men are often stigmatized. Raced standards of beauty include blonde, blue-eyed, skin color standards for both men and women, along with requirements for particular body build and facial types.

Discuss the ways that ableism affects standards of beauty, asking participants to cite specific examples of ways that attitudes toward ageism and disabilities impact assessments of beauty. Ask participants to name ways that classism or access to resources affects who can attain the characteristics typically associated with beauty. Identify these standards of beauty through an examination of contemporary magazines including fashion magazines, health magazines, textbooks, etc. Refer back to examples from the "Ageism and Adultism in the Media Gallery" (from earlier in this module) as instances of standards of beauty presented in the media (such as stories on how to avoid aging). Discuss the implications of these standards of beauty for the life experience of young people and elders.

Conclude by asking participants to share in pairs or triads their own experience with contemporary standards of beauty, how these standards affected them as young people, and how they anticipate managing these standards as elders.

### Facilitation Issues

Bring a collection of magazines and materials for this activity with you to class.

### 6. Ageism, Adultism, and Violence: Child Abuse and Elder Abuse (40 minutes)

Ask participants to think of examples of methods through which violence is perpetrated against young people and elders in society. Some examples include discipline, rape, kidnapping, withholding of resources, child abuse (shaken baby syndrome, for instance), and elder abuse. Other forms of violence are less direct but no less invasive such as the tobacco industry's targeted advertising to children and youth.

In groups of three, ask participants to share ways that they experienced or witnessed violence directed toward young people or elders. Ask participants to share out from the triads. Post sharing on newsprint. Close this activity with a phenomenological listening exercise where participants share any feelings that they noticed during this activity. Remind participants of the confidentiality agreement, reinforcing the importance of participants sharing any feeling that they experience without fear of having their comments repeated outside the class.

### 7. Closing (15 minutes)

Ask five participants to share one key point each from this module.

### Module 4: Transformation and Change

Time needed: 3 hours

### Goals (distribute Appendix 15T)

- Identify and analyze manifestations of internalized adultism and ageism in the life experience of young people and elders.
- Describe strategies for interrupting internalized ageism and internalized adultism.
- Describe an environment that is free of ageism and adultism.
- Develop and reflect on a vision of a liberatory society.
- Identify and describe actions that can be taken to transform society and eliminate ageism and adultism.
- Discuss the elements of a liberatory consciousness and how this might be applied to the elimination of ageism and adultism.
- Develop a personal action plan aimed toward increasing participants' capacity and readiness to take action to eliminate ageism and adultism.

**Key concepts**: internalized oppression, internalized adultism, internalized ageism, collusion, liberatory society, liberatory consciousness, transformation of society (see Appendix 15T).

### 1. Introduction and Manifestations of Internalized Ageism and Adultism (30 minutes)

Ask participants to briefly share reactions and thoughts since the last class. Review the agenda and goals for this module, in Appendix 15A and Appendix 15T. Indicate that we will continue our strategy of examining oppression with a focus on liberation and that this discussion of internalized ageism and internalized adultism will help to inform our discussion of liberation and strategizing for the transformation of society. Go over the definitions of internalized oppression, internalized subordination, internalized domination, and collusion that are included in Appendix 15T.

Post two sheets of newsprint on which to list examples generated by the group of internalized subordination and domination for ageism and adultism. Label one sheet "Ageism" and the second sheet "Adultism." Draw two columns on each sheet, and label column 1 "Internalized Domination" and column 2 "Internalized Subordination."

Ask participants to suggest some examples of internalized ageism and internalized adultism. Present the information on internalized ageism and internalized adultism described in Appendices 15U and 15V. Ask participants to give some examples of internalized ageism, followed by examples of internalized adultism. Provide the examples listed in Appendices 15U and 15V if they are not mentioned by participants. Post the examples in the two columns on the newsprint for internalized domination and internalized subordination.

## 2. Developing a Liberatory Consciousness (15 minutes)

Make the transition from the discussion of internalized ageism and adultism to a discussion of liberation and transformation by discussing notions of personal responsibility for making change. Review the concepts of empowerment and ally (see Appendix 15T) and developing a liberatory consciousness (Appendix 15W). Discuss Freire's (1970) idea that people have the capacity to transform oppression. Refer to Freire's *conscientização* or critical consciousness as a context for this discussion. Discuss the elements of a liberatory consciousness—awareness, analysis, action, and accountability (Love, 2000)—described in Appendix 15W. Point out that members of all groups, those advantaged by oppression as well as those targeted by oppression, have a role to play in eliminating oppression and transforming society. Give examples of empowerment actions and ally actions: An adult interrupts a store clerk who is treating a youth disrespectfully, students participate in a youth leadership group and advocate for reforms in their school, adults who run a nonprofit organization learn more about how to work in a respectful way with young people and include youth as board members with meaningful decision-making power, elders challenge patronizing behaviors, and doctors in a health group analyze data on health care for elders and work together with elders to make changes in their policies and protocols.

Ask participants to think about a situation as a young person or as an elder in which they have acted in an empowered way, or acted as an ally to interrupt the oppression of a young person or elder. Discuss examples in pairs, with each person having 2 minutes. Distribute and ask participants to refer to "Characteristics of an Ally" (Appendix 6G). Have five or six participants each share an example.

## 3. Envisioning a Society Free From Adultism and Ageism (40 minutes)

This activity allows participants to extend and deepen their reflection on a society free of ageism and adultism. Review the newsprint from the first day listing participants' ideas about a society free of ageism and adultism. See if there are additional ideas that participants can now add to this list. Distribute and review the guidelines for transformation of society (Appendix 15X). See if there are additional ideas that participants can now add to either list.

Ask participants to form groups of three, and then ask each person to take 3 minutes to share his or her vision of a society free of ageism and adultism. Ask participants in the groups to focus on homes, schools, and one other institution in their reflections. After each person has shared his or her vision, ask each group of three to join another group to form a group of six and, together, write two guidelines that would establish ways in which homes, schools, and one other institution could be made free of ageism and adultism. At the end of 5 minutes, ask the groups to post their lists. Have participants walk around, review the guidelines, and place a check next to any guideline that any participant wishes to discuss in more detail.

## 4. Strategies for Interrupting and Eliminating Ageism and Adultism (60 minutes)

Distribute and explain the "Spheres of Influence" (Appendix 4B), which include self; close friends and family; social, school, and work relationships; and community. Ask participants to brainstorm strategies for interrupting ageism and adultism in each area. For example, actions in the area of self could focus on changing internalized beliefs and behaviors, gaining new skills such as how to use the youth development framework in working with youth, and educating oneself more about ageism. List all ideas. Refer to "parking lot" lists created initially during Module 1, and distribute Appendix 15H for additional ideas or resources. Participants can also do this activity in small groups, in which each group post their ideas, and participants conduct a "transformation idea" gallery walk to review each group's ideas.

Ask participants to work together in groups of three or four to share their ideas for actions they could take, the barriers or obstacles they might encounter, support they would need, and ways they could evaluate any successes. Ask participants to return to the large group to share insights or hints that they have gained in the small-group discussions about choosing and planning a liberatory action. Have those who are considering an action that would be best undertaken collectively share their ideas and see if anyone else wants to work with them.

Have participants commit to at least one action by completing the "Action Planning Worksheet" (use Appendix 6I or Appendix 11X), working individually or in groups, to discuss and complete their action plan.

## 5. Summary and Closing (30 minutes)

Seated or standing in a circle, ask each participant, including the facilitators, to state one action they will commit to making to combat ageism and/or adultism. Then have each person, including the facilitators, state one appreciation for another person in the group and one highlight of the class.

## 6. Distribute the Evaluation Form

Ask participants to write their feedback about the class.

# Conversations Among Facilitators

# 16

# Knowing Ourselves as Social Justice Educators

LEE ANNE BELL,
BARBARA J. LOVE,
SHARON WASHINGTON,
GERALD WEINSTEIN*

Although much has been written about the content of social justice education courses, and some about how to engage students in learning about social justice, little attention has been paid to helping social justice educators cope with the emotional and intellectual challenges of this kind of teaching. Yet few would claim that raising issues of oppression and social justice in the classroom is a dispassionate activity. Content as cognitively complex and socially and emotionally charged as social justice inevitably challenges both personal and intellectual knowledge and commitments. In the social justice classroom, we often struggle alongside participants in our classes with our own social identities, biases, fears, and prejudices. We, too, need to be willing to examine and deal honestly with our values, assumptions, and emotional reactions to oppression issues. Accordingly, the self-knowledge and self-awareness that we believe are desirable qualities for any teacher become indispensable in social justice education.

For most faculty, our professional training has not prepared us to deal with emotionally and socially charged issues in the classroom. Social justice education is not simply new content but also often a radical change in process as well, one that requires

---

* Revised by L. A. Bell, based on the earlier 1997 chapter version. We ask that those who cite this work always acknowledge by name all of the authors listed rather than either only citing the first author or using "et al." to indicate coauthors. All collaborated on the conceptualization, development, and writing of the original chapter.

us to expand beyond traditional models of teaching. This shift in standpoint can be a fearful and anxiety-producing experience. "There has to be an acknowledgement that any effort to transform institutions so that they reflect a multicultural standpoint must take into consideration the fears teachers have when asked to shift their paradigms" (hooks, 1994, p. 36).

To examine teaching fears more closely, Weinstein and Obear (1992) invited a group of 25 university faculty colleagues from different disciplines to respond anonymously to the question "What makes you nervous about raising issues of racism in your classroom?" Faculty respondents expressed several concerns that are relevant to our topic. Below, we examine these and other concerns identified in taped discussions among the authors of this chapter. Sometimes, we use a common voice in which "we" refers to the authors. Other times, we use a single voice, identified as Barbara, Jerry, Lee or Sharon.

Below, we discuss faculty fears and concerns about teaching social justice content providing examples of how we grapple with them in our own classes. Although we treat each issue separately, they do in fact overlap and constantly interact. Moreover, the strategies we discuss are not formulaic responses applicable to any teaching situation. Raising oppression issues in the classroom can be exciting and rewarding, but never entirely comfortable or predictable, especially since group interaction is such a central part of the process.

## Awareness of Our Own Social Identities

In traditional classrooms, the particular social and cultural identities of teachers usually remain in the background, but in the social justice classroom, where social identity is central to the content, the significance of who we are often takes center stage. In the study by Weinstein and Obear (1992), faculty expressed heightened awareness about their social identities when teaching social justice content, requiring them to be more conscious of the attitudes and assumptions they convey in their teaching. We are not immune as faculty to feelings of guilt, shame, or embarrassment that arise in discussions of social injustice. Often we are likely to be self-conscious about our own positions in the privileged or targeted group and concerned about how participants are likely to perceive us as we react to material under discussion.

*Jerry:*    Even though I come into the classroom as a professional teacher, I do not leave my social identities at the door. I am a blend of such identities, for example, white, male, Jewish, heterosexual, beyond middle age, working-class background, now middle class. Especially when I am conducting antisemitism courses, I am constantly reminded of my conflicts about being at the same time a member of a group that is targeted by antisemitism and a member of the dominant white, male group in this society, with all of the inequities and privileges associated with each status.

As facilitators, we can offer our experience with both advantaged and targeted identities as a way to join with participants, model openness to exploring our own relative positions of power and privilege in relation to different oppression issues and expand the boundaries in the room for discussing these subjects.

*Barbara:*  African American students often express difficulty in seeing themselves in the role of dominant or agent of oppression. They are so closely identified with the role of target or victim of oppression that they fail to see how they benefit from agent aspects of their identity. I grew up with a keen awareness of myself as a black person, but with no understanding at all of the ways I benefit from my status as a Christian. I gathered lots of information about disability oppression, but gained a much deeper understanding of systematic exclusion of people with disabilities when I suffered an injury that left me temporarily disabled.

Awareness of social identity is further complicated by historical and experiential contexts. The meaning of social group membership will vary for people who are from the same social group but from different geographic regions, historical periods, and family experiences, or who view their experiences through different social identity positions. As facilitators, we need to be conscious of how individual members of a social group experience oppression in diverse ways and be cautious about rigid categorizations.

*Barbara:* Being Black means different things to different African heritage people. A light-skinned middle- or upper-class African heritage person growing up in the Northeast in the 1990s will describe the experience of being Black very differently from a dark-skinned working-class person raised in the South in the 1950s. Neither experience is any more or less authentically Black. While different, both experiences interact with a system of racism that extends through time, geographic region, and particular individual/family locations.

Though we experience the oppression directed toward our group as individuals, no one individual can ever embody the totality of group subjugation. This is one of the central limitations of identity politics. We are constantly balancing the broad strokes of group oppression with the finer shadings of individual experience. If we can be conscious of our own identity explorations, we may be more likely to remember that our students too come from a range of different places and experiences as they struggle to define an individual identity in the context of a variety of differently positioned group memberships.

*Sharon:* What may be in the forefront for a student of color at a particular moment may not be race, but sexual orientation, physical ability, or age. Just because a participant is in a wheelchair does not mean disability is the issue that is currently primary. At any given moment a participant may be more engaged with issues of gender, race, or sexual orientation.

As facilitators, we find it helpful to reflect on the experiences that have shaped our various identities and note the particular issues with which we feel most comfortable and those we tend to avoid, distort, or fear. This self-knowledge can be helpful preparation for engaging with student discomfort with these issues and enable us to respond thoughtfully to participants even when we ourselves feel exposed or uncertain.

*Lee:* As a white woman, racism is an ongoing learning process for me. I keep realizing new areas where I'm unaware, learning, and hopefully growing, but it is never closed and finished content. If I acknowledge my own ongoing learning, I can be more open to what participants in my classes raise for me to look at. Being aware of my own struggles to be honest with myself and open to new information hopefully also helps me to be more empathetic and supportive of their struggles.

As teachers, we can keep learning and be thoughtful about our levels of knowledge and awareness of particular issues, realizing that our own consciousness is likely to shift and change through ongoing discovery of the various forms and manifestations oppression takes in our society. We, too, are life long learners in this process.

## Confronting Previously Unrecognized Prejudices

A second issue noted by faculty in the Weinstein and Obear (1992) study had to do with fear of being labeled racist, sexist, and so on, and discovering previously unrecognized prejudices within ourselves. This concern included having our assumptions called into question in front of our students, being corrected or challenged publicly (especially by members of targeted groups), and encountering our own fears and romanticized notions about members of targeted groups.

No one who has taken on the task of teaching about oppression wants to be thought of as homophobic, racist, sexist, classist, antisemitic, ableist, ageist, and so on. Yet we know that recognizing and rooting out deeply socialized, and often unconscious, prejudices and practices is not likely to be easy or completed work. Educators understandably feel a sense of vulnerability that what is out of our awareness will rise up to confront us as we engage these issues in our classrooms.

*Lee:* I grew up in the Midwest and didn't meet a Jewish person, or at least was not aware I had, until I went to college. I thought that meant I couldn't be antisemitic. Slowly I came to realize all the assumptions and stereotypes I breathe in just living in this culture. I still have unexpected moments of new learning when I suddenly become aware of something I have missed or overlooked that is tied to antisemitism. And I think, "Oh no, how could I not have seen this?" I can berate myself for not noticing, or try to avoid the discomfort of this awareness, or I can try to be grateful that at least now I can do something about it.

An example of one activity that went awry because of unexamined assumptions is illustrative. Lee had planned an activity to elicit discussion of gender socialization, using a fishbowl format in which first men and then women would talk about their experiences in a homogeneous group so that each group could listen to each other without interruption.

*Lee:* I was so intent on gender issues in my planning that I didn't anticipate the discomfort a gay man might feel in the rather raucous male-bonding discussion that took place among the men in the fishbowl emphasizing sports and heterosexual dating. I had not anticipated the way a gay man might have a very different relationship to his experiences of maleness. I noticed the student's discomfort and began to guess my mistake, which he confirmed when we talked about it later.

This lesson serves as a helpful reminder for instructors to continually ask, "Who are the participants I imagine as I do this planning?" and "Who might I be leaving out or forgetting to include?"

Barbara notes that encountering previously unrecognized prejudice enables her to be more effective and empathetic with her students:

*Barbara:* An important part of my own learning has been to recognize the ways I have internalized oppression and how it permeates my consciousness without my awareness. For example, learning to confront the homophobia at the heart of my own religious tradition has been vital to being able to support students who are seeking to learn about heterosexism and homophobia while remaining loyal to their own religious beliefs.

Self-examination about the effects of oppressive socialization in our lives is a never-ending learning process. We all have areas of limited vision, particularly where we are members of the advantaged group and have been taught to assume our own experiences as normative. When we stay open to ongoing learning, and accept the inevitable mistakes as we uncover new areas of ignorance or lack of awareness, our students can learn to do so as well. Such self-awareness supports the long view needed to sustain our commitments and not retreat from this difficult but vital work.

## Responding to Biased Comments in the Classroom

Faculty anxiety about how to respond sensitively and effectively to biased comments in the classroom is understandable, yet such comments invariably arise once we open up the topic. Those interviewed by Weinstein and Obear (1992) worried most about dealing with biased comments from privileged group members in the presence of targeted group members, especially when made by members of their own socially advantaged group.

Language plays such a central role in perpetuating oppression that miscommunication and misunderstanding can easily arise. Targeted group members usually have a long history with and have developed sensitivity to negative cues that signal oppressive attitudes. They have been subjected to, have suffered from, have discussed, and have thought about such cues throughout the course of their lives and so are highly tuned to note them in the language used by members of the advantaged group. Advantaged group members, on the other hand, are often oblivious to, and quite often shocked to realize, the injury they can cause to members of the targeted group. Thus, the potential for breakdown in communication, hurt feelings, defensiveness, and recrimination is high. As educators, we want to create an atmosphere where all participants feel included, and where we can address hurtful language without inhibiting honest discussion. We have found that setting ground rules and establishing mutually agreed upon procedures for addressing offensive statements when they arise can be productive in creating an atmosphere of honesty and support. (see Chapters 5, 12 and 13; Appendix 12K).

As social justice educators, we are not immune to triggering cues either, thus we find it helpful to recognize beforehand the comments and signals to which we are most susceptible.

*Jerry:*    As a Jew, particularly when I am teaching about antisemitism, I am vulnerable to all the dominant signals concerning my group. Some version of all the stereotyped statements and attitudes that have pursued me my entire life are bound to be expressed. I always experience those expressions and attitudes with some degree of pain, for they restimulate past fears. When I hear those expressions, I may get angry and want to retaliate, but I know that acting directly on my feelings would be inappropriate and counterproductive to the goals of the session and my role as teacher and facilitator. By anticipating typical responses that I have experienced before, I can prepare myself to address these triggers intentionally and constructively during the class.

Careful analysis of how we typically react in situations of tension can lead to more options for responding in thoughtful ways when conflicts arise. For example, we can examine motives for avoiding conflict, proving ourselves as unprejudiced, or wanting people to like us. Through paying attention to our internal dialogue in these situations, we can make more conscious choices in the moment:

*Sharon:*    I make sure that I know myself in relation to the material and the particular issues that give me the most discomfort or anxiety. If I feel like a well of emotion, I remind myself this class is for the students. Once I had someone co-teaching a particular session, and this person just lost it and raged at the class. I went away thinking, "Wow, she just threw up all over the class!"

To avoid responding in ways we might later regret, we can build in ways beforehand to deal with and respond effectively when we are triggered by what participants say in class. For example, creating a support system, a person or group with whom we can discuss these issues, share feelings, and get support, can be extremely helpful. Sharon regularly meets with a friend and colleague, another African American woman, to debrief and talk about her classes. She has also at times used a journal to note her feelings and reactions as the class progresses. This process is a helpful reminder, at points in a course where resistance is particularly high or she is feeling down on herself, that these are predictable parts of the process rather than flaws in the class or her own teaching. Such realizations can be very reassuring.

An appreciation for the process people go through in developing awareness about oppression can also help us acquire patience and understanding when dealing with our own frustrations and feelings toward students.

*Lee:*    I can feel very impatient sometimes. But when I shift my frame of reference to one of trying to understand the process by which people can be engaged in unlearning oppressive attitudes, it kind of unhooks me. Then it becomes a challenge to figure out, "Okay, how is this person thinking about these issues now, and what is going to be the way to help them to try out a different perspective?"

Attention to process in the moment occurs on two levels. One level relates to noticing how participants may be thinking about or experiencing what is going on in the classroom: "Why does that person say or think that? What is getting triggered for him or her?" On a parallel track, we can also note and try to understand our own reactions to what is occurring in the moment: "Why am I so annoyed at this person? What does it trigger for me?"

We often hold romanticized notions that those who are themselves victimized by bigotry and discrimination will naturally be more sensitive and vigilant when groups other than their own are targeted or victimized. Unfortunately, the experience of oppression does not automatically render one an expert or liberate one from bias toward another group. It can be quite disillusioning when such expectations are shattered.

*Jerry:*    I have been exposed to Jewish racism and sexism, African American antisemitism and sexism, and white, Gentile women who are racist and antisemitic. I always harbor the wish that all targeted group members would be allies in interrupting bias in all of its forms. However, wishing doesn't make it so. When I am confronted with bias toward my group from other targeted people, I have to overcome my fear of alienating those whom I thought were "on my side" and challenge their beliefs in the same way I would anyone else. However, in the process I try to provide continuous evidence that I am also sensitive to their target group issues.

The challenge for us as educators is to stay open both to our own internal process and to what may be going on for our students, so that we can respond to biased comments clearly and directly, but also with compassion and understanding for what it means to discover and challenge oppressive beliefs and behaviors in ourselves (see Chapter 5 for further discussion of triggers).

## Doubts and Ambivalence About One's Own Competency

Weinstein and Obear (1992) found that faculty members often worry about having to expose struggles, uncertainty, or mistakes because we are assumed, as college faculty, to be experts. To the degree that we expect ourselves to appear certain about what we know, we may find it difficult to encounter hot spots or knowledge gaps exposed through our interactions with participants in our social justice classes.

*Jerry:*    This is especially true when targeted group members other than my own describe perspectives to which I am not yet sensitive. Unless I can admit to students that I am still in the process of learning and that there are areas about which I still need to be educated, I may give the impression that there are simple solutions to which I have access. This places great pressure on me to have "the answer." One way of diminishing the pressure is to disclose my own uncertainties to students. It also models that unlearning prejudice is a lifelong process in which there are rarely simple answers.

The issues participants raise that challenge our awareness and sensitivity can create a valuable space for opening up the learning process. As we confront our own misinformation, ignorance, and the blind spots of privilege, we create the possibility for modeling honesty and openness to what can be learned by listening to others who are different from us, especially those who have been targets of stereotypes and assumptions from members of advantaged groups.

In our discussions for this chapter, Lee recalled a course in which classism was a central focus. Because most of the students were teachers or human service professionals, she had assumed a predominantly middle-class perspective and focused the course accordingly, only to discover the simmering anger at the cost of textbooks and the amount of time outside of class needed to complete the homework among participants working two jobs and struggling to make ends meet. Once Lee realized her mistake, she acknowledged the false assumptions she had made and initiated a discussion about how to address the problems participants were experiencing in ways that would be supportive and promote learning. The discussion with her students provided an opportunity for them to explore the issue of classism and the unexamined assumptions that reinforce class privilege. The discussion also gave Lee useful new ideas about how to select texts for courses, develop a library of books to loan to students, and think about new ways to construct assignments and build supportive classroom community.

*Sharon:*    You can't come into the class saying, in effect, "I know everything there is to know about this and let me tell you." When you make a mistake, you have to be willing to say, "Well, that was a mistake" or "I've learned something about this now, and I'll do it differently next time." I don't know how comfortable most teachers are with doing this, but there is a way to say, "It didn't occur to me" or "I didn't notice, I'm sorry."

Teaching in ways that invite challenge and model ongoing learning conveys a different definition of competence than the traditional one of mastery and expertise. *Competence* here means skill in creating an atmosphere where difficult dialogues can occur (Goodman, 1995), developing processes that enable people (including the teacher) to expose and look critically at their own assumptions and biases, and building a community that encourages risk taking and action to challenge oppressive beliefs and behaviors within and beyond the classroom.

## Need for Learner Approval

Most educators hope that their students will like and respect them, and leave class feeling positively about their experience. Those interviewed by Weinstein and Obear (1992) revealed fear of making students frustrated, frightened, or angry. Such encounters often leave faculty feeling shaken and confused, and uncertain of how to respond.

*Lee:*     I think I'm good at creating community in the classroom and making people feel welcome and supported. Where I have to push myself is to introduce and not smooth over conflict, to challenge students, and risk their not liking me. I do it, but I realize I'm much more comfortable with the community-building part. It makes me feel good. I want students to like me. But there are times when that can get in the way of productive learning.

In social justice teaching, we intentionally create tension in order to disrupt participants' complacent and unexamined attitudes about social life. These very conditions can cause participants to dislike or feel hostile toward us at various points in the course. Confronting oppression invariably involves feelings ranging from anxiety, confusion, anger, and sadness, to exhilaration and joy. We need to remind ourselves that as much as we crave approval from our students, a sense of well-being is not always conducive to long-lasting learning, especially with regard to issues of oppression. A better indication of our effectiveness might be whether participants leave with more questions than they when they entered, are unsettled by what they have learned, are pushed to know more about core assumptions in their own socialization, or feel a need to get more actively involved in the world around them.

*Jerry:*     When participants left feeling frustrated, upset, and confused I used to regard it as evidence of my failure as a facilitator. It was not until we ran a racism workshop for a community college in which the entire faculty and administration were involved that my concept of what constituted successful teaching began to change. On finishing the weekend-long session the participants were not smiling. On the way home my co-leader and I felt that the workshop had been a failure. Over the next 3 to 5 years, however, we kept getting reports of systematic changes in that institution that promoted greater racial equity and awareness and that were directly attributed to the workshop.

## Dealing With Emotional Intensity and Fear of Losing Control

Faculty worry they won't know how to respond to angry comments, discussions that blow up, participant anger directed at them, or their own strong emotions engendered by the discussion (Weinstein & Obear, 1992). Johnella Butler describes this process well:

> All the conflicting emotions, the sometimes painful movement from the familiar to the unfamiliar, are experienced by the teacher as well. We have been shaped by the same damaging, misinformed view of the world as our students. Often, as we try to resolve their conflicts, we are simultaneously working through our own. (1989, p. 160)

Many educators have been taught that emotions have no place in academia. However, traditionally dispassionate modes of teaching can distance us from the core issues and conflicts that are central to social justice education and can often result in simply skimming the surface. Ultimately, it is questionable whether intellectual and abstract reflection alone can effectively change oppressive attitudes and behaviors. Emotions and experience must inevitably be engaged for social justice learning to be meaningful or have a lasting impact on how we and our students act in the world.

Tension, anger, and conflict in the classroom are truly challenging and often exhausting to handle. However, avoiding the feelings that are stimulated by oppression ignores how deeply it is embedded in our psyches, and reinforces norms of silence and discounting that ultimately sustain oppression (Aguilar & Washington, 1990). Often, the disequilibrium that direct confrontation with feelings and contradictory information generate leads to the most significant learning (see Chapter 4; see also Keil, 1984; Zaharna, 1989).

Barbara notes how helpful it can be to examine our own personal history with emotional expression to understand our responses to emotion in the classroom.

*Barbara:* I have had to examine how anger and other intense emotions were handled in my household to get a better understanding of my current response to emotions in the classroom. Quite apart from my professional training to be carefully neutral and suppress any display of emotion, I was raised in a household where feelings were denied until they erupted. My response has been to deny feelings any place in discussions, and especially to disallow loud voices. Learning to listen to loud voices and to encourage others to be receptive to them has been important for my ability to facilitate authentic discussion. Reminding learners that loud voices sometimes indicate that a person cares a lot about an issue can provide a context that allows "heated" discussion to take place.

Once we accept emotional expression as a valid and valuable part of the learning process, we can turn our focus to finding effective ways to enable its expression in the service of learning.

*Sharon:* I actually don't really try to control emotions, but I do try to manage outlets for expressing emotions through dyads or journals, for example. If people are upset, I say, "Be upset! Be angry, whatever, and we'll just notice it." And I just sort of acknowledge that it's part of the process.

Simply acknowledging when we feel overwhelmed and uncertain about what to do can be a powerful step. When emotions are running high and we are uncertain about how to proceed, one useful strategy is to acknowledge that and create time-out for the whole class to reflect before deciding on next steps.

*Jerry:*    There have been a number of times during my antibias teaching when I have felt totally helpless in dealing with certain interactions. A participant may say something that stimulates great tension and anxiety, and a dense silence overtakes the group. I may feel upset and paralyzed as all eyes turn to me to see what I will do, expecting me to take care of the situation. I cannot think of any helpful intervention. I am too upset to think clearly. It is a fearsome moment, one I anticipate with dread.

Over the years, Jerry has accumulated a few emergency procedures that help him survive these moments:

- Give participants a brief time-out.
- Ask people to record their own immediate responses in their notebooks.
- Invite each participant to share his or her responses with one other person.
- Return to the whole-group discussion to consider what has occurred and what can be learned as a result.

Such strategies change the focus momentarily from public to private, allow time for participants and instructor to assess how they are feeling, and regroup. Often, it then becomes more possible to return to the discussion with greater clarity, thoughtfulness, and honesty.

When a supportive climate has been previously established, losing control or facing strong emotions can be a constructive event, one from which both facilitators and participants learn. In fact, participants often make fundamental shifts in perspective after they have experienced someone "losing" control, revealing the deeper feelings, fears, and experiences surrounding oppression that are always operating but rarely expressed.

*Barbara:*    I teach social justice education from a position of hope and belief that our efforts can make a difference in the elimination of oppression. I was co-teaching an antisemitism course with a Jewish colleague who said that she did not think antisemitism would ever be entirely eliminated and that other holocausts were and are possible. Before I could catch them, tears coursed down my face as I felt the enormity of the task before me and the challenge to my own optimism. Several students later told me that this was a powerful learning moment for them.

## Personal Disclosure and Using Our Experience As Example

As social justice educators, we are in many ways texts for our students. Our social group identities, behavior in the classroom, and openness about our own process of learning can all be significant aspects of course content, as who we are affects student perceptions of the issues we raise. In some respects, we are both the messenger and the message. Asking participants to engage experientially with oppression-related material also requires that we be willing to take the risks we ask of them.

*Lee:*    If we want to create an environment where our students can be vulnerable enough to look at painful issues that challenge our faith in a fair society and ourselves as good human beings, then we have to give ourselves the same permission to be vulnerable and confused. I'm constantly struggling against this image that teachers are supposed to be perfect, in control, totally aware. Which is ridiculous! Nobody can be that. The question is how can I try to be skillful, and at the same time give myself permission to be a fallible human being? If I'm going to ask my students to disclose something, then I should be willing to do that too. I try to disclose ways in which I've made mistakes and where I felt really stupid when I realized what I was saying, to let students know there's not perfection. We're just human beings trying to be humane with each other and not perpetuate this bloody system.

Sharing our own struggles with issues of oppression gives permission for our students to engage in this difficult process themselves. Acknowledging that we cannot know everything, but can commit to persistent effort to learn about oppression, helps us and participants in our classes let go of expectations of perfection that often block action. Better to take imperfect action and continue to engage with these crucial issues than to avoid responsibility for action altogether while we search for perfect knowledge.

*Sharon:*    I want students to understand that learning about social justice is part of a lifelong process. I will share with them stories of my own development, both in areas where I was a target of oppression, or stood in the shoes of an agent of oppression with the accompanying privileges.

The amount, context, and nature of personal information that we disclose are always a matter of judgment, depending on the learning purposes of disclosure, nature and size of the group, relationships we have established, and amount of time we have together. What we choose to disclose as facilitators should have a clear relationship to the topic under discussion and serve a learning purpose.

For many social justice educators, especially from targeted groups, the risks of self-disclosure, however, need to be thoughtfully weighed. For example, self-disclosure by a gay or lesbian facilitator can be a significant boon to learning, especially if the topic is heterosexism, but can also backfire. The instructor should be aware of the homophobia and misinformation sure to exist among her students and plan carefully how and when she will come out and the educational purposes this will serve.

*Sharon:*    I know that for myself I'm always conscious about when it is that I'll come out in class, or even if I will. Because I want them to still see me as credible and I believe that as soon as I come out, that piece of knowledge looms in their eyes over everything else. Like all of a sudden their teacher is sexual, and they have to deal with the internal contradictions of respect for teacher along with societal messages that gay men and lesbians are bad, perverse, immoral, etc. So I know that I'm very conscious about when to share that information. I try to wait until after I've gotten their trust so that any trust I lose during that time period can hopefully be reestablished before the end of the semester. I have had students deny my being lesbian and think I was only saying it to create a learning opportunity for them!

A facilitator's purpose and role in disclosing personal experiences differ in important ways from those of participants. Participants draw on their experiences to probe and understand the personal implications of a specific issue. Facilitators often use personal experience to illustrate a point, push the discussion forward, challenge mis-information, or support a particular learning goal. Our role is to be comprehensive, so we also need to understand the limits of our own experience and to consciously develop examples that go beyond our own personal range.

## Negotiating Authority Issues

In the social justice classroom, we deliberately interrupt the traditional classroom hierarchy in order to build a community of learning in which the teacher participates as a facilitator of process rather than an authority delivering knowledge (Tompkins, 1990). Issues of authority in the classroom are especially complicated for faculty who are members of targeted groups. Much has been written, for example, about the dilemmas faced by faculty of color and by female and gay/lesbian faculty who often cope with both institutional and student devaluation of their professional status (Aguilar & Washington, 1990; Ahlquist, 1991; Arnold, 1993; hooks, 1994; Ladson-Billings, 1996; Maher & Tetreault, 1994). Students sometimes perceive them as less authoritative and may discount the legitimacy of what they teach or accuse them of pushing their own agenda. A professor of color and a white professor teaching about racism, for example, are likely to be perceived quite differently by students of color and white students. Sharon describes the various issues she often juggles and the common student perceptions she faces as an African American woman teaching about racism.

*Sharon:*    The fact that my students are often 99 percent white means that I have to set up an environment where they can talk about their perceptions of reverse discrimination, quotas, affirmative action, etc. I also don't want to come off appearing like it's only my issue, or it's my personal thing, or that I've got a chip on my shoulder. And if I do have students of color in the class, then I'm also concerned about trying to keep them from having to be the authority on all issues of race.

Gender also casts authority issues in particular ways. We are socialized to expect females to defer to male authority, not to be authorities themselves. Women who achieve professional roles often juggle negative social messages about women in power with an internal sense of being imposters in these roles (Bell, 1990; McIntosh, 1988). When we are dealing with emotional issues and feelings in the classroom, female professors can easily be typecast in unfair and distorting ways. Students, for example, often expect female teachers to be warm and nurturing and may become angry or challenge our authority when we do not fulfill their expectations (see Culley, 1985).

## Institutional Risks and Dangers

One additional concern relates to the institutional risks involved when we depart from traditional teaching formats and content. As we engage with social justice issues and change our classrooms accordingly, we often come into conflict with institutional norms of professed objectivity, authority, and professorial distance in ways that can undermine our confidence, lose the support of some of our colleagues, and in some cases jeopardize our positions as faculty.

When we take on the challenge of teaching social justice content and developing a democratic, participatory process in our classrooms, we run the very real risk of getting in trouble with our institutions because we are challenging traditional content, teaching processes, and norms about the teacher–student relationship. We may also encounter problems with grading and evaluation not typical for traditional instructors.

*Sharon:*   A student's mother wrote to the dean and told him that I was a bad teacher and that if her daughter didn't get a B, she was going to take this to the provost and the president of the university and have them call me on the carpet. And it was really hard holding my own ground. [Did the dean support you?] The dean *did* support me but not without questioning me.

In this example, we see multiple vulnerabilities: the jeopardy facing an African American teacher in a predominantly white institution where she cannot necessarily count on the support on which white faculty can usually rely. Also, she is introducing subject matter that may not be supported by the institution. Finally, she is engaging in a process of teaching that also may not be valued institutionally.

Faculty who teach social justice courses are commonly from underrepresented groups, often women and the few people of color on a faculty, and frequently untenured. Thus, the most vulnerable groups take on the most difficult and institutionally risky teaching. Faculty who teach social justice courses sometimes receive lower ratings on teaching evaluations than those who teach traditional courses, adding yet another layer of institutional danger to an already exposed position. Such teachers, especially if they are members of targeted groups, are often left in an extremely vulnerable position institutionally.

Team teaching, particularly with a tenured faculty member, can be a valuable way to build support for untenured faculty. Other support systems also need to be developed and nurtured so that faculty who teach social justice education can survive and hopefully thrive in institutions that benefit from their perspectives and experiences.

## Conclusion

Too often, people who write about social justice education fail to share their own struggles in the classroom. We hope that through naming and discussing the fears and concerns faced by faculty who teach about oppression, we can begin a dialogue of support and encouragement that will enable teachers to sustain their commitment to social justice education and contribute to the ongoing development of effective social justice pedagogy and practice. We recognize that we are part of a much larger process of change, and we want to affirm the importance of the small but essential role each of us can play in the quest for a more just and inclusive society. What we do counts, often in ways that will not come back to us for validation.

*Sharon:*   I just think it's helpful to know that I am doing the best I can do and not to be too wedded to the here and now. I know ancestors who came before fought for freedom, equality, and justice and made it possible for me to live this life. Even if I don't change the world for me, I have faith that my work can contribute to a better world for the generations yet to come. That's what keeps me doing it, keeps me grounded, being grateful and knowing that my little part counts.

We hope that nurturing this perspective in our students will make it possible for them to see the meaningful role they too can play in envisioning and working to create a just society.

# 17

# Knowing Our Students

## MAURIANNE ADAMS, JOANNE JONES, BEVERLY DANIEL TATUM*

This chapter originated in audiotaped conversations among the three authors as we reflected upon our combined years of teaching experience, and set ourselves the following questions: Why do we want to know our students? What do we need to know about them? How do we get to know our students? What theory and knowledge bases help us to understand them? What do we want students to know about themselves, about each other, and about us?

These questions are addressed in this chapter by interweaving narrative descriptions, examples, and excerpts from our conversational reflections on what "knowing our students" has meant for our practice. Sometimes, we use a common voice in which "we" refers generally to the three authors; at other times, each of us is expressed in her voice, identified as Beverly, JoAnne, or Maurianne. We offer examples of how to gather and then make use of information about our students, and we describe experiences that illustrate successful strategies or, in some cases, the mistakes we have made when we didn't practice what we preach.

## Why Do We Want to Know Our Students?

Some background knowledge about student learning styles (discussed this volume, Chapter 4) and prior familiarity with course content are generally helpful in any teaching situation. However, when the content involves issues of social justice, to which students bring strongly held opinions and beliefs, this knowledge becomes essential. Regardless of age or experience, participants do not enter the social justice classroom

---

* We ask that those who cite this work always acknowledge by name all of the authors listed rather than either only citing the first author or using "et al." to indicate coauthors. All collaborated on the conceptualization, development, and writing of this chapter.

as blank slates. They bring information and opinions about gender roles, racial stereotypes, "normal" ability, or "appropriate" sexual behavior as part of their socialization. What they have learned, and from whom, affects their attitude about everything presented in our social justice education courses.

In our conversation, we identified six specific reasons why we want to know the participants in our classes. First, we want to be able to match our curricular goals, and the instructional activities that support them, to what we anticipate or learn about our students. Early assessments provide information about students' past experiences and beliefs about social differences. JoAnne recounts an example of beginning a course on issues of oppression with a group of human service professionals. During an opening discussion designed to elicit information about prior experiences with the topic, one participant said emphatically, "I want to tell you this: I don't want any lectures. I'm tired of being lectured to! I want to be able to talk to people here and learn from each other." If JoAnne had started with something didactic, this participant would probably have tuned out. By carefully assessing expectations and remaining flexible, JoAnne was able to alter her design and return to important conceptual material at a time when participants were more able to listen responsively.

Second, we want to know enough about our participants in our social justice education classes to be able to anticipate questions or areas of confusion. We need to think about who our students are as we decide how to introduce key terms and concepts. Some participants may hesitate to ask us what the words we use mean; they may speak English as a second language, or feel embarrassed by their lack of understanding and sensitive to public humiliation. Beverly recounts a training for college staff that focused on racism but inadvertently excluded people through the use of undefined key terms.

*Beverly:*    Among the staff in attendance was a group of five women from housekeeping who sat together during the workshop. On the last day of the training, they came up to us, and one of them said she was totally lost. She didn't have a college degree, she said, and the material we had given them to read was difficult. She then said that when someone in the group referred to "nepotism," she didn't even know what the word meant and had been too embarrassed to say this in the group. She had tears in her eyes when she was talking to us. She was embarrassed to admit that so much had gone over her head, but she also didn't want to lose more.

A third reason we want to know our students is to be able to teach to their current levels of awareness, assumptions, expectations, and information. For example, we sometimes forget how quickly student generational culture changes, and assume that issues such as sexism are readily apparent to most of our female participants. Some younger women insist that the women's movement has already solved all issues of gender inequity in the workplace and that sexual harassment is "no big deal."

Knowing or learning about our students does not occur all at once, or just at the beginning of a course. The nature of social justice courses is such that along the way, participants may discover beliefs, assumptions, and feelings they did not know they held. Participants also change as they engage with social justice content, putting old beliefs behind them and embracing new ways of thinking. We want our teaching strategies to also change as we, along with our students, make new discoveries about their beliefs and values.

*Beverly:*    I change things all the time! I think flexibility is a major resource. I'm constantly assessing my educational goals and asking myself whether what we are doing is moving in a useful direction.

*Maurianne:*  I tend to have backup strategies—depending on where I think the group may go with a particular topic and what the dynamics may be. Although I always give out a written "agenda" for a class, students know I am likely to change activities, such as break them into small groups or ask them to write a page on their thoughts or provide a short impromptu lecture on missing information or conceptual links for clarification. The fact that I revise the agenda during the class tells participants that I'm trying to be responsive to who they are and what they seem to need in the moment.

A fourth reason we want to know our students is to be able to judge whether we are using appropriate and realistic learning goals. Even the fairly basic instructional goals of awareness, knowledge, and action (noted in Chapter 4, this volume) may be unrealistic, if we find that generating awareness and providing missing information on a topic consume most of our class time, and we are left with insufficient time or participant readiness to think about intervention skills or action strategies until somewhat later in a semester.

*Maurianne:*  Often, there's a sharp difference between how I may prioritize my teaching objectives and what I discover is actually possible for my students, given the limitations of time, the number of other courses they are taking, and their actual "learning edge" for a specific social justice issue. In planning our general education "diversity" course, we sometimes overestimate the awareness level and readiness of many of our students. We find we can't introduce personal interventions or action until students actually care about these issues and feel personally implicated in them.

Group size also affects one's teaching goals and is important to plan for in advance. Teaching about racism or heterosexism in a class with more than 100 students might call for more of a lecture format rather than raising awareness through experiential learning.

*JoAnne:*    I might give some experiential taste to provide a frame for the information in a large class of 100 students located in a lecture hall, but it certainly wouldn't be the "get to know yourself" kind of experience used in a smaller class of 20 or 30. I think we must be very clear to not raise questions when there is not sufficient time to answer them. If there's only a limited time with a large group of people, I wouldn't want to open people up to self-disclosure.

Still, an introductory activity such as "I am" (described below) can be done with a large group in row seating if students fill out the worksheet individually, turn and pair with the person next to them, or form groups of four with people sitting in front and in back. The benefits of self-reflection and learning about each other in this case can be augmented by the instructor who reads the "I am" worksheets after class and reports back on the overall group demographics in a later class.

*Beverly:*    The "I am" exercise I use asks participants to fill in as many or as few descriptors as they choose. When students have finished writing, I ask for volunteers to read their lists and then ask people to talk about any patterns they notice.

Usually, somebody will notice that the white people have not mentioned being white but that the people of color have mentioned their ethnicity; the men have not mentioned being male, but the women have mentioned something about being female. I often use this exercise as an introduction to a lecture presentation on the topic of racial identity development.

A fifth reason we want to know our students is to be able to anticipate participant reactions to our own specific social group identities as instructors, an issue presented at greater length in the preceding chapter, but relevant to our discussion here as well. We have experienced contradictory reactions among participants to our various target identities as female, lesbian, Jewish, or black. Sometimes, participants grant us an expertise on "our" issues that enables them to avoid exposing their own views or struggles with their own experiences. Other times, they discount what we present as overly subjective or self-interested, and write us off as lacking expertise or authority. Either side of this paradox diminishes our effectiveness as facilitators in ways that may not hold true for facilitators perceived as belonging to dominant groups.

Sixth, we try to know our participants well enough to plan for their likely reactions to and interactions with each other in a culturally diverse class setting. We have observed white participants who become silenced by their own participation in the larger system of racism. We have seen participants of color become frustrated by the slow pace of discussion or by the level of white denial.

*Beverly:*    One of the things I might be thinking about is "Well, do we need to break up into small groups? Or, can this continue as a large-group discussion?" If there seems to be a lot of animation in the classroom, everybody wants to talk, and yet we don't have enough time to let everybody talk, does that mean I should put people in pairs, so that everybody can say something to someone, even if they're not participating as a large group? Does it mean that we need to make a change in the order of the content? Those are some of the things I'm prepared to think about on the spot in terms of what's happening in the class: *process* as well as *content*.

## What Do We Need to Know about Our Students?

With which social identities are students most or least comfortable? What issues are of greatest concern to them, and what is their motivation for being in this class? What is their prior experience with the range of social justice issues, and what are their expectations? We have learned that within any group, there will be a range of experiences, familiarity with the material, and emotional comfort. We also anticipate that everyone, including the facilitator, will bring a certain amount of misinformation and ignorance to any discussion about social justice issues. These are assumptions that we make explicit for participants at the start of the educational experience.

## Social Identity Mixture in the Class and Multiple Social Identities of Individual Participants

Prior to the start of a class or during the first class or introductory module, we ask for specific information about social identities to help us assess the racial and ethnic diversity, gender mix, and age ranges of the group. Revealing personal information about one's social identities may be emotionally difficult for many people, so creating a climate of safety and comfort is important. Beverly tells the story of a man visibly identifiable as black, who had grown up in a mostly white community and identified culturally with the white community when she divided the class into caucus groups. The people of color caucus group was assigned to a room in one building and the white caucus group in another building, and she found this man in the breezeway between the two buildings.

*Beverly:*   He stood there, unsure of which way to go. We stood in the breezeway and talked about it. I didn't say you need to be in this group or that group, but I asked him what it would mean for him to go one way or the other. He said, "I know I'm black, but I still identify with being white." I told him that I knew a lot of folks in his situation, who had grown up in white communities, that I had grown up in a similar situation, and I guessed that there were other people of color in that room with a similar experience. I suggested it might be helpful for him to be in the room with the people of color and talk about his dilemma and what it meant for him. In the end, that's what he chose to do.

Sometimes, merely posing a provocative question creates a crisis of meaning for participants that in turn leads to new levels of understanding. The following example illustrates an unexpected response to the introductory "I am" activity (described earlier) and illustrates the strong feelings that can attach to one's social identities, especially when those identities may be in transition, turmoil, or disguise.

*Beverly:*   At the end of my presentation, a woman came up to me in tears. She had left the room for a period of time during my lecture, because she had been overcome by emotion. At the end, she apologized for leaving and said, "It was because when you asked us to do the 'I am' exercise, I didn't know what to put." She had been raised in a Cuban family, but she was not visibly identifiable as Hispanic and had been taught to pass as white. She felt she could not put down white, but was terrified at the idea of writing down that she was Cuban. I had not asked them to write down anything in particular. I had asked them to simply complete the sentence, "I am ..." But this was what she was experiencing. By the end of my presentation, she realized that she had internalized a lot of racism herself. She said she realized the biggest racist was the one inside of her, and that she really wanted to explore and reclaim her identity as Cuban. She said, "I know it doesn't matter, nobody cares, nobody in this room cares if I'm Cuban or not, but I feel like I'm going to be found out." I had never anticipated that this brief exercise would be so powerful for a particular individual in the room.

One reason it is important to know our participants is that we are able to then be sensitive and responsive to the ways in which social identity can be so internal and ambivalent that what seems obvious to a viewer is far from obvious or simple to the self.

## Prior Experience with and Reactions to Social Justice Education

We try to find out whether participants have had prior experiences with social justice courses, and if so, to hear about their reactions to these experiences.

*Beverly:*   Some students relaxed visibly when I said, "I know you know this material, and so I would appreciate it if there's a different way you understand it or a different language you use. Please speak up. I also know there are some people here for whom this is all new." Some know a lot, some know very little, and both will feel anxious unless you acknowledge some way they can move forward together.

In addition to finding out what participants already know, we try to learn about their attitudes and beliefs, their expectations for the experience, and their motivation for participating. Gathering some of this information can be a fairly straightforward process. A written assessment of participant expectations and concerns about the course can be conducted prior to the start of a class or during the first session. Informally asking participants why they are taking the class and what they hope to learn can accomplish this goal as well.

The level of resistance is likely to be quite high if participants are attending a required course or workshop they believe they have been unfairly mandated to attend. Knowing this information in advance allows the facilitator to acknowledge the ways people might be feeling and plan activities to help a resistant group move forward in their understanding of the content and their acknowledgment of its importance.

## How Do We Find Out the Information We Need to Know Our Students?

### Prior Assessments

There are countless formal and informal ways to collect assessment information before the start of a class or during its initial stages. One productive strategy, already noted, is to distribute a questionnaire or needs assessment prior to the start of the learning experience. Participants might be asked to describe themselves in terms of the issues to be covered in the course. For example, if the course is on racism, questions regarding racial identity are appropriate. Questions about expectations, particular learning needs, and previous experiences with similar courses or workshops are useful. Often, asking questions about areas of worry or concern will provide insight into the perspectives and issues participants bring.

Sometimes, it is possible to have information in advance about the participants in one's course (if they are staff members at one's institution or if an academic course has a prerequisite with which one is familiar). One can make some assessments on the basis of known demographics of an established group of participants (entering students in a geographic area, transfer students from certain schools, faculty members at a neighboring institution), although mere demographics cannot convey the personal meanings participants may attach to their age cohort, race, ethnicity, gender, sexual orientation, class, religion, ability or disability.

### Introductory Activities

We have learned always to confirm prior demographic or attitudinal assessments with information generated face-to-face during the opening segments of classes or workshops. Also, because it is often not possible to obtain critical information in advance, participants can be asked to fill out a questionnaire as an opening exercise or the facilitator can pose some questions for open discussion. Alternatively, the facilitator can engage participants in experiential exercises that bring out information about group membership. For example, during the initial module of a racism course, Beverly has used an exercise called "Common Ground" during the beginning phase of a class or workshop.

*Beverly:*    In this exercise, I ask participants to line up on one side of the room and to remain silent throughout the exercise. Before beginning, I assure them that they always have the right not to participate at any point in the exercise and can simply remain where they are or stand aside. Then, I read a series of statements and ask them to step to the other side of the room if the statement is true for them. For example, I might say, "Please step to the other side of the room if you are a woman." Those women who choose to participate cross over to the other side of the room and stand facing the remaining participants. I ask everyone to look and see who is in your group and who is not. Notice what thoughts and feelings you have as you look across the room. After people have had some time to observe who has crossed the room and who has not, those who crossed the room return to the original group. Then I read another statement, for example, "Please cross the room if you are Asian, Asian Indian, or Pacific Islander."

I may read as many as 15 or 20 social group identifications, some of which may be visibly identifiable, some of which may not be. I ask questions such as "Cross the room if you have a visible or hidden disability, or if neither parent attended college, or if you have ever been homeless, or if you have an alcoholic parent, or if you are an immigrant to this country." When no one crosses the room in response to one of the requests, the group can pause to notice. These moments are often very powerful reminders of whose voices are not represented in the class. We did this activity recently at a Catholic college, and there was no one Jewish in the room. That was a powerful statement about who's not here, so we said, please take note, and then went on to the next question. Or a person of Native American descent may cross the room by herself and it is powerful to see her standing there by herself and then move back again. When you ask for people who grew up poor, white people cross the room with people of color, but often there are still people of color who did not grow up poor standing on the other side.

Afterwards, when we process this exercise, people often talk about their surprise to see that sometimes those who crossed and those who did not fit with their expectations. It brings out one's assumptions. For example, when it comes to disabilities, sometimes people cross whose disabilities are not visible. It is a powerful, nonverbal experience. It shows, I'm not just what I look like on the outside. An opening exercise like this one, though not without risks, can quickly and powerfully bring issues for discussion to the surface, allow the group to feel a sense of intimacy, and provide valuable background information to the teacher as well as to the members of the class.

There are many other activities like this that can provide valuable information about participants. Some of these activities are public, such as the activity described above; others are more private, such as asking participants to write to the instructor.

*Maurianne:*    At the end of the first class, I give students time to write to me, telling me whatever they want me to know about themselves, such as their background or preparation for the class, their goals for themselves in this class, any worries they may have about the class, or any physical or other disabilities they want me to know about so I can adjust assignments or activities. These are confidential. Then, during the semester, I ask them to write again, telling me how they're doing, what they're struggling with, what questions or problems they have, what aspects of my teaching they find helpful, what they wish I would change. This lets me know what I need to spend more time on and what I should think about changing. I find out about the students on day 1 and keep learning more throughout the semester.

Another strategy might be to have students call out the identities that are important to them personally and begin conversations in homogeneous caucus groups.

*Beverly:*    Midway through the course, I ask people to choose an aspect of their identity they would like to talk about, and it is interesting to see that some of the women of color chose the fact of growing up poor, in which they meet with white women who have also grown up poor. Asking class members to name the identities that are important to them allows the group to decide how they are going to caucus without my imposing the important identity on them.

These activities affirm the multiple and interactive nature of social identities; they cue the instructor into the important issues for particular students; they enable paticipants to probe their own experiences and personal meanings more deeply, and they enable participants to get beyond each others' surface appearance or skin.

A variant JoAnne uses as a frame for her graduate courses invites students to meet together in generationally defined groups (those born between 1960 and 1970, between 1970 and 1980, and so on) to identify their heroes, favorite music, and memorable public events.

*JoAnne:*    It was interesting how the historic moment becomes clear and how social forces shape people's understanding of a range of things. We then walk around the room and read newsprinted presentations of what each others' generational groups have talked about and use these as metaphors and identifiers for the rest of the semester. It doesn't take much of an age range to have a powerful impact. Between 20 and 35, you have three generations; between 20 and 45, there are many worlds.

## Feedback Mechanisms throughout the Course

The small- and large-group discussions, the various ways of processing activities, and our responses to writing assignments can simultaneously serve as teaching, self-reflection, and information-generating tools. Processing can mean something as simple as asking, "How are you doing? Does this make sense to you? What was the hardest part of this activity for you? What was the easiest?"

*Beverly:*    I try to structure in some processing time at the beginning and end of classes. If it's an ongoing class, frequently other people will begin to help with that responsibility. Sometimes I'll check with people privately, and sometimes it can be helpful to do that kind of checking publicly: "I noticed that this was really upsetting for you and I wondered how you're doing with it now?"

Similarly, walking around and listening during small-group discussions is another useful way for facilitators to stay attuned to participants' thoughts, concerns, and level of understanding. We may notice feelings or questions that members of the class can then share. This information can be used as a point of departure for the next segment.

*JoAnne:*  When people are in small groups and you're moving around the room from group to group, you can listen to what's being said about what's just taken place. Sometimes I'll ask the members of group, "Do you mind if I say something about this question that came up?" Sometimes I share it in an anonymous way and say, "As I was circulating, I heard several of you talking about such and such, and this looks like an issue we need to respond to."

We can also notice how the group is coalescing and what issues are central, peripheral, or unmet. What is the learning climate of the group? Who is speaking? Who is silent? What issues are being avoided? Where is the tension? What are the strengths of the group?

We use journals or reflective writing activities as feedback and response mechanisms and to guide future sessions.

*Beverly:*  I have, in a classroom setting, required writing assignments, reflection papers, or journal writing that will be coming back to me the next time so that I have an ongoing source of information. I have used index cards on which I asked people to write down a burning question or something that has come up for them. And, have them do it anonymously. Often, people will put down a question they would be embarrassed to ask otherwise. Then, I collect the index cards, leaf through them, and read off samples. This allows me to see right away what issues or points of clarification need to be discussed and share some with the group.

A version of this activity occurred one time when it seemed as if my co-facilitator and I had been talking too much and the group was sort of dead. We were trying to think what to do. So, we distributed these index cards, and students wrote down their questions, and we read the questions to the group for the group to answer. We said, "Who thinks they can answer this question?" It got very lively! It was a very useful thing to do both in getting questions from them and, also, increasing their own participation.

Maurianne also asks participants to bring to class whatever "burning" open-ended questions (questions for which there is are simple or correct answers) they have after completing homework reading assignments. These can be used to start the next class or as questions for small-group discussions. Or, as a variation, each person's question can be passed along for one or more written responses, before reading aloud a sampling of questions and responses. This lets everyone know what the key questions are and how various participants are thinking about the same issues.

JoAnne invites visual or dramatic symbolic representations of students' experience to draw on different learning styles:

*JoAnne:*  So far, most of the feedback devices we've been talking about are paper-and-pencil or talk. I think those are excellent, and they work for some people. But, then, I think there are other media as well that can get at different ways that people express themselves, such as symbolically representing things that are happening for them. I like to use colors and papers. It also gets people physically into different configurations. They may huddle on the floor. All kinds of changes in structure will bring out different interactions, such as music or silence.

## Feedback Strategies at Various Endpoints

We also want to know what participants have learned at the end of a given class session or the end of the course. What knowledge and awareness have been gained? What questions or tensions remain? What type of support system is available to participants as they apply what they have learned?

Written statements, action plans, and presentations synthesizing a participant's learning represent various methods for assessing the impact of the course. We also ask direct questions such as "What have you learned? What has changed in your understanding of these issues? What next steps would you like to take to continue to learn about and address these issues?"

Particularly with social justice content, application to real-world contexts is an important goal for our teaching. Depending on the duration of a course, participants may choose to implement these strategies and report the results back to the class. When time is more limited, a written or verbal description of a proposed action plan helps transfer the learning from classroom to daily life (see Module 4 in Chapters 6–15, for examples).

It is important to acknowledge the obstacles inherent in confronting issues of oppression without a community of like-minded people. For some participants, there may be limited safety outside the classroom for engaging with social justice issues. A gay student may not yet be able to speak with dorm mates or family. A woman in an abusive family relationship may not be able to act upon gender politics at home. Action plans must be tempered by the real-life conditions for participants. Issues of safety, risk, comfort, and the legitimization of feelings are important to consider as the learning experience ends. Participants need to understand that as their consciousness shifts, they may experience new tensions with friends, family, or colleagues. Discussions about ways to develop an ongoing support network or to maintain whatever supportive relations have been developed within the class are often useful as the semester reaches its close.

## What Theory and Knowledge Sources Help Us Understand Our Students?

We and our colleagues have written elsewhere about the ways in which theories about learning styles, social identity, and cognitive development inform our overall curriculum, our in-the-moment facilitative judgments, and the ways we devise and respond to various writing assignments (Adams & Love, 2005; Adams & Marchesani, 1992; Adams & Zhou-McGovern, 1994; Anderson & Adams, 1992; Hardiman, 1994; Hardiman & Jackson, 1992, 1997; Marchesani & Adams, 1992; Romney, Tatum, & Jones, 1992; Tatum, 1992, 1994). The major guiding social identity, cognitive development, and learning style theories we use to anticipate and understand participant reactions to social justice subject matter are presented in this volume, Chapters 2-5. Here, we will say something of how we draw upon and use specific theories to help us better understand the participants in our social justice education classes.

## Learning Style Models

Kolb's learning style model (Kolb, 1984) helps us understand students' differing modalities for taking in new information (concrete experience or abstract conceptualization) and for processing or applying new information (reflective observation or active experimentation) (Anderson & Adams, 1992; Smith & Kolb, 1986; Svinicki & Dixon, 1987; see also Chapter 4, this volume). Maurianne informally introduces Kolb's learning style and experiential learning theory early in the semester and explains its relevance to the experiential dimensions of the course.

*Maurianne:*   I ask students to brainstorm (while I chalkboard) their various learning and study behaviors. Some prefer to study alone, take notes, and draw diagrams; others work in study groups, make telephone calls, stop by each others' dorm rooms. Some look for the big picture; others take detailed notes of the facts. I then ask about their most and least preferred teaching styles, and again their responses are wide-ranging and sometimes situationally quite specific. In these discussions, examples of all four learning styles keep coming up, so I then have students' personal examples to draw upon to illustrate the range of learning styles in the classroom, using Kolb's model.

I then talk about my two major learning style objectives for this class. First, I want to make sure that everyone's preferred learning style is matched at least some of the time (so I use Kolb's model as a checklist for my weekly instructional design), and, second, I want everyone's learning style repertoire to be stretched by trying out and developing new skills in relation to their less preferred learning styles. This gives me the transition I need to show how Kolb's experiential learning theory rests on the importance of all four learning modalities for a complete process of learning. As a result, the relatively "odd" interactive and experiential things we sometimes do in class—unusual when compared to what goes on in other classes at our large research university—make sense and are supported by an established theory of how people learn.

Other learning style models, such as Witkin's bipolar model of field sensitivity and field independence (Witkin & Moore, 1975), have been adapted to describe culturally and linguistically based learning style differences (Anderson, 1988; Cushner, McClellan, & Safford, 2006; Gay, 2000; Hale-Benson, 1986; Nieto, 2004; Ramírez & Castañeda, 1974; Shade, 1989) and to differentiate connected and separate learning styles in relation to socialized gender differences (Belenky, Clinchy, Goldberger, & Tarule, 1986; Lyons, 1983). Learning style models help facilitators to acknowledge and understand that intergroup learning style differences are not deficits for one group and indices of superiority for another. We learn to respect cultural and linguistic as well as individual learning style differences, and to recognize their existence within groups as well as among groups (Anderson & Adams, 1992; Shade, 1989). At the same time, we try to avoid any tendency to restereotype our students through the uncritical, careless, or simplistic application of learning style templates (Tharp, 1989).

As facilitators, we also use the various learning style models as self-correcting devices to call attention to learning style limits in our own instructional designs, and to remind us to plan curricular and facilitative strategies that both match and stretch the variety of learners in our classes.

## Social Identity Development Models

Social identity development models (Cross, 1991; Hardiman & Jackson, 1992, 1997; Helms, 1990; Jackson, 2001; Tatum, 1992) provide road maps for participants as they grapple with who they and others are in relation to racism, sexism, heterosexism, and other forms of oppression (discussed in Chapter 2, this volume). The social identity models prove especially helpful for understanding the various ways in which the anger, denial, or pain evoked by social justice subject matter may be expressed by participants and felt by ourselves as facilitators (see Cross, 1995; Hardiman & Jackson, 1992, 1997; Tatum, 1992).

*Beverly:*    If you're talking about race, some white students will feel guilty and will wonder whether they are bad people, and what does living in a racist society mean for who they are? Some students of color will feel angry or agitated because of an increased awareness of victimization. They express impatience with slow progress on obvious problems. The clash of their anger and the white students' guilt is predictable. Both groups of students reach a saturation point where they don't want to hear about racism any more. It feels too overwhelming. They pull back, avoid coming to class perhaps, or don't complete the reading assignments.

For me, I need to know, *Is it happening yet?* I have strategies in place to address these issues. I forewarn people that these things are likely to happen. My experience has been that telling people ahead of time is a helpful thing to do. Sometimes, students will tell me, "Oh, that thing you said would happen, is happening now."

It helps to remember that participants in our classes are likely to have different understandings of racism, sexism, and other social identities, depending in part on their levels of identity development with relation to specific social justice topics and on their identity status, that is, whether their identities are advantaged or targeted. The Jackson-Hardiman social identity development model (reprinted this volume Appendix 2A; 1992, 1997) provides a valuable tool for anticipating and understanding these different between-group and within-group social identity perspectives. For example, we note different perspectives among men or women of color on topics in racism and among men and women of color on sexism, which derive in part from their different life experiences and in part from the lens or filters on their experiences created by their social identity development locations. These perspectives expand and become more multifaceted as they learn more, for example, in the context of these courses. This expansion is itself a developmental process. The social identity development models help us anticipate and plan for the potential collision in the classroom of contradictory but strongly held worldviews among participants across social identity groups and also within social identity groups. As with the learning style models, these social identity development models also serve to remind us as facilitators that we, too, have our own social identity perspectives that both characterize and limit our worldviews and from which we tend to generalize what we believe that participants in our courses ought to do, feel, and think.

### Cognitive Development Models

Social cognitive theory (Belenky, Clinchy, Goldberger, & Tarule, 1986; Perry, 1981) helps facilitators anticipate the tendency of many participants who are new to social justice course content to dichotomize complex questions, reduce multiple perspectives to simple either/or choices, or not see relations between concrete examples of personal experience and broader theoretical principles. Another cognitive development indicator is whether participants are willing to listen to one another as sources of knowledge rather than insisting that the facilitator be the classroom authority. With these concerns in mind, we as facilitators attempt to moderate the sources of complexity and contradiction by emphasizing one issue, one perspective, or one theoretical construct at a time. We start with the concrete, personal, and experiential before moving to the abstract and conceptual, and process the sources of contradiction and conceptual confusion. For example, rather than starting out with the notion of multiple identities, we gradually and incrementally build multiple perspectives as a semester-long enterprise (Adams & Marchesani, 1992; Adams & Zhou-McGovern, 1994).

For dualistic thinkers, our authority as facilitators can be used to support new and more complex modes of thinking.

*Maurianne:* I use my authority to model respect and appreciation for peer perspectives as a valid source of knowledge about social diversity. Gradually, over a semester, authority and leadership are taken over by students in the class. Initially, however, I have found that if I don't use my authority, there is a power vacuum that leads to many lost learning opportunities. The more complex thinkers seem readier to pick up different perspectives from a range of sources, including other students.

## What Do We Want Students to Know about Themselves and about Each Other?

### Multiple Identities

One limitation of social identity models is the tendency to describe social identities as if they existed in equally weighted either/or categories: male/female, Jewish/Gentile, people of color/white. These binary categories obscure the complex identities experienced by biracial, bisexual, and multiethnic people, and oversimplify the interactions in all people among their own multiple social identities, and in many cases, their different advantaged or targeted social identity statuses. Further, a participant is often more conscious of his or her target identities than advantaged identities.

*Beverly:* One of the most important things I want students to know about themselves is that they are both advantaged and targeted. Almost everybody can think of themselves in both these ways, although they tend not to. So, in a course on racism, students of color tend to think of themselves as victimized by racism and white students as unwitting agents of oppression. For students in the advantaged group, whatever that area of advantage is, one of the things I want them to become aware of is the power they have to reconceptualize their area of advantage as victimizer into being one of ally, someone who has the power to interrupt racist or sexist or antisemitic acts, for example. Similarly, students who think of themselves primarily as victims need to reconceptualize their target area into one of empowerment, taking pride in that aspect of their identity.

But this leads to multiple identities as well. For instance, there are areas of privilege unacknowledged by students who feel victimized by race. The black male student needs to be aware of his sexism, the Latina woman of her dominance as a Christian perhaps, the heterosexual black woman of the privilege she has because of her sexual orientation.

We have met participants for whom membership in targeted groups seems preferable, almost a badge of honor. For them, it seems more desirable and socially acceptable to be a "victim" than to be an agent of oppression in order to avoid the guilt, pain, and responsibility of advantaged-group status. Participants who do acknowledge their membership in a advantaged group often struggle not to be reduced to a stereotype in other people's eyes. Facilitators need to be understanding and help participants recognize and name these feelings as part of their learning process.

Participants who experience themselves exclusively through their targeted identities may be newly grappling with personal experiences of discrimination and oppression for the first time, and unable to explore other aspects of their identity. They may never before have questioned accepted ways of thinking and find it conceptually difficult to balance the many layers of a complex issue, especially when those layers have deeply personal and sometimes contradictory meanings.

*Maurianne:*  One of my students, a Jamaican American man, was vehemently and openly sexist and homophobic, as well as believing the derogatory stereotypes about Jews to be factually based and true. As a black man, he didn't see how race and gender could possibly be disentangled. But gradually, by associating gender issues with his mother and grandmother, both of whom he admired, he was able to wonder whether sexism had affected them as women. He also learned a lot from interviews he conducted with black women about their experiences of sexism.

This man's homophobia came from his church minister, a man whom he credited with saving him from the streets. As part of his classroom learning, he agreed to try to separate his beliefs (about homosexuality) from his behavior (toward gay, lesbian, or bisexual students), and to change his "unfair" behavior toward gays, lesbians, and bisexuals, especially since he hoped to be hired as a residence assistant in student residence halls. As a residence assistant, he knew that he would have to treat *all* people fairly.

His breakthrough on antisemitism came after a long segment on Jewish history, highlighted by the films *Genocide* and *Courage to Care*. He told the class that he now understood that not all white folks had the same history or life chances. This breakup of a single concept, "all white folks," was powerful for him. By my not pushing too hard, this young man begin to disentangle for himself a set of beliefs that had been based on personal experiences of racism, revered authorities, and efforts to survive.

## The Challenge of Inclusivity

The challenge of inclusivity refers to finding ways that enable each participant to feel safe while on a learning edge as part of a classroom community, without diminishing the reality of the rage, fear, and shame.

*Beverly:*  After we had done the "Common Ground" activity and were processing it, a white mother of biracial children explained that she didn't cross when I asked for people of racially mixed heritage, because the question was about parentage, although she wanted to cross because she had African American children. The next time we used the exercise, we added, "If you are a member of a multiracial family, please cross the room." This would have included her experience.

Making it possible for participants to speak up about our unintentional omissions provides opportunities to fill in missing information.

A common example of inclusivity occurs when white participants say, "I have no culture," and attempt to find something in their background that will afford them "victim status." Maurianne offers the example of a white, heterosexual man who recently discovered a fraction of Native American ancestry and wanted to focus on exploring this racial heritage rather than his white privilege. Although it may be important that he explore a distant Native American ancestry, it is more important in the social justice curricular context that he explore his advantaged identities and recognize his corresponding privileges. Only in this way might he be able to understand the hostility felt by other participants who struggle with their target identities on a daily basis.

## What Do Students Need to Know About Us and Our Own Struggles With Social Justice Issues?

In conversations that led to this chapter, we could not separate our discussion about knowing the participants in our classes and workshops from the need to understand ourselves as facilitators. This raised the related question, "What do participants need to know about us?" The amount, context, and nature of personal information that we disclose are matters of judgment in planning or in the moment. We believe that particularly in the early moments of a course, important modeling takes place. Self-disclosure may seem unusual to many participants, especially in an academic climate. We try to make the relation of our own self-disclosure to the topic under discussion clear. We offer our own experience with both advantaged and targeted identities as a way to join with participants, expand the boundaries for discussing these subjects, and model how such discussions can happen. For example, Beverly usually describes herself sometime during the first session as an able-bodied, African American, heterosexual, Christian female, raised in a middle-class family. She talks about the fact that she is targeted by racism and sexism because she is a black female, but she also acknowledges her struggle to become aware of the daily privileges she receives as a heterosexual, as a Christian, as an able-bodied person, and with the education she received as the result of her middle-class status. In this way, she establishes connections with participants whose primary identification may be with a targeted or advantaged group, and encourages her students to consider the range of positions of privilege and marginality they occupy in relation to others.

Beverly:   In a recent workshop, I noticed a number of highly verbal black men who talked a lot about racism but interrupted the women all the time. I said we need to look at our ally behavior not only in relation to racism but also to sexism, and I referred to my previous impatience with white people around not understanding white privilege. How can you not notice that? I got less impatient when I became aware of how ignorant or unobservant I was about my heterosexual privilege. Recognizing my own learning process regarding heterosexual privilege helped me be more generous in terms of my understanding of the way white people can struggle around understanding white privilege, or black men can struggle around their sexism.

Maurianne recounts how she talks with her students about her efforts to disentangle her Jewish identity and her white privilege in ways that feel honest and authentic. She does this to help all her students think about their ethnic family histories in relation to race and to help Jewish students balance their conscious experience as targets of antisemitism with their largely unconscious assumptions about white privilege.

*Maurianne:*   One of my challenges in class is to talk about how I grew up thinking of Jews as a race, partly because of my ancestry in Europe where Jews were stigmatized racially. But I also talk about how I had "passed" as a non-Jew, by ignoring that aspect of my identity and assuming that Jews, like other white ethnic groups, could assimilate if we worked hard and ignored our differences.

This is obviously not a strategy that works for people of color. Acknowledging my personal struggle with these issues, and talking about the similarities and differences among differently racialized ethnic groups in different historical contexts, shows how my own analysis was reshaped over many years to fit my emerging understanding of my experience as a Jew and as a white woman. It's often easier for participants to acknowledge their racial privilege, as Whites in this society, if we've already acknowledged where they and their families may have been targeted due to social class, ethnicity, religion, or sexual orientation.

This chapter is about the importance of knowing the participants in our social justice education classes. We identify such needs as knowing how students are processing and making sense of social justice information, and how they are relating to each other and the instructor. We close this chapter with the acknowledgment that social diversity and social justice education involves journeying into life experiences that are often fraught with fear, suspicion, lies, and shame. Questions that may seem innocuous, such as "List your strengths" or "Describe your social identities," can pose a crisis to a participant. To know the participants in our classes means to maintain an attitude of respectful awe at the range, diversity, and elasticity of human experience.

# References

Abbott, S., & Love, B. (1973). *Sappho was a right-on woman: A liberated view of lesbianism*. New York: Stein & Day.

Abdelkarim, R. Z. (2003). Surge in hate crimes followed by official U.S. targeting of Muslim, Arab men. Retrieved July 21, 2005, from http://www.washington-report/archives/April03/030.

About Not Dead Yet and the resistance. (2006). Retrieved September 2, 2006, from http://www.notdeadyet.org.

Abrams, D., & Hogg, M. A. (Eds.). (1990). *Social identity theory: Constructive and critical advances*. New York: Springer-Verlag.

Adams (2001). Core processes of racial identity development. In C. Wijeyesinghe & B. W. Jackson (Eds.), *New perspectives on racial identity development: A theoretical and practical anthology* (pp. 209-242). New York: New York University Press.

Adams, M. (Ed.). (1992). *Promoting diversity in college classrooms: Innovative responses for the curriculum, faculty, and institutions* (New Directions for Teaching and Learning, No. 52). San Francisco: Jossey-Bass.

Adams, M., Abraham, S., Burrell, S., & Whitlock, E. (2003). Review of the year's publications for 2002: Social justice education. *Equity & Excellence in Education, 36*(4), 285-299.

Adams, M., Allen, S. D., Runell, M., Varghese, R., Whitlock, E., & Williams, T. (2004). Review of the year's publications for 2003: Social justice education. *Equity & Excellence in Education, 37*(4), 360-376.

Adams, M., Bell, L. A., & Griffin, P. (Eds.). (1997). *Teaching for diversity and social justice: A sourcebook*. New York: Routledge.

Adams, M., Blumenfeld, W., Castañeda, R., Hackman, H., Peters, M., & Zúñiga, X. (2000). *Readings for diversity and social justice*. New York: Routledge.

Adams, M., & Bracey, J. (Eds.). (1999). *Strangers & neighbors: Relations between Blacks & Jews in the United States*. Amherst: University of Massachusetts Press.

Adams, M., Briggs, R. R., Catalano. D. C., Núñez, J., Wagner, R., & Whitlock, E. R. (2006). Review of the year's publications for 2005: Social justice education. *Equity & Excellence in Education, 39*(4), 345-361.

Adams, M., Briggs, R. R., Catalano. D. C., Whitlock, E. R., & Williams, T. (2005). Review of the year's publications for 2004: Social justice education. *Equity & Excellence in Education, 38*(4), 342-366.

Adams, M., & Love, B. J. (2005). Teaching with a social justice perspective: A model for faculty seminars across academic disciplines. In M. L. Ouellett (Ed.), *Teaching inclusively: Resources for course, department & institutional change in higher education* (pp. 586-620). Stillwater, OK: New Forums.

Adams, M., & Marchesani, L. S. (1992). Curricular innovations: Social diversity as course content. In M. Adams (Ed.), *Promoting diversity in college classrooms: Innovative responses for the curriculum, faculty, and institutions* (New Directions for Teaching and Learning, No. 52, pp. 85–98). San Francisco: Jossey-Bass.

Adams, M., & Zhou-McGovern, A. (1994, April). *The sociomoral development of undergraduates in a "social diversity" course: Developmental theory, research, and instructional applications.* Paper presented at the American Educational Research Association annual meeting, New Orleans, LA. (ERIC # ED 443 739)

Advancement Project and the Civil Rights Project, Harvard University. (2000). *Opportunities suspended: The devastating consequences of zero tolerance and school discipline policies, a report from a national summit on zero tolerance, June 15–16, 2000.* Washington, DC, and Cambridge, MA: Author.

Afridi, S. (2001). *Muslims in America: Identity, diversity, and the challenge of understanding.* New York: Carnegie Corporation of New York.

Aguilar, T., & Washington, S. (1990). Towards an inclusion of multicultural issues in leisure studies curricula. *Schole: A Journal of Leisure Studies and Recreation Education, 5,* 41–52.

Ahlquist, R. (1991). Position and imposition: Power relations in a multicultural foundations class. *Journal of Negro Education, 60,* 158–169.

Ahlstrom, S. E. (2004). *A religious history of the American people* (2nd ed.). New Haven, CT: Yale University Press.

Alamillo, L., Palmer, D., Viramontes, C. & Garcia, E. G. (2005). California's English-only policies: An analysis of initial effects. In A. Valenzuela (Ed.), *Leaving children behind: How "Texas-style" accountability fails Latino youth.* Albany: State University of New York Press.

Albanese, C. L. (1999). *America: Religions and religion* (3rd ed.). Belmont, CA: Wadsworth.

Albrecht, L., & Brewer, R. M. (1990). *Bridges of power: Women's multicultural alliances.* Philadelphia: New Society Press.

Allen, A. (2005). Portray me in silence: Teaching for justice. In R. A. Pena, K. Guest, & L. Y. Matsuda (Eds.), *Community and difference: Teaching, pluralism, and social justice* (pp. 77–108). New York: Peter Lang.

Almaguer, T. (1994). *Racial fault lines: The historical origins of white supremacy in California.* Berkeley: University of California Press.

Altman, D. (1973). *Homosexual: Oppression and liberation.* New York: Avon.

American Council on Education. (1949). *Intergroup relations in teaching materials: A survey and appraisal.* Washington, DC: American Council on Education.

Americans with Disabilities Act of 1990. 42 U.S.C. §12101 *et. seq.*

Amir, Y. (1969). Contact hypothesis in ethnic relations. *Psychological Bulletin, 71,* 319–342.

Anderson, J. (1988). Cognitive styles and multicultural populations. *Journal of Teacher Education, 39* (1), 2–9.

Anderson, J., & Adams, M. (1992). Acknowledging the learning styles of diverse student populations: Implications for instructional design. In L. L. B. Border & N. V. N. Chism (Eds.), *Teaching for diversity* (New Directions for Teaching and Learning, No. 49, pp. 19–33). San Francisco: Jossey-Bass.

Anderson, S., Cavanagh, J., Lee, T., & The Institute for Policy Studies (2000). *Field guide to the global economy* (Revised & updated). New York: New Press.

Anti-Defamation League. (2004). *Religion in the public schools.* Retrieved September 4, 2006, from http://www.adl.org/religion_ps_2004/.

Antonio, A. L., Chang, M. J., Hakuta, K., Kenny, D. A., Levin, S., & Milem, J. F. (2004). Effects of racial diversity on complex thinking in college students. *American Psychological Society, 15*(8), 507–510.

Anzaldúa, G. (1987). *Borderlands/La frontera: The new mestiza.* San Francisco: Aunt Lute Books.

Aptheker, H. (1993). *Anti-racism in U.S. history: The first 200 years.* Westport, CT: Praeger.

Argyris, C. (1970). *Intervention theory & method: A behavioral science view.* Reading, MA: Addison-Wesley.

Argyris, C. (1975). Dangers in applying results from experimental social psychology. *American Psychologist, 30*(4), 469–485.

Arnold, M. S. (1993, October). *Breaking the pot: Melting student resistance to pluralism in counseling programs.* Paper presented at the Association for Counselor Education and Supervision annual meeting, San Antonio, TX.

Arnold, R., Burke, B. James, C., D'Arcy, M., & Thomas, B. (1991). *Educating for a change.* Toronto: Between the Lines and the Doris Marshall Institute for Education and Action.

Asahina, R. (2006). *Just Americans: How Japanese Americans won a war at home and abroad: The story of the 100th Battalion/442d Regimental Combat Team in World War II.* New York: Gotham.

Astin, A. W. (2003). *What matters in college: Four critical years revisited.* San Francisco: Jossey-Bass.

Auvine, B., Densmore, B., Extrom, M., Poole, S., & Shanklin, M. (1978). *A manual for group facilitators.* Madison, WI: Center for Conflict Resolution.

Axtell, J. (1985). *The invasion within: The contest of cultures in colonial North America.* New York: Oxford University Press.

Ayers, W., Hunt, J. A., & Quinn, T. (1998). *Teaching for social justice: A democracy and education reader.* New York: New Press.

Bagdikian, B. H. (2004). *The new media monopoly.* Boston: Beacon Press.

Bakhtin, M. (1981). *The dialogic imagination.* Austin: University of Texas Press.

Balka, C., & Rose, A. (Eds.). (1989). *Twice blessed: On being lesbian, gay, and Jewish.* Boston: Beacon Press.

Banks, J. A. (1996). The African American roots of multicultural education. In *Multicultural education, transformative knowledge, and action: Historical and contemporary perspectives* (pp. 30–45). New York: Teachers College Press.

Banks, J. A. (1991). *Teaching strategies for ethnic studies.* 5ᵗʰ edition. Boston: Allyn & Bacon.

Banks, J. A., & Banks, C. A. M. (Eds.). (1995). *Handbook of research on multicultural education.* New York: Macmillan.

Bargad, A., & Hyde, J. S. (1991). Women's studies: A study of feminist identity development in women. *Psychology of Women Quarterly, 15,* 181–210.

Barker, P. (1993). *Regeneration.* New York: Plume.

Barkun, M. (2004). Religious violence and the myth of fundamentalism. In L. Weinberg, & A. Pedahzur (Eds.), *Religious fundamentalism and political extremism* (pp. 55–70). London: Frank Cass.

Barlow, A. L. (2003). *Between fear & hope: Globalization and race in the United States.* Lanham, MD: Rowman & Littlefield.

Batchelder, D., & Warner, E. G. (Eds.). (1977). *Beyond experience: The experiential approach to cross-cultural education.* Brattleboro, VT: Experiment Press.

Baxter-Magolda, M. B. (1992). *Knowing and reasoning in college: Gender-related patterns in students' intellectual development.* San Francisco: Jossey-Bass.

Baylor Religion Study (2006). *American piety in the 21st century: New insights to the depth and complexity of religion in the United States.* Baylor Institute for Studies of Religion. www.bylor.edu/religion

Bazin, M., Tamez, M., & the Exploratorium Teacher Institute. (2002). *Math and science across cultures: Activities and investigations from the exploratorium.* New York: New Press.

Beaman, L. G. (2002). Aboriginal spirituality and the legal construction of freedom of religion. *Journal of Church and State, 44*(1), 135–149.

Belenky, M. F., Clinchy, M. B., Goldberger, N. R., & Tarule, J. M. (1986). *Women's ways of knowing: The development of self, voice, and mind.* New York: Basic Books.

Bell, D. (1987). *And we are not saved: The elusive quest for racial justice.* New York: Basic Books.

Bell, D. (1992a). *Faces at the bottom of the well: The permanence of racism.* New York: Basic Books.

Bell, D. (1992b). *Race, racism, and American law* (3rd ed.). Boston: Little, Brown.

Bell, D. (2004). *Silent covenants:* Brown v. Board of Education *and the unfulfilled hopes for racial reform.* New York: Oxford University Press.

Bell, J. (2000). Understanding adultism: A key to developing positive youth–adult relationships. Retrieved June 20, 2006, from http://freechild.org/bell.htm.

Bell, L. A. (1990). Changing our ideas about ourselves: Group consciousness raising with elementary school girls as a means to empowerment. In Christine Sleeter (Ed.) *Empowerment through multicultural education.* NY: SUNY Press.

Bell, L. A. (1990). The gifted woman as imposter. *Advanced Development, 2,* 55–64.

Bell, L. A. (2003a). Sincere fictions: The challenges of preparing White teachers for diverse classrooms. *Equity and Excellence in Education, 35*(3), 236–245.

Bell, L. A. (2003b). Telling tales: What stories can teach us about racism. *Race Ethnicity and Education, 6*(1), 8–25.

Bell, L. A., & Roberts, R. A. (Unpublished manuscript). The storytelling project: Teaching about race and racism through storytelling and the arts.

Bell, L. A., & Schniedewind, N. (1987). Reflective minds, intentional hearts: Joining humanistic education and critical theory for liberating education. *Journal of Education, 169*(2), 55–77.

Bell, M. (1995). What constitutes experience? Rethinking theoretical assumptions. In R. J. Kraft & J. Kielsmeier (Eds.), *Experiential learning in schools and higher education* (pp. 9–17). Dubuque, IA: Kendall/Hunt.

Bellah, R. N. (1967). Civil religion in America. *Daedalus, 134*(4), 40–55.

Bellah, R. N. (1970). Civil religion in America. In *Beyond belief: Essays on religion in a post-traditional world* (pp. 168–189). New York: Harper & Row.

Benjamin, H. (1966/1977). *The transsexual phenomenon.* New York: Warner Books.

Benne, K. D. (1964). History of the T-Group in the laboratory setting. In L. P. Bradord, J. Gibb, and K. D. Benne (Eds.), *T-Group theory and laboratory method: Innovation in re-education* (pp. 80–136). New York: John Wiley.

Bennett, J.M. (2006) *History matters: Patriarchy and the challenge of feminism.* Philadelphia: University of Pennsylvania Press.

Berlak, A., & Moyenda, S. (2001). *Taking it personally: Racism in the classroom from kindergarten to college.* Philadelphia: Temple University Press.

Berlin, I. (1998). *Many thousands gone: The first two centuries of slavery in North America.* Cambridge, MA: Harvard University Press.

Biale, D., Galchinsky, M., & Heschel, S. (Ed.). (1998). *Insider/outsider: American Jews and multiculturalism.* Berkeley: University of California Press.

Bidell, T. R., Lee, E. M., Bouchie, N., Ward, C., & Brass, D. (1994). Developing conceptions of racism among young white adults in the context of cultural diversity
coursework. *Journal of Adult Development, 1*(3), 185–200.

Bigelow, B. (2006). *The line between us: Teaching about the border and Mexican immigration*. Milwaukee, WI: Rethinking Schools.

Block, G., & Drucker, M. (1987). *Rescuers: Portraits of moral courage in the Holocaust*.
New York: Holmes & Meier.

Blood, P., Tuttle, A., & Lakey, G. (1983). Understanding and fighting sexism: A call to me.
In P. Blood., A. Tuttle, and G. Lakey (Eds.), *Off their backs ... and on our own two
feet* (pp. 1–16). Philadelphia: New Society.

Bloom, B. S. (Ed.). (1956). *Taxonomy of educational objectives: Vol. 1. Cognitive domain*.
New York: McKay.

Blum, E. J. (2005). *Reforging the white republic: Race, religion and American nationalism, 1865–1898*. Baton Rouge: University of Louisiana Press.

Blumenfeld, W. J. (2006). Christian privilege and the promotion of "secular" and not-
so-"secular" mainline Christianity in public schooling and in the larger society.
*Equity & Excellence in Education*, (3), 195–210.

Boal, A. (1985). *Theater of the oppressed* (C. A. McBridge & M-O. L. McBridge, Trans.).
New York: Theatre Communications Group.

Boal, A. (1992). *Games for actors and non-actors* (A. Jackson, Trans.). New York: Routledge.

Bochenek, M., & Brown, A. W. (2001). *Hatred in the hallways: Violence and discrimination against gay, lesbian, bisexual, and transgender students in U.S. schools*. New
York: Human Rights Watch.

Bockting, W. O. (1997). Transgender coming out: Implications for the clinical management of gender dysphoria. In B. Bullough, V. Bullough, & J. Elias (Eds.), *Gender
blending* (pp. 48–52). Amherst, NY: Prometheus Books.

Bogle, D. (2001). *Toons, coons, mulattoes, mammies and bucks: An interpretive history of
Blacks in American film*. New York: Continuum.

Bolgatz, J. (2005). *Talking race in the classroom*. New York: Teachers College Press.

Bolin, A. (1997). Transforming transvestism and transsexualism: Polarity, politics, and
gender. In B. Bullough, V. Bullough, & J. Elias (Eds.), *Gender blending* (pps. 25–32).
Amherst, NY: Prometheus Books.

Bonilla-Silva, E. (2003). *Racism without racists: Color blind racism and the persistence of
inequality in the United States*. Lanham, MD: Rowman & Littlefield.

Boonstra, J., Jansen, H., & Kniesmeyer, J. (1993). *Antisemitism: A history portrayed* (2nd
rev. ed.). 's-Gravenhage, Holland: SDU Uitgeverij Knoninginnegracht.

Bornstein, K. (1994). *Gender outlaw: On men, women and the rest of us*. New York:
Routledge.

Borton, T. (1970). *Reach, touch, and teach*. New York: McGraw-Hill.

Bourdieu, P. (1986). The forms of capital. In J. Richardson (Ed.), *Handbook of theory and
research for the sociology of education*. New York: Greenwood Press.

Bourdieu, P., & Passeron, J-C. (1977). *Reproduction in education, society and culture*.
Thousand Oaks, CA: Sage.

Bourke, A., Strehorn, K. C., & Silver, P. (2000). Faculty members' provision of instructional accommodations to students with learning disabilities. *Journal of Learning
Disabilities, 33*(1), 26–32.

Bowles, S., & Gintis, H. (1987). *Democracy and capitalism: Property, community, and the
contradictions of modern social thought*. New York: Basic Books.

Bowser, B., & Hunt, R. G. (Eds.). (1981). *Impacts of racism on white Americans*. Beverly
Hills, CA: Sage.

Boykin, K. (1996). *One more river to cross: Black and gay in America*. New York: Anchor Books/Doubleday.

Boys, M. C. (2004, Summer). "I didn't see any anti-Semitism": Why many Christians don't have a problem with *The passion of the Christ. Cross Currents*, 8–15.

Braden, A. (1999). *The wall between* (2nd ed., with new epilogue). Knoxville, TN: The University of Tennessee Press.

Bradford, L. P., Gibb, J. R., & Benne, K. D. (Eds.). (1964). *T-Group theory and laboratory method: Innovation in re-education*. New York: John Wiley.

Branco, K. J., & Williamson, J. B. (1982). Stereotyping and the life cycle: Views of aging and the aged. In A. G. Miller (Ed.), *In the eye of the beholder: Contemporary issues in stereotyping* (pp. 364–410). New York: Praeger.

Brandt, E. (Ed.). (1999). *Dangerous liaisons: Blacks & gays and the struggle for equality*. New York: New Press, dist. by Norton.

Brantlinger, E. (2003). *Dividing classes: How the middle class negotiates and rationalizes school advantage*. New York: RoutledgeFalmer.

Brettschneider, M. (Ed.). (1996). *The narrow bridge: Jewish views on multiculturalism*. New Brunswick, NJ: Rutgers University Press.

Brewer, M. B., & Brown, R. J. (1998). Intergroup relations. In D. T. Gilbert, S. T. Fiske, & G. Lindzey (Eds.), *The handbook of social psychology* (Vol. 2, 4th ed., pp. 554–594). Boston: McGraw-Hill.

Bricker-Jenkins, M., & Hooyman, N. (1986). Feminist pedagogy in education for social change. *Feminist Teacher, 2*(2), 36–42.

Briggs, M. (Ed.). (1995, September). *Connections, 1* (6), 2. Washington, DC: Alliance for a Global Community.

Brodkin, K. (1998). *How Jews became white folks and what that says about race in America*. Brunswick, NJ: Rutgers University Press.

Brodkin Sacks, K. (1994). How did Jews become white folks? In S. Gregory & R. Sanjek (Eds.), *Race* (pp. 78–101). New Brunswick, NJ: Rutgers University Press.

Bronner, S. E. (2000). *A rumor about the Jews: Antisemitism, conspiracy, and the Protocols of Zion*. New York: Oxford University Press.

Brooks-Harris, J., & Stock-Ward, S. (1999). *Workshops: Defining and facilitating experiential learning*. Thousand Oaks, CA: Sage.

Brown, M. K. (2003). *Whitewashing race*. Berkeley: University of California Press.

Brugge, D. (2006). *The anti-immigrant backlash*. Retrieved September 3, 2006, from http://www.publiceye.org/magazine/v09n2/immigran.html.

Bunch, C., & Powell, B. (1983). Charlotte Bunch and Betty Powell talk about feminism, Blacks and education as politics. In C. Bunch & S. Pollack (Eds.), *Learning our way: Essays in feminist education* (pp. 302–317). Trumansburg, NY: Crossing Press.

Bureau of Labor Statistics. (2006). Union members in 2005. Retrieved September 6, 2006, from http://www.bls.gov/news.release/union2.nr0.htm.

Burke, P. (1997). *Gender shock*. New York: Anchor.

Butler, J. (1990). *Gender trouble: Feminism and the subversion of identity*. New York: Routledge.

Butler, J. (2004). *Undoing gender*. London: Taylor & Francis.

Butler, J., Wacker, G., & Balmer, R. (2003). *Religion in American life: A short history*. New York: Oxford University Press.

Butler, J. E. (1985). Toward a pedagogy of Everywoman's Studies. In M. Culley & C. Portuges (Eds.), *Gendered subjects: The dynamics of feminist teaching* (pp. 230–240). Boston: Routledge & Kegan Paul.

Butler, J. E. (1989). Transforming the curriculum: Teaching about women of color. In J. A. Banks & C. A. M. Banks (Eds.), *Multicultural education: Issues and perspectives* (pp. 145–163). Boston: Allyn & Bacon.

Butler, R. N. (1969). Age-ism: Another form of bigotry. *Gerontologist, 9*, 243–246.

Butler, R. N. (1975). *Why survive? Being old in America.* New York: Harper & Row.

Calasanti, T. M., & Slevin, K. F. (2001). *Gender, social inequalities and aging.* Walnut Creek, CA: AltaMira Press.

Califia, P. (1997). *Sex changes: The politics of transgenderism.* San Francisco: Cleis Press.

California Newsreel. (2003a). California Newsreel. Retrieved October 30, 2006, from http://www.newsreel.org.

California Newsreel. (2003b). *Race: The power of an illusion.* Retrieved October 30, 2006, from http://www.newsreel.org/nav/title.asp?tc=CN0149.

Campaign for Fiscal Equity. (N.d.). CFE news. Retrieved October 29, 2006, from http://www.cfequity.org.

Canadian Broadcasting Corporation. (1987). *Old like me* [Video]. New York: Filmmakers Library.

Cannon, L. W. (1990). Fostering positive race, class and gender dynamics in the classroom. *Women's Studies Quarterly, 18*(1–2), 126–134.

Carew, D., Carew, E., & Blanchard, K. (1990). *Group development and situational leadership II: The color model.* Escondido, CA: Blanchard Training and Development.

Carey, K. (2004). *The funding gap 2004: Many states still shortchange low-income and minority students.* New York: Education Trust.

Carlisle, L. R., Jackson, B. W., & George, A. (2006). Principles of social justice education: The social justice education in schools project. *Equity & Excellence in Education, 39*(1), 55–64.

Carnes, T., & Yang, F. (2004). *Asian American religions: The making and remaking of borders and boundaries.* New York: New York University Press.

Carroll, B. E. (2000). *The Routledge historical atlas of religion in America.* New York: Routledge.

Cashin, S. (2005). *The failures of integration: How race and class are undermining the American dream.* New York: Perseus.

Cass, V. C. (1996). Sexual orientation identity formation: A western phenomenon. In R. P. Cabaj & T. S. Stein (Eds.), *Textbook of homosexuality and mental health.* Washington, DC: American Psychiatric Press.

Cavanagh, J., Mander, J., Anderson, S., & Barker, D. (2002). *Alternatives to economic globalization.* San Francisco: Barrett-Koehler.

Center on Crime, Communities & Culture. (1997, September). Education as crime prevention (Center on Crime, Communities & Culture Research Brief, Occasional Paper Series, No. 2). : New York: Open Society Institute.

Chacon, J. A., & Davis, M. (2006). *No one is illegal: Fighting racism and state violence on the U.S.–Mexico border.* Chicago: Haymarket Books.

Chaffee, C. C. (1978). Cross-cultural training for Peace Corps volunteers. In D. S. Hoopes, P. B. Pedersen, & G. W. Renwick (Eds.), *Overview of intercultural education, training, and research: Vol. 4. Education and training* (pp. 104–126). Washington, DC: Society for Intercultural Education, Training, and Research (SIETAR).

Chan, C. S. (1995). Issues of sexual identity in an ethnic minority: The case of Chinese American lesbians, gay men, and bisexual people. In A. R. D'Augelli & C. J. Patterson (Eds.), *Lesbian, gay, and bisexual identities over the lifespan: Psychological perspectives* (pp. 87–100). New York: Oxford University Press.

Chang, M. J., Hakuta, K., & Jones, J. (2002). *Compelling interest: Examining the evidence on racial dynamics in colleges and universities.* Palo Alto, CA: Stanford University Press.

Charlton, J. (2000). *Nothing about us without us.* Berkeley: University of California Press.

Cherry, C. (Ed.). (1971). *God's new Israel: Religious interpretations of American destiny.* Englewood Cliffs, NJ: Prentice Hall.

Chesler, M., Lewis, A. E., & Crowfoot, J. E. (2005). *Challenging racism in higher education: Promoting justice.* New York: Rowman & Littlefield.

Chickering, A. K., & Gamson, Z. (1987). Seven principles of good practice. *AAHE Bulletin, 39,* 3–7.

Ching Yoon Louie, M. (2001). *Sweatshop warriors: Immigrant women workers take on the global factory.* Boston: South End Press.

Cho, H. E., Paz y Puente, F. A., Ching Yoon Louie, M., & Khokha, S. (2004). *Bridge: Building a race and immigration dialogue in the global economy.* Oakland, CA: National Network for Immigrant and Refugee Rights.

Chodorow, N. (1978). *The reproduction of mothering: Psychoanalysis and the sociology of gender.* Berkeley: University of California Press.

Christensen, L. (2000). *Reading, writing and rising up.* Milwaukee, WI: Rethinking Schools.

Churchill, W. (1995). *Since predator came: Notes from the struggle for American Indian liberation.* Littleton, CO: Aigis.

Clark, C., Brimhall-Vargas, M., Schlosser, L. Z., & Alimo, C. (2002, Winter). It's not just "secret Santa" in December: Addressing educational and workplace climate issues linked to Christian privilege. *Multicultural Education,* 52–57.

Clinchy, B. M. (1993). Ways of knowing and ways of being: Epistemological and moral development in undergraduate women. In A. Garrod (Ed.), *Approaches to moral development: New research and emerging themes* (pp. 180–201). New York: Teachers College Press.

Coch, L., & French, J. R. P., Jr. (1948). Overcoming resistance to change. *Human Relations, 1*(4), 512–532.

Cochran-Smith, M. (2004). *Walking the road: Race, diversity and social justice in teacher education.* New York: Teachers College Press.

Cohen, M. R. (1994). *Under crescent and cross: The Jews in the Middle Ages.* Princeton, NJ: Princeton University Press.

Cohn-Sherbok, D. (2002). *Anti-Semitism: A history.* Phoenix Mill, UK: Sutton.

Cohn-Sherbok, D., & El-Alami, D. (2003). *The Palestine–Israeli conflict: A beginner's guide* (Rev. ed.). Oxford: Oneworld.

Colby, A., & Damon, W. (1992). *Some do care: Contemporary lives of moral commitment.* New York: Free Press.

Cole, J. B. (1991). Black Studies in liberal arts education. In J. E. Butler & J. C. Walter (Eds.), *Transforming the curriculum: Ethnic studies and women's studies* (pp. 131–147). Albany: State University of New York Press.

Coleman-Burns, P. (1993). The revolution within: Transforming ourselves. In J. James & R. Farmer (Eds.), *Spirit, space & survival: African American women in (White) academe* (pp. 139–157). New York: Routledge.

Collins, C., & Yeskel, F., with United for a Fair Economy and Class Action. (2005). *Economic apartheid in America: A primer on economic inequality & insecurity* (2nd ed.). New York: New Press.

Collins, P. H. (1990). *Black feminist thought: Knowledge, consciousness and the politics of empowerment.* New York: Routledge.

Condon, J. C. (1986). The ethnocentric classroom. In J. M. Civikly (Ed.), *Communicating in college classrooms* (New Directions in Teaching and Learning, No. 26). San Francisco: Jossey-Bass.

Conly, S.R., & Chaya, N. (1998). The global gender gap in education. In *Educatoing girls: Gender gaps and gains*. Washington, D.C.: Population Action International Retrieved November 13, 2006 from http://www.populationaction.org/resources/publications/educating_girls/ggp_find06.htm

Cook, L. A. (1954). *Intergroup education*. New York: McGraw-Hill.

Cooper, M. (2000). The heartland's raw deal: How meatpacking is creating a new immigrant underclass. In M. Adams, W. Blumenfeld, R. Castañeda, H. Hackman, M. Peters, & X. Zúñiga (Eds.), *Readings for diversity and social justice* (pp. 99–104). New York: Routledge.

Correctional Association of New York. (2004, October). *Juvenile detention in New York City*. New York: Author.

Cortes, C. E. (2000). *The children are watching: How the media teach about diversity*. New York: Teachers College Press.

Cose, E. (1993). *The rage of a privileged class*. New York: HarperPerennial.

Coven, Martha. (2006). *An introduction to TANF*. Washington, DC: Center for Budget and Policy Priorities. Retrieved August 25, 2006, from http://www.cbpp.org.

Covey, H. (1998). *Social perspectives of people with disabilities in history*. Springfield, IL: Charles Thomas.

Cowan, D. E. (2003). Theologizing race: The construction of "Christian Identity." In C. R. Prentiss (Ed.), *Religion and the creation of race and ethnicity* (pp. 112–124). New York: New York University Press.

Coward, H. G., Hinnells, J. R., & Williams, R. B. (2000). *The south Asian religious diaspora in Britain, Canada, and the United States*. Albany: State University of New York Press.

Cox, S., & Gallois, C. (1996). Gay and lesbian identity development: A social identity perspective. *Journal of Homosexuality, 30*(4), 1–30.

Cramer, E. P., & Gilson, S. F. (1999). Queers and crips: Parallel identity development processes for persons with nonvisible disabilities and lesbian, gay, and bisexual persons. *Journal of Gay, Lesbian, and Bisexual Identity, 4*(1), 23–37.

Crenshawe, K., Gotanda, N., Peller, G., & Thomas, K. (1995). *Critical race theory: The key writings that formed the movement*. New York: New Press.

Cromwell, J. (1999). *Transmen and FTMs: Identities, bodies, genders, and sexualities*. Chicago: University of Illinois Press.

Cross, T., Klein, F., Smith, B., & Smith, B. (1982). Face-to-face, day-to-day: Racism CR. In G. T. Hull, P. B. Scott, & B. Smith (Eds.), *All the women are white, all the blacks are men, but some of us are brave*. New York: Feminist Press.

Cross, W. E. (1971). The Negro-to-black conversion experience: Toward a psychology of black liberation. *Black World, 20*(9), 13–27.

Cross, W. E., Jr. (1991). *Shades of black: Diversity in African-American identity*. Philadelphia: Temple University Press.

Cross, W. E., Jr. (1995). In search of blackness and Afrocentricity: The psychology of Black identity change. In H. W. Harris, H. C. Blue, & E. E. H. Griffith (Eds.), *Racial and ethnic identity: Psychological development and creative expression* (pp. 53–72). New York: Routledge.

Cross, W. E., Jr., & Phagen-Smith, P. (2001). Patterns of African American identity development: A life span perspective. In B. W. Jackson & C. L. Wijeyesinghe (Eds.), *New perspectives on racial identity development: A theoretical and practical anthology*. New York: New York University Press.

Cross, W. E., Jr., Smith, L., & Payne, Y. (2002). Black identity: A repertoire of daily enactments. In P. B. Pedersen, J. G. Draguns, W. J. Lonner, & J. E. Trimble (Eds.), *Counseling across cultures* (5th ed., pp. 93–107). Thousand Oaks, CA: Sage,

Crumpacker, L., & Vander Haegen, E. M. (1987). Pedagogy and prejudice: Strategies for confronting homophobia in the classroom. *Women's Studies Quarterly, 15*(3–4), 65–79.

Culley, M. (1985). Anger and authority in the introductory women's studies classroom. In M. Culley & C. Portuges (Eds.), *Gendered subjects: The dynamics of feminist teaching* (pp. 209–217). Boston: Routledge & Kegan Paul.

Culley, M., & Portuges, C. (1985). *Gendered subjects: The dynamics of feminist teaching*. Boston: Routledge & Kegan Paul.

Daloz, L.A.P., Keen, C.H., Keen, J.P., & Parks, S.D. (1996). *Common fire: Lives of commitment in a complex world*. Boston: Beacon Press.

Damarin, S. (1994). Equity, caring and beyond: Can feminist ethics inform educational technology? *Educational Technology, 34*(2), 34–39.

Daniels, R. (1997). *Not like us: Immigrants and minorities in America, 1890–1924*. Chicago: Ivan R. Dee.

Daniels, R. (2002). *Coming to America: A history of immigration and ethnicity in American life* (2nd ed.). Princeton, NJ: HarperPerennial.

Darder, A. (1991). *Culture and power in the classroom: A critical foundation for bicultural education*. Westport, CT: Bergin & Garvey.

Darling-Hammond, L. (2006). Securing the right to learn: Policy and practice for powerful teaching and learning. *Educational Researcher, 35*(7), 13-24.

Darling-Hammond, L., French, J., & García-Lopez, S. P. (Eds.). (2002). *Learning to teach for social justice*. New York: Teachers College Press.

Das Gupta, M. (1997). "What is Indian about you?" A gendered, transnational approach to ethnicity. *Gender & Society, 11*(5), 572–596.

Davis, A., & Wing, A. K. (2000). *Global critical race feminism*. New York: New York University Press.

Davis, D. H. (2004). Explaining the complexities of religion and state in the United States: Separation, integration, and accommodation. In D. Odell-Scott (Ed.), *Democracy and religion: Free exercise and diverse visions* (pp. 33–47). Kent, OH: Kent State University Press.

de Beauvoir, S. (1972). *The coming of age*. New York: Putman.

Decent Schools for California. (N.d.). Decent Schools for California: *Williams v. State of California*. Retrieved October 29, 2006, from http://www.decentschools.org.

De Danaan, L. (1990). Center to margin: Dynamics in a global classroom. *Women's Studies Quarterly, 18*(1–2), 135–144.

Degraaf, J., Wann, D., & Naylor, T. H. (2001). *Affluenza: The all-consuming epidemic*. San Francisco: Barrett-Koehler.

Delgado, R. (1984). The imperial scholar: Reflections on a review of civil rights literature. *University of Pennsylvania Law Review, 133*, 561.

Delgado, R. (1995). *Critical race theory: The cutting edge*. Philadelphia: Temple University Press.

Delgado, R., & Stefancic, J. (1999). *Critical race theory: The cutting edge*. Philadelphia: Temple University Press.

Delgado, R., & Stefancic, J. (2001). *Critical race theory: An introduction.* New York: New York University Press.

Deloria, V. (1999). Missionaries and the religious vacuum (1969). In J. Treat (Ed.), *For this land: Writings on religion in America* (pp. 22–30). New York: Routledge.

Delpit, L. (1988). The silenced dialogue: Power and pedagogy in educating other people's children. *Harvard Educational Review, 58*(3), 280–298.

D'Emilio, J. (1983). *Sexual politics, sexual communities: The making of a homosexual minority in the United States, 1940–1970.* Chicago: University of Chicago Press.

D'Emilio, J., & Freedman, E. (1997). *Intimate matters: A history of sexuality in America.* New York: Harper & Row.

Derber, C. (2002). *People before profit: The new globalization in an age of terror, big money, and economic crisis.* San Francisco: Barrett-Koehler.

Dever, W. G. (2003). *Who were the early Israelites, and where did they come from?* Grand Rapids, MI: William B. Eerdmans.

Devor, H. (1989). *Gender blending: Confronting the limits of duality.* Bloomington: Indiana University Press.

Dillon, J. (1994). *Using discussions in classrooms.* Philadelphia: Open University Press.

Dillon, M. (Ed.). (2003). *Handbook of the sociology of religion.* Cambridge: Cambridge University Press.

Dillon, S. (2006, August 27). In schools across U.S., the melting pot overflows. *New York Times,* p. 1.

Diner, H. (2004). *The Jews of the United States: 1654–2000.* Berkeley: University of California Press.

Dinges, W. D. (2004). On naming religious extremists: The "fundamentalist" factor. In D. Odell-Scott (Ed.), *Democracy and religion: Free exercise and diverse visions* (pp. 243–266). Kent, OH: Kent State University Press.

Dinnerstein, D. (1976). *The mermaid and the minotaur: Sexual arrangements and human malaise.* New York: Harper & Row.

Dinnerstein, L. (1994). *Antisemitism in America.* New York: Oxford University Press.

Dirlik, A. (1997). *The post-colonial aura: Third World criticism in the age of global capitalism.* Boulder, CO: Westview Press.

Dixon, A. D., & Rousseau, C. K. (Eds.). (2006). *Critical race theory in education: All God's children got a song.* New York: Routledge.

Dovidio, J. F., Gaertner, S. L., Stewart, T. L., Esses, V. M., ten Vergert, M., & Hodson, G. (2004). From intervention to outcome: Processes in the reduction of bias. In W. Stephan & W. Vogt (Eds.), *Education programs for improving intergroup relations: Theory, research, & practice* (pp. 243–265). New York: Teacher's College Press.

Downing, N. E., & Roush, K. L. (1985). From passive acceptance to active commitment: A model of feminist identity development for women. *Counseling Psychologist, 13*(4), 695–709.

Downs, J. F. (1978). Intercultural training for government employees and military personnel for overseas assignments. In D. S. Hoopes, P. B. Pedersen, & G. W. Renwick (Eds.), *Overview of intercultural education, training and research: Vol. 2. Education and training.* Washington, DC: Society for Intercultural Education, Training, and Research (SIETAR).

Draut, T. (2006). *Strapped: Why America's 20- and 30-somethings can't get ahead.* New York: Doubleday.

Duany, J. (1998). Reconstructing racial identity: Ethnicity, color, and class among Dominicans in the United States and Puerto Rico. *Latin American Perspectives, 25*(3), 147–172.

Duhaney, L. G. (2000). Culturally sensitive strategies for violence prevention. *Multicultural Education*, 7(4), 9–17.

Duncan, C., & Loretto, W. (2004). Never the right age? Gender and age-based discrimination in employment. *Gender, Work & Organization*, 11(1), 95–115.

Duncan, G. A. (2002). Beyond love: A critical race ethnography of the schooling of adolescent black males. *Equity & Excellence in Education*, 35(2), 131–144.

Ebaugh, H. R., & Chafetz, J. S. (Eds.). (2000). *Religion and the new immigrants: Continuities and adaptations in immigrant congregations.* Walnut Creek, CA: Altamira Press.

Echo-Hawk, W. R. (1993). Native American religious liberty: Five hundred years after Columbus. *American Indian Culture and Research Journal*, 17(3), 33–53.

Echols, A. (1989). *Daring to be bad: Radical feminism in America.* Minneapolis: University of Minnesota Press.

Eck, D. L. (2001). *A new religious America: How a "Christian country" has become the world's most religiously diverse nation.* San Francisco: HarperSanFrancisco.

*The Economist.* (2004, December 29). Special report: Meritocracy in America.

Eitington, J. (1984). *The winning trainer.* Houston, TX: Gulf.

Ellsworth, E. (1989/1994). Why doesn't this feel empowering? Working through the repressive myths of critical pedagogy. *Harvard Educational Review*, 59(3), 297–234. (Reprinted in L. Stone (Ed.) (1994), *The education feminism reader,* pp. 300–327. New York: Routledge.)

Emerson, M. O., & Smith, C. (2000). *Divided by faith: Evangelical religion and the problem of race in America.* Oxford: Oxford University Press.

Endelman, T. M. (2005). Antisemitism in Western Europe today. In D. J. Penslar, M. R. Marrus, & J. G. Stein (Eds.), *Contemporary antisemitism* (pp. 64–79). Toronto: University of Toronto Press.

Engberg, M. E. (2004). Improving intergroup relations in higher education: A critical examination of the influence of educational interventions on racial bias. *Review of Educational Research*, 74(4), 473–524.

Enns, C. Z., & Sinacore, A. L. (Eds.). (2005). *Teaching and social justice: Integrating multicultural and feminist theories in the classroom.* Washington, DC: American Psychological Association.

Ensign, J. (2005). A story of complexity: Identity development, difference, and teaching for social justice. In R. A. Pena, K. Guest, & L. W. Matsuda (Eds.), *Community and difference: Teaching, pluralism, and social justice.* New York: Peter Lang.

Entman, R. M., & Rojecki, A. (2001). *The black image in the white mind: Media and race in America.* Chicago: University of Chicago Press.

Epstein, S. (1987). Gay politics, ethnic identity: The limits of social constructionism. *Socialist Review*, 17(3–4), 9–54.

Erikson, E. H. (1964). *Insight and responsibility.* New York: Norton.

Erikson, E. H. (1968a). Identity, psychosocial. In D. L. Sills (Ed.), *International encyclopedia of the social sciences* (Vol. 7, pp. 65–66). New York: Macmillan.

Erikson, E. H. (1968b). *Identity: Youth and crisis.* New York: Norton.

Erikson, E. H. (1968c). Life cycle. In D. L. Sills (Ed.), *International encyclopedia of the social sciences* (Vol. 9). New York: Macmillan.

Evans, S. (1979). *Personal politics: The roots of women's liberation in the Civil Rights movement and the New Left.* New York: Random House.

Faderman, L. (1991). *Odd girls and twilight lovers: A history of lesbian life in twentieth century America.* New York: Columbia University Press.

Falicov, C. J. (2005). *Ambiguous loss: Risk and resilience in Latino immigrant families*. In M. M. Suarez-Orozco, C. Suarez-Orozco, & D. B. Qin (Eds.), *The new immigration: An interdisciplinary reader* (pp. 197–206). New York: Routledge.

Fanon, F. (1967). *Black skin, white masks*. New York: Grove Press.

Fanon, F. (1968). *The wretched of the earth*. New York: Grove Press.

Fausto-Sterling, A. (2000). *Sexing the body: Gender politics and the construction of sexuality*. New York: Basic.

Feagin, J. R. (1997). Old poison in new bottles: The deep roots of modern nativism. In J. F. Perea (Ed.), *Immigrants out! The new nativism and the anti-immigrant impulse in the United States*. New York: New York University Press.

Feagin, J. R. (2001). *Racist America: Roots, current realities, and future reparations*. New York: Routledge.

Feagin, J. R., & Sikes, M. P. (1994). *Living with racism: The black middle-class experience*. Boston: Beacon Press.

Feinberg, L. (1993). *Stone butch blues: A novel*. Ithaca, NY: Firebrand Books.

Feinberg, L. (1997). *Transgender warriors: Making history from Joan of Arc to Dennis Rodman*. New York: Routledge.

Feinberg, L. (1999). *Trans liberation: Beyond pink and blue*. Boston: Beacon Press.

Feldman, S. M. (1997). *Please don't wish me a merry Christmas: A critical history of the separation of Church and State*. New York: New York University Press.

Felman, J. L. (2001). *Never a dull moment: Teaching and the art of performance—feminism takes center stage*. New York: Routledge.

Femia, J. (1987). *Gramsci's political thought: Hegemony, consciousness and the revolutionary process*. New York: Oxford University Press.

Fernandez, L. (2002). Telling stories about school: Using critical race and Latino critical theories to document Latina/Latino education and resistance. *Qualitative Inquiry, 8*(1), 45–65.

Fine, M., Roberts, R. A., & Torre, M. E. (2004). *Echoes of Brown: Youth documenting and performing the legacy of Brown v. Board of Education*. New York: Teachers College Press.

Finkelstein, N. G. (2005). *Beyond chutzpah: On the misuse of anti-Semitism and the abuse of history*. Berkeley: University of California Press.

Firestone, S. (1970). *The dialectic of sex: The case for feminist revolution*. New York: Morrow.

Fischman, G. E., McLaren, P., Sünker, H., & Lankshear, C. (Eds.). (2005). *Critical theories, radical pedagogies, and global conflicts*. Lanham, MD: Rowman & Littlefield.

Fishel, D. (Dir.). (2003). *Still doing it: The intimate lives of women over 65* [Video]. Harriman, NY: New Day Films.

Fisher, B. (1987). The heart has its reasons: Feeling, thinking, and community-building in feminist education. *Women's Studies Quarterly, 15*, 47–58.

Fleischer, D., & Zames, F. (2001). *The disability rights movement*. Philadelphia: Temple University Press.

Folbre, N. (2001). *The invisible heart: Economics and family values*. New York: New Press.

Foner, E. (2005). *Forever free: The story of emancipation and reconstruction*. New York: Knopf.

Foner, N. (2005). *In a new land: A comparative view of immigration*. New York: New York University Press.

Foner, N., & Frederickson, G. (2004a). Immigration, race and ethnicity in the United States: Social constructions and social relations in historical and contemporary perspective. In N. Foner & G. Frederickson (Eds.), *Not just black and white: Historical and contemporary perspectives on immigration, race and ethnicity in the U.S.* (pp. 1–19). New York: Russell Sage Foundation.

Foner, N., & Frederickson, G. (2004b). *Not just black and white: Historical and contemporary perspectives on immigration, race, and ethnicity in the U.S.* New York: Russell Sage Foundation.

Fosl, C. A. (2002). *Subversive Southener: Anne Braden and the struggle for racial justice in the Cold War South.* Lexington, KY: University of Kentucky Press.

Foucault, M. (1980). *The history of sexuality.* New York: Vintage Books.

Foucault, M. (1995). *Discipline and punishment: The birth of the prison* (A. Sheridan, Trans.). New York: Vintage.

Foundation for Child Development. (2004). *New American children: Immigrant children's initiative.* New York: Author.

Fox, J. (2002). *Ethnoreligious conflict in the late twentieth century: A general theory.* Lanham, MD: Lexington Books.

Frank, R. (1999). *Luxury fever.* Princeton, NJ: Princeton University Press.

Frankenberg, R. (1990). White women, racism, and anti-racism: A women's studies course exploring racism and privilege. *Women's Studies Quarterly* (1–2), 145–153.

Franklin, J. H., & Moss, A. A. (2000). *From slavery to freedom: A history of African Americans.* New York: McGraw-Hill.

Franklin, M. (1992). Culturally sensitive practices for African American learners with disabilities. *Exceptional Children, 59*(2), 115–122.

Fraser, J. W. (1999). *Between church and state: Religion and public education in a multicultural America.* New York: St. Martin's Press.

Fredrickson, G. M. (2002a). *Racism: A short history.* Princeton, NJ: Princeton University Press.

Fredrickson, G. M. (2002b). Religion and the invention of racism. In G. M. Fredrickson (Ed.), *Racism: A short history* (pp. 17–95). Princeton, NJ: Princeton University Press.

Freedman, E. B. (1994). Small-group pedagogy: Consciousness raising in conservative times. In L. Garber (Ed.), *Tilting the tower* (pp. 35–50). New York: Routledge.

Freeman, L. (2006). *There goes the 'hood: Views of gentrification from the ground up.* Philadelphia: Temple University Press.

Freire, P. (1970/1994). *Pedagogy of the oppressed.* New York: Continuum.

Freire, P. (1973). *Education for critical consciousness.* New York: Seabury.

Friedan, B. (1965). *The feminine mystique.* New York: Penguin.

Frommer, M. K., & Frommer, H. (1995). *Growing up Jewish in America: An oral history.* Lincoln: University of Nebraska Press.

Frye, M. (1983). *The politics of reality: Essays in feminist theory.* Freedom, CA: Crossing Press.

Fulbright-Anderson, K., Lawrence, K., Sutton, S., Susi, G., & Kubisch, A. (2005). *Structural racism and youth development: Issues, challenges, and implications.* Aspen Institute Roundtable on Community Change. Washington, DC: Aspen Institute.

Fulop, T. E., & Raboteau, A. J. (Eds.). (1997). *African-American religion: Interpretive essays in history and culture.* New York: Routledge.

Gallagher, H. (1995). *By trust betrayed: Patients, physicians, and the license to kill in the Third Reich.* Arlington, VA: Vandamere.

Gaultieri, S. (2001). Becoming "white": Race, religion & the foundations of Syrian/Lebanese ethnicity in the United States. *Journal of American Ethnic History, 20*(4), 29–59.

Gay, G. (2000). *Culturally responsive teaching: Theory, research, & practice.* New York: Teachers College Press.

Geller, T. (Ed.). (1990). *Bisexuality: A reader and sourcebook.* Hadley, MA: Common Wealth Printing.

Gender Public Advocacy Coalition. (N.d.). Gender Public Advocacy Coalition. Retrieved October 30, 2006, from http://www.genderpac.org.

Gibson, P. (2004). Gay male and lesbian suicide. Retrieved August 30, 2006, from http://www.lambda.org/youth_suicide.htm.

Giecek, T. S., with United for a Fair Economy (2000). *Teaching economics as if people mattered: A high school curriculum guide to the new economy.* Boston: United for a Fair Economy.

Gilbert, M. (2003). *The righteous: The unsung heroes of the Holocaust.* New York: Henry Holt.

Gitlin, T. (1987). *The sixties: Years of hope, days of rage.* New York: Bantam.

Goldberg, D. T., & Krausz, M. (Eds.). (1993). *Jewish identity.* Philadelphia: Temple University Press.

Goldberg, C. (2005, June 27). Tests reveal gender early in pregnancy: Ethicists fear use in sex selection. *Boston Globe*, p. 1.

Goldberg, M. (2006). *Kingdom coming: The rise of Christian nationalism.* New York: Norton.

Goldenberg, D.M. (2006). *The curse of Ham: Race and slavery in early Judaism, Christianity, and Islam.* Princeton, NJ: Princeton University Press.

Goldenberg, I. (1978). *Oppression and social intervention: Essays on the human condition and the problems of change.* Chicago: Nelson-Hall.

Goldschmidt, H., & McAlister, E. (Eds.). (2004). *Race, nation, and religion in the Americas.* New York: Oxford University Press.

Golembiewski, R. T., & Blumberg, A. (1977). *Sensitivity training and the laboratory approach: Readings about concepts and applications.* Itasca, IL: F. E. Peacock.

Gonzalez, J. (2000). *Harvest of empire: A history of Latinos in America.* New York: Viking.

Gonzalez, J., & Torres, J. (2004). How long must we wait? The fight for racial and ethnic equality in the American News Media. Retrieved August 23, 2006, from http://images.democracynow.org/howlong.pdf.

Goodman, D. (1995). Difficult dialogues: Enhancing discussions about diversity. *College Teaching, 43*(2), 47–52.

Gordon, J. (2005). *Suburban sweatshops: The fight for immigrant rights.* Cambridge, MA: Belknap Press.

Gosse, V. (2005). *Rethinking the new left: An interpretive history.* New York: McMillan.

Gransci, A. & Forgacs. D. (2000). *The Antionio Gransci reader: Selected writings 1916-1935.* New York: New York University Press.

Grande, S. (2004). *Red pedagogy: Native American social and political thought.* Lanham, MD: Rowman & Littlefield.

Grant, C. A. (Ed.). (1992). *Research and multicultural education.* London: Falmer.

Gray, D. (1982). *Patriarchy is a conceptual trap.* Wellesly, MA: Roundtable Press.

Grayson, P. J. (1995, July). Universal design—Environments for everyone: Usable spaces, places, and products. *Architecture and Society*, 33–39.

Green, J. (2004). *Becoming a visible man.* Nashville, TN: Vanderbilt University Press.

Greenawalt, K. (2002). Teaching about religion in the public schools. *Journal of Law & Poliltics, 18*, 329.

Gregory, S. & Sanjek, R. (Eds.) (1994). *Race.* New Brunswick, NJ: Rutgers University Press.

Grew, R. (1997). On seeking the cultural context of fundamentalism. In M. Marty & R. S. Appleby (Eds.), *Religion, ethnicity, & self-identity: Nations in turmoil* (pp. 19–34). Hanover, NH: University Press of New England.

Griffin, C., & Mulligan, J. (Eds.). (1992). *Empowerment through experiential learning: Explorations of good practice.* London: Kogan Page.

Griffin, P. (2003). LGBTQ issues in K–12 schools [Special issue]. *Equity & Excellence in Education*, *36*(2).

Griffin, P., & Harro, R. (1997). Heterosexism curriculum design. In P. Griffin, M. Adams, & L. Bell (Eds), *Teaching for diversity and social justice: A sourcebook* (pp. 141–169). New York: Routledge.

Griffiths, M. (Ed.). (2003). *Action for social justice in education: Fairly different*. Philadelphia: Open University Press.

Grossman, L. (1998). Jewish religion in America. In N. Linzer, D. J. Schnall, & J. A. Chanes (Eds.), *A portrait of the American Jewish community* (pp. 77–115). Westport, CT: Praeger.

Gudykunst, W. (1994). *Bridging differences: Effective intergroup communications*. Thousand Oaks, CA: Sage.

Guglielmo, T. A. (2003). Rethinking whiteness historiography: The case of Italians in Chicago, 1890–1945. In A. W. Doane & E. Bonilla-Silva (Eds.), *White out: The continuing significance of racism* (pp. 49–67). New York: Routledge.

Guglielmo, J. & S. Salerno (2003) (Eds.), *Are Italians white? How race is made in America*. New York: Routledge.

Guinier, L. & Torres, G. (2002). *The miner's canary: Enlisting race, resisting power, transforming democracy*. Cambridge, MA: Harvard University Press.

Gupta, H. (2003). Staking a claim on American-ness: Hindu temples in the United States. In J. N. Iwamura & P. Spickard (Eds.), *Revealing the sacred in Asian and Pacific America* (pp. 193–208). New York: Routledge.

Gurin, P., Dey, E. L., Hurtado, S., & Gurin, G. (2002). Diversity and higher education: Theory and impact on educational outcomes. *Harvard Educational Review*, *72*(3), 330–366.

Gurin, P., Lehman, J., & Lewis, S. (Eds.). (2004). *Defending diversity: Michigan's affirmative action cases*. Ann Arbor: University of Michigan Press.

Gutiérrez, K., Asato, J., Santos, M., and Gotanda, N. (2002). Backlash pedagogy: Language and culture and the politics of reform. *The Review of Education, Pedagogy, and Cultural Studies, 24* (4), 335-351.

Gutstein, E., & Peterson, B. (2005). *Rethinking mathematics: Teaching social justice by the numbers*. Milwaukee, WI: Rethinking Schools.

Hacker, A. (1992). *Two nations: Black and white, separate, hostile, unequal*. New York: Ballantine.

Hackman, H. (2005). Five essential components for social justice education. *Equity & Excellence in Education*, *38*(2), 103–110.

Haddad, Y. Y. (2002). *Muslims in the West: From sojourners to citizens*. New York: Oxford University Press.

Halberstam, J. (1998). *Female masculinity*. Durham, NC: Duke University Press.

Hale-Benson, J. E. (1986). *Black children: Their roots, culture, and learning styles* (Rev. ed.). Baltimore: Johns Hopkins University Press.

Haney Lopez, I.F. (2006). Colorblind to the reality of race in America. *The Chronicle of Higher Education, 53* (11), B6.

Haney Lopez, I. F. (1996). *White by law: The legal construction of race*. New York: New York University Press.

Hans, T.A., & Sangrey, T. (2001). Genderbread activity. In *Trans Activist Network facilitators' guide*. Self-published: Amherst, MA. Available pdf www.riseconsulting.org

Hardiman, R. (1994). White racial identity development in the United States. In E. P. Salett & D. R. Koslow (Eds.), *Race, ethnicity, and self: Identity in multicultural perspective*. Washington, DC: National Multicultural Institute.

Hardiman, R. (2001). Reflections on white identity development theory. In C. Wijeyesinghe & B. W. Jackson (Eds.), *New perspectives on racial identity development: A theoretical and practical anthology* (pp. 108–128). New York: New York University Press.

Hardiman, R., & Jackson, B. W. (1992). Racial identity development: Understanding racial dynamics in college classrooms and on campus. In M. Adams (Ed.), *Promoting diversity in college classrooms: Innovative responses for the curriculum, faculty, and institutions* (New Directions for Teaching and Learning, No. 52, pp. 21–37). San Francisco: Jossey-Bass.

Hardiman, R. & Jackson, B. W. (1997). Conceptual foundations for social justice courses. In M. Adams, L. A. Bell, & P. Griffin (Eds.), *Teaching for diversity and social justice: A sourcebook* (pp. 16–29). New York: Routledge.

Harding, S. (1991). *Whose science, whose knowledge?* Ithaca, NY: Cornell University Press.

Harding, S. (1993). Rethinking standpoint epistemology. In L. Alcoff & E. Potter (Eds.), *Feminist epistemlologies* (pp. 49–82). New York: Routledge.

Harris, M. (1988). *Women and teaching.* New York: Paulist Press.

Harrison, O. (2004). As disability is emerging globally, so is advocacy for full participation for people with disabilities. *Access New England, 9*(1), 1. Retrieved June 25, 2006, from http://www.adaptenv.org/newsletter/pdf/Access_Fall_2004.pdf.

Hart, M. U. (1991). Liberation through consciousness raising. In J. Mezirow (Eds.), *Fostering critical reflection in adulthood: A guide to transformative and emancipatory learning.* San Francisco: Jossey-Bass.

Hartsock, N. (1983). *Money, sex and power: Toward a feminist historical materialism.* New York: Longman.

Hatfield, S. R. (Ed.). (1995). *The seven principles in action: Improving undergraduate education.* Bolton, MA: Anker.

Harvey, P. (2003). "A servant of servants shall he be": The construction of race in American religious mythologies. In C. R. Prentiss (Ed.), *Religion and the creation of race and ethnicity* (pp. 13–27). New York: New York University Press.

Hayles, R. (1978). Inter-ethnic and race relations education and training. In D. S. Hoopes, P. E. Pedersen, & G. W. Renwick (Eds.), *Overview of intercultural education, training, and research: Vol. 2. Education and training.* Washington, DC: Society for Intercultural Education, Training and Research (SIETAR).

Haynes, S.R. (2002). *The biblical justification of American slavery.* New York: Oxford University Press.

Heintz, J., & Folbre, N. (2000) *The ultimate field guide to the U.S. economy: A compact and irreverent guide to economic life in America.* New York: New Press.

Helms, J. E. (1990). *Black and white identity: Theory, research and practice.* Westport, CT: Greenwood Press.

Helms, J. E. (1995). An update of Helms's white and people of color racial identity models. In J. G. Ponterotto, J. M. Casas, L. A. Suzuki, & C. M. Alexander (Eds.), *Handbook of multicultural counseling* (pp. 181–198). Thousand Oaks, CA: Sage.

Hendricks, J. (2004). Public policies and old age identity. *Journal of Aging Studies, 18*(3), 245–260.

Henry, P. (1981). "And I don't care what it is": The tradition-history of a civil religion proof text. *Journal of the American Academy of Religion, 49*(1):35–49.

Herek, G. (2004). Beyond homophobia: Thinking about sexual prejudice and stigma in the twenty-first century. *Sexuality Research & Social Policy, 1*(2), 6–24.

Herman, D. (1998). *The anti-gay agenda: Orthodox vision and the religious right.* Chicago: University of Chicago Press.

Hertz, T. (2006). *Understanding mobility in America*. Washington, DC: Center for American Progress.

Higham, J. (2004). *Strangers in the land: Patterns of American nativism*. New Brunswick, NJ: Rutgers University Press.

Hilberg, R. (1961). *The destruction of the European Jews*. New York: HarperTorchbooks.

Hilberg, R. (1992). *Perpetrators, victims, bystanders: The Jewish catastrophe 1933–1945*. New York: HarperPerennial.

Hill, M. (1997). *Whiteness: A critical reader*. New York: New York University Press.

Hin, S. L. (2006). *May Day 2006: We have made history!* Retrieved September 2, 2006, from http://www.immigrantsolidarity.org.

Hochschild, J., & Scovronick, N. (2003). *The American dream and the public schools*. New York: Oxford University Press.

Hoffman, N. J. (1985). Breaking silences: Life in the feminist classroom. In M. Culley & C. Portuges (Eds.), *Gendered subjects: The dynamics of feminist teaching* (pp. 147–154). Boston: Routledge & Kegan Paul.

Hogg, M. A. (1995). Social identity theory. In A. S. R. Manstead & M. Hewstone (Eds.), *The Blackwell encyclopedia of social psychology* (pp. 555–560). Cambridge, MA: Blackwell.

Holt, J. (1967). *How children learn*. New York: Pitman.

Hondagneu-Sotelo, P. (1994). *Gendered transitions: Mexican experiences of migration*. Berkeley: University of California Press.

Hondagneu-Sotelo, P. (Ed.). (2007). *Religion and social justice for immigrants*. New Brunswick, NJ: Rutgers University Press.

hooks, b. (1984). *Feminist theory: From margin to center*. Boston: South End Press.

hooks, b. (1989). *Talking back: Thinking feminist, thinking black*. Boston: South End Press.

hooks, b. (1994). *Teaching to transgress: Education as the practice of freedom*. New York: Routledge.

hooks, b. (2000). *Feminist theory: From margin to center* (2nd ed.). Cambridge, MA: South End Press.

Horton, M., & Freire, P. (1991). *We make the road by walking: Conversations on education and social change* (Reprint ed.). Philadelphia: Temple University Press.

Howard, G. R. (1999). *We can't teach what we don't know: White teachers, multiracial schools*. New York: Teachers College Press.

Howe, F. (1984). Mississippi's Freedom Schools: The politics of education. In F. Howe (Ed.), *Myths of coeducation: Selected essays, 1964–1983* (pp. 1–17). Bloomington: Indiana University Press.

Hull, G. T., Scott, P. B., & Smith, B. (Eds.). (1982). *All the women are white, all the blacks are men, but some of us are brave*. New York: Feminist Press.

Human Rights Campaign. (2002). *HRC releases ground-breaking public opinion research on transgender issues*. Washington, DC: Human Rights Campaign.

Human Rights Campaign. (2006). Human Rights Campaign: Working for lesbian, gay, bisexual and transgender equal rights. Retrieved October 30, 2006, from http://www.hrc.org.

Human Rights Watch. (2002, February 27). Race and incarceration in the United States. Human Rights Watch Backgrounders. Retrieved October 30, 2006, from http://hrw.org/backgrounder/usa/race.

Hunt, J. S., Jr. (1995). Dewey's philosophical method and its influence on his philosophy of education. In K. Warren, M. Sakofs, & J. S. Hunt, Jr. (Eds.), *The theory of experiential education*. Dubuque, IA: Kendall/Hunt.

Huntington, S. P. (1993). The clash of civilizations. *Foreign Affairs, 72*(3), 22–49.

Huntington, S. P. (1996). *The clash of civilizations and the remaking of the world order.* New York: Simon & Schuster.

Hurtado, A. (1997). Understanding multiple group identities: Inserting women into cultural transformations. *Journal of Social issues, 53*(2), 299–328.

Hurtado, A., Gurin, P., & Peng, T. (1994). Social identities—a framework for studying the adaptations of immigrants and ethnics: The adaptations of Mexicans to the United States. *Social Problems, 41*(1), 129–151.

Hutchins, L., & Kaahumanu, L. (Eds.). (1991). *Bi any other name: Bisexual people speak out.* Boston: Alyson.

IFSW (International Federation of Social Workers) (2005, November 25 last update). *International Policy on Women.* Retrieved November 14, 2006, from http://ifsw.bestsite.ch/en/p38000218.html

Ignatiev, N. (1995). *How the Irish became white.* New York: Routledge.

International Forum on Globalization. (N.d.). International Forum on Globalization. Retrieved October 29, 2006, from http://www.ifg.org.

Intersex Society of North America. (1993–2005). Our mission. Retrieved October 30, 2006, from http://www.isna.org.

Irvine, J. J. (2002). *In search of wholeness: African American teachers and their culturally specific classroom practices.* New York: Palgrave.

Irvine, J. J. (2003). *Educating teachers for diversity: Seeing with a cultural eye.* New York: Teachers College Press.

Islam for Today. (2006). *Islam in the United States: Official State Department fact sheet.* Retrieved September 5, 2006, from http://www.islamfortoday.com/historyusa4.htm.

Iwamura, J. N., & Spickard, P. (2003). *Revealing the sacred in Asian and Pacific America.* New York: Routledge.

Iyer, D. (2003). A community on the front lines: Pushing back the rising tide of anti-immigrant policy since September 11th. *Subcontinental: The Journal of South Asian American Public Affairs, 3*(1), 35–53.

Jackins, H. (1997). *The list.* Seattle, WA: Rational Island.

Jackson, B. W. (2001). Black identity development: Further analysis and elaboration. In C. Wijeyesinghe & B. W. Jackson (Eds.), *New perspectives on racial identity development: A theoretical and practical anthology* (pp. 8–31). New York: New York University Press.

Jackson, B. W. (2005). The theory and practice of multicultural organization development in education. In M. L. Ouellett (Ed.), *Teaching inclusively: Resources for course, department & institutional change in higher education* (pp. 3–20). Stillwater, OK: New Forums.

Jackson, B. W. (Ed.). (1976). *Black identity development.* Dubuque, IA: Kendall/Hunt.

Jackson, B. W., & Hardiman, R. (1994). Multicultural organization development. In E. W. Cross, J. H. Katz, F. A. Miller, & E. W. Seashore (Eds.), *The promise of diversity* (pp. 231–239). Arlington, VA: National Training Laboratories.

Jacobs, J. L. (2002). *Hidden heritage: The legacy of the Crypto-Jews.* Berkeley: University of California Press.

Jacobs, S. (Ed.). (1997). *Two Spirit people: Native American gender identity, sexuality and spirituality.* Champaign: University of Illinois Press.

Jacobson, M. F. (1998). *Whiteness of a different color: European immigrants and the alchemy of race.* Cambridge, MA: Harvard University Press.

Jagose, A. (1996). *Queer theory: An introduction.* New York: New York University Press.

James, J., & R. Farmer (Eds.). (1993). *Spirit, space & survival: African American women in (white) academe.* New York: Routledge.

Jamison, K. (1978). Affirmation action: Springboard for a total organizational change effort. *OD Practitioner, 10*(4), 1-9.

Jasso, G., Massey, D. S., Rosenzweig, M. R., & Smith, J. P. (2003). Exploring the religious preferences of recent immigrants to the United States: Evidence from the New Immigrant Survey Pilot. In Y. Y. Haddad, J. I. Smith, & J. L. Esposito (Eds.). *Religion and Immigrationi: Christian, Jewish, and Muslim experiences in the United States* (pp. 217-254). Lanham, MD: Altamira Press.

Jay, K., & Young, A. (Eds.). (1992). *Out of the closets: Voices of gay liberation.* London: Gay Men's Press.

Jensen, B. (2004). Across the great divide: Crossing classes and clashing cultures. In Michael Zweig (Ed.), *What's class got to do with it?* Ithaca, NY: Cornell University Press.

Jensen, R. (2005). *The heart of whiteness: Confronting race, racism and white privilege.* San Francisco: City Light Books.

Johnson, A. (2005). *The gender knot: Unraveling our patriarchal legacy* (revised ed.) Philadelphia: Temple University Press.

Johnson, A. (2005). *Privilege, power and difference.* New York: Prentice Hall.

Johnson, A. (1997). Where are we? In *The gender knot: Unraveling our patriarchal legacy* (pp. 3-26). Philadelphia: Temple University Press.

Johnson, D., & Johnson, F. (1987). *Joining together: Group theory and group skills.* Englewood Cliffs, NJ: Prentice Hall.

Johnson, K. A., Delgado Bernal, D., Ramirez Wiedeman, C., & Knight, M. G. (2002). The struggle for equity and social justice education: Theories, policies, and practices [Special issue]. *Equity & Excellence in Education, 35*(3).

Johnson, S. A. (2004). *The myth of Ham in nineteenth-century American Christianity: Race, heathens, and the people of God.* New York: Palgrave Macmillan.

Johnstone, R. L. (2004). *Religion in society: A sociology of religion* (7th ed.). Upper Saddle River, NJ: Prentice Hall.

Jones, J. (1998). *American work: Four centuries of black and white labor.* New York: Norton.

Joplin, L. (1995). On defining experiential education. In K. Warren, M. Sakofs, & J. S. Hunt, Jr. (Eds.), *The theory of experiential education.* Dubuque, IA: Kendall/Hunt.

Joshi, K. Y. (2006a). *New roots in America's sacred ground: Religion, race, and ethnicity in Indian America.* New Brunswick, NJ: Rutgers University Press.

Joshi, K. Y. (2006b). The racialization of Hinduism, Islam, and Sikhism in the United States. *Equity & Excellence in Education, 39*(3), 211-226.

Juergensmeyer, M. (2000). *Terror in the mind of God: The global rise of religious violence* (3rd ed.). Berkeley: University of California Press.

Juergensmeyer, M. (2004, November 1). *Religious terror and the secular state* (Global & International Studies Program. Paper 22). Retrieved September 4, 2006, from http://repositories.cdlib.org/gis/22.

Kamenetz, A. (2006). *Generation debt: Why now is a terrible time to be young.* New York: Riverhead Books.

Kanpol, B. (1994). *Critical pedagogy: An introduction.* Westport, CT: Bergin & Garvey.

Kao, G., & Tienda, M. (2005). *Optimism and achievement: The educational performance of immigrant youth.* In M. M. Suarez-Orozco, C. Suarez-Orozco, & D. B. Qin (Eds.), *The new immigration: An interdisciplinary reader* (pp. 331-343). New York: Routledge.

Kaplan, E. (2004). *With God on their side: How Christian fundamentalists trampled science, policy, and democracy in George W. Bush's White House.* New York: New Press.

Katz, J. (1978). *White awareness: A handbook for anti-racism training.* Norman: University of Oklahoma Press.

Katz, J. N. (1976). *Gay American history: Lesbians and gay men in the USA.* New York: Avon.

Katz, J. N. (1995). *The invention of heterosexuality*. New York: Dutton.

Katznelson, I. (2005). *When affirmative action was white: An untold history of racial inequality in the twentieth century*. New York: Norton.

Kaye/Kantrowitz, M. (1992). *The issue is power: Essays on women, Jews, violence and resistance*. San Francisco: Aunt Lute Books.

Kaye/Kantrowitz, M. (1996). Jews in the U.S.: The rising cost of Whiteness. In B. Thompson & S. Tyagi (Eds.), *Names we call home: Autobiography on racial identity* (pp. 121–137). New York: Routledge.

Kegan, R. (1982). *The evolving self*. Cambridge, MA: Harvard University Press.

Keil, F. C. (1984). Mechanisms of cognitive development and the structure of knowledge. In R. J. Sternberg (Ed.), *Mechanisms of cognitive development*. New York: W. H. Freeman.

Kennedy, E. L., & Davis, M. D. (1994). *Boots of leather, slippers of gold: The history of a lesbian community*. New York: Penguin.

Kershaw, B. (1992). *The politics of performance: Radical theatre as cultural intervention*. New York: Routledge.

Kessler, S. (1998). *Lessons from the intersexed*. New Brunswick, NJ: Rutgers University Press.

Khanga, Y. (1992). *Soul to soul: A black Russian American family 1865–1992* (W. S. Jacoby, Trans.). New York: Norton.

Khazzoum, L. (2003). *The flying camel: Essays on identity by women of North African and Middle Eastern Jewish heritage*. New York: Seal Press.

Khosla, D. (2006). *Both sides now: One man's journey through womanhood*. New York: Tarcher.

Kim, J. (2001). Asian American identity development. In B. W. Jackson & C. Wijeyesinghe (Eds.), *New perspectives on racial identity development: A theoretical and practical anthology* (pp. 67–90). New York: New York University Press.

King, P. M., & Kitchener, K. S. (1994). *Developing reflective judgment: Understanding and promoting intellectual growth and critical thinking in adolescents and adults*. San Francisco: Jossey-Bass.

King, P. M., & Shuford, B. C. (1996). A multicultural view is a more cognitively complex view: Cognitive development and multicultural education. *American Behavioral Scientist, 40*(2), 153–164.

Kirk, G., & Okazawa-Rey, M. (2003). *Women's lives: Multicultural perspectives*. New York: McGraw-Hill.

Kitchener, K. (1982). Human development and the college campus: Sequences and tasks. In G. Hanson (Ed.), *Measuring student development* (New Directions for Student Services, No. 20). San Francisco: Jossey-Bass.

Kitwana, B. (2002). *The hip-hop generation: Young Blacks and the crisis in African-American culture*. New York: Basic Books.

Kivel, P. (2004). *You call this a democracy? Who benefits, who pays, and who really decides?* Croton-on-Hudson, NY: Apex Press.

Klug, B. (2004, February 2). The myth of the new anti-Semitism. *The Nation*. Retrieved September 3, 2006, from www.thenation.com/doc/20040202/klug.

Kochman, T. (1981). *Black and white styles in conflict*. Chicago: Chicago University Press.

Kohl, M. (Ed.). (1978). *Infanticide and the value of life*. New York: Prometheus Books.

Kolb, D. A. (1984). *Experiential learning: Experience as the source of learning and development*. Englewood Cliffs, NJ: Prentice-Hall.

Koliba, C., O'Meara, K., & Seidel R. (2000). Social justice principles for experiential education [Special issue]. *National Society of Experiential Education Quarterly, 26*(1).

Kosciw, J. G. (2002). *The GLSEN 2001 National School Climate Survey: The school-related experiences of our nation's lesbian, gay, bisexual and transgender youth*. New York: Office for Public Policy of the Gay, Lesbian and Straight Education Network.

Kosciw, J. G. & Diaz, E. (2006). *The 2005 National School Climate Survey: The experiences of gay, lesbian, bisexual and transgender youth in our nation's schools*. New York: Office for Public Policy of the Gay, Lesbian and Straight Education Network.

Kozol, J. (1992). *Savage inequalities*. New York: Crown.

Kozol, J. (2005). *The shame of the nation: The restoration of apartheid schooling in America*. New York: Random House.

Krauss, I. K. (1987). Environmental psychology. In G. L. Maddox (Ed.), *The encyclopedia of aging* (pp. 213–215). New York: Springer.

Kreisberg, S. (1992). *Transforming power: Domination, empowerment, and education*. Albany: State University of New York Press.

Krueger, A. (2002, November 14). The apple falls close to the tree, even in the land of opportunity. *New York Times*, p. C2.

Kumashiro, K. K. (2000). Toward a theory of anti-oppressive education. *Review of Educational Research, 70*(1), 25–53.

Kumashiro, K. K. (2001). *Troubling intersections of race and sexuality: Queer students of color and anti-oppressive education*. Lanham, MD: Rowman & Littlefield.

Kumashiro, K. K. (2002). *Troubling education: Queer activism and antioppressive pedagogy*. New York: RoutledgeFalmer.

Kumashiro, K. K. (Ed.). (2003). *Restoried selves: Autobiographies of queer Asian-Pacific-American activists*. New York: Harrington Park.

Kumashiro, K. K. (Ed.). (2004). *Against common sense: Teaching and learning toward social justice*. New York: RoutledgeFalmer.

Kurien, P. (1998). Becoming American by becoming Hindu: Indian Americans take their place at the multicultural table. In R. S. Warner & J. G. Wittner (Eds.), *Gatherings in diaspora: Religious communities and the new immigration*. Philadelphia: Temple University Press.

Kushner, T., & Solomon, A. (Eds.). (2003). *Wrestling with Zion: Progressive Jewish-American responses to the Israeli-Palestinian conflict*. New York: Grove Press.

Ladson-Billings, G. (2004). Culture vs. citizenship: The challenge of racialized citizenship in the United States. In J. A. Banks (Ed.), *Diversity and citizenship education: Global perspectives* (pp. 99–126). San Francisco: Jossey-Bass.

Ladson-Billings, G. (1994). *The dreamkeepers: Successful teachers of African American children*. San Francisco: Jossey-Bass.

Ladson-Billings, G. (1996). Silence as weapons: Challenges of a black professor teaching White students. *Theory into Practice, 35*(2), 79–85.

Ladson-Billings, G., & Tate, W. F. (1995). Toward a theory of culturally relevant pedagogy. *American Educational Research Journal, 32*(3), 465–491.

Landau, S. (Ed.). (2003). *Cambridge Dictionary of American English*. Cambridge, England: Cambridge University Press.

Langman, P. F. (1995). Including Jews in multiculturalism. *Journal of Multicultural Counseling and Development, 23*, 222–236.

Langmuir, G. I. (1990). *Toward a definition of antisemitism*. Berkeley: University of California Press.

Lankford, H., Loeb, S., & Wyckoff, J. (2002). Teacher sorting and the plight of urban schools: A descriptive analysis. *Educational Evaluation and Policy Analysis, 24*(1), 37–62.

Laquer, W., & Rubin, B. (Eds.). (1995). *The Israel–Arab reader: A documentary history of the Middle East conflict* (5th rev. and updated ed.). New York: Penguin.

Larson, L. M. (2005). The necessity of feminist pedagogy in a climate of political backlash. *Equity & Excellence in Education, 38*(2), 135–144.

Lather, P. (1991). *Getting smart: Feminist research and pedagogy within the postmodern.* New York: Routledge.

Lawrence, K., Sutton, S., Kubisch, A., Susi, G., & Fulbright-Anderson, K. (2004). *Structural racism and community building.* Washington, DC: Aspen Institute Roundtable on Community Change.

Lawrence-Lightfoot, S. (2000). *Respect: An exploration.* New York: Perseus.

Lee, D. B. (2004). A great racial commission: Religion and the construction of White America. In H. Goldschmidt & E. McAlister (Eds.), *Race, nation, and religion in the Americas* (pp. 85–111). New York: Oxford University Press.

Lee, E. (2004). American gatekeeping: Race and immigration law in the twentieth century. In N. Foner & G. Frederickson (Eds.), *Not just black and white: Historical and contemporary perspectives on immigration, race and ethnicity in the U.S.* New York: Russell Sage Foundation.

Lee, J., & Bean, F. D. (2003). America's changing color lines: Immigration, race/ethnicity, and multiracial identification. *Annual Review of Sociology, 30*, 221–242.

Lee, R. G. (1999). *Orientals: Asian Americans in popular culture.* Philadelphia: Temple University Press.

Lee, S. (1994). Behind the model minority stereotype: Voices of high- and low-achieving Asian American students. *Anthropology and Education Quarterly, 25*(4), 413–429.

Lee, S. (1996). *Unraveling the "model minority" stereotype.* New York: Teachers College Press.

Lee, W. H. (2001). *My country versus me.* New York: Hyperion.

Leonardo, Z. (Ed.). (2005). *Critical pedagogy and race.* Malden, MA: Blackwell.

Leondar-Wright, B. (2005). *Class matters: Cross-class alliance building for middle-class activists.* Gabriola Island, BC: New Society.

Leong, R. (1996). *Asian American sexualities: Dimensions of the gay and lesbian experience.* New York: Routledge.

Lerner, G. (1986). *Women and history.* New York: Oxford University Press.

Lerner, M. (1992). Zionism: Its legitimacy and tragic flaws; Israel: Legitimate criticisms vs. Israel-bashing and anti-Semitism. In *The socialism of fools: Anti-Semitism on the left* (pp. 1–21). Oakland, CA: Tikkun Books.

Levitt, P., & Waters, M. C. (2002). *The changing face of home: The transnational lives of the second generation.* New York: Russell Sage Foundation.

Levin, K. (1951). *Field theory in social science: Selected theoretical papers.* New York: Harper & Brothers Publishers.

Lewin, K. (1948). *Resolving social conflicts: Selected papers on group dynamics.* New York: Harper & Row.

Lewis, B. (1984). *The Jews of Islam.* Princeton, NJ: Princeton University Press.

Lewis, M. G. (1993). *Without a word: Teaching beyond women's silence.* New York: Routledge.

Lincoln, C. E., & Mamiya, L. H. (1990). *The black church in the African American experience.* Durham, NC: Duke University Press.

Linton, S. (2005). *My body politic: A memoir.* Ann Arbor: University of Michigan Press.

Lippitt, R. (1949). *Training in community relations.* New York: Harper & Brothers

Lipsitz, G. (1998). *The possessive investment in whiteness: How white people profit from identity politics.* Philadelphia: Temple University Press.

Lipsky, S. (1977). Internalized oppression. *Black Re-Emergence*, 2, 5–10.

Lipton, M., & Oakes, J. (2003). *Teaching to change the world*. New York: McGraw-Hill.

Little, D. (Ed.). (2007). *Peacemakers in action: Profiles of religion in conflict resolution*. New York: Cambridge University Press & Tanenbaum Center for Religious Understanding.

Loewen, J. W. (1995). *Lies my teacher told me: Everything your American history textbook got wrong*. New York: Simon & Schuster.

Long, C. N. (2000). *Religious freedom and Indian rights: The case of* Oregon v. Smith. Lawrence: University Press of Kansas.

Longmore, P., & Umanski, L. (Eds). (2001). *The new disability history: American perspectives*. New York: New York University Press.

Lopez, G. E., Gurin, P., & Nagda, B. A. (1998). Education and understanding structural causes for group inequalities. *Political Psychology*, 19(2), 305–329.

Lorde, A. (1983). There is no hierarchy of oppressions. *Interracial Books for Children Bulletin*, 14(3–4), 9.

Lorde, A. (1984). *Sister outsider*. Trumansburg, NY: Crossing Press.

Lovato, R. (2005). *Far from fringe: Minutemen mobilizes white men left behind by globalization*. Retrieved September 3, 2006, from http://www.publiceye.org/magazine/v19n3/lovato fringe.html.

Love, B. (2000). Developing a liberatory consciousness. In M. Adams, W. J. Blumenfeld, R. Castañeda, H. W. Hackman, M. Peters, & X. Zúñiga. (Eds.), *Readings for diversity and social justice* (pp. 470–474). New York: Routledge.

Love, B. J. (2004). *Brown* plus 50 counter-storytelling: A critical race theory analysis of the "majoritarian achievement gap" story. *Equity & Excellence in Education*, 37(3), 227–246.

Lubrano, A. (2003). *Limbo: Blue-collar roots, white-collar dreams*. Hoboken, NJ: John Wiley.

Lui, M. (2005, February 3). Doubly divided: The racial wealth gap. *Black Commentator* (124). Retrieved October 30, 2006, from http://www.blackcommentator.com.

Lui, M., Robles, B., Leondar-Wright, B., Brewer, R., & Adams, R., with United for a Fair Economy (2006). *The color of wealth: The story behind the U.S. racial wealth divide*. New York: New Press.

Luke, C., & Gore, J. (Eds). (1992). *Feminisms and critical pedagogy*. New York: Routledge.

Lunatics' Liberation Front. (2006). Lunatics' Liberation Front. Retrieved October 30, 2006, from http://walnet.org/llf/.

Lynn, M., & Adams, M. (2002). Critical race theory and education: Recent developments in the field [Special issue]. *Equity & Excellence in Education*, 35(2).

Lynn, M., Yosso, T., Solórzano, D. G, & Parker, L. (2002). Critical race theory and qualitative research [Special issue]. *Qualitative Inquiry*, 8(1).

Lyons, N. P. (1983). Two perspectives on self, relationships, and morality. *Harvard Education Review*, 55, 124–146.

MacDonald-Dennis, C. (2005). *Competing narratives: The interplay between racial and ethno-religious identity among Ashkenazi Jewish undergraduate anti-racist peer educators*. Unpublished doctoral dissertation, University of Massachusetts Amherst.

MacDonald-Dennis, C. (2006). Understanding anti-Semitism and its impact: A new framework for conceptualizing Jewish identity. Equity & Excellence in Education, (3), 267–278.

Macedo, D., & Gounari, P. (Eds.). (2006). *The globalization of racism*. Boulder, CO: Paradigm.

MacKinnon, C. A. (1991). *Toward a feminist theory of the state*. Cambridge, MA: Harvard University Press.

Maddigan, M. M. (1993). The establishment clause, civil religion, and the public church. *California Law Review, 81*, 293.

Maher, F. A. (1985). Pedagogies for the gender-balanced classroom. *Journal of Thought, 20*(3), 48–64.

Maher, F. A., & Tetreault, M. K. T. (1994). *The feminist classroom: An inside look at how professors and students are transforming higher education for a diverse society.* New York: Basic Books.

Males, M. (2004, February). Coming of age in America. *Youth Today*, 1–2.

Mamdani, M. (2004). *Good Muslim, bad Muslim: America, the Cold War, and the roots of terror.* New York: Pantheon Books.

Mann, G. S. (2000). Sikhism in the United States. In H. Coward, J. Hinnells, & R. B. Williams (Eds.), *The South Asian religious diaspora in Britain, Canada, and the United States* (pp. 259–276). Albany: State University of New York Press.

Marabel, M. (1984). *Race, reform, and rebellion: The second reconstruction in black America, 1945–1982.* Jackson: University of Mississippi Press.

Marabel, M. (2002). *The great wells of democracy: The meaning of race in American life.* New York: Basic Books.

Marchesani, L., & Adams, M. (1992). Dynamics of diversity in the teaching-learning process: A faculty development model for analysis and action. In M. Adams (Ed.), *Promoting diversity in college classrooms: Innovative responses for the curriculum, faculty and institutions* (New Directions for Teaching and Learning, No. 52, pp. 9–21). San Francisco: Jossey-Bass.

Marchesani, L. M., & Jackson, B. W. (2005). Transforming higher education institutions using multicultural organizational development: A case study of a large northeastern university. In M. L. Ouellett (Ed.), *Teaching inclusively: Resources for course, department & institutional change in higher education* (pp. 241–251). Stillwater, OK: New Forums.

Marcus, E. (1992). *Making history: The struggle for gay and lesbian equal rights.* New York: Harper Perennial.

Marrow, A. J. (1969). *The practical theorist: The life and work of Kurt Lewin.* New York: Basic Books.

Marshall, C., & Oliva, M. (Eds.). (2006). *Leadership for social justice: Making revolutions in education.* Boston: Pearson.

Martin, J. (2003). Almost White: The ambivalent promise of Christian missions among the Cherokees. In C. R. Prentiss (Ed.), *Religion and the construction of race and ethnicity* (pp. 43–60). New York: New York University Press.

Martin, W. (2005). *With God on our side: The rise of the religious right in America.* New York: Broadway.

Martinez, R. (2004). *The new Americans: Seven families journey to another country.* New York: New Press.

Marty, M. E., & Appleby, R. S. (Eds.). (1997). *Religion, ethnicity, and self-identity: Nations in turmoil.* Hanover, NH: University Press of New England.

Marx, S. (2006). *Revealing the invisible: Confronting passive racism in teacher education.* New York: Routledge.

Massachusetts Department of Education. (2004). *2003 Youth Risk Behavior Survey results.* Retrieved September 21, 2005, from http://www.doe.mass.edu/hssss/yrbs/03/results.pdf.

Mathisen, R. R. (2001). *Critical issues in American religious history: A reader.* Waco, TX: Baylor University Press.

Mazur, E. M. (1999). *The Americanization of religious minorities: Confronting the constitutional order*. Baltimore: Johns Hopkins University Press.

McCarthy, L. (2005). Special theme issue: Recent issues in social justice education. *Equity & Excellence in Education, 38*(2), 101-167.

McCarthy, L., & Whitlock, E. R. (2002). Review of the year's publications in social justice education. *Equity & Excellence in Education, 35*(1), 79–85.

McChesney, R. W. (2004). *The problem of the media: U.S. communication politics in the 21st century*. New York: Monthly Review Press.

McCloud, A B. (2003). Islam in America: The mosaic. In Y. Y. Haddad, J. I. Smith, & J. L. Esposito (Eds.). *Religion and immigration: Christian, Jewish, and Muslim experiences in the United States* (pp. 159-174). Lanham, MD: AltaMira Press.

McGuire, P. (1993). *Taps for a Jim Crow army: Letters from Black soldiers in WWII*. Lexington: University Press of Kentucky.

McIntosh, P. (1988). *White privilege and male privilege: A personal account of coming to see correspondences through work in women's studies*. Working paper No. 189. Wellesley, MA: Wellesley College Center for Research on Women.

McIntosh, P. (1989, July–August). White privilege: Unpacking the invisible knapsack. *Peace and Freedom*, 10–12.

McIntosh, P. (1992). White privilege and male privilege: A personal account of coming to see correspondences through work in women's studies. In M. L. Andersen and R H. Collins (Eds.), *Race, class, and gender: An anthology*. Belmont, CA: Wadsworth.

McIntosh, P. (1998). White privilege: Unpacking the invisible knapsack. In *Beyond heroes and holidays: A practical guide to K–12 anti-racist, multicultural education and staff development* (pp. 79–82). Wellesley, MA: Network of Educators on the Americas.

McIntyre, A. (1997). *Making meaning of whiteness: Exploring racial identity with white teachers*. New York: State University of New York Press.

McKeachie, W. J., & Svinicki, M. (2006). *McKeachie's teaching tips: Strategies, research, and theory for college and university teachers*. New York: Houghton Mifflin.

McLemore, S. D. (1993). *Racial and ethnic relations in America* (4th ed.). Boston: Allyn & Bacon.

McNamee, S. J., & Miller, R. K., Jr. (2004). *The meritocracy myth*. New York: Rowman & Littlefield.

McNeil, L. M. (2005). Faking equity: High stakes testing and the education of Latino youth. In A. Valenzuela (Ed.), *Leaving children behind*. Albany: State University of New York Press.

McWhorter, G. A. (1969). Deck the ivy racist halls: The case of Black Studies. In A. L. Robinson, C. C. Foster, & D. H. Ogilvie (Eds.), *Black Studies in the university: A symposium*. New Haven, CT: Yale University Press.

Memmi, A. (1967/1991). *The colonizer and the colonized*. Boston: Beacon Press.

Memmi, A. (1975). Who is an Arab Jew? *Jimena: Jews indigenous to the Middle East and North Africa*. Retrieved 3/3/2005. www.jemena-justice.org/faq/memmi.htm.

Memmi, A. (2000). *Racism*. Minneapolis: University of Minnesota Press.

Merithew, C. W. (2003). Making the Italian other: Blacks, Whites, and the inbetween in the 1895 Spring Valley, Illinois, race riot. In J. Guglielmo & S. Salerno (Eds.), *Are Italians White? How race is made in America*. New York: Routledge.

Meyers, C., & Jones, T. B. (1993). *Promoting active learning: Strategies for the college classroom*. San Francisco: Jossey-Bass.

Michael, R. (2005). *A concise history of American antisemitism*. Lanham, MD: Rowman & Littlefield.

Mill, C. R. (1974). Working with hostile groups. *Social Change: Ideas and Applications*, *4*(1), 1–5.

Miller, F. A., & Katz, J. H. (2002). *The inclusion breakthrough: Unleashing the real power of diversity*. San Francisco: Barrett-Koehler.

Miller, J. B. (1976). *Toward a new psychology of women*. Boston: Beacon Press.

Miller, S. M., & Savoie, A. J. (2002). *Respect and rights: Class, race and gender today*. New York: Rowman & Littlefield.

Min, P. G. (1996). The entrepreneurial adaptation of Korean immigrants. In S. Pedraza & R. G. Rumbaut (Eds), *Origins and destinies: Immigration, race, and ethnicity in America* (pp. 302–314). Belmont, CA: Wadsworth.

Min, P. G., & Kim, J. H. (2002). *Religions in Asian America: Building faith communities*. Walnut Creek, CA: AltaMira Press.

Mindell, A. (1995). *Sitting in the fire: Large group transformation using conflict and diversity*. Portland, OR: Lao Tse Press.

MindFreedom. (2003). MindFreedom: Win human rights in the mental health system! Retrieved October 30, 2006, from http://www.mindfreedom.org.

Mirsky, Y. (1986). Civil religion and the establishment clause. *Yale Law Journal, 95*, 1237.

Mohanty, C. T. (2003). *Feminism without borders: Decolonizing theory, practicing solidarity*. Durham, NC: Duke University Press.

Mohanty, C. T., Russo, A., & Torres, L. (1991). *Third world women and the politics of feminism*. Bloomington: Indiana University Press.

Moosbruker, J. (1987). Using a stage theory model to understand and manage transitions in group dynamics. In W. B. Reddy & C. Henderson (Eds.), *Training theory and practice*. La Jolla, CA: University Associates.

Moraga, C., & Anzaldúa, G. (Eds.). (1981/1983). *This bridge called my back: Writings by radical women of color*. New York: Kitchen Table/Women of Color Press.

Morgan, R. (Ed.). (1970). *Sisterhood is powerful: An anthology of writings from the women's liberation movement*. New York: Vintage.

Morris, J. (1991). *Pride against prejudice: Transforming attitudes to disability*. Philadelphia: New Society.

Morrow, R. A., & Torres, C. A. (1995). *Social theory and education: A critique of theories of social and cultural reproduction*. New York: State University of New York Press.

Moser, B. (2005). *The battle of "Georgiafornia."* Retrieved September 3, 2006, from http://www.splcenter.org/intel/intelreport/article.jsp?aid=505.

Moses, R. P., & Cobb, C. E., Jr. (2001). *Radical equations: Math literacy and civil rights*. Boston: Beacon Press.

Mosse, G. L. (1985). *Toward the final solution: A history of European racism*. Madison: University of Wisconsin Press.

Muska, S., & Olafsdóttir, G. (1998). *The Brandon Teena story* [Video]. New York: Docurama.

Nagda, B. A., Gurin, P., & Lopez, G. (2003). Transformative pedagogy for democracy and social justice. *Race, Ethnicity and Education, 6*(2), 165–191.

Namaste, V. (K.). (2000). *Invisible lives: The erasure of transsexual and transgendered people*. Chicago: University of Chicago Press.

*The Nation*. (2006, August 28–September 4). White heat: What's fueling the new nativism? [Special issue] 11–32.

National Asian Pacific American Legal Consortium. (2002). *Backlash final report*. Washington, DC: Author.

National Council for Social Studies. (1998). Study about religions in the social studies curriculum. Retrieved Sept 26, 2006, from http://www.socialstudies.org/positions/religion/.

National Network for Immigrant and Refugee Rights. (2001). *Uprooted: Refugees of the global economy* [Video]. http://www.nnir.org.

National Organization on Disability. (2000). Harris Survey of Americans with Disabilities. Retrieved August 25, 2006, from http://www.nod.org.

National Research Council. (1998). *Children of immigrants: Health adjustment and public assistance*. Washington. DC: Author.

National Urban League. (2006). *State of black America 2006: Opportunity compact*. New York: Author.

Nelson, G. (1982). Social class and public policy for the elderly. *Social Service Review, 56*(1), 85–107.

Nelson, T. E. (Ed.). (2002). *Ageism: Stereotyping and prejudice against older persons*. Cambridge, MA: MIT Press.

Nelson-Laird, T. F. (2005). Modeling accentuation effects: Enrolling in a diversity course and the importance of social action engagement. *Journal of Higher Education, 76*(4), 448–476.

Nestle, J., Howell, C., & Wilchins, R. (Eds.). (2002). *Genderqueer: Voices from beyond the sexual minority*. New York: Routledge.

Newton, E. (1972). *Mother camp: Female impersonators in America*. Chicago: University of Chicago Press.

*New York Times* correspondents. (2005). *Class matters*. New York: Henry Holt.

Nieto, S. (1999). *The light in their eyes: Creating multicultural learning communities*. New York: Teachers College Press.

Nieto, S. (2003a). *Affirming diversity: The sociopolitical context for multicultural education* (4th ed.). White Plains, NY: Longman.

Nieto, S. (2003b). *What keeps teachers going?* New York: Teachers College Press.

Nieto, S. (2004). *Affirming diversity: The sociopolitical context of multicultural education* (4th ed.). New York: Longman.

Nieto, S. (2005). *Why we teach*. New York: Teachers College Press.

Nimer, M. (2001). *The status of Muslim civil rights in the United States*. Washington, DC: Council on American Islamic Relations.

Noddings, N. (1999a). Care, justice, and equity. In M. S. Katz, N. Noddings, & K. A. Strike (Eds.), *Justice and caring: The search for common ground in education* (pp. 7–20). New York: Teachers College Press.

Noddings, N. (1999b). Caring and competence. In G. Griffen (Ed.), *The education of teachers* (pp. 205–220). Chicago: National Society of Education.

Noddings, N. (2003). *Caring: A feminine approach to ethics and moral education*. Berkeley: University of California Press.

Noguera, P.A. (2003). *City schools and the American dream. New* York: Teachers College Press.

Noronha, J. (1992). International and multicultural education: Unrelated adversaries or successful partners? In M. Adams (Ed.), *Promoting diversity in college classrooms: Innovative responses for curriculum, faculty, and institutions* (New Directions for Teaching and Learning, No. 52, pp. 53–61). San Francisco: Jossey-Bass.

Obear, K. H. (2000). Exploring the phenomenon of triggering events for social justice educators. *Dissertation Abstracts International, 61* (07), 2563A. (UMI No. 9978535)

Oboler, S. (1995). *Ethnic labels, Latino lives*. Minneapolis: University of Minnesota Press.

Odell-Scott, D. (Ed.). (2004). *Democracy and religion: Free exercise and diverse visions*. Kent, OH: Kent State University Press.

Office of Immigration Statistics. (2004). *Yearbook of immigration statistics 2004.* Retrieved September 4, 2006, from http://www.uscis.gov/graphics/shared/statistics/yearbook/YrBk04Im.htm.

Okihiro, G. Y. (1994). *Margins and mainstreams: Asian American history and culture.* Seattle: University of Washington Press.

Oliver, M. L., & Shapiro, T. M. (1997). *Black wealth/White wealth: A new perspective on racial inequality.* New York: Routledge.

Omi, M., & Winant, H. (1986). Racial formation. In *Racial formation in the United States from the 1960s to the 1980s* (pp. 57–69). New York: Routledge.

Omolade, B. (1987). A black feminist pedagogy. *Women's Studies Quarterly, 15*(3–4), 32–39.

O'Neil, J. H. (1996). *The golden ghetto: The psychology of affluence.* Center City, MN: Hazelden.

Orfalea, G. (2006). *The Arab Americans: A history.* Northampton, MA: Olive Branch Press.

Orfield, G. (1998). Commentary on the education of Mexican immigrant children. In M. Suarez-Orozco (Ed.), *Crossings: Mexican immigration in interdisciplinary perspectives.* Cambridge, MA: Harvard University Press.

Orfield, G., & Eaton, S. E. (1996). *Dismantling desegregation: The quiet reversal of* Brown v. Board of Education. New York: New Press.

Orfield, G., & Kurlaender, M. (Eds.). (2001). *Diversity challenged: Evidence on the impact of affirmative action.* Cambridge, MA: Civil Rights Project, Harvard Education Publishing Group.

Orfield, G., & Lebowitz, H. J. (1999). *Religion, race and justice in a changing America.* New York: Century Foundation Press.

Orfield, G., & Lee, C. (2006). *Racial transformation and the changing nature of segregation.* Cambridge, MA: Civil Rights Project, Harvard University.

Orfield, G., Marin, P., & Horn, C. (2005). *Higher education and the color line.* Cambridge, MA: Harvard University Press.

Oser, F. K., Andreas, D., & Patry, J-L. (Eds.). (1992). *Effective and responsible teaching: The new synthesis.* San Francisco: Jossey-Bass.

O'Shea, S. (2006). *Sea of faith: Islam and Christianity in the medieval Mediterranean world.* New York: Walker.

Ouellett, M. (2000). *Disabilities resources for teaching inclusively.* Amherst, MA: Center for Teaching.

Ouellett, M. (Ed.). (2005). *Teaching inclusively: Resources for course, department & institutional change in higher education.* Stillwater, OK: New Forums.

Ouellett, M., & Fraser, E. (2005). Teaching together: Interracial teams. In M. Ouellett (Ed.), *Teaching inclusively: Resources for course, department and institutional change in higher education.* Stillwater, OK: New Forums Press.

Oyler, C., Hamre, B., & Bejoian, L. M. (2006). Narrating disability: Pedagogical imperatives [Special issue]. *Equity & Excellence in Education, 39*(2).

Palmer, P. (1998). *The courage to teach: Exploring the inner landscape of a teacher's life.* San Francisco: Jossey-Bass.

Palmore, E. B., Branch, L., & Harris, D. K. (Eds.). (2005). *Encyclopedia of ageism.* New York: Haworth Press.

Parker, L., Deyhle, D., & Villenes, S. (1999). *Race is ... race isn't: Critical race theory & qualitative studies in education.* Boulder, CO: Westview.

Pascarella, E. T., & Terenzini, P. T. (1991). *How college affects students: Findings and insights from twenty years of research.* San Francisco: Jossey-Bass.

Pedraza, S. (1996). Origins and destinies: Immigration, race and ethnicity in contemporary America. In S. Pedraza & R. G. Rumbaut (Eds.), *Origins and destinies* (pp. 21–42). Belmont, CA: Wadsworth.

Peña, R. (2005). Water is clear like me: A story about race, identity, teaching, and social justice. In R. A. Peña, K. Guest, & L. W. Matsuda (Eds.), *Community and difference: Teaching, pluralism, and social justice* (pp. 1–24). New York: Peter Lang.

Pensler, D. J. (2005). Antisemitism and anti-Zionism: A historical approach. In D. J. Pensler, M. R. Marrus, & J. G. Stein (Eds.), *Contemporary antisemitism* (pp. 80–95). Toronto: University of Toronto Press.

Perea, J. F. (Ed.). (1997). *Immigrants out! The new nativism and the anti-immigrant impulse in the United States.* New York: New York University Press.

Perez, L., (2002, April 23). Suit alleges predatory lending: FTC seeks unfair loan stories. *(Syracuse, NY) Post Standard.*

Perlmutter, P. (1991). The teaching of contempt. In *Divided we fall: A history of ethnic, religious, and racial prejudice in America* (pp. 259–305). Ames: Iowa State University Press.

Perrucci, R., & Wysong, E. (2002). *The new class society.* Lanham, MD: Rowman & Littlefield.

Perry, M., & Schweitzer, F. M. (2002). *Antisemitism: Myth and hate from antiquity to present.* New York: Palgrave Macmillan.

Perry, W. G. (1970). *Forms of intellectual and ethical development in the college years.* New York: Holt, Rinehart & Winston.

Perry, W. G. (1981). Cognitive and ethical growth: The making of meaning. In A. Chickering (Ed.), *The modern American college* (pp. 76–116). San Francisco: Jossey-Bass.

Petillo-McCoy, M. (1999). *Black picket fences: Privilege and peril among the black middle class.* Chicago: University of Chicago Press.

Pettigrew, T.F. (1998). Intergroup contact theory. *Annual Review Psychology, 49*:65-85.

Pew Forum on Religion & Public Life (2006, August 24). *Many Americans uneasy with mix of religion and politics.* http://pewforum.org/docs/index.php?DocID=153.

Pfeiffer, J. W., & Jones, J. E. (Eds.). (1974). *Handbook of structured experiences for human relations training* (Vols. 1-2, revised. edition)., La Jolla, CA: University Associates.

Pharr, S. (1988). *Homophobia: A weapon of sexism.* Inverness, CA: Chardon Press.

Pharr, S. (1996). *In the time of the right: Reflections on liberation.* Berkeley, CA: Chardon Press.

Pheterson, G. (1990). Alliances between women: Overcoming internalized oppression and internalized domination. In L. Albrecht and R. Brewer (Eds.), *Bridges of power: Women's multicultural alliances* (pp. 34–48). Philadelphia: New Society.

Philbrick, N. (2006). *Mayflower: A story of community, courage and war.* New York: Viking.

Phillips, C. (1987). The trainer as person: On the importance of developing your best intervention. In W. B. Reddy & C. Henderson (Eds.), *Training theory and practice* (pp. 29–35). La Jolla, CA: University Associates.

Phillips, K. (2006). *American theocracy: The peril and politics of radical religion, oil, and borrowed money in the 21st century.* New York: Viking.

Pittelman, K., & Resource Generation. (2005). *Classified: How to stop hiding your privilege and use it for social change.* Brooklyn, NY: Soft Skull Press.

Piven, F. F., & Cloward, R. (1982). *The new class war: Reagan's attack on the welfare state and its consequences.* New York: Pantheon.

Pizzigati, S. (2004). *Greed and good: Understanding and overcoming the inequality that limits our lives.* Croton-on-Hudson, NY: Apex Press.

Pliner, S. (2004). Universal instructional design and higher education [Special issue]. *Equity & Excellence in Education, 37*(2).

Pluralism Project. (2006). Statistics. Retrieved October 30, 2006, from http://www.pluralism.org/resources/statistics.

Polk, W. (2006). *The birth of America.* New York: HarperCollins.

Porter, L. (1982). Giving and receiving feedback: It will never be easy, but it can be better. In L. Porter & B. Mohr (Eds.), *The NTL reading book for human relations training.* Alexandria, VA: National Training Laboratories Institute.

Portes, A., & Rumbaut, R. G. (2001). *Legacies: The story of the immigrant second generation.* Berkeley: University of California Press.

Portes, A., & Zhou, M. (1993). The new second generation: Segmented assimilation and its variants. *Annals of the American Academy of Political and Social Science, 530,* 74–96.

Postman, N. (1982). *The disappearance of childhood.* New York: Vintage Books.

Powell, A. B., & Frankenstein, M. (1997). *Ethnomathematics: Challenging Eurocentrism in mathematics education.* Albany: State University of New York Press.

Prager, D., & Telushkin, J. (2003). *Why the Jews? The reason for antisemitism* (Rev. and updated ed.). New York: Touchstone.

Prejudice Institute. (2005). *What is ethnoviolence?* Retrieved July 21, 2005, from http://www.publiceye.org/prejinst/factsheet1.html.

Prentiss, C. R. (2003). *Religion and the creation of race and ethnicity.* New York: New York University Press.

Preves, S. (2003). *Intersex and identity: The contested self.* New Brunswick, NJ: Rutgers University Press.

Prewitt, K. (2004). The census counts, the census classifies. In N. F. Foner & G. M. Frederickson (Eds.), *Not just Black and White: Historical and contemporary perspectives on immigration, race, and ethnicity in the United States* (pp. 145–164). New York: Russell Sage Foundation.

Proudman, B. (1995). AEE adopts definition. *AEE Horizon, 15,* 1, 21.

Raboteau, A. J. (2001). *Canaan land: A religious history of African Americans.* New York: New York University Press.

Rachal, J. R. (1998). We'll never turn back: Adult education and the struggle for citizenship in Mississippi's Freedom Summer. *American Educational Research Journal, 35*(2), 167–198.

Ramírez, M., & Casteñada, A. (1974). *Cultural democracy, bicognitive development, and education.* New York: Academic Press.

Ramos, J. (Ed.). (1994). *Campañeras: Latina lesbians.* New York: Routledge.

Ratti, R. (Ed.). (1993). *A lotus of another color: An unfolding of the South Asian gay and lesbian experience.* Boston: Alyson.

Rawls, J. (1971). *A theory of justice.* Cambridge, MA: Harvard University Press.

Raymond, J. (1979) *Transsexual empire: The making of the she-male.* Boston: Beacon Press.

Reagon, B. J. (1983). Coalition politics: Turning the century. In B. Smith (Ed.), *Home girls: A black feminist anthology* (pp. 356–368). New York: Kitchen Table Press.

Reason, R. D., Broido, E. M., Davis, T. L., & Evans, N. J. (Eds.). (2005). *Developing social justice allies* (Vol. 110). San Francisco: Jossey-Bass.

Regenspan, B. (2002). *Parallel practices: Social justice–focused teacher education and the elementary school classroom* (Vol. 206). New York: Peter Lang.

Rehabilitation Act Amendments of 1973. 29 U.S.C. §701 *et. seq* (also known as Section 504).

Remba, G. D., & Klug, B. (2004, April 12). Anti-Semitism: New or old? *The Nation.* Retrieved September 3, 2006, from www.thenation.com/doc/20040412/exchange.

Rethinking Schools. (2002). Rethinking Schools online. Retrieved October 30, 2006, from http://www.rethinkingschools.org.

Rich, A. (1979). *On lies, secrets, and silence*. New York: Norton.

Richie, R. E., & Jones, D. G. (Eds.). (1974). *American civil religion*. New York: Harper & Row.

Riley, M. W., & Foner, A. (1968). *Aging and society: Vol. 1. An inventory of research finding*. New York: Russell Sage Foundation.

Risen, J. (2006). *The secret history of the CIA and the Bush administration*. New York: Free Press.

Ritzer, G., & Goodman, D. (2003). *Sociological theory*. New York: McGraw-Hill.

Road Map Foundation. (2002–2003). At Conversation Cafés, you are the talk show! Retrieved October 30, 2006, from http://www.conversationcafe.org.

Roberts, R.A., Bell, L.A., & Murphy, B. (unpublished manuscript). Flipping the script: Analyzing youth responses to race and racism.

Rodriguez, N. M., & Villaverde, L. E. (Eds.). (2000). *Dismantling white privilege: Pedagogy, politics, and whiteness*. New York: Peter Lang.

Roediger, D. R. (1991). *The wages of whiteness: Race and the making of the American working class*. London: Verso.

Roediger, D. R. (2005). *Working toward whiteness: How America's immigrants became white—the strange journey from Ellis Island to the suburbs*. New York: Basic Books.

Rogoff, B. (2003). *The cultural nature of human development*. New York: Oxford University Press.

Rohd, M. (1998). *Theatre for community, conflict and dialogue: The Hope Is Vital training manual*. Portsmouth, NH: Heinemann.

Romney, P., Tatum, B., & Jones, J. (1992). Feminist strategies for teaching about oppression: The importance of process. *Women's Studies Quarterly, 20*(1–2), 95–110.

Rose, T. (1994). *Black noise: Rap music and black culture in contemporary America*. Middletown, CT: Wesleyan University Press

Rosenblatt, R. (July 3, 1994). Their finest minute. *New York Times Magazine, 143* (49746). 22–33.

Rosenbaum, R. (Ed.). (2004). *Those who forget the past: The question of anti-Semitism*. New York: Random House.

Ross, M., Tait, R., Brandeberry, L., Grossberg, G., & Nakra, R. (1986, May). Age differences in emotional and physical health. Poster presentation, Midwest Psychological Association, Chicago.

Rothenberg, P. (1985). Teaching about racism and sexism: A case history. *Journal of Thought, 20*(3), 122–136.

Rothenberg, P. (2004). *White privilege: Essential readings on the other side of racism*. New York: Worth.

Rumbaut, R. D. (1995). Comparative research findings on the educational progress of immigrant children. In R. D. Rumbaut and W. Cornelius (Eds), *California's immigrant children*. La Jolla, CA: Center for U.S.-Mexican Studies.

Rumbaut, R. G. (1996). Origins and destinies: Immigration, race, and ethnicity in contemporary America. In S. Pedraza and R. G. Rumbaut (Eds.), *Origins and destinies: Immigration, race, and ethnicity in America* (pp. 21–42). Belmont, CA: Wadsworth.

Russell, J. (2005, September 11). At regional malls, a teen test. *Boston Globe*, p. A1.

Russell, M. G. (1983). Black-eyed blues connections: From the inside out. In C. Bunch & S. Pollack (Eds.), *Learning our way: Essays in feminist education* (pp. 272–284). Trumansburg, NY: Crossing Press.

Russo, A. (2001). *Taking back our lives: A call to action for the feminist movement*. New York: Routledge.

Ryan, W. (1972). *Blaming the victim*. New York: Vintage.

Saalfield, C., & Phipps, C. (Dirs.). (1993). *Sacred lies, civil truths* [Video]. Black Planet Productions. http://www.planetout.com/popcornq/movies.

Sacher, H. M. (1992). *A history of the Jews in America*. New York: Vintage Books.

Sacher, H. M. (2005). *A history of the Jews in the modern world*. New York: Knopf.

Sadker, M., & Sadker, D. (1992). Ensuring equitable participation in college classes. In L. L. B. Border & N. V. N. Chism (Eds.), *Teaching for diversity* (New Directions for Teaching and Learning, No. 49). San Francisco: Jossey-Bass.

Saha, S. C. (Ed.). (2004). *Religious fundamentalism in the contemporary world: Critical social and political issues*. Oxford: Lexington Books.

Said, E.W. (1978). *Orientalism*. New York: Vintage Books.

Said, E. W. (1979/1992). *The question of Palestine* (New preface ed.). New York: Vintage.

Said, E. W. (1993). *Culture and imperialism*. New York: Knopf.

Said, E. W., & Hitchens, C. (Eds.). (2001). *Blaming the victims: Spurious scholarship and the Palestinian question*. London: Verso.

Sandler, B. R., & Hall, R. M. (1982). *The campus climate revisited: Chilly for women faculty, administrators, and graduate students*. Washington, DC: Project on the Status and Education of Women, Association of American Colleges.

Sandoval, C. (2000). *Methodology of the oppressed*. Minneapolis: University of Minnesota Press.

Sarachild, K. (1975). Consciousness-raising: A radical weapon. In Redstockings (Ed.), *Feminist revolution* (pp. 144–150). New York: Random House.

Sassen-Koob, S. (1987). Formal and informal associations: Dominicans and Colombians in New York. In C. R. Sutton & E. M. Chaney (Eds.), *Caribbean life in New York City: Sociocultural dimensions* (pp. 261–277). Staten Island: Center for Migration Studies of New York.

Satloff, R. (2006). *Among the righteous: Lost stories from the Holocaust's long reach into Arab lands*. New York: Public Affairs [Perseus].

Sayres, S. (1984). *The 60's without apology*. Minneapolis: University of Minnesota Press.

Schaefer, G. (1990, November 25). Ultrasound tests determine sex of fetus. *The (Vancouver, BC) Province*. Retrieved August 30, 2006, from http://www.holysmoke.org/fem/fem0305.htm.

Schepers, E. (2005). Harvesting hatred: Anti-immigrant racism today. Retrieved July 21, 2005, from http://www.politicalaffairs.net/article/articleview/995/1/90/.

Schlosser, L. Z. (2003). Christian privilege: Breaking a sacred taboo. *Journal of Multicultural Counseling and Development, 31*, 44–51.

Schniedewind, N. (1985). Cooperatively structured learning: Implications for feminist pedagogy. *Journal of Thought, 20* (3), 74-87.

Schniedewind, N. (1993). Teaching feminist process in the 1990's. *Women's Studies Quarterly*, 3 & 4, 17-30.

Schoem, D., Frankel, L., Zuñiga, X., & Lewis, E. A. (Eds.). (1993). *Multicultural teaching in the university*. Westport, CT: Praeger.

Schoem, D., & Hurtado, S. (Eds.). (2001). *Intergroup dialogue: Deliberative democracy in school, college, community, and workplace*. Ann Arbor: University of Michigan Press.

Scholinski, D. (1998). *The last time I wore a dress*. New York: Riverhead Books.

Schultz, D. L. (2001). *Going south: Jewish women in the Civil Rights movement*. New York: New York University Press.

Schutzman, M., and Cohen-Cruz, J. (1994). *Playing Boal: Theatre, therapy, activism*. Routledge: London.

Schwarz, R. M. (1994). *The skilled facilitator: Practical wisdom for developing effective groups*. San Francisco: Jossey-Bass.

Seabrook, J. (2002). *Class, caste & hierarchies*. London. Verso.

Segrest, M. (1994). *Memoirs of a race traitor*. Boston: South End Press.

Sennett, R., & Cobb, J. (1972). *The hidden injuries of class*. New York: Vintage Books/ Random House.

Shade, B. J. R. (Ed.). (1989). *Culture, style and the educative process*. Springfield, IL: Charles C. Thomas.

Shaheen, J. G. (1984). *The TV Arab*. Bowling Green, OH: Bowling Green State University Popular Press.

Shaheen, J. G. (2001). *Reel bad Arabs: How Hollywood vilifies a people*. New York: Olive Branch Press.

Shapiro, J. P. (1993). *No pity: People with disabilities forging a new civil rights movement*. New York: Random House.

Shapiro, T. (2004). *The hidden cost of being African American: How wealth perpetuates inequality*. New York: Oxford University Press.

Shaw, B. (Ed.). (1994). *The ragged edge: The disability experience from the pages of the first fifteen years of The Disability Rag*. Louisville, KY: Avocado Press.

Shepard, B. (2004). Sylvia and Sylvia's children: A battle for a queer public space. In M. Bernstein (Ed.), *That's revolting: Queer strategies for resisting assimilation* (pp. 97–112). Brooklyn, NY: Soft Skull Press.

Sherif, M. (1967). *Group conflict and co-operation*. London: Routledge and Kegan Paul.

Sherif, M., & Sherif, C. (1970). Black unrest as a social movement toward an emerging self-identity. *Journal of Social and Behavioral Sciences*, *15*(3), 41–52.

Sherover-Marcuse, R. (1981, Fall). Towards a perspective on unlearning racism: Twelve working assumptions. *Issues in Cooperation and Power*, *7*, 14–15.

Sherrod, L. (Ed.). (2005). *Youth activism: An international encyclopedia*. Westport, CT: Greenwood Press.

Shiva, V. (2005). *Earth democracy: Justice, sustainability and peace*. Philadelphia: South End Press.

Shneer, D., & Aviv, C. (Eds.). (2000). *Queer Jews*. New York: Routledge.

Shohat, E. (1997/1988). Sephardim in Israel: Zionism from the standpoint of its Jewish victims. In A. McClintock, A. Mufti, & E. Shohat (Eds.), *Dangerous liaisons: Gender, nation, and postcolonial perspectives* (pp. 39–68). Minneapolis: University of Minnesota Press.

Shor, I. (1992). *Empowering education: Critical thinking for social change*. Chicago: University of Chicago Press.

Shor, I. (1993). Education is politics: Paulo Freire's critical pedagogy. In P. McLaren & P. Leonard (Eds.), *Paulo Freire: A critical encounter* (pp. 25–35). New York: Routledge.

Shor, I. (Ed.). (1987). *Freire for the classroom: A sourcebook for liberatory teaching*. Portsmouth, NH: Heinemann.

Shor, I., & Freire, P. (1987). What is the "dialogical method" of teaching? *Journal of Education*, *169*(3), 11–31.

Sickinger, T. (1999, February 28). American dream denied: When the door is locked to buying a home. *Kansas City Star*.

Silberstein, L. J. (Ed.). (2000). *Mapping Jewish identities*. New York: New York University Press.

Silver, P., Bourke, A., & Strehorn, K. C. (1998). Universal instructional design in higher education: An approach for inclusion. *Equity & Excellence in Education*, *2*, 47–51.

Singh, J. (2003). The racialization of minoritized religious identity: Constructing sacred sites at the intersection of White and Christian supremacy. In J. N. Iwamura & P. Spickard (Eds.), *Revealing the sacred in Asian and Pacific America* (pp. 87–106). Routledge: New York.

Sleeter, C. (1993). How white teachers construct race. In C. McCarthy and W. Crichlow (Eds.), *Race, identity, and representation in education*. New York: Routledge.

Sleeter, C. E., & Grant, C. A. (1994). Education that is multicultural and social reconstructionist. In C. E. Sleeter & C. A. Grant (Eds.), *Making choices for multicultural education: Five approaches to race, class, and gender* (2nd ed., pp. 243–251). New York: Macmillan.

Smelser, N. J., Wilson, W. J., & Mitchell, F. (2001). *Becoming: Racial trends and their consequences: Vol. 1. National Research Council.* Washington, DC: National Academies Press.

Smith, B. (1998). *The truth that never hurts: Writings on race, gender and freedom.* New Brunswick, NJ: Rutgers.

Smith, D. M., & Kolb, D. A. (1986). *User's guide for the learning style inventory: A manual for teachers and trainers.* Boston: McBer.

Smith-Maddox, R. & Solórzano, D.G. (2002). Using critical race theory, Paulo Freire's problem-posing method, and case study research to confront race and racism in education. *Qualitative Inquiry* 8(1): 66-84.

Snopes.com. (1995–2006). Photo gallery. Retrieved October 29, 2006, from http://www.snopes.com/photos/Katrina.

Snow, D. A., & Anderson, L. (1987). Identity work among the homeless: The verbal construction and avowal of personal identities. *American Journal of Sociology, 92*(6), 1336-1771.

Snow, J. (2004). The civilization of white men: The race of the Hindu in *United States v. Bhagat Singh Thind*. In H. Goldschmidt & E. McAlister (Eds.), *Race, nation, and religion in the Americas* (pp. 259–281). New York: Oxford University Press.

Solórzano, D. G., & Bernal, D. D. (2001). Examining transformational resistance through a critical race and Latcrit theory framework: Chicana and Chicano students in an urban context. *Urban Education, 36*(3), 308–342.

Solórzano, D.G. & Yosso, T.J. (2002). Critical Race methodology: Counter-storytelling as an analytical framework for education research. *Qualitative Inquiry* 8(1): 23-44.

Southern Poverty Law Center. (2001a). Anti-immigration groups. Retrieved September 3, 2006, from http://www.splcenter.org/intel/intelreport/article.isp?sid=17.5.

Southern Poverty Law Center. (2001b). Blood on the border. Retrieved September 3, 2006, from www.splcenter.org/intel/intelreport/intrep.jsp?iid=15.

Southern Poverty Law Center. (2003). Supporters send 10,000 petitions on behalf of immigrant children. Retrieved September 4, 2006, from http://splcenter.org/center/splcreport/article.jsp?aid=27.

Spelman, E. (1988). *Inessential woman: Problems of exclusion in feminist thought.* Boston: Beacon Press.

Spelman, E. V. (1985). Combating the marginalization of black women in the classroom. In M. Culley & C. Portuges (Eds.), *Gendered subjects: The dynamics of feminist teaching* (pp. 240–244). Boston: Routledge & Kegan Paul.

Spring, J. (2003). *Deculturalization and the struggle for equality: A brief history of the education of dominated cultures in the United States* (4th ed.). Boston: McGraw-Hill.

Spring, J. (2007). *Deculturalization and the struggle for equality: A brief history of the education of dominated cultures in the United States* (5th ed.). Boston: McGraw-Hill.

Stannard, D. E. (1992). *American holocaust: The conquest of the new world*. New York: Oxford University Press.

Stearns, P. J. (1986). Old age family conflict: The perspective of the past. In K. A. Pillemer & R. S. Wolf (Eds.), *Elder abuse: Conflict in the family* (pp. 3–24). Dover, MA: Auburn House.

Steinberg, S. (1981/1989). *The ethnic myth: Race, ethnicity, and class in America* (Updated ed.). Boston: Beacon Press.

Stephan, W. G., & Stephan, C. W. (1996). *Intergroup relations*. Boulder, CO: Westview.

Stephan, W. G., & Stephan, C. W. (2001). *Improving intergroup relations*. Thousand Oaks, CA: Sage.

Stephan, W. G., & Vogt, W. P. (Eds.). (2004). *Education programs for improving intergroup relations: Theory, research, and practice*. New York: Teachers College Press.

Stryker, S. (Ed.). (2006). *The transgender reader*. New York: Routledge.

Suarez-Orozco, C. (2005). Identities under siege: Immigration stress and social mirroring among the children of immigrants. In M. M. Suarez-Orozco, C. Suarez-Orozco, & D. B. Quin (Eds.), *The new immigration: An interdisciplinary reader*. New York: Routledge.

Suarez-Orozco, M. M. (2005). "Right moves"? Immigration, globalization, utopia, and dystopia. In M. M. Orozco-Suarez, C. Orozco-Suarez, & D. B. Quin (Eds.), *The new immigration: An interdisciplinary reader*. New York: Routledge.

Sultan, C. (2006). *Israeli and Palestinian voices: A dialogue with both sides*. Minneapolis, MN: Scarletta Press.

Suzuki, B. H. (1984). Curriculum transformation for multicultural education. *Education and Urban Society, 16*(3), 294–322.

Suzuki, B. H. (1979). Multicultural education: What's it all about? *Integrated Education, 17*, 97-98.

Svinicki, M. D., & Dixon, N. M. (1987). The Kolb model modified for classroom activities. *College Teaching, 35*(4), 141–146.

Swarns, R. (2006, May 4). Growing unease from some Blacks on immigration. *New York Times*, p. 1.

Takaki, R. (1990). *Iron cages: Race and culture in 19th century America*. New York: Oxford University Press.

Takaki, R. (1993). *A different mirror: A history of multicultural America*. Boston: Little, Brown.

Takaki, R. (1998a). *A larger memory: A history of our diversity with voices*. Boston: Little Brown.

Takaki, R. (1998b). *Strangers from a different shore: A history of Asian America* (Rev. and updated ed.). Boston: Back Bay Books.

Tanenbaum Center for Interreligious Understanding (2003). *Religion in the Workplace*. www.tanenbaum.org/programs/

Tatum, B. D. (1992). Talking about race, learning about racism: The application of racial identity development theory in the classroom. *Harvard Educational Review, 62*(1), 1–24.

Tatum, B. D. (1994). Teaching white students about racism: The search for white allies and the restoration of hope. *Teacher's College Record, 95*(4), 462–476.

Taylor, A. (2006). *The divided ground: Indians, settlers, and the northern borderland of the American Revolution*. New York: Knopf.

Teller-Elsberg, J., Folbre, N., Heintz, J., & The Center for Popular Economics (2006). *U.S. economy: A compact and irreverent guide to economic life in America*. New York: The New Press.

Terry, R. (1975). *For Whites only.* Grand Rapids, WI: William B. Eerdmans.

Tessman, L., & Bar On, B-A. (Eds.). (2001). *Jewish locations: Traversing racialized land-scapes.* Lanham, MD: Rowman & Littlefield.

Tharp, R. G. (1989). Psychocultural variables and constraints: Effects on teaching and learning in schools. *American Psychologist, 44*(2), 349–359.

Themba-Nixon, T. M. (2006, July 3). Co-opting consumers of color. *The Nation.* Retrieved August 23, 2006, from http://www.thenation.com/doc/20060703/thembanixon.

Thompson, B., & Disch, E. (1992). Feminist, anti-racist, anti-oppression teaching: Two white women's experiences. *Radical Teacher, 41,* 1–10.

Thompson, C., Schaefer, E., & Brod, H. (2003). *White men challenging racism.* Durham, NC: Duke University Press.

Tobin, D. K., Tobin, G. A., & Rubin, S. (2005). *In every tongue: The racial & ethnic diversity of the Jewish people.* San Francisco: Institute for Jewish & Community Research.

Tobocman, S. (2003). *Portraits of Israelis & Palestinians, for my parents.* Brooklyn, NY: Soft Skull Press.

Tolan, S. (2006). *The lemon tree: An Arab, a Jew, and the heart of the Middle East.* New York: Bloomsbury.

Tompkins, J. (1990). Pedagogy of the distressed. *College English, 52*(6), 653–660.

Tong, R. (1989). *Feminist thought: A comprehensive introduction.* Boulder, CO: Westview Press.

Transgender Law and Policy Institute: Home Page. www.transgenderlaw.org

Trinh, T. M. H. (1989). *Woman, native, other.* Bloomington: Indiana University Press.

Truong, J. (2004). *Homeless LGBT youth and LGBT youth in foster care.* Retrieved September 21, 2005, from http://www.safeschoolscoalition.org/RG-homeless.html.

Tuan, M. 2001. *Forever foreigners or honorary Whites? The Asian ethnic experience today.* New Brunswick, NJ: Rutgers University Press.

Tusmith, B., & Reddy, M. T. (Eds.). (2002). *Race in the college classroom: Pedagogy and politics.* New Brunswick, NJ: Rutgers University Press.

Tuveson, E. L. (1968). *Redeemer nation: The idea of America's millenial role.* Chicago: University of Chicago Press.

U.S. Census Bureau. (2000). The changing shape of the nation's income distribution: 1947–1998. Retrieved September 4, 2006, from http://www.census.gov/prod/2000pubs/p60-204.pdf

U.S. Census Bureau. (2004). Current population survey, income limits for each fifth and top 5 percent of families (Tables F-1 and F-3). Retrieved October 30, 2006, from http://www.census.gov/hhes/www/income/histinc/f01x1.html.

U.S. Department of Education, National Center for Education Statistics. (2000). *National Education Longitudinal Study of 1988 (NEL S:88/2000), "Fourth Follow-up," and Postsecondary Education Transcript Study (PETS).* Washington, DC: Author.

U.S. Department of Education, National Center for Education Statistics. (2004). *Digest of Education Statistics, 2004.* Washington, DC: Author.

U.S. Department of Health and Human Services, Health Resources and Services Administration. (2005). *Women's Health 2005.* Rockville, MD: Author.

U.S. Department of State. (2005). *Report on global anti-Semitism.* Retrieved September 4, 2006, from http://www.state.gov/g/drl/rls/40258.htm.

Urban Institute. (2006). *Children of immigrants: Facts and figures.* Washington, DC: Author.

Valenzuela, A. (1999). *Subtractive schooling: U.S.-Mexican youth and the politics of caring.* Albany: State University of New York Press.

Van Hook, J. (2003). *Poverty grows among children of immigrants in the U.S.* Washington, DC: Migration Policy Institute.

V-Day. (n.d.). V-Day is a global movement to stop violence against women and girls. Retrieved October 29, 2006, from http://www.vday.org.

Ventrell, M. (1998). Evolution of the dependency component of the juvenile court. *Juvenile and Family Court Journal, 49*(4), 17–38.

Villegas, A. M., & Lucas, T. (2002). *Educating culturally responsive teachers: A coherent approach.* Albany: State University of New York Press.

Vincent, C. (Ed.). (2003). *Social justice, education and identity.* New York: Routledge.

Vygotsky, L. (1978). *Mind in society.* Cambridge, MA: Harvard University Press.

Waldinger, R., & Feliciano, C. (2004). Will the new second generation experience "downward assimilation"? Segmented assimilation reassessed. *Ethnic and Racial Studies, 27*(3), 376–402.

Walker, R. (1995). *To be real: Telling the truth and changing the face of feminism.* New York: First Anchor Books.

Walker, R. (2001). *Black, White and Jewish: Autobiography of a shifting self.* New York: Riverhead Books.

Wallerstein, N. (1987). Problem-posing education: Freire's method for transformation. In I. Shor (Ed.), *Freire for the classroom: A sourcebook* (pp. 33–44). Portsmouth, NH: Heinemann.

Walter, S., & Stephan, C. (1996). *Intergroup relations.* Boulder, CO: Westview Press.

Warner, M. (Ed.). (1993). *Fear of a queer planet.* Minneapolis: University of Minnesota Press.

Warner, R. S., & Wittner, J. G. (1998). *Gatherings in diaspora: Religious communities and the new immigration.* Philadelphia: Temple University Press.

Warren, J., & Twine, F. W. (1997). White Americans, the new minority? Non-Blacks and the ever expanding boundaries of whiteness. *Journal of Black Studies, 28*(2), 200–218.

Warren, K. (2005). A path worth taking: The development of social justice in outdoor experiential education. *Equity & Excellence in Education, 38*(1), 89–99.

Warren, K. (Ed.). (1996). *Women's voices in experiential education.* Dubuque, IA: Kendall/Hunt.

Washington, M. H. (1985). How racial differences helped us discover our common ground. In M. Culley & C. Portuges (Eds.), *Gendered subjects: The dynamics of feminist teaching* (pp. 221–230). Boston: Routledge and Kegan Paul.

Watkins, S. C. (2006). *Hip hop matters: Politics, pop culture and the struggle for the soul of a movement.* Boston: Beacon Press.

Weiler, K. (1991). Freire and a feminist pedagogy of difference. *Harvard Educational Review, 61*(4), 449–474.

Weinberg, G. (1973). *Society and the healthy homosexual.* New York: Doubleday.

Weinberg, L., & Pedahzur, A. (Eds.). (2004). *Religious fundamentalism and political extremism.* London: Frank Cass.

Weinberg, M. (1986). *Because they were Jews: A history of antisemitism.* Westport, CT: Greenwood Press.

Weinstein, G., & Mellen, D. (1997). Antisemitism curriculum design. In M. Adams, L. A. Bell, & P. Griffin (Eds.), *Teaching for diversity and social justice: A sourcebook* (pp. 170–197). New York: Routledge.

Weinstein, G., & Obear, K. (1992). Bias issues in the classroom: Encounters with the teaching self. In M. Adams (Ed.), *Promoting diversity in college classrooms: Innovative responses for the curriculum, faculty, and institutions* (New Directions for Teaching and Learning, No. 52 pp. 39–50). San Francisco: Jossey-Bass.

Wellman, D.T. (1977). *Portraits of white racism.* New York: Cambridge University Press.

Welton, N., & Wolf, L. (2001). *Global uprising: Confronting the tyrannies of the 21st century: Stories from a new generation of activists.* Philadelphia: New Society.

Wendell, S. (1996). *The rejected body: Feminist philosophical reflections on disability.* New York: Routledge.

West, C. (2004). *Democracy matters: Winning the fight against imperialism.* New York: Penguin.

Whitlock, E., & Adams, M. (2004). Special theme issue: Brown + 50. *Equity & Excellence in Education, 37* (3), 175-315.

Wigginton, E. (Ed.). (1992). *Refuse to stand silently by: An oral history of grass roots social activism in America, 1921–1964.* New York: Doubleday.

Wijeyesinghe, C., & Jackson, B. W. (Eds.). (2001). *New perspectives on racial identity development: A theoretical and practical anthology.* New York: New York University Press.

Wilchins, R. A. (1997). *Read my lips: Sexual subversion and the end of gender.* Ithaca, NY: Firebrand Books.

Wildman, S. (Ed.). (1996). *Privilege revealed: How invisible preference undermines America.* New York: New York University Press.

Williams, R. M., Jr. (1947). *The reduction of intergroup tensions: A survey of research on problems of ethnic, racial, and religious group relations.* New York: Social Science Research Council

Wills, D. W. (2002). *Christianity in the United States: A historical survey and interpretation.* Notre Dame, IN: University of Notre Dame Press.

Wills, G. (2006, November 16). A country ruled by faith. *The New York Review of Books, LIII* (18), 8-12.

Wilson, C. C., Gutierrez, F., & Chao, L. M. (2003). *Racism, sexism and the media: The rise of class communication in multicultural America.* Thousand Oaks, CA: Sage.

Wilson, J. E., & Drakeman, D. L. (2003). *Church and state in American history: Key documents, decisions, and commentary from the past three centuries* (3rd ed.). Boulder, CO: Westview.

Winant, H. (1997). Behind blue eyes: Contemporary white racial politics. In M. Fine, L. Weis, L. C. Powell, & L. M. Wong (Eds.). *Off white: Readings on race, power, and society* (pp. 40–53). New York: Routledge.

Winant, H. (2001). *The world is a ghetto: Race and democracy since World War II.* New York: Basic Books.

Winant, H. (2004). *The new politics of race: Globalism, difference, justice.* Minneapolis: University of Minnesota Press.

Winerip, M. (2005). For immigrant students, math is one road to success. *New York Times.* Retrieved May 30, 2005, from http://web.lexis-nexis.com/universe/printdoc.

Wing, A. K. (2003). *Critical race feminism: A reader.* New York: New York University Press.

Wink, J. (2000). *Critical pedagogy: Notes from the real world* (2nd ed.). New York: Longman.

Winnick, L. (1990). America's "model minority." *Commentary, 90*(2), 22–29.

Wistrich, R. S. (1991). Introduction. In *Antisemitism: The longest hatred.* New York: Pantheon.

Witkin, H. A., & Moore, C. A. (1975). *Field-dependent and field-independent cognitive styles and their educational implications.* Princeton, NJ: Educational Testing Service.

Wong, E. (2005, August 9). Swift road for U.S. citizens soldiers already fighting in Iraq. *New York Times*, p. A11.

Woolf, L. (2005). An in-depth look at ageism. Retrieved June 20, 2006, from http://www.webster.edu/~woolflm/ageism.html.

Wright, R. (1992). *Stolen continents: The "New World" through Indian eyes*. Boston: Houghton/Mifflin.

Wuthnow, R. (1996). *Christianity and civil society: The contemporary debate*. Valley Force, PA: Trinity Press International.

Wuthnow, R. (2005). *America and the challenges of religious diversity*. Princeton, NJ: Princeton University Press.

Yoo, D. K. (Ed.). (1999). *New spiritual homes: Religion and Asian Americans*. Honolulu: University of Hawai'i Press.

York, D. E. (1994). *Cross-cultural training programs*. Westport, CT: Bergin & Garvey.

Yosso, T. (2006). *Critical race counterstories along the Chicana/Chicano educational pipeline*. New York: Routledge.

Young, E. (1992). *Keepers of the history: Women and the Israeli-Palestinian conflict*. New York: Teachers College Press.

Young, I. M. (1990a). Five faces of oppression. In *Justice and the politics of difference* (pp. 39–65). Princeton, NJ: Princeton University Press.

Young, I. M. (1990b). *Justice and the politics of difference*. Princeton, NJ: Princeton University Press.

Zaharna, R. S. (1989). Self-shock: The double-binding challenge of identity. *International Journal of Intercultural Relations, 13*(4), 501–525.

Zames Fleischer, D., & Zames, F. (2001). *The disability rights movement: From charity to confrontation*. Philadelphia: Temple University Press.

Zandy, J. (1996). Decloaking class: Why class identity and consciousness count. *Race, Gender & Class, 4*(1), 7–23.

Zhou, M. (1997). Segmented assimilation: Issues, controversies, and recent research on the new second generation. *International Migration Review, 31*(4), 975–1008.

Ziedenberg, J., & Schiraldi, V. (2002). *Cellblocks or classrooms? The funding of higher education and corrections and its impact on African American men*. Washington, DC: Justice Policy Institute.

Zine, J. (2003). Dealing with September 12: Integrative anti-racism and the challenge of anti-Islamophobia education. *Orbit, 33*(3), 39–41.

Zinn, H. (1980/1995). *A people's history of the United States* (Rev. and updated ed.). New York: Harper & Row.

Zinn, H. (2004). *Voices of a people's history of the United States*. New York: Seven Stories Press.

Zirkel, S., Lopez, G. E., & Brown, L. M. (2004). Special theme issue: The 50th anniversary of *Brown v. Board of Education*: Interethnic contact and change in education in the 21st century. *Journal of Social Issues, 60*(1).

Zúñiga, X., Nagda, B. A., Chesler, M., & Cytron-Walker, A. (2007) *Intergroup dialogues in higher education: Meaningful learning about social justice* (ASHE-ERIC Report Series, 32(4). San Francisco: Jossey-Bass.

Zúñiga, X., Nagda, B. A., & Sevig, T. D. (2002). Intergroup dialogues: An educational model for cultivating engagement across differences. *Equity & Excellence in Education, 35*(1), 7–17.

# About the Contributors

**Maurianne Adams** is Professor of Education at the University of Massachusetts Amherst in the Social Justice Education concentration. She is co-editor of *Strangers and Neighbors: Relations Between Blacks and Jews in the United States* and *Readings for Diversity and Social Justice* and editor of *Equity & Excellence in Education.*

**Lee Anne Bell** is Barbara Silver Horowitz Director of Education at Barnard College, Columbia Univeristy. Her current activities include the *Storytelling Project*, a collaboration with artists and educators to create anti-racist curriculum for youth in urban schools and designing social justice approaches to teacher education. Recent articles address race talk in education.

**Steven D. Botkin,** Executive Director of Men's Resources International, is an educator and organizer of men on gender justice, positive masculinity and violence prevention for over 25 years, and founder/former director of the Men's Resource Center of Western Massachusetts. He presents lectures/trainings on men's issues throughout the world.

**Chase Catalano** received his B.A. in American Studies from Dickinson College and his M.Ed. in Higher Education Administration from the University of Massachusetts Amherst. As a current doctoral student in Social Justice Education at the University of Massachusetts Amherst, his primary research is focused on FTM identity at all-female colleges.

**Katja Hahn d'Errico** an adjunct faculty member in Social Justice Education and lecturer for Commonwealth College at the University of Massachusetts Amherst, was born and raised in Germany where she became aware of social justice issues. She is currently interested in the connection between social justice education and spirituality.

**Pat Griffin** is Professor Emerita in Social Justice Education at the University of Massachusetts Amherst. She is Director of *It Takes A Team! Education Campaign for Lesbian, Gay, Bisexual, Transgender Issues in Sport* and author of *Strong Women, Deep Closets: Homophobia and Lesbians in Sport.*

**Rita Hardiman** has been a practitioner in the field of multicultural organizational development for over 25 years. Rita's work focuses on developing diverse, socially just and equitable workplaces and learning environments. She has published articles on multicultural organizations, managing diversity, racial identity development, and facilitating dialogue groups on diversity.

**Bobbie Harro**, professor at the School of Human Services Springfield College, teaches adults in human services professions about issues of social justice and social change. She works with pre-service and in-service teachers in multicultural urban settings and consults with non-profit organizations on issues of white racism, privilege, sexism, and heterosexism.

**Bailey Jackson** is Chair of the Social Justice Education Graduate Concentration, School of Education, University of Massachusetts Amherst. Dr. Jackson's research interests include Social Identity Development, Black Identity Development, Multicultural Organizational Development and Change. He is co-editor of *New Perspectives on Racial Identity Development: A Theoretical and Practical Anthology.*

**JoAnne Silver Jones** has maintained for 35 years a passion for teaching and learning about how to use educational method-ologies to create a more socially and economically just world. She is now a full professor at Springfield College's School of Human Services.

**Khyati Y. Joshi** is Assistant Professor of Education at Fairleigh Dickinson University. She is author of the book *New Roots in America's Sacred Ground: Religion, Race, and Ethnicity in Indian America*. She works with teachers and school admin-istrators on multicultural curriculum development and the needs of immigrant and second-generation students.

**Tanya Kachwaha** is an experienced educator and group facil-itator who has worked with intergroup dialogues, women's groups, psycho-educational groups, and youth empowerment groups. She has a CAGS in Feminist Studies, an MEd in Social Justice Education and currently works at a rape crisis center as director of community education.

**Betsy Leondar-Wright** is co-author of *Class Matters: Cross-Class Alliance Building for Middle Class Activists* (www.class-matters.org) and *The Color of Wealth: The Story Behind the U.S. Racial Wealth Divide*. She was the Communications Director at United for a Fair Economy from 1998-2006 and she is on the board of Class Action.

**Barbara J. Love** is Associate Professor of Education at the University of Massachusetts Amherst in Social Justice Edu-cation. She writes on the achievement gap as an opportunity gap, the phenomenon of internalized racism, and critical theory of liberation. She works with organizations in the U.S. and internationally on racial and gender equity, empower-ment, liberation and community development.

**Linda McCarthy** earned her doctorate in Social Justice Education from the University of Massachusetts Amherst, where her dissertation research focused on transgender identity. Former Associate Editor for the School of Education journal, *Equity & Excellence in Education*, Linda is Assistant Professor of Sociology at Greenfield Community College in Greenfield, Massachusetts.

**Mathew L. Ouellett** directs the Center for Teaching,UMASS-Amherst and lectures in Educational Policy and Social Justice Education. He taught courses on racism in social work practice at Smith College School for Social Work and is editor of *Teaching Inclusively: Resources for Course, Department and Institutional Change in Higher Education* (2005).

**Madeline L. Peters**, Director of Disability Services at the University of Massachusetts, Amherst and co-editor of *Reading for Diversity and Social Justice,* is a 20 year veteran in the field of disabilities, presenter at national conferences social justice workshops, and has also won a national law suit for the disabled.

**Kathleen J. Phillips,** has nearly 40 years experience leading youth empowerment organizations, including an award winning community youth leadership program and a comprehensive educational and family support program for young parents; conducting research in adult literacy and self-knowledge education; and, teaching at all grades levels and in teacher education programs.

**Rosemarie A. Roberts,** is a Social Psychologist and Assistant Professor at John Jay College of Criminal Justice. She also directs the *Storytelling Project* at Barnard College. Her research interests are in the areas of social justice and the ways in which social institutions create conditions of inclusion and exclusion.

**Tom Schiff,** a Health Educator and Adjunct Professor in Social Justice Education at UMass-Amherst has over twenty years experience as an educator, counselor, trainer, and consultant on organization development and human relations and particular expertise working with men on issues of health, violence prevention, sexism, and homophobia.

**Davey Shlasko** is an educator/activist whose work focuses on trans/gender issues, queer community building, and youth leadership development. Ze also has written on queer pedagogy for *Equity and Excellence in Education.* Davey currently coordinates an HIV prevention outreach/education program in Western Massachusetts.

**Robin M. Smith,** is an Associate Professor of Special Education at the State University of New York at New Paltz in the Department of Educational Studies/Special Education Program. Her research and writing interests are in the areas of disability studies, inclusion, and social justice teaching.

**Beverly Daniel Tatum** is President of Spelman College in Atlanta, the country's oldest historically black college for women. She is author of the highly acclaimed book, *Why are all the black kids sitting together in the cafeteria? and other conversations about race* (Basic Books, 1999).

**Sharon J. Washington** has worked on social equity for 20 years. Previously Special Assistant to the President for Diversity Initiatives at Bennett College for Women, Spelman College Provost, and faculty at Kent State and Springfield College, she currently works on faculty equity at University of California Office of the President.

**Gerald Weinstein** is Professor Emeritus at the University of Massachusetts/Amherst where he developed his theory of self-knowledge development. His lifetime of work on anti-racism included studying desegregation in the South in the 1950s, public school and university teaching about racism, and developing the first campus workshops on antisemitism.

**Felice Yeskel** is Director of Class Action, (www.classism.org), a national, non-profit focusing on issues of social class. Felice is a Founder of United for a Fair Economy. She is the co-author of *Economic Apartheid in America*. She comes from a Jewish, working-class family from New York City's lower east side.

**Ximena Zúñiga**, Associate Professor of Education, UMASS-Amherst, writes about pedagogy, intergroup dialogue, diversity and learning in higher education. She is coeditor of *MulticulturalTeaching in the Univer*sity (Praeger) and *Readings for Diversity and Social Justice* (Routledge), and coauthor of *Intergroup dialogues in higher education: Meaningful learning about social justice* (Jossey Bass).

# Index